THE GLOBAL ECONOMY
Contemporary Debates

THE GLOBAL ECONOMY

Contemporary Debates

THOMAS OATLEY

University of North Carolina at Chapel Hill

PEARSON
Longman

New York   San Francisco   Boston
London   Toronto   Sydney   Tokyo   Singapore   Madrid
Mexico City   Munich   Paris   Cape Town   Hong Kong   Montreal

Executive Editor: Eric Stano
Acquisitions Editor: Ed Costello
Marketing Manager: Elizabeth Fogarty
Production Manager: Ellen MacElree
Project Coordination, Text Design, and Electronic Page Makeup: Stratford
Publishing Services
Cover Design Manager: John Callahan
Cover Designer: Maria Illardi
Cover Image: Courtesy of Getty Images, Inc.
Manufacturing Manager: Mary Fischer
Cover Printer: Phoenix Book Tech

Library of Congress Cataloging-in-Publication Data

Oatley, Thomas
    The global economy : contemporary debates/Thomas Oatley.
        p.   cm.
      ISBN 0-321-24377-3
    1. Globalization—Economic aspects.   2. International trade.   3. Inter-
national economic relations.   I. Title.
HF1359.0247 2004
337—dc22   2004019676

Copyright © 2005 by Pearson Education, Inc.

ISBN 0-321-24377-3

  3 4 5 6 7 8 9 10—PBT—07 06

For my students, who have taught me much.

◼◯ CONTENTS

 **PREFACE**

An undergraduate trying to understand the global economy must clear three hurdles. First, she must become familiar with a broad range of theories from both political science and economics that have been developed to study the global economy. Second, she must become familiar with the historical development of the global economic system. Third, she must become familiar with the issues and debates that are at the center of contemporary discussion among governments, international economic organizations, think tanks, and academics.

Existing textbooks and edited International Political Economy readers provide faculty with a wealth of options of material that promotes the development of core theoretical knowledge and historical background. Professors have fewer options when it comes time to select a textbook that introduces students to contemporary issues and debates in the global economy. For this purpose, I suspect that most teachers rely on infrequently revised textbooks and a set of photocopied (or more commonly now, scanned or on-line) readings taken from some of the more policy-oriented journals.

This book makes available—in a convenient format—a collection of recent articles addressing many of the more prominent and controversial issues in the contemporary global economy. Selection of the articles was governed by five broad considerations.

1. The book should cover all of the traditional IPE issue areas: trade, multinational corporations, finance and exchange rates, and development. This approach ensures that students are exposed to contemporary issues across the whole spectrum of the global economy.
2. The articles should focus on issues that are the subject of current debate and discussion, rather than focus on issues that are of largely historical interest. Consequently, most articles have been published recently, with few written and published prior to the year 2000.
3. The articles should focus primarily on topics that lie at the intersection between contemporary issues and enduring problems in the global economy. Such an approach enables faculty to place the topics covered and the specific articles included in a broader historical and theoretical context.
4. The book should introduce students to contending positions on the issues included. Therefore, each issue is examined through the lens of two articles each of which adopts a distinct perspective. In some cases the two

articles represent an explicit debate; in others the debate is more implicit. In all cases, however, students are exposed to quite different ways of thinking about the issue at hand.

5. The book should help students place the debates in context, encourage them to think critically about the arguments and the broader debate, and provide a gateway to further study. Consequently, each debate is preceded by a brief introduction that places the issue in a historical and theoretical context, and ends with a set of discussion questions and suggestions for further reading.

Using these criteria, I have selected a set of readings that should be integrated easily into most undergraduate IPE courses. Moreover, the book's broad scope and debate-oriented format should enable students to develop a sophisticated understanding of contemporary policy issues and global economy debates.

In assembling this book, I have benefited from Eric Stano's initial enthusiasm for the project and then from Ed Costello. The selections were strengthened by the very helpful comments I received from external reciewers, including

Steven Livingston (Middle Tennessee St. University)
Jaroslav Tir (University of Georgia)
Waltraud Queiser Morales (University of Central Florida)
Charles R. Boehmer (University of Texas at El Paso)
Linda Petrou (High Point University)
A. L. Morgan (University of Tennessee)
Gordon Bennett (University of Texas)
Peter B. Heller (Manhattan College)
Daniel Gibran (Tennessee State University)
Ian Hurd (Northwestern University)
John A. C. Conybeare (University of Iowa)
William M. Downs (Georgia State University)

Finally, I owe my students a large debt for helping to convince me that sometimes one can grasp abstract theoretical concepts more easily by approaching them through the more familiar territory of contemporary issues and debates.

—*Thomas Oatley*

THE GLOBAL ECONOMY

Contemporary Debates

PART

I

Introduction

INTRODUCTION

The last decades of the twentieth century brought tremendous growth in global economic activity and a consequent deepening of economic interdependence, often referred to as "globalization." Economic globalization can be defined as "the integration of national economies into the international economy through trade, direct foreign investment (by corporations and multinationals), short term capital flows, international flows of workers and humanity generally, and flows of technology."[1] This definition highlights two distinct aspects of globalization. On the one hand, globalization is a *process*. As a process, globalization refers to the growth of the cross-border economic activities listed in the definition offered above. On the other hand, globalization is an *outcome*. As an outcome, globalization refers to the emergence of highly interdependent national economies. Countries that may have once enjoyed considerable economic independence or autonomy find that they are now enmeshed in interdependent relationships in which economic conditions at home depend heavily upon economic developments in the rest of the world.

Globalization as a process is clearly evident in many of the standard statistics of international economic activity. Between 1980 and 2000, for example, world trade grew at an average rate of 5.1 percent per year, more than twice as fast as the average annual rate of growth of the world economy as a whole.[2] Consequently, total world merchandise trade rose from about $84 billion in 1953 to $3.7 trillion in 1993 and then to about $6.3 trillion in 2002.[3] Foreign direct investment (FDI), the process by which a firm based in one country gains an ownership stake in a company based in a second country, has also grown at historically unprecedented rates during this period. According to the United Nations Conference on Trade and Development (UNCTAD), which assembles the most authoritative statistics on the activities of multinational corporations (MNCs), annual FDI inflows amounted to about $62.2 billion in 1985. In 2000, FDI inflows equaled just less than $1.4 trillion.[4]

Not surprisingly, the number of MNCs operating in the global economy has also grown sharply. UNCTAD estimates that in 1969 there were about 7,258 MNCs operating in the global economy. By 1988 the number of MNCs had doubled to about 18,500. Between 1988 and 2000 the number of MNCs operating in the global economy tripled, reaching 63,000 by 2000.[5]

International financial transactions experienced similar growth. To provide just one indicator, total foreign claims held by banks based in the advanced industrialized countries rose from $755 billion at the end of 1983 to more than $14.7 trillion at the end of 2003.[6] This is a clear indication that over the last 20 years foreign lending has become an increasingly important counterpart to banks' loans to domestic businesses. While the rate of growth of all of these international economic transactions slowed in the first decade of the twenty-first century, this reflects the worldwide slowdown in economic growth rather than a more profound retreat from globalization. The pace of globalization is likely to pick up again as soon as the global economy recovers fully.

Globalization as an outcome is also evident in statistics and in the events of the day. Trade openness provides one standard statistical measure of globalization. Trade openness measures each country's total trade (its imports plus its exports) as a percentage of its total domestic economic production (its gross domestic product, or GDP). Because world trade has grown more rapidly, on average, than world production, we can conclude that each year the world as a whole is becoming more open to trade—a larger share of the world's economic output crosses at least one national border between the time it is produced and the time it is consumed. Consequently, whether a company based in your hometown continues to produce, and therefore continues to hire local residents, depends in no small part on whether people living in other countries remain willing to purchase the company's products. Economic conditions in your hometown thus increasingly come to depend on developments in other parts of the world. When you consider where many of the products that you own were produced, it becomes evident that such dependence is a two-way street. The fortunes of workers and businesses in foreign countries depend in part on your willingness to continue to buy the goods that they produce. This situation—your dependence on foreigners and their dependence on you— is what the economic interdependence generated by the dynamic process of globalization is all about.

Because globalization strengthens connections between national economies, and because the economic dynamics that are at the core of globalization can be disruptive for individuals, communities, and nations, globalization has given rise to a number of debates among academics, nongovernmental organizations, and policymakers. One can place these debates into three broad categories. The first category features debates that revolve around the basic dynamics of the global economy. How far has globalization progressed? Has the world entered an unprecedented era of global markets, or is the current world economy still less deeply integrated than it was in the late nineteenth century (at the end of the so-called "first wave of globalization")? What are the consequences of globalization for individuals, groups, governments, and nations? Is the life of the typical person (if indeed there is a typical person) improved or worsened by globalization? Are governments losing the capacity to govern in the face of global markets, or do they retain the capability to use national policies to achieve most of their desired domestic objectives? Are global markets undermining the nation-state, and is political authority therefore gradually being transferred to international economic organizations like the World Trade Organization (WTO), the Internatinal Monetary Fund (IMF), and the European Union (EU)? Each of these debates involves contending perspectives about how to characterize the depth and the consequences of globalization.

The second category includes debates that focus on the foreign economic policies that governments use to manage the relationship between their national economies and the global economy. Should a government pursue additional trade liberalization or should it take steps to protect certain domestic industries from trade? If more liberalization is desired, is it best to achieve it through the World Trade Organization's multilateral process or is it better to proceed through regional free trade agreements? Should governments, particularly in developing countries, liberalize capital flows as well as trade, or should they continue to control and regulate capital flows? Should governments attempt to maintain fixed exchange rates, or should they allow their currency to float? Should they strive to maintain a strong national currency, or is it better to keep the currency a bit undervalued? Debates of this type involve contending perspectives about the extent to which a particular country should participate in the global economy, and about the terms under which it should do so.

The final category includes debates that revolve around broader issues of governance. These debates focus on the political institutions and rules that have been established to govern the global economy, as well as on the possible need for new global rules in areas where they do not currently exist. For example, should the WTO decision-making process be reformed, perhaps by opening participation to nongovernmental organizations? Should the WTO and regional trade arrangements like the North American Free Trade Agreement (NAFTA) incorporate explicit rules concerning labor and the environment? Should governments establish a set of international rules that would govern the activities of MNCs? Debate on these issues involves distinct perspectives on *how*—and in some cases *whether*—various aspects of the global economy should be governed.

This book presents a sample of the debates that have arisen out of the dynamics of globalization. While the articles focus on contemporary issues and events, the deeper issue at the center of each debate tends to be more enduring. In one exchange, for example, the authors debate whether the United States should pursue regional free trade agreements in the wake of the failure to reach agreement at the WTO Ministerial Conference in Cancun, Mexico in the fall of 2003. Yet, this contemporary debate reflects a more enduring disagreement about the respective roles of multilateralism and regionalism in American trade policy that has been taking place for at least 15 years. In another debate, the participants disagree about the contribution that international trade can make to economic development in the South. While each article reflects current thinking on this question, the debate itself has been raging for more than 50 years, and will likely continue into the future. Thus, while the articles focus on contemporary issues, these contemporary debates typically have quite a long history.

One important reason why these debates endure is that most lack clear answers. Some debates, such as those that involve contending perspectives about how far globalization has progressed and what its consequences are, could be resolved through careful empirical research. We could engage in research that measures the extent of trade and financial integration over time, and then come to some conclusion about how far globalization has progressed. We could develop indicators to measure the quality of life for the typical individual and then examine whether globalization is improving or worsening living standards. In other words, such debates are largely about what the world looks like, and presumably can be settled with evidence. Debates arise about these issues because empirical research is not always easily conducted and does not always yield clear conclusions. To take just one example, is globalization widening or narrowing world income inequality? One might think that this question could be answered relatively easily. Most governments collect data on the incomes of their citizens on a regular basis. We need only assemble this data over a reasonable period of time and then examine what it tells us. Yet, this debate has proven remarkably difficult to resolve. In part this is because people do not agree about what data one should collect (should we examine income or consumption expenditures?), and the conclusion one reaches appears to depend on the kind of data one uses. The lack of resolution also reflects the difficulties associated with getting accurate data about individual incomes in developing societies. Consequently, there remains a debate between scholars, some of whom believe that globalization has widened global income inequality, and others who believe that globalization has narrowed this gap.[7]

The fact that empirical debates are not always easily resolved should not blind us to the fact that correct answers do exist. World income inequality has either widened or it has not; it cannot have done both. One should, therefore, be cautious about arguing too strongly when the issue at hand is an empirical question.

Other debates are long-lasting because they have no right or wrong answer. This type of debate revolves around different values and priorities. Most of the policy-related debates fall into this category. For example, should the U.S. government maintain a strong (overvalued) dollar or should it instead maintain a weak (under-valued) dollar? We could begin to answer this question with empirical research. We could investigate the impact that a strong and a weak currency have on the American economy. We would discover that a strong dollar has costs (it makes it more difficult for American firms to export and reduces the income of people employed in the traded-goods sector) and benefits (it reduces the cost of imports and raises the income of people employed in the non-traded-goods sector). A weak dollar has the opposite effect. The research could not tell us how individuals, not to mention governments, should weigh the costs and benefits of each strategy. In order to do so, we must place a value on the costs and benefits associated with each option, and there is no single correct weighting to attach. Consequently, perfectly reasonable people are quite likely to disagree about such issues.

Most of the debates about broad issues of global governance also fall into this category. For example, should governments establish international rules to regulate the activities of multinational corporations? Again, we could engage in empirical research to begin to answer this question. We could explore the wages that MNCs pay and the impact of these jobs and wages on the countries that host MNCs. We could investigate the impact of MNC activity on the environment. With enough time and money we could catalog everything that MNCs do. Yet, would such a project help us determine whether MNC activities should be regulated? Suppose we found that MNCs producing in developing countries damage the environment. Would this finding necessarily imply that MNC activities should be regulated? Some people will argue that a bit of environmental damage is a reasonable price to pay for the benefits that MNCs bring to developing countries. Others likely would argue that MNCs should be prevented from engaging in any activities that harm the environment. The answer that one proposes, therefore, has less to do with the facts concerning the impact of MNCs on the environment, and more to do with the relative weight that different people attach to the protection of the environment and to economic development. Again, perfectly reasonable people can easily reach quite different, and yet equally legitimate conclusions about the same issue.

I encourage you to keep these categories in mind as you read the articles presented in this volume, and as you discuss and debate them with your colleagues inside and outside of class. Ask yourself whether the debate at hand is one that empirical research can resolve. If it is, then ask yourself whether you are willing to accept conclusions that emerge from careful research, even when the conclusion contradicts some of your prior beliefs. If the issue at hand cannot be resolved through empirical research, then I ask something different. Try to become conscious of how your values shape your position on such issues, and be willing to listen to and respect those whose views differ from your own. In short, debate these issues, but recognize that on such issues reasonable people can disagree. Please disagree reasonably.

ENDNOTES

1. Jagdish Bhagwati, *In Defense of Globalization* (New York: Oxford University Press, 2004), page 3.
2. World Trade Organization, "Long Term Trends—World Exports, Production, GDP, From 1950," Available at http://www.wto.org/english/res_e/statis_e/its2003_e/section2_e/ii01.xls (accessed March 13, 2004).
3. World Trade Organization. *International Trade Statistics 2003* (Geneva: World Trade Organization, 2003), page 32. Available at http://www.wto.org/english/res_e/statis_e/its2003_e/its03_toc_e.htm (accessed March 18, 2004).
4. UNCTAD, "FDI Database." Available at http://www.unctad.org/Templates/ Page.asp?intItemID=1923&lang=1 (accessed March 13, 2004).
5. Medard Gabel and Henry Bruner. *Global Inc.: An Atlas of the Multinational Corporation* (New York: The New Press, 2003), page 3.
6. Bank for International Settlements, *Consolidated Claims by Maturity and Sector, Historical Time Series*. Available at http://www.bis.org/publ/hcsv/hanx9a_for.csv (accessed March 13, 2004).
7. See "More of Less Equal?" *The Economist*, March 13, 2004: 69–71. For a more detailed discussion see Angus Deaton, "Measuring Poverty in a Growing World (or measuring growth in a poor world)," *Research Paper in Development Studies*, Woodrow Wilson School, Princeton University. Available at http://www.wws.princeton.edu/%7Erpds/downloads/deaton_measuringpoverty_204.pdf (accessed June 14, 2004).

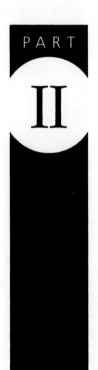

PART

II

The Economic Impact of International Trade

CHAPTER 1

TRADE AND JOBS IN THE UNITED STATES

The United States has run persistent trade and current account deficits since the early 1970s. Each year, residents of the United States import more goods and services from residents of other countries than they sell to residents of foreign countries. The U.S. trade deficit averaged $94 billion per year between 1980 and 1999. In 2002, it rose to its highest level ever, peaking at $435 billion, about four percent of U.S. gross domestic product. Most of this deficit arises in the U.S. trade account, which measures imports and exports of goods. In 2002, the U.S. trade account registered a deficit of $484.4 billion. The United States ran a $49.1 billion surplus in internationally traded services, producing an overall current account deficit of $435.2 billion. And while the slower economic growth that has characterized the early part of this decade should reduce the trade deficit, figures from the first half of 2003 suggest that the deficit continues to widen. Persistent current account deficits have translated into growing foreign indebtedness as the United States borrows from the rest of the world to pay for its imports in excess of its exports. Indeed, in 1980 the United States was the world's largest creditor nation; the United States had more financial claims on the rest of the world than the world had on the United States. By the end of the 1980s, the United States had become the world's largest debtor nation.

Such deficits raise a number of issues that have been at the center of policy debate during the last 20 years. What causes the United States to run such persistent trade deficits? What impact does the trade deficit have on job creation and destruction in the American economy? Are such large deficits sustainable, or must the United States change its policies in order to reduce, if not fully eliminate them? If the United States must adjust, what policies are most likely to work, and what consequences will such adjustment have on the American economy? While all of these issues have received considerable attention in the policymaking arena, discussion has thus far failed to produce a consensus view that the deficit is an urgent problem that needs attention.

The two readings presented in this chapter examine two issues generated by the current account deficit: its causes and its impact on employment. Robert E. Scott, an economist based at the Washington DC think tank The Economic Policy Institute, argues that the trade deficit eliminates American jobs. He estimates that between 1994 and 2000 as many as three million jobs, most in well-paying manufacturing industries, were lost as a direct consequence of American trade deficits. According to Scott, the trade deficit, and thus the large number of lost jobs, are caused by American trade policy. In particular, he argues that the terms under which the United States has participated in the North American Free Trade Agreement and the World Trade Organization are the chief cause of the imbalance in America's trade account. Without quite saying so, he asks the reader to conclude that additional trade liberalization will further worsen the deficit and therefore eliminate additional jobs.

Douglas A. Irwin, an economist who teaches at Dartmouth College, challenges the logic of Scott's analysis, as well as Scott's conclusions. Irwin argues that the trade deficit has no net effect on the number of jobs available in the United States. In his view, one can't focus solely on the trade deficit. One must also look at how the United States pays for these trade deficits. Once you do, you begin to notice that although some jobs are no doubt lost as a consequence of trade deficits, others are created by the capital inflows that the United States attracts to finance the deficit. Irwin also argues that American trade policy is not the underlying cause of the current account deficit. The deficit, he argues, is caused by an imbalance between domestic savings and domestic investment, and has nothing whatsoever to do with how open the United States is to international trade. Thus, raising tariffs or adopting other protectionist barriers will do little to eliminate the deficit, and engaging in additional trade liberalization will not increase the deficit. The implication of Irwin's analysis, therefore, is that the United States can engage in additional trade liberalization without concern that such policies will reduce the number of jobs available to American workers.

Fast Track to Lost Jobs: Trade Deficits and Manufacturing Decline are the Legacies of NAFTA and the WTO

ROBERT E. SCOTT

The U.S. has experienced steadily growing trade deficits for nearly three decades, and these deficits have accelerated rapidly since the North American Free Trade Agreement took effect in 1994 and the World Trade Organization was created in 1995. The toll on U.S. employment has been heavy: from 1994 to 2000, growing trade deficits eliminated a net total of 3.0 million actual and potential jobs from the U.S. economy.[1]

Yet despite substantial evidence that current trade policies have resulted in massive trade deficits and job losses, the Bush Administration is pressing Congress for "fast track" trade negotiating authority, by which the President could submit trade agreements to Congress for a yes or no vote without amendment.[2] Fast-track promoters want this authority to make it easier to extend NAFTA throughout the hemisphere in a proposed Free Trade Area of the Americas (FTAA) agreement and to expand the WTO in a new round of multilateral negotiations. Promotion of fast track has even made its way into the post-September 11 debate over an economic stimulus. House Appropriations Committee Chairman Bill Thomas has repeatedly urged that Congress include fast track authority in any economic stimulus plan.

The dismal U.S track record in negotiating trade agreements since the mid-1990s, as indicated by the nation's growing trade deficit and the attendant economic problems, suggests that a fast track is exactly what the nation does not need:

- While gross U.S. exports rose 61.5% between 1994 and 2000, imports rose much more, by 80.5%.
- Job losses associated with the trade deficit increased six times more rapidly between 1994 and 2000 than they did between 1989 and 1994.
- Every state and the District of Columbia suffered significant job losses due to growing trade deficits between 1994 and 2000. Ten states, led by California, lost over 100,000 net jobs.
- The manufacturing sector, where the trade deficit rose 158.5% between 1994 and 2000, shouldered 65% of the surge in job losses during that period.

From Robert E. Scott, 2002. "Fast Track to Lost Jobs," *Economic Policy Institute Briefing Paper*, Economic Policy Institute, Washington, DC.

- U.S. trade deficits with NAFTA partners Canada and Mexico increased nearly four-fold between 1993 and 2000, driven primarily by direct U.S. investment in Mexican and Canadian factories that export to the United States. The sustained appreciation of the U.S. dollar also encouraged investors around the world to build new and expanded production capacity at home to export more goods to the U.S. As a result, U.S. markets have been flooded with imports from Asia, Europe, Central and South America, and Africa since 1994.

Fast track by itself, a procedural rule designed to facilitate passage of new trade agreements, will have no effect of any kind on the economy. It is unlikely that the U.S. can negotiate and submit for approval any new agreements for at least three years, and it will take even longer for these agreements to affect the economy. Moreover, if past trade deals are any indication, fast track and new trade deals are likely to curtail growth, not increase it.

Between August 1998 and September 2001 the U.S. manufacturing sector had already lost 1.4 million jobs (BLS 2001c). In the wake of the attacks of September 11, unemployment is likely to grow. As a result, the underlying employment problems related to trade, especially in the manufacturing sector, will be much costlier and more visible over the next few years than they were in the 1990s, when the U.S. economy was generating two to three million jobs per year.

If the U.S. had achieved balanced trade in this period, as was predicted by the advocates of NAFTA and the WTO, U.S. manufacturing would be much stronger today and in a much better position to weather the downturn that is now under way. But the fact that 25 steel-producing companies, now including Bethlehem Steel, have declared bankruptcy reveals that rapidly growing trade deficits have had corrosive effects on the U.S. industrial base (Nag and Goldfarb 2001). Rather than putting new trade deals on a fast track, policy makers should step back for a strategic pause, during which they can review the structure, enforcement, and effectiveness of U.S. trade policies.[3]

GROWING TRADE DEFICITS AND JOB LOSSES

Supporters of NAFTA and the WTO frequently tout the benefits of exports while remaining silent on the impact of rapid import growth (Zoellick 2001). But any evaluation of the impact of trade on the domestic economy must look at both imports and exports. When the United States exports 1,000 cars to Germany or Mexico, plants in this country employ U.S. workers in their production. If, however, the U.S. imports 1,000 cars from Germany or Mexico rather than building them domestically, then a similar number of U.S. workers who would have otherwise been employed in the auto industry will have to find other work. Ignoring imports and counting only exports is like balancing a checkbook by counting only deposits but not withdrawals.

U.S. trade deficits and job losses increased much more rapidly between 1994 and 2000 than they did between 1989 and 1994, as illustrated in Figure A. Indeed,

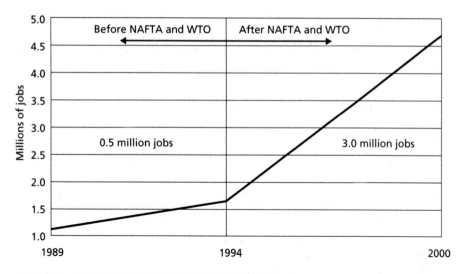

FIGURE A ■ NET U.S. JOB LOSSES DUE TO TRADE DEFICITS, 1989–2000
Sources: U.S. Census Bureau; Bureau of Labor Statistics; Bureau of Economic Analysis.

persistent barriers to U.S. exports (as well as overvaluation of the U.S. dollar) have contributed to these growing deficits, but NAFTA and the WTO were supposed to overcome those barriers. These agreements, and globalization more generally, have also contributed to rising income inequality, depressed real wages for production workers, and increased numbers of companies using threats to move plants to China, Mexico, and other countries to reduce wages, eliminate benefits and work rules, and thwart union organizing campaigns (Scott 2001).

The impact of trade on employment is one of the most widely used measures of the costs and benefits of trade policies, but also one of the least understood. The top half of Table 1 reports the amounts of, and changes in, goods trade (not including services), measured in constant 2000 dollars.[4] The bottom half of Table 1 estimates the employment impact of trade. These estimates utilize a detailed, 192-sector model that is prepared annually by the U.S. Bureau of Labor Statistics (see the methodology section for more details).

The net employment impact of trade is determined by the relationships between imports, exports, and the domestic labor requirements for each type of good. An increase in exports creates demands for U.S. workers to produce those goods, while an increase in imports reduces demand for U.S. workers, either because imports displace comparable U.S. products or because new demand is satisfied with foreign rather than domestic products.

Although gross U.S. exports increased 61.5% between 1994 and 2000, those increases were overshadowed by the growth in imports, which rose 80.5%, as shown in top half of Table 1. As a result, the 1994 U.S. trade deficit of $182 billion increased 141.6% to $439 billion by 2000 (all figures in inflation-adjusted 2000 dollars).

As shown in Table 1, total U.S. exports rose from $583 billion to $942 billion between 1994 and 2000. This net increase of $359 billion created 2.8 million jobs

TABLE 1 ■ U.S. TRADE AND TRADE-RELATED JOB CREATION, 1989–2000

Changes in U.S. Trade, 1989–2000 (billions of constant 2000 dollars)

	1989	1994	2000	Changes since 1994	
				Dollars	%Change
U.S. exports	422	583	942	359	61.5%
U.S. imports	560	765	1381	616	80.5
U.S. trade balance	−138	−182	−439	−257	141.6

U.S. trade-related job creation, 1989–2000

	1989	1994	2000	Changes since 1994	
				No. of jobs	%Change
U.S. exports	4,131	5,723	8,494	2,771	48.4%
U.S. imports	−5,244	−7,371	−13,186	−5,815	78.9%
U.S. trade balance	−1,113	−1,648	−4,692	−3,044	184.8%

Sources: U.S. Census Bureau; Bureau of Labor Statistics; Bureau of Economic Analysis

or job opportunities. On the other hand, the $616 billion rise in imports eliminated 5.8 million jobs. Thus, the $257 billion increase in the trade deficit eliminated a net of 3.0 million jobs or job opportunities in this period. By contrast, between 1989 and 1994 growing trade deficits eliminated approximately 500,000 jobs. Thus, the number of jobs lost since 1994, after implementation of NAFTA and then the WTO, was six times larger than in the previous period.

JOB LOSSES ACROSS THE UNITED STATES

In all 50 states and the District of Columbia, imports more than offset exports between 1994 and 2000, with associated job losses. Net job loss figures range from a low of 6,838 in North Dakota to a high of 364,197 in California. Other hard-hit states include Texas, New York, Pennsylvania, Michigan, North Carolina, Illinois, Ohio, Tennessee, Florida, Indiana, Georgia, and New Jersey, each with more than 100,000 net jobs lost.

While job losses in most states are modest relative to the size of the economy, the promise of new jobs was the principal justification for NAFTA and the WTO. According to the agreements' promoters, the predicted new jobs would compensate for the increased environmental degradation, economic instability, and public health dangers that the agreements would bring (Lee 1995, 10–11). If NAFTA and the WTO have not delivered net new jobs, they cannot provide enough benefits to offset the costs imposed on the American public.

Table 2B, which presents job losses as a share of the total labor force in each state, identifies several smaller states that have been hard hit by trade-related

TABLE 2A ■ TRADE-RELATED JOB LOSSES BY STATE, 1994–2000

State	Jobs	State	Jobs lost
Alabama	63,239	Montana	7,521
Alaska	6,972	Nebraska	15,312
Arizona	32,461	Nevada	16,493
Arkansas	37,469	New Hampshire	12,936
California	309,762	New Jersey	84,749
Colorado	34,982	New Mexico	16,733
Connecticut	31,431	New York	179,288
Delaware	6,467	North Carolina	133,219
District of Columbia	6,558	North Dakota	5,788
Florida	100,047	Ohio	135,139
Georgia	89,736	Oklahoma	42,266
Hawaii	7,116	Oregon	41,124
Idaho	11,021	Pennsylvania	142,221
Illinois	139,537	Rhode Island	19,164
Indiana	102,873	South Carolina	54,233
Iowa	31,770	South Dakota	8,458
Kansas	23,248	Tennessee	96,355
Kentucky	50,948	Texas	227,559
Louisiana	44,940	Utah	22,523
Maine	22,357	Vermont	6,283
Maryland	31,057	Virginia	66,083
Massachusetts	64,434	Washington	45,739
Michigan	152,061	West Virginia	14,458
Minnesota	49,925	Wisconsin	73,476
Mississippi	41,338	Wyoming	6,977
Missouri	68,392	Total	3,044,241

Source: U.S. Census Bureau; U.S. Bureau of Labor Statistics

TABLE 2B ■ JOBS LOST AS PERCENT OF STATE LABOR FORCE

State	Jobs lost	Percent of labor force
Rhode Island	19,164	5.8
North Carolina	133,219	3.7
Maine	22,357	3.6
Tennessee	96,355	3.6
Indiana	102,873	3.4
Mississippi	41,338	3.3
Michigan	152,061	3.2
Alabama	63,239	3.1
Arkansas	37,469	3.1

(continued)

TABLE 2B ■ CONTINUED

State	Jobs lost	Percent of labor force
South Carolina	54,233	3
Kentucky	50,948	2.8
Wyoming	6,977	2.8
Oklahoma	42,266	2.7
Wisconsin	73,476	2.6
Georgia	89,736	2.5
Missouri	68,392	2.5
Oregon	41,124	2.5
Ohio	135,139	2.4
Pennsylvania	142,221	2.4
Texas	227,559	2.4
Alaska	6,972	2.3
Illinois	139,537	2.3
Louisiana	44,940	2.3
Utah	22,523	2.3
District of Columbia	6,558	2.2
New Mexico	16,733	2.2
South Dakota	8,458	2.2
Nevada	16,493	2.1
New Hampshire	12,936	2.1
New Jersey	84,749	2.1
New York	179,288	2.1
California	309,762	2
Iowa	31,770	2
Massachusetts	64,434	2
Vermont	6,283	2
Idaho	11,021	1.9
Minnesota	49,925	1.9
Virginia	66,083	1.9
Connecticut	31,431	1.8
West Virginia	14,458	1.8
Colorado	34,982	1.7
Delaware	6,467	1.7
Kansas	23,248	1.7
Montana	7,521	1.7
Nebraska	15,312	1.7
North Dakota	5,788	1.7
Washington	45,739	1.7
Arizona	32,461	1.6
Florida	100,047	1.5
Hawaii	7,116	1.2
Maryland	31,057	1.2
Total	3,044,241	2.3

Sources: U.S. Census Bureau; U.S. Bureau of Labor Statistics

job losses in the late 1990s, including Rhode Island (job losses equivalent to 5.8% of the workforce), Maine (3.6%), Mississippi (3.3%), Alabama (3.1%), and Arkansas (3.1%).

The impacts of NAFTA and the WTO on the U.S. job market were obscured by the boom-and-bust cycle that has driven domestic consumption, investment, and speculation in the mid- and late 1990s. Although there was net job loss in the international sector of the economy between 1994 and 2000, total employment rose rapidly in the U.S., causing overall unemployment to fall to record low levels. However, with the bursting of the stock market bubble, unemployment has risen from 3.9% in October 2000 to 4.9% in September 2001 (BLS 2001c).

Table 3 summarizes the direct and indirect effects of trade on employment in all U.S. industries, including primary commodities and services that provide inputs for traded goods. Changes in the numbers of jobs lost (shown in the last two columns) illustrate several key effects of trade policies on the U.S. The U.S. deficit in manufacturing trade increased 158.5% between 1994 and 2000, and the manufacturing sector was responsible for the vast majority of all job losses: 1.9 million jobs lost in manufacturing compared with 3.0 million overall jobs lost between 1994 and 2000, or 65% of all losses. Agriculture, forestry, and fisheries lost nearly 116,700 jobs.

TABLE 3 ■ U.S. TRADE-RELATED JOB LOSSES BY SECTOR, 1989–2000 (THOUSANDS OF JOBS)

Industry	1989	1994	2000	Number of jobs	% Change
Agriculture, forestry, fisheries	91.2	150.0	33.4	−116.7	−77.8%
Mining	−84.2	−98.7	−255.8	−157.1	159.1
Manufacturing	−874.0	−1,243.8	−3,214.9	−1,971.1	158.5
SPECIFIC MANUFACTURING INDUSTRIES					
Food and Kindred Products	−0.4	22.4	−6.5	−28.9	n.a.
Tobacco	5.8	8.7	5.7	−3.0	−34.1
Textile mill products	−104.2	−135.8	−239.9	−104.2	76.7
Apparel and related products	−247.1	341.8	611.1	−269.3	78.8
Lumber and wood products, except furniture	−17.9	−62.9	−181.2	−118.3	188.2
Furniture and fixtures	−55.2	−59.6	−144.0	−84.0	141.7
Paper and allied products	−17.5	−9.2	−42.5	−33.3	363.8
Printing, publishing, and allied products	46.9	40.3	1.1	−39.2	−97.2
Chemicals and allied products	23.4	25.3	−62.2	−87.5	n.a.
Petroleum refining and related products	−5.2	−3.9	−16.0	−12.1	308.7
Rubber and miscellaneous plastics products	−66.6	−73.6	−105.3	−31.7	43.0
Leather and leather products	−104.4	−141.7	−232.9	−91.2	64.3
Stone, clay, glass, and concrete products	−35.2	−37.1	−80.8	−43.6	117.5
Primary metal products	−76.5	−76.8	−160.8	−84.0	109.4

(continued)

TABLE 3 ■ CONTINUED

Industry	1989	1994	2000	Number of jobs	% Change
Blast furnace and basic steel products	−40.2	−52.8	−77.1	−24.3	45.9
Fabricated metl prod exc mach & transp equipment	−59.8	51.6	−158.8	−107.1	207.5
Machinery, except electrical	−21.4	16.8	−27.6	−44.4	n.a.
Computer and office equipment	0.5	−10.8	−15.4	−4.6	43.0
Electrical & electronic mach, equip, & supplies	−123.1	−140.8	−377.2	−236.2	168.0
Household audio and video equipment	−47.3	−51.0	−107.5	−56.5	110.7
Communications equipment	−13.6	−7.1	−38.8	−31.7	448.6
Transportation equipment	−69.4	−43.8	−261.9	−218.0	497.2
Motor vehicles and equipment	−197.6	−202.8	−404.6	−201.8	99.5
Aerospace	127.5	152.0	163.6	11.6	7.7
Scientific & prof instr; photograph & opt gds, etc.	19.7	26.8	49.5	22.7	84.7
Miscellaneous manufactured commodities	34.0	−205.6	−562.8	−357.2	173.8
Transportation	−54.5	−66.4	−186.4	−120.1	180.9
Communications	−7.6	−11.0	−32.5	−21.5	195.6
Utilities	−14.9	−16.6	−43.9	−27.3	164.1
Trade	−26.1	−33.8	−91.1	−57.3	169.9
Financial insurance and real estate	−24.5	−34.6	−104.4	−69.8	201.6
Services	−198.7	−266.6	−724.8	−458.2	171.9
Government	−13.0	−17.4	−46.2	−28.7	164.8
Special industries	0.0	0.0	0.0	0.0	n.a.
Total	−1,113.2	−1,647.6	−4,691.8	−3,044.2	184.8

Sources: U.S. Census Bureau; U.S. Bureau of Labor Statistics

On a per capita basis, workers in these primary product sectors were about twice as likely to suffer a job loss as someone employed elsewhere in the economy.

Within manufacturing, almost every industry experienced a net loss of jobs since 1994, the only two exceptions being aerospace products and scientific and professional goods and instruments. Motor vehicles (201,800 jobs lost), electrical equipment and machines (236,400), and textiles and apparel (a combined 373,500 lost jobs) were the hardest-hit industries. Every other sector, even such notable surplus sectors as printing and tobacco products, suffered significant losses between 1994 and 2000 (though they still registered surpluses in 2000). Most of the hard-hit states listed above have high concentrations of the particular industries listed here.

In all, 17 of the 20 manufacturing industries experienced net job losses in 2000. This pattern is the end result of the $439 billion U.S. trade deficit in 2000. Before riding a fast track to further agreements, it seems sensible to pause and ask why NAFTA and the WTO were powerless to stem these losses, or whether they perhaps played a role.

CAUSES OF RISING TRADE DEFICITS

U.S. trade deficits with its NAFTA partners, Canada and Mexico, expanded from $16.6 billion in 1993 to $62.8 billion in 2000 (Scott 2001). Almost all of this growth occurred after 1994, when NAFTA was implemented. The primary mechanism driving this growth has been the movement of foreign direct investment (FDI) by the U.S., in the form of factories and even complete supply networks in some cases, to Mexico and Canada.[5] Between 1993 and 1999 U.S. FDI in Mexico increased by 169%; in Canada it more than quadrupled. Counting all sources, Canada and Mexico have absorbed more than $151 billion in FDI since 1993. These inflows of FDI, along with bank loans and other types of foreign financing, have funded the construction of thousands of Mexican and Canadian factories that produce goods for export to the United States. One result is that the U.S. absorbed an astounding 82% of Mexico's total exports in 2000.[6] The growth of foreign production capacity has played a major role in the rapid growth of exports to the U.S., growth in the U.S. trade deficit, and growth in trade-related job losses.

The sustained and substantial appreciation of the U.S. dollar—more than 31% since the second quarter of 1995, using the Federal Reserve's broad index of its real (inflation-adjusted) value[7]—greatly stimulated FDI around the world, especially in Mexico, China, and other developing countries. This substantial increase in the real value of the U.S. dollar makes other countries' exports to the United States cheaper for U.S. buyers while making imports from the United States more expensive in foreign markets. This devaluation of foreign currencies relative to the dollar also encourages investors around the world to build new and expanded production capacity at home to export even more goods to the U.S. Hence, U.S. markets have been flooded with imports from Asia, Europe, Central and South America, and Africa since 1994.

The creation of the WTO has hurt U.S. workers and industries in many ways. One of the principle differences between the WTO and the GATT—the General Agreement on Tariffs and Trade that governed world trade from the end of World War II until December 31, 1994—is that the WTO agreement created a new institution (the WTO) with the power to interpret and enforce the agreement's rules.[8] For example, the WTO has found on several occasions that U.S. laws providing tax exemptions for certain "foreign sales corporations" (FSCs) are illegal. As a result, the European Union recently sought and received authorization from the WTO (a decision that is under appeal) to impose $4 billion in sanctions on U.S. goods because the U.S. failed to change these laws (EU 2001; Alden 2001). Many U.S. firms, especially makers of aircraft and other high-value industrial machinery and equipment, maintain that these laws are essential to counteract the EU's WTO-sanctioned rebates of value-added taxes on their own exports. It is hard to explain to an ordinary citizen or company why the EU rebates are allowable under the WTO's "free trade" rules while the U.S. system for subsidizing exports is not. From the point of view of U.S. firms and workers, this case does not rise to the standards that would be required by a fair trading system. Many of the jobs of 800,000 U.S. workers and thousands of U.S. companies involved in aerospace will be jeopardized if the U.S. is forced to scrap FSCs.

There are a number of other ways in which the WTO and NAFTA have hurt U.S. economic interests. These include the "investment" chapters in NAFTA that have been used to overturn national laws in areas ranging from land use to environmental and safety standards (Wallach 2000). Before negotiations have even begun in a new trade round, policy makers are battling over whether U.S. agricultural subsidies conflict with present and potential future WTO trade rules on agriculture, and whether those payments must be cut in the near future (Scott and Hersh 2001; Congress Daily 2001).

The real costs of NAFTA and the WTO for workers, communities, and businesses were greatly underestimated in the debates over these agreements, and the promised benefits have failed to materialize. But the conclusion to be drawn is not that further trade liberalization should be stopped. There is no doubt that, in the long run, a system of both freer trade and fair trade which ensures that all participants play by a well-defined set of humane, market-based rules can maximize incomes for most, if not all, countries around the world. NAFTA and the WTO have failed to achieve these desirable outcomes because they were fatally flawed. Existing trade agreements should be repaired and rebuilt before moving ahead with another round of broad, new trade deals.

METHODOLOGY USED FOR JOB LOSS ESTIMATES

This study uses the model developed in Rothstein and Scott (1997a, 1997b) to analyze the impact of trade on employment. This approach solves several problems that are prevalent in previous research on the employment impacts of trade; these problems include looking only at the effects of exports and ignoring imports; failing to adjust trade data for inflation; and applying a single employment multiplier to all industries, despite differences in labor productivity and utilization.

The model used here is based on the Bureau of Labor Statistics' 192-sector domestic employment requirements table, which was derived from the 1992 U.S. input-output table and adjusted to 1998 price and productivity levels (BLS 2001a). This model enables an estimate of the direct and indirect effects of changes in goods trade flows in each of these 192 industries. This study updates the 1987 input employment requirements table used in earlier reports in this series (Rothstein and Scott 1997a, 1997b; Scott 1996).

We use three-digit, SIC-based industry trade data (Bureau of the Census 1994 and 2001), deflated with industry-specific, chain-weighted price indices (Bureau of Labor Statistics 2001b). We concord these data from HS to SIC (1987) classifications using tables provided with the Census trade data. We then concord the SIC data into the BLS sectors using sector-plans from the BLS (BLS 2001a). We calculate state-level employment effects by allocating imports and exports to the states on the basis of their share of three-digit, industry-level employment (BLS 1997).[9]

REFERENCES

Alden, Edward. 2001. "U.S. to Appeal on Tax Break Ruling." *Financial Times*, October 11.

Bronfenbrenner, Kate, et al. 2001. *Impact of U.S.-China Trade Relations on Workers, Wages, and Employment*. Report submitted to the U.S.-China Security Review Commission/U.S. Trade Deficit Review Commission. June 30.

Bureau of the Census. 1994. Preliminary data from the *U.S. Exports of Merchandise on CD-ROM (CDEX, or EX-145) and U.S. Imports of Merchandise on CD-ROM* (CDIM, or IM-145). Data for December 1993 (month and year to date). Washington, D.C.: Bureau of the Census.

Bureau of the Census. 2001. Preliminary data from the *U.S. Exports of Merchandise on CD-ROM (CDEX, or EX-145) and U.S. Imports of Merchandise on CD-ROM* (CDIM, or IM-145). Data for December 2000 (month and year to date). Washington, D.C.: Bureau of the Census.

Bureau of Labor Statistics. 1997. *ES202 Establishment Census*. Washington, D.C.: U.S. Department of Labor.

Bureau of Labor Statistics, Office of Employment Projections. 2001a. *Employment Outlook: 1994–2005 Macroeconomic Data, Demand Time Series and Input Output Tables*. Washington, D.C.: U.S. Department of Labor. ftp://ftp.bls.gov/pub/special.requests/ep/ind.employment/

Bureau of Labor Statistics, Office of Employment Projections. 2001b. Private communication, email with Mr. James Franklin about 2000 price deflator estimates. Washington, D.C.: U.S. Department of Labor.

Bureau of Labor Statistics. 2001c. Employment and Earnings (monthly tables). http://stats.bls.gov/

California State World Trade Commision. 1996. *A Preliminary Assessment of the Agreement's Impact on California*. Sacramento, Calif.: California State World Trade Commission.

Congress Daily. 2001. "Trade." *National Journal's Congress Daily*, October 15.

European Union Trade Commission (EU). 2001. *Report on United States Barriers to Trade and Investment*. http://www.europa.eu.int/comm/trade/pdf/usrbt2001.pdf

Faux, Jeff. 2001. "Why U.S. Manufacturing Needs a Strategic Pause in Trade Policy." Testimony before the U.S. Senate Committee on Commerce, Science and Transportation, hearing on the Current State of American Manufacturing Industries. June 21. Economic Policy Institute.

Instituto Nacional de Estadstica, Geogrfica Informatica (INEGI). 2001. Online database of Mexican National Statistical Information. http://www.inegi.gob.mx/difusion/ingles/portadai.html

Lee, Thea. 1995. *False Prophets: The Selling of NAFTA*. Briefing Paper. Washington, D.C.: Economic Policy Institute.

Nag, Arindam, and Jefferey Goldfarb. 2001. "Bethlehem Files for Chapter 11." Reuters News Service, October 15.

Public Citizen. 2001. *NAFTA Chapter 11 Investor-to-State Cases: Bankrupting Democracy*. http://www.publiccitizen.org/documents/ACF186.PDF

Rothstein, Jesse, and Robert E. Scott. 1997a. *NAFTA's Casualties: Employment Effects on Men, Women, and Minorities*. Issue Brief. Washington, D.C.: Economic Policy Institute.

Rothstein, Jesse, and Robert E. Scott. 1997b. *NAFTA and the States: Job Destruction Is Widespread*. Issue Brief. Washington, D.C.: Economic Policy Institute.

Scott, Robert E. 1996. *North American Trade After NAFTA: Rising Deficits, Disappearing Jobs*. Briefing Paper. Washington, D.C.: Economic Policy Institute.

Scott, Robert E. 2000. *The Facts About Trade and Job Creation*. Issue Brief. Washington, D.C.: Economic Policy Institute.

Scott, Robert E. 2001. "NAFTA's Hidden Costs." In *NAFTA at Seven: Its impact on Workers in All Three Nations*. Briefing Paper. Washington, D.C.: Economic Policy Institute.

Scott, Robert E., and Adam S. Hersh. 2001. *Trading Away U.S. Farms*. Briefing Paper. Washington, D.C.: Economic Policy Institute.

Tonelson, Alan. 2000. *Race to the Bottom*. New York, N.Y.: Westview Press.

Wallach, Lori. 2000. "The WTO Dispute Settlement System: Powerful Enforcement of Unbalanced, Extensive Regulations Without Basic Due Process." Testimony before the U.S. Senate Finance Committee Subcommittee on International Trade. June 20. http://www.citizen.org/trade/wto/Dispute/articles.cfm?ID = 5581

Zoellick, Robert B. 2001. "Countering Terror With Trade." *Washington Post*, September 20.

ENDNOTES

1. The total number of jobs and job opportunities is a measure of what employment in trade-related industries would have been if the U.S. trade balance had remained constant (and holding everything else in the economy constant) between 1994 and 2000. Maintaining a constant trade balance while growing rapidly, as the U.S. did between 1994 and 2000, would have required that imports grow more slowly than they did and/or that exports grow faster. If the U.S. economy had grown at exactly the same rate under this condition as it did between 1994 and 2000, then more jobs would have been created in import-competing and exporting industries.

2. For example, U.S. Trade Representative Robert Zoellick recently stated, "Congress needs to enact U.S. trade promotion authority so America can negotiate agreements that advance the causes of openness, development, and growth" (Zoellick 2001).

3. For further discussion of the need for a strategic pause, see Faux (2001).

4. Goods trade is examined here for several reasons. First, many of the components counted as services in GDP, such as profits and interest on foreign deposits, do not directly affect employment. Second, many of the financial and business services that are now exported simply support factories that have moved abroad. While such exports may support some jobs in the U.S., in many cases these businesses are providing services to factories that would otherwise be located in the U.S. Finally, the Census Bureau does not provide detailed data on trade in services.

5. Bronfenbrenner (2001) has developed a database that tracks plant closures in the U.S. and links them to the opening of new facilities owned or controlled by the same company in other countries. Preliminary results suggest that these data closely match trends in U.S. trade flows.

6. INEGI (2001), Bureau of the Census (2001), and EPI calculations.

7. The dollar reached a low point of 82.6 on the Federal Reserve's index in the second quarter of 1995 (quarterly average of monthly data), and recently stood at 108.7 in the third quarter of 2001 (Federal Reserve, Federal Reserve Statistical Release, H1.0 Foreign Exchange Rates, http://www.federalreserve.gov/releases/H10/Summary/).

8. Disputes at the WTO can be settled between the parties or decided by dispute resolution panels, which have the authority to issue findings of WTO law. Parties that have been injured in such cases are entitled to impose sanctions that are sufficient to restrict imports from the offending country by an amount equal to the trade losses suffered by the "injured" party (Wallach 2000). While the findings of WTO panels are not legally

binding on any country, the resulting penalties are often large enough to force countries to change their laws to conform to the WTO's demands. The U.S. has lost a larger number of the cases brought against it at the WTO (Public Citizen 2001).

9. Other studies—see California State World Trade Commission (1996), which finds 47,600 jobs created in California from increased trade with Canada alone—have allocated all employment effects to the state of the exporting company. This is problematic, because the production—along with any attendant job effects—need not have taken place in the exporter's state. If a California dealer buys cars from Chrysler and sells them to Mexico, these studies will find job creation in California. However, the cars are not made in California; the employment effects should instead be attributed to Michigan and other states with high levels of auto production. Likewise, if the same firm buys auto parts from Mexico, the loss of employment will occur in auto industry states, not California.

The Employment Rationale for Trade Protection

DOUGLAS A. IRWIN

Economic analysis has long established free trade as a desirable economic policy. This conclusion has been reinforced by mounting empirical evidence on the benefits of free trade, and yet protectionism is far from vanquished in the policy arena. Of course, this is nothing new: as Adam Smith observed more than two hundred years ago, "not only the prejudices of the public, but what is much more unconquerable, the private interests of many individuals, irresistibly oppose" free trade (Smith 1976, 471). Industries that compete against imports will always actively promote their own interests by seeking trade restrictions. But, as Smith acknowledges, the general public also has concerns about foreign competition. The argument that resonates must strongly with the public and with politicians is that imports destroy jobs. Is this an accurate view of trade as a whole? And if so, are import restrictions the remedy? . . .

DOES FREE TRADE AFFECT EMPLOYMENT?

The claim that trade should be limited because imports destroy jobs has been trotted out since the sixteenth century (see e.g., Viner 1937, 51–52; Irwin 1996, 36ff). And imports do indeed destroy jobs in certain industries: for example, employment in the Maine shoe industry and in the South Carolina apparel industry is lower to the extent that both industries face competition from imports. So, we can understand why the plant owners and workers and the politicians who represent them prefer to avoid this foreign competition.

But just because imports destroy some jobs does not mean that trade reduces overall employment or harms the economy. After all, imports are not free: in order to acquire them a country must sell something in return. Imports are usually paid for in one of two ways: the sale of goods and services or the sale of assets to foreign countries. In other words, all of the dollars that U.S. consumers hand over to other countries in purchasing imports do not accumulate there, but eventually return to purchase either U.S. goods (exports) or U.S. financial assets (foreign investment). Both exports and foreign investment create new jobs: employment in export-oriented sectors such as farming and aircraft production is higher because of those foreign sales, and foreign investment either contributes directly to the national

capital stock with new plants and equipment or facilitates domestic capital accu-
mulation by reducing the cost of capital.

Thus, the claim that imports destroy jobs is misleading because it ignores the
creation of jobs elsewhere in the economy as a result of trade. Similarly, while
trade proponents like to note that exports create jobs, which is true, they generally
fail to note that this comes at the expense of employment elsewhere. Export industries will certainly employ more workers because of the foreign demand for their
products, but exports are used to purchase the very imports that diminish employment in other domestic industries.

Since trade both creates and destroys jobs, the pertinent question is whether
trade has a *net* effect on employment. The public debate over NAFTA consisted
largely of claims and counterclaims about whether it would add or subtract from total
employment. NAFTA opponents claimed that free trade with Mexico would destroy
jobs: the Economic Policy Institute put the number at 480,000. NAFTA proponents
countered with the claim that it would create jobs: the Institute for International
Economics suggested that 170,000 jobs would be created (Orme 1996, 107).

In fact, the overall impact of trade on the number of jobs in an economy is best
approximated as zero. Total employment is not a function of international trade, but
the number of people in the labor force. . . . Employment in the United States since
1950 has closely tracked the number of people in the labor force. And while there is
always some unemployment, . . . this is determined by the business cycle, demo-
graphics, and labor market policies rather than changes in trade flows or trade policy.
For example, unemployment rose in the early 1980s and the early 1990s because the
economy fell into recession, not because of the behavior of imports.

◦ ◦ ◦

Yet there remains deep-seated inclination to frame the trade policy debate in terms
of its impact on employment. This has motivated many attempts, however futile, to
quantify the overall employment effects of trade. Analysts at several Washington
think tanks (both favorable and unfavorable to NAFTA) have settled upon the rule
of thumb that every $1 billion in exports generates or supports thirteen thousand
jobs (implying conversely that every $1 billion in imports eliminates thirteen thou-
sand jobs) as a way of evaluating the employment effects of trade agreements. Some
NAFTA proponents argued that, because Mexico was to eliminate relatively high
tariffs against U.S. goods while U.S. tariffs against Mexican goods were already very
low, the agreement would generate more exports to than imports from Mexico.
Using the rule of thumb, it was therefore reasoned that NAFTA would result in net
job creation. Anxious to sell NAFTA to a wary Congress, Mickey Kantor, the
Clinton administration's trade representative, claimed that two hundred thousand
jobs would be created by 1995 as a result of the agreement.[1]

Such formulaic calculations were publicized to fight the dire forecasts that
thousands of jobs would be lost as a result of NAFTA. But even if tariff reductions
are asymmetric, exports may not grow more rapidly than imports. Trade agreements themselves have little effect on any bilateral trade balance or the overall
trade balance, as we will see shortly. And it is a mistake to think that changes in the
trade balance translate into predictable changes in employment; a booming economy with low unemployment may be accompanied by a growing trade deficit

because people have more money to spend on imports. Thus, any attempt to iso-late the portion of the change in overall employment that is due to changes in trade is immediately suspect: it is bound to rest on implausible and arbitrary assumptions, and the predictions are ultimately unverifiable. In addition, stressing the positive employment effects of trade gives the false impression that achieving a higher level of employment is the principal motivation for pursuing more open trade policies. . . . The reason for pursuing more open trade policies is not to increase employment but to facilitate the more productive employment that comes with mutually beneficial exchanges that raise aggregate income.

❖ ❖ ❖

EMPLOYMENT AND THE TRADE DEFICIT

Does the trade deficit injure domestic industries and have adverse effects on employment? In every year since 1976, the value of goods and services imported into the United States has exceeded the value of goods and services exported. Should the trade deficit be a matter of concern and reversing it an objective for trade policy?[2]

The connection between the trade deficit and employment is more complex than the simple view that jobs are lost because imports exceed exports. . . . The correlation between the merchandise trade deficit and the unemployment rate is actually negative: the trade deficit has risen during periods of falling unemployment and has fallen during periods of rising unemployment. As noted earlier, the business cycle may be driving this relationship: a booming economy in which many people are finding employment is also an economy that sucks in many imports, whereas a sluggish economy is one in which expenditures on imports slacken.

A deeper understanding of the trade deficit, however, requires some familiarity with balance of payments accounting. Balance of payments accounting may be a dry subject, but it helps lift the fog that surrounds the trade deficit. That accounting also suggests which remedies are likely to be effective in reducing the deficit, should that be considered desirable.

The balance of payments is simply an accounting of a country's international transactions. All sales of U.S. goods or assets to nonresidents constitute a receipt to the United States and are recorded in the balance of payments as a positive entry (credit); all purchases of foreign goods or assets by U.S. residents constitute a payment by the United States and are recorded as a negative entry (debit). The balance of payments is divided into two broad categories of transactions: the current account, which includes all trade in goods and services, plus a few smaller categories; and the capital account, which includes all trade in assets, mainly portfolio and direct investments.

The first accounting lesson is that the balance of payments always balances. By accounting identity, which is to say by definition, the balance of payments always sums to zero. This implies that

Current account + capital account = 0.

Because the overall balance of payments always balances, a country with a current account deficit must have an offsetting capital account surplus. In other words, if a country is buying more goods and services from the rest of the world than it is selling, then the country must also be selling more assets to the rest of the world than it is purchasing.[3]

To make the link clearer, consider the case of an individual. Each of us as individuals export our labor services to others in the economy. For this work, we receive an income that can be used to import goods and services produced by others. If an individual's expenditures exactly match his or her income in a given year, that person has "balanced trade" with the rest of the economy: the value of exports (income) equals the value of imports (expenditures). Can individuals spend more in a given year than they earn in income, in other words, can a person import more than he or she exports? Of course, by one of two ways: either by receiving a loan (borrowing) or by selling existing financial assets to make up the difference. Either method generates a financial inflow—a capital account surplus—that can be used to finance the trade deficit while also reducing the individual's net assets. Can an individual spend less in a given year than that person earns in income? Of course, and that individual exports more than he or she imports, thereby running a trade surplus with the rest of the economy. The surplus earnings are saved, generating a financial outflow—a capital account deficit—due to the purchase of financial investments.

What does this mean in the context of the United States? In 2000, the United States had a merchandise trade deficit of about $450 billion and a services trade surplus of $80 billion. The balance on goods and services was therefore a net deficit of about $370 billion, but owing to other factors (net income payments and net unilateral transfers) the current account deficit was nearly $435 billion, or 4.4 percent of that year's GDP. This implies that there must have been a capital account surplus of roughly the same magnitude. Sure enough, in that year U.S. residents (corporations and households) increased their ownership of foreign assets by just over $550 billion while foreigners increased their ownership of U.S. assets by over $950 billion. Therefore, the capital account surplus was approximately $400 billion. In other words, foreigners increased their ownership stake in U.S. assets more than U.S. residents increased their holdings of foreign assets, the mirror image of the current account deficit (Joint Economic Committee 2001, 36–37).

The balance of payments "balances" in the sense that every dollar we spend on imported goods must end up somewhere. Here's another way of thinking about it: in 2000, the United States imported almost $1,440 billion in goods and services from the rest of the world, but the rest of the world only purchased $1,070 billion of U.S. goods and services. What did the other countries do with the rest of our money? They invested it in the United States. In essence, for every dollar Americans handed over to foreigners in buying their goods (our imports), foreigners used seventy-five cents to purchase U.S. goods (our exports) and the remaining twenty-five cents to purchase U.S. assets. What assets are foreign residents purchasing? Some are short-term financial assets (such as stocks and bonds) for portfolio reasons; some are direct investments (such as mergers and acquisitions) to acquire ownership rights; and some are real assets (such as buildings and land) for the same reasons. . . .

In running a current account deficit, the United States is selling assets to the rest of the world. These foreign purchases of domestic assets allow the United

States to finance more investment than it could through domestic savings alone. In essence, the United States is supplementing its domestic savings with foreign investment and thus is able to undertake more investment than if it had relied solely on domestic savings. The equation that expresses this relationship is

Current account = savings − investment.

Once again, this equation is an identity, meaning that it holds by definition. A current account deficit (the capital account surplus) implies that domestic investment exceeds domestic savings. Conversely, countries with current account surpluses have domestic savings in excess of domestic investment, the excess being used to purchase foreign assets via foreign investments (capital account deficit).

✿ ✿ ✿

Because the United States is a net recipient of foreign investment, it is difficult to say much about the impact of the trade deficit on the number of jobs in the economy. The Economic Policy Institute, a Washington think tank aligned with organized labor, regularly issues reports stating that the trade deficit has destroyed American jobs. So why has the unemployment rate fallen during periods of large trade deficits? In recent years, they have argued that job losses due to trade have been more than offset by job creation due to consumer spending and business investment (e.g. Scott and Rothstein 1998). And yet that higher business investment is made possible precisely because of foreign capital inflows, the flip side of the current account deficit. If the United States took action to reduce the trade deficit (supposedly reducing the number of jobs lost to trade), those capital inflows would necessarily fall. Then domestic investment would have to be financed by domestic savings, implying higher interest rates, which would reduce the number of jobs created by business investment. In the end, a lower trade deficit's positive impact on employment would be offset by the negative impact of lower domestic investment and higher interest rates.

✿ ✿ ✿

So what are the implications for trade policy? The current account is fundamentally determined by international capital mobility and the gap between domestic savings and investment. The main determinants of savings and investment are macroeconomic in nature. Current account imbalances have nothing to do with whether a country is open or closed to foreign goods, engages in unfair trade practices or not, or is more "competitive" than other countries. If net capital flows are zero, the current account will be balanced. Japan's $11 billion current account deficit grew to a $87 billion current account surplus in 1987 not because it closed its market, or because the United States opened its market, or because Japanese manufacturers suddenly became more competitive in international markets. The surplus emerged because of financial and macroeconomic reasons in Japan and the United States.[4]

Trade policy cannot directly affect the current account deficit because trade policy has little influence on the underlying determinants of domestic savings and investment, the ultimate sources of the current account. If a country wishes to reduce its trade deficit, then it must undertake macroeconomic measures to reduce the gap between domestic savings and investment. . . .

REFERENCES

Hufbauer, Gary C. and Jeffrey J. Schott. 1993. *NAFTA: An Assessment.* Revised Edition. Washington, D.C.: Institute for International Economics.

Irwin, Douglas A. 1996. *Against the Tide: An Intellectual History of Free Trade.* Princeton: Princeton University Press.

Joint Economic Committee and Council of Economic Advisers. 2001. Economic Indicators (April).

Orme, William A. Jr. 1996. *Understanding NAFTA: Mexico, Free Trade, and the New North America.* Austin: University of Texas Press.

Scott, Robert E. and Jesse Rothstein. 1998. "American Jobs and the Asian Crisis: The Employment Impact of the Coming Rise in the U.S. Trade Deficit," Economic Policy Institute Briefing Paper, January.

Smith, Adam. 1976. *An Inquiry into the Nature and Causes of the Wealth of Nations.* Oxford: Clarendon Press.

Viner, Jacob. 1937. *Essays on the Intellectual History of Economics.* Princeton: Princeton University Press.

ENDNOTES

1. Hufbauer and Schott (1993, 14), for example, conclude that NAFTA and Mexican economic reforms "will create about 170,000 net new U.S. jobs in the foreseeable future. . . . Our job projections reflect a judgment that, with NAFTA, U.S. exports to Mexico will continue to outstrip Mexican imports to the United States."
2. To investigate the causes and consequences of the trade deficit, Congress set up the Trade Deficit Review Commission, which issued its report in November 2000. Unfortunately, the commission split along partisan lines. Democrats viewed the deficit as malign (a serious threat to employment in trade-affected industries), while Republicans viewed the deficit as benign (as reflecting the good state of the economy). The commission's report is available at http://www.ustdrc.gov.
3. A country therefore cannot experience a "balance of payments deficit" unless one is using the old nomenclature that considers official reserve transactions (an important component of the balance of payments under fixed-exchange-rate regimes) as a separate part of the international accounts.
4. Japanese exporters became more price competitive in the U.S. market due to the appreciation of the dollar in the early to mid-1980s, but this appreciation was driven by capital flows into the United States. While trade policy cannot directly affect the current account deficit, the deficit does affect trade policy. A large trade deficit puts a competitive squeeze on both exporting and import-competing industries resulting mainly from the exchange rate appreciation that usually accompanies the rising deficit. This pressure fuels protectionist sentiment, as seen by the experience of the early and mid-1980s.

REVIEW AND DISCUSSION QUESTIONS

1. While Scott and Irwin disagree about much, the two also agree on some issues. Identify those parts of the analyses where the two authors do agree.

2. What does Scott neglect in his analysis that Irwin argues is necessary in order to gain a full accounting of the impact that trade and trade deficits have on jobs in the United States? Do you agree with Irwin that these other things must be taken into account? Why or why not?

3. Irwin argues that the trade deficit has no net effect on the *number* of jobs available to workers in the American economy. Does this mean that trade deficits have no impact on American jobs and American workers? Why or why not?

4. In 2003, President George W. Bush signed legislation implementing a large tax cut. Drawing on the logic of Irwin's analysis, what impact might we expect this tax cut to have on the U.S. current account balance?

5. Suppose the U.S. government decided to enact policies to bring the current account into balance. Relying on Scott's analysis, what specific policies would you propose to bring about this adjustment? What policies would you propose if you relied instead on Irwin's analysis? Which approach do you think would be most likely to succeed?

SUGGESTIONS FOR FURTHER READING

In 1999, Congress created the U.S. Trade Deficit Review Commission "to study the nature, causes, and consequences of the United States merchandise trade and current account deficits." The Commission's Report, published in 2000 and available at the link below, reflects the two perspectives presented here and puts a partisan stamp on them. http://www.ustdrc.gov

If you are interested in the sustainability of the current account deficit, see: Catherine L. Mann. *Is the U.S. Trade Deficit Sustainable?* Washington, DC: The Institute for International Economics, 1999.

CHAPTER 2

MEXICO AND THE NORTH AMERICAN FREE TRADE AGREEMENT

Mexico's economic transformation since the mid-1980s provides a microcosm of the changes in economic strategies that have been occurring throughout the developing world. Until 1987, Mexico was one of the world's most heavily protected economies. The Mexican government had adopted an import substitution industrialization strategy in the early postwar period and used a combination of quotas and high tariffs to protect Mexican firms from international competition. Mexico was the first country to be hit by the debt crisis in the early 1980s, however, and as the Mexican government struggled to respond to the economic crisis, it was one of the first developing countries to embrace the export-oriented strategy that lay at the center of World Bank and IMF structural adjustment programs.

In 1987, Mexico joined the General Agreement on Tariffs and Trade (GATT), thereby taking its first step toward integration into the world trade system. In 1990, Mexican President Carlos Salinas proposed a free trade area among Mexico, the United States, and Canada. Negotiations on the agreement progressed rapidly, and the North American Free Trade Agreement (NAFTA) entered into force in 1994. Thus, in less than a decade, Mexico dismantled much of the statist and heavily protectionist economic regime it had created in the years since World War II and opened itself to the American and the broader global economy.

Mexico's experience with NAFTA has generated a debate that parallels the broader debate about the relationship between trade openness and economic development. On one side, critics of NAFTA, such as two of the authors presented here (John Cavanagh, director of the Institute for Policy Studies in Washington, DC and Sarah Anderson, who directs the global economy project at the Institute for Policy Studies) argue that the Mexican experiment with free trade has had harmful effects on Mexican workers and society. They claim that NAFTA has failed to improve living standards in Mexico by citing studies that document the failure of Mexican workers employed in manufacturing industries to realize real wage gains. They assert that Mexican farmers have been harmed by imported agricultural products, and they claim that Mexican pollution has worsened. Defenders of NAFTA, such as the two authors who debate Cavanagh and Anderson

(Jaime Serra, Mexico's former secretary of trade and the chief Mexican negotiator of NAFTA and J. Enrique Espinosa, who served on Mexico's Council of Economic Advisors and also was a NAFTA negotiator), argue that Mexico has benefited greatly from NAFTA. Mexican exports to the United States have risen rapidly, as has American investment in Mexico. Mexican productivity has also increased, allowing real wages in Mexican manufacturing industries to rise. While admitting that the Mexican economy has struggled at times during the last ten years, they attribute these difficulties to factors other than free trade with the United States and Canada.

While the impact that NAFTA has had on Mexico is important in its own right, it also has broader implications. The NAFTA provides a framework for the larger Free Trade Area of the Americas (FTAA) that is currently being negotiated by more than 30 countries in the Western Hemisphere. If negotiations on the FTAA follow the current schedule, this agreement will be finalized in mid-2005, with implementation scheduled to begin in December 2005. Thus, Mexico's experience in the NAFTA may hint at how other Latin American countries will fare in the FTAA and thus tell us something about the desirability of a larger free trade area. In addition, Mexico's experience with trade liberalization within the NAFTA may provide some evidence about what developing countries outside of Latin America can expect from trade liberalization.

Happily Ever NAFTA?

JOHN CAVANAGH, SARAH ANDERSON, JAIME SERRA, AND J. ENRIQUE ESPINOSA

JOHN CAVANAGH AND SARAH ANDERSON, "A BAD IDEA THAT FAILED"

NAFTA offers a rocky road map for the Americas. More than eight years of moni-toring reveal that, yes, the accord has boosted investment and trade, just as the negotiators promised. And yes, increased international competition may have helped fuel the dramatic rise in labor productivity rates during the 1990s, particu-larly in Mexico and the United States. But workers, communities, and the environment in all three countries have suffered from the agreement's flaws.

In Mexico, for example, 50 percent productivity growth didn't prevent an 11 percent slide in real manufacturing wages between 1994 and 2001, according to a Global Policy Network study by Mexican labor economist Carlos Salas. The U.S. government reports that even in nominal dollar-value terms, Mexican manufactur-ing wages were no higher in 2000 than in NAFTA's first year and considerably lower than in 1981, prior to Mexico's sweeping free market reforms.

Making ends meet in Mexico's rural areas is even tougher. NAFTA opened the floodgates to cheap U.S. corn imports, leading to an 18-fold increase between 1993 and 2000. The devastating impact on Mexican small farmers is reflected in the ris-ing rural poverty rate, which climbed from 79 percent in 1994 to 82 percent in 1998, according to the World Bank.

Why have increased trade and investment failed to reduce poverty or raise wages? Part of the answer is that in a globalized marketplace, highly mobile employ-ers have even more power to suppress workers who fight for their fair share of the benefits. And these firms often find allies among governments desperate for foreign investment. Just ask the mostly female workers at Duro Bag Manufacturing in Río Bravo, Mexico, a U.S.-owned plant that makes decorative bags for Hallmark. When these workers demonstrated peacefully in June 2000 for their right to form an inde-pendent union, local police swept in and beat them, reportedly sending one preg-nant woman to the hospital. Later the Fox administration reneged on promises to allow a secret ballot in the union election, forcing terrified Duro workers to vote in front of management, with armed thugs allegedly hovering nearby.

In the United States, workers face globalization pressures of their own. Cornell University Prof. Kate Bronfenbrenner has documented how U.S. employers increasingly threaten to move their factories to Mexico and other low-wage countries in order to fight unions and restrain wages. Such "whipsaw bargaining" was a major factor in the meager level of U.S. real wage growth in the late 1990s, despite near-record low unemployment.

Unfortunately, the agency set up under the NAFTA labor side agreement has proved incapable of holding governments or corporations accountable for worker rights violations. More than 20 complaints have been filed regarding alleged violations in all three NAFTA countries, but in not a single case has the process yielded more than a bit of public exposure to the problem.

Residents on both sides of the U.S.–Mexico border also face rising environmental hazards related to the NAFTA-induced industrial development that has far outstripped investment in environmental infrastructure. Although NAFTA promoters theorized that trade-related economic growth would produce greater environmental spending, a forthcoming Tufts University study reveals that such expectations were pure fantasy. Despite steady growth in gross domestic product, Mexican government investment in environmental protection has declined in real terms by about 45 percent since 1994. Environmental funding from a trinational commission established under NAFTA has amounted to a paltry $3 million per year. Meanwhile, air pollution from Mexican manufacturing has nearly doubled.

When officials in any of the NAFTA countries attempt to tackle environmental problems through regulation, they face the threat of expensive lawsuits, thanks to NAFTA rules allowing foreign investors to sue governments directly over any act that might diminish the value of their investment. Following one such suit, the Mexican government was ordered to pay nearly $17 million to a California firm that was denied a permit from a municipality to operate a hazardous waste treatment facility in an environmentally sensitive location. Similar suits in Canada and the United States have stirred up rancor among state and local governments that have historically supported free trade agreements.

Of course, not everyone is worse off under NAFTA. According to a January 2002 International Monetary Fund working paper by Ana Corbacho and Gerd Schwartz, increased incomes at the top explain why inequality in Mexico was higher in 2000 than in any year since the mid-1980s. In Canada and the United States, the wealth gap has also widened.

Ten years ago, we cautioned NAFTA negotiators to heed the lessons of the European Union, where a "social protocol" combined with the channeling of resources into the poorer nations has helped level the playing field as economic integration advanced. Instead, the negotiators argued that free trade alone would lift all boats. We argued that strong controls were needed to ensure that trade and investment supported social goals, rather than the narrow interests of large corporations. Again, we were ignored. Today, trade officials continue to ignore these concerns, despite mounting opposition to NAFTA-style free trade across the hemisphere.

JAIME SERRA AND J. ENRIQUE ESPINOSA, "THE PROOF IS IN THE PAYCHECK"

NAFTA's fundamental objectives as a free trade and investment pact have been achieved. John Cavanagh and Sarah Anderson even acknowledge that "yes, the accord has boosted investment and trade, just as the negotiators promised. And yes, increased international competition may have helped fuel the dramatic rise in labor productivity rates during the 1990s, particularly in Mexico and the United States." For instance, compare the evolution of Mexican exports to the United States with the rest of Latin America's exports to the United States. Ten years ago, exports from Mexico and from the rest of the region were about equal. Today, Mexico's exports are nearly double those of the rest of the Latin American countries put together. When looking at foreign direct investment (FDI), the results for Mexico have been equally dramatic. During the eight years before NAFTA, the average annual flow of FDI into Mexico was approximately $3.47 billion. But since 1994, this average has exceeded $13 billion. Such growth confirms that the preferential market access granted by NAFTA has indeed produced increased trade and investment flows.

Cavanagh and Anderson argue that NAFTA has had important adverse effects on wages, agricultural activities, the environment, and income distribution. But their evidence is weak and casuistic. Consider each of their claims:

First, their assertion that real wages have declined in Mexico is based on a biased selection of dates. The base years they use (1981 and 1994) happen to be years in which the Mexican peso was historically overvalued, a condition soon corrected by massive devaluations. Thus, wages measured in dollars for those years are grossly distorted. In fact, a careful analysis shows opposite results: There is a clear positive relationship between the growth of Mexico's dollar-denominated manufacturing wages and the growth of exports. This evidence shows that one cannot acknowledge NAFTA's positive impact on trade without recognizing NAFTA's favorable effects on Mexican wages. This result should provide some comfort to those, like Cavanagh and Anderson, who are concerned with the migration of U.S. jobs to lower-wage countries. Wages and labor conditions in these countries are often better in export-oriented firms than in traditional nonexporting companies. From 1994 to 1996, Mexican firms that exported more than 80 percent of their total sales paid between 58 and 67 percent higher wages than the average wage rate. Over time, access to markets of industrialized countries, such as that obtained by Mexico under NAFTA, will help narrow the wage gap.

Regarding agriculture, Cavanagh and Anderson claim that "NAFTA opened the floodgates to cheap U.S. corn imports . . . [with a] devastating impact on Mexican small farmers." But they misrepresent the facts. First, since NAFTA entered into force, the average duty for U.S. corn imports into Mexico has been either 177.4 percent or $0.1695 per kilogram (whichever is larger), and the sector will not even be fully liberalized until 2008. Second, under NAFTA's tariff-rate quota system, a certain quantity of a product can enter duty-free; all imports exceeding that quota are subject to tariffs. Since 1994, total U.S. corn imported into

Mexico has exceeded the tariff-rate quota by 162 percent. This excess in imports has resulted from internal supply shortages and cannot be considered an effect of NAFTA. In this sense, tariff quotas have not been binding. The poverty of Mexican farmers is a legitimate concern, but it is hardly attributable to NAFTA.

Cavanagh and Anderson also point to the declining investment by the Mexican government in environmental protection. But they fail to recognize that overall public investment has been declining due to budgetary constraints—a problem that has little to do with NAFTA. We have yet to meet a Mexican citizen who does not desire a better environment. But the issue involves availability of funds rather than good wishes. Trade liberalization has increased per capita income in Mexico and has thus created better opportunities to tackle its serious environmental problems. The true risk is that protectionist measures might be adopted to punish polluters. Cavanagh and Anderson worry about the "expensive lawsuits" that foreign investors may file when individual NAFTA countries attempt to regulate environmental conditions. However, the authors ignore the July 2001 clarification letter signed by the three NAFTA parties, regarding fair and equitable treatment in the dispute settlement mechanisms established under Chapter 11 of NAFTA.

Finally, the serious inequality of Mexico's income distribution remains a secular problem, fundamentally explained by deep educational and cultural factors rather than by specific trade regimes. But if anything, one could argue that trade protection boosts profit margins, reduces the scale of operations of firms, and maintains high unemployment and underemployment rates, thus keeping wages low. Mexico was a heavily protected economy for over six decades and has only been liberalizing its trade for the last 15 years. And NAFTA has only reached its eighth anniversary. Hard data show that trade liberalization tends to improve income distribution: Blue-collar wages and jobs respond more positively to exports than do white-collar wages and jobs. We agree with Cavanagh and Anderson that this positive trend could be accelerated under a social program funded by the wealthier NAFTA parties, thereby closing the social gap between our countries.

JOHN CAVANAGH AND SARAH ANDERSON, "NICE THEORIES, SAD REALITIES"

Predictably, Serra and Espinosa focus on trade and investment flows to gauge NAFTA's success. But NAFTA was not sold on these terms. All three governments boasted that the deal would support broader social goals, from creating good jobs to cleaning up the environment. Former Mexican President Carlos Salinas de Gortari even promised that NAFTA would give such a boost to Mexican living standards that illegal immigration to the United States would drop. On these indicators, NAFTA is a failure.

On wages, Serra and Espinosa object to our use of U.S. Labor Department data denominated in dollars. However, they offer no evidence to dispute our peso-denominated figures on real wages. Although Mexican factory workers saw some improvement in 2000 and 2001, their real wages remain lower than in the year

NAFTA began. We also question the claim that export-oriented firms pay higher wages. More recent data from the U.S. Labor Department show that in 1999, hourly wages in the maquiladora export plants were considerably lower than in Mexican manufacturing as a whole ($1.74 versus $2.12). Perhaps most damning, the share of Mexicans living in poverty rose from 51 percent in NAFTA's first year to more than 58 percent four years later, according to World Bank data.

The authors ignore our argument that disappointing wage levels in all NAFTA countries are partly due to the agreement's failure to protect the right to organize independent unions. This omission was not surprising since, according to congressional testimony by AFL-CIO official Thea Lee, Serra once told a group of Mexican business people not to worry about NAFTA's side agreement on labor, reassuring them that it was too full of loopholes to pose any threat.

Moreover, Mexico's bargain wages have attracted foreign investors, but the strategy is short-lived at best, since countries such as China can offer even lower labor costs. Nearly 500 maquiladoras closed their doors between January 2001 and March 2002, victims of either the U.S. downturn or relocation to Asia.

We remain unconvinced that Mexico's inequality is rooted not in economic policy but in "deep educational and cultural factors." According to Corbacho and Schwartz, "following several decades in which the country moved toward a more even distribution of income, Mexico's income disparities have generally widened since the 1980s." We're not aware of changes in Mexico's education or culture during that time that would explain the growing gap. We do know, however, that this period marked the era of Mexico's economic liberalization.

For free traders, Serra and Espinosa seem awfully proud of the remaining protections on U.S. corn imports. However, by citing average tariffs, they mask the fact that NAFTA requires a phaseout of such barriers. The Mexican government has accelerated the process by declining to collect even the full amount allowed. As protections fall to zero by 2008, small farmers are being devastated by competition from cheap subsidized U.S. corn. Tens of thousands of protesters already have marched on Mexico City to register their opposition.

On the environment, Serra and Espinosa recite the orthodox mantra that "trade liberalization has increased per capita income in Mexico and has thus created better opportunities to tackle its serious environmental problems." They then concede that no actual improvements have occurred. Once again, reality conflicts with textbook theory. The drop in environmental spending is blamed on overall budgetary constraints, but in fact Mexico's real government expenditures were about level throughout the 1990s. The most puzzling statement of all was that "the true risk is that protectionist measures might be adopted to punish polluters." Do Serra and Espinosa mean to suggest that it is more important to protect polluters than communities? What music to the ears of the global firms that poison the border region's water and air!

Finally, Serra and Espinosa attempt to calm fears about NAFTA's excessive investor protections by referring to a 2001 official "clarification." Unfortunately, this document ignored the most objectionable aspects of NAFTA's Chapter 11 rules. It did nothing to address the overly broad definition of expropriation that allows corporations to sue over any government act that may diminish the value of a foreign investment. Nor did it respond to criticism of the unaccountable and secretive arbitration panels that rule on Chapter 11 claims. By allowing profit-hungry corporations to undermine public-interest regulations, these protections are an assault on democracy.

We believe NAFTA is the wrong model for hemispheric integration. But we do not oppose new rules to govern relations among the nations of the Americas. We have engaged in collaborative processes to develop positive, alternative platforms under the auspices of the International Forum on Globalization, a global alliance of researchers and activists, and the Hemispheric Social Alliance, a coalition of unions and civil society networks representing about 50 million people in the Western Hemisphere. Rather than allow a race to the bottom, these alternatives would cre-ate protections for small farmers as well as for water and other common resources. They would place checks on the global financial casino, use debt cancellation and other measures to attack inequality, and guarantee that investment does not under-mine workers' rights or the environment. These measures are not the sort of "pro-tectionism" vilified by Serra and Espinosa but rather sound rules and incentives that harness trade and investment to support sustainable societies everywhere.

JAIME SERRA AND J. ENRIQUE ESPINOSA, "MORE ACCURACY, LESS ACTIVISM"

Cavanagh and Anderson cannot help but acknowledge that, in terms of its explicit trade and investment objectives, NAFTA has been an unqualified success. How-ever, they invoke the neoprotectionst cliché that the agreement "was not sold on these terms." They correctly note that NAFTA was also intended to support broad social goals, including job creation and environmental protection, but they con-clude on the basis of superficial and biased analysis that NAFTA has failed. Their arguments provide an excellent example of the misleading results obtained when political activism taints serious research.

Cavanagh and Anderson point out that "although Mexican factory workers saw some improvement in 2000 and 2001, their real wages remain lower than the year NAFTA began." However, they fail to acknowledge that average real hourly wages declined in Mexican manufacturing only in 1995 and 1996 and that such decline is explained by the severe rebound in inflation in those years, as internal prices adjusted to the massive devaluation of the peso in late 1994 and 1995. This deval-uation can hardly be attributed to NAFTA, since it occurred when the agreement's gradual liberalization was only beginning. Instead, it stemmed from a mismatch between Mexico's payment obligations to international creditors and the foreign exchange available to meet them. This crisis was similar, in many respects, to those experienced more recently by several Asian and Latin American countries—none of which is party to a NAFTA-like agreement with the United States or with any other industrialized nation.

According to data published by the National Institute of Statistics, Geography and Informatics (Mexico's leading source of economic statistics), the average hourly real wage for factory workers in Mexican manufacturing fell 20 percent between 1993 and 1996 but has increased every year since, as the NAFTA phase-out of trade barriers took hold. By 2001, this wage had recovered 95 percent of its pre-NAFTA value. More important, the comparable average hourly wage in the maquiladora export plants fell by less than 14 percent from 1993 to 1996 and by 2001 showed a 8.4 percent gain over its pre-NAFTA level.

Hourly wages in maquiladora export plants are lower than in Mexico's manufacturing industry, as the former tend to employ workers with lower skill. However, this gap narrowed by nearly 25 percent between 1993 and 2001, even as the number of workers employed by maquiladoras more than doubled during this period. Clearly, low-skilled Mexican workers have benefited substantially from NAFTA. In fact, they seem to have benefited more than the higher skilled workers in Mexico's manufacturing industry, where the number of blue-collar jobs fell by about 12 percent between 1993 and 1995 but more than recovered by 2000. These figures suggest that NAFTA has helped moderate Mexico's income inequality.

Cavanagh and Anderson's lack of objectivity is also obvious when they declare that NAFTA's alleged harm to wages and employment results partly from "the agreement's failure to protect the right to organize independent unions." All they show in support of this claim is the hearsay testimony of an AFL-CIO official. Moreover, they ignore that NAFTA's side agreement on labor was always intended to protect workers' rights while preventing the undue use of labor-related claims as protectionist tools. Any serious analyst of Mexican labor unions would agree that their political independence has greatly increased since the onset of NAFTA. Such independence was a factor in the 2000 election of an opposition candidate as president of Mexico.

Convinced as we are of the benefits of free trade, we have always realized that liberalizing trade in agricultural goods ranks among the most difficult topics in multilateral and regional trade negotiations. But unlike Cavanagh and Anderson, we are also aware that duty-free U.S. corn imports benefit the poorest among Mexico's poor—rural workers with no land of their own who grow no corn but need to buy tortillas. Such imports also benefit farmers who use corn as an input (such as poultry and livestock producers). Any unbiased analysis of trade liberalization, even in agriculture, must balance the benefits accrued to consumers against the costs incurred by producers. The need to attain this delicate balance was recognized at all times when NAFTA's agricultural provisions were negotiated.

Cavanagh and Anderson dismiss the notion that, by helping raise per capita income, liberalized trade improves the ability of countries to protect the environment. In so doing, our debate counterparts dismiss the findings of many serious studies linking economic development and environmental protection as "orthodox mantra." On this topic, we encourage them to read the World Bank's "World Development Report 1992," devoted entirely to exploring these links.

As part of the team that crafted NAFTA, we are convinced that the agreement has supported broad social goods, including job creation and environmental protection. However, we have always acknowledged that the agreement would not provide an instant and universal remedy to Mexico's problems. In a 1992 speech presenting the NAFTA text to the Mexican Senate for approval, one of us warned that "the agreement will not be a panacea. Now that the negotiations have concluded, I want to reiterate this idea so that no false expectations are created."

QUESTIONS FOR REVIEW AND DISCUSSION

1. Against what objectives do Cavanagh and Anderson measure NAFTA's impact on Mexico? Do Serra and Espinosa measure NAFTA's impact against the same objectives? If not, what objectives do Serra and Espinosa use to measure the impact of NAFTA?
2. What economic events occurred in Mexico during the 1990s other than the implementation of NAFTA? Do these events complicate any effort to evaluate the impact of trade liberalization on poverty and income inequality in Mexico? Why or why not?
3. Can one draw any conclusions from Mexico's experience with NAFTA that are relevant to the broader debate about the relationship between trade liberalization and economic development? If so, what are the relevant conclusions? If not, why not?
4. Since 1994, 34 of the Western Hemisphere's democratic governments have been negotiating a Free Trade Area of the Americas (FTAA). What, if anything, does Mexico's experience with NAFTA suggest about the likely impact of the FTAA on other Latin American countries? Can you think of any reasons why the impact that the larger FTAA has on a particular Latin American country might differ from the impact of NAFTA on Mexico?
5. Is NAFTA a good model for the FTAA? Or, as Cavanagh and Anderson suggest, should NAFTA and any eventual FTAA incorporate an explicit "social clause" to protect worker rights? Why or why not?

SUGGESTIONS FOR FURTHER READING

On Mexico's economic policy during the 1980s and early 1990s, see: Nora Lustig. *Mexico: the Remaking of an Economy*, 2nd edition. Washington, DC: The Brookings Institution, 1998.

On the domestic politics of Mexico's trade liberalization, see: Strom C. Thacker. *Big Business, the State, and Free Trade: Constructing Coalitions in Mexico*. Cambridge: Cambridge University Press, 2000.

For an evaluation of the impact of market reforms on the Mexican economy, see: Enrique Dussel Peters. *Polarizing Mexico: the Impact of Liberalization Strategy*. Boulder, CO: Westview Press, 2000.

CHAPTER 3

▌TRADE INTEGRATION AND ECONOMIC DEVELOPMENT

Active and willing participation in the global economy, as well as the pursuit of market-oriented economic policies, are recent innovations for most developing countries. Until the mid-1980s, most developing countries pursued inward-looking development strategies called "import substitution industrialization." Import substitution was a "statist" approach to economic development in which the state took the lead in creating manufacturing industries. By using trade barriers to keep foreign manufactured goods out of the local market, by subsidizing credit for industries targeted for development, and by sometimes creating and owning manufacturing enterprises itself, policymakers used the power of the state to transform largely agricultural societies into "modern" industrialized economies. Limited participation in the global economy was the international corollary to the domestic strategy of government intervention. Governments tightly controlled imports to minimize foreign competition with domestic producers. Because the strategy emphasized production for the domestic market, governments did little to encourage exports. As a consequence, developing countries participated little in GATT negotiations, and certainly did not keep pace with the tariff reductions being negotiated by the advanced industrialized countries. In the mid-1980s, most developing country markets remained tightly protected.

This policy orientation changed dramatically beginning in the 1980s. Facing internal problems with import substitution, accumulating large foreign debts that they could not easily service, and confronting a deteriorating international economic climate, many developing countries were forced to turn to the International Monetary Fund and the World Bank for financial assistance. By the middle of the decade, the price of this assistance was the adoption of a set of far-reaching economic reforms known as "structural adjustment." Under this broad reform agenda, developing-country governments were encouraged to scale back the state's role in the domestic economy and to increase the role of the market. To that end, governments were encouraged to deregulate the domestic economy, reduce trade barriers, make it easier for multinational corporations to invest in the domestic economy, privatize state-owned enterprises, and establish and maintain a stable macroeconomic environment. The overarching rationale for these reforms was the deeply held belief of officials at the World Bank, International Monetary Fund, and in the U.S. government, that the economic problems that developing countries faced stemmed from inefficient economic structures that had been established during 30 years or more of import substitution industrialization. For growth to resume in the developing world, this policy consensus argued, governments would have to dismantle the existing economic structure and establish markets in its place. The market would then ensure that resources were allocated to productive uses.

Throughout the developing world, governments heeded the advice embodied in this so-called "Washington Consensus" and began to implement market-based reforms. They did so in part because the IMF and World Bank gave them little choice: developing countries needed IMF and World Bank finance, and structural reforms were the price of this aid. It was also clear to many governments in the developing world that import substitution industrialization did play a role in their poor economic performance and consequently that some change in strategy was necessary. It appeared that the newly industrializing countries in East Asia, South Korea, Singapore, Taiwan, and Hong Kong, had used a market-based and export-oriented development strategy to achieve rapid industrialization. If market-based, export-oriented strategies could work for Asian countries, it might also work for countries in Latin American and sub-Saharan Africa. The collapse of the socialist economies in the former Soviet bloc in 1989 delivered a final blow to the statist model. Thus, the late 1980s and the early 1990s brought extensive policy reforms throughout the developing world. Governments reduced their trade barriers, privatized state-owned enterprises, deregulated the domestic market, and began to produce for export markets. In less than a decade developing countries fundamentally changed their economic orientation. No longer did they insulate themselves from the global economy. Instead, many were strengthening their linkages to the global economy.

By the late 1990s scholars and policymakers were beginning to evaluate the consequences of market-oriented reforms. Were the countries that had moved furthest on the reform trajectory established by the World Bank and IMF performing better than countries that had adopted fewer reforms? More broadly, was it correct to claim that deeper integration into the global economy, and particularly into the international trade system, would produce sustainable growth and help alleviate poverty? The two articles presented in this chapter reflect this debate over the consequences of market reforms in the developing world.

David Dollar and Aart Kraay, economists at the World Bank, summarize the results of a recent World Bank research project. They argue that the preponderance of evidence illustrates a positive relationship between trade openness and economic growth. Developing countries that removed barriers to trade and foreign direct investment experienced more rapid economic growth than countries that remained insulated from the global economy. For Kraay and Dollar, therefore, developing countries intent on reducing poverty should take further steps to strengthen their participation in the global economy.

Dani Rodrik, a political economist at Harvard University, claims that market-oriented policy reforms have failed to deliver on their promises. Rodrik argues that countries that opened most to the global economy during the 1980s and 1990s, such as many in Latin America, have subsequently realized slower economic growth than they experienced during the 1960s and 1970s. He also claims that countries that have experienced long periods of rapid economic growth recently, such as China and India, liberalized trade gradually and only after growth had taken off. Moreover, he argues that in most cases government policies played an important role in generating the initial period of high growth.

Spreading the Wealth

DAVID DOLLAR AND AART KRAAY

A RISING TIDE

One of the main claims of the antiglobalization movement is that globalization is widening the gap between the haves and the have-nots. It benefits the rich and does little for the poor, perhaps even making their lot harder. As union leader Jay Mazur put it in these pages, "globalization has dramatically increased inequality between and within nations" ("Labor's New Internationalism," January/February 2000). The problem with this new conventional wisdom is that the best evidence available shows the exact opposite to be true. So far, the current wave of globalization, which started around 1980, has actually promoted economic equality and reduced poverty.

Global economic integration has complex effects on income, culture, society, and the environment. But in the debate over globalization's merits, its impact on poverty is particularly important. If international trade and investment primarily benefit the rich, many people will feel that restricting trade to protect jobs, culture, or the environment is worth the costs. But if restricting trade imposes further hardship on poor people in the developing world, many of the same people will think otherwise.

Three facts bear on this question. First, a long-term global trend toward greater inequality prevailed for at least 200 years; it peaked around 1975. But since then, it has stabilized and possibly even reversed. The chief reason for the change has been the accelerated growth of two large and initially poor countries: China and India.

Second, a strong correlation links increased participation in international trade and investment on the one hand and faster growth on the other. The developing world can be divided into a "globalizing" group of countries that have seen rapid increases in trade and foreign investment over the last two decades—well above the rates for rich countries—and a "nonglobalizing" group that trades even less of its income today than it did 20 years ago. The aggregate annual per capita growth rate of the globalizing group accelerated steadily from one percent in the 1960s to five percent in the 1990s. During that latter decade, in contrast, rich countries grew at two percent and nonglobalizers at only one percent. Economists are cautious about drawing conclusions concerning causality, but they largely agree that openness to foreign trade and investment (along with complementary reforms) explains the faster growth of the globalizers.

From *Foreign Affairs*, Vol. 91, No. 1, January/February, 2002, pp. 120–133. © 2002 by the Council on Foreign Relations, Inc. Reprinted by permission of *Foreign Affairs*.

Third, and contrary to popular perception, globalization has not resulted in higher inequality within economies. Inequality has indeed gone up in some countries (such as China) and down in others (such as the Philippines). But those changes are not systematically linked to globalization measures such as trade and investment flows, tariff rates, and the presence of capital controls. Instead, shifts in inequality stem more from domestic education, taxes, and social policies. In general, higher growth rates in globalizing developing countries have translated into higher incomes for the poor. Even with its increased inequality, for example, China has seen the most spectacular reduction of poverty in world history—which was supported by opening its economy to foreign trade and investment.

Although globalization can be a powerful force for poverty reduction, its beneficial results are not inevitable. If policymakers hope to tap the full potential of economic integration and sustain its benefits, they must address three critical challenges. A growing protectionist movement in rich countries that aims to limit integration with poor ones must be stopped in its tracks. Developing countries need to acquire the kinds of institutions and policies that will allow them to prosper under globalization, both of which may be different from place to place. And more migration, both domestic and international, must be permitted when geography limits the potential for development.

THE GREAT DIVIDE

Over the past 200 years, different local economies around the world have become more integrated while the growth rate of the global economy has accelerated dramatically. Although it is impossible to prove causal linkage between the two developments—since there are no other world economies to be tested against—evidence suggests the arrows run in both directions. As Adam Smith argued, a larger market permits a finer division of labor, which in turn facilitates innovation and learning by doing. Some of that innovation involves transportation and communications technologies that lower costs and increase integration. So it is easy to see how integration and innovation can be mutually supportive.

Different locations have become more integrated because of increased flows of goods, capital, and knowledge. From 1820 to 1914, international trade increased faster than the global economy. Trade rose from about 2 percent of world income in 1820 to 18 percent in 1914. The globalization of trade took a step backward during the protectionist period of the Great Depression and World War II, and by 1950 trade (in relation to income) was lower than it had been in 1914. But thanks to a series of multilateral trade liberalizations under the General Agreement on Tariffs and Trade (GATT), trade dramatically expanded among industrialized countries between 1960 and 1980. Most developing countries remained largely isolated from this trade because of their own inward-focused policies, but the success of such notable exceptions as Taiwan and South Korea eventually helped encourage other developing economies to open themselves up to foreign trade and investment.

International capital flows, measured as foreign ownership of assets relative to world income, also grew during the first wave of globalization and declined during the Great Depression and World War II; they did not return to 1914 levels until 1980. But since then, such flows have increased markedly and changed their nature as well. One hundred years ago, foreign capital typically financed public infrastructure projects (such as canals and railroads) or direct investment related to natural resources. Today, in contrast, the bulk of capital flows to developing countries is direct investments tied to manufacturing and services.

The change in the nature of capital flows is clearly related to concurrent advances in economic integration, such as cheaper and faster transportation and revolutionary changes in telecommunications. Since 1920, seagoing freight charges have declined by about two-thirds and air travel costs by 84 percent; the cost of a three-minute call from New York City to London has dropped by 99 percent. Today, production in widely differing locations can be integrated in ways that simply were not possible before.

Another aspect of integration has been the movement of people. Yet here the trend is reversed: there is much more international travel than in the past but much less permanent migration. Between 1870 and 1910, about ten percent of the world's population relocated permanently from one country to another; over the past 25 years, only one to two percent have done so.

As economic integration has progressed, the annual growth rate of the world economy has accelerated, from 1 percent in the mid-nineteenth century to 3.5 percent in 1960–2000. Sustained over many years, such a jump in growth makes a huge difference in real living standards. It now takes only two to three years, for example, for the world economy to produce the same amount of goods and services that it did during the entire nineteenth century. Such a comparison is arguably a serious understatement of the true difference, since most of what is consumed today—airline travel, cars, televisions, synthetic fibers, life-extending drugs—did not exist 200 years ago. For any of these goods or services, therefore, the growth rate of output since 1820 is infinite. Human productivity has increased almost unimaginably.

All this tremendous growth in wealth was distributed very unequally up to about 1975, but since then growing equality has taken hold. One good measure of inequality among individuals worldwide is the mean log deviation—a measure of the gap between the income of any randomly selected person and a general average. It takes into account the fact that income distributions everywhere are skewed in favor of the rich, so that the typical person is poorer than the group average; the more skewed the distribution, the larger the gap. Per capita income in the world today, for example, is around $5,000, whereas a randomly selected person would most likely be living on close to $1,000—80 percent less. That gap translates into a mean log deviation of 0.8.

Taking this approach, an estimate of the world distribution of income among individuals shows rising inequality between 1820 and 1975. In that period, the gap between the typical person and world per capita income increased from about 40 percent to about 80 percent. Since changes in income inequality within countries were small, the increase in inequality was driven mostly by differences in growth rates across countries. Areas that were already relatively rich in 1820 (notably, Europe and the United States) grew faster than poor areas (notably, China and India). Global inequality peaked sometime in the 1970s, but it then stabilized and even began to decline, largely because growth in China and India began to accelerate.

Another way of looking at global inequality is to examine what is happening to the extreme poor—those people living on less than $1 per day. Although the percentage of the world's population living in poverty has declined over time, the absolute number rose fairly steadily until 1980. During the Great Depression and World War II, the number of poor increased particularly sharply, and it declined somewhat immediately thereafter. The world economy grew strongly between 1960 and 1980, but the number of poor rose because growth did not occur in the places where the worst-off live. But since then, the most rapid growth has occurred in poor locations. Consequently the number of poor has declined by 200 million since 1980. Again, this trend is explained primarily by the rapid income growth in China and India, which together in 1980 accounted for about one-third of the world's population and more than 60 percent of the world's extreme poor.

UPWARD BOUND

The shift in the trend in global inequality coincides with the shift in the economic strategies of several large developing countries. Following World War II, most developing regions chose strategies that focused inward and discouraged integration with the global economy. But these approaches were not particularly successful, and throughout the 1960s and 1970s developing countries on the whole grew less rapidly than industrialized ones. The oil shocks and U.S. inflation of the 1970s created severe problems for them, contributing to negative growth, high inflation, and debt crises over the next several years. Faced with these disappointing results, several developing countries began to alter their strategies starting in the 1980s.

For example, China had an extremely closed economy until the mid-1970s. Although Beijing's initial economic reform focused on agriculture, a key part of its approach since the 1980s has involved opening up foreign trade and investment, including a drop in its tariff rates by two-thirds and its nontariff barriers by even more. These reforms have led to unprecedented economic growth in the country's coastal provinces and more moderate growth in the interior. From 1978 to 1994 the Chinese economy grew annually by 9 percent, while exports grew by 14 percent and imports by 13 percent. Of course, China and other globalizing developing countries have pursued a wide range of reforms, not just economic openness. Beijing has strengthened property rights through land reform and moved from a planned economy toward a market-oriented one, and these measures have contributed to its integration as well as to its growth.

Other developing countries have also opened up as a part of broader reform programs. During the 1990s, India liberalized foreign trade and investment with good results; its annual per capita income growth now tops four percent. It too has pursued a broad agenda of reform and has moved away from a highly regulated, planned system. Meanwhile, Uganda and Vietnam are the best examples of very low-income countries that have increased their participation in trade and investment and prospered as a result. And in the western hemisphere, Mexico is noteworthy both for signing its free-trade agreement with the United States and Canada in 1993 and for its rapid growth since then, especially in the northern regions near the U.S. border.

These cases illustrate how openness to foreign trade and investment, coupled with complementary reforms, typically leads to faster growth. India, China, Vietnam, Uganda, and Mexico are not isolated examples; in general, countries that have become more open have grown faster. The best way to illustrate this trend is to rank developing countries in order of their increases in trade relative to national income over the past 20 years. The top third of this list can be thought of as the "globalizing" camp, and the bottom two-thirds as the "nonglobalizing" camp. The globalizers have increased their trade relative to income by 104 percent over the past two decades, compared to 71 percent for rich countries. The nonglobalizers, meanwhile, actually trade less today than they did 20 years ago. The globalizers have also cut their import tariffs by 22 percentage points on average, compared to only 11 percentage points for the nonglobalizers.

How have the globalizers fared in terms of growth? Their average annual growth rates accelerated from 1 percent in the 1960s to 3 percent in the 1970s, 4 percent in the 1980s, and 5 percent in the 1990s. Rich countries' annual growth rates, by comparison, slowed to about 2 percent in the 1990s, and the nonglobalizers saw their growth rates decline from 3 percent in the 1970s to 1 percent in the 1980s and 1990s.

The same pattern can be observed on a local level. Within both China and India, the locations that are integrating with the global economy are growing much more rapidly than the disconnected regions. Indian states, for example, vary significantly in the quality of their investment climates as measured by government efficiency, corruption, and infrastructure. Those states with better investment climates have integrated themselves more closely with outside markets and have experienced more investment (domestic and foreign) than their less-integrated counterparts. Moreover, states that were initially poor and then created good investment climates had stronger poverty reduction in the 1990s than those not integrating with the global economy. Such internal comparisons are important because, by holding national trade and macroeconomic policies constant, they reveal how important it is to complement trade liberalization with institutional reform so that integration can actually occur.

The accelerated growth rates of globalizing countries such as China, India, and Vietnam are consistent with cross-country comparisons that find openness going hand in hand with faster growth. The most that these studies can establish is that more trade and investment is highly correlated with higher growth, so one needs to be careful about drawing conclusions about causality. Still, the overall evidence from individual cases and cross-country correlation is persuasive. As economists Peter Lindert and Jeffrey Williamson have written, "even though no one study can establish that openness to trade has unambiguously helped the representative Third World economy, the preponderance of evidence supports this conclusion." They go on to note that "there are no anti-global victories to report for the postwar Third World."

Contrary to the claims of the antiglobalization movement, therefore, greater openness to international trade and investment has in fact helped narrow the gap between rich and poor countries rather than widen it. During the 1990s, the economies of the globalizers, with a combined population of about 3 billion, grew more than twice as fast as the rich countries. The nonglobalizers, in contrast, grew only half as fast and nowadays lag further and further behind. Much of the discussion of global inequality assumes that there is growing divergence between the developing world and the rich world, but this is simply not true. The most important development in global inequality in recent decades is the growing divergence within the developing world, and it is directly related to whether countries take advantage of the economic benefits that globalization can offer.

THE PATH OUT OF POVERTY

The antiglobalization movement also claims that economic integration is worsening inequality within countries as well as between them. Until the mid-1980s, there was insufficient evidence to support strong conclusions on this important topic. But now more and more developing countries have begun to conduct household income and consumption surveys of reasonable quality. (In low-income countries, these surveys typically track what households actually consume because so much of their real income is self-produced and not part of the money economy.) Good surveys now exist for 137 countries, and many go back far enough to measure changes in inequality over time.

One way of looking at inequality within countries is to focus on what happens to the bottom 20 percent of households as globalization and growth proceed apace. Across all countries, incomes of the poor grow at around the same rate as GDP. Of course, there is a great deal of variation around that average relationship. In some countries, income distribution has shifted in favor of the poor; in others, against them. But these shifts cannot be explained by any globalization-related variable. So it simply cannot be said that inequality necessarily rises with more trade, more foreign investment, and lower tariffs. For many globalizers, the overall change in distribution was small, and in some cases (such as the Philippines and Malaysia) it was even in favor of the poor. What changes in inequality do reflect are country-specific policies on education, taxes, and social protection. It is important not to misunderstand this finding. China is an important example of a country that has had a large increase in inequality in the past decade, when the income of the bottom 20 percent has risen much less rapidly than per capita income. This trend may be related to greater openness, although domestic liberalization is a more likely cause. China started out in the 1970s with a highly equal distribution of income, and part of its reform has deliberately aimed at increasing the returns on education, which financially reward the better schooled. But the Chinese case is not typical; inequality has not increased in most of the developing countries that have opened up to foreign trade and investment. Furthermore, income distribution in China may have become more unequal, but the income of the poor in China has still risen rapidly. In fact, the country's progress in reducing poverty has been one of the most dramatic successes in history.

Because increased trade usually accompanies more rapid growth and does not systematically change household-income distribution, it generally is associated with improved well-being of the poor. Vietnam nicely illustrates this finding. As the nation has opened up, it has experienced a large increase in per capita income and no significant change in inequality. Thus the income of the poor has risen dramatically, and the number of Vietnamese living in absolute poverty dropped sharply from 75 percent of the population in 1988 to 37 percent in 1998. Of the poorest 5 percent of households in 1992, 98 percent were better off six years later. And the improved well-being is not just a matter of income. Child labor has declined, and school enrollment has increased. It should be no surprise that the vast majority of poor households in Vietnam benefited immediately from a more liberalized trading system, since the country's opening has resulted in exports of rice (produced by most of the poor farmers) and labor-intensive products such as footwear. But the experience of China and Vietnam is not unique. India and Uganda also enjoyed rapid poverty reduction as they grew along with their integration into the global economy.

THE OPEN SOCIETIES

These findings have important implications for developing countries, for rich countries such as the United States, and for those who care about global poverty. All parties should recognize that the most recent wave of globalization has been a powerful force for equality and poverty reduction, and they should commit themselves to seeing that it continues despite the obstacles lying ahead.

It is not inevitable that globalization will proceed. In 1910, many believed globalization was unstoppable; they soon received a rude shock. History is not likely to repeat itself in the same way, but it is worth noting that antiglobalization sentiments are on the rise. A growing number of political leaders in the developing world realize that an open trading system is very much in their countries' interest. They would do well to heed Mexican President Vicente Fox, who said recently,

> We are convinced that globalization is good and it's good when you do your homework, . . . keep your fundamentals in line on the economy, build up high levels of education, respect the rule of law. . . . When you do your part, we are convinced that you get the benefit.

But today the narrow interests opposed to further integration—especially those in the rich countries—appear to be much more energetic than their opponents. In Quebec City last spring and in Genoa last summer, a group of democratically elected leaders gathered to discuss how to pursue economic integration and improve the lives of their peoples. Antiglobalization demonstrators were quite effective in disrupting the meetings and drawing media attention to themselves. Leaders in developed and developing countries alike must make the proglobalization case more directly and effectively or risk having their opponents dominate the discussion and stall the process.

In addition, industrialized countries still raise protectionist measures against agricultural and labor-intensive products. Reducing those barriers would help developing countries significantly. The poorer areas of the world would benefit from further openings of their own markets as well, since 70 percent of the tariff barriers that developing countries face are from other developing countries.

If globalization proceeds, its potential to be an equalizing force will depend on whether poor countries manage to integrate themselves into the global economic system. True integration requires not just trade liberalization but wide-ranging institutional reform. Many of the nonglobalizing developing countries, such as Myanmar, Nigeria, Ukraine, and Pakistan, offer an unattractive investment climate. Even if they decide to open themselves up to trade, not much is likely to happen unless other reforms are also pursued. It is not easy to predict the reform paths of these countries; some of the relative successes in recent years, such as China, India, Uganda, and Vietnam, have come as quite a surprise. But as long as a location has weak institutions and policies, people living there are going to fall further behind the rest of the world.

Through their trade policies, rich countries can make it easier for those developing countries that do choose to open up and join the global trading club. But in recent years, the rich countries have been doing just the opposite. GATT was originally built around agreements concerning trade practices. Now, institutional harmonization, such as agreement on policies toward intellectual property rights, is a requirement for joining the WTO. Any sort of regulation of labor and environmental standards made under the threat of WTO sanctions would take this requirement for harmonization much further. Such measures would be neoprotectionist in effect, because they would thwart the integration of developing countries into the world economy and discourage trade between poor countries and rich ones.

The WTO meeting in Doha was an important step forward on trade integration. More forcefully than in Seattle, leaders of industrial countries were willing to make the case for further integration and put on the table issues of central concern to developing nations: access to pharmaceutical patents, use of antidumping measures against developing countries, and agricultural subsidies. The new round of trade negotiations launched at Doha has the potential to reverse the current trend, which makes it more difficult for poor countries to integrate with the world economy.

A final potential obstacle to successful and equitable globalization relates to geography. There is no inherent reason why coastal China should be poor; the same goes for southern India, northern Mexico, and Vietnam. All of these locations are near important markets or trade routes but were long held back by misguided policies. Now, with appropriate reforms, they are starting to grow rapidly and take their natural place in the world. But the same cannot be said for Mali, Chad, or other countries or regions cursed with "poor geography"—i.e., distance from markets, inherently high transport costs, and challenging health and agricultural problems. It would be naive to think that trade and investment alone can alleviate poverty in all locations. In fact, for those locations with poor geography, trade liberalization is less important than developing proper health care systems or providing basic infrastructure—or letting people move elsewhere.

Migration from poor locations is the missing factor in the current wave of globalization that could make a large contribution to reducing poverty. Each year, 83 million people are added to the world's population, 82 million of them in the developing world. In Europe and Japan, moreover, the population is aging and the labor force is set to shrink. Migration of relatively unskilled workers from South to North would thus offer clear economic benefits to both. Most migration from South to North is economically motivated, and it raises the living standard of the migrant while benefiting the sending country in three ways. First, it reduces the South's labor force and thus raises wages for those who remain behind. Second, migrants send remittances of hard currency back home. Finally, migration bolsters transnational trade and investment networks. In the case of Mexico, for example, ten percent of its citizens live and work in the United States, taking pressure off its own labor market and raising wages there. India gets six times as much in remittances from its workers overseas as it gets in foreign aid.

Unlike trade, however, migration remains highly restricted and controversial. Some critics perceive a disruptive impact on society and culture and fear downward pressure on wages and rising unemployment in the richer countries. Yet anti-immigration lobbies ignore the fact that geographical economic disparities are so strong that illegal immigration is growing rapidly anyway, despite restrictive policies. In a perverse irony, some of the worst abuses of globalization occur because there is not enough of it in key economic areas such as labor flows. Human traffic, for example, has become a highly lucrative, unregulated business in which illegal migrants are easy prey for exploitation.

Realistically, none of the industrialized countries is going to adopt open migration. But they should reconsider their migration policies. Some, for example, have a strong bias in their immigration rules toward highly skilled workers, which in fact spurs a "brain drain" from the developing world. Such policies do little to stop the flow of unskilled workers and instead push many of these people into the illegal category. If rich countries would legally accept more unskilled workers, they could address their own looming labor shortages, improve living standards in developing countries, and reduce illegal human traffic and its abuses. In sum, the integration of poor economies with richer ones over the past two decades has provided many opportunities for poor people to improve their lives. Examples of the beneficiaries of globalization can be found among Mexican migrants, Chinese factory workers, Vietnamese peasants, and Ugandan farmers. Many of the better-off in developing and rich countries alike also benefit. After all the rhetoric about globalization is stripped away, many of the policy questions come down to whether the rich world will make integrating with the world economy easy for those poor communities that want to do so. The world's poor have a large stake in how the rich countries answer.

Trading in Illusions

DANI RODRIK

Advocates of global economic integration hold out utopian visions of the prosperity that developing countries will reap if they open their borders to commerce and capital. This hollow promise diverts poor nations' attention and resources from the key domestic innovations needed to spur economic growth.

A senior U.S. Treasury official recently urged Mexico's government to work harder to reduce violent crime because "such high levels of crime and violence may drive away foreign investors." This admonition nicely illustrates how foreign trade and investment have become the ultimate yardstick for evaluating the social and economic policies of governments in developing countries. Forget the slum dwellers or *campesinos* who live amidst crime and poverty throughout the developing world. Just mention "investor sentiment" or "competitiveness in world markets" and policymakers will come to attention in a hurry.

Underlying this perversion of priorities is a remarkable consensus on the imperative of global economic integration. Openness to trade and investment flows is no longer viewed simply as a component of a country's development strategy; it has mutated into the most potent catalyst for economic growth known to humanity. Predictably, senior officials of the World Trade Organization (WTO), International Monetary Fund (IMF), and other international financial agencies incessantly repeat the openness mantra. In recent years, however, faith in integration has spread quickly to political leaders and policymakers around the world.

Joining the world economy is no longer a matter simply of dismantling barriers to trade and investment. Countries now must also comply with a long list of admission requirements, from new patent rules to more rigorous banking standards. The apostles of economic integration prescribe comprehensive institutional reforms that took today's advanced countries generations to accomplish, so that developing countries can, as the cliché goes, maximize the gains and minimize the risks of participation in the world economy. Global integration has become, for all practical purposes, a substitute for a development strategy.

This trend is bad news for the world's poor. The new agenda of global integration rests on shaky empirical ground and seriously distorts policymakers' priorities. By focusing on international integration, governments in poor nations divert human resources, administrative capabilities, and political capital away from more urgent development priorities such as education, public health, industrial

From Dani Rodrik, *Foreign Policy,* March/April 2001, pp. 55–62. © 2001 by *Foreign Policy.* Reproduced with permission of *Foreign Policy* in the format Textbook via Copyright Clearance Center..

capacity, and social cohesion. This emphasis also undermines nascent democratic institutions by removing the choice of development strategy from public debate.

World markets are a source of technology and capital; it would be silly for the developing world not to exploit these opportunities. But globalization is not a shortcut to development. Successful economic growth strategies have always required a judicious blend of imported practices with domestic institutional innovations. Policymakers need to forge a domestic growth strategy by relying on domestic investors and domestic institutions. The costliest downside of the integrationist faith is that it crowds out serious thinking and efforts along such lines.

EXCUSES, EXCUSES

Countries that have bought wholeheartedly into the integration orthodoxy are discovering that openness does not deliver on its promise. Despite sharply lowering their barriers to trade and investment since the 1980s, scores of countries in Latin America and Africa are stagnating or growing less rapidly than in the heyday of import substitution during the 1960s and 1970s. By contrast, the fastest growing countries are China, India, and others in East and Southeast Asia. Policymakers in these countries have also espoused trade and investment liberalization, but they have done so in an unorthodox manner—gradually, sequentially, and only after an initial period of high growth—and as part of a broader policy package with many unconventional features.

The disappointing outcomes with deep liberalization have been absorbed into the faith with remarkable aplomb. Those who view global integration as the prerequisite for economic development now simply add the caveat that opening borders is insufficient. Reaping the gains from openness, they argue, also requires a full complement of institutional reforms.

Consider trade liberalization. Asking any World Bank economist what a successful trade-liberalization program requires will likely elicit a laundry list of measures beyond the simple reduction of tariff and nontariff barriers: tax reform to make up for lost tariff revenues; social safety nets to compensate displaced workers; administrative reform to bring trade practices into compliance with WTO rules; labor market reform to enhance worker mobility across industries; technological assistance to upgrade firms hurt by import competition; and training programs to ensure that export-oriented firms and investors have access to skilled workers. As the promise of trade liberalization fails to materialize, the prerequisites keep expanding. For example, Clare Short, Great Britain's secretary of state for international development, recently added universal provision of health and education to the list.

In the financial arena, integrationists have pushed complementary reforms with even greater fanfare and urgency. The prevailing view in Washington and other Group of Seven (G-7) capitals is that weaknesses in banking systems, prudential regulation, and corporate governance were at the heart of the Asian financial crisis of the late 1990s. Hence the ambitious efforts by the G-7 to establish international codes and standards covering fiscal transparency, monetary and financial policy, banking supervision, data dissemination, corporate governance, and accounting standards. The Financial Stability Forum (FSF)—a G-7 organization with minimal representation from developing nations—has designated 12 of these standards as essential for creating sound financial systems in developing countries. The full FSF compendium includes an additional 59 standards the agency considers "relevant for sound financial systems," bringing the total number of codes to 71. To fend off speculative capital movements, the IMF and the G-7 also typically urge developing countries to accumulate foreign reserves and avoid exchange-rate regimes that differ from a "hard peg" (tying the value of one's currency to that of a more stable currency, such as the U.S. dollar) or a "pure float" (letting the market determine the appropriate exchange rate).

A cynic might wonder whether the point of all these prerequisites is merely to provide easy cover for eventual failure. Integrationists can conveniently blame disappointing growth performance or a financial crisis on "slippage" in the implementation of complementary reforms rather than on a poorly designed liberalization. So if Bangladesh's freer trade policy does not produce a large enough spurt in growth, the World Bank concludes that the problem must involve lagging reforms in public administration or continued "political uncertainty" (always a favorite). And if Argentina gets caught up in a confidence crisis despite significant trade and financial liberalization, the IMF reasons that structural reforms have been inadequate and must be deepened.

FREE TRADE-OFFS

Most (but certainly not all) of the institutional reforms on the integrationist agenda are perfectly sensible, and in a world without financial, administrative, or political constraints, there would be little argument about the need to adopt them. But in the real world, governments face difficult choices over how to deploy their fiscal resources, administrative capabilities, and political capital. Setting institutional priorities to maximize integration into the global economy has real opportunity costs.

Consider some illustrative trade-offs. World Bank trade economist Michael Finger has estimated that a typical developing country must spend $150 million to implement requirements under just three WTO agreements (those on customs valuation, sanitary and phytosanitary measures, and trade-related intellectual property rights). As Finger notes, this sum equals a year's development budget for many least-developed countries. And while the budgetary burden of implementing financial codes and standards has never been fully estimated, it undoubtedly entails a substantial diversion of fiscal and human resources as well. Should governments in developing countries train more bank auditors and accountants, even if those investments mean fewer secondary-school teachers or reduced spending on primary education for girls?

In the area of legal reform, should governments focus their energies on "importing" legal codes and standards or on improving existing domestic legal institutions? In Turkey, a weak coalition government spent several months during 1999 gathering political support for a bill providing foreign investors the protection of international arbitration. But wouldn't a better long-run strategy have involved reforming the existing legal regime for the benefit of foreign and domestic investors alike?

In public health, should governments promote the reverse engineering of patented basic medicines and the importation of low-cost generic drugs from "unauthorized" suppliers, even if doing so means violating WTO rules against such practices? When South Africa passed legislation in 1997 allowing imports of patented AIDS drugs from cheaper sources, the country came under severe pressure from Western governments, which argued that the South African policy conflicted with WTO rules on intellectual property.

How much should politicians spend on social protection policies in view of the fiscal constraints imposed by market "discipline"? Peru's central bank holds foreign reserves equal to 15 months of imports as an insurance policy against the sudden capital outflows that financially open economies often experience. The opportunity cost of this policy amounts to almost 1 percent of gross domestic product annually—more than enough to fund a generous antipoverty program.

How should governments choose their exchange-rate regimes? During the last four decades, virtually every growth boom in the developing world has been accompanied by a controlled depreciation of the domestic currency. Yet financial openness makes it all but impossible to manage the exchange rate.

How should policymakers focus their anticorruption strategies? Should they target the high-level corruption that foreign investors often decry or the petty corruption that affects the poor the most? Perhaps, as the proponents of permanent normal trade relations with China argued in the recent U.S. debate, a government that is forced to protect the rights of foreign investors will become more inclined to protect the rights of its own citizens as well. But this is, at best, a trickledown strategy of institutional reform. Shouldn't reforms target the desired ends directly—whether those ends are the rule of law, improved observance of human rights, or reduced corruption?

The rules for admission into the world economy not only reflect little awareness of development priorities, they are often completely unrelated to sensible economic principles. For instance, WTO agreements on anti-dumping, subsidies and countervailing measures, agriculture, textiles, and trade-related intellectual property rights lack any economic rationale beyond the mercantilist interests of a narrow set of powerful groups in advanced industrial countries. Bilateral and regional trade agreements are typically far worse, as they impose even tighter prerequisites on developing countries in return for crumbs of enhanced "market access." For example, the African Growth and Opportunity Act signed by U.S. President Clinton in May 2000 provides increased access to the U.S. market only if African apparel manufacturers use U.S.-produced fabric and yarns. This restriction severely limits the potential economic spillovers in African countries.

There are similar questions about the appropriateness of financial codes and standards. These codes rely heavily on an Anglo-American style of corporate governance and an arm's-length model of financial development. They close off alternative paths to financial development of the sort that have been followed by many of today's rich countries (for example, Germany, Japan, or South Korea).

In each of these areas, a strategy of "globalization above all" crowds out alternatives that are potentially more development-friendly. Many of the institutional reforms needed for insertion into the world economy can be independently desirable or produce broader economic benefits. But these priorities do not necessarily coincide with the priorities of a comprehensive development agenda.

ASIAN MYTHS

Even if the institutional reforms needed to join the international economic community are expensive and preclude investments in other crucial areas, pro-globalization advocates argue that the vast increases in economic growth that invariably result from insertion into the global marketplace will more than compensate for those costs. Take the East Asian tigers or China, the advocates say. Where would they be without international trade and foreign capital flows?

That these countries reaped enormous benefits from their progressive integration into the world economy is undeniable. But look closely at what policies produced those results, and you will find little that resembles today's rule book.

Countries like South Korea and Taiwan had to abide by few international constraints and pay few of the modern costs of integration during their formative growth experience in the 1960s and 1970s. At that time, global trade rules were sparse and economies faced almost none of today's common pressures to open their borders to capital flows. So these countries combined their outward orientation with unorthodox policies: high levels of tariff and nontariff barriers, public ownership of large segments of banking and industry, export subsidies, domestic-content requirements, patent and copyright infringements, and restrictions on capital flows (including on foreign direct investment). Such policies are either precluded by today's trade rules or are highly frowned upon by organizations like the IMF and the World Bank.

China also followed a highly unorthodox two-track strategy, violating practically every rule in the guidebook (including, most notably, the requirement of private property rights). India, which significantly raised its economic growth rate in the early 1980s, remains one of the world's most highly protected economies.

All of these countries liberalized trade gradually, over a period of decades, not years. Significant import liberalization did not occur until after a transition to high economic growth had taken place. And far from wiping the institutional slate clean, all of these nations managed to eke growth out of their existing institutions, imperfect as they may have been. Indeed, when some of the more successful Asian economies gave in to Western pressure to liberalize capital flows rapidly, they were rewarded with the Asian financial crisis.

That is why these countries can hardly be considered poster children for today's global rules. South Korea, China, India, and the other Asian success cases had the freedom to do their own thing, and they used that freedom abundantly. Today's globalizers would be unable to replicate these experiences without running afoul of the IMF or the WTO. The Asian experience highlights a deeper point: A sound overall development strategy that produces high economic growth is far more effective in achieving integration with the world economy than a purely integrationist strategy that relies on openness to work its magic. In other words, the globalizers have it exactly backwards. Integration is the result, not the cause, of economic and social development. A relatively protected economy like Vietnam is integrating with the world economy much more rapidly than an open economy like Haiti because Vietnam, unlike Haiti, has a reasonably functional economy and polity.

Integration into the global economy, unlike tariff rates or capital-account regulations, is not something that policymakers control directly. Telling finance ministers in developing nations that they should increase their "participation in world trade" is as meaningful as telling them that they need to improve technological capabilities—and just as helpful. Policymakers need to know which strategies will produce these results, and whether the specific prescriptions that the current orthodoxy offers are up to the task.

TOO GOOD TO BE TRUE

Do lower trade barriers spur greater economic progress? The available studies reveal no systematic relationship between a country's average level of tariff and nontariff barriers and its subsequent economic growth rate. If anything, the evidence for the 1990s indicates a positive relationship between import tariffs and economic growth. The only clear pattern is that countries dismantle their trade restrictions as they grow richer. This finding explains why today's rich countries, with few exceptions, embarked on modern economic growth behind protective barriers but now display low trade barriers.

The absence of a strong negative relationship between trade restrictions and economic growth may seem surprising in view of the ubiquitous claim that trade liberalization promotes higher growth. Indeed, the economics literature is replete with cross-national studies concluding that growth and economic dynamism are strongly linked to more open trade policies. A particularly influential study finds that economies that are "open," by the study's own definition, grew 2.45 percentage points faster annually than closed ones—an enormous difference.

Upon closer look, however, such studies turn out to be unreliable. In a detailed review of the empirical literature, University of Maryland economist Francisco Rodriguez and I have found a major gap between the results that economists have actually obtained and the policy conclusions they have typically drawn. For example, in many cases economists blame poor growth on the government's failure to liberalize trade policies, when the true culprits are ineffective institutions, geographic determinants (such as location in a tropical region), or inappropriate macroeconomic policies (such as an overvalued exchange rate). Once these misdiagnoses are corrected, any meaningful relationship across countries between the level of trade barriers and economic growth evaporates.

The evidence on the benefits of liberalizing capital flows is even weaker. In theory, the appeal of capital mobility seems obvious: If capital is free to enter (and leave) markets based on the potential return on investment, the result will be an efficient allocation of global resources. But in reality, financial markets are inherently unstable, subject to bubbles (rational or otherwise), panics, shortsightedness, and self-fulfilling prophecies. There is plenty of evidence that financial liberalization is often followed by financial crash—just ask Mexico, Thailand, or Turkey—while there is little convincing evidence to suggest that higher rates of economic growth follow capital-account liberalization.

Perhaps the most disingenuous argument in favor of liberalizing international financial flows is that the threat of massive and sudden capital movements serves to discipline policymakers in developing nations who might otherwise manage their economies irresponsibly. In other words, governments might be less inclined to squander their societies' resources if such actions would spook foreign lenders. In practice, however, the discipline argument falls apart. Behavior in international capital markets is dominated by mood swings unrelated to fundamentals. In good times, a government with a chronic fiscal deficit has an easier time financing its spending when it can borrow funds from investors abroad; witness Russia prior to 1998 or Argentina in the 1990s. And in bad times, governments may be forced to adopt inappropriate policies in order to conform to the biases of foreign investors; witness the excessively restrictive monetary and fiscal policies in much of East Asia in the immediate aftermath of the Asian financial crisis. A key reason why Malaysia was able to recover so quickly after the imposition of capital controls in September 1998 was that Prime Minister Mahathir Mohamad resisted the high interest rates and tight fiscal policies that South Korea, Thailand, and Indonesia adopted at the behest of the International Monetary Fund.

GROWTH BEGINS AT HOME

Well-trained economists are justifiably proud of the textbook case in favor of free trade. For all the theory's simplicity, it is one of our profession's most significant achievements. However, in their zeal to promote the virtues of trade, the most ardent proponents are peddling a cartoon version of the argument, vastly overstating the effectiveness of economic openness as a tool for fostering development. Such claims only endanger broad public acceptance of the real article because they unleash unrealistic expectations about the benefits of free trade. Neither economic theory nor empirical evidence guarantees that deep trade liberalization will deliver higher economic growth. Economic openness and all its accouterments do not deserve the priority they typically receive in the development strategies pushed by leading multilateral organizations.

Countries that have achieved long-term economic growth have usually combined the opportunities offered by world markets with a growth strategy that mobilizes the capabilities of domestic institutions and investors. Designing such a growth strategy is both harder and easier than implementing typical integration policies. It is harder because the binding constraints on growth are usually country specific and do not respond well to standardized recipes. But it is easier because once those constraints are targeted, relatively simple policy changes can yield enormous economic payoffs and start a virtuous cycle of growth and additional reform.

Unorthodox innovations that depart from the integration rule book are typically part and parcel of such strategies. Public enterprises during the Meiji restoration in Japan; township and village enterprises in China; an export processing zone in

Mauritius; generous tax incentives for priority investments in Taiwan; extensive credit subsidies in South Korea; infant-industry protection in Brazil during the 1960s and 1970s—these are some of the innovations that have been instrumental in kick-starting investment and growth in the past. None came out of a Washington economist's tool kit.

Few of these experiments have worked as well when transplanted to other settings, only underscoring the decisive importance of local conditions. To be effective, development strategies need to be tailored to prevailing domestic institutional strengths. There is simply no alternative to a homegrown business plan. Policymakers who look to Washington and financial markets for the answers are condemning themselves to mimicking the conventional wisdom *du jour*, and to eventual disillusionment.

QUESTIONS FOR REVIEW AND DISCUSSION

1. What are the elements of the development strategy that Rodrik recommends? Does this differ from what Dollar and Kraay advocate? If so, in what specific ways is it different from the policy advice advanced by Dollar and Kraay?
2. How do you think Dollar and Kraay would respond to Rodrik's argument and to the policies Rodrik recommends?
3. What particular countries do Dollar and Kraay point to in order to highlight their posited relationship between trade openness and economic growth? Does Rodrik agree with their interpretation of the reasons for rapid growth in these countries? Why or why not?
4. What factors do you think complicate any attempt to evaluate the relationship between trade openness and other policy reforms and economic development?
5. What is at stake in the debate about the relationship between trade openness and economic development? Is it possible to have a definitive solution to the problem of development; that is, a single development strategy that will work in every country? What would Dollar and Kraay say? How about Rodrik?

SUGGESTIONS FOR FURTHER READING

You can read an exchange between David Dollar, Aart Kraay, and three of their critics that was triggered by the article presented above in *Foreign Affairs* July/August 2002.

David Dollar further develops the argument presented above in a recent World Bank study: David Dollar and Paul Collier. *Globalization, Growth, and Poverty: Building an Inclusive World Economy.* Oxford: Oxford University Press, 2001. This publication is also available online at: http://econ.worldbank.org/prr/globalization/

Dani Rodrik elaborates on the views presented above in a number of publications. See, for example: Dani Rodrik. *The New Global Economy and Developing Countries: Making Openness Work.* Washington, DC: Overseas Development Council, 1999, and Dani Rodrik. *The Global Governance of Trade as if Development Really Mattered.* United Nations Development Programme, October 2001. Available online at: http://www.undp.org/mainundp/propoor/docs/pov_globalgovernancetrade_pub.pdf

The World Trade Organization

CHAPTER 4

THE DOHA DEVELOPMENT ROUND

In September 2003, the members of the WTO gathered in Cancún, Mexico for the fifth Ministerial Conference. The primary goal of the Cancún Ministerial Conference was to "take stock of progress" made in the negotiations that had been initiated in Doha, Qatar in November 2001.[1] Negotiations between national governments on the so-called Doha Development Agenda had been under way within the WTO's Trade Negotiations Committee in Geneva since early 2002. These negotiations, typically run by national civil servants rather than politicians, had explored the issues on the Doha Development Agenda, outlining areas of potential agreement and identifying areas where national positions remained far apart. At Cancún, the hope was that trade ministers from each member government would be able and willing to make concessions that would bridge gaps between distant national positions, thereby making agreement possible. Once the major differences in national positions had been narrowed, negotiations would return to Geneva where civil servants could work out the final details. Any serious differences that remained could then be resolved at a special session of the Ministerial Conference to be held in late 2004 or early 2005.

The hopes for agreement were not realized. In five days of discussions and negotiations, WTO member governments proved unwilling to make any major concessions and the Cancún Ministerial Conference ended without bringing a final agreement any closer. The collapse of the Ministerial Conference was followed by acrimonious charges and countercharges by the United States, the EU, and a number of developing countries, each accusing the others of being unwilling to make the concessions necessary for a successful round. It is now generally accepted that the current round of negotiations cannot be concluded by the scheduled date of January 31, 2005, and some wonder whether the round will be concluded at all.

What went wrong at Cancún, and how will this failure affect the rest of the bargaining round? The two articles presented in this chapter explore these questions in some depth, looking in particular at what happened in Cancún and what impact this will have on the trade system moving forward. Understanding what went wrong in Cancún, however, requires us to take a step back to look at some of the issues in broader context.

One of the most significant factors contributing to the failure of the Cancún Ministerial Conference is the growing role played by developing countries in the WTO. Until the Uruguay Round (1986–1994), developing countries played a small role in the world trade system. Many belonged to the GATT, but few were willing to engage in reciprocal trade negotiations. During the Uruguay Round, some developing countries began to participate in trade negotiations, but were not particularly successful in shaping the bargaining agenda or shaping the rules being negotiated.

During the last ten years, developing countries have begun to exert more coordinated and more powerful influence in the WTO. In part, this greater influence is a function of numbers—more than two-thirds of current WTO members are developing countries. Of equal importance, however, has been the ability of developing countries to coordinate their WTO activities and translate their greater numbers into a coherent coalition capable of formulating and supporting a unified position. Observers saw initial signs of this at Ministerial Conferences throughout the 1990s, and particularly at the Doha Ministerial in 2001. At Doha, the Brazilian representative remarked that for the first time the conclusion of a trade bargaining round would require agreement from the developing world.

The increasing influence of developing countries has translated into greater pressure to liberalize trade in products that developing countries export (especially agriculture), and greater resistance to efforts by the United States and the European Union to add new issues to the agenda. The growing influence of developing countries in the WTO, in other words, has generated conflict between the developed and developing world over the direction that trade liberalization should take. At the 1999 WTO Ministerial Conference, held in Seattle, Washington, this conflict prevented agreement on an agenda for a new round of trade negotiations. The EU wanted to begin negotiations on new WTO rules to govern investment, competition (or antitrust) policy, government procurement, and trade facilitation (issues known collectively as "the Singapore issues" because they first arose as potential topics for WTO negotiations at the Singapore Ministerial Conference in 1996). The United States pushed to add global labor standards and the relationship between trade and the environment to the negotiating agenda. Developing countries were unwilling to begin negotiations on the Singapore issues, insisting instead that commitments that the developed world had accepted under the Uruguay Round, particularly in textiles and agriculture, be fully implemented before negotiations on new issues began.

Developing countries also opposed negotiations on labor standards and resisted the attempt by the advanced industrialized countries to link their ability to gain access to foreign markets to the adoption of commonly-agreed environmental regulations. Developing countries also insisted that the new round focus on dismantling existing barriers to international trade in agricultural commodities. They placed particular emphasis on eliminating the export subsidies that governments in the industrialized countries provided to their farmers.

At the Doha Ministerial Conference in 2001, WTO members reached agreement on a broad negotiating agenda.[2] At the core of the agenda were negotiations aimed at further liberalization of trade in industrial products, services, and agricultural goods. In addition, negotiations focused on a number of "implementation" issues, which in WTO-speak is "shorthand for developing countries' problems in implementing the . . . agreements arising from the Uruguay Round negotiations."[3] Members also agreed to continue discussion about the Trade-Related Intellectual Property Rights (TRIPS), with a particular focus on the problems arising from compulsory licensing in the pharmaceutical industry. Governments also agreed to begin negotiations on a number of WTO rules, including antidumping rules, the dispute settlement mechanism, WTO rules concerning regional trading agreements, and to continue to discuss the relationship between trade and the environment.

Success in Doha was achieved in part through resolving some of the problems that had blocked agreement in Seattle. An agreement was reached on the TRIPS that made it easier for developing countries to gain access to pharmaceutical products at low prices. In addition, all governments, including those in the advanced industrialized world, emphasized that the interests of developing countries would be placed at the forefront of negotiations. Consequently, the Doha Round came to be called "the Development Round." Success was achieved also, however, by papering over some of the more profound disagreements. Disagreement about the Singapore issues was resolved by delaying the decision about whether to begin negotiations until the Ministerial Conference in Cancún. Disagreement about whether to cut export subsidies to agricultural producers was resolved by vague wording that lent itself to different interpretations. At Cancún, governments were once again forced to confront the fact that successful negotiations require someone to make concessions in these areas. The failure of Cancún indicates that none are yet willing to do so.

The two articles presented in this chapter examine why Cancún failed and what this failure implies for the current round and the WTO more broadly. The first article, which appeared in the British weekly magazine *The Economist* the week after the Cancún Ministerial Conference, argues that the EU, the United States, developing countries, and even antiglobalization nongovernmental organizations all share the blame for the failure at Cancún. The article is somewhat pessimistic about the future, suggesting that the momentum in favor of a successful round may now be lost. The second article, written by Columbia University economist Jagdish Bhagwati, is more optimistic. Bhagwati agrees with *The Economist* about the reasons for the failure in Cancún, but suggests that the WTO is the only forum in which developing countries can achieve what they are seeking—greater market access for their agricultural and labor-intensive exports.

ENDNOTES

1. WTO. 2003. "What is the Cancún Ministerial Conference?" http://www.wto.org/english/thewto_e/minist_e/min03_e/min03_whatis_e.htm
2. See the full agenda at WTO Doha Ministerial 2001. "Ministerial Declaration," WT/MIN(01)/DEC/1,20 November 2001. Available at: http://www.wto.org/english/thewto_e/minist_e/min01_e/mindecl_e.htm
3. WTO. 2001. "The Doha Declaration Explained." http://www.wto.org/english/tratop_e/dda_e/dohaexplained_e.htm (accessed January 23, 2004)

The Doha Round: The WTO Under Fire

WHY DID THE WORLD TRADE TALKS IN MEXICO FALL APART? AND WHO IS TO BLAME?

Some poor countries' politicians seemed to revel in the collapse of the World Trade Organisation's ministerial meeting on September 14th. The Philippine trade minister, for instance, told Reuters news agency that he was "elated" by it. Tanzania's delegate claimed to be "very happy" that poor countries had stood up to rich-country "manipulation." But others were upset and shocked. According to one observer, the trade minister of Bangladesh had tears in his eyes. "I'm really disappointed," he is reported to have said. "This is the worst thing we poor countries could have done to ourselves."

Disappointment is the right reaction. For the Doha round of trade talks run by the WTO was geared specifically to help poor countries. They will be the biggest victims if the talks cannot be revived, and there seems to be scant prospect of that. The negotiations have not been officially abandoned. Diplomats pledged to continue talking in Geneva, the WTO's headquarters, with a formal meeting to be held no later than December 15th. But momentum has clearly been lost. No one now expects the round to finish by its original deadline of December 31st 2004. Some trade officials privately wonder whether it will ever finish, or whether Cancún's collapse—coming less than four years after the Seattle ministerial meeting broke down in December 1999—marks the end of the WTO as an effective negotiating forum.

THE PRICE OF POSTURING

According to the World Bank, a successful Doha round could raise global income by more than $500 billion a year by 2015. Over 60% of that gain would go to poor countries, helping to pull 144 million people out of poverty. While most of the poor countries' gains would come from freer trade among themselves, the reduction of rich-country farm subsidies and more open markets in the north would also help. That prize is now forgone.

As the scale of this lost opportunity becomes clear, the post-mortems and recriminations are beginning. Three big questions stand out: Why did the talks collapse? Who was to blame? And where does the WTO go from here?

Though the speed of the collapse caught even seasoned trade negotiators by surprise, the seeds of disaster were sown long before September 14th. The launch of the

From *The Economist* 368, no. 8342 (September 20, 2003): pp. 26–28. © 2003 The Economist Newspaper, Ltd.

Doha round in the eponymous capital of Qatar in November 2001 was itself a nail-biting negotiation marked by acrimony between rich and poor. The rhetoric was grand: Doha would reduce trade-distorting farm support, slash tariffs on farm goods and eliminate agricultural-export subsidies; it would cut industrial tariffs, especially in areas that poor countries cared about, such as textiles; it would free up trade in services; and it would negotiate global rules (subject to a framework to be decided at Cancún) in four new areas—in competition; investment; transparency in government procurement; and trade facilitation. These four new areas are referred to as the "Singapore issues" after the trade meeting at which they were first raised.

From the start, countries disowned big parts of the Doha agenda. The European Union, for instance, denied it had ever promised to get rid of export subsidies. Led by India, many poor countries denied that they ever signed up for talks on new rules. Other poor countries spent more time moaning about their grievances over earlier trade rounds than they did in negotiating the new one. Several rich countries too showed little interest in compromise. Japan, for instance, seemed content simply to say no to any cuts in rice tariffs.

This kind of posturing meant the trade round stagnated for 22 months between the meetings in Doha and Cancún. All self-imposed deadlines were missed; all tough political decisions were put off. That placed a needlessly heavy burden on the Cancún meeting. But it was not an overloaded agenda that killed the talks last weekend. It was that too many countries continued grandstanding at the Mexican resort, rather than seeking the compromises on which trade talks depend.

FOCUS ON FARMING

Agriculture was the toughest issue dividing negotiators both before and during the Cancún meeting. After months of stalemate, and at the behest of many developing countries, in August America and the EU drew up a framework for freeing farm trade. Though it involved some reform, the plan was much less ambitious than Doha had implied. Export subsidies, for example, were not to be eliminated after all.

Angered by this lack of ambition, a new block of developing countries emerged just before the Cancún meeting to denounce the EU/US framework as far too timid. Led by Brazil, China and India, this so-called G21 became a powerful voice. It represented half the world's population and two-thirds of its farmers. It was well organised and professional.

Although it spanned diverse interests—India, for instance, is terrified of lowering tariffs on farm goods, while Brazil, a huge and competitive exporter, wants free trade as fast as possible—the G21 stood together and hammered one message home: rich countries, as the most profligate agricultural subsidisers, should make bigger efforts to cut subsidies and free farm trade. The level of support given to farmers by the rich countries of the OECD has remained more or less unchanged (at over $300 billion) for the past 15 years.

While the fight between Europe, America and the G21 received most attention, another alliance of poor countries, most of them from Africa, was also worried about agriculture, but for different reasons. They feared that freeing farm trade would mean losing their special preferences. (Europe's former colonies, for instance, get special access to the EU's markets for their bananas.) They were even more worried about cutting tariffs than India, fretting that imports would ruin their small farmers. And many, particularly a small group of countries in West Africa, worried most of all about cotton.

Prodded and encouraged by non-governmental organisations (NGOs), especially Oxfam, a group of four West African countries—Benin, Burkina Faso, Chad and Mali—managed to get cotton included as an explicit item on the Cancún agenda. Their grievances were simple, and justified. West African cotton farmers are being crushed by rich-country subsidies, particularly the $3 billion-plus a year that America lavishes on its 25,000 cotton farmers, helping to make it the world's biggest exporter, depressing prices and wrecking the global market.

The West African four wanted a speedy end to these subsidies and compensation for the damage that they had caused. Though small fry compared with the overall size of farm subsidies, the cotton issue (like an earlier struggle over poor-country access to cheap drugs) came to be seen as the test of whether the Doha round was indeed focused on the poor.

But the draft text that emerged halfway through the Cancún meeting was a huge disappointment. The promises on cotton were vague, pledging a WTO review of the textiles sector, but with no mention of eliminating subsidies or of compensation. Worse, it suggested that the West African countries should be encouraged to diversify out of cotton altogether.

This hardline stance had American fingerprints all over it. Political realities in Congress (the chairman of the Senate agriculture committee is a close ally of the cotton farmers) made American negotiators fiercely defensive of their outrageous subsidies. For the Africans, the vague text was a big blow. It caused "anger and bitterness" said one delegate. As a result, the poorest countries dug in their heels when it came to the other big controversial area: that of extending trade negotiations into the four new Singapore issues. Along with many other poor countries, the Africans had long been leery about expanding the remit of the trade talks at all.

Some of their concerns, such as the fear of overloading their few negotiators, were reasonable. Others made less sense, such as the worry (fanned by many NGOs) that rich countries would use these rules to trample on poor countries' sovereignty. Two days into the conference, over 90 countries signed a letter saying that they were not ready to move into these areas.

Unfortunately, the EU and others who cared about the Singapore issues (a group that did not include the Americans) refused to compromise. Only 24 hours before the meeting was due to end, Pascal Lamy, the EU's chief negotiator, reiterated that negotiations had to proceed in all four areas. Only on Cancun's final morning did he budge, offering to give up two of the Singapore issues. There were even hints that Europe could jettison three, leaving only negotiations on trade facilitation on the table.

Rationally, no country should have objected to that, least of all poor countries. The trade blockages that these rules are designed to minimise cost them far more than tariffs. According to the World Bank, the costs of transporting African exports to foreign markets are five times higher, on average, than the tariffs paid on those goods. Complex, inefficient and corrupt customs procedures make up a big share of these transport costs.

By this time, however, reason was playing little role in the progress of the meeting. The group of embittered African countries refused to negotiate on any of the four Singapore issues. South Korea, by contrast, said it could only accept negotiations on all four. At that point, Luis Ernesto Derbez, Mexico's foreign minister and chairman of the Cancún gathering, said he saw no basis for compromise and declared the meeting over. At the centre of all the negotiations between the different factions, Mr. Derbez was better placed than anyone to make that judgment.

Within minutes, delegates who had been set to argue all night over agriculture scrambled to catch earlier flights home. Within hours, the Mexican technicians were dismantling the equipment at the conference centre.

THE BLAME GAME

Who bears responsibility for this? Some delegates, especially from Europe, blamed Mr. Derbez for cutting off discussion too hastily. One British politician claimed his action was "utterly unexpected" and "premature." Conspiracy theorists claimed that Mexico ended debate at the behest of the Americans who wanted the meeting to fail all along.

That is nonsense. Given the Mexicans' determination to finish the Cancún meeting on time, the Europeans probably made a tactical mistake in retreating so late on the Singapore issues. But Cancún's failure goes deeper than miscalculations on timing. It happened because of intransigence and brinkmanship by both rich and poor countries; because of irresponsible and inflammatory behaviour by NGOs; and because of the deeply flawed decision-making system of the WTO itself.

The instant post-mortems blamed rich countries most. NGOs accused them of wrecking the talks by pushing poor countries too far on the Singapore issues and giving too little on agriculture. There is much truth to both claims. Europe's ideological attachment to negotiations on investment and competition is hard to fathom, particularly since no European industries were clamouring for them.

On agriculture, moreover, the rich world's concessions were too timid and too grudging. America's bold promises were belied by its actions. Last year's outrageous increase in American farming subsidies, and the cave-in at Cancún by American negotiators to their domestic cotton growers, made far more of an impression on poor countries than Washington's high-minded words about freer farm trade—and rightly so.

Europe was stymied not just by its desire to mollycoddle its own farmers, but by the EU's cumbersome decision-making process. Only after its own internal reforms were agreed to in June could Brussels offer concessions on agriculture, and even then they were meagre. Given the mess that their farm policies create, rich countries should have done far more.

But poor countries, too, bear some responsibility for Cancún's collapse. Although a few emerging economies were tireless negotiators, too many others did no more than posture. Some of the posturing was tactical: for all their public rhetoric, for instance, the G21 group was actively negotiating with both America and Europe. But others, particularly some African countries, could not get beyond their radical public positions. Anti-rich-country rhetoric became more important than efforts to reach agreement.

NGOs, who were at Cancún in force, deserve much of the blame for this radicalisation. Too many of them deluged poor countries with muddle-headed positions and incited them to refuse all compromise with the rich world. The NGOs' main mistake, however, was to raise poor countries' expectations implausibly high. Shout loudly and long enough, they seemed to suggest, and you will get your way. That proved a big miscalculation.

Finally, blame belongs to the WTO's own decision-making procedures, or rather the lack of them. Mr. Lamy, with reason, called the WTO a "medieval" organisation whose rules could not support the weight of its tasks. Its predecessor, the old GATT system (which was folded into the WTO in 1995), was run by rich countries. Poor countries had little power, but also few responsibilities.

The WTO, by contrast, is a democratic organisation that works by consensus, but with no formal procedures to get there. Any one of the organisation's 148 members can hold up any aspect of any negotiation. Efforts to create smaller informal groups are decried as "non-transparent" by those left out. Not surprisingly, this lends itself more to grandstanding than to serious negotiation. The worst problem, though, is that the WTO's requirement for consensus makes it virtually impossible for it to be reformed.

HEADED FOR OBLIVION?

Can any of these failures be addressed and the Doha round be revived? Some countries are more optimistic than others. The G21, for instance, left Cancún determined to stick together and fight another day. Brazil, in particular, is convinced that sooner or later rich countries will be forced to reform their outrageous farm policies. One weapon it points to is the expiration of the "peace clause."

As part of the trade round before Doha, the Uruguay round, countries pledged not to file formal WTO complaints over the dumping of farm products as long as each country stuck to its (limited) farm-trade commitments. That peace clause runs out at the end of this year. The ensuing flood of disputes, claim some Brazilians, will at last force the Americans and Europeans to negotiate seriously on farm trade.

Optimists also point to the fact that previous trade rounds all took far longer to finish than planned. The Uruguay round, for instance, took eight years rather than three. According to this view, Cancún's collapse is just par for the course. Maybe. But the risk is that trade momentum will simply move elsewhere.

Even before Cancún's failure, the global trade-negotiating process faced unprecedented competition from bilateral and regional trade deals. Last week-end's events can only reinforce that trend. Bob Zoellick, America's top trade nego-tiator, claimed that countries were approaching him to push for bilateral deals even as the meeting was crumbling. From a global economic perspective, a tangle of such deals is far inferior to freer multilateral trade. For the poorest countries in particular, the chances of getting from a bilateral deal with America what they failed to get from the Doha round are nil.

If the momentum in trade negotiations moves away from the WTO, the con-sequences for the organisation itself could be grave. There would then be little political impetus to make it more effective, and the WTO's Geneva headquarters could quickly become no more than a court where disputes on existing trade rules are slowly adjudicated. Far from building a stronger multilateral system, the WTO would quietly sink into oblivion as a negotiating forum. Everyone would lose from this but, once again, the biggest losers would be the poor countries.

Cancún's collapse does not make any of these outcomes inevitable, but it does make them much more likely. That is why it is such a tragedy.

Don't Cry for Cancún

JAGDISH BHAGWATI

AFTER THE FALL

Once, when asked by a student radical whether he agreed with Mao Zedong's assertion that a statement could be both true and false, the philosopher Sidney Morgenbesser famously replied, "I do and I don't." Something similar could be said about the recent trade talks in Cancún, which collapsed in acrimony: they were truly both a failure and a success. The failure lay in the here and now, in the bad press and in the fact that no actual agreement was reached. But the talks also represented a success, which will soon become apparent: Cancún will serve as a stepping stone to a successful conclusion of the Doha Round of trade negotiations, underway since November 2001.

The Cancún talks collapsed abruptly on September 14 of last year, when Mexico's foreign minister, Luis Ernesto Derbez, pulled the plug following a stormy meeting. Immediately, nongovernmental organizations (NGOs) began to celebrate, and TV screens worldwide flashed scenes of Walden Bello, an eminent Filipino sociologist, dancing joyfully with fellow activists.

Less joyful were the two major players at the talks, the United States and the European Union, who responded to the breakdown by letting recriminations fly. The heads of both delegations—Robert Zoellick, the U.S. trade representative (USTR), and the EU's trade commissioner, Pascal Lamy—had hoped for an agreement at Cancún that would let the Doha Round finish on time, in January 2005, when they both expect to still be in office. When no such agreement occurred, both rushed their grievances into print. Zoellick threatened in the *Financial Times* to shift Washington's focus away from multilateral pacts and toward bilateral agreements with "will-do" nations instead—a threat that made him sound like the Donald Rumsfeld of trade policy, intent on forgoing multilateral institutions in favor of ad hoc coalitions of the willing. Zoellick laid blame for the breakdown of Cancún on the "Group of 22" developing countries (G-22) that had emerged at the talks, deploring their "transformation of the World Trade Organization into a forum for the politics of protest."

Meanwhile, Lamy responded to the end of the Cancún negotiations by suggesting darkly that the EU would not return to the trade talks anytime soon. As the *Financial Times* reported six weeks later, Lamy warned against a "rush to relaunch talks" and suggested that the World Trade Organization (WTO) negotiating

From *Foreign Affairs*, Vol. 83, No. 1, January/February, 2004, pp. 52–63. Reprinted by permission of *Foreign Affairs*. © 2004 by the Council on Foreign Relations, Inc.

process was deeply flawed. With both major players deploring multilateralism and many NGOs celebrating the collapse of Cancún, parallels with the disastrous WTO meeting held in Seattle, Washington, in late 1999 were perhaps inevitable.

Yet these comparisons were entirely inappropriate. Cancún was no Seattle. The latter will go down in the history of the WTO and of free trade as a failure. The collapse of Cancún, on the other hand, will soon be forgotten, overshadowed by the successes that still should come.

THREE CONTRASTS

Three main differences can be drawn between the breakdowns in Seattle and Cancún. To begin with, Seattle was paralyzed by protests, whereas Cancún was not. To be fair, many observers (including myself) had feared that Cancún would get mired in street protests the way that Seattle had. After all, Cancún, like Seattle—and unlike Doha, Qatar, where the current negotiating round was launched—was readily accessible to agitators. Mexico also has a longstanding tradition of student and rural radicalization; in fact, early reports suggested that the Zapatistas would come to Cancún. Moreover, Mexico's president, Vicente Fox, had run the country's Coca-Cola operation before going into politics, a career that invited the caricature that he was a tool of international big business. To make matters worse, his left-leaning foreign minister, Jorge Castañeda, had just resigned before the talks began.

Many also expected the huge reservoir of anger left over from agitations against the war in Iraq—which was hugely unpopular in Mexico—to be redirected against the trade talks. Prior to Cancún, the antiwar movement had already begun to build bridges with antiglobalization groups. Even Howard Dean, the leading Democratic presidential candidate in the United States, had responded to this growing link between the two issues, taking a number of anti-WTO, anti-free trade positions that would have made Representative Dick Gephardt (D-Mo.) blush.

In the end, however, Cancún never witnessed the kind of wild scenes that had disrupted the Seattle talks. The most dramatic events were the suicide of a South Korean farmer (who actually opposed the agricultural liberalization that several NGOs wanted), a nude "happening" on the beach that turned out to be more diverting than a diversion, and some street theater by Oxfam demonstrators wearing masks to represent the leaders of the G-7 group of leading industrialized countries.

There are at least two reasons why the protests in Cancún never matched the size or intensity of those in Seattle. First, the more strident antiglobalization groups appear to have suffered from what the economists call "the law of diminishing returns." At first, their tactics had been brilliant. Whereas guerrillas traditionally strike where they are least expected, the protesters had appeared exactly where they were expected the most: at big international meetings, where thousands from the media had gathered looking for colorful stories to file. At first, the protesters had provided just that, a welcome contrast to the gray delegates inside the conference centers. But by Cancún, the novelty that marked Seattle had worn off. Second, prior to Cancún, the most energetic antiglobalization groups had created their own playground: in Pôrto Alegre, Brazil, which now hosts the World Social Forum (a counterpoint to the World Economic Forum usually held in Davos, Switzerland).

A second major difference between the Seattle talks and those in Cancún was that the stakes at the former meeting were much higher. Seattle represented the attempt to launch a whole new round of multilateral trade negotiations. And the proposed round would have been the first to be held under the WTO, which had replaced and incorporated the General Agreement on Tariffs and Trade (GATT) in 1995, following the conclusion of the Uruguay Round. For these reasons, the abortion of the Seattle talks was a much bigger deal and had far more symbolic meaning than the collapse of Cancún. The failure to properly start a new round of trade talks (at Seattle) was much more traumatizing than lack of agreement in the midst of an ongoing round (at Cancún). After all, the preceding Uruguay Round, which took more than seven years to complete, had suffered collapses of its own, in Montreal (1988) and Brussels (1990). Cancún fell into this more benign category—more of a hiccup than a permanent end to the Doha process.

Finally, the politics of Cancún were very different from those of Seattle. At Seattle, the U.S. leadership was less than exemplary. President Bill Clinton, who had fought heroically to win passage of the North American Free Trade Agreement (NAFTA) and for support for the Uruguay Round, had been reluctant to push hard for new WTO talks at Seattle. The bruising fight over NAFTA had left him exhausted. Moreover, the Democratic Party was divided over trade, and one of its key constituencies—organized labor—had been deeply offended by Clinton's support for NAFTA.

Clinton had also worked hard to secure normal trade status for China and to smooth its entry into the WTO; in fact, Charlene Barshefsky, then USTR, had arrived breathless in Seattle just two weeks after concluding a marathon trade negotiation in Beijing. She and Clinton seemed far more focused on China than on the talks in Washington State. And Clinton failed to do the spadework necessary to get important countries on board for the Seattle talks, going into overdrive only when it was already too late. According to one story, his administration could not find hotel rooms in Seattle for foreign leaders to stay in; as a result, they had to resort to last-minute tactics such as telling the Canadian prime minister, Jean Chretien, to fly down in the morning and back to Ottawa that night.

Clinton also made a serious error by telling an interviewer, just before he arrived in Seattle, that maintaining high labor standards should eventually become mandatory for trade-treaty-guaranteed access to markets. This statement angered developing countries, which were already distressed by the spectacle of union activists from rich countries claiming that such measures were meant to protect workers in poor countries, when they appeared to have been designed to shelter jobs in rich countries instead.

Cancún, by contrast, was a very different story for the United States. With President Bush strongly behind him, Zoellick had cleverly exploited the tragedy of September 11, 2001, to get the new trade round launched at Doha. Nonetheless, the Bush administration then proceeded to harm the cause by taking a number of protectionist actions. For example, in March 2002 it succumbed to the steel industry's demands for protection and enacted steel tariffs, invoking the safeguards provisions of the WTO. Two months later, it also increased government support for American farmers under the U.S. farm bill. Washington claimed that both measures were compatible with WTO rules and within its rights. But even if they were (and the steel tariffs have since been declared illegal by the WTO), the symbolism was bad: one cannot start negotiations to reduce protection and then follow immediately by raising subsidies and trade barriers.

To give it credit, however, the Bush administration recognized that the hostile foreign reaction to its protectionist actions undermined its free trade credentials. Unless they were reestablished, the Doha Round would have been jeopardized. Had the United States persisted in asking for freer trade while taking protectionist measures, many countries would have retreated behind their own trade barriers rather than join an effort to dismantle them.

And thus, as this danger sank in, Washington turned its policy around in a remarkable fashion. The administration had not realized how badly its earlier missteps would be received elsewhere; once it did, Washington beat a rapid retreat on the most damaging of these measures—specifically, those relating to agriculture. Together, Zoellick and U.S. Agriculture Secretary Ann Veneman secured political support for a substantial offer in June 2002 to reduce agricultural subsidies and trade protection, putting the ball in the EU's court. That summer, Zoellick also managed to get the president's fast-track negotiating authority renewed, something Clinton had failed to achieve in two attempts.

The favorable contrast between Cancún and Seattle was also evident in the controversial issue of the "trade-related aspects of intellectual property rights" (TRIPS) regime in the WTO. At Seattle, the pharmaceutical industry and the U.S. government were attacked by NGOs for having added TRIPS to the WTO agreement that concluded the Uruguay Round. This criticism was fair: after all, intellectual property protection is a matter of collecting royalties, and including them in a trade institution such as the WTO seriously distorted what that organization should accomplish. But by Cancún, the NGOs had muted their criticism on this subject. Washington had managed to get the pharmaceutical industry to agree to relaxed patent protections right before Cancún, which not only removed a contentious issue from the scene but also cast the United States in a favorable light.

NOW FOR THE BAD NEWS

Why, then, did the talks at Cancún fail? Failure, like success, has many fathers, and there has already been a plethora of official explanations of what went wrong—or, more accurately, complaints. Zoellick's and Lamy's grievances have already been mentioned. Other principals also publicly weighed in, including Celso Amorim, Brazil's foreign minister and chief negotiator, who published his version in *The Wall Street Journal,* and Alec Erwin, South Africa's trade minister and a favorite to become the next director-general of the WTO, who published his in the *Financial*

Times. Most of these players, however, were too close to the scene to provide an objective assessment.

In fact, the most likely explanation for the failure of Cancún lies in a multitude of mistakes made by all parties. To begin with, Zoellick and the United States made two clear errors. First, although the most controversial items on the agenda at Cancún were TRIPS and agriculture, the United States made its concession on TRIPS before the conference started. It presumably hoped that the gesture would demonstrate Washington's eagerness to achieve accord at Cancún. But a concession made can no longer be used as a bargaining chip. Countries such as Brazil and South Africa, which had benefited from the TRIPS concession, nonetheless remained tough on agriculture—to Zoellick's surprise and chagrin.

As for agriculture itself, Washington had been prepared to offer major concessions at Cancún. But as Claude Barfield and James Glassman of the American Enterprise Institute (no foes of the current administration) have pointed out, Zoellick erred by reducing this offer at Cancún in order to bring it in line with the far less ambitious concessions proposed by the EU. This move allowed Washington to make common cause with Brussels. But it left the Cairns Group of 17 agricultural exporters and the G-22 hugely dissatisfied and disappointed, especially since their hopes had been raised by the ambitious original U.S. offer. A better strategy, according to Barfield and Glassman, would have been "for the United States to isolate Europe" and to negotiate separately with the G-22 on agriculture. Would this strategy have worked? Could Europe have been cowed into yielding some ground, despite the traditional French intransigence? Perhaps; Lamy did compromise at Cancún on other issues, although agriculture raises exceptional difficulties.

Still, if the United States made strategic errors, so did the mid-level developing countries of the G-22, led by Brazil, South Africa, India, and China. Zoellick has correctly blamed them for being unwilling to offer to reduce their own agricultural trade barriers. After all, Zoellick could not have sustained a significant offer on agriculture, or improved the general U.S. position at Cancún, unless he could have convinced both the EU and the G-22 to make their own moves toward freer trade. The U.S. farm lobby and the members of Congress who represent it insisted on it, demanding that there be a "level playing field" before they agreed to abandon their insistence on domestic protections. Why, then, was the G-22 so adamant?

The answer seems to be that policymakers in developing countries have fallen victim to two fallacies, one of description and one of prescription. The first fallacy is that protection is greater in rich countries than in poor ones, that Brussels and Washington are guilty of double standards, practicing protectionism at home while pressing for free trade abroad. Such arguments are remarkably prevalent, and are not confined to NGOs such as Oxfam; they are shared by some leaders of multilateral institutions as well, who should know better. Even such a splendid economist as Nicholas Stern, the World Bank's senior vice president, has observed, "It is surely hypocritical of the rich countries to encourage poor nations to liberalize trade, whilst at the same time succumbing to powerful groups in their own countries that seek to perpetuate narrow self-interest."

Such comments are remarkable, for if one looks at average trade protections in rich versus poor countries, the facts show that the latter nations are more protectionist than the former, not less so—and not just in industrial products, but also in labor-intensive goods such as textiles and garments and in agriculture as well. Rich nations' industrial tariffs now average close to 3 percent. But the figure is 13 percent for poor countries. As for agricultural tariffs, these average 112 percent in India and 37 percent in Brazil but only 12 percent in the United States.

Of course, agricultural subsidies are a different matter: few among even midlevel developing countries can afford to match the money governments pay to farmers in rich countries today, which amount to an average of $300 billion annually. But farm subsidies are not exactly small in countries such as India either, which heavily underwrite the costs to farmers of electricity, irrigation, and fertilizers by having state-owned providers supply them at reduced prices.

Although it may be groundless, this fallacy of description has had a major impact, making it more comfortable for leaders of developing countries to ignore their own protectionism and to reject rich countries' demands for reciprocity in trade liberalization. Reinforcing this attitude is a fallacy of prescription: that it is fine to condemn rich-country protectionism while leaving one's own trade barriers in place. This fallacy is linked to the old notion popular in many developing countries in the quarter-century after World War II: that protectionism is actually a good thing, since the freeing of trade would be either impractical or downright deadly for their development. By this logic, any level of reciprocity of trade liberalization would imperil development, and poor countries are therefore justified in rejecting it.

Again, however, the facts tell a different story. Countless studies over the last three decades have demonstrated that trade protection makes it harder to achieve prosperity, whether a country is rich or poor. Reciprocity, moreover, is a useful tool—whether developing countries recognize this fact or not. After all, reciprocity gives export industries a stake in trade liberalization, thereby handing leaders who want to break down barriers a powerful counterweight to those sectors of their economies that want to keep trade barriers in place. Moreover, except when it comes to outright aid payments, few countries are willing to give something for nothing; they rarely do so, at least, in trade matters.

In the context of Cancún, the fact that NGOs such as Oxfam encouraged developing countries to maintain their trade protections shows how such groups, despite their good intentions, can do a lot of damage—particularly when they wander into areas in which they have little expertise. This goes for the World Bank as well, which, despite the excellence of its technical staff, has occasionally indulged in unhelpful populist comments on the subject. Such mission creep is not a good thing. One solution to the problem would be to help the cash-strapped WTO develop expertise on questions relating to the world trading system; after all, the WTO is the institution devised to address such matters, and it is hard to imagine its director-general (unlike the World Bank's) ever forgetting the uses of reciprocity. Even if he did, his staff, who would be familiar with the academic literature on trade and the history of trade liberalization, would surely remind him.

FALSE CHARGES

Other divisive issues at Cancún included the infamous cotton question and the insistence of the EU, joined by South Korea and Japan, on putting the so-called Singapore issues into the Cancún text. Both of these matters have been over-played, however; neither were really deal-breakers.

The Singapore issues are a mixed bag, relating to investment, competition policy, trade facilitation, and transparency. The EU had been pushing them as a package since the time of the WTO ministerial conference in Singapore in 1995, and Lamy inherited the issues from his predecessor, Sir Leon Brittan. Both the EU and Japan have been very keen on the investment provisions in particular, although their business lobbies have not pushed this agenda—at least not as hard as have their NGOs, which, in contrast, oppose the measures and helped derail a multilat-eral agreement on investment at the Organization for Economic Cooperation and Development some years ago.

On competition policy, the United States and the EU had several disagree-ments, with the U.S. antitrust division under Bill Clinton opposed to pursuing competition policy in the WTO, while the EU wanted matters handled there. Trade facilitation (in customs) and transparency (in procurement) were the least objectionable issues, although several of the poor countries would have found their resources strained to implement better administrative regimes. But then more funds could have been made available for this purpose.

In the end, although South Korea continued to insist on the four Singapore issues being packaged together, Lamy walked away from this position and indi-cated that he would have been willing to let go of investment and competition policy. Thus the issue was not a sticking point, as some have charged. Lamy has been blamed for waiting too long before showing he was ready to compromise. But that is not a credible charge: he gave way well before the end of Cancún.

As for the cotton question, much has been made of the fact that the African and Caribbean countries walked out of the Cancún talks as a measure of solidarity with four cotton-exporting countries (Benin, Burkina Faso, Chad, and Mali)—a walkout that, some have claimed, caused the meeting to collapse. Both cotton subsidies and sugar tariffs have long been denounced by trade economists as harmful to poor countries. But the demand by the four African countries that they be immediately compensated for this harm with between $250 million and $1 billion annually was simply unrealistic and inappropriate. Rarely do countries compensate others for the effects of economic policies that they pursue; doing so would open up a Pandora's box. The issue is better handled by asking the World Bank and other aid agencies to redirect some funds to assist countries in need. This should be done while Zoellick works, as he has promised to, on eliminating production subsidies to U.S. cotton within a total package that would be part of the conclusion of the Doha Round.

If Zoellick goes to work on some form of multilateral support for the four cotton-producing nations and tries to include the reduction of cotton subsidies in Doha's total agricultural package, these countries should return to the table. This would be in everyone's interest; the wound is too small to let it fester until it destroys an otherwise healthy organism.

DERBEZ AND DENOUEMENT

Luis Derbez, Mexico's foreign minister, has been widely criticized for his inexperience as the chairman of the talks at Cancún—especially for terminating the conference without consulting a wide group of trade ministers. But it is hard to believe that Derbez halted the proceedings without consulting Zoellick first. After all, although Mexico has had problems with the Bush administration, it remains part of NAFTA and a strong U.S. ally. And even Zoellick's angry statements after the end of the conference suggest that he approved, if not proposed, the meeting's termination: "As Derbez . . . closed the session, representatives of influential developing countries *finally* rushed forward to say they wanted to keep going . . . *yet they were too late*" (italics added). Zoellick evidently was so angered and frustrated by the impasse that he pulled the plug.

But Zoellick was likely confident that such hardball tactics, along with the threat that the United States would turn to bilateral trade negotiations, would force recalcitrant nations back to the multilateral table. He did not actually plan on leaving the poker game; rather, he hoped that it would resume as soon as the other players returned with more chips.

He may well be proven right. Chances are high that negotiations will resume and that, when they do, a successful outcome will be reached. None of the players, now that their passions are spent, have any interest in a failed Doha Round. True, there are reasons for pessimism. The United States is now entering an election season and the Democratic candidates are staking out fiercely irresponsible anti-trade positions. President Bush will probably see this as an opportunity to make a case for trade, accusing the Democrats of putting politics above the national interest. Bush almost never indulged the cause of "fair trade" during his first campaign, and there is little evidence that he lost any votes on this account; thus he is unlikely to endorse the issue this time. Of course, a weak economy could weaken support for serious trade liberalization and make it difficult politically. But the economy's growth in the third quarter of 2003, which exceeded 7 percent, has lifted Bush's hopes and dampened those of his opponents.

Even if the situation were to deteriorate on these fronts, all it would mean is that the Doha Round will not be completed by its original January 2005 deadline. But that would not be fatal; this deadline has always been regarded in private, although never acknowledged publicly, as overambitious. After all, the Tokyo Round took more than five years to complete, and the Uruguay Round that followed took more than seven. For Doha to finish in three would be a heroic achievement.

What matters most is that the negotiators keep talking, beyond the original deadline if necessary. And the chances are high that they will, for at least one overriding reason. If the G-22 and the Cairns Group really want agriculture to be liberalized, they are unlikely to achieve this except in the context of a multilateral agreement. Bilateral deals are simply not up to the task. Most of them today exempt agriculture, and few exist between countries with competing farm sectors. Besides, production subsidies cannot be cut preferentially for favored nations. So the G-22, the EU, the United States, and Japan have only one real option: multilateralism.

QUESTIONS FOR REVIEW AND DISCUSSION

1. To what extent do *The Economist* and Bhagwati focus on the same factors in explaining why the Cancún Ministerial Conference failed? Where do they disagree? What do you think is the single most significant cause of the failure to reach agreement at Cancún?
2. According to *The Economist*, what role did NGOs play in the failure at Cancún? Does Bhagwati agree or disagree with this analysis?
3. The European Union appears reluctant to reduce agricultural subsidies. How do politics in the EU make it difficult for it to do so?
4. What are Bhagwati's "fallacies of description and prescription?" What role does Bhagwati think they played in the failure to reach agreement in Cancún?
5. In what way did American cotton subsidies contribute to the failure at Cancún? Do you think that four small countries should be able to block agreement in the WTO?
6. *The Economist* and Bhagwati reach quite different conclusions about how the failure at Cancún will affect the current round and, more broadly, the WTO. What are these conclusions, and which one do you think is likely to be proven correct? Why?

SUGGESTIONS FOR FURTHER READING

For the full Doha Development Agenda, as well as discussion of the negotiations, visit the WTO Web site: http://www.wto.org/english/tratop_e/dda_e/dda_e.htm

For a detailed, if rather critical, examination of the establishment of the Doha Development Agenda, see: Fatoumata Jawara and Aileen Kwa. *Behind the Scenes at the WTO: the Real World of International Trade Negotiations*. London: Zed Books, 2003.

BRIDGES Weekly Trade News Digest is a valuable resource for following current developments. You can browse this on-line journal at: http://www.ictsd.org/weekly/

You can get a sample of national responses to the failure of the Cancún Ministerial Conference in three editorials that appeared in the weeks following the Conference. See: Robert B. Zoellick. "America Will Not Wait For The Won't-Do Countries." *Financial Times* September 22, 2003, p. 23; Celso Amorim. "The Real Cancun." *The Wall Street Journal* September 25, 2003, A18; and Alec Erwin. "Developing Countries Were Held To Ransom In Cancun." *Financial Times* September 30, 2003, p. 23.

CHAPTER 5

THE WORLD TRADE ORGANIZATION AND THE ENVIRONMENT

The relationship between trade and the environment, and the question of whether WTO rules should be reformed to make it easier to use trade restrictions to protect the environment, have been hotly debated issues during the last ten years. At the core of this debate lies a broader question concerning the role of trade restrictions in correcting negative externalities caused by economic activity. It is widely accepted that legitimate economic activity can have unintended harmful consequences for the environment. To take just one example, shrimpers kill many sea turtles when harvesting shrimp. Of course, shrimping is a legitimate activity, but one unintended consequence of this activity is that turtles become entangled in shrimp nets and drown. Shrimping therefore has a cost—dead turtles—that is not reflected in the market price of shrimp. Because the full cost to society of shrimp fishing is not reflected in the price of shrimp, more shrimp is consumed, more resources are allocated to harvesting shrimp, and more turtles are killed than would be if shrimpers were forced to take into account the full cost of their activity. This externality, therefore, reduces social welfare.

Government regulation can correct externalities. Some such regulations work through the price mechanism. A tax imposed on a certain good, for example, will raise its cost, thereby reducing demand for the good. Lower demand will lead to less production and thus to less of the externality-generating activity. Other regulations instruct producers to adopt certain production techniques or technologies that would reduce the unintended harm. For example, the U.S. government requires coal-burning power plants to install scrubbers in their smokestacks to reduce sulfur emissions. To protect sea turtles, the U.S. government now requires American shrimpers to use Turtle Exclusion Devices (TEDs) on their shrimp nets. By adopting such regulations, governments force producers and consumers to limit the environmental harm caused by their activities.

WTO rules do not limit the ability of governments to apply such regulations on domestic firms. WTO rules begin to constrain action when governments attempt to extend such regulations beyond their national borders through either unilateral or multilateral initiatives. Suppose, for example, that the U.S. government, having required American shrimpers to use TEDs, then banned shrimp imports from countries that did not require their shrimp fleets to use similar technology. In doing so, the U.S. has restricted trade in pursuit of an environmental objective. Is this restriction consistent with WTO rules? Should such trade restrictions be consistent with WTO rules? Or, suppose that a number of governments conclude a multilateral environmental agreement (MEA) that incorporates trade restrictions that are inconsistent with a particular WTO rule. There are currently approximately 200 such MEAs, about 25 of which contain trade-restricting measures that are potentially inconsistent with WTO rules. In cases of conflict, which rules should apply— WTO rules prohibiting such restrictions or MEA rules requiring them? More broadly, to what extent do and should WTO rules allow governments to use trade restrictions as one among many policies to protect the natural environment?

Politics further complicate the issue. Governments must balance the demands of the environmental movement, which would like to see environmental concerns take precedence over trade liberalization, and those of businesses, workers, and consumers who benefit greatly from trade liberalization and may be more cautious about the costs of environmental protection. Consequently, it is unlikely that governments can elaborate a general principle that gives trade precedence over the environment, or the converse. Instead, governments must try to strike a balance between protecting the environment and promoting higher standards of living.

Thinking about where this balance should be struck, and who should strike it, raises further complications. The WTO is the most likely forum for such decisions, if only because no other international organization exists to consider the issue. However, WTO members do not agree on whether, much less how, to bring environmental concerns more fully into the trade organization. In some instances, disagreement falls along North–South lines. The advanced industrialized countries, including the United States and the European Union, have pushed to make the WTO more sensitive to environmental concerns, and have proposed rule changes for doing so. Many developing countries, however, are skeptical about the need for such changes and wary of the motivations behind them. In other instances, conflict falls along North–North lines, as the EU and United States disagree about the precautionary principle and other issues. Such conflicts have shaped how the WTO has addressed the environment in the past, and even moderate reforms to WTO rules in the future will require solutions to these conflicts among WTO members.

The two articles presented in this chapter focus on this debate. The first article, written by Lori Wallach and Michelle Sforza, both researchers at the Washington, DC–based NGO Public Citizen, argue that the GATT and WTO have had a negative impact on the environment. The authors argue that GATT/WTO rules, and the WTO dispute panels' interpretation of these rules, threaten to undermine existing environmental regulations, make it difficult for governments to adopt new environmental regulations, and weaken the incentive for governments to negotiate MEAs. They suggest that the WTO has done little to improve its treatment of the environment during the last ten years.

The second article, written by Michael M. Weinstein, a BP Senior Fellow for International Economics at the Council on Foreign Relations, and Steve

Charnovitz, a former director of the Global Environment and Trade Study at Yale University, focuses on the evolution of environmental issues in the GATT/WTO since the late 1980s. The authors argue that during the last ten years the WTO has become increasingly sensitive to environmental concerns and increasingly willing to take such concerns into account when ruling on trade disputes. They conclude by suggesting a number of moderate reforms that would further strengthen the environmental component of the WTO.

The WTO's Environmental Impact
LORI WALLACH AND MICHELLE SFORZA

When the legislation implementing the GATT Uruguay Round and establishing the World Trade Organization was approved in the U.S. Congress in 1994, it was done without the support of a single environmental, conservation or animal welfare group.

While the year before, several environmental groups had split away from the majority of U.S. nongovernmental organizations to support NAFTA, environmentalists were unified in opposition to the Uruguay Round Agreements. Then-U.S. Trade Representative Mickey Kantor claimed that no U.S. environmental or health laws would be undermined by the WTO, testifying, "The . . . [WTO] clearly recognizes and acknowledges the sovereign right of each government to establish the level of protection of human, animal and plant life and health deemed appropriate by that government."[1] But these assurances failed to persuade the environmental community.

The environmentalists' skepticism was not surprising. Some of the groups that had supported NAFTA the year before—in exchange for an environmental "side agreement"—felt betrayed. First, early indications were that the side agreement would be ineffective.[2] Second, the groups had been promised by the Clinton administration that the NAFTA model would establish a "floor" for environmental protection in trade agreements that would be strengthened in subsequent trade pacts.[3] Instead, NAFTA's environmental side pact turned out to be the high water mark. The next year it became clear that the Uruguay Round Agreements contained numerous provisions limiting the actions governments could take to protect the public and the environment—but included no environmental safeguards at all.

In addition, environmentalists had witnessed the negative impacts of GATT provisions in effect *before* the Uruguay Round. In several instances, countries had challenged environmental laws as violating GATT rules. GATT dispute resolution tribunals had agreed that the environmental laws violated GATT rules and also made extremely narrow interpretations of several GATT "exception" provisions that theoretically could be relied upon to protect environmental safeguards from such challenges.

Environmentalists feared that the expansive new powers of enforcement that were granted to the WTO, combined with the anti-environmental bias already

From Lori Wallach and Michell Sforza, "The WTO's Environmental Impact," *Whose Trade Organization? Corporate Globalization and the Erosion of Democracy*, Washington, DC: Public Citizen, © 1999.

evident in the GATT, would produce dire consequences for global environmental protection. Environmentalists implored the Uruguay Round negotiators to refashion their approach to environmental issues.[4]

These entreaties were ignored by the negotiators, who produced an agreement that built upon the GATT's foundation of rules prioritizing commercial prerogatives over conservation and environmental protection. In an effort to counter the potential political problems that environmental concerns could cause with parliaments faced with approval of the Uruguay Round, the future WTO Member countries made a last-minute decision at the Marakesh, Morocco, WTO signing ceremonies to establish a Committee on Trade and Environment (CTE). The committee was given the mandate to study ways to make trade and environmental goals mutually compatible. The CTE was designated a WTO study group (not a negotiating group, meaning it was not empowered to develop new WTO rules for environmental protection). It has proven entirely ineffective as a mechanism for promoting environmental interests within the WTO.

Five years of experience under the WTO have confirmed environmentalists' fears. In case after case, the WTO is being used to threaten or has upheld formal challenges to environmental safeguards, doing far more damage than occurred under the pre-Uruguay Round regime.

Threats—often by industry but with government support—of WTO illegality are being used to chill environmental innovation. Increased trade flows also are leading to greater biodiversity problems caused by invasive species infestations, and the status of multilateral environmental agreements is being undermined by the WTO. . . .

Through the threat of sanctions, the WTO has compelled countries to repeal or rewrite key environmental laws or has chilled innovations. Particularly disturbing, most challenges to date have merely involved the application of the WTO's new enforcement powers to long-standing, anti-environmental GATT rules. The new, stronger, anti-environmental provisions developed through the Uruguay Round have, with limited exceptions, only been brought to bear in the context of threats. These new agreements, as they are fully implemented, will provide new, far broader opportunities for anti-environmental interests to use the WTO to attack environmental safeguards—a process already under way.

GATT AND THE ENVIRONMENT: PRE-URUGUAY ROUND

The GATT's anti-environmental bent was apparent prior to negotiations of approval of the Uruguay Round, as exemplified by high-profile challenges to two key U.S. environmental laws—the Marine Mammal Protection Act (MMPA) and the Corporate Average Fuel Efficiency (CAFE) standards for automobiles.

In 1991, GATT Article III on National Treatment (nondiscrimination) was interpreted to prohibit governments from treating goods differently based on the way they are produced or harvested. This interpretation arose from a successful

GATT challenge by Mexico to the MMPA—an effective, long-standing U.S. statute banning the U.S. sale of tuna caught by domestic or foreign fishers using purse seines. Purse seines are massive nets that are laid over schools of dolphins to catch tuna swimming below. The technique had resulted in millions of dolphin nets.[5] A GATT tribunal rules that the U.S. law violated GATT rules by distinguishing tuna caught in a dolphin-safe manner from tuna caught using deadly encirclement seines.

Then, in 1994, a GATT panel ruled against U.S. CAFE regulations on a challenge brought by the European Economic Community (EEC). The GATT panel concluded that although the CAFE rules were facially neutral—i.e., they treated domestic and foreign cars alike—they had a discriminatory effect on European cars. Under the regulation, a manufacturer's entire fleet of cars sold in the U.S. was required to meet a combined average fuel efficiency. European auto manufacturers had made the marketing decision to sell only the larger, high-end (and thus more profitable) models of their cars in the U.S. An unintended consequence of that marketing decision was the requirement under the CAFE standards that such models be more fuel efficient than comparable American or Japanese luxury cars, whose efficiency could be averaged against smaller, cleaner models that the American and Japanese makers also sold on the U.S. market.

In both the dolphin and the automobile fuel efficiency cases, the U.S. tried to invoke exceptions to the GATT that are contained in Article XX of the agreement. Article XX "exceptions" are supposed to allow countries to adopt and/or maintain laws that contradict GATT rules in certain narrowly defined circumstances.[6] In theory, the exceptions protect countries from inappropriate infringements on the capacity of policymakers to protect the public interest in vital areas such as national security and, theoretically, health or environmental protection. However, in both of these cases, the exceptions were so narrowly interpreted as to render them moot.

Thus, before the Uruguay Round talks were complete, environmentalists had witnessed successful attacks on environmental laws using GATT rules and had seen that the existing GATT exceptions provided no protection for such laws.

THE WTO AND THE ENVIRONMENT: STRONG ENFORCEMENT OF ANTI-ENVIRONMENTAL LAWS

Mindful of this disturbing pre-Uruguay Round track record, environmentalists urged Uruguay Round negotiators to strengthen the weak Article XX exceptions so that they might be used effectively to safeguard WTO-challenged environmental laws. They also sought to amend GATT provisions that had been—or could be—the basis for attacks on environmental policies. Since a central objective of the Uruguay Round was to make the GATT and other related agreements strongly enforceable through the WTO by use or threat of trade sanctions, environmentalists considered it to be critical that the new regime not include provisions that could undermine domestic and international environmental laws and policy.

Uruguay Round negotiators refused to remedy the existing problems. Rather, in the Uruguay Round Agreements, they added a vast array of new anti-environment, anti-conservation provisions to the existing GATT rules. These new rules subject a wider array of hard-won environmental laws to scrutiny as so-called "non-tariff barriers" to trade. . . .

The WTO agreement on Sanitary and Phytosanitary Measures (SPS) explicitly restricts the actions that governments can take relating to food and agriculture in an effort to protect the environment, human, plant, and animal health, and the food supply. As a result, many policies that governments use to avoid or contain invasive species infestations from undermining biodiversity can run afoul of SPS rules. The WTO agreement on Technical Barriers to Trade (TBT) requires that product standards—a nation's rules governing the contents and characteristics of products—be the least restrictive version and, with extraordinarily limited exceptions, be based on international standards. The WTO agreement on Government Procurement (AGP) requires that governments take into account only "commercial considerations" when making purchasing decisions. The agreement on Trade Related Aspects of Intellectual Property Rights (TRIPS) requires that WTO Members provide property rights protection to genetically modified plant varieties even though their long-term environmental impacts have not been established. All of these agreements are enforceable, by threat of sanction, through the WTO's dispute resolution system.

A crucial difference between the GATT and the WTO trade regimes is the legal status of their respective dispute settlement panel rulings. Both systems include the possibility of challenging other countries' laws before trade tribunals, when one country thinks another's law violates GATT rules. Under GATT, however, the emphasis was on cooperation and negotiated settlements to trade agreements. The WTO, in contrast, is "self-executing," which means its panels are empowered to make binding decisions, enforceable through trade sanctions.

Under pre-Uruguay Round rules, a dispute panel report was adopted only if there was consensus by all GATT Contracting Parties. Requiring consensus for action is a typical sovereignty protection found in many international agreements. Under the previous GATT rules, a country whose domestic regulations were under fire could essentially block the enforcement of a ruling (although, in order to avoid undermining GATT's legitimacy, countries rarely exercised this option).

The Uruguay Round Agreements turned the sovereignty safeguard of consensus on its head by requiring unanimous consensus to stop adoption of any WTO panels' ruling. This would require 134 [now 155] WTO Members, including the victorious country, to all agree to stop adoption of a panel ruling. The intention of this change was to create a rule-based system in which all WTO Members were equal, since the former cooperative system was seen to give too much negotiating power to the financially stronger countries who had more political ability to decide to follow or ignore rulings. Unfortunately, the effect of the new binding system has been to consolidate the dominant position of countries that can afford permanent representation at the WTO and expert help at the panel hearings.[7] Worse still, the outcomes of trade battles are now being sold to the public as technical, legal interpretations of commercial law and not recognized as what they are: political and policy decisions.

While the WTO publicly states its support for the principles of sustainable development in the WTO ("the [environment] has been given and will continue to be given a high profile on the WTO agenda"),[8] the track record suggests an altogether different set of priorities. Indeed, in a revealing attack of candor, then-WTO Secretary General Renato Ruggiero stated that environmental standards in the WTO are "doomed to fail and could only damage the global trading system."[9]

WTO'S NEW BINDING RULES HAVE WEAKENED ENVIRONMENTAL SAFEGUARDS

❊ ❊ ❊

Case 2: Clinton Administration Guts Dolphin Protection

Under amendments to the U.S. Marine Mammal Protection Act (MMPA), the sale by domestic or foreign fishers of tuna caught with encirclement nets, known as purse seines, was banned in the U.S. in 1988 because the nets killed millions of dolphins in the Eastern Tropical Pacific.[10] For reasons marine biologists have never determined, schools of tuna in that region congregate under schools of dolphins. Thus, the fishing industry began using mile-long nets deployed by speed-boats to encircle the dolphins on the surface. In this method, the weighted bottoms of the massive nets are drawn short, creating huge sacks in which both the dolphins and tuna are trapped. Over 30 years, seven million dolphins were drowned, crushed or otherwise killed as a result of purse seine tuna fishing.[11]

The slaughter was captured on videotape by an environmentalist who slipped aboard a fishing boat as a cook.[12] The resulting furor—including millions of children writing to Congress to "Save the Dolphins"—led to the dolphin-safe tuna provisions of the MMPA.[13] Two of the four affected species of dolphin, the eastern spinner and northeastern offshore spotted dolphins, have been designated "depleted" under the MMPA due to purse seine fishing methods.[14]

The GATT Dolphin Cases

In 1991, a GATT panel ruled against Section 101(a)(2) of the U.S. MMPA[15]—which excluded from the U.S. market tuna caught by domestic or foreign fishers using purse seines. The panel interpreted language in GATT's Article III, which prohibits discrimination between products on the basis of *where* they are produced to also forbid distinguishing between products based on *how* they are produced (called production processes and methods or PPMs). Specifically, the GATT panel interpreted language in GATT Article III requiring "like products" produced domestically or abroad to be given equal treatment. By deciding that the notion of "like product" only pertained to a product's physical characteristics, the panel ruling placed a long list of U.S. and other countries' laws that focus on *how* tuna is caught or *how* paper is manufactured in violation of GATT rules. Thus, unless there is literally dolphin meat in a can of tuna, making it physically different, a can of tuna caught with dolphin-deadly nets must be treated exactly the same as one caught by dolphin-safe methods.

The next year the European Community, which sought to export prepared tuna processed from fish obtained from Pacific Ocean stocks, launched its own challenge to the law.[16] In its 1994 ruling, the GATT panel on the European challenge again ruled against dolphin protection.[17]

In both cases, the U.S. argued that because dolphin protection is a legitimate environmental objective and the embargo was applied to both the domestic and foreign tuna industries, the law would fall well within the protections of GATT Article XX. Both GATT panels rejected this argument. The first panel found that the law was not "necessary" to protect dolphin health because, in the panel's opinion, the U.S. could have attempted to protect dolphins through other measures that would not have violated GATT.[18] It also found that the U.S. law targeted tuna fishing largely outside U.S. borders and ruled that Article XX applied only to actions taken inside a nation's borders.[19] This ruling is astounding, given that fish are migratory and are not confined to the territory of one country.

The panel in the European challenge disagreed with the first panel's conclusion that a country can never, under GATT rules, protect resources outside of its territory if such protections limit trade. However, it agreed with the first panel that the dolphin-safe law was not "necessary" to protect dolphin health and thus that the U.S. law was GATT-illegal.

In addition, the panel in the European challenge concluded that a nation cannot require another country to change domestic laws—in this case adopt regulations on tuna fishing to protect dolphins—in exchange for market access.[20] The U.S. could pressure individual tuna producers to change their behavior but could not condition access to the U.S. market for these producers on their home country governments' taking concrete action to enforce U.S. dolphin protection standards. This line of reasoning would be recycled in a similar WTO case involving a U.S. embargo on shrimp from countries that do not require fishers to protect sea turtles (see below).

Given that the rulings against the U.S. dolphin-safe law were issued by GATT—and not WTO—panels, they were not automatically enforceable. Indeed, worried that implementation of the controversial 1991 GATT case that had been dubbed *GATTzilla vs. Flipper* could threaten NAFTA's 1993 congressional approval, the U.S. and Mexico originally agreed to block further GATT action.

However, in 1995, with NAFTA already implemented and the WTO enforcement mechanism now in effect, Mexico threatened a WTO enforcement case against the U.S. for continuing failure to implement the 1991 GATT dolphin ruling. In order to avoid the political embarrassment of having the WTO order the U.S. to rescind the highly popular dolphin protection (or face millions of dollars in trade sanctions) the Clinton administration launched a two-year campaign that ultimately resulted in the gutting of the MMPA.

Clinton Administration Guts Dolphin Law to Comply with GATT

President Clinton was so anxious to avoid the public spectacle of a dolphin protection law being eviscerated again by the WTO, he sent a letter to Mexican President

Ernesto Zedillo declaring that the weakening of the standard "is a top priority for my Administration and for me personally."[21] Clinton promised to take action within the first thirty days of his second term.[22] It would not prove easy to comply with the ruling or this promise, as this required the U.S. to amend the Marine Mammal Protection Act through an act of Congress.

The administration recruited several members of Congress with notoriously bad environmental voting records, such as Rep. Randy "Duke" Cunningham, a California Republican, and Sen. John Breaux, a Louisiana Democrat, to introduce a bill weakening the MMPA to make it conform to the GATT ruling. That legislation was quickly nicknamed the "Dolphin Death Act" by many environmental groups.[23]

Under the leadership of the Marine Mammal Protection Act's original champions, such as Sen. Barbara Boxer and Rep. George Miller, both California Democrats, a coalition of environmental, consumer, and other public interest groups—the Dolphin Safe Fair Trade Campaign—was able to stall the Dolphin Death Act in 1996. However, a slightly different version of the legislation was passed in August 1997[24] after a huge push by the Clinton administration, led by then-Undersecretary of State Timothy Wirth and Vice President Al Gore. The amendment would allow tuna caught with the deadly nets to be sold in the U.S. Moreover, it would even allow tuna caught with such nets to carry the "dolphin safe" label that consumers have come to know and trust—provided the tuna is certified as coming from a catch where a single monitor on a football field-length fishing boat did not observe any dolphin deaths.

On April 29, 1999, the Commerce Department announced that based on the results of a study by the National Marine Fisheries Service (NMFS)[25] in consultation with the Marine Mammal Commission and the Inter-American Tropical Tuna Commission (IATTC), it would implement the 1997 law and weaken the labeling standard for "dolphin safe" tuna.[26] The study, mandated by the 1997 legislation, concluded that dolphin mortality has declined in areas where purse seines are used when monitors are aboard fishing fleets.[27] The study also found, however, that the dolphin population in the Eastern Tropical Pacific was not recovering, despite the use of monitors. The study showed that although mortality rates declined *relative* to unmonitored purse seine fishing, the decline was not sufficient to replace the damage that purse seines had already wrought on the dolphin population. Nonetheless, the Commerce Department decided to move ahead, and tuna caught with purse seines was slated to be back on the U.S. market by the fall of 1999—for the first time in over a decade. (Meanwhile, the IATTC will continue to study dolphin mortality until 2002, at which time, if the results are the same, the U.S. will make the new U.S. standard permanent.)[28]

The U.S. Commerce Department claims that the new regulation will allow only tuna from catches during which no dolphin deaths were observed to bear the "dolphin safe" label.[29] However, tuna boats are a football field in length, the nets are miles in circumference, and only one observer is required per ship—making it physically impossible to monitor thoroughly. Moreover, to enforce this policy, the U.S. would have to track all tuna imports from the moment they are caught in the Eastern Tropical Pacific to the time they enter the U.S. consumer market. This presents an enormous task for regulators, which is why the old law operated on a country-by-country basis, not on a catch-by-catch basis. It remains unclear how the U.S. can, with any confidence, distinguish among tuna shipments that have involved the death of dolphins and those that have not. Instead, regulators will have to rely on the "dolphin safe" reports of the producers themselves—those with the greatest incentive to downplay dolphin deaths. Consumer and environmental groups say that this new policy degrades the "dolphin safe" label from an effective way in which to hold the tuna industry accountable to consumers to a cynical marketing ploy rewarding unsafe fishing practices.[30]

The precedent set in the GATT panel's ruling has widespread implications.[31] It declares import bans designed to further a legitimate social or environment aim by eliminating objectionable production methods to be outside GATT/WTO permissible policy. Under such reasoning, prohibiting the use of fur harvested by clubbing of harp seals could be GATT-illegal. Similarly, bans on products involving child labor or even slave labor could be prohibited by the WTO.

Case 3: The WTO Rules Against Endangered Species Act

Provisions of the Endangered Species Act allow sale of shrimp in the U.S. only if the shrimp is caught in nets equipped with turtle excluder devices, or TEDs.[32] These devices are designed to allow sea turtles to escape from shrimp nets. In late 1998, a WTO panel ruled that the U.S. law violated trade rules and ordered the U.S. to rewrite its turtle protection policy. Worldwide, the turtle population has plummeted, and all sea turtles that inhabit U.S. waters are listed as endangered or threatened.[33] Shrimp nets entangle, drown, dismember and kill as many as 55,000 endangered or threatened sea turtles each year.[34] Indeed, shrimping kills more sea turtles than all other human threats to turtles combined.[35]

In an effort to minimize the decline in the sea turtle populations, the National Marine Fisheries Service promoted the use of TEDs to U.S. shrimpers. After few shrimpers installed TEDs in their nets, U.S. law was changed in 1980 to require shrimpers to operate in a manner that did not harm turtles.[36] Under section 609 of the Endangered Species Act,[37] all shrimp sold in the U.S. must be caught using TEDs, any of several trapdoor-like devices that shunt sea turtles out of shrimp nets before they drown. Costing from $50 to $400, TEDs are a relatively inexpensive way to reduce sea turtle deaths by as much as 97%—without appreciably decreasing shrimp catches.[38]

The governments of India, Malaysia, Pakistan, and Thailand joined forces to challenge the U.S. law, arguing that WTO rules prohibit limitations on imports based on the way products are produced.[39] Australia, El Salvador, the EU, Guatemala, Hong Kong, Japan, Nigeria, the Philippines, Singapore, and Venezuela made third-party submissions to the WTO panel arguing that the U.S. law violated WTO rules.

Under the argument used by these nations—the same one used in the tuna-dolphin case—all shrimp are "like products" and therefore must be allowed into the U.S. market, regardless of whether the shrimp are caught using methods that kill sea turtles.

The U.S. argued that it was allowed under WTO rules to protect animal life, as long as the law was applied equally to U.S. and foreign shrimp producers. Indeed, unlike the MMPA challenge in the tuna-dolphin case, which had a potential for technical discrimination in how one aspect was implemented, the turtle policy was *exactly* the same for foreign and domestic fishers. Thus, the U.S. argued that the shrimp law qualified for an exception under Article XX.

The WTO panel disagreed. "We note that the issue in dispute was not the urgency of protection of sea turtles, . . . It was not our task to review generally the desirability or necessity of the environmental objectives of the U.S. policy on sea turtle conservation. In our opinion, Members are free to set their own environmental objectives. However, they are bound to implement these objectives in such a way that is consistent with their WTO obligations, not depriving the WTO Agreement of its object and purpose."[40]

The panel ruled that the U.S. law was designed to interfere with trade and thus the Article XX exceptions were inapplicable. Of course, this interpretation eviscerates the entire exceptions clause of GATT. The panel also declared that because the regulations were unilaterally imposed on U.S. trading partners, the law deprived the WTO of its object and purpose of establishing a multilateral trade regime, regardless of the non-trade related objective that was being pursued and the lack of discrimination between domestic and foreign fisheries.

Major U.S. environmental organizations quickly denounced the decision and urged the Clinton administration to continue to implement the sea turtle protections and attempt to reform the WTO substantially—or withdraw from it.[41] Even the pro-WTO *New York Times* editorialized about the "Sea Turtles Warning," contradicting its past admonitions about WTO critics' unfounded concerns by urging the WTO to reconsider and the U.S. not to change the law.[42] The U.S. government appealed the WTO decision.[43]

In October 1998, the WTO Appellate Body reaffirmed the decision that the U.S. law is WTO-illegal.[44] However, the Appellate Body reversed the lower panel as to whether the Endangered Species Act theoretically could be covered by Article XX exceptions.[45] Reaching impressive heights of legal sophistry, the panel held that the law could indeed have qualified for an environmental exception under Article XX but did not do so in this case because the law was implemented in a way that was unjustifiably and arbitrarily discriminatory.[46]

The Appellate Body's ruling has been viewed as an attempt to defuse the criticism of environmentalists while still advancing the GATT agenda of primacy of trade over all other policy goals. The panel acknowledged that sea turtles are endangered and that there is a legitimate interest in protecting and preserving them. It also acknowledged the appropriateness of the U.S. turtle excluder device policy. The ruling included language aimed at pacifying environmentalists, stating, "We have not decided that the protection and preservation of the environment is of no significance to the Members of the WTO. Clearly, it is. We have not decided that the sovereign nations that are Members of the WTO cannot adopt effective measures to protect endangered species, such as sea turtles. Clearly they can and should."[47] Despite the positive sounding political rhetoric, the WTO Appellate Body ultimately ruled that the measure violated WTO rules.

The Appellate Body recommended that the U.S. change its turtle protection measures to comply with the ruling, leading one trade policy expert to quip, "Good dicta for environmentalists, but I wouldn't want to be a sea turtle."[48]

If implemented, the WTO ruling against the Endangered Species Act could severely hamper efforts to protect sea turtles. Perversely, it could also put the U.S. producers who have already invested in TEDs technology at a competitive disadvantage for having complied with the law of the land. According to one shrimper, "We are the ones who have to pay the price to save the turtle. I thought we were going to have a level playing field to compete, but apparently not."[49]

As domestic industry learns the lesson that the WTO is hostile to strong environmental safeguards affected domestic industries will question environmental legislation on the basis that it disadvantages them vis-à-vis their foreign competitors, whose noncompliance is effectively sanctioned by the WTO. The combination of WTO environmental hostility and related industry pressure will make it increasingly difficult for countries to assert environmental leadership in the absence of often slow or impossible international consensus.

Initially, the U.S. agreed to comply with the WTO ruling against the Endangered Species Act by revising regulations to allow shipment-by-shipment certification of TEDs use. Under the original regulation, a country seeking to send shrimp to the U.S. was responsible for requiring its shrimp fleet to have sea turtle protections comparable to the Endangered Species Act standard. Environmental groups charged that the new regulation would violate the Endangered Species Act. In April 1999, the U.S. Court of International Trade (CIT) sided with environmental groups, interpreting Section 608 of the ESA as requiring countries to have fleet-wide TEDs regulations in place before any boat could export shrimp to the U.S.[50] That would stop shrimpers who don't use TEDs from evading U.S. law by purchasing export permits that say they do or by shipping their product on boats that do use TEDs.[51]

The Clinton administration faces a stark choice. The administration agreed to comply with the WTO ruling by taking regulatory action, thus limiting the role of Congress and the public. The Court of International Trade ruling removes this option. Now, the administration must bow to the WTO and prepare for a bruising congressional battle to change the Endangered Species Act or face WTO sanctions.

MULTILATERAL ENVIRONMENTAL AGREEMENTS RUN AFOUL OF WTO

The negotiation of multilateral environmental agreements (MEAs) represents a recognition of the fact that natural resources like air, water, and wildlife are not constrained by national borders. When these resources are threatened by pollution or with extinction, nations must cooperate to forestall the damage. These are numerous multilateral efforts under way to address global environmental issues such as climate change, air pollution, endangered species and the trade in hazardous waste.

MEAs are the embodiment of global progress toward, and commitment to, the preservation of the environment. Yet many WTO rules explicitly contradict

MEAs, including those in effect long before the WTO's formation. As a matter of international law, the WTO automatically supersedes MEAs signed before the WTO. Uruguay Round negotiators refused to include language in the WTO to make MEAs and their domestic enforcement immune to WTO challenge.

There are several ways in which MEAs can run afoul of WTO rules. First, some of the international environmental agreements explicitly restrict trade. For instance, the Convention on International Trade in Endangered Species (CITES) bans trade in endangered species; the Basel Convention on the Transboundary Movement of Hazardous Waste bans the export of toxic waste from rich countries—which produce 98% of the world's hazardous waste—to developing nations; and the Montreal Protocol bans trade in ozone-depleting chemicals and also products made with those chemicals. Second, these treaties and others sometimes employ the use of trade sanctions to enforce their objectives. Still other multilateral environmental agreements do not involve trade sanctions but may require countries to adopt policies that affect the potential products (asbestos, for example) of one country more than those of another. Thus, MEAs of all stripes have a significant chance of coming into conflict with GATT/WTO rules.

Finally, unlike the WTO, which is self-executing, . . . the MEAs provide commitments that each country agrees to enforce. For instance, CITES lists species for which its signatory countries have agreed that protection is needed. But, the enforcement of CITES comes not through a central CITES tribunal but rather under the domestic laws of each signatory. Thus, many U.S. CITES obligations are enforced through the Endangered Species Act (ESA). ESA provisions ban import of CITES-listed species and products made from them and endorse embargoes against countries that violate the rules.[52] Other countries have similar domestic laws implementing their CITES obligations. Yet, under WTO rules, such domestic laws can—and have—been challenged as illegal trade barriers.

WTO dispute panels are not required to interpret the existence of MEAs as evidence in favor of environmental laws that are challenged as WTO violations. Indeed, the rules of international law stipulate that the "latest in time" of international obligations trumps previous obligations unless an exception is taken.[53] While a very limited "saving" clause—giving some precedence to the three MEAs over conflicting rules—was forced in the North American Free Trade Agreement,[54] it is conspicuously absent in the WTO or other Uruguay Round Agreements. To date there have been several rulings both under GATT and the WTO that have been detrimental to domestic efforts to implement obligations undertaken under MEAs.

❖ ❖ ❖

MISGUIDED WTO COMMITTEE
ON THE ENVIRONMENT

Environmentalists had hoped that the WTO's Committee on Trade and the Environment (CTE) would provide a forum for WTO Members to devise new WTO rules to safeguard MEAs. Indeed, the original CTE work plan prioritized the issue.

But when the European Union offered proposals in 1996 for WTO recognition of MEAs that allow the imposition of trade sanctions, the U.S. neither supported the EU nor produced any proposals of its own.[55] Other countries grew bitter at the lack of leadership from the U.S., the country that had called for the creation of the CTE in the first place.[56]

Indeed, in its somewhat beleaguered four years of operation, the CTE has failed to agree to any recommendations for pro-environment changes to the GATT/WTO system. Some environmentalists criticize it as being used primarily to identify environmental measures that distort trade and to propose ways to get rid of them.[57]

Recently, the CTE has shifted the entire approach to its work. Dubbed the "win-win" strategy, the new approach abandons the goal of protecting environmental regulations from WTO challenge and instead focuses on identifying and eliminating trade barriers (like subsidies for fisheries) that are also bad for the environment.

At the March 1999 high-level WTO meeting on the environment in Geneva, WTO officials sought out environmental groups to give this strategy their support.[58] A few groups such as World Wildlife International did issue positive statements on the idea of cutting fisheries subsidies,[59] but the environmental community as a whole criticized the WTO's failure to make progress on the issue of safeguarding existing environmental policies coming under increasing WTO attack worldwide.[60]

Now the Clinton administration is shifting its environmental strategy for WTO in the same direction, specifically as regards to its position in the WTO's Seattle Ministerial, where the WTO's future agenda will be set.[61] Indeed, some environmental groups view the shift to the so-called "win-win" strategy as a way to buy off environmental opposition to the European proposal to launch further liberalization talks and to make use of environmentalists to further aspects of the WTO's agenda.[62] Ironically, even as the WTO staff and now the Clinton administration are calling for such a "win-win" strategy, the U.S. is moving forward with its efforts to make liberalization in forest products—which is vigorously opposed by environmentalists and has been estimated by the industry to increase depletion of forests by 3–4%[63]—a high priority for future WTO negotiations.[64]

ENDNOTES

1. U.S. Trade Representative Michael Kantor, Testimony to the House Ways and Means Committee, Jan. 26, 1994.
2. The North American Agreement on Environmental Cooperation (NAAEC) is ancillary to NAFTA, meaning its terms are not binding over any of NAFTA's core provisions. The NAAEC created the Commission for Environmental Cooperation (CEC), which can investigate citizens' complaints that a NAFTA member-country is not enforcing its environmental laws. The side agreement does not cover environmental problems caused by the *absence* of regulation. The NAFTA environmental side agreement also specifically excludes laws on natural resources, endangered species and other vital environmental issues. The process for seeking review of the limited areas covered is long and tortured. In the five years that NAFTA has been in effect, the CEC has issued a total of two fact-finding reports out of over 20 citizen submissions alleging government non-enforcement of environmental laws. The first report took the CEC over two years to complete,

and though it found that Mexico was not enforcing its environmental laws in allowing the construction of a pier requiring the destruction of ecologically critical coral reefs in the port of Cozumel, the pier had been built and the reefs had been destroyed for over a year before the report was even issued. See "NAFTA Environmental Agreement: A Paper Tiger?", *News-Journal Wire Services*, Jul. 29, 1988. All petitions to use the limited provision that could result in actual enforcement actions (versus the issuance of reports on the matter) have been refused to date.

3. The Clinton Administration, *The NAFTA: Expanding U.S. Exports, Jobs, and Growth*, U.S. Government Printing Office, Nov. 1993, at 1.

4. Letter to President Clinton, April 21, 1998, Signed by the Center for International Environmental Law, Center for Marine Conservation, Community Nutrition Institute, Defenders of Wildlife, Earth Island Institute, Earthjustice Legal Defense Fund, Friends of the Earth, Humane Society of the United States, National Audubon Society, National Wildlife Federation, Natural Resources Defense Council, Sierra Club, on file at Public Citizen.

5. Between 1958 and 1994, at least 6 million dolphins in the Eastern Tropical Pacific have been killed by purse seine nets. See Shannon Brownlee, "A Political Casserole of Tuna and Greens," *U.S. News and World Report*, Aug. 11, 1997, at 53.

6. [Note deleted. See original article for note.]

7. American Electronics Association (AEA), *Legality Under International Trade Law of Draft Directive on Waste From Electrical and Electronic Equipment*, Mar. 1999, prepared by Rod Hunter and Marta Lopez of Hunton & Williams, Brussels, on file with Public Citizen.

8. See Chapter 8 [of *Whose Trade Organization? Corporate Globalization and the Erosion of Democracy*] on the WTO's Dispute Resolution System.

9. Robert Evans, "Green Push Could Damage Trade Body—WTO Chief," *Reuters*, May 15, 1998.

10. Shannon Brownlee, "A Political Casserole of Tuna and Greens," *U.S. News and World Report*, Aug. 11, 1997, at 53.

11. John Malek and Dr. Peter Bowler, *Dolphin Protection in the Tuna Fishery, Interdisciplinary Minor in Global Sustainability*, Seminar, Irvine: University of California Press (1997), at 1.

12. *Id.*

13. The key provision that was the target of challenges under GATT is 16 U.S.C. Section 1371(a)(2), prohibiting the importation of tuna from countries that harvest tuna using purse seine nets.

14. See Statement for the Inter-American Tropical Tuna Commission Meeting, Oct. 21–23, 1996.

15. GATT, United States—Restrictions on Imports of Tuna (DS21/R), Report of the Panel, Sep. 3, 1991.

16. See GATT, United States—Restrictions on Imports of Tuna (DS29/R), Report of the Panel, Jun. 1994.

17. See *id.* at Para. 6.0.

18. See GATT, Findings on U.S. Tuna Ban, Report of Dispute Panel, Aug. 16, 1991 at Paras. 5.24–5.29.

19. See *id.* at Paras. 5.30–5.34.

20. GATT, United States—Restrictions on Imports of Tuna (DS29/R), Report of the Panel, Jun. 1994, at Para. 5.24.

21. "Clinton Pledges Early, Renewed Effort to Pass Tuna-Dolphin Bill," *Inside U.S. Trade*, Oct. 1996.

22. *Id.*

23. See 104th Congress, H.R. 2179, Sponsor: Rep. "Duke" Cunningham (R-CA); see also S.1420, Sponsors: Sen. Ted Stevens (R-AK), Co-sponsor: Sen. John Breaux (D-LA).

24. See 105th Congress, H.R. 408, Sponsor: Rep. Gilchrest (R-MO); see also S.39, Sponsor: Sen. Ted Stevens (R-AK).

25. See 64 *Fed. Reg.* 24590, May 7, 1999. In its initial finding NMFS concluded that there was insufficient evidence to show that catching tuna by encircling dolphins has a significant adverse impact on dolphin stocks.

26. See U.S. Department of Commerce, "Commerce Department Issues Initial Finding on Tuna/Dolphin Interactions—Will Adopt New Dolphin-Safe Label Standard," Press Release, Apr. 29, 1999

27. 64 *Fed. Reg.* 24590, May 7, 1999.

28. *Id.*

29. See U.S. Department of Commerce, "Commerce Department Issues Initial Finding on Tuna/Dolphin Interactions—Will Adopt New Dolphin-Safe Label Standard," Press Release, Apr. 29, 1999.

30. Scott Harper, "Rule Revised for Tuna Fishing, Encirclement Will be Allowed with Oversight to Help Protect Dolphins," *The Virginian Pilot*, May 18, 1999. A campaign by Earth Island Institute has resulted in commitments by some major tuna canners to use only tuna caught without purse seine nets.

31. A WTO Appellate Body has stated that adopted reports of either GATT or WTO "create legitimate expectations among Members and, therefore, should be taken into account where they are relevant to a dispute." Japan—Taxes on Alcoholic Beverages, (WT/DS10/AB/R), Report of the Appellate Body, Oct. 4, 1996, at 14. In practice, panels have cited previous reports as precedents and have supported subsequent rulings by referring to previous decisions.

32. Public Law 93–205, 16 U.S.C. 1531 *et.seq*; see also 52 *Fed. Reg.* 24244, Jun. 29, 1987.

33. 52 *Fed. Reg.* 24244, Jun. 29, 1987. Five species of sea turtles fell under the Endangered Species Act regulations: loggerhead (Caretta caretta), Kemp's ridley (Lepidochelys kempi), green (Chelonia mydas), leatherback (Dermochelys coriacea) and hawksbill (Eretmochelys imbricate).

34. National Research Council, Committee on Sea Turtle Conservation, *Decline of the Sea Turtle: Causes and Prevention* (1990) at 5.

35. *Id.*

36. *Id.* at 17–18.

37. Pub. L. 101–162.

38. National Research Council, Committee on Sea Turtle Conservation, *Decline of the Sea Turtle: Causes and Prevention* (1990) at 11.

39. WTO, United States—Import Prohibition of Certain Shrimp and Shrimp Products (WT/DS58), Complaint by India, Malaysia, Pakistan, and Thailand.

40. WTO, United States—Import Prohibition of Certain Shrimp and Shrimp Products (WT/DS58/R), Final Report, May 15, 1998, at Para 9.1 (Concluding Remarks).

41. See Letter to President Clinton, Apr. 21, 1998, signed by the Center for International Environmental Law, Center for Marine Conservation, Community Nutrition Institute, Defenders of Wildlife, Earth Island Institute, Earthjustice Legal Defense Fund, Friends of the Earth, Humane Society of the United States, National Audubon Society, National Wildlife Federation, Natural Resources Defense Council, and Sierra Club, on file at Public Citizen.

42. "The Sea Turtles Warning," *The New York Times*, Apr. 10, 1998.

43. WTO, United States—Import Prohibition of Certain Shrimp and Shrimp Products (WT/DS58), Appealed on Jul. 13, 1998.

44. WTO, United States—Import Prohibition of Certain Shrimp and Shrimp Products (WT/DS58/AB/R), Report of the Appellate Body, Oct. 12, 1998, at Para. 187.

45. *Id*. at Para. 122.

46. *Id*. at Para. 184.

47. *Id*. at Para. 185.

48. Jock Nash, Trade Analyst, written communication with Michelle Sforza, Research Director, Public Citizen's Global Trade Watch, Oct. 13, 1998.

49. "Louisiana Shrimpers Threatened By Ruling on Turtle Excluder," *States News Service*, Apr. 14, 1998.

50. *Earth Island Institute vs. William M. Daley*, U.S. Court of International Trade, Case No. 98–09–02818, Apr. 2, 1999, at 35.

51. The U.S. government had initially refused to implement the shrimp-turtle policy's country-based certification requirements in favor of shipment-by-shipment certification. In 1996, three environmental groups sued to force implementation of the law as written. The U.S. Court of International Trade (ICT) ruled in 1997 for the environmentalists, and ordered the State Department to rewrite the rule to require country-based certification. This CIT ruling triggered the WTO challenge. The CIT overturned its earlier ruling on a technicality in 1998, but in April 1999, an appellate judge ruled that the law allowed the U.S. sale of shrimp only from countries that have regulations mandating TEDs. If the CIT affirms its interim ruling, the State Department will have no choice but to scrap its proposal to certify shrimp on a shipment-by-shipment basis.

52. 16 U.S.C. Chapter 35, Section 1538.

53. 1969 Vienna Convention on the Law of Treaties at Article 30(2).

54. North American Free Trade Agreement (NAFTA) at Para. 104.

55. Dan Seligman, *Broken Promises: How the Clinton Administration is Trading Away our Environment*, Sierra Club Responsible Trade Campaign, May 13, 1998.

56. *Id*.

57. See "U.S. Business, Environmental Groups Divided on Shrimp-Turtle Case," *BRIDGES Weekly Trade News Digest*, vol. 2, no. 15, Apr. 27, 1988.

58. "WTO Enviro Groups Getting Closer Together," *Washington Trade Daily*, Mar. 17, 1999.

59. "Green Groups Challenge WTO," *Financial Times*, Mar. 17, 1999.

60. "Cuts Urged in Fishing and Farm Aid," *Financial Times*, Mar. 16, 1999.

61. Statement by the U.S. delegation to the WTO General Council Session, Geneva, Switzerland, Jul. 29, 1999.

62. See e.g., Friends of the Earth International. The U.S. government was speaking about reconciling the WTO and the environment at the WTO high-level environmental meeting while it was negotiating with other countries in an attempt to secure a final forestry deal as an "early harvest" at the Seattle Ministerial.

63. The American Forest & Paper Association, "Forest Industry Leader Urges Worldwide Tariff Elimination," Press Release, Apr. 28, 2000, citing study by the international consultant firm of Jaakko Poyry.

64. Statement by the U.S. delegation to the WTO General Council Session, Geneva, Switzerland, Jul. 29, 1999.

The Greening of the WTO

MICHAEL M. WEINSTEIN AND STEVE CHARNOVITZ

SAVE THE TURTLES

Anyone who has followed the negative press coverage of the World Trade Organization over the last few years would be shocked to learn that the WTO has started to develop an environmental conscience. With only a few tweaks, it can turn greener still.

The most memorable assault on the WTO's environmental record came at its 1999 meeting in Seattle, where antiglobalization demonstrators dressed as sea turtles to highlight the alleged damage wrought by the organization's policies. Similar protests have dogged multilateral trade meetings ever since. But a careful look at the WTO's record shows that such attacks are unwarranted. The organization is in fact developing constructive principles for accommodating both trade and environmental concerns. A series of rulings by the WTO's dispute-resolution bodies—judicial panels that settle conflicts among member states—has established the principle that trade rules do not stand in the way of legitimate environmental regulation.

The gradual greening of the WTO throughout its seven-year life reflects changes made to international rules when the organization was created in 1994. In particular, the preamble to the WTO agreement noted the importance of protecting the environment and the need for enhanced means of doing so. Environmental sensitivity has also been heightened by the stalwart efforts of environmentalists in and out of government to influence the system of global trade. The environmental movement has, in fact, achieved most of the goals it pursued in the early 1990s—although the need to keep their supporters energized makes some groups loath to say so.

Moreover, and contrary to what protesters often claim, further progress can take place within the current system. This is reassuring, because modest reform is the only politically realistic way to further the green agenda. The WTO's rules can be changed only by a consensus of its 142 [now 147] members, and many developing nations want no part of a costly environmental program they regard as an imposition by the wealthy industrialized powers. Radical demands in this area would increase friction between rich and poor countries and sabotage efforts to start a new round of global trade negotiations—a round that the WTO's director-general proposes be focused on the needs of the poorest countries. Moderate proposals, backed by sound public explanations, have a much better chance of achieving significant results.

From *Foreign Affairs*, Vol. 80, No. 6, November/December, 2001, pp. 147–156. Reprinted by permission of *Foreign Affairs*. © 2001 by the Council on Foreign Relations, Inc.

As the WTO struggles to handle environmental concerns, one issue looms above all others: the organization needs to figure out how to manage the clash between its open trade agenda and unilateral attempts by some member governments to protect the environment through trade restrictions. The WTO must strike a balance between two extremes. Cracking down too hard on the use of environmental trade restrictions invites environmental damage. But excessive leniency in imposing sanctions invites two other abuses: pressure on poorer countries to adopt standards that are ill suited to their strained economies, and suppression of trade that will lead to higher prices and stunted growth.

SEDUCTIVE SANCTIONS

Trade policy must have an environmental dimension because the environment is a global collective resource. To manage it properly, governments must cooperate on all policies—including trade—that can threaten fisheries, forests, air quality, and endangered species. Without collective agreements, countries will be tempted to lower their environmental standards in an effort to increase their competitive advantage. The question is not whether there should be some form of international cooperation on environmental issues, but what kind of cooperation there should be, and under what institutional auspices.

Purists want environmental regulations left to specialized agencies, whereas many environmentalists want them enforced by the WTO. The argument for using the WTO is simple, for unlike most other international organizations, the WTO has a mechanism for enforcing its rulings: trade sanctions. The WTO convenes panels of experts to rule on trade disputes among member governments. If the losing government refuses to comply with the ruling, the panel authorizes the winning government to impose trade sanctions.

The recent transatlantic flap over hormones shows how the system works. Claiming that beef from cows fed with artificial hormones posed a health hazard, the European Union (EU) blocked imports of such beef from the United States in 1989. The U.S. government brought the dispute before a WTO panel, which ruled in Washington's favor. The panel, however, had no power to change Europe's laws. All it could do was authorize the United States to retaliate—which Washington did, by imposing stiff tariffs on meat products, cheeses, and several other European exports. Punishment through sanctions was quick and easy. That is why environmentalists, along with organized labor and many other groups, want to use the international trading system to advance their missions.

Trade sanctions come at a cost, however. They often backfire, hurting a country's own consumers while aiding a politically powerful group of domestic producers. They can drive up prices and threaten the living standards of workers in both rich and poor countries, as well as provide cover for protectionists. In the beef-hormone case, for example, U.S. sanctions did indeed hurt European farmers and ranchers. But they also raised food prices in the United States, punishing American consumers. And the sanctions have not forced the Europeans to back down. They continue to ban beef produced with artificial hormones.

Trade sanctions are at best crude weapons, and environmentalists should reconsider their enthusiasm for them. Sanctions are ill suited to the subtleties of environmental policymaking and unlikely to persuade developing countries to undertake environmentally sensitive policies. Even if sanctions might ultimately play some role in a few unusual cases, in general environmentalists ought to focus primarily on education, persuasion, and mediation.

LOSING BATTLES, WINNING THE WAR

According to its critics, the WTO interferes with legitimate efforts by the United States and other countries to block imports that harm the environment. For example, Lori Wallach and Michelle Sforza of Public Citizen, a group affiliated with Ralph Nader, argue that "in case after case, the WTO is being used to threaten or has upheld formal challenges to environmental safeguards, doing far more damage than occurred under the [pre-WTO] regime." Using similar arguments, the Humane Society of the United States has labeled the WTO "the single most destructive international organization ever formed" when it comes to animals.

To prove their case, critics point to several controversial decisions made over the past decade by trade panels, each of which ruled against attempts by the United States to protect the environment through unilateral measures. Reading just the headlines, these decisions may indeed appear to have undermined conservation. But closer inspection reveals a different picture. As Professor John Jackson of the Georgetown University Law Center has said, environmentalists "lost the battles but won the war."

In the first set of cases, known as tuna-dolphin, two pre-WTO trade panels in 1991 and 1994 rejected U.S. bans on imports of tuna caught with nets that unintentionally also trapped dolphins, a threatened (although not endangered) species. Environmental advocates howled. But the decisions were never formally adopted by the then governing body and therefore established no legal precedent. Besides, the tuna-dolphin panels predate the creation of the WTO and its improved recognition of environmental concerns. Nevertheless, critics of the WTO cite this case as evidence of the threat that trade-dispute panels continue to pose to the environment.

In the second case, a WTO trade panel ruled that the United States had wrongfully blocked imports of Venezuelan and Brazilian gasoline, which the United States claimed violated its clean-air laws. The United States appealed the decision to the organization's Appellate Body, where it lost again. Environmental activists angrily accused the WTO of trampling Washington's right to protect the American environment. But the appellate decision was actually a step forward because it rejected some of the key findings of the lower panel. The appellate jurists found no problem with the U.S. clean-air law itself, declaring it legitimate under the provision of the WTO agreement that permits trade barriers "relating to the conservation of exhaustible natural resources." They merely disapproved of the regulations the United States used to administer the law, in particular the fact that the rules subjected foreign gasoline suppliers to tougher standards than were applied to domestic suppliers. All that Washington had to do to bring its policy into compliance was correct its administrative procedures, and it has since done so.

In the third case, known as shrimp-turtle, a WTO trade panel in 1998 ruled that the United States was wrongfully blocking imports of shrimp from countries that did not require fishing fleets to use devices designed to safeguard endangered sea turtles. Once again the WTO's Appellate Body upheld the ruling—but once again it rejected some of the lower panel's key arguments. The appellate judges acknowledged that an import ban might sometimes be justified and thus found nothing inherently wrong with the U.S. law in question. But it sharply criticized Washington for using administrative procedures that lacked due process and for making insufficient efforts to negotiate a conservation agreement with the Asian governments filing the complaint. As in the gasoline case, the WTO ruled that the United States needed to change only its procedures, not its law, to bring itself into compliance, and the United States has done so. Last year Malaysia challenged the revised U.S. regulations, but this time the WTO panel sided with the United States. Indeed, the judges went so far as to declare that "sustainable development is one of the objectives of the WTO agreement." This decision is now under appeal.

The Appellate Body's judgment in the shrimp-turtle case demonstrates that trade law may permit a nation to impose an import ban even when the primary purpose of the ban is to safeguard an endangered species found outside that nation's territory. In terms of environmental protection, that stance is light-years ahead of the tuna-dolphin ruling from ten years ago. Another milestone was reached this year in a dispute over asbestos, a carcinogen. The WTO Appellate Body upheld France's policy of blocking imports from Canada that contain the material—the first time the WTO has approved the use of a trade restriction to protect human health.

PRECAUTIONARY PUZZLE

Although the WTO has begun to embrace environmental protection, it certainly can and should do more. The challenge will be to find an effective middle ground among the rival parties in this debate: environmentalists and free traders, the United States and the EU, and the industrialized and developing worlds.

One proposal favored by European governments and environmental advocates on both sides of the Atlantic is to write a "precautionary principle" into WTO rules. This measure would protect the right of countries to block imports of products they deem a threat to public health, safety, or the environment even when no existing scientific evidence supports the feared threat. Had this concept prevailed when the beef-hormone case was decided, the Europeans would have won. Lurking behind the proposal to adopt the precautionary principle is the dispute over genetically modified organisms (GMOs). The United States is a large producer of food products incorporating GMOs, and American industry, citing a lack of evidence to the contrary, insists that they are safe. Europeans respond that GMOs are too new for scientists to know what their long-term consequences might be.

Two aspects of the WTO framework bear on this issue. First, the Agreement on the Application of Sanitary and Phytosanitary Measures (SPS) governs a country's rules for protecting the health of its people, animals, and plants from listed risks such as toxins, disease, and pests. The SPS requires that these rules be based on scientific evidence showing that a risk to health exists, although scientific certainty is not required. Once a risk has been established, individual countries can set their standards as high as they like. In the beef-hormone case the SPS agreement was invoked successfully against the Europeans because the EU did not produce scientific evidence to support its claims. Another accord, the Agreement on Technical Barriers to Trade (TBT), governs general health and safety standards. The TBT does not require a country to produce a scientifically backed assessment of risk, but it does insist, among other conditions, that standards be set in a way that restricts trade as little as possible to achieve the intended goal.

Neither the SPS nor the TBT threatens legitimate environmental or health measures. Neither puts environmental restrictions into a scientific straitjacket. Both permit countries to set high standards even when the scientific evidence on risk is uncertain. For example, the SPS calls for making the standards provisional and subject to modification once more evidence becomes available. That approach provides for balance and is the reason that the Appellate Body ruled that the precautionary principle already "finds reflection" in the SPS.

Explicitly embedding a precautionary principle in the SPS or TBT sections of the WTO framework would, by contrast, allow countries to block imports on environmental or health grounds in the absence of any scientific evidence of a significant risk. This would be a step backward. The current WTO rules have not been abused to undermine any country's legitimate environmental or health standards. Furthermore, no one has determined how to define a precautionary principle that would not provide a gaping loophole for protectionism, health fads, or environmental zealotry. Finally, because of the provisions in the SPS and the TBT, the WTO does not need an explicit precautionary principle. What the EU and others should pursue instead is getting future judicial panels to provide plenty of legal room for countries to set high health standards when scientific evidence of risk exists but is uncertain.

IT'S EASY BEING GREEN

The WTO can take several concrete steps to answer its critics. These need not be dramatic policy modifications, such as an ill-considered adoption of a precautionary principle. Instead, a series of measured, incremental changes could pass the twin tests of environmental effectiveness and political viability.

First, the organization should make some accommodation for multilateral environmental agreements—treaties among groups of countries that can call for trade restrictions to protect the environment. For example, the Montreal Protocol blocks trade in ozone-depleting chemicals with nonsignatory countries, and the Convention on International Trade in Endangered Species (often referred to by its acronym, CITES) bans trafficking in endangered species. Europe has lobbied within the WTO for giving deference to these agreements, a step that could lead the WTO to bless trade restrictions that would otherwise violate its rules.

The European position makes good sense in cases where trade controls are imposed by one signatory against another according to rules set out in a multilateral agreement both have ratified. But the issue becomes knottier when a signatory applies trade restrictions to a nonparty. Permitting this type of sanction would turn the WTO into a tool for coercing nonsignatory countries to join, or at least adhere to, the agreement in question. Complicating the matter further is the question of what precisely constitutes a multilateral environmental agreement. If two countries form a cartel and erect import barriers to protect domestic industry, should the WTO go along blindly so long as the countries label their agreement "environmental"? Although such shenanigans cannot be allowed, the EU makes a strong case for putting the WTO on the side of multilateral environmental cooperation. But a complete plan for doing so remains elusive.

Another needed step would open the WTO dispute-resolution process to public participation. The WTO's newfound sensitivity toward the environment has shallow roots. Several times the Appellate Body has had to overrule misguided judgments by lower panels, and nothing guarantees that future appellate jurists will be as wise or as shrewd as their predecessors. Environmentalists have been able to pull WTO jurisprudence away from the tuna-dolphin rulings, but advocates need to remain vigilant and fight any sign of backtracking if the trade body is to continue on its green trend. Yet WTO rules make public oversight difficult by keeping most deliberations secret, thereby breeding distrust. The organization has made some efforts to answer its critics. Recently, panels have been permitted to review unsolicited "friend of the court" briefs submitted by nongovernmental organizations. Yet this practice is hotly contested within the organization and may not continue. For reasons of both sound jurisprudence and sound public relations, the WTO ought to routinely accept briefs by independent experts.

Additionally, the WTO needs procedures specially crafted to handle environmental disputes. The shrimp-turtle case showed that the United States exploited its market power too quickly by imposing unilateral sanctions, and that the Asian plaintiffs complained to the WTO too quickly rather than examining their own fishing practices. When environmental disputes are brought to the WTO, the organization's director-general should push the parties, publicly if necessary, toward mediation. If that fails, then the WTO should steer the dispute to an appropriate environmental forum before getting involved itself.

The WTO should also explicitly authorize "eco-labeling." The EU wants to clarify WTO rules for labeling goods, protecting a country's right to require disclosure of potential health, safety, or environmental threats so that consumers can decide for themselves what risks to take. But labeling can create problems. For example, simply telling consumers when beef contains artificial hormones suggests that the hormones are dangerous, even though the scientific evidence says otherwise. For this reason, the U.S. Food and Drug Administration carefully regulates labels on food and drugs and prohibits claims that it deems misleading or scare-mongering. On balance, however, giving countries wide latitude to label products would be a smart reform that would keep markets open while allowing countries to respect the wishes of concerned citizens.

The WTO should also appoint a commission of experts to monitor future trade negotiations in order to inform countries of the potential environmental impact of the measures under discussion. The goal would be to press negotiators to take account of environmental consequences before trade accords are signed. Such a review process would increase public confidence that environmental concerns had not been ignored.

Pressuring countries to adopt clean technologies would be another effective measure. This step would require member countries to lower tariffs and remove needless regulations that impede imports of pollution-control equipment and other environmental technologies and services. In addition, the industrialized countries should comply with an existing WTO rule calling for the transfer of technology to the developing world.

The WTO also needs to root out environmentally harmful national subsidies. Government subsidies to domestic fishing industries worsen the depletion of fishery stocks. Subsidies to other sectors, such as agriculture, can cause harm by encouraging overuse and excessive consumption of other natural resources. In 1999, the U.S. government joined several other countries in proposing that the WTO consider curbing fishing subsidies. The proposal was shelved after the failed Seattle conference. The initiative needs to be relaunched, and the WTO should combat other subsidies that harm both trade and the environment.

Defer to multilateral environmental agreements. Invite legal briefs from outside experts. Mediate before litigating disputes. Monitor the environmental impacts of proposed trade agreements. Allow eco-labeling. Promote technology transfer and trade in environmental services. Curb environmentally damaging subsidies. None of these ideas sounds earth-shattering, because none is. Radical steps are not needed. For seven years, the WTO has moved toward a responsible environmental posture. The best way to continue that green trend is for the industrialized powers to latch onto a modest set of reforms that are affordable for developing nations, protect the environment and public health, and keep zealots and protectionists at bay.

QUESTIONS FOR REVIEW AND DISCUSSION

1. What specific aspects of the WTO do Wallach and Sforza focus on to develop their argument? Do they think the WTO is becoming more sensitive to and concerned about the environmental aspects of international trade?
2. Weinstein and Charnovitz argue that while the environmentalists have lost many of the key battles in the WTO, they have won the war. What do they mean by this? How can two sets of authors reach such different conclusions about the same policy process?
3. What aspects of the WTO–environment relationship do you think are most in need of development and clarification? Do the authors of the two articles agree on the aspects that most need attention? Would the reforms that Weinstein and Charnovitz propose

to address their concerns satisfy the concerns advanced by Wallach and Sforza? Why or why not?

4. What do you think is the right balance to be struck between economic activity and environmental protection? More concretely, how many turtles or dolphins is it acceptable to kill in the process of harvesting shrimp or tuna?

5. What is the Precautionary Principle? How has this principle become central to the WTO's handling of environmental issues? What do you think is the best approach to the risk associated with such issues?

6. Assuming that the WTO should take environmental concerns more into account, should it do so by allowing the Dispute Settlement Body to make decisions that gradually develop an appropriate balance, or through governments negotiating explicit and mutually agreed rules? What are the advantages and disadvantages of each approach?

7. Why are developing countries wary of bringing environmental issues into the WTO? How should these concerns be addressed by the United States and the European Union?

SUGGESTIONS FOR FURTHER READING

For two in-depth treatments on current thinking about the relationship between trade and the environment, see: Gary P. Sampson and W. Bradnee Chambers, Eds. *Trade, Environment, and the Millennium.* Tokyo: United Nations University Press, 1999; and Gary P. Sampson. *Trade, the Environment, and the WTO: the Post-Seattle Agenda.* Washington, DC: Overseas Development Council, 2000.

For an in-depth examination of the history of the environment under the GATT, see: Daniel Esty. *Greening the GATT: Trade, Environment, and the Future.* Washington, DC: Institute for International Economics, 1994.

To follow current WTO developments visit the Committee on Trade and the Environment at http://www.wto.org/english/tratop_e/envir_e/envir_e.htm

CHAPTER 6

THE WORLD TRADE ORGANIZATION AND POLITICAL LEGITIMACY

The World Trade Organization has been at the center of controversy since it was established in 1995. Controversy arises in part from a widespread perception that the WTO has widened substantially the reach of global trade rules, and in part from the equally widespread belief that these rules are created through a process that systematically excludes the interests and concerns of a large segment of society.

It is true that global trade rules reach further today than they did 20 years ago. Throughout most of the postwar period, work undertaken within the General Agreement on Tariffs and Trade (GATT), which was the WTO's institutional fore-runner, focused principally on the progressive reduction of tariffs. While GATT negotiations did occasionally foray into nontariff aspects of trade, including rules governing such things as antidumping investigations, government procurement practices, and the use of product standards, most negotiations focused principally on selecting the industries in which, as well as the amount by which, tariffs would be reduced. The Uruguay Round, during which the WTO was created, extended global trade rules beyond tariffs and began to address many nontariff barriers to trade as well. Governments agreed to rules on the protection of intellectual property, to common practices concerning the use of trade restrictions on products that harm human health, and created a dispute-settlement mechanism to enforce compliance with these rules.

The shift in emphasis from tariffs to nontariff barriers raises the potential for international trade rules to conflict with domestic policies designed to achieve other legitimate social objectives. Many of the more prominent recent disputes in the WTO, such as the shrimp-turtle dispute, as well as the current disputes over the European Union's import bans on hormone-treated beef and genetically modifed foods illustrate the real potential for such conflict.

For some, the fact that obligations that governments have accepted as WTO members sometimes conflict with domestic policies adopted to achieve other important goals is made more worrisome by the nature of the WTO decision-making process. The postwar trade regime, under the GATT as well as within the WTO, has made decisions and established new rules through intergovernmental bargaining. Membership in the WTO, and therefore participation in WTO negotiations, is restricted to national governments. National governments in turn appoint trade ministers to act on their behalf in these negotiations. For the last 50 years, negotiations between trade ministers have taken place behind closed doors in a process that has come to be called the "club model" of decision making. As a result, nongovernmental actors, whether firms, trade unions, or public-interest groups, have little access to or influence over the WTO bargaining process through which new rules are established. While of little concern when GATT bargaining focused narrowly on tariffs, the exclusive nature of WTO decision making became a source of concern as the WTO began to extend its reach beyond tariffs. Critics argue that trade ministers can now reach agreements in the WTO that limit the ability of national governments to protect the environment, safeguard health, or pursue a multitude of other potentially desirable goals, and there is little that public-interest groups can do to prevent it. As a consequence, many hard-won victories on issues ranging from environmental safeguards to consumer-protection regulations will be undermined by the WTO. More extreme critics suggest that democracy itself may be jeopardized.

Widespread concern about what is seen as the increasingly intrusive nature of WTO rules and the overly restrictive nature of WTO decision making has generated demands for changes to the WTO decision-making process. The two articles presented in this chapter consider the case for and against such reforms. Daniel Esty, a professor at Yale Law School and an expert on environmental law and policy, argues that the WTO is facing a crisis of legitimacy that can be resolved only through fundamental reforms of the Organization's decision-making process. According to Esty, the club model of bargaining was appropriate in an age when the trade regime's attention was restricted to tariffs. Now, however, as WTO rules extend into other areas, the club model deprives the organization of needed legitimacy among the broader public. The solution, he argues, is a number of reforms that would "democratize" the WTO and restrict the Organization's jurisdiction to international trade.

David Henderson, a fellow at the Hoover Institution and a professor of economics at the Naval Postgraduate School, challenges Esty's claim that the WTO is facing a crisis of legitimacy and criticizes the reforms that Esty proposes. According to Henderson, international organizations like the WTO are not designed to be, and should not be designed to be accountable to the general public. Instead, they derive their legitimacy from their member governments. Giving nongovernmental organizations the right to participate in the WTO would do little to increase the Organization's legitimacy and greatly limit its ability to achieve its principal mission.

The World Trade Organization's Legitimacy Crisis

DANIEL C. ESTY

Turmoil surrounds the international trading system and especially the World Trade Organization (WTO). The 1999 WTO Ministerial Meeting in Seattle broke down in chaos. Other international gatherings to promote economic integration, including the European Union's 2000 Summit Meeting in Gothenburg and the 2001 Summit of the Americas in Quebec City, have triggered similar protests and violent clashes between demonstrators and the police. Undoubtedly, the anti-globalization backlash and the rioting in the streets has a number of causes (Blackurst 2001; Esty 2000). And, while some commentators have dismissed the demonstrations as mere "noise," I believe a "signal" can be extracted from the current difficulties of the trade regime. Simply put, the international trading system has not adapted to a rapidly changing global scene and now faces a serious legitimacy crisis (Keohane and Nye 2001). This article explores the origins and implications of this crisis.

I argue that the WTO stands at a watershed. The post-World War II inter-national order centered on issue-based "decomposable hierarchies" has begun to break down (Simon 1996; Keohane and Nye 2001).[1] A new, more complex and fluid international system is beginning to emerge. But the new architecture has structural flaws. In particular, little attention has been paid to what is required to establish the *legitimacy* of international organizations in general and the WTO in particular (Bodansky 1999; Hurd 1999; Stephan 1999).

The WTO appears simultaneously to be at the leading edge of the economic integration process and yet curiously old-fashioned and out of step with some modern norms, particularly those involving good public decisionmaking. As recent events have demonstrated, coherently managing interdependence is of vital importance. This need makes the resolution of the legitimacy issues surrounding the WTO of even greater urgency.

Many of those who criticize the WTO and other elements of international eco-nomic structure have little foundation for the charges they make. Indeed, many of the attacks on the WTO are off-base and deeply confused. The suggestion, for instance, that freer trade leads to greater poverty disregards the enormous gains that have been made by hundreds of millions of people across the planet over the last several decades in countries that have opened themselves up to world markets (Bhagwati 1993; Anderson and Blackhurst 1992). Those chanting "no WTO" really

From Daniel C. Esty, "The World Trade Organization's Legitimacy Crisis," *World Trade Review*, vol. 1, no. 1, 2002, pp. 7–22; Cambridge University Press, New York, NY.

do not want an international marketplace without structure or rules in which multinational corporations operate without constraints.

LEGITIMATE CONCERNS

While much of the criticism of the WTO is analytically unfounded and some of it is positively upside down and backwards, there are a number of kernels of truth in the general angst about the future that is manifested in anti-globalization rhetoric. First, trade liberalization creates losers as well as winners. There can be no doubt, furthermore, that we live in a time of considerable turbulence. Fears about job insecurity and the prospect of wages being bid down in the globalized labor market have some foundation, even if the long-term broader economic trend is positive for most people.

Second, economic integration and the broader forces of globalization threaten some traditions and local cultures. But these changes—for example, the evolving rhythms of rural life in France, which Jose Bové decries—are not the product of some grand conspiracy but rather choices by everyday people about how they want to lead their lives (Jeffress and Mayanobe 2001). Similarly, the urbanization of countries across the world, the commercial prominence of global brands and multinational corporations, and the powerful presence of a worldwide media and entertainment culture are driven largely by public preferences. But the fear that an overemphasis on materialism and economic growth will result in policies that run roughshod over other values about which people care has an underlying logic. It may, for example, be more difficult to follow through on concerns about the environment or human rights within the context of an economic dynamic of global competition (Esty 1996; Esty and Geradin 2001).

Third, the benefits of trade liberalization and economic integration may not be fairly distributed. In many countries the general public benefits from access to a greater variety of goods at lower prices (Gilpin 1987). But in some nations, elite groups dominate both political processes and the economy, allowing them to claim a vastly disproportionate share of the "spoils" of freer trade and economic growth more generally (O'Rourke 2001). Thus, distributional questions cannot be ignored.

Too often the trade community leaders duck these concerns, arguing that economic transactions always result in some dislocation, that environmental harms are not related to trade, and that equity issues should be dealt with in other fora. But to disregard these issues damages the credibility of those pressing the trade liberalization agenda—and may mean that economic integration proceeds in ways that do not maximize social welfare (Esty 2001).

THE UNDERLYING LEGITIMACY CRISIS

Beyond these broad sources of concern about trade liberalization lie a set of questions about the WTO specifically. In fact, the WTO's very legitimacy has been called into question (Weinstein and Charnovitz 2001; Stokes and Choate 2001; Bodansky 1999). Public acceptance of the authority and decisions that emerge from the World Trade Organization can no longer be taken for granted in many countries.

Legitimacy is a complex concept in the context of governance. It can be derived through elections and a majority vote for representatives who reflect the political will of a community (in the spirit of Rousseau) (Franck 1990). Alternatively, a governing body may gain authority and public acceptance based on reason and the efficacy of the outcomes it generates (in the Kantian tradition) (Kahn 1989). Popular sovereignty and efficacy are to some extent fungible. Thus, some governments maintain their hold on power because they continue to win elections even though their results in office are not outstanding (consider the regimes in Argentina over the past century). In other cases, governments fall short of full democratic practices (think of Singapore), but maintain public support and acceptance by their effectiveness and their capacity to deliver on public expectations. As a general rule, people appear more willing to cede authority to "expert" decisionmaking in realms that are perceived to be technical or scientific (Kahn 1989; Weber 2000). The American public, for example, has seemed quite willing to leave monetary policy in the hands of the not-too-democratic Federal Reserve Board under the leadership of Alan Greenspan so long as the economy remained strong.[2]

Legitimacy also has a *systemic* dimension. The authority of a particular decisionmaking body depends not only on the electoral accountability of those making decisions or the perceived rationality of the choices that emerge but also on the popular sovereignty and efficacy of the broader system within which a decisionmaking entity is lodged (Breton 1996; Hurd 1999). Thus, for example, the US Supreme Court has a high degree of legitimacy although its justices are not elected and its decisions sometimes appear to fall short of full rationality. But the US Supreme Court is embedded in a broader structure of legislative, executive, and judicial decisionmaking bodies that provide a dense web of checks and balances (Strauss 1984; Eskridge and Ferejohn 1992). Taken as a whole, this system provides a reasonably strong connection between the American public and their political leadership and delivers generally good results over time (Ackerman 2000).

Historically, the trade regime has not been managed by elected officials accountable to a defined public. Instead, its legitimacy derived almost entirely from its perceived efficacy and value as part of the international economic management structured.[3] Indeed, the GATT-WTO system may represent the high water mark of the twentieth-century commitment to technocratic decisionmaking (Charnovitz 1994; Howse 1999; Shaffer 2001) and belief in a governance model centered on bureaucratic rationality (Frug 1984; Weber 1994). Until recently, the trade regime benefited from a sense that international economics and trade policy making were highly technical realms best left in the hands of an elite cadre of qualified experts. To the extent that links to elected officials were required, the connection between appointed trade officials (both at the national level and in the international domain) and the elected governments to which they reported seemed sufficient.

But public perceptions about trade and trade policy making have changed. Trade is no longer considered to be an obscure policy domain best left to technical experts. Instead, trade issues and initiatives are now a major focus of public attention and discussion across the world. The trade regime can no longer function on the basis of technocratic rationality and quiet accomplishments. As I discuss in more detail below, with its efficacy-based claim to legitimacy under attack and lacking any undergirding in true popular sovereignty, the WTO needs a new foundation for its legitimacy. The organization needs to reestablish its reputation for efficacy and to build new connections to the publics around the world in whose name trade policy is advanced as well as to strengthen the broader institutional structure of checks and balances within which the WTO operates.

THE "CLUB MODEL" TRADE REGIME

From its origins in the General Agreement on Tariffs and Trade (GATT), a cornerstone of the Bretton Woods system that undergirded the post-World War II international economic order (Ruggie 1983), the trade regime was long operated as a tight-knit "club" (Keohane and Nye 2001). This Club Model persisted because it was successful. In fact, the World Trade Organization (and the forerunner structure created under GATT auspices) generated an enviable record of accomplishment with regard to trade liberalization and successful settlement of international economic disputes. Through eight successive rounds of multilateral negotiations, the GATT provided a forum for coordinated commitment to significant tariff reductions and the creation of a system of rules to guide international commerce (Jackson 1996).

For a long period of time, the trade regime's clubbishness, low profile, and obscure workings were seen as a virtue. A clique of committed economists and diplomats and a small Secretariat in Geneva toiled quietly in pursuit of a vision of open markets and deeper economic integration as both a path to prosperity and a bulwark against the chaos and war that plagued the world through the first half of the twentieth century (Gilpin 1987; Jackson 1994). The closed and secretive nature of the regime isolated—and insulated—the trade policymaking process from day-to-day politics, keeping at bay the protectionist interests that are active in many countries (Schott 1996).

As a matter of theory, asymmetries of interest and commitment to political activity between the beneficiaries of liberalized trade (the broad public which often neither recognizes the benefits of free trade nor is willing to invest much political energy in defending the gains from open markets) and the losers from trade liberalization (special interests who face new competition and are highly motivated to intervene politically to protect their monopoly rents) create a powerful "public choice" logic for such a structure (Petersmann 1992). The international trade regime, as Robert Hudec has described it, serves as a mechanism by which governments can tie their hands to the mast and avoid protectionist siren calls (Hudec 1971). Under the Club Model, governments operating behind closed doors can cut deals to lower tariff barriers and to open markets for the benefit of the general public out of sight of rent seekers, protectionists, and other special interests (van Dijck and Faber 1996; Jackson 1996).

But the "insulation" advantages of the Club Model of trade policy making come at a price. Unable to gain any real appreciation for how the trade regime worked, the public sees the WTO as a "black box" where insiders take advantage of their access to the levers of power. Fears of special interest domination are now prevalent. And these worries are not limited to the public; many developing countries share the concern (Blackhurst 2001). The belief that the WTO is dominated by multinational corporations and other elite interests cannot be assuaged without a more transparent policymaking process (Goldman 1994). The Club Model no longer represents therefore a viable management structure for the international economic system. The days of major agreements being hammered out in Geneva hotels by a trade cognoscenti operating under the radar of public view are gone forever. Whatever the virtues of keeping special interests off balance and out of the way, the closed-door style of negotiations that lies at the heart of the Club Model is no longer workable. After years on the periphery of the global scene, trade policy now occupies center stage.

Indeed, for all their confusion (and there has been a great deal), the anti-globalization street protestors have one thing right: the WTO matters. The trade regime stands at the center of the emerging structure of global governance. While there have been many rounds of trade negotiations over the past 50 years, the central focus of the process has shifted from tit-for-tat reductions to the identification of rules and procedures to manage economic interdependence.

In important respects, the next round of negotiations will resemble a Global Constitutional Convention. The process of global constitutionalism—defining core principles, establishing international standards, and creating institutions to manage interdependence—is likely to involve decades or even centuries of discussions and refinements. Nevertheless, the WTO mission must be understood as fundamentally an exercise in global-scale regime building with profound effects for every person on the planet. Such an exercise inherently touches on big questions about how to structure the world in which we want to live and the mechanisms by which we will be governed. In this regard, we must find more robust modalities and substantive principles by which to square the economic gains of more efficient markets with other public priorities, such as poverty alleviation, environmental protection, or the promotion of human rights. The importance of the work of the WTO—including the goals defined, agenda pursued, rules of participation advanced, and the values and assumptions that underpin the discussions—cannot be gainsaid and must be undergirded by a strong foundation of legitimacy.

It is with good reason therefore that the whole world is now watching the WTO and asking questions about the organization's purpose, structure, representation, decision processes, and *legitimacy* (Bodansky 1999; Stephan 1999). Progress in opening markets is no longer justification enough for the organization's existence. Moreover, as I noted earlier, doubts are now being raised in many quarters about whether the WTO is delivering on its mission and promise of greater economic efficiency and prosperity. In the past, only the close-knit trade community—united by a common vision of a world of open markets, a commitment to a well-defined set of core principles (for example, non-discrimination), and common traditions of education (particularly a belief in the centrality of economics)—paid attention to the work of the WTO. Today, a broader community that does not share this cultural affinity and understanding stands in judgment on the organization. Different standards of efficacy are being applied. As a result, the WTO's marks are coming in much lower, eroding the organization's legitimacy. Fundamentally, the closed-door approach to decisionmaking that was a virtue under the Club Model has now emerged as an obstacle to popular understanding of and support for the WTO.

Simultaneously, the WTO's efficacy-based claim to legitimacy has been undermined by the trade system's ever-broader reach (Dunoff 1994; Esty 1998; Keohane and Nye 2001). The seeds of the WTO's current troubles were planted dialectically in the furrows of its success. Because the international trade regime is perceived to be effective, increasing numbers of people have come to see the WTO as a key decisionmaking body and an important point of policy leverage (Mearsheimer 1994/5). Environmentalists, for example, have focused on "greening the GATT" because there are no international environmental bodies or structures of comparable strength available for advancing pollution control and natural resource management initiatives (Esty 1994). Similarly, the relative vitality of the WTO's dispute resolution procedures has meant that a wide range of conflicts that involve trade (but other policy domains as well) have ended up being settled within the confines of the WTO (Wofford 2000). A number of these matters—involving, for instance, the protection of dolphins and sea turtles or the implementation of the reformulated gasoline provisions of the United States 1990 Clean Air Act—have forced the WTO to render judgments that go beyond the scope of its core competence. With its small trade-oriented staff, the WTO is not well positioned to make endangered species or air pollution policy decisions. As a result, there has been substantial unhappiness about the impacts of trade regime decisions in other arenas, such as the environment. Every time the WTO makes "trade and . . ." decisions, it is perceived as over-reaching and its claim to legitimacy based on 'reason' gets strained (Dunoff 1997).

Acceptance of a decisionmaking process based on bureaucratic rationality can only persist to the extent that the public is convinced that the decisions that are made are "technical" in nature and undergirded by "science." The WTO's impact has clearly moved beyond the narrow realm of trade economics; its decisions inescapably involve trade-offs with other policy goals, broadly affect other realms, and clearly require value judgments.[4] Under such circumstances, the presumption in favor of technocratic rationality cannot be sustained. And the problem is not merely one of perception. Insofar as the trade agenda intersects with other policy domains such as environmental protection, trade logic and principles cannot be counted upon to reconcile appropriately the competing policy pressures. In sum, while in some policy domains, there continues to be a push for more "science" as a way of reducing disputes and over-politicization, in trade policy making, the tide is flowing the other way. As the public learns more about the choices to be made, demands for open debate and more "politics" rise.

To the extent that legitimacy based on rationality erodes, the need for legitimacy based on democracy and links to the public whose interests are being affected mounts. But, here again, the former virtues of the Club Model WTO have become serious detriments. In particular, the WTO's "membership" policy has emerged as a source of strain. The old Club does not seem adequately representative. For example, the exclusion in Seattle of most developing country representatives from the "green rooms," where an inner circle of key countries did the real negotiating, raised hackles among many delegates (Blackhurst 2001). Similarly, the WTO'S long-standing exclusion of nongovernmental organizations (NGOs) from its decision processes has become a bone of contention. In addition to developing country negotiators and NGOs, a series of government officials, representing other issue areas (for example, Environment Ministers) were pushed to the fringes of the Seattle convocation. Their presence—and distress—at being marginalized provides further testament to the fissures in the old international regime and the strain on the traditional, issue-based hierarchical structures.

The trade regime's evolving mission has added to the legitimacy crisis. The central focus of trade negotiations is no longer tit-for-tat tariff reductions. Trade policy making now centers on creating a rules-based system to manage international economic interdependence. Moreover, as economic integration deepens, the trade agenda inevitably touches more often and more directly on other issue domains and values (Esty 2001). Thus, the WTO's recent trouble can, in part, be traced to the failure of many participants in the trade community to recognize the shift that has occurred in their goals over the last decade.

Many free traders argue that their ambition does not go beyond advancing a narrow trade-liberalizing agenda. But as the scope of GATT rules and the other elements of the trade regime have expanded—driven by a shift from a shallow integration model toward a much deeper integration program (Rodrik 1997; Lawrence et al. 1996)—the WTO's reach has extended into intellectual property, environment, competition rules, and health care policy. Some of these inter-connections are not only inevitable, they are desirable. For example, a failure to take account within the trade regime of the possibility of transboundary pollution spillovers would render the international economic system open to market failures resulting in diminished allocative efficiency, reduced gains from trade, and lost social welfare, not to mention environmental degradation. Other interactions have exposed the narrowness of the trade agenda. The clash between the trade system's intellectual property rules as applied to AIDS drugs and the need to treat a major public health crisis in Africa provides one such example (Harrelson 2001).

Deeper economic integration cannot be sustained without a concomitant deepening of political integration (Dua and Esty 1997). Some commentators recognize this economics-politics connection but believe there exists a degree of "useful inefficiency" in the trading system that reduces harmonization pressures and permits divergent domestic policy differences to persist (Cooper 1968), insulating politicians from the pressures of globalization (Garrett 1998; Keohane and Nye 2001). Clearly, there are some buffers which allow some elements of national policy autonomy. Borders do matter (Helliwell 1998). But those who highlight the ongoing vitality of national authorities do little to reconcile their vision of a trade policy buffer with the reality of growing "sensitivity" created by higher trade-to-GDP ratios and the fact of ever-diminishing inefficiency in international trade.

Economic integration and political integration are interactive and iterative. Progress depends on a deepening sense of community. For the public to be comfortable opening its markets to goods from other jurisdictions, they must believe that these other jurisdictions generally share their core values. And shared values define a community. As the scope and depth of common values expands, so does the sense of community, which makes the public more willing to accept further economic integration. As I explain in more detail below, what is lacking at the WTO is any recognition of the need for more politics—more dialogue and debate, and engagement with civil society—as a way of building the political foundation needed to support the economic structure that is being erected.

The "democratic deficit" of the WTO goes deeper (Stokes and Choate 2001). We live in a world where state power has been weakened, and powerful new actors have emerged (Talbott 1997; Keohane and Nye 2001). The theory that a small set of trade officials and representatives—even if appointed by legitimately elected national governments—can appropriately "represent" the diverse global public has come under strain. National governments simply cannot mediate all global-scale politics. Even duly elected national governments cannot fully represent all of the voices that should be heard in the global-scale policymaking process (Esty 1998). The diversity of views is simply too great. Moreover, some of the regimes of WTO members are not fully democratic. Even where elections are held, corruption and elite domination may result in less than fully representative leadership. Derivative legitimacy built on the popular sovereignty of unelected Trade Ministries in distant national governments is simply no longer adequate (Harms 2000).

Individual identity is also more textured and multi-layered than the traditional model of representation reflects, making geographic electoral constituencies an inadequate foundation for robust public decisionmaking. Many people identify with communities of interest defined by an issue focus (for example, animal lovers, human rights activists, trade union members) as much as they do with geographically defined communities (Esty 1996). Thus, to limit their participation in global politics to electing national representatives who will designate trade ministry officials to represent the nation in a narrowly confined intergovernmental dialogue produces a terribly thin reed of popular sovereignty on which to build the legitimacy of the WTO.

The distinction here is between representation and representativeness. While it is useful to legitimacy to have the public perceive that it chose (by voting) the decisionmaker, a more powerful sense of comfort with the decision process is generated when individuals feel that not only their votes but their views were taken seriously in the course of policy making. Thus, the process by which public decisions are made always matters (Fiss 1993). And given the constitutional implications of the current WTO agenda, procedural fairness and an open dialogue are of even greater importance (Fiss 2001).

The idea of global-scale participatory democracy is often dismissed as a Utopian dream (Keohane and Nye 2001). Clearly, with six billion people on the planet, international trade policy decisions cannot be made in a "town meeting" format. But the WTO policymaking process can be enriched by a shift toward more transparency and open debate that engages non-governmental interests and the spectrum of views from civil society more fully (Habermas 2001). This does not mean that NGOs will—or should—get to vote when the time comes to make a decision. But it is useful to have the governmental decisionmakers exposed to a range of views, questions, data, analyses, and options. Not only does such a full-scale dialogue provide a forum for intellectual "competition" that strengthens the ultimate outcome, the legitimacy of the choice will be enhanced to the extent that the process is perceived as more representative (Esty 1998).

Modern norms of good public decisionmaking furthermore demand transparency (Florini 2001; Hansen 1999). Public acceptance of governmental authority depends on having a clear view of who is making the decision and on what basis they are deciding. This entails administrative law and procedures that reveal the informational foundation for the decision (a public docket) and who has tried to shape the outcome (disclosure of lobbying) (Aman 2001; Shapiro 2001). The WTO has some distance to go in adopting such norms of modern policy making.

AN ALTERNATIVE MODEL OF LEGITIMACY

Some commentators trace the legitimacy crisis at the WTO to a lack of political accountability. Keohane and Nye (2001, p. 280), for example, conclude that "politicians are needed who can link specific organizations and policies with a broader range of public issues through electoral accountability." I see a more granular world. Legitimacy is not simply a function of popular sovereignty and decisionmaking by majority vote. Institutions also win legitimacy and authority because of their capacity to deliver good results and from their systemic ties to other institutions (checks and balances) which provide an indirect link to those who have legitimacy derived through democratic elections. The WTO needs to move forward on all of these fronts.

Popular sovereignty

While global elections and thus directly accountable WTO "politicians" seem a long way off, the trade regime could dramatically improve the quality, authoritativeness, and representativeness of its decisionmaking and, in doing so, enhance its legitimacy. Lacking any global "demos," there will inescapably be limits to the accountability of WTO decisionmakers, but improved connections to the national (and sub-national) publics across the world can be established. In particular, non-governmental organizations (NGOs) can provide a degree of "connective tissue," linking distant citizens with the WTO (Esty 1998).[5] NGOs can pass information "down" from the WTO to their constituencies, ensuring better public understanding of the workings of the trade regime. A commitment to transparency and to greater involvement of civil society groups within the WTO would provide trade policymakers with access to fresh thinking, more diverse information sources, and a wide range of viewpoints coming "up" to Geneva from across the world. The presence of NGO-provided intellectual "competition" would produce a more vigorous WTO policy dynamic and add to the trade regime's capacity to reflect popular will and to generate well-reasoned outcomes.

To improve its accountability and connection to those with electoral legitimacy, the WTO might also engage more directly with national-scale politicians. One idea would be for legislators from a diverse set of countries to hold joint "oversight hearings" on the WTO's performance. While the WTO cannot gain the full credibility that might be generated by having directly elected leaders, more outreach and more vigorous policy debates would go some distance towards enhanced legitimacy.

Reason

Trade policy making in its current form is not a technocratic science but rather a broad-gauged realm in which values inevitably play a role and through which the balancing of trade goals with other policy aims must be worked out. The Seattle fiasco marks the death knell of the WTO as a technocratic decisionmaking body operating out of sight. But the trade regime can reclaim a degree of legitimacy based on the rationality of its outputs if its capacity for generating "right" answers is restored.

As a critical first step, the WTO must trim its sails and reserve its strength for core trade liberalization activities. By retreating from its current role as dispute resolution mechanism to the world, perhaps the WTO can reestablish its reputation for authoritativeness, efficiency, and fairness. Whenever possible, the WTO should avoid making decisions that are viewed as extending beyond its scope of trade competence. The WTO's authoritativeness and legitimacy would be enhanced to the extent that "trade and environment" problems, for example, could be redirected to a functioning Global Environmental Organization (GEO).[6] Where decisions inescapably touch other policy domains, more effort should be made to draw in relevant expertise. A more virtual WTO that places itself within a web of global public policy networks would be more effective and durable (Reinecke 1997; Slaughter 1999).

Authoritativeness is also established by the breadth and depth of the debate that takes place when difficult decisions must be made. Especially where there are high degrees of uncertainty over issues, it is important to triangulate on the truth. To ensure the requisite spectrum of viewpoints, the WTO needs more robust, transparent and participatory decisionmaking processes (Weinstein and Charnovitz 2001). To the extent that the WTO makes decisions that reinforce a narrow set of values (for example, economic efficiency) and ignore other critical values (environmental protection, human rights, etc.), its credibility and authority suffer damage. The trade community today needs to bend over backwards to recognize the validity of the other policy goals and values that are impinged upon by the trading system.

The WTO's claim to reason-based legitimacy also depends on its perceived fairness and commitment to justice. Fairness has both procedural and substantive elements. A fundamental tenet of procedural fairness or "due process" is openness—identification of who is making decisions; disclosure of the assumptions on which the process turns; and an explanation of the values, influences, and information sources that are being brought to bear. Procedural fairness also requires appropriate opportunities for interested parties to contribute to the decision process as well as guarantees (enforced through a system of administrative law) that special interests will not be able to manipulate outcomes (Joerges and Dehousse 2002; Fiss 1993).

Substantive fairness is a function of consistency across circumstances and time as well as the generation of outcomes that comport a community's values and traditions (Fiss 2001). For the WTO there is a need to ensure that, in addition to getting the right answer from the trade perspective, the institution is capable of cross-issue balancing where other values (for example, environmental concerns) are at play.

Systemic reinforcement

WTO decisionmaking would also be strengthened to the extent it were embedded in a broader structure of "checks and balances."[7] As noted above, institutions draw strength from the broader systems of which they are a part. Multiple institutions occupying the same governance "space" can cross-check and reinforce each other. They can compete and cooperate in pursuit of optimal public decisionmaking (Esty 1998).

Such an architecture would entail a multi-tier system of international governance that provides a degree of "vertical" competition between international and national decisionmakers (Esty 1999; Esty and Geradin 2001). Simultaneously, the WTO would benefit from greater "horizontal" reinforcement from other international bodies that have policymaking authority and legitimacy. The presence of a Global Environment Organization would, for example, serve as a useful counterweight and counterbalance to the World Trade Organization. Similarly, a revitalized International Labor Organization (ILO) would help to broaden the institutional base of international economic management (Charnovitz 2000).

CONCLUSION

The WTO is capable of regaining broad public acceptance and legitimacy. But a restructuring of the trade regime's substantive rules and procedures will be required. Effective global institutions whose decisionmaking processes are understood and accepted are essential in a world of complex interdependence. While there may not be a coherent political community at the global scale nor any immediate prospect of accountability in international organizations provided by direct electoral processes, it is possible to envision more representative international decisionmaking bodies, including a revitalized World Trade Organization. Broadening the base of global governance and creating a system of checks and balances that spreads authority horizontally across international organizations as well as vertically across the global and national (and local) scales promises to deliver better results over time. Beyond strengthening its legitimacy through a commitment to more transparent procedures and to providing a forum for broader global-scale political dialogue, the WTO needs to rebuild its reputation for efficacy. To do this, the trade community must show that it recognizes the broader context of the choices made at the WTO and build sensitivity to the stresses of poverty, environmental concerns, human rights issues, and other matters into the trading system. Good governance almost always involves optimization across multiple criteria—and the WTO needs rules and procedures that better balances the (sometimes) competing goals of economic integration, trade, and investment liberalization, and economic efficiency on the one hand, with environmental protection, human rights, equity, and other virtues on the other.

Wistfulness about the disappearance of the Club Model trade regime, the old post-war economic order, and its implied shallow integration should be put aside. Such a vision is both dated and undesirable. Instead, the WTO must be seen as a crucial element of the emerging international governance system. We should acknowledge the challenge—whether we call it global constitutionalism or not—of defining the core principles, rules, and procedures for managing interdependence. Getting the structure of this new international regime right is an important challenge. As a number of commentators on globalization have observed, it is essential that "space" be reserved for separate domestic political processes (Keohane and Nye 2001), just as the US Constitution reserves important elements of authority to the states. The trading regime must not over-reach and should maintain the "escape clauses" and other safety valves (Hudec 2001) which protect against too much domestic political pressure building up. But it would be a mistake to think that the future of the international economic regime would be on solid footings if we ignore the cry for reform or try to shift the focus of the trade debate to domestic fora. Revitalizing the WTO—and reestablishing its legitimacy—must be a high priority.

REFERENCES

Ackerman, B. (2000), "The New Separation of Powers," *Harvard Law Review*, 113: 633.

Aman, A. C. (2001), "Globalization, Accountability, and the Future of Administrative Law: The Limits of Globalization and the Future of Administrative Law: From Government to Governance," *Indiana Journal of Global Legal Studies*, 8 (Spring): 379, 383–384, 396–401.

Amar, A. R. (1987), "Of Sovereignty and Federalism," *Yale Law Journal*, 96: 1492–1519.

Anderson, K. and R. Blackhurst (1992), *The Greening of World Trade Issues*, Ann Arbor, MI: University of Michigan Press.

Bhagwati, J. (1993), "The Case for Free Trade," *Scientific American*, 269 (November): 42.

Bhagwati, J. and T. N. Srinivasan (1996), "Trade and Environment," in J. Bhagwati and R. E. (eds.), *Fair Trade and Harmonization: Prerequisites for Free Trade*, Cambridge, MA: MIT Press.

Blackhurst, R. (2001), "Reforming WTO Decisionmaking: Lessons from Singapore and Seattle," in K. G. Deutsch and B. Speyer (eds.), *The World Trade Organization Millennium Round: Freer Trade in the Twenty-First Century*, London: Routledge.

Bodansky, D. (1999), "The Legitimacy of International Governance: A Coming Challenge for International Environmental Law," *American Journal of International Law*, 93 (July): 596.

Breton, A. (1996), *Competitive Governments: An Economic Theory of Politics and Public Finance*, Cambridge: Cambridge University Press.

Charnovitz, S. (1994), "The World Trade Organization and Social Issues," *Journal of World Trade*, 28 (October): 17.

Charnovitz, S. (2000), "The International Labour Organisation in Its Second Century," in J. A. Frowein and R. Wolfrum, *Max Planck Yearbook of United Nations Law—Volume IV*, The Hague: Kluwer Law International.

Cooper, R. M. (1968), *The Economics of Interdependence: Economic Policy in the Atlantic Community*, New York: McGraw-Hill.

Dua, A. and D. C. Esty (1997), *Sustaining the Asia Pacific Miracle*, Washington DC: Institute for International Economics, pp. 109–10, 120–127.

Dunoff, J. L. (1994), "Institutional Misfits: The GATT, the ICJ, and Trade-Environment Disputes," *Michigan Journal of International Law*, 15: 1043.

Dunoff, J. L. (1997), " 'Trade And': Recent Developments in Trade Policy and Scholarship—And Their Surprising Political Implications," *Northwestern Journal of International Law and Business*, 17 (Winter–Spring): 759.

Eskridge, Jr., William N. and John Ferejohn (1992), "The Article I, Section 7 Game," *Georgetown Law Journal*, 80: 523–64.

Esty, D. C. (1994), *Greening the GATT: Trade, Environment, and the Future*, Washington DC: Institute for International Economics.

Esty, D. C. (1996), "Revitalizing Environmental Federalism," *Michigan Law Review*, 95: 570.

Esty, D. C. (1998), "Nongovernmental Organizations at the World Trade Organization: Cooperation, Competition, or Exclusion," *Journal of International Economic Law*, 1: 123.

Esty, D. C. (1999), "Toward Optimal Environmental Governance," *New York University Law Review*, 74: 1495.

Esty, D. C. (2000), "An Environmental Perspective on Seattle," *Journal of International Economic Law*, 3: 176.

Esty, D. C. (2001), "Bridging the Trade-Environment Divide," *Journal of Economic Perspectives*, 15: 113.

Esty, D, C. and D. Geradin (2001), "Regulatory Co-opetition," in D. C. Esty and D. Geradin (eds.), *Regulatory Competition and Economic Integration: Comparative Perspectives*, Oxford: Oxford University Press.

Fiss, O. M. (2001), "The Autonomy of Law," *Yale Journal of International Law*, 26 (Summer): 517, 520, 525–526.

Fiss, O. M. (1993), "The Allure of Individualism," *Iowa Law Review*, 78: 970–971, 978–979.

Florini, A. (2001), "Decent Exposure," *World Link* (July/August): 12–13.

Franck, T. M. (1990), *The Power of Legitimacy Among Nations*, New York: Oxford University Press.

Frug, G. E. (1984), "The Ideology of Bureaucracy in American Law," *Harvard Law Review*, 97: 1276.

Garrett, G. (1998), *Partisan Politics in the Global Economy*, Cambridge: Cambridge University Press.

Goldman, P. (1994), "The Democratization of the Development of the United States Trade Policy," *Cornell International Law Journal*, 27: 631.

Gilpin, R. (1987), *The Political Economy of International Relations*, Princeton, NJ: Princeton University Press.

Habermas, J. (2001), *The Postnational Constellation*, Cambridge, MA: MIT Press.

Hansen, P. I. (1999), "Transparency, Standards of Review and the Use of Trade Measures to Protect the Global Environment," *Virginia Journal of International Law*, 39 (Summer): 1017, 1021, 1061–1068.

Harms, B. C. (2000), "Holding Public Officials Accountable in the International Realm: A New Multi-Layered Strategy to Combat Corruption," *Cornell International Law Journal*, 33: 159, 180–181.

Harrelson, J. A. (2001), "TRIPS, Pharmaceutical Patents and the HIV/AIDS Crisis: Finding the Proper Balance Between Intellectual Property Rights and Compassion," *Widener Law Symposium Journal*, 7 (Spring): 175.

Helliwell, J. (1998), *How Much Do National Borders Matter?* Washington DC: Brookings Institution Press.

Howse, R. (1999), "The House That Jackson Built: Restructuring the GATT System," *Michigan Law Review*, 20: 107.

Hudec, R. E. (1971), "GATT or GABB? The Future Design of the General Agreement on Tariffs and Trade," *Yale Law Journal*, 80: 1299.

Hudec, R. E. (2001), "Covenent," in Roger Porter et al. (eds.), *Efficiency, Equity and Legitimacy: The Multilateral Trading System at the Millennium*, Washington DC: Brookings Institution Press, pp. 295–300.

Hurd, I. (1999), "Legitimacy and Authority in International Politics," *International Organization*, 53 (Spring): 379.

Jackson J. (1994), *World Trade and the Law of GATT*, New York: Bobbs-Merrill.

Jackson J. (1996), "Reflections on Constitutional Challenges to the Global Trading System," *Chicago Kent Law Review*, 72: 511, 519–521.

Jeffress, L. and J.-P. Mayanobe (2001), "A World Struggle is Underway: An Interview with Jose Bove," *Z Magazine*, June.

Joerges, C. and R. Dehousse (eds.) (2002), "Good Governance in an Integrated Market," *The Collected Courses of the Academy of European Law*, Vol. XI, Book 2.

Kahn, P. (1989), "Reason and Will in the Origins of American Constitutionalism," *Yale Law Journal*, 98: 449.

Keohane, R. O. and J. S. Nye, Jr. (2001), "The Club Model of Multilateral Cooperation and Problems of Democratic Legitimacy," in Roger Porter et al. (eds.), *Efficiency, Equity and Legitimacy: The Multilateral Trading System at the Millennium*, Washington DC: Brookings Institution Press.

Kobrin, S. (1998), "Back to the Future: Neomedievalism and the Postmodern Digital World Economy," *Journal of International Affairs*, 51: 362–386.

Ku, C. (2001), "Global Governance and the Changing Face of International Law," *ACUNS Reports and Papers* 2: 1–4.

Lawrence, R. et al. (1996), *A Vision of the World Economy: Openness, Diversity, and Cohesion*. Washington DC: Brookings Institution Press.

Mearsheimer, J. (1994/5), "The False Promise of International Institutions," *International Security*, 19 (Winter): 3.

Nichols, P. M. (1996), "Realism, Liberalism, Values, and the World Trade Organization," *Pennsylvania Journal of International Economic Law*, 17: 851, 856–860.

O'Rourke, K. H. (2001), "Globalization and Inequality: Historical Trends," National Bureau of Economic Research, Working Paper 8339.

Petersmann, E.-U. (1992), "National Constitutions, Foreign Trade Policy, and European Community Law," *European Journal of International Law*, 3: 15.

Reinecke, W. (1997), *Global Public Policy*, Washington DC: Brookings Institution Press.

Rodrik, D. (1997), *Has Globalization Gone Too Far?* Washington DC: Institute for International Economics.

Ruggie, J. V. (1983), "International Regimes, Transactions, and Change: Embedded Liberalism in the Post-War Economic Order," in Stephen D. Krasner (ed.), *International Regimes*, Ithaca: Cornell University Press.

Shaffer, G. C. (2001), "The World Trade Organization Under Challenge: Democracy and the Law and Politics of the WTO's Treatment of Trade and Environment Matters," *Harvard Environmental Law Review*, 25: 1.

Schott, J. J. (ed.) (1996), *The World Trading System: Challenges Ahead*, Washington DC: Institute for International Economics.

Shapiro, M. (2001), "Administrative Law Unbounded: Reflections on Government and Governance," *Indiana Journal of Global Legal Studies*, 8: 369.

Simon, H. A. (1996), *The Sciences of the Artificial*, 3rd ed., Cambridge, MA: MIT Press.

Slaughter, A.-M. (1999), "The Long Arm of the Law," *Foreign Policy*, 114 (Spring): 34.

Spiro, P. J. (1996), "New Global Potentates: Nongovernmental Organizations and the 'Unregulated' Marketplace," *Cardozo Law Review*, 19: 957.

Stephan, P. B. (1999), "Part IV Relationship of the United States to International Institutions: The New International Law—Legitimacy, Accountability, Authority and Freedom in the New Global Order," *University of Colorado Law Review*, 70 (Fall): 1555.

Stokes, B. and P. Choate. (2001), *Democratizing US Trade Policy*, New York: Council on Foreign Relations.

Strauss, P. (1984), "The Place of Agencies in Government: Separation of Powers and the Fourth Branch," *Columbia Law Review*, 84: 573.

Talbott, S. (1997), "Globalization and Diplomacy: A Practitioner's Perspective," *Foreign Policy*, 108 (Fall): 69.

van Dijck, P. and G. F. Faber (1996), *Challenges to the New World Trade Organization (Legal Aspects of International Organization*, 28), The Hague: Kluwer Law International.

Weber, M. (1994), "The Profession and Vocation of Politics," in P. Lassman and R. Speirs (eds.), *Political Writings*, Cambridge: Cambridge University Press.

Weber, S. (2000), "International Organizations and the Pursuit of Justice in the World Economy," *Ethics and International Affairs*, 4.

Webster, D. and D. Bell (1997), "First Principles of Constitutional Revision," *Nova Law Review*, 22: 391.

Weinstein, M. M. and S. Charnovitz (2001), "The Greening of the WTO," *Foreign Affairs*, 80: 147.

Wilson, J. Q. (1989), *Bureaucracy: What Government Agencies Do and Why They Do It*, United States: Basic Books.

Wofford, C. (2000), " A Greener Future at the WTO: The Refinement of WTO Jurisprudence on Environmental Exceptions to the GATT," *Harvard Environmental Law Review*, 24: 563.

ENDNOTES

1. As Keohane and Nye explain, we are shifting from a mode of international relations in which people interact only through governments and where tightly controlled inter-governmental regimes facilitate international cooperation with regard to particular issues. This system can be seen as "decomposable" to the extent that the specific regimes operate quite independently, with rules and traditions developed by a tight-knit "community" (that is, national government officials and a small number of officials serving as the staff to the relevant international organization) in the issue-area, making it hard for "outsiders" (NGOs, new state actors, etc.) to participate.

2. It will be interesting to see whether this acceptance of "expert" control over an important realm of policy continues with a faltering economy.

3. When I speak here of the trade "regime," I mean not only the small Secretariat that works within the World Trade Organization in Geneva but the entire set of trade ministry officials in all of the national capitals who contribute to the WTO policymaking process.

4. Courts similarly have their greatest legitimacy when they address issue-specific concerns raised by particularized parties and rule narrowly (on what might be considered a "negative" basis—that is, you cannot do . . .). Affirmative rulings that demand sweeping actions (for example, new laws or regulations) create much more stress and raise legitimate concerns.

5. Some critics of a more open WTO fear that a greater NGO presence within the WTO would expose the organization to greater special interest pressures and exacerbate the North-South imbalance because of the likely preponderance of Northern NGOs (Nichols 1996; Spiro 1996; Bhagwati and Srinivasan 1996). But, in fact, the logic runs the other way. Northern NGOs spend most of their time criticizing Northern governments, thereby ameliorating existing imbalances.

6. Of course, today we lack a functioning international environmental regime. For information on ongoing research into the possible structure of a GEO, see the Yale University Global Environmental Governance Web site (http://www.yale.edu/envirocenter/research).

7. The literature on the benefits of checks and balances runs deep (see, for example, Amar 1987; Strauss 1984; Webster and Bell 1997; Ackerman 2000).

WTO 2002: Imaginary Crisis, Real Problems

DAVID HENDERSON

INTRODUCTION

In his challenging article in the inaugural issue of *World Trade Review*, Daniel Esty takes the position that the international trading system, and with it the World Trade Organization, face "a serious legitimacy crisis." He argues that the world has changed profoundly, in ways that put in question the present status, objectives, and procedures of the WTO: hence the Organization now "stands at a watershed." He puts forward some radical proposals for reforming it.

While I agree with Esty that the trading system and the WTO currently face serious problems, I see the nature and origins of these problems in different terms from his. I believe that both his diagnosis and his prescription are wide of the mark.

Esty's thesis has three main interrelated elements.

The first of these concerns the issue of legitimacy which features in his title. The argument here runs as follows. The WTO's justification and effectiveness depend on its recovering, through far-reaching measures of reform, a legitimacy which it no longer possesses. The twin foundations of legitimacy for international agencies are "popular sovereignty" and "efficacy," and it is in relation to the former in particular that the present crisis has arisen, the WTO, like the GATT before it, is run by officials who are not elected, and whose allegiance is to member governments. Such official ties to governments provide only an indirect link with popular sovereignty; and given the now extended responsibilities of the Organization, and the increase in public concern about what it does, the time has come to establish a formal and direct connection. Efficacy alone is no longer enough to furnish legitimacy, and in any case, the efficacy of the Organization has now itself been put in question by its critics in 'civil society.' Hence the WTO should now make "a commitment to transparency and to greater involvement of civil society groups" (p. 17) so as to establish the foundation of popular sovereignty which it can no longer do without and regain the legitimacy that it has lost.

A second element concerns the objectives of the Organization. Here Esty argues (p. 7) that "the trade regime needs to pursue its economic goals in a fashion that shows sensitivity to other goals and values, such as poverty alleviation, environmental protection, and the promotion of public health." This is a strange form

From David Henderson, "WTO 2002: Imaginary Crisis, Real Problems," *World Trade Review*, vol. 1, no. 3, 2002, pp. 277–296; Cambridge University Press, New York, NY.

of words, since poverty alleviation is unmistakably an economic goal, and the same is true of both environmental protection and public health in so far as, under both headings, monetary values can be attributed to alternative states of affairs and outcomes. But the underlying idea can be expressed in a different way. Essentially, what Esty proposes is that in relation to trade rules and trade policies the WTO should explicitly weigh and take into account what could be their full effects, both economic and non-economic, and in particular their possible impact on the state of the environment and the distribution of income within and between countries. It should not treat trade liberalization as its sole purpose and concern.

A third element relates to global governance. Like many other observers, Esty takes the view that globalization has brought with it a need for new forms and mechanisms of international collective action: "Effective global institutions . . . are essential in a world of complex interdependence" (p. 19), and (p. 12) "the trade regime stands at the center of the emerging structure of global governance." In this new structure, "more representative international decision-making bodies, including a revitalized World Trade Organization," would play a larger role. In the case of the WTO, it is the two proposed changes in its functioning—the greater involvement of "civil society," and the conscious adoption of broader objectives— that would provide the necessary "revitalization." By embracing wider aims and ensuring closer ties with popular sovereignty, the Organization would gain acceptance and support, improve its efficacy, and enlarge its capacity to contribute to the stronger global governance that the world now stands in need of. The different elements of radical reform are thus presented as mutually reinforcing.

In what follows I focus mainly on Esty's thesis, but refer also to some related lines of thought. I begin by examining the issue of legitimacy in relation to international agencies in general and the WTO in particular.

INTERNATIONAL AGENCIES, GOVERNMENTS AND "POPULAR SOVEREIGNTY"

Since Esty is so much concerned with the legitimacy of organizations, it is worth asking how this term is to be interpreted. His treatment of the issue has a missing dimension. Although he rightly notes (p. 9) that legitimacy "is a complex concept in the context of governance," he considers only one aspect of it. Both in his text and in an article that he draws on by Keohane and Nye (2001), the legitimacy of an institution is implicitly defined in terms of its acceptability to public opinion in a democratic society and the attributes that make for acceptability. But this is not the only possible interpretation; one can also think of the concept in more straightforward formal terms. The Oxford English Dictionary provides a form of words that gives expression to this alternative—or additional—interpretation. It offers, as one meaning of legitimacy, "the condition of being in accord with law or principle" (1989, Vol. VIII, p. 811).[1] Admittedly, it can be argued that, at any rate in relation to political institutions, such an interpretation captures only a part of what is involved. But formal legitimacy, even if no more than a starting point, is neither irrelevant nor unimportant for international agencies as for other institutions of governance. In this restricted but pertinent sense of the term, the legitimacy of an organization such as the WTO does not derive from, nor depend on, public acceptability or support. It comes from governments alone.

This direct link with governments rather than peoples is inherent in the nature of institutions such as the WTO. It was the governments of national states that created the Organization, as they had created the GATT before it. In the same way, it is governments that have established an array of international organizations including the International Monetary Fund (IMF), the World Bank (IBRD), the regional development banks, the International Labour Organisation (ILO), the Organisation for Economic Cooperation and Development (OECD), and the various agencies that directly make up the United Nations (UN) system. All such organizations are, and can only be, the creatures of sovereign nation-states. It is their member governments that bring them into existence, lay down their initial roles and terms of reference, decide their future membership, finance their current activities (whether directly or indirectly), and exercise continuing control over what they do and how they do it. Admittedly there is no set pattern of relationships and procedures, and different agencies may acquire, or be granted, different degrees of initiative and autonomy. But whatever pattern may evolve, and whatever the differences between the agencies which are indeed substantial, it is the member governments that determine these matters and have the sole right to change them. Except by winding up an agency, a course of action which only they can decide on, its governments cannot escape these responsibilities. So long as an international agency continues to be maintained and financed by member governments, its right to exist, and to carry out the functions which those members have collectively assigned to it, is clear. To this extent, and in this sense, its legitimacy derives from governments alone. Questions of public acceptability and "direct links with popular sovereignty" do not enter in.

What is more, the formal legitimacy of an agency does not necessarily depend on its having the "indirect links with popular sovereignty" which are made possible by democratic processes within member states. Most existing international agencies include among their members governments which are far from democratic, and this is neither an oversight nor an anomaly. Now, as in the past, it is unusual for the observance of democratic forms to be made a condition of eligibility; generally speaking, the right of a member state to join an agency, and to participate in its affairs, does not depend on whether or how far the government of that state is democratically elected, accountable to its citizens, and concerned to safeguard civil and political rights.[2] This is most obviously the case with the United Nations, where Article 3 of the Charter specifies that membership is open "to all peace-loving states which accept the obligations contained in the present Charter and, in the judgement of the Organization, are able and willing to carry out these obligations." The reason for this is clear: insistence on the observance of democratic forms as a condition of membership would not only have created from the start huge and divisive problems of interpretation, but also put in question the principle of universality which is widely viewed as essential to the legitimacy of the UN system.

Forms of government were likewise not taken into account in defining eligibility for membership of the GATT, and this continues to be the case in the WTO.

Thus—to take a recent leading instance—China was not barred from consideration for membership of the Organization on the grounds that its political system does not provide for free elections or protect basic liberties. As in other applications for membership, and in accordance with the WTO Articles of Agreement, the pre-conditions were more technical and specific to the Organization. Most people, including some though not all of today's critics of the WTO in "civil society," would take the view that the legitimacy of the WTO was not undermined by the accession of China. As to the future, extending the criteria for accession, so as to include within them the observance of democratic forms, would strengthen the Organization's claim to formal legitimacy only if it were agreed by the existing member governments. It is for them to determine the basis of eligibility.

Esty notes (p. 15) that "some of the regimes of WTO members are not fully democratic." Although he views this as one of the reasons why the Organization now lacks legitimacy in his sense of the term, he does not argue for a tightening of the conditions for WTO membership. He simply by-passes the aspect of formal legitimacy, to argue that those of the Organization's member governments that are democratic should now take effective steps to strengthen its claims to public acceptability, through new or stronger links to "popular sovereignty."

Whether such direct links would in fact make the WTO more legitimate is open to question. The notion that they make the democratic process within nations more legitimate has been questioned by Robert Hudec in the context of the history of trade policy in the United States. Hudec makes the point that the notorious Smoot-Hawley tariff of 1930 was a product of "direct democracy:" "Seldom has so much of the US electorate had so much direct impact on so many details of a major US statute" (Hudec 1999, p. 217). He argues (p. 220) that such episodes, as also the handling of present-day issues of sanitary and phyto-sanitary standards, cast doubt on what he terms "the simplistic notion that democratic participation is a one-dimensional phenomenon measured by the distance between the voter and the decision-maker."

In Esty's treatment of the issues, this "simplistic notion" goes unquestioned; legitimacy and "popular sovereignty" march together. Moreover, it is not sufficient for democratic participation to be achieved by actions taken, and procedures followed, within the boundaries of member states; the "diverse global public" has to be effectively brought into the processes of the WTO. Hence (he argues) the official machinery of trade policy must give more scope, in the WTO as well as at national level, to non-governmental organizations which directly represent the people of a country, and in some cases, arguably, the people of the world.

THE STATUS AND CLAIMS OF NON-GOVERNMENTAL ORGANIZATIONS

Esty's proposals for the WTO can be set against a wider background of institutions and events. In sketching out this background, I use the lower-case term "non-governmental organizations" in a broad sense, so that it covers unofficial associations of all kinds, national and international. Among non-governmental organizations thus broadly defined, two groups are especially relevant in relation to the constitution and working of international agencies. One comprises representatives of the "social partners"—that is, the organizations that represent businesses and trade unions. The second is the "public interest" groups which have grown in number and influence in recent years. Following general current practice, I refer to these latter as the (upper-case) NGOs. They stand for particular causes, rather than sectional or professional interests. They include consumer associations, conservation and environmental groups, societies concerned with economic development in poor countries, human rights groups, movements for social justice, humanitarian societies, organizations representing indigenous peoples, and church groups from all denominations. They are often classed together under the label of "civil society"; but this is a misuse of language, since the term should be, and historically has been, given a much broader meaning. It would appear that, in referring to "civil society," it is the NGOs that Esty has in mind.

The principle of non-official involvement in the proceedings of international agencies is neither new nor controversial. Right from the start, the UN system assigned a role to non-governmental organizations. Article 71 of the Charter authorized the Economic and Social Council "to make suitable arrangements for consultation with non-governmental organizations which are concerned with matters within its competence," and a recent text notes that there are now over 1,500 such organizations that are recognized as having consultative status within ECOSOC (Archer 2001, pp. 26–27). Well before the UN Charter was drafted, a much closer involvement of particular non-governmental organizations, going beyond consultation, had already been established by its member governments within the ILO, which was set up after the First World War. The ILO is now, and always has been, an agency in which "the trade union and employers' representatives . . . have an equal voice [with member governments] in formulating its policies" (ILO, 2002, opening page of text). In the OECD as in its predecessor agency, labour and business organizations have throughout been formally represented by advisory committees which have offices and staff in Paris. The committees function as channels for information, consultation, and exchange of views.

More recently, the NGOs, as distinct from business organizations and trade unions whose participation has a much longer history, have acquired a more prominent role in the working of many international agencies. In the main UN system, some notable steps towards involving them more closely were taken in the context of the 1992 UN Conference on Environment and Development (the 'Rio Summit'). Since then they have continued to grow in numbers, influence and (thanks largely to the Internet) in the ability to act in concert; and all the main international agencies, at varying stages and in different ways and degrees, and with the approval or acquiescence of their member governments, have made provision for enlarged NGO participation in their proceedings. The WTO is among these.

The question now is how much further, and in what ways, the involvement of non-governmental organizations should be taken; and though this aspect is rarely mentioned, and is not explicitly referred to by Esty, it applies not only to "public interest" NGOs but also to representatives of business and labour organizations. I begin with some general observations, and then turn to aspects that are more specific to the WTO.

Participation: the general aspect

It is possible to distinguish broadly between two forms of participation, both of which can be provided for within national states as well as—or possibly, rather than—within international agencies. Under the first, governments can involve non-governmental organizations more closely by making non-sensitive information widely and promptly available to them and by establishing, and treating seriously, procedures for consulting them. In such a process, the distinction between insiders and outsiders—the official participants and the non-governmental organizations—is fully maintained, though the outsiders are given more time, attention and opportunities to be heard. A second form of participation goes further, and brings closer interaction between the two worlds. It can cover active involvement of non-governmental organizations in intergovernmental meetings, substantive discussions, negotiations and decisions, and also in operations where—as with the IMF, the IBRD and the European Commission–an agency has major operational responsibilities.

The first form of participation is relatively straightforward and uncontroversial, at intergovernmental as well as national level. As noted above, governments have been taking this path in the WTO and elsewhere, with NGOs especially in mind. The Guidelines established in 1996 by the General Council of the WTO "mention the need to make documents more readily available than in the past, require the Secretariat to engage actively with NGOs, and recommend the development of new mechanisms for fruitful engagement, including symposia on WTO-related issues" (Loy 2001, p. 122); and since then, recent Directors-General have made clear their commitment to act on these lines. Gary Sampson has noted (Sampson 2001, p. 12) that "In the run-up to the [1999] Seattle meeting, all negotiating proposals were posted on the WTO website with no apparent ill effects. This would have been considered unthinkable to many delegations even in the recent past." In the OECD, the 1999 ministerial communiqué said that "Ministers . . . looked to the Organisation to assist governments in the important task of improving communication and consultation with civil society."

Since making agencies more open and consultation processes fuller and more intensive gives rise to costs as well as benefits, there will always be questions as to how far to go. Again, there may be problems in judging the claims to recognition of NGOs in particular, and in deciding which of them are to be brought into formal consultations; the issues of credentials and "modalities" are not to be seen as trivial. But the general principles of transparency and closer consultation are widely accepted, with good reason, and accepting them does not change or obscure the boundaries between insiders and outsiders. "Popular sovereignty" is not given serious expression.

For Esty and those who share his views, this does not meet the main problem, which is that even democratic governments and those who work for them are insufficiently representative of their peoples. The remedy is (to use Esty's wording, p. 19) "to establish more representative international decisionmaking bodies." Non-governmental organisations would then have a recognized place of their own, alongside ministers and officials, in the substantive work and the decisions of an agency such as the WTO. This would supposedly ensure popular sovereignty and the legitimacy that depends on it.

I believe that this conception of legitimacy is at fault.[3] The whole notion of a 'civil society' which has claims of its own to speak for the people of a country has no basis when that country has a democratically elected and responsible government: persons who are not elected, and who are not accountable to a duly elected and broadly representative legislature, can have no such representative status. This is not to argue that democracy is only a matter of elections, nor that the notion of 'civil society' is without meaning or value, despite the questionable use that is now often made of it. The issue is one of defining admissible roles and claims, and here the main point is contained in the view that Gary Sampson attributes to WTO member states, that "the WTO is an intergovernmental organization and governments should represent the collectivity of their constituents" (Sampson 2000, p. 1114).

The above argument applies to all non-governmental organizations. It is sometimes argued, or simply assumed, that the NGOs have a special claim to represent society as a whole, which is not possessed by business or professional groups, because they speak for the "public interest." This is doubly mistaken. For one thing, the contrast is overdrawn. The involvement of groups representing special interests, including business organizations, may serve to promote better informed and more satisfactory outcomes. At the same time, the distinction between "sectional" and "public interest" groups is blurred in practice; there is no reason to presume that all NGOs, particularly those with large organizations and budgets, are free from self-regarding motives. Second, it may be that arguments typically advanced by NGOs are open to question, and that their recommendations for action, if taken seriously, would be contrary to the interests of people in general. (Esty himself notes [p. 8] that "Many of those who criticize the WTO and other elements of international economic structure have little foundation for the charges they make.") Fundamentally, though, what is in question is not the motives or wisdom of non-governmental organizations, including NGOs, but their status as bodies that are neither elected nor politically accountable.

This does not mean that involvement of these organizations cannot properly or usefully go beyond consultation—as witness the very different cases of the ILO, with its long-established tripartite structure, and the IBRD where, with the consent of member governments, NGOs are now closely keyed into operational work. But two principles should bear on such involvement. First, its nature and extent is for governments to decide, case by case. Second, no non-governmental organization, whether speaking for businesses, trade unions, professional groups, "public interest" concerns or any other constituency, has a valid claim to active participation in its own right in proceedings where the responsibility for outcomes rests, and has to rest, with the governments of member states, and is therefore exercised by political leaders and the officials who are authorized, qualified and paid to act on their behalf and in support of their role.[4]

The qualifying phrase, "in its own right," needs to be underlined. My contention is that "civil society" has no claim, on grounds of democratic legitimacy alone, to have a governing voice in international agencies, or even to close involvement in their substantive work. But the member governments are free to choose: it is for them to decide whether and how far to go down such a path. While they cannot shed their status or responsibilities, they can, if they so wish, assign to representatives of non-governmental organizations roles and tasks within the agencies alongside, or even in place of, official participants. I turn now to consider the case for moving in this direction within the WTO.

Participation: the WTO today

Up to now, member governments of the WTO have drawn a fairly clear line between the two forms of participation described above. While the Organization has made itself more accessible and open to the non-official world, through informing and consulting non-governmental organizations more fully, governments have not been prepared to sanction more active outside involvement. It is true that a few governments sometimes include representatives of non-governmental organizations in their delegations to biennial WTO Ministerial Conferences, but to the best of my knowledge none are directly involved in the day-to-day operations of the Organization. To quote Sampson (2000, p. 11) again, "Unlike a number of other international organizations, the WTO permits only representatives of governments and selected intergovernmental organizations to participate in or observe the processes of its regular activities."

There are sound reasons for retaining these restrictions on outside participation in the activities of the Organization.

One reason, and arguably the most decisive, concerns the Organization's agenda, As Sampson notes (p. 11 again), "WTO members justify their reluctance on the grounds that the WTO is both a legally binding instrument and a forum for negotiations." The latter aspect is especially telling. More than any other international agency, the work of the WTO is linked to intergovernmental negotiations, with the national delegates chiefly acting as actual or potential negotiators and the Secretariat assisting them in that capacity. Few governments, if any, would welcome the active and regular participation of outsiders in negotiating processes, and there are valid reasons for this. An essential part of the GATT/WTO's *raison d'etre* is that governments can negotiate the exchange of market-opening concessions in order to overcome the opposition of protectionist interests at home. It would hardly make sense to bring such outsiders inside the negotiating tent. The same argument applies to negotiations relating to revising existing rules or making new ones, where "protectionist capture" is an ever-present threat.

Second, many if not most of the NGOs which aspire to greater influence in the WTO either do not share or actually reject the objectives of the Organization. They are opposed to freedom of cross-border trade and capital flows, suspicious of further moves in that direction, and preoccupied with what they see as the damaging effects of globalization. These attitudes typically go with a generalized hostility to capitalism, multinational enterprises, and the idea of a market economy.[5]

Third, the issue is a divisive one. The support for closer NGO involvement has largely come from some of the OECD member countries, while it is firmly opposed by the governments of most developing countries.

For all these reasons, the active formal involvement in the substantive work of the WTO of non-governmental organizations in general, and NGOs in particular, would make it a less effective institution for achieving the objectives that its member governments have assigned to it. Esty's proposals for constitutional change, however, go together with the view that these objectives should now be broadened. I therefore turn to this second element of his thesis.

OBJECTIVES, AGENDA, AND THE ENSEMBLE OF POLICIES

Esty believes that trade officials, national and international, need to change their ways, and hence the ways of the WTO. They should recognize that "The WTO's impact has clearly moved beyond the narrow realm of trade economics; its decisions inescapably involve trade-offs with other policy goals, broadly affect other realms, and clearly involve value judgements" (p. 13). This recognition should go together with an administrative reorientation. They should no longer work within the now outdated "club model" of international cooperation, under which groups of like-minded specialists conduct negotiations behind closed doors, and arrive at agreements largely in isolation from government policies in general, within what Robert Keohane and Joseph Nye (who invented the concept of the club model) refer to as "decomposable issue areas" (Keohane and Nye 2001, p. 291).

It is true that trade officials, like other specialists, live much of the time in a world of their own. Up to a point, however, such things are inevitable, and serve a useful purpose: one might expect that the same situation would soon prevail, in large part for valid reasons, in the new Global Environment Organization which Esty would like to see established. In any case, isolation is not the whole story: in most areas, including that of trade policies, the working environment is far from wholly closed. Governments remain responsible for the "ensemble of policies," in economic affairs as elsewhere, and in reviewing and deciding the economic ensemble they typically try to take account of a broad range of objectives and concerns including those that Esty lists. The fact that in a particular area of policy ministers and officials engage with limited and specific issues does not mean that they are required, expected or allowed to do so in isolation or without regard to wider aspects.

Esty gives an oversimplified picture of the work of trade officials, and of the WTO and the GATT before it. He portrays those involved as single-mindedly pursuing the cause of freer trade, with "economic efficiency" alone as their guiding principle. But the trade policies of member governments have never conformed to such a pattern. In a brilliant dissection of the draft Havana Charter of 1947, Jacob Viner showed that the International Trade Organisation (ITO) then proposed was a complex compromise reflecting the prevailing political realities of the time: it certainly was not a blueprint for free trade (Viner 1947). The GATT, which then emerged as a pared-down version of the ITO, was likewise a delicate political balancing act: rules were established to liberalize trade in goods, but these were circumscribed by other rules which allowed contracting parties wide leeway to continue existing protectionist measures and even to adopt new ones.

This balancing act was maintained throughout the history of the GATT, and has now been transferred to the WTO. Trade liberalization in the GATT/WTO process has throughout been gradual, patchy and laborious, sometimes reluctant, and always subject to limitations, reservations, and even on occasion reversals. With one surprising exception, which brought with it no tangible result, no WTO member has formally endorsed free trade.[6] Over the 55 years since the GATT came into existence, even those of its member governments that have participated fully in the various "trade rounds," and brought down their tariff rates accordingly, have pursued policies only of heavily qualified liberalism. This is hardly surprising, since in all of them trade policies have been, and continue to be, strongly influenced by considerations other than "efficiency," such as concern for particular interests and groups, and conceptions of national interest which can be viewed as justifying protectionist measures. The picture of trade ministers and officials as unconditional and narrowly focused proponents of trade liberalization, allowed by governments to do their will in obscurity, is a caricature.

Admittedly, to recognize these facts does not dispose of the case for a broadening of the objectives of the WTO—nor, more generally, for discarding the "club model." The main aims and concerns that governments assigned to the GATT, and which they have carried over into the WTO, are indeed restricted in scope: they relate specifically to the conduct of trade policies, where they give expression to liberal principles of quota abolition, tariff reduction, and non-discrimination. While the Organization is instructed, in its Articles of Agreement, to have regard to broader objectives, which now include "sustainable development" and ensuring that developing countries participate fully in the benefits of economic growth, these objectives form a background for officials and Secretariat, rather than serving directly as a basis for action. They do not meet the need that Esty perceives in the WTO of today, for "rules and procedures that better balance the (sometimes) competing goals of economic integration, trade, and investment liberalization, and economic efficiency on the one hand, with environmental protection, human rights, equity and other virtues on the other" (p. 19).

It is understandable that Esty's concerns relate specifically to the WTO of today rather than the GATT of old. As a result of the Uruguay Round agreements, the WTO provides market access rules for the bulk of international trade, not just trade in (some) industrial goods; it deals more extensively with non-tariff barriers, going deeper into domestic regulations that increasingly bear upon trade flows, it covers intellectual property (substantially) and trade-related investment measures (partially); nearly all agreements now form part of a "single undertaking," by which the obligations entered into by countries in different areas are linked; and these obligations have been made enforceable through a much stronger dispute settlement procedure. "New issues," such as labour and environmental standards, and rules governing competition and foreign direct investment, have swirled around the Organization for the last few years. With the exception of labour standards, all these form part of the agenda for the new WTO round launched at the Doha Ministerial Conference last year. Finally, the WTO membership has greatly increased, with the accession of many developing and transitional countries.

Overall, the WTO in 2002 is more politicized and legalized than the diplomacy-oriented GATT. It is *politicized* in the sense that it is in the spotlight of public heat and controversy, to a far greater extent than was ever the case with the GATT, It is *legalized* through what is in effect a quasi-automatic dispute settlement mechanism charged with interpreting and enforcing increasingly complicated legal agreements. The combination has manifestly put the squeeze on traditional GATT-style diplomacy. The WTO thus operates in a changed environment. Internally, it has wider though still limited scope; and partly in consequence, it faces strong and growing external pressures.

Even granting the differences between the GATT then and the WTO now, however, it does not follow that Esty's programme of change should be adopted. For one thing, it is far from clear what form his new "rules and procedures" (or alternatively, as on p. 19, "new modalities and substantive principles") might take. In this connection, his two specific proposals for the Organization fit uneasily with the idea of broadening its concerns. On the one hand, he suggests (p. 17) that "As a critical first step, the WTO must trim its sails and reserve its strength for core liberalization activities," which would involve "retreating from its current role as dispute resolution mechanism to the world." At the same time, he wishes to involve the NGOs more closely in the Organization's work, even though the great majority of these are concerned with particular issues and causes rather than the ensemble of policies. More fundamentally, the whole notion of broadening the goals and concerns of the Organization is open to question.

In my view, it would be unwise for the WTO to be charged, in all its proceedings, with the duty of taking explicit account of a wide range of other objectives that governments have endorsed, but which are not directly related to the goal of a more liberal trade system. As David Robertson has noted, the fact that environment and development objectives have now been incorporated in the Organization's terms of reference does not mean that its distinctive role and purposes have to be redefined. Now as in the GATT, "the means specified in the WTO for achieving these objectives are limited to reciprocal and mutually advantageous reductions in tariffs and other barriers to trade, and the elimination of discriminatory treatment in trade relations" (Robertson 2000, p. 1119). The reason for retaining this focused agenda for the Organization is simply that (to quote Martin Wolf) "experience suggests that the opening of trade . . . flows enriches most citizens in the short run and virtually all citizens in the long run" (Wolf 2001a, p. 182). If anything, the WTO needs to re-emphasize, not redefine, the GATT's *raison d'etre*, albeit with a wider agenda of trade liberalization—in agriculture and services as well as industrial goods—and of rule-strengthening, especially in relation to anti-dumping measures and subsidies.

More broadly, and in relation to economic policies as a whole, it is going well beyond the evidence to argue that globalization has rendered obsolete the notion of "decomposable issue areas," with its corresponding division of labour between different specialists and different international agencies. Coordination problems are present today, as always, but they have not built up in a way that requires a jettisoning of the "club model" as a basis for international economic cooperation. There is no compelling reason to redraw the boundaries of the leading international agencies, and much to be said for the view that "at present the world does best by constructing regimes designed to achieve specific and limited ends" (Wolf 2001b, pp. 201–202).

This however raises the more general issue of "global governance," and leads onto the third element in Esty's thesis.

"GLOBAL GOVERNANCE" AND THE ROLE OF THE WTO

Two closely related arguments are now brought to bear, by Esty and many others, to support the view that the world now requires, and is in course of developing, a stronger system of global governance in which international agencies, including the WTO, would play a leading part. Both arguments relate to the supposed effects of globalization, and both are without foundation.

Argument Number One, in its most basic form, is that the huge size and rapid growth of international trade and capital flows establishes *in itself* the case for more effective global governance: such flows, it is presumed, cannot be left unmanaged. For some commentators, globalization has brought the dawn of a new era. One of these international dawnists is the present Secretary-General of the UN: "Today, networks of production and trade have broken free from national borders and become truly global. But they have left the rest of the system far behind" (Annan 2001, p. 27).

A similarly melodramatic view is taken . . . by Peter Sutherland, John Sewell, and David Weiner: "It is obvious to many observers that the development of the world economy is out-pacing the capacity to govern it, at both the national and international level . . . The impact of globalization has made the 'logic' of the post-war period obsolete" (Sutherland et al. 2001, pp. 102, 103).

Argument Number Two is that (to quote Esty, p. 15) "We live in a world where state power has been weakened, and powerful new actors have emerged." It is now widely held, and endlessly reiterated on all sides, that globalization has deprived national governments of their ability to control events. This is often joined with a belief that the powers thus lost have passed in large part to multinational enterprises (MNEs), and indeed the MNEs may be among the "powerful new actors" that Esty refers to.

A presumption that globalization has had these effects often leads on to the thesis that increasingly there will be, and should be, greater involvement of NGOs and international businesses in shouldering the now heavier burdens of global governance. For example, the World Economic Forum, in a document issued after its annual meeting for 2002, advances the view that "Transparent multi-stakeholder networks will likely emerge as the most legitimate form of global problem solving in the 21st century. Governments must join with business, international organizations and the emerging transnational civil society to form coalitions around critical challenges on the global agenda and collaborate in flexible frameworks to resolve them" (World Economic Forum 2002). Other business spokespersons and organizations have voiced the same idea.

These twin arguments, or assumptions, take no account of the fact that closer international economic integration, both in recent years and farther back—for it is by no means a new phenomenon—has in large part resulted from decisions voluntarily taken by national governments. Generally speaking, governments have made their economies more open not because they were forced to but because, with good reason, they considered such actions to be in the interests of their citizens. In taking this course, they accepted specific constraints on their freedom of action; and in some cases, most notably the members and would-be members of the European Union, they have even ceded the right to determine their own trade policies. But they have done these things of their own accord. More than technological advance, national policies and institutions have determined the pace and depth of globalization, and governments remain free to decide how much further to go towards fuller economic integration with the rest of the world.

Aside from such constraints on external economic policies as they have freely accepted and wish to maintain, national states today remain almost as free to act and decide today as they were 10, 20 or 30 years ago.[7] Even small states, provided they have stable governments, retain in full the power to run their affairs in relation to such matters as defence, foreign policy, constitutional arrangements, the electoral system and voting rights, residence, citizenship, the legal system, public provision for health, pensions and welfare, and the status of the national language or languages. Even in relation to the choice of taxation rates, the evidence clearly shows that there remains substantial freedom of choice. The notion that today's more economically integrated world is one of "post-sovereign governance" has no basis.[8] As to the dreaded MNEs, the freeing of cross-border trade and investment flows tends to weaken such economic power as they may possess, because it widens the scope for competition.

For some commentators, globalization enhances the role of international agencies; thus Miles Kahler writes that "Growing international integration points to greater delegation" to the agencies (Kahler 2001, p. 104), while Keohane and Nye (2001, p. 265) begin a sentence with the words "As these institutions become more important . . ." There is in fact no such general tendency for the power of the agencies to increase. Both the IMF and the IBRD are less influential than they were 20 or 30 years ago, the Fund because its lending operations are now limited in practice to developing countries, and the Bank because of the growth of private lending to an increasing range of its borrowing countries. All the agencies, now as before, are the servants and instruments of their member governments. There is little or no evidence of any wish or tendency to delegate powers to them.

The WTO and Global Governance

It is true that the WTO can be portrayed as an exception to this generalization. At the time when the Organization was set up, John Jackson observed that its establishment marked "a watershed in the international economic system," resulting from "the mere fact of creating a definitive international arrangement, combined with the extraordinary expanse of the Uruguay Round negotiations." As noted above, the formal establishment of the WTO as an international agency (as distinct from a mere agreement), the extension of its concerns to a range of new areas, the notion of a "single undertaking," and, most notably, the enormous strengthening of the dispute settlement mechanism, have between them created a new political-legal situation for the agency and its members.

However, there is another side to the picture. It is also possible to take the view that, to quote from a recent book by Douglas Irwin, "The World Trade Organization is something more, but not much more, than the GATT . . ." (Irwin 2002, p. 186) and that both agencies should be seen as closely restricted in their capacity to act independently and to influence events. Four aspects of the WTO's inherited limitations are worth noting.

First, like the GATT, the Organization has a notably small Secretariat with a strictly limited role. Its complement of 575 permanent staff, plus some 200 persons on short term contracts, compares with a figure of over 2,800 for the IMF (counting "contractual employees" as well as regular staff), and some 11,000 staff names listed in the IBRD's current directory. The difference reflects the fact that both the Fund and the Bank, and especially the latter, have large operational responsibilities. By contrast, the primary role of the WTO Secretariat is to service national delegations. In this it resembles the OECD, where however Secretariat numbers are much larger, both absolutely and—still more—in relation to the numbers of national officials in permanent delegations, and where the scope for the Secretariat to do independent work is greater than in the WTO.

Second, the WTO like the GATT is an organization where decisions are made by consensus. The limits that this tends to impose are reinforced by a third factor, which is that, like most international agencies but unlike the Fund and the Bank, the Organization is financed by direct contributions from member governments which are subject each year to prolonged, detailed and often contentious scrutiny. Agreement on the budget is subject to consensus.

The last and most fundamental factor is that those who make up the Organization, whether in the Secretariat or the permanent delegations, have virtually no power to act independently. Generally speaking, though exceptions can occur, national delegations to the WTO are under close and continuous control from their capital cities. They are not independent actors, but persons under instruction.

Despite its enlarged scope and capacity to act, therefore, the Organization is not a powerful instrument of global governance, nor is it in course of becoming so, because this is not what its members wish or require of it. Here as elsewhere, national governments remain in charge, and show little tendency to cede or delegate authority.

Twin Illusions of Globalization

In so far as the WTO is required by its members to act in ways that constrain or put in question their conduct, the need for this does not mainly arise from globalization. To the contrary, the main activities of the Organization, and most of the debates and disputes that take place within it, arise from the fact that member governments have not fully liberalized their trade. Their failure and reluctance to do so gives rise to the rich and varied array of exceptions, qualifications, derogations, reservations and outright departures which go along with the rules, the handling of which accounts for a substantial part of the Organization's proceedings. If and in so far as member countries were prepared to liberalise unilaterally, as many of them have in fact done in the past, this would both increase the extent of globalization and reduce the WTO's present restricted role in global governance.

The notion that closer international economic integration demands new forms of collective action rests on a misconception, a distorted picture of what such integration involves.[9] In this picture, the growth of cross-border trade and capital flows, in response to liberalization, appears as an anarchic melee or tidal wave, which puts hapless people and governments at the mercy of events and forces which they cannot control. Alternatively, or even simultaneously, it is depicted as a means through which human lives are made subject to dictation by impersonal and uncaring markets. A recent and striking instance of this second line of thinking is to be found in a document issued by the European Commission; "Existing international economic and social rules and structures are unbalanced at the global level. *Global market governance* has developed more quickly than global social governance" (European Commission 2001, p. 3, italics added).[10] More justly seen, the freeing of trade and capital flows is a source of neither disorder nor constraints. It is first and foremost a means by which people and enterprises, and even governments themselves as purchasers of goods and services, are enabled to realize more fully their legitimate goals and desires. Everywhere, it widens opportunities and enlarges the domain of individual freedom. There is no reason to treat it as a generalized threat, nor to suppose that it is inherently a subject for new forms or extensions of official regulation through mechanisms of "global governance."

CONCLUSIONS: THE CHALLENGES FACING THE WTO

Historians often treat events with reference to two contrasting but ever-present elements, continuity and change. In the case of the WTO today, as compared with the GATT, both elements are very much in evidence. Like many commentators, Esty gives too much weight to the element of change; and in particular, he overstates the extent to which the external environment of the Organization has been transformed. Now as in the past, international agencies derive their legitimacy from their member governments; and in the case of the WTO, the fact that it is today more subject to attack, by NGOs especially, does not establish the existence of a genuine "legitimacy crisis." Now as in the past, WTO members are committed to freer trade only with many and substantial reservations: they are not subject to a narrow preoccupation with an "efficiency" criterion which has outlived its usefulness. Now as in the past, national governments possess substantial powers of action and decision. Globalization has not deprived them of these powers, and it does not render necessary, or even advisable, the creation of new modes of "global governance" in which they hand over responsibilities to international agencies. All three related elements of Esty's case for radical reform have little or no foundation of fact.

All the same, substantial changes have taken place in the role and status of the WTO, as compared with the GATT before it, and it is clear that these have brought with them problems as well as opportunities, The main problems that have emerged are summarized by David Robertson (p. 1131) as follows; "Extension of the GATT rules to services, government procurement and intellectual property has already stretched the system dangerously . . . With the dispute settlement process generating new rules which also extend the scope of the WTO into new areas, the cohesion of the membership is weakening." In addition, two recent developments have given rise to procedural problems. One is the large influx of new members. A second is the growing desire on the part of many members to participate more actively in WTO business as the Organization's agenda expands to include new and often potentially divisive subjects. As a result, changes in internal structure may well be needed in order to improve the conduct of business. One possibility, which has been proposed by Richard Blackhurst, is the creation of a formally constituted Consultative Board (Blackhurst 2001).

Last but not least among the problems that the Organization now faces is the growth in numbers, activity and influence of anti-liberal NGOs. This too is a relatively recent development, though it is linked, not with globalization as such, but with mistaken notions as to its meaning and effects.

I believe that the main threat today to the WTO, and still more to the purposes for which it and its predecessor were created by member governments, does not come from an erosion of democratic legitimacy. It arises from several sources, some old and some new. As ever, there is the combined influence of protectionist ideas and pressures, which remain strong almost everywhere, and the inherent and continuing sensitivity of trade policy questions. Alongside and reinforcing these are some newer interrelated elements. Internally, there are the problems that now arise from the combination of the Organization's expanded agenda and membership. More disturbing are external factors: the hostility of many NGOs to its aims and even its continued existence, the disposition of many member governments, as also of large and growing numbers of multinational enterprises, to fail to contest, or to make substantial concessions to, the dubious or unfounded arguments and claims of these organizations;[11] and the tendency of some member countries, including the US and the EU, to lend support to notions of "global governance" through which common international norms and standards could be defined and imposed without due regard for differing local circumstances, so that they became elements of disintegration in the world economy.

On this diagnosis, the way ahead for the Organization is not that prescribed by Esty—involving the NGOs in its substantive discussions and decisions, broadening its objectives and concerns, and extending its powers in the name of global governance. Rather, its future usefulness depends on the member governments consulting effectively with non-governmental organizations in general, especially though not only within their own borders, devising better ways of conducting the internal business of the WTO; using the now enlarged scope of the Organization in ways that are not unduly ambitious or divisive; and above all, being ready to defend the idea of trade liberalization against its many opponents and to give expression to it in their actions.

REFERENCES

Annan, K. (2001), "Laying the Foundations of a Fair and Free World Trade System," in Sampson (ed.), *The Role of the World Trade Organization in Global Governance*, Chapter 1.

Archer, C. (2001), *International Organizations*, Third Edition, London and New York: Routledge.

Blackhurst, R. (2001), "Reforming WTO Decision Making: Lessons from Singapore and Seattle," in K. G. Deutsch and B. Speyer (eds.), *The World Trade Organization Millennium Round: Freer Trade in the Twenty-first Century*, London and New York: Routledge.

Commission of the European Communities (2001), "Promoting Core Labour Standards and Improving Social Governance in the Context of Globalisation," a Communication from the Commission to the Council, the European Parliament, and the Economic and Social Committee, Brussels.

Esty, D. C. (2002), "The World Trade Organization's Legitimacy Crisis," *World Trade Review*, I (March): 7–22.

Halfon, R. (1998), *Corporate Irresponsibility: Is Business Appeasing Anti-business Activists?*, London: Social Affairs Unit.

Henderson, D. (1998), "International Agencies and Cross-Border Liberalization: The WTO in Context," in A. Krueger (ed.), *The WTO as an International Organization*, Chapter 3, Chicago: University of Chicago Press.

Henderson, D. (1999), *The MAI Affair: A Story and Its Lessons*, London: Royal Institute of International Affairs.

Henderson, D. (2001), *Misguided Virtue: False Notions of Corporate Social Responsibility*, London: Institute of Economic Affairs.

Hudec, R. E. (1999), *Essays on the Nature of International Trade Law*, London: Cameron and May.

International Labour Organisation (2002), *The ILO at Work: Factpack*, London: ILO.

Irwin, D. A. (2002), *Free Trade under Fire*, Princeton: Princeton University Press.

Jackson, J. (1995), "The World Trade Organization: Watershed Innovation or Cautious Small Step Forward ?" *The World Economy*.

Kahler, M. (2001), *Leadership in the Major Multilaterals*, Washington, DC: Institute of International Economics.

Keohane, R. O. and J. S. Nye (2001), "The Club Model of Multilateral Cooperation and Problems of Democratic Legitimacy," in R. Porter et al. (eds.), *Efficiency, Equity and Legitimacy: The Multilateral Trading System at the Millennium*, Chapter 12, Washington, DC: Brookings Institution Press.

Letwin, W. A. (1989), "American Economic Policy, 1865–1939," in P. Mathias and S. Pollard (eds.), *The Cambridge Economic History of Europe*, Chapter IX, Vol. VIII, Cambridge: Cambridge University Press.

Loy, F. (2001), "Public Participation in the World Trade Organization," in Sampson (ed.), *The Role of the World Trade Organization in Global Governance*, Chapter 6.

Oxford English Dictionary (1989), Second Edition, Oxford: Clarendon Press.

Robertson, D. (2000), "Civil Society and the WTO," *The World Economy* 23 (September): 1119–1134.

Sally, R. (1998), *Classical Liberalism and International Economic Order: Studies in Theory and Intellectual History*, London and New York: Routledge.

Sampson, G. P. (2000), "The World Trade Organization after Seattle," *The World Economy* 23 (September): 1097–1117.

Sampson, G. P. (ed.) (2001), *The Role of the World Trade Organization in Global Governance*, Tokyo: United Nations University Press.

Schoulte, J. A., with R. O'Brien and M. Williams (1999), "The WTO and Civil Society," *Journal of World Trade* 33(1): 107–123.

Sutherland, P., J. Sewell and D. Weiner (2001), "Challenges Facing the WTO and Policies to Address Global Governance," in Sampson (ed.), *The Role of the World Trade Organization in Global Governance*, Chapter 5.

United Kingdom Government, Foreign and Commonwealth Office and Department of Trade and Industry (1996), *Free Trade and Foreign Policy: A Global Vision*, London: Her Majesty's Stationery Office.

Viner, J. (1947), "Conflicts of principle in drafting a trade charter," *Foreign Affairs*, XXV (July).

Webster's Third New International Dictionary (1961), Springfield: G. and C. Merriam.

Wolf, M. (2001a), "Will the Nation-State Survive Globalization?" *Foreign Affairs*, 80 (January–February): 178–190.

Wolf, M. (2001b), "What the World Needs from the Multilateral Trading System," in Sampson (ed.), *The Role of the World Trade Organization in Global Governance*, Chapter 9.

World Economic Forum (2002), *Annual Meeting 2002*, Cologny-Geneva: World Economic Forum.

ENDNOTES

1. Oxford's main American rival, *Webster's Dictionary*, offers a similar though more explicit wording: "possession of title or status as a result of acquisition by means that are held to be in accordance with law or custom" (1961, p. 1291).

2. There are of course exceptions. Thus in the case of the OECD today, it is clear that new candidates for accession would have to establish democratic credentials as well as meeting other tests. (The fact that the criteria for OECD membership are notably more restrictive than the UN agencies is sometimes viewed, mistakenly, as weakening the Organization's claims to legitimacy.) In the case of the European Union, achieving membership is formally dependent on demonstrating "stability of institutions guaranteeing democracy"; but the EU is not an international agency, though the European Commission is.

3. The argument here draws on Henderson (1999, pp. 57–60).

4. As noted above, Esty appears uneasy about the fact that national and international civil servants are not elected persons. But any notion that they should be elected would be absurd.

5. In this connection, David Robertson has reported (Robertson 2000, p. 1132) his experience that "A search of NGOs' websites that claim to be part of 'civil society' does not reveal any that support liberal trade." The anti-liberal role of the NGOs in connection with the ill-fated Multilateral Agreement on Investment is reviewed in Henderson (1999).

6. In a White Paper issued in November 1996, the then (Conservative) British government formally endorsed the goal of global free trade by 2020. However, a different government came into office soon afterwards, and in any case the external trade regime of the UK has long been, aside from a few residual elements, that of the European Union as a whole. The White Paper appears to have left no trace on thinking or events.

7. Arguments and evidence in support of this statement are set out in Wolf (2001), in Chapter 5 of Henderson (2001), and in the final chapter of Sally (1998).

8. Such an assertion is to be found in a journal article on the WTO (Schoulte et al. 1999), where it is also stated that "Recent intensified globalization has broken the Westphalian mould of politics." All of this is pure fantasy.

9. Of course, today's argument for stronger global governance rests in part on the need to deal with external effects that are global rather than local, and in particular, to handle problems that could arise in connection with climate change. It is widely believed that greenhouse gas emissions should be substantially curbed, and the argument that this would require some form of binding international agreement is hard to question. But greenhouse gas emissions are not a product of closer international economic integration: they are generated in closed as well as open economies.

10. The Commission goes on to say that "global social governance" should take effect mainly through "the universal application of core labour standards."

11. The readiness of many MNEs to engage in appeasement of their critics and enemies has been treated in an incisive essay by Robert Halfon (1998), and in Henderson (2001) which further argues (1) that endorsement as well as appeasement may be involved, and (2) that generally speaking the contribution of the international business world to public debate on leading current issues of economic policy has been inadequate or worse.

QUESTIONS FOR REVIEW AND DISCUSSION

1. What does Esty mean by political legitimacy? What does Henderson mean by political legitimacy? Which understanding of political legitimacy do you think should be used in relation to the WTO? Defend your choice.

2. On what grounds does Henderson criticize Esty's claim that public interest NGOs should be given a more prominent role in the WTO? How do you think Esty would respond? Based on your answers, do you think that allowing NGOs to participate in the WTO gives the Organization more legitimacy? Why or why not?

3. Suppose you accept the force of Esty's critique and thus agree on the need for reforms of the WTO. Do you think the reforms that Esty proposes would add legitimacy to the WTO? How would you change these reform proposals? What incentives, if any, do governments have to adopt such reforms?

SUGGESTIONS FOR FURTHER READING

For collections of articles that focus especially on governance in the world trade system, see: Gary P. Sampson (ed.). *The Role of the World Trade Organizaton in Global Governance.* Tokyo: United Nations University Press, 2001, and Roger Porter et al. (eds.). *Efficiency, Equity and Legitimacy: The Multilateral Trading System at the Millennium* Washington, DC: Brookings Institution Press, 2001. For a recent article calling for greater participation in global governance by civil society, see: Patrizia Nanz and Jens Steffek. "Global Governance, Participation and the Public Sphere,' *Government & Opposition* 39 (Spring): 314-335. For a collection of recent papers that examine global governance from a broader context, see: Miles Kahler and David Lake (eds.). *Governance in a Global Economy: Political Authority in Transition.* Princeton: Princeton University Press, 2003.

CHAPTER 7

REGIONALISM AND MULTILATERALISM IN AMERICAN TRADE POLICY

In the last 15 years, we have seen a fairly dramatic expansion in regional trading agreements. Regional trading arrangements (RTAs), also referred to as preferential trading arrangements (PTAs) are trade agreements in which tariffs discriminate between members and nonmembers. RTAs come in two basic forms. In a free trade area, or FTA, such as the North American Free Trade Agreement, governments eliminate tariffs on goods entering their markets from other FTA members, but each member government retains independent tariffs on goods entering their market from nonmembers. In a customs union, like the European Union, member governments eliminate all tariffs on intra-union trade and create a common tariff for goods entering the union from nonmembers.

While RTAs have been a feature of the global economy throughout the post-war period, the number of such agreements, as well as their geographic coverage, accelerated rapidly during the 1990s. More than 190—and perhaps as many as 250—RTAs are currently in force, and all WTO members except Macau China, Mongolia, and Chinese Taipei belong to at least one RTA.[1] The WTO estimates that as many as 300 RTAs could be in effect by 2005 if all agreements currently being planned or negotiated are completed successfully.

The proliferation of RTAs has generated debate within the academic and policy communities concerning the impact that RTAs will have on the multilateral trade system. Are RTAs a stepping-stone toward global free trade, in which case they complement multilateral trade liberalization within the WTO? Or, are they stumbling blocks that introduce new forms of discrimination into world trade and divert the energy of governments from WTO negotiations, in which case they represent a challenge to the multilateral trade system? Some analysts argue that RTAs provide a useful mechanism for global trade liberalization. Liberalizing trade is often difficult in a 150-member organization like the WTO, so why not pursue a "second best" strategy of liberalization among smaller groups of like-minded countries? Even where the discrimination inherent in such arrangements does divert trade, the resulting welfare losses are likely to be quite small.[2] Moreover, once an RTA is established it might exert a gravitational force that pulls additional countries into its orbit. Over time, this gravitational force can attract so many additional members that what began as a small regional RTA could evolve into a much larger free trade area. The EU, for example, has expanded from an initial membership of only six Western European countries to more than twenty countries in Western, Central, and Eastern Europe. In the Western Hemisphere, NAFTA began as an agreement between the United States and Canada, was then extended to incorporate Mexico, and now, under the proposed Free Trade Area of the Americas, could be extended to all of South and Central America. In this optimistic scenario, RTAs are useful building blocks that will help push world trade to more open multilateral trade.

Others argue that RTAs represent a serious challenge to the multilateral system. Some argue that RTAs are discriminatory regional trade blocs that can lead to trade wars. The creation of an RTA in one region could encourage governments in other regions to form rival RTAs. According to this logic, the NAFTA, and its extension into the Free Trade Area of the Americas, might be seen as an American response to the creation and deepening of the EU. The emerging free trade area in Pacific Asia might in turn be a response to regional trade agreements in Europe and the Western Hemisphere. Once regional trading blocs have formed, each bloc might raise tariffs in an attempt to limit trade with nonmembers. A tariff increase by one RTA could provoke retaliation by the others, leading to a rising spiral of protection that undermines global trade liberalization.[3] Others argue that even if interbloc trade wars do not arise, RTAs threaten to reverse the decades-long process of trade liberalization achieved under the GATT and WTO. As economist Jagdish Bhagwati, a prominent critic of RTAs, has written, the proliferation of RTAs "creates a world of preferences . . . which increases transactions costs and facilitates protectionism. In the guise of freeing trade, PTAs have managed to recreate the preferences-ridden world of the 1930s as surely as protectionism did at the time."[4] In this more pessimistic scenario, the proliferation of RTAs threatens to undermine the trade liberalization achieved under the multilateral trade system.

The question of whether RTAs complement or challenge the multilateral trade system has taken on additional importance over the last 15 years as the United States has embraced RTAs in its trade policy. Until the late 1980s, American trade policy focused exclusively on the multilateral trade system. While the United States encouraged and supported efforts by European governments to create and strengthen the European Union, the United States did not negotiate or belong to any RTAs. Policy changed in the late 1980s; the United States concluded a free trade agreement with Canada in 1989, then extended this agreement to Mexico in the early 1990s. Since then, the United States has concluded bilateral free trade agreements with Singapore, Chile, and Jordan, as well as a regional free trade agreement with El Salvador, Guatemala, Honduras, and Nicaragua (the Central American Free Trade Area or CAFTA). The U.S. continues to negotiate the Free Trade Area of the Americas, and has recently proposed negotiations for a free trade area with Australia, another with several Middle Eastern countries, and still another with the South African Customs Union.

Current American enthusiasm for RTAs sharpens concerns about how such agreements affect the multilateral trade system. If the United States, traditionally the world's largest importer and exporter and historically the strongest supporter of the multilateral system, embraces RTAs, who will be left to support the WTO? And will American enthusiasm for RTAs initiate a strategic dynamic that generates a world trade system composed of antagonistic trade blocs?

The two articles presented in this chapter focus on the American embrace of RTAs and the impact this change will have on the multilateral trade system. The first article, written by current U.S. trade representative Robert B. Zoellick provides a forthright justification for an American trade strategy that liberalizes trade through multilateral, regional, and bilateral agreements. This strategy of "competitive liberalization," Zoellick argues, will create "a web of mutually reinforcing trade agreements to meet diverse commercial, economic, developmental and political challenges. The United States is combining this building-block approach to free trade with a clear commitment to reducing global barriers to trade through the WTO." For Zoellick, in other words, RTAs are a stepping-stone to global free trade.

In the second article, Bernard K. Gordon, a Professor of Political Science Emeritus at the University of New Hampshire, challenges Zoellick's claim that RTAs provide a building block to global free trade. Gordon argues that regional trading agreements are inconsistent with American economic interests and are already generating opposing regional blocs that will make it harder for American producers to capture foreign markets. For Gordon, therefore, RTAs are a stumbling block to global free trade.

ENDNOTES

1. World Trade Organization, "Regionalism: Friends or Rivals?" http://www.wto.org/english/thewto_e/whatis_e/tif_e/bey1_e.htm (accessed January 20, 2004).
2. See Lawrence Summers, "Regionalism and the World Trading System," in *Policy Implications of Trade and Currency Zones* (Wyoming: Federal Reserve Bank of Kansas City, 1991), 295–301.
3. See Jeffrey Frankel, *Regional Trading Blocs in the World Economic System* (Washington, DC: Institute for International Economics, 1997), 210.
4. Jagdish Bhagwati, "The FTAA is Not Free Trade." In *The Wind of the One Hundred Days: How Washington Mismanaged Globalization* (Cambridge, MA: MIT Press, 2001), 244.

Unleashing the Trade Winds: A Building-Block Approach

AMBASSADOR ROBERT B. ZOELLICK

As President Bush's first term approaches its midpoint, the commentary about American trade policy has shifted. The debate is now over how—not whether—the United States is advancing free trade.

America has stated its intentions plainly. We will promote free trade globally, regionally and bilaterally, while rebuilding support at home. By moving forward on multiple fronts, the United States can exert its leverage for openness, create a new competition in liberalization, target the needs of developing countries, and create a fresh political dynamic by putting free trade onto the offensive.

America's trade policies are connected to our broader economic, political, and security aims. This intellectual integration may confound some trade scholars, but it follows in the footsteps of the architects of reconstruction after 1945. In fact, its roots extend to the protesters who dumped English tea in Boston harbor. To be sustainable at home, our trade strategy needs to be aligned with America's values and aspirations—as well as with our economic interests. And to be influential abroad, we seek to listen and learn from our trading partners, large and small. To lead globally, President Bush recognized that he had to reverse the retreat on trade policy at home. Any American president building support for trade must overcome protectionists, special interests, anti-globalization nihilists and partisanship against the President. Nevertheless, the President was not diverted by an economic slowdown or terrorism. He pressed Congress to enact the Trade Act of 2002, which re-established the vital trade authority ("fast track") that had lapsed for eight years. Republicans compromised with pro-trade Democrats on an environmental and labor trade agenda, without overstepping concerns about sovereignty and protectionism. The act included a large, immediate down payment on open trade for the neediest, cutting tariffs to zero for an estimated $20 billion in American imports from the developing world.

To rebuild a congressional coalition, the administration had to demonstrate that the United States would use international rules to pursue its interests. Since American trade-weighted tariffs average only about 1.6 percent, congressional support for lower barriers depends on the Executive's willingness to use the same rules employed by other countries. One Republican leader in the Senate told me that the

From Ambassador Robert B. Zoellick, "Unleashing the Trade Winds: A Building-block Approach," *U.S. Foreign Policy Agenda: An Electronic Journal of the U.S. Department of State* 8 August 2003, pp. 16–20.

administration's record of enforcing international rules was the most persuasive argument for granting the president more negotiating authority. By leading the fight at home for freer trade within a system of enforceable international rules, President Bush has strengthened America's power to promote free commerce abroad.

THE TASK AT DOHA

Coming to office as it did in the wake of the Seattle debacle for the World Trade Organization, the Bush administration recognized the importance of launching a new global trade round. Working with the European Union (EU) and others, and against long odds, we helped to launch the Doha Development Agenda (DDA). The WTO itself has been strengthened by adding China and Taiwan as members, and efforts are in train to add Russia before long.

The United States is fully committed to completing the DDA by the agreed deadline of 2005. We have already tabled far-reaching proposals in agriculture, industrial and consumer goods, and services, to highlight the primary goal of the WTO: to open access to markets and to spur growth and development.

America's goal in the farm negotiations is to harmonize subsidies and tariffs while slashing them to much lower levels, on a path toward elimination. The last global trade negotiation—the Uruguay round—accepted high and asymmetrical levels of subsidies and tariffs just to get them under some control. For example, the United States accepted a cap for the European Union's production-distorting subsidies that was three times the size of America's, even though agriculture represents about the same proportion of our economies.

The farm bill—which authorized up to $123 billion in all types of food-stamp, conservation and farm spending over six years, amounts within WTO limits—made clear that America will not cut agricultural support unilaterally. But America's farmers and Congress back our proposal that all nations should cut together. The United States wants to eliminate the most egregious and distorting agricultural payments, export subsidies. We would cut global subsidies that distort domestic farm production by some $100 billion, slashing our own limit almost in half. We would cut the global average farm tariff from 60 percent to 15 percent, and the American average from 12 percent to 5 percent. The United States also advocates agreeing on a date for the total elimination of agricultural tariffs and distorting subsidies.

The American proposal for manufactured goods would free the world of tariffs on these products by 2015. This was the trade sector first targeted by the founders of the General Agreement on Tariffs and Trade (GATT) in 1947; after more than 50 years of work, about half the world's trade in goods has been freed from tariffs. It is time to finish the job.

With zero tariffs, the manufacturing sectors of developing countries could compete fairly. The proposal would eliminate the barriers between developing countries, which pay 70 percent of their tariffs on manufactured goods to one another. By eliminating barriers to the farm and manufactured-goods trade, the income of the developing world could be boosted by over $500 billion.

The American proposal on trade in services would broaden opportunities for growth and development in a sector that is just taking off in the international economy. Services represent about two-thirds of the American economy and 80 percent of our employment, but account for only about 20 percent of world trade. The World Bank has pointed out that eliminating services barriers in developing countries alone would yield them a $900 billion gain.

The United States listens to the concerns of developing countries striving towards free trade. This year, we devoted $638 million to help such countries build the capacity to take part in trade negotiations, implement the rules and seize opportunities. We have acted in partnership with the Inter-American Development Bank to integrate trade and finance, and we are urging the World Bank and the IMF to back their rhetoric on trade with resources.

We agreed at Doha that the flexibility in the global intellectual-property rules could be used to allow poor countries to license medicines compulsorily to deal with HIV/AIDS, tuberculosis, malaria and other epidemics. We are also committed to helping those poor regions and states obtain medicines produced abroad—if they cannot manufacture them locally—as long as other countries with pharmaceutical industries do not carve these special terms into loopholes to circumvent the intellectual-property protection that rewards research on the medicines of the future.

The Doha negotiations include customized treatment for developing countries. Yet flexible transitions and special needs should not degenerate into perpetual protectionism. "Good intentions" that cover up trade barriers raise prices for the poorest people, profit cosseted interests, increase costs for competitive businesses and block exports from productive firms and workers to other developing countries. We are pleased that nongovernmental organizations (NGOs) such as Oxfam now recognize the benefits of trade for development, but they need to acknowledge that these benefits flow from removing barriers to imports as well as from promoting exports and competition at home. The WTO can foster export-driven growth for developing countries without reviving the neo-colonialist trade patterns promoted by an earlier generation.

EUROPE AS PARTNER

As one African minister told me recently, when the United States and the EU agree on a course in the WTO, we cannot ensure success, but we make it much more likely. Fortunately, I have no doubt that my respected and close colleague Pascal Lamy, the EU trade commissioner, is just as committed to completing the Doha negotiation on time.

The United States and the EU share a common aim of trade liberalization, but have pursued different approaches. In the lexicon of the EU, the United States is pressing to "deepen" the WTO by freeing trade across the core agenda of market access. The EU's distinguishing agenda is to "widen" the WTO mandate by developing new rules to cover more topics. As one Asian colleague observed, the EU sees the world through the lens of recent European experience: it wants gradually to achieve a supranational system of governance for globalization. Yet many developing countries have no wish to add new topics to the WTO, believing our priority should be to spur more trade and investment. There is a risk that the EU will trade off cuts in barriers in order to add rules and institutions.

At Doha, the United States helped bridge the gap between "deepeners" and "wideners" because the EU needs progress on its broader agenda to achieve movement on agriculture, which is critical for many developing countries. The United States will continue to work to accommodate the EU's objectives, as long as the EU is committed to liberalizing trade in agriculture, goods and services. We need to ensure that any new negotiating topics and rules enhance free markets, strengthen transparency in the WTO and facilitate trade, while respecting the prerogatives of sovereign states. Another European perspective might also be borne in mind— Hayek's "spontaneous order," which advises that rules should be forged first through markets, rather than through government controls.

Even if America and Europe cooperate, the Doha agenda will still be hard to achieve. (Sadly, Japan's mercantilist, zero-sum approach to trade is typified by its recent agriculture proposal, which argued for cutting its quota on imported rice.) It is encouraging to find a network of trade ministers, in both developing and developed countries, working together.

Yet any decision by the WTO requires a consensus among its 144 members. Any one country—for whatever political or economic reason—can stop the Doha agenda in its tracks. We will not passively accept a veto over America's drive to open markets. We want to encourage reformers who favor free trade. If others do not want to move forward, the United States will move ahead with those who do. It is time for others to tell us when they are ready to open their markets, to table proposals to liberalize and to match their criticism with commitment.

Some trade specialists cavil about America's use of leverage to push for greater openness. I urge them to broaden their perspective. We want to strengthen the hand of the coalition pressing for freer trade. It would be fatal to give the initiative to naysayers abroad and protectionists at home. As we have seen in the League of Nations, the U.N., the International Monetary Fund and the World Bank, international organizations need leaders to prod them into action.

NAFTA AND ITS IMITATORS

To multiply the likelihood of success, the United States is also invigorating a drive for regional and bilateral free-trade agreements (FTAs). These agreements can foster powerful links among commerce, economic reform, development, investment, security and free societies. The North American Free-Trade Agreement (NAFTA) not only almost tripled American trade with Mexico and nearly doubled its trade with Canada, but also made all three members more competitive internationally. NAFTA proved definitively that both developed and developing countries gain from free-trade partnerships. It enabled Mexico to bounce back quickly from its 1994 financial crisis, launched the country on the path of becoming a global economic competitor, and supported its transformation to an open democratic society.

Ironically, a number of European publications that have criticized America's "competitive liberalization" through regional and bilateral free-trade negotiations were noticeably silent when the EU negotiated 30 such pacts; the United States only has three, but we are hard at work.

Since Congress granted the president fast-track authority, the United States has signed FTAs with Singapore and Chile and started talks for FTAs with the five nations of the Central American Economic Community, the five countries of the Southern African Customs Union, Morocco and Australia. We helped push forward the negotiations among 34 democracies for a Free-Trade Area of the Americas. We will co-chair this effort, with Brazil, until it is successfully concluded.

Our free-trade agenda conveys signals. We are open to free trade with all regions—Latin America, sub-Saharan Africa, Asia-Pacific, the Arab world—and with both developing and developed economies. We want to expand commercial links with these countries. Equally important, all our free-trade partners, though varying greatly in size and development, are showing political courage at home by making the case for open markets and connecting those ideas to economic reforms. These are governments we want to help.

One Europe-based publication recently claimed that the United States "has little to offer other countries" because America's barriers are relatively low already. But the "market test" is proving such commentaries mistaken, as countries are lining up to negotiate FTAs. Countries recognize that assured access to the huge, dynamic American market is a valuable economic asset. Because American FTAs are comprehensive, with high standards, our FTA partners stand out as good places to invest, as strong links in a global sourcing chain, or simply as promising markets in which to do business.

We will work with our FTA partners—through the U.S. Agency for International Development (USAID) and with the multilateral development banks—to link liberalization to sectoral reforms. For example, we have been discussing with Morocco how to support its shift, backed by the World Bank, from the production of cereals to fruits and vegetables for export. For Southern Africa and Central America, our FTAs can encourage regional integration, the reduction of local barriers to regional competitiveness, the development of a larger market for investment, and greater political cooperation. Many other countries are working with us on market and trade reforms simply to prepare for an FTA.

As our FTA negotiation with Singapore showed, our agreements can also serve as models by breaking new ground and setting higher standards. The United States-Singapore FTA will help advance areas such as e-commerce, intellectual property, labor and environmental standards, and the burgeoning services trade. As we work more intensively with nations on FTAs, the United States is learning about the perspectives of good trading partners. Our FTA partners are the vanguard of a new global coalition for open markets.

These partners are also helping us to expand support for free trade at home. Each set of talks enables legislators and the public to see the practical benefits of more open trade, often with societies of special interest for reasons of history, geography, security, or other ties. There is an old adage in American politics: "You can't beat something with nothing." We want the American debate to be focused on our agenda of opening markets, not on the protectionists' defensive dogma of closing them.

Whether the cause is democracy, security, economic integration or free trade, advocates of reform often need to move toward a broad goal step by step—working with willing partners, building coalitions, and gradually expanding the circle of cooperation. Just as modern business markets rely on the integration of networks, we need a web of mutually reinforcing trade agreements to meet diverse commercial, economic, developmental and political challenges. The United States is combining this building-block approach to free trade with a clear commitment to reducing global barriers to trade through the WTO. By using the leverage of the American economy's size and attractiveness to stimulate competition for openness, we will move the world closer toward the goal of comprehensive free trade.

A High-Risk Trade Policy

BERNARD K. GORDON

A STEP IN THE WRONG DIRECTION

Robert Zoellick, the U.S. trade representative and the main force shaping U.S. for-eign trade policy today, combines prodigious negotiating skills with an equally solid background in realpolitik. Nevertheless, the current American approach to trade, over which he has presided, promises to severely damage U.S. foreign policy and trade. At the heart of the problem is Washington's unwise return to economic "regionalism"—an approach evident in the many U.S. efforts now underway to build new bilateral or regional trade agreements with a number of small trading partners.

Washington's regionalism aims, in principle, to induce the world's major trade actors, especially Europe and Japan, to complete the broader, multilateral agenda of the World Trade Organization (WTO). This strategy is no secret; in fact, it has been publicly discussed several times. In a letter to the author in late 2001, for example, Zoellick wrote,

> I believe a strategy of trade liberalization on multiple fronts—globally, regionally, and bilaterally—enhances our leverage and best promotes open markets. As Europeans have pointed out to me, it took the completion of NAFTA [North American Free Trade Agreement] and the first APEC [Asia-Pacific Economic Cooperation] Summit in 1993–94 to persuade the EU to close out the Uruguay Round. I favor a "competition in liberalization" with the U.S. at the center of the network.

Zoellick's description of events in the early 1990s is dead on. That was a time when the former main framework for world trade, the General Agreement on Tariffs and Trade (GATT), was notoriously in trouble—"GATT is dead," economist Lester Thurow declared at the time—and its weaknesses led to the establishment of the considerably more institutionalized WTO. American efforts were key to that change, and the WTO's present Doha Round of negotiations likewise owes much to Washington. Two recent and very bold American proposals—dealing with trade in agricultural goods and industrial products—could make the Doha Round the most successful round thus far.

Yet at the same time the United States has also accelerated its "free trade areas" policy, and these FTAs—precisely because they are not broadly multilateral—are bound to cause serious problems. Aside from the conceptual and practical challenge they pose to the WTO (a point its leaders recognize and often condemn), regional FTAs are also fundamentally incompatible with America's national interests.

From Bernard K. Gordon, "A High-Risk Trade Policy," *Foreign Affairs*, Vol. 82, No. 4, July/August, 2003, pp. 105–118. Reprinted by permission of *Foreign Affairs*. © 2003 by the Council on Foreign Relations, Inc.

Nowhere is that incompatibility clearer than in East Asia, where local FTAs are proliferating, and where all are justified as a necessary response to American initiatives.

China, for example, since 2001 has embarked on a mission to achieve a free trade area with all of Southeast Asia and has begun work on a similar arrangement in Northeast Asia. In direct response to that Chinese initiative, Japan has announced that it is ending its 50-year commitment to multilateral trade. Recognizing how large is its policy shift, Japan frankly calls it a "departure." Yet both countries, to explain and justify their new emphasis on regionalism, regularly blame the United States for starting the trend.

The Japanese shift dates to 1999, when the director of the Japan External Trade Organization (JETRO), Japan's foreign trade body, wrote that in a world of regional trading blocs, "we cannot prevail alone. We have to face reality. . . . 26 of the world's 30 main economies were or would be partners in such [regional] accords—the European Union, the North American Free Trade Agreement and the Association of Southeast Asian Nations' planned Free Trade Agreement (AFTA)."

Since then, and especially in light of China's economic successes and its announced FTA with the Association of Southeast Asian Nations (ASEAN), Tokyo has hardened its rhetoric still further. Old rivalries between Japan and China, among Asia's longest-standing, have resurfaced. Today, however, the antagonism is marked by an ascendant China and a possibly declining Japan. A Tokyo official put the issue simply: "If Japan does nothing, its economic leadership in East Asia would be taken over by the Chinese."

This new and developing competition between Beijing and Tokyo is not something Washington could possibly want. Nor would American interests be served by the most likely alternative: formal collaboration between China and Japan on East Asia's trade. Yet that is precisely the pattern now forming. Since early last year, and culminating in November 2002—when the foreign ministers of China, Japan, and South Korea met on the fringes of the annual ASEAN meetings—evidence of such cooperation has proliferated, coming under the rubric of "ASEAN + 3" (or the reverse), which combines the ten ASEAN countries with Japan, China, and South Korea.

As many will remember, "ASEAN + 3" is exactly the model first proposed in the mid-1980s by Malaysian Prime Minister Mahathir bin Mohamad. He called at the time for an "East Asian Economic Caucus," a proposal that was quickly resisted and successfully put down by U.S. Secretary of State James Baker, who believed the Mahathir plan would in effect draw a line down the Pacific separating the United States from East Asia. Because the grouping would also have excluded Australia, New Zealand, and Canada, it was quickly labeled a "caucus without Caucasians," and those racist overtones have been perpetuated by the fact that ASEAN continues to rebuff Australia's membership.

LESS IS LESS

The growth in regionalism was thrown into new and urgent focus earlier this year, when preliminary 2002 trade data were released. Most attention centered on

Japan because, for the first time since 1961, Japan imported more from China than from the United States. Similar dramatic changes were reported by the other East Asian economies. Taiwan and South Korea, along with the principal ASEAN nations, all recorded 50 percent increases in their exports to China in 2002, while their exports to the United States remained flat.

This was sobering news, but it should not have been surprising. Signs of change, particularly of a relatively reduced U.S. trade presence in East Asia, have been evident since at least the mid-1990s. Those signs were discounted or ignored by many observers because they ran counter to the widespread belief that large and growing exports from Asia to the United States were a reliable fixture of the environment. Indeed, the "Asian miracle" analysis identified exports to the United States as a key element in East Asia's growth, so much so that they were taken for granted.

Many American observers were so blinded that they ignored the evidence and dismissed as naive any suggestion that Asia's economies were intensifying their regional interactions and becoming less reliant on the U.S. market. Whenever that suggestion was made, the common rejoinder was that "the Japanese [or the Koreans, or the Chinese] would never do anything so foolish and so much opposed to their own interests." The response recalls a comment made by John Foster Dulles when he was supervising the end of America's occupation of Japan in the early 1950s. In a memorable remark on Japan's economic future, he urged that Tokyo concentrate on nearby Asian markets because Japanese products would never be attractive to Americans. Needless to say, the seeds had already been planted that would soon become known to Americans as Honda and Sony.

Incipient trends are once again present in U.S.-East Asian trade, but this time in the reverse direction. As the accompanying charts illustrate, the rise of China and the relative decline of the United States—the two events that raised eyebrows in 2002—have already been evident for a number of years. The chart on the facing page shows that Japan's imports from China rose from $36 billion to almost $60 billion between 1995 and 2001, while its imports from the United States fell, from $76 billion to $63 billion. It is hardly surprising, then, that in the year following, Japan's imports from China exceeded those from the United States.

Although Japan's shift is the most dramatic in absolute dollar terms among the several East Asian economies, there were similar striking trends across the board. South Korea's exports to China rose by 100 percent (from $9 billion to $18 billion), while its exports to the United States grew by just 30 percent. Likewise for its imports: from China they nearly doubled, to $13 billion, while from the United States they fell by a quarter. Again, in absolute dollar terms, South Korea's trade with the United States still remains larger than its trade with China, but the very different growth rates are not promising—and the same applies to Thailand, Singapore, and Malaysia. For each of these four countries, trade with China has been rising much faster than trade with the United States. In three out of four, imports from China rose by more than 70 percent, while imports from the United States fell. Singapore's experience is particularly dramatic: its imports from China rose by 120 percent, while those from the United States fell by 6 percent.

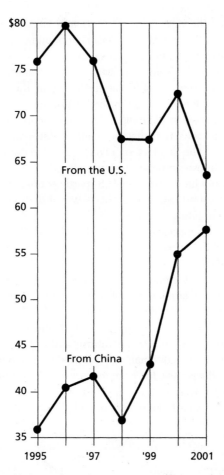

JAPAN'S IMPORTS FROM THE UNITED STATES AND FROM CHINA, 1995–2001 *(IN BILLIONS)*
Source: Calculated from data in the International Monetary Fund's Direction of Trade Statistics Yearbook, *2002.*

These trends, to borrow a Wall Street reminder, do not necessarily predict the future, but they do highlight several important realities. One is the mammoth size of U.S. exports to East Asia. In 2001, precisely a quarter of the United States' total exports of goods went to the Pacific Rim. Their value, at $182 billion, was identical to the value of the United States' exports to Europe. In 2002, U.S. exports to the Pacific Rim rose still further, to 26 percent of the U.S. total, while Europe's share dropped slightly, to 24 percent.

The sharply different trade growth rates underline a second reality: East Asia's tightening economic ties. That process was accelerated by the region's financial crisis in 1997–98 and reinforced by Washington's initially cool response. Tokyo, in contrast, stepped up to the plate with several imaginative offers of help, including its sponsorship of the "Asian Monetary Fund," an idea quickly—and, some would say, brutally—crushed by then Treasury Secretary Lawrence Summers. The contrast in behavior strengthened the view, especially in Southeast Asia, that the United States was prepared to write off several of the Asian economies; some even believed that Americans were anxious to benefit from Asia's plight.

A good reflection of this sentiment were the statements of a senior official in Thailand's Foreign Ministry. In 1997, at the onset of the crisis, he complained that while the United States benefited from globalization, Thailand suffered. Three years later, when Bangkok was planning to host an economic conference, his bitterness had ripened to a conviction that the United States was simply unconcerned with Southeast Asia: "The leaders of eight ASEAN countries have confirmed participation. The Japanese prime minister will attend. . . . EU leaders will . . . attend [but] I am a bit disappointed with the U.S. participation. . . . The U.S. domestic economy is large and sound, which is probably why it does not attach much importance to participation in international forums."

Much the same disappointment with the United States was reflected this past March, in a Washington speech given by Emil Salim, one of Indonesia's most prominent economists. Salim co-chairs the United States-Indonesia Society, and in remarks there, he spoke of a fundamental change in Indonesia's future economic orientation. Gone was the familiar talk of first-rung manufacturing progress, of the sort typified by Nike footwear and garments destined for the United States. Instead Salim spoke of how Indonesia must now fit in with "China's role in Asia's economies," of "ASEAN + 3," and of how Indonesia's future must depend not on manufactured exports but on exports of its traditional "tropical products." His statements, like those of many others in Southeast Asia today, reflect a shift away from the region's 30-year effort to integrate with America and the West. They signal instead a turn toward planning for prosperity as part of a resurgent and postcrisis Asia.

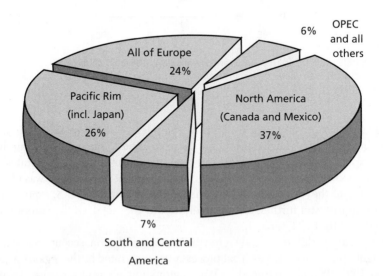

GLOBAL SHARES OF U.S. MERCHANDISE EXPORTS IN 2002; *TOTAL $693.5 BILLION*
Source: Calculated from data in U.S. Commerce Dept., Census Bureau, *Exhibit 14 in FT900, Exports of Goods, December 2002.*
Note: OPEC share excludes Venezucla and Indonesia.

The third reality these illustrations point to is the global distribution of U.S. exports. As the chart on the facing page demonstrates, half of American exports are divided almost equally between Europe and Asia, and more than a third go to immediate neighbors, Canada and Mexico. Putting this another way, almost 90 percent of U.S. exports are directed, in roughly equal proportions, to the globe's three main economic regions: North America, East Asia, and the EU. None of the world's other major economic players, whose exports go mainly to nearby markets, has a distribution even approaching this U.S. record. The EU export pattern is the least diversified, with two-thirds of the exports staying within the EU, and Japan's exports are almost as concentrated.

ONE AFTA THE OTHER

These contrasts are a reminder of the enormity of the United States' stake in all of the world's regions, and of the corollary U.S. need to strengthen and maintain its commitment to the global trade system symbolized by the WTO. Yet both recent presidents have undermined that goal by their insistence on new regional or bilateral free trade agreements. None of those agreements is remotely analogous to NAFTA, the creation of which was justified by the political and strategic advantages it brought to the United States. The items on today's FTA agenda represent no such political or economic gain to Washington.

The most recent, a proposed "Central American Free Trade Area," can hardly be taken seriously from a U.S. perspective, in part because Central America is a tiny market, but more important because U.S. exports there already account for at least 40 percent of Central America's imports. In contrast, the United States' supposed "competitors," the EU and Japan, have less than 10 and 5 percent of the Central American market, respectively. Yet so strong is today's FTA fetish that when President George W. Bush called for a Central American FTA, all perspective (and humor) went out the window. The White House solemnly announced that U.S. exports to Central America were "more than to Russia, Indonesia, and India combined"—conveniently forgetting that those three have long ranked at the bottom of America's markets.

How to explain this belief in the future of FTAs? Zoellick hopes that they will act as "building blocks" of global free trade, but that has always been a debatable proposition, and now there is clear evidence that trade blocs in one region simply beget trade blocs in other regions. This is the real lesson of the Asian experience and Asia's new FTA proposals. Whether under Chinese or Japanese sponsorship, these proposals are responses to burgeoning FTAs elsewhere—especially those in the western hemisphere, which are U.S.-sponsored—and they will likewise have two consequences for the United States. The first, as the above data demonstrate, will be to threaten the United States' major economic stake in East Asia. The second will be to help build a political and strategic counterweight to Washington's long-term security interests in the Pacific.

Critics will object that there is no tradeoff between the two: that East Asia and the western hemisphere are quite separate, and that U.S. policy can readily handle that separation. But events in the two regions are far from separate, as Henry Kissinger was forcefully reminded when he visited Tokyo in the early 1990s. Kissinger spoke with Ryutaro Hashimoto, who was then Japan's finance minister and would soon become its prime minister. In his book Vision of Japan, Hashimoto reported on their conversation and recalled that its background was two policy questions that directly connected the western hemisphere and East Asia.

The first issue was Malaysia's proposal for an "East Asia Economic Caucus" (EAEC). The second was the debate then current in the United States about NAFTA, specifically its possible expansion to Central and South America. Those developments, which of course later led to President Bill Clinton's call for a hemisphere-wide Free Trade Area of the Americas (FTAA), were closely monitored by Asian leaders, who worried that an enlarged NAFTA would give South Americans preferential treatment in the enormous U.S. market and that those preferences would come at Asia's expense. Some also feared that this FTAA talk in the western hemisphere would give added support and justification to those Asians who had long contemplated establishing their own regional trade bloc in the Pacific.

It was in that context that Hashimoto spoke with Kissinger about the link between the EAEC proposal, which Japan was being pressed to support, and the possibility of NAFTA expansion, which the United States was considering. When Kissinger asked whether Tokyo's posture would be influenced by American plans to extend NAFTA southward, Hashimoto answered, "Yes, that is what would happen":

> As a member of the cabinet I do not highly regard the Mahathir plan. But if the United States strengthens its posture towards forming a protectionist bloc by extending NAFTA and closing off South America and North America, then Japan will have to emphasize its position as an Asia-Pacific country. This will inevitably alter the Japan-U.S. relationship. . . . So please do not force us into such a corner.

In the years since that blunt advice, Japan's posture has moved substantially along the lines of Hashimoto's warning, as two recent developments suggest. The first is the reemergence of what Hashimoto called Japan's "position as an Asia-Pacific country." In part this revival stems from Japan's perennial debate about whether it is truly "Western," and in part it derives from the passing of the generation that directly (and usually favorably) experienced the American occupation. Equally important, however, are the views of Japan's most senior and sophisticated observers, in which a central strand holds that U.S. primacy has become somewhat suffocating and must be loosened. A good example is Ogura Kazuo, one of Japan's most senior Foreign Ministry officials, and hardly an elderly right-wing "nationalist." Now ambassador to France, he has a graduate degree in economics from Cambridge, was ambassador to both South Korea and Vietnam, and has been his ministry's director-general for economic affairs. He writes often on Asian affairs in influential Japanese journals, and in a 1999 essay titled "Creating a New Asia," Ogura argued that it is "necessary for a united Asia, along with Western Europe, to be prepared to check America. Asia must act in a unified way and . . . Japan must shoulder a large part of the leadership needed to achieve that. One reason has to do with America's world dominance, the concentration of power in the hands of the United States."

Hashimoto's prediction has also come to pass in Japan's decision to end its exclusive reliance on the GATT-WTO system. The Japanese government's 2000 white paper on trade signaled the change, and China's announcement of its ASEAN free trade plan prompted an immediate Japanese response. Within weeks of Beijing's initiative, Prime Minister Junichiro Koizumi went to Southeast Asia to stake out Japan's claim. In Singapore, he conceded that "China is an attractive market" but insisted nevertheless that Japan's trade approach is better: "Cooperation among Japan, China, and South Korea is essential; and in the future, it would only be natural to add Australia and New Zealand." The prime minister's rhetoric led quickly to action: Tokyo signed its first-ever free trade agreement, with Singapore, and in early 2002, Japan and South Korea announced they too were talking about an FTA.

In practice, and because of the power of Japan's agricultural interests, both steps will result in less than meets the eye. The agreement with Singapore, for example, excludes agriculture, even though Singapore has no pastureland and its "agricultural" exports are mainly its tropical fish. An agreement with South Korea will face similar hurdles. Even so, Japan is engaged in ongoing talks with both New Zealand and Mexico, and elsewhere in the region other FTA negotiations are in progress. They include talks between Thailand and China, between New Zealand and Singapore, and reportedly even between the United States and Thailand and Japan.

It is certainly true that this flurry of activity does not mean imminent change, as Beijing acknowledged with its ten-year ASEAN time frame. But more important is the question of whether Asia should be moving in this direction at all. Today's competing Chinese and Japanese models remind us why, thanks largely to Cordell Hull, U.S. secretary of state from 1933 to 1944, the early postwar vision of regions and economic blocs promoted by Winston Churchill was rejected, and why multilateralism was adopted instead. Political rivalries inevitably develop within and among the blocs, and protectionist walls, by whatever name, necessarily rise between them.

A good example is Northeast Asia today, where an FTA is being actively discussed by specialists and governments, and where its advocates expect it to result in a "huge trading bloc." That outcome, which implies a dividing line in the Pacific, would hardly be in the interests either of the global economy or of the United States. It is tempting to believe that, given the history and consequences of regional blocs between the two world wars, no policymaker today would deliberately repeat such folly, but the historical record provides no such assurance or comfort.

A WINNING RECORD

Much of the current trade dilemma and its U.S. foreign policy consequences stem from a widespread American belief that the United States has not been a successful player in world trade. This perception is found both at the local level and in Washington, and it is rooted in a long-standing mercantile tradition, which teaches that exports are better than imports. That lesson is regularly reinforced when monthly trade figures are released because they are always accompanied by reports of the nation's "growing trade deficit." The genuine importance of that deficit is debated among economists, but what is not in doubt is that Americans commonly believe that they are a "soft touch" on trade and that the United States has not done too well as an exporter.

Nothing could be further from the truth. A long look back at the record of the last 100 years, illustrated below shows that the United States has largely held a steady 12–13 percent share of world exports. That was the case at the beginning of the twentieth century, when farm products and commodities dominated U.S. exports (and Europe dominated global exports), and at the century's very end, when U.S. exports of aircraft, jet engines, medical equipment, and other high-technology and industrial products had replaced those earlier commodities.

Only in the periods that followed the two world wars did America's exports account for more than their rock-steady 12–13 percent. In those years, as a result of wartime devastation, few other nations were left on the trade scene, and American suppliers briefly and very temporarily had the export field to themselves. In all other periods, 12–13 percent was the norm; indeed it is remarkable that both in 1913 and 1998, two years that are worlds apart in almost every other respect, the U.S. share of world exports was the same: 12.6 percent.

The years since 1980 are worth a second look because that period witnessed an explosion in world trade and the arrival of major new economic actors. Both factors are essential for understanding America's role in world trade because most of those new actors either simply did not exist as independent players when the century began or—as in Japan's case—had just entered global export markets. In 1913, Japan's share of world exports was just 2 percent; since then it has more than tripled. The other new actors—Singapore, South Korea, Taiwan, and Hong Kong—played no separate role at all as export economies before World War II, but today their

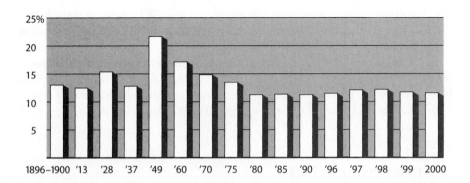

U.S. EXPORTS AS A PERCENTAGE OF THE WORLD MARKET, 1896–2000
Sources: Historical Statistics of the United States; *League of Nations, UN, IMF,* Direction of Trade Statistics; *U.S. Commerce Dept.*

combined global share is more than 10 percent. Add to that China, the newest major Asian exporter, and the global share of these newcomers becomes more than 13 percent. Japan's inclusion brings the figure to more than 20 percent.

The meaning of this arithmetic is that more than a fifth of today's global export market is now held by economies that had little or no international significance when the century began. Yet despite those new arrivals, and in the face of the overall explosion in world trade, America has continued to hold a steady global share. That has been the one constant factor in a world of otherwise enormous change; it should help demonstrate that the United States, far from having been "disadvantaged" in world trade, instead has a clear winning record.

Believing the opposite, that the field is not level but is tilted against the United States, has led to two troublesome consequences. One is the kind of protectionist "safeguards" the United States is often led to adopt: antidumping measures and countervailing duties, spurred by the self-serving demands for Washington's protection that regularly come from America's steel, textile, and farming sectors. The second and now more dangerous consequence is the belief that the United States needs to build special bilateral or regional FTAs. The reality is that the United States not only does not need any such special FTAs, but is precisely in the opposite situation: because it has the world's most evenly distributed pattern of exports, U.S. interests would be harmed were regional FTAs to flourish.

To avoid that outcome, Washington should take two main steps. One is to end the promotion of regional blocs. For the United States that will mean recognizing that its own trade policies, especially its quixotic insistence on a western hemisphere FTA, have helped bring about what it cannot want: the emergence of an East Asian economic bloc. The FTAA has long been in trouble in any case, especially and increasingly with Brazil, and its aims would best be met at the WTO. Second, the United States must resume in practice as well as in rhetoric its postwar role as world trade leader. It must reject, and be seen to reject, whatever short-term advantages regionalism or bilateralism might seem to offer. That will be no easy task for an administration now in serial FTA mode: witness Australia, which was moved to the top of the list of FTA candidates following its support for the United States in Iraq, and the president's recent call for a "Free Trade Area for the Middle East." Instead, the United States must act intensively and single-mindedly to champion the multilateral system of trade, which means principally to ensure that the U.S.-inspired WTO and its Doha Round offshoot are vigorously maintained and strengthened.

Many will argue that because of its recent actions on steel, textiles, and timber, the United States cannot now enter that fray with clean hands. Paradoxically, however, since the United States clearly is not about to reverse those actions, and has already been subjected to worldwide criticisms for them, its situation contains an important tactical and strategic advantage, namely that any positive trade steps it now takes will be welcomed as acts aimed at redemption. The United States has already begun to seize that advantage with its call for the elimination of all tariffs on industrial goods traded among the nations of the Organization for Economic Cooperation and Development. More broadly, however, what is called for is a trade-policy initiative that will restore to center stage the multilateral trading system represented by the WTO.

Such an initiative will mean sparing no effort to complete, by its scheduled 2005 date, the WTO's Doha Development Round, and to meet its important milestones before then. One opportunity has already slipped by, when negotiators failed in March to agree on agricultural "modalities." The next test will be the September ministerial meeting in Cancun, Mexico, and if that chance too is missed, the prospects for 2005 will be bleak indeed. The administration should therefore now concentrate its energies on Cancun and on the core agricultural and market-access issues. In the overlapping trading format represented by the WTO's 146 members, the onus will be on several key actors: the EU, Japan, South Korea, Brazil, India, and of course the United States. All stand to gain, as the GATT's 50-year trade explosion has shown, but all will have to give in order to get.

For that reason, Zoellick—acutely sensitive to Congress' constitutional power in trade matters and already an avid counter of congressional votes—will need to hear from business, agriculture, and industry, along with consumers, that their interests require success in the Doha Round. The WTO is not as strong as it needs to be, but from the perspective of American national interests it is better than any realistic alternative. It is time, in other words, to recall that in the 1930s and 1940s, the massive contribution of U.S. policymakers was to aim for a world not of regional economic blocs, but a single world trade system. That is what we now have, and that is what could now be lost.

QUESTIONS FOR REVIEW AND DISCUSSION

1. Based on Zoellick's article, what is the relative importance that the U.S. administration places on negotiations within the WTO versus negotiations for RTAs? Is this an appropriate balance? Why or why not?
2. Do you think that competitive liberalization is likely to push the Doha Round of WTO negotiations forward? Why or why not?
3. Does Zoellick see any danger in pursuing "competitive liberalization"? Based on the two articles presented here, do you see any dangers in this strategy?
4. What two features of the contemporary global economy does Gordon point to in order to justify his opposition to the strategy of competitive liberalization?
5. What evidence does Gordon provide to support his claim that RTAs are not stepping-stones toward global free trade? Do you find this evidence convincing? Why or why not?

SUGGESTIONS FOR FURTHER READING

For a comprehensive examination of RTAs in the contemporary global economy, see: OECD. *Regionalism and the Multilateral Trading System*. Paris: Organisation for Economic Cooperation and Development, 2003; The World Bank. *Trade Blocs*. Washington, DC: Author, 2000; and Jeffrey Frankel. *Regional Trading Blocs in the World Economic System*. Washington, DC: Institute for International Economics, 1997.

For a more academic treatment of RTAs, see: Jagdish Bhagwati, Pravin Krishna, and Arvind Panagariya. *Trading Blocs: Alternative Approaches to Analyzing Preferential Trade Agreements*. Cambridge, MA: MIT Press, 1999.

Jagdish Bhagwati and his frequent co-author Arvind Panagariya have been two of the most vocal opponents of RTAs. Together they have produced a number of articles and books that are critical of RTAs. See, for example: Jagdish Bhagwati and Arvind Panagariya. *The Economics of Preferential Trade Agreements*. Washington, DC: American Enterprise Institute, 1996; and Jagdish Bhagwati. *The Wind of the Hundred Days: How Washington Mismanaged Globalization*. Cambridge, MA: MIT Press, 2000, pp. 225–250.

For a political economy analysis of RTAs, see: Edward D. Mansfield and Helen V. Milner (eds.). *The Political Economy of Regionalism*. New York: Columbia University Press, 1997.

The WTO maintains a Web site dedicated to regional trading arrangements. You can access this page at http://www.wto.org/english/tratop_e/region_e/region_e.htm. The United States Trade Representative's Website also contains valuable information about regional trading agreements and American trade policy. Visit this site at www.ustr.gov and follow the links to "World Regions."

Multinational Corporations in the Global Economy

CHAPTER 8

MULTINATIONAL CORPORATIONS AND THE RACE TO THE BOTTOM

Multinational corporations (MNCs) sit at the intersection of production, international trade, and cross-border investment. They are also at the center of the debate about globalization. A multinational corporation, sometimes called a transnational corporation (TNC) or a multinational enterprise (MNE), is an "enterprise that controls and manages production establishments—plants—in at least two countries" (Caves 1996, p. 1). According to the United Nations Conference on Trade and Development (UNCTAD), there are more than 63,000 MNC parent firms that together own close to 700,000 foreign affiliates. Together, these parent firms and their foreign affiliates account for about 25 percent of the world's economic production and employ some 86 million people worldwide (UNCTAD 1999). MNC activities are not limited to production, however. MNCs are also important actors in international trade, responsible for almost two-thirds of the world's exports of goods and services (Dunning 1996, p. 77). A large portion of this trade is intrafirm trade, that is, trade that takes place between an MNC parent and its affiliates located in other countries. In the United States, for example, one-third of all exports are intrafirm exports, and as much as 40 percent of imports are intrafirm imports (Grimwade 2000, p. 134). For the world as a whole, it has been estimated that intrafirm trade accounts for 30 to 40 percent of world trade (Dunning 1996, p. 77).

The role that MNCs play in the global economy has grown sharply over the last 20 years. While MNCs have operated in the global economy for more than 100 years, the amount of foreign direct investment (FDI), as well as the number of MNCs operating in the global economy, grew sharply between 1985 and 2000. During the mid-1980s, annual flows of FDI amounted to about $180 billion. In 2000, FDI totaled more than $1 trillion (UNCTAD 2001). And while slower world economic growth has caused annual flows of FDI to fall sharply since 2000, with only $651 billion of FDI in 2002, the total stock of FDI was valued at slightly more than $7.1 trillion in 2002, up from $802 billion in 1982 (UNCTAD 2003).

The sharp increase in MNC activity during the last 20 years has its roots in a number of changes. Technological change has made it substantially easier, and less costly, to organize production globally. The cost of communicating over long distances has fallen sharply during the last 20 years. Charges for long-distance telephone calls, for example, are now a small fraction of what they were in the 1970s. The Internet has also reduced the cost of organizing production globally, as it allows companies to send large volumes of data and text across long distances rapidly and at a very low cost. Transportation costs—the cost of shipping goods by sea or by air—have also fallen sharply. Consequently, it is now feasible to organize production efficiently on a global scale.

The last 20 years also have brought sweeping changes in government policies toward MNCs, particularly in the developing world. During the 30 years immediately following World War II, most developing country governments were extremely wary of MNCs. As a consequence, most governments regulated MNC activity, thereby making it difficult for MNCs to invest in developing economies. During the last 20 years, developing country governments have come to believe that, on balance, MNCs contribute importantly to economic development. As this belief has spread, governments have reduced the restrictions they had previously imposed on MNCs operating within their economies.

The growth of MNCs has brought renewed scrutiny of how these large firms operate and what impact they have on the societies in which they operate. One issue that has received considerable attention is whether the rapid growth in MNC activity has given rise to a "race to the bottom" dynamic in government regulation. Governments maintain different regulatory standards. In some countries, governments enact fairly stringent laws that regulate how firms can treat workers, how they must handle their toxic waste and other environmental pollutants, and other business activities. Other countries maintain less stringent regulatory environments, thereby allowing firms to engage in activities that are illegal in other countries. Many of these regulations affect a firm's cost of production. It is more expensive, for example, for a firm to treat chemical waste before it is disposed than to simply dump the raw waste in a landfill. Consequently, even if all other production costs that a firm faces in two countries are the same, different regulatory standards can make production in the lower-standard country less costly. MNCs might thus be expected to shift their production out of countries with stringent regulatory standards and into countries with relatively lax regulatory standards. Governments in high-standard countries might then feel pressure to relax their standards in order to eliminate the cost disadvantage that leads firms to move production to other countries. Over time, regulatory standards throughout the world might then converge around the regulatory practices of the least restrictive country. More broadly, the race-to-the-bottom logic suggests that governments will dismantle regulations designed to protect workers, the environment, and the public good as they compete to attract and keep MNC investments.

It is not clear whether MNCs have generated a race-to-the-bottom dynamic in the contemporary global economy. The two articles presented in this chapter examine this debate in detail. The first article, written by Debora Spar and David Yoffie, who both teach at the Harvard Business School, develops a conceptual framework to help us think about when we are most and least likely to see a race-to-the-bottom dynamic. Using this same conceptual framework, they also suggest that under certain conditions, one might also see a race-to-the-top dynamic in which national regulations converge around the more, rather than less, stringent regulations.

The second article, written by Daniel W. Drezner, a political scientist at the University of Chicago, challenges the idea that a race-to-the-bottom dynamic exists, arguing that there is little evidence to support the idea. He suggests that the claim has become popular because it is politically convenient for both opponents and proponents of globalization.

REFERENCES

Caves, Richard E. *Multinational enterprise and economic analysis.* Cambridge: Cambridge University Press, 1996.

Dunning, John H. "Re-evaluating the Benefits of Foreign Direct Investment." In *Companies without Borders: Transnational Corporations in the 1990s,* edited by UNCTAD. London: International Thomson Business Press, 1996, pp. 73–101.

Grimwade, Nigel. *International trade: new patterns of trade, production & investment.* London: Routledge, 2000.

United Nations Conference on Trade and Development. *World Investment Report.* Geneva: The United Nations, 2003.

United Nations Conference on Trade and Development. *World Investment Report.* Geneva: The United Nations, 2001.

United Nations Conference on Trade and Development. *World Investment Report.* Geneva: The United Nations, 1999.

Multinational Enterprises and the Prospects for Justice

DEBORA SPAR AND DAVID YOFFIE

One of the defining features of the modern era is the spread of business enterprises across international borders. Markets once considered peripheral or exotic are now often viewed as integral to a firm's success; and a global corps of businesses has replaced the once-scattered legion of expatriate firms. As corporations increasingly define their markets to encompass wide swathes of the globe, cross-border flows of capital, technology, trade and currencies have skyrocketed. Indeed, cross-border activities of multinational firms are an integral piece—perhaps the integral piece— of globalization. They are also, in some quarters at least, highly controversial.

One of the controversies centers on the impact of global mobility. According to some scholars, the corporate scramble for ever-wider markets has a dark side. In addition to creating economies of scale and enhancing efficiency, globalization may create a deleterious "race to the bottom," a downward spiral of rivalry that works to lower standards among all affected parties. As described by proponents of this view, the dynamic behind such races is straightforward and compelling. As corporations spread throughout the international economy, their constant search for competitive advantage drives down all those factors that the global players seek to minimize. Tax and labor rates are pushed down, and health and environmental regulation are kept to a bare minimum. In the process, crucial functions of governance effectively slip from the grasp of national governments, and corporations and capital markets reap what societies and workers lose. Since justice is hardly a central concern of the modern corporate enterprise, it presumably gets lost in the shuffle.

Does corporate expansion necessarily lead to such race-to-the-bottom behavior? Or are there situations in which multinational enterprises might actually contribute to the pursuit of international justice? Common wisdom would probably suggest that because corporations are motivated solely by the desire to maximize profits, it would be unrealistic to expect them to play any positive role in the pursuit of international justice. This paper seeks to unbundle such arguments and looks in greater detail at races to the bottom and their impact on affected nations. In particular, it seeks to examine when such races really do occur and when they do not; when corporate expansion is liable to drive global standards to rock-bottom lows; and when it can, paradoxically perhaps, actually enhance prospects for global governance and international justice. . . .

From Debora Spar and David Yoffie, "Multinational Enterprises and the Prospects for Justice," *Journal of International Affairs* 52, Spring 1999, pp. 557–581.

When we speak of justice, we are referring to the basic conditions of human livelihood, to the political and economic factors that expand the realm of human choice and possibility. Our definition of justice, based on the United Nations' description of human development, is the process of enlarging people's choices, ensuring access to basic resources and providing citizens with education and the ability to live a healthy life.[1] One might argue that these factors are more directly linked to political concerns for justice: civil liberties, for example, only become plausible once the citizens of a particular state have reached a basic level of economic subsistence and political sophistication. In this article, however, such claims are neither made nor drawn upon. Rather, we confine our analysis to a much more limited, preliminary sphere. We try to examine whether multinational expansion always leads to race-to-the-bottom behavior, with all of its presumed ill effects, or whether, under some circumstances, multinationals can actually lead the charge toward higher global standards and greater concern for the lives and livelihoods of affected populations.

In a very preliminary way, this article proposes a series of hypotheses about the impact of corporate mobility on international standards and international governance. Specifically, we suggest that races to the bottom only occur when border controls are minimal and regulation and factor costs differ across national markets. Once these preconditions are met, races will most likely occur when products are relatively homogeneous, cross-border differentials are significant and both sunk costs and transaction costs are minimal. Likewise, we suggest that "governance from the top" will be facilitated by the strong presence of externalities within a particular issue area, by a cascading process that affects several states (racing that occurs in steps), by the presence of cross-cutting and powerful domestic coalitions and, occasionally, by incentives for self-governance among the racing firms.

Taken together, these hypotheses imply a more nuanced combination of races to the bottom and governance from the top. They describe globalization as a complex process with no determinate outcome and few clear winners. Sometimes, the integration of capital flows and corporate structures can indeed produce a deleterious spiral and an erosion of governance mechanisms. Yet sometimes it can also culminate in increased governance and more stringent international standards. The challenge for both scholars and policymakers is to separate these effects and probe their disparate causes.

GLOBAL RACES

In an influential 1994 *Foreign Affairs* article, Terry Collingsworth, J. William Goold and Pharis J. Harvey laid forth a bleak logic of globalization. According to the authors, the advent of the global economy has enabled multinational companies to escape from developed countries' labor standards and to depress working conditions and wages around the world. As corporations have ventured abroad, they have encouraged a fierce rivalry among the developing countries that seek to win their investment capital. In the process of wooing multinationals, countries "compete against each other to depress wages."[2] As a result: "First World components are assembled by Third World workers who often have no choice but to work under any conditions offered them. Multinational companies have turned back the clock, transferring production to countries with labor conditions that resemble those in the early period of America's own industrialization."[3]

In other words, a race to the bottom occurs with global standards forced ever lower by the centripetal forces of multinational rivalry. In the process, human rights and justice suffer.

Similar arguments characterize much of the literature on globalization.[4] At the broadest level, scholars such as Philip Cerny, Susan Strange and Richard Falk have suggested that the expansion of new global actors, and particularly of global corporate actors, is serving to erode and transform the policymaking power of states. As Cerny writes: "[T]he capacity of industrial and financial sectors to whipsaw the state apparatus by pushing state agencies into a process of competitive deregulation or what economists call competition in laxity . . . has both undermined the control span of the state from without and fragmented it from within."[5]

Falk echoes these sentiments, suggesting that as a result, in part, of market forces and technology, "[t]erritorial sovereignty is being diminished on a spectrum of issues in such a serious manner as to subvert the capacity of states to control and protect the internal life of society."[6] In all three authors' work, there is a clear link between the globalization of firms and capital and the restriction of state power. This link is forged by the pressures that competing firms are able to exert on state policy: in other words, by a race-to-the-bottom effect.[7]

More specific arguments focus on the impact of globalization on labor, suggesting that, in a bid to attract multinational investment, countries may race to the regulatory bottom, lowering wages and abandoning any labor protection they might have offered in the past. In the process, international economic justice is almost certainly compromised, as labor demands give way to corporate rivalry.[8] In the environmental realm, numerous studies have likewise suggested that international competition for investment will compel governments to create "pollution havens," lowering their environmental regulations far below socially desirable levels.[9] These havens will, in turn, lure multinational firms, causing them to flee from more stringent environments. The result of this migration will be more lax standards around the world, increased environmental degradation and a massive migration of jobs and capital from the industrialized states.

Though "justice" is not an explicit theme in this work, the implications in its direction are clear: as corporations race around the world, they weaken the ability of governments to address social issues. Concerns about income distribution, for example, will be muted by a desire to retain multinational investment, and demands for unionization or free association will fall prey to corporate preferences for low wages and docile labor pools. As a result, society at large is bound to suffer and justice will take a back seat to profits. This is the basic logic that connects globalization with race-to-the-bottom effects.

Empirically, evidence of races is more difficult to discern.[10] Indeed, most of the research done tends to dispute the race-to-the-bottom hypothesis, arguing that firms do not actually trawl around the global economy looking for lower labor standards or weaker environmental regimes.[11] Admittedly, finding empirical evidence of race-to-the-bottom effects is bound to be a difficult endeavor since so many variables and motives are involved. Firms choose locations for a wide variety of reasons: to expand markets, to be close to customers, to follow competitors and to reduce factor and regulatory costs. In most instances, it will be difficult to discern from aggregate data which motives predominate and how important cost or regulatory reduction has been in prompting firms' overseas movements. Even if aggregate data suggest, for instance, a major influx of foreign direct investment to lower-wage states, or an outflow from states that unilaterally raise their tax rates or regulatory standards, it is difficult to demonstrate that corporate movements were actually prompted by the wage rates or regulatory change. Case studies or survey data may be able to reveal the importance of these motives in slightly finer detail, but even here the results will be clouded by the source upon which they rely. Aware of race-to-the-bottom accusations, most firms will probably be reluctant to admit to motives that they sense will be perceived as unsavory.

Yet even if the empirical evidence is somewhat dismissive, races to the bottom remain a troubling element of the global economy. Theoretically, they are also quite plausible. Firms undeniably seek to increase profits and create a competitive advantage, and if moving to less expensive or less onerous locations would serve these aims, then it is only logical to expect them to do so. It is also reasonable to expect these cross-border movements to increase as globalization tears down old barriers to international flows of capital, people and technology. If these movements occur, and if they force governments to restrict their own policy options, then the outcomes will be distinctly troubling. In short, even the possibility of race-to-the-bottom effects are important enough to demand continued attention and rigorous inquiry.

At the same time, though, such inquiries must also not lose sight of a parallel possibility. Sometimes it appears that the very same forces that lead to downward spirals can simultaneously produce pressures for higher standards and increased levels of international governance.[12] In other words, some races to the bottom have let loose a countervailing force: supranational regulation, either by governments or by the firms themselves. Rather than directly competing for multinational investment, countries can sometimes agree to common standards for the treatment of multinationals and protocols for taxation. Rather than using wage differentials to compete in the trading arena, national governments can negotiate agreements that regulate their trade and promote more just outcomes. In at least a few cases, governance from the top has mitigated races to the bottom.

In the discussion below, we try to separate out these two effects and the relationship between them. What factors lead, theoretically, to a race to the bottom, and what factors can transform this dynamic into governance from the top?

RACING TO THE BOTTOM

We begin with a definition. For our purposes, a race to the bottom is characterized by the progressive movement of capital and technology from countries with relatively high levels of wages, taxation and regulation to countries with relatively lower levels. We then pose the central question of this inquiry: under what conditions, and in what areas, is a race to the bottom most likely to occur? Logically, the answers seem to fall into two distinct tiers: necessary conditions and facilitating factors.

Necessary Conditions

The necessary conditions for races to the bottom are fairly obvious. The first is simply mobility. As with any race, races to the bottom depend critically on the participants' ability to move. Corporations can only launch a race to the bottom once they are free to move across national borders.[13] This essential assumption is evident in many more formal treatments of races.[14] Practically, it also implies that races to the bottom can occur only where border controls are minimal. As countries remove barriers to trade and, particularly, investment, they fire the starting gun that allows corporations to race abroad. This general progression aligns with the empirical patterns of the industrial era. Initially, overseas operations were the province of only a small handful of firms, most of which went abroad primarily in search of scarce resources such as oil. Then, in the wake of the Second World War, the international community launched a series of initiatives and institutions designed to open nations to the vicissitudes and rewards of expanded international trade. Global tariffs were gradually reduced under the auspices of the General Agreement on Tariffs and Trade (GATT); capital controls decreased first in the developed world and then in the developing nations; and the protection of intellectual property rights was extended through a combination of bilateral pressure and multilateral rules appended to the GATT's Uruguay Round. As these controls were dismantled, foreign investment skyrocketed, rising from $58 billion in 1985 to $318 billion by 1996.[15] Only against the backdrop of such mobility did races to the bottom become a realistic possibility. By itself, however, the freedom to move is not sufficient to launch a full-scale race. For a race to occur, corporations must also have some incentives to search for lower cost or more attractive locations: there must be lower taxes and/or lower wage costs in an overseas location, less expensive inputs and/or less onerous regulations. If these factors are the same across borders, then there is little incentive for firms to race across them.[16] Firms race only when regulation and factor costs are heterogeneous—and when this heterogeneity leaves gaps that can be turned to the firms' competitive advantage.

At a minimum, racing to the bottom demands that two necessary conditions be met. Firms must be mobile and markets must be heterogeneous; there must either be differential factor costs or regulatory differences that affect product costs. Without these conditions, firms either will not be able to move across international borders or will have no incentive to do so. Yet does the mere existence of these conditions ensure that such races will occur? Empirically, it seems not. As mentioned above, numerous studies have demonstrated that even when the conditions for racing are met, races do not necessarily occur.[17] Less formally, we can observe that races simply do not happen everywhere and in every industry. In today's global economy, most firms are able to move across international borders with relative ease and governments employ heterogeneous policies across a wide spectrum of issues. Yet, accusations of racing are rife in some industries, such as footwear, and virtually nonexistent in others, such as semiconductors. Clearly, there are other factors at work.

Facilitating Factors

We hypothesize that four variables raise the incentives for races to occur: homogeneity of products, regulatory differentials, transaction costs and sunk costs. While all four capture different elements of the interaction between firms and states in a global economy, we believe that races are more likely when multiple combinations of these variables are present.

Homogeneity of Products

The first variable is what we label as homogeneity of products. In some industries, firms compete across a wide range of dimensions. They may have sharply different products, marketing operations or research foci. For these firms, marginal cost differentials are unlikely to be all that important to their competitive performance. Intel, for example, does not compete with other semiconductor manufacturers by shaving a few pennies off the price of its Pentium chip. Merck does not undercut its rivals through cut-throat pricing on cancer drugs. These firms still compete, and they still worry about relative cost structures, but they are probably not predisposed to race across the world in order to seize either a cost or a regulatory advantage.

By contrast, firms that manufacture homogeneous products will be more inclined to leap for any advantages that location hopping might bring. If firms produce essentially the same product, and if their internal cost structures are similar, they will feel obligated to compete more at the margin, seizing whatever relative advantage they can find. Thus, firms such as Sony and Matsushita, which produce television sets, may well be tempted to search for lower labor costs in their assembly plants, bulk chemical producers may look for regulatory gaps that help to reduce their relative costs. The more homogeneous the products in any industry, the more we would expect to see competition lured by races toward the bottom.

An interesting twist here concerns the homogeneity of products within a firm's production chain. In developed economies many firms produce high-profile brand goods: Nike shoes or Izod shirts, for example. At the product level, these goods are not homogeneous. A customer may refuse, for example, to purchase anything but Air Jordan shoes. Yet if we separate the marketing and distribution of these brand goods from their production, homogeneity becomes relevant once more. Only here homogeneity exists at the level of the supplier. Nike and Izod, after all, essentially still produce homogeneous goods—sneakers and t-shirts—that are sourced and assembled by a range of virtually interchangeable suppliers. Nike, for example, purchases nearly all its footwear from relatively small suppliers scattered across Asia. From Nike's perspective, these suppliers are basically homogeneous. Nike can pick and choose among them, chasing whatever cost advantages a particular subcontractor might provide. Nike can then act as an oligopolist in its own market, and can pocket the profit differential that lower-cost suppliers can offer. This combination of oligopolistic industry structure at home combined with homogeneity of international suppliers sharply increases the incentives for Nike (and indeed any firm from the apparel or footwear industries) to pursue lower-cost suppliers—that is, to race toward the bottom. Thus, races can occur not only when final products are homogeneous, but also when the producers of non-homogeneous products can disaggregate their own supply chain and wring advantages from the homogeneous components they employ.

Regulatory Differentials

A second factor concerns the relative cost of regulatory differentials. The logic here is largely intuitive. If factor and regulatory costs vary widely across borders, and if these costs are important to the affected firms, then firms will have an incentive to follow these costs to their lowest possible point. If the differences are small and/or unimportant, firms will generally be more content to remain where they are or base any relocation decisions on a range of other factors. Consider, for example, the impact of regulatory variation on firms from two very different industries: toys and paper. For the paper firm, environmental regulation is a critical component of doing business. Under certain circumstances, therefore, it may be in the paper firm's interest to search the globe for more lax regulatory regimes and to invest wherever environmental regulation is least stringent. In this case, a race to the bottom is likely to occur. For a toy producer, however, environmental regulation is generally not that important. If being in a more lax regulatory regime does not affect a firm's way of doing business—or if this effect is minimal—a firm is unlikely to race toward a more lax country, in which case no race to the bottom will ensue. This dynamic may help to explain why evidence of industrial flight to "pollution havens" is limited, despite the obvious logic behind such proposed flights. In most industries, it appears that the costs of complying with pollution control measures are simply not that high.[18]

Transaction Costs and Sunk Costs

The third and fourth factors relate to the economists' well-worn notion of stickiness. In most cases, empirical evidence indicates that firms do not move with the ease suggested by economic models. Changes in production costs do not instantaneously manifest themselves in price changes, wage increases do not create instant layoffs and firms do not change suppliers or supply patterns to accord perfectly with their relative prices. Such stickiness is particularly relevant for investment decisions, since investment involves a considerable outlay of firm resources. In the race-to-the-bottom literature, there is an underlying sense that firms move at the speed of relative cost change: they hop across borders as soon as they perceive a financial advantage. Yet the stickiness of investment is bound to slow the pace of relocation. Most firms cannot switch plant locations at will as most will incur substantial costs from any move across borders. The higher these costs, the stickier existing investments will prove to be—and stickier investments will decrease the momentum for any race to the bottom.

In particular, we can imagine two kinds of stickiness that would affect firms' propensity to engage in a race to the bottom. The first is that which arises from sunk costs: the more expensive and capital-intensive an operation is, the less likely its parent firm will be to relocate.[19] The second comes from transaction costs: the more difficult and time-consuming a move will be, the less likely it is to occur. Both of these points are largely intuitive, yet they explain considerable differences in industry structure and incentives.

Consider again the gap that separates apparel firms from paper mills. An apparel firm is a highly labor-intensive venture, with only a limited amount of in-the-ground capital investment. It may lease a building or a few floors and own some machinery, the total cost of which can be as low as $100,000. Neither relocating its operations nor opening additional facilities in a new location is particularly daunting. The sunk costs are low and the stickiness of the investment is thus minimal. Similar characteristics would adhere to firms in the footwear industry and many low-technology assembly operations. A paper mill, by contrast, has much lower levels of labor intensity and correspondingly higher levels of capital intensity. Instead of housing primarily laborers and easily duplicated machinery, a paper plant (or a chemical processing plant or semiconductor fabrication facility) typically contains highly specific machinery and complex interlocked processes. Such plants can be moved; they can also be closed in one location and supplanted by newer facilities elsewhere. Yet the propensity for such changes is significantly lower than in the apparel industry, since the sunk costs of any particular plant are much greater. We should expect, therefore, that paper mills are less likely to race abroad than apparel firms. They may still race, especially if regulatory gaps or lower input costs were to open up competitive advantages, but the threshold for their race will be undeniably higher. In industries with high sunk costs, the lure of pursuing lower-cost locations must be extremely high in order to incite a race to the bottom.

A similar logic adheres to the stickiness created by transaction costs. As the literature on institutional economics makes clear, not all costs borne by firms are explicitly financial. There are also invisible costs such as the costs of hiring and training new employees, suffering productivity losses after introducing new technologies and building contacts and reputation. All of these costs will be present, and frequently heightened, as firms move to new locations. The higher these costs, the more reluctant firms should be to engage in race-to-the-bottom behavior.[20] Logically, we might also expect some variation along with the size and market presence of a given firm. In most cases, large multinational firms will be better positioned to absorb the transaction costs entailed by a cross-border move. Smaller firms, with less international experience and fewer overseas contacts, will incur relatively higher transaction costs for identical foreign investments. Firms with more sophisticated training needs or more specific production technologies will also tend to move more slowly. In general, though, the relationship here is directly parallel to that described with regard to sunk costs: as transaction costs diminish, the propensity for racing should increase.

Taken together, these hypotheses sketch a two-tiered view of races and an argument that industry structure matters. In any industry, races can occur only when two key necessary conditions are met: corporations must be free to move their capital and technology across borders, and government regulation and factor costs must be heterogeneous across those borders. Once these conditions are in place, though, industry variation comes into play, meaning that not all firms will be equally predisposed to chase each other toward the lowest common denominator. Firms will be most inclined to race when they produce homogeneous, commodity-type products; when the costs that matter most to them are sharply divergent across national borders; and when their sunk costs of investment and transaction costs of relocation are both relatively low. When these conditions are not in place, races to the bottom are less likely to occur.

RACING TOWARD JUSTICE?

Thus far, we have described only how races to the bottom might be forestalled by the internal dynamics of various industries. Yet, as mentioned at the outset, there exists another realm of possibilities: races, once launched, might be curtailed by the imposition of external standards. A race to the bottom, in other words, can be transformed into governance from the top.[21] In the process, the prospects for justice are bound to increase.

To imagine how this transformation might occur, consider the dynamics of the race. Essentially, regulatory and/or factor arbitrage facilitates a downward spiral. In the absence of high sunk or transaction costs, firms chase competitive advantage to the lowest possible point; they will move investment to whatever location will support their operations at the lowest cost. Countries can reinforce the game by depressing the cost of factors under their control (taxes, regulation, minimum wages) and watering down standards in order to compete for scarce capital.

What would slow the race down, then, is any constraint that either prevents the firm from seizing the arbitrage opportunity or prevents the state from creating it. Theoretically, such possibilities are relatively easy to imagine. Consider the situation from the firm's perspective. What drives the race here is rivalry and relative costs. Firms need to chase lower costs primarily to keep (or get) a cost advantage relative to their competitors. If everyone were to stop chasing, then no one would be at a particular disadvantage. It is precisely the dynamic that describes cartels, the dynamic captured in Rousseau's classic parable of the stag hunt.[22] If firms were to cooperate and hold to a common standard, the race would stop. The problem, though, is that firms are rarely able to form this kind of collective endeavor. Indeed, as we know, the record of cartels is dismally poor: most succumb early on to the pressures of competition and defection.[23]

Where national governments are concerned, however, the prospects are considerably brighter. As the vast literature on international organizations and regimes makes clear, it is eminently possible for governments not only to govern effectively at home, but also to establish governance structures that stretch across borders. Especially in the postwar era, governments have forged a wide and ever-expanding array of international organizations, most designed to enforce a set of common rules across the international arena. Indeed, it is precisely these organizations and their rules that have enabled the mobility that now characterizes the global business environment. Could these rules also be used to limit the races that they have facilitated? Theoretically at least, there should be no difficulty. States, after all, are responsible for having lowered standards in the first place. They are the ones that compete for multinational investment by lowering one or more of the following: minimum wage rates, tax rates and regulations. While corporations benefit from this scramble to the bottom, states lose.[24] Some lose tax revenues that they might have been able to generate; others lose the cleaner air or safer conditions that more stringent regulation could have produced. This is the basis of the criticism against race-to-the-bottom effects. It is also the logical corollary of the processes entailed in these races.

What the process also suggests, however, is that in the abstract states have a clear incentive to cooperate around common norms of governance. If they could, they would all like to have their cake and eat it too—to win the investors they seek without having to depress their standards or limit their own realm of governance. Once again, there is a classic problem of collective action. All parties are better off if they cooperate; but competition leads predictably to defection and suboptimal outcomes.[25] Yet we know from the international relations literature that, in numerous cases, governments have triumphed over these collective action problems. They have agreed on common, higher standards; and they have achieved (varying) degrees of compliance with the rules they set. The GATT, the World Trade Organization, the Nuclear Nonproliferation Treaty and the European Union all clearly do this. They all enforce common standards that collectively enhance their members' well-being while simultaneously denying these members the advantages of certain unilateral actions. Conceptually, there is no reason to suspect that the global playing field could not be similarly leveled with regard to multinational investment and corporate mobility.

More challenging, though, is to imagine the precise conditions under which this "race to the top" might emerge to regulate races to the bottom. As a first cut, we might expect that a necessary condition for any kind of international governance is the strong presence of externalities within a particular issue area. Realistically, governance efforts are likely to cluster where state borders are most porous. The more that events in one country affect outcomes or welfare in another, the greater the need for cross-border governance to address any problems that might arise. Where autarchy reigns, international governance is irrelevant. It becomes important only as interdependence increases cross-border externalities in a particular issue area and decreases the effectiveness of national policies. A related point is that negative externalities are more likely to spawn governance efforts than are their positive counterparts. Recall again the dynamics of the race. As countries scramble to woo corporations, they compete by progressively raising incentives and lowering regulation. As the race proceeds, some contenders are left worse off than others. They are the countries that fail to attract new investment or even lose some of their current investors. They are also the ones most likely to seek remedies beyond the confines of their own borders. States, in short, will be more inclined to pursue international governance when the effect of races to the bottom is to damage their own domestic economy. The greater the damage, the greater their incentive to stop the race.

A final point along these lines, though, is that state identity matters. While all states may have similar interests in stopping races or forging governance structures, not all states will be similarly equipped to address these issues. Returning to the basic tenets of realism, it seems reasonable to assume that some states will be better positioned to create and enforce arrangements of international governance. States that are more powerful in the international arena simply will carry more clout in the formation of cross-border rules. They will be better able to set higher standards, abide by them and persuade others to do likewise. They will also generally be better prepared to perform the duty of enforcer, punishing those who wander too far from the rules established at the international level.[26] The importance of particular states is amply demonstrated throughout the history of international organizations and the literature that describes them. The United States took the lead in ushering in postwar institutions such as the GATT and the International Monetary Fund; Germany and France have been the driving force behind the European Monetary Union; and Saudi Arabia was for many years the dominant voice in Organization of the Petroleum Exporting Countries. A similar pattern marks the more limited history of state interventions in ongoing corporate races. The major international agreements regarding textile trade (the Long-Term Arrangement Regarding International Trade in Cotton Textiles and the Multifiber Arrangement) were launched largely by the United States and Europe, which saw their textile operations slipping away to lower-cost Asian operations and feared the domestic ramifications of higher unemployment in this key sector.[27] Capital adequacy standards were the work of American, British and Japanese negotiators who worried that more lax standards at foreign banks were destined, not only to damage the security of the global financial system, but also to draw business away from their domestic banks.[28] Note that in all these cases, international governance stemmed from the self-interest of key states, particularly the large industrialized democracies. Governance occurred and races stopped once some subset of these states felt the adverse effect of a race to the bottom and made a commitment to halt the spiral.

A second hypothesis concerns what might be labeled "cascading." When races occur, they rarely sweep downwards in a single motion. Rather, firms move through a series of steps: from their home country to a less expensive, less onerous foreign location; from that spot to an even more lax alternative; then on to the next contender; and so forth. This is the process by which the spiral is widened and accelerated. Governments are most likely to get involved only after the process has already moved down several of the early steps. If firms move only from their home market to an overseas facility, pressure for governance will be muted by the inherent ambiguities described earlier. The firms may have moved for a whole range of reasons, and the state is unlikely to get involved. If these same firms move on from destination to destination, then the pressure for governance is likely to mount. There are more states that feel the negative consequences of their movement, and more evidence that the movement is being driven by a race-to-the-bottom rivalry. Critically, in order for international governance to succeed, multiple states must share a common interest in arresting the race at any particular point and preventing any further downward movement. We should therefore expect to see more concerted efforts at international governance as the race cascades beyond its initial stages.

This hypothesis tracks rather well with the available evidence. The original regime in cotton textiles and apparel, for example, did not occur until the global textile industry had migrated not just to Japan, but also to Hong Kong, Korea and

Taiwan in the late 1950s. When textile production began to further migrate to Bangladesh, Sri Lanka and other lower-cost Asian countries, pressure mounted to strengthen the international agreement, which ultimately culminated in the Multi-fiber Arrangement in 1974. Indeed, countries such as Taiwan and Korea preferred a multilateral solution because they feared losing production to lower-cost states. Similarly, although the United States feared an outflow of investment after stringent pollution controls were first introduced in the early 1970s, pressure for international governance did not really mount until more than a decade later, when the corporations that were thought to have fled to Canada, and then Mexico, were perceived to be heading even further afield. Similarly, concern for international codes of taxation has been prompted by corporate expansion beyond the traditional havens of Bermuda and Luxembourg to more far-flung (and increasingly less restrictive) locales.

A third hypothesis brings domestic politics back into the global picture. Once the black box of the state is opened to scrutiny, it quickly becomes apparent that domestic groups typically put international governance issues on the state's agenda. The Multifiber Arrangement is the end result of extensive lobbying by U.S. textile firms and (particularly) their labor unions; pressure for environmental regulation has for decades been the work of concerted activist groups such as Greenpeace and the Environmental Defense Fund; and pressure for international labor standards comes from human rights groups, as well as labor organizations.[29] When these domestic groups have already forged their own alliances at the international level, the political pressure is likely to be even more effective and the governance swifter. The more that domestic groups care about a particular issue, and the more powerful these groups are, the higher levels of international governance we should expect to see.

A final hypothesis returns us to the role of firms. While it is easy to paint firms as the malevolent drivers of these downward spirals, it is also conceivable that firms could play some role in redirecting their races back toward the top—that is, toward global regulation and higher international standards. Under some circumstances, firms might choose to self-regulate, settling upon common standards rather than competing for relative advantage along these lines. Admittedly, these circumstances are bound to be rare. Given the collective action dilemma described above, firms generally will be wary of defection and thus not eager to bind themselves to a set of prescribed rules. Nevertheless, in some cases rules may triumph over races. If firms suspect that formal international governance is imminent, then they may choose to self-regulate in the hopes of pre-empting a more onerous set of restrictions. Likewise, if the race is becoming too costly for all of the players, or even for a solid and powerful majority of them, then they may choose again to self-regulate and set a common floor below which none of the players will compete.

Cases of this sort are actually quite common, more common by far than the race-to-the-bottom literature would suggest. As early as 1981, for example, when pressure for environmental regulation was just beginning to spread around the world, the International Chamber of Commerce (a private business group) passed its own set of environmental guidelines supporting the harmonization of global pollution regulations. After the 1984 disaster in Bhopal, India, the U.S.-based

Chemical Manufacturers Association (CMA) enacted a set of environmental guidelines known as "Responsible Care" that applied to all of the association's 180 member firms. Consisting of ten "guiding principles" and six management codes, Responsible Care specifies requirements for many different aspects of the chemicals business, from community awareness and emergency response to pollution control and employee health and safety. While the initiative was largely a response to negative public opinion within the United States, its effects have ranged far beyond national borders. By mandating that Responsible Care be extended to cover the numerous foreign manufacturing facilities of member firms, the CMA has successfully exported United States environmental standards to developing nations.[30] Similar guidelines were adopted subsequently by the European Chemical Industries Council (CEFIC).[31] More recently, major producers of chemicals and pesticides adopted a voluntary and apparently highly effective system to ensure that exports of these substances follow certain well-defined rules and procedures.[32]

In the area of human rights and labor standards, private initiatives are also playing an increasingly important role. In 1997, for example, both the World Federation of Sporting Goods Industry and the U.S.-based Sporting Goods Manufacturers Association pledged to eradicate child labor in the Pakistani soccer ball industry. Spurred by Reebok, a U.S. firm that had been hard hit by accusations that it had purchased balls made by 12-year-old workers, all members of the private industry associations eventually agreed to establish a system of independent monitors to ensure that no children were involved in the production of soccer balls. The firms also joined forces in establishing schools and other programs for the former child workers.[33] Similarly, public pressure in the United States has recently led to the formation of a private Apparel Industry Partnership, under which firms such as Liz Claiborne and L.L. Bean have agreed to ensure that all of their suppliers comply with specific workplace codes of conduct.[34] In the rug industry, importers in both the United States and Germany have agreed to monitor the source of the products they sell, affixing a "Rugmark" label to those carpets that are guaranteed to have been made without the use of child labor.[35] At the most general level, a number of major multinationals such as Toys 'R Us and Avon announced in the spring of 1998 that their suppliers will henceforth need to comply with the provisions of SA8000, a certifiable set of labor and human rights standards. Modeled on the International Organization for Standardization system for ensuring compliance with technical and environmental standards, SA8000 is an ambitious attempt to create private standards for social accountability.[36] Under this system, corporations voluntarily agree to adhere to a list of social standards: for example, provisions regarding the use of child labor, the right to collective bargaining, nondiscrimination and so forth. Independent auditors then visit the firms and their suppliers to ensure compliance with the SA8000 code.

Like all the examples just mentioned, SA8000 is purely a private scheme. There is no formal regulation involved, and no coercion on the part of either national governments or international bodies. Instead, the "regulation" occurs in the marketplace and through the coordinated activities of private firms. In some cases, these firms may be acting out of a deep-seated sense of responsibility.

They may operate under the guidance of leaders who care about social issues and are even willing, under some circumstances, to sacrifice profit maximization to other goals. Yet, realistically, such motives and corporate leaders are bound to be the exception rather than the rule. The beauty of the arrangements just described, however, is that they enable corporations to pursue both financial and social goals. By creating common standards, these arrangements level the proverbial playing field at a higher-than-usual plane. Corporations can still compete freely—they just cannot race to the bottom of a regulatory pit.

Clearly, any scheme for private corporate governance must be regarded with some degree of caution. None of these arrangements have any formal structure around them, and all lack stringent enforcement mechanisms. They can all easily disintegrate into public relations efforts and will always bear the stigma of this possibility. Yet private corporate arrangements also have a number of advantages. They appear easier to forge than governmental structures, since the negotiation process involves fewer parties and does not have the same measure of public accountability as would a governmental initiative.[37] According to some evidence, they also actually have higher rates of compliance over a harder range of issues.[38]

Finally, from the firms' perspective, self-regulation can be an effective means of restoring or enhancing profitability. If racing becomes too costly, or if firms fear that governments are prepared to impose collective regulation upon them, then self-regulation can make sense. By leveling the playing field, firms can solve the collective action dilemma that binds them all. They can also use harmonized policies to shift the cost of compliance from producers to consumers: if all producers are held to the same standard, then the world price of their good is likely to rise. Finally, if firms are already adhering to their own cross-national standards (a common practice for many firms from industrialized countries), then encouraging other firms to agree to these same standards can convey a significant advantage. As one American CEO recently commented in response to a U.S. proposal to include environmental standards in trade legislation: "We already have environmental standards . . . we want a level playing field."[39] Cooperation under these circumstances can prove a powerful competitive weapon.

FIRMS, STATES, AND THE PURSUIT OF JUSTICE

Drawing a connection between multinational enterprises and international justice is no easy task. As stated at the outset, corporations are not designed as emissaries of justice and the pursuit of justice will often run counter to their basic financial motivation. Still, the picture is far from bleak. Even though multinational firms are not designed to further the cause of international justice, they may nevertheless be able to gradually advance it. At a minimum, it appears that the most deleterious effects of corporate activity are not necessarily as pernicious as many critics claim. Corporations can exploit host countries and peoples; they can capitalize on whatever advantages a location offers to them; and they can chase each other round the globe in a downward spiraling search for more lax regulations and lower costs. Yet they also can eschew all of these activities—not because they find them unsavory, but because it may be in their own best interest to do so. Under some circumstances, corporations may even act to raise global standards. Working either through national governments or private associations, corporations may cooperate to enact tougher environmental standards, bans on child labor and tighter health and safety regulations. While none of these measures can be seen as solving the problem of global justice, they do nevertheless enhance the quality of workers' lives in the developing world. A higher quality of life, though clearly not akin to justice itself, certainly seems a step in the right direction. As a policy issue, of course, the key question is "how?" How can governments prod multinational firms into a race to the top rather than the bottom? How can they compel multinationals to work toward justice rather than against it? Several possibilities emerge from the discussion presented here. First, if governments seriously want to prevent any possibility of a corporate race to the bottom, they simply could close their borders, for without mobility, races are impossible. Clearly, though, such draconian policies are no longer a real option for most national governments since the historical record strongly demonstrates the benefits of open borders and free capital flows. Second, as races thrive only in an environment of policy heterogeneity, steps toward harmonization might reduce the incentives for corporate racing. Though governments may individually be tempted to use lower standards to attract corporate investment, refusing to play the game can yield even greater collective gains.

The dilemma for government policy is that races to the bottom are largely driven by factors inherent in industry structure. Some industries—footwear, apparel and toys, for example—are more likely to engage in this type of behavior than others. If countries explicitly woo these industries, then they should expect, eventually, that they will either be outbid by countries offering even more attractive terms, or that they will progressively have to lower their own standards in order to compete. Not surprisingly, it is also these industries that have witnessed some of the greatest allegations of labor abuse and unjust practices. If countries truly want to end corporate racing (and this, after all, remains an open question), they would be wise to promote investment in other spheres and to resist the temptation of using competitive deregulation as a sustainable policy tool.

Finally, if the arguments laid forth in this paper are correct, then multinationals may hold the most powerful key to their own regulation. To forestall racing to the bottom and enhance the prospects for corporate self-governance, states may want to facilitate a process in which multinationals forge their own common standards. They may wish, for example, to host or encourage intra-industry negotiations, perhaps even conducting these negotiations under governmental auspices. Such has been the case with the U.S. Apparel Industry Partnership, which was launched by (though not controlled by) the U.S. Department of Labor. Governments may also want to keep regulation as an everready possibility, since a concern for impending formal regulation seems often to coalesce industry interest in informal self-regulation.

Lastly, if governments wish to push corporations toward higher standards and a concern for social issues, then they should focus on maintaining freedom of expression and an active civic debate. What often drives corporations toward higher standards is pressure from public voices and concerned shareholders.

The Responsible Care initiative sprang from public outrage at the Bhopal disaster; the Apparel Industry Partnership formed after media revelations of sweatshop labor and abusive conditions, and Shell became an active participant in a series of social and environmental programs after suffering repeated attacks over its activities in Nigeria and the North Sea. Some corporations, admittedly, will choose to pursue social goals and international justice simply because they care to do so. The bulk, however, need to see how concern for these issues (or lack of concern) can affect their bottom lines. Public pressure is a blunt instrument in this direction.

Ultimately, it is unrealistic to expect that corporations will be leaders in the pursuit of international economic justice. Yet corporations are neither an impediment to justice nor an irrelevant instrument in its pursuit. Under certain conditions and with the prodding of concerned voices in both the public and private arenas, multinational enterprises may be surprisingly forceful means for pushing global standards to a higher, and more just, plateau.

ENDNOTES

1. This definition is given by the United Nations Development Programme, *Human Development Report 1990*, http://www.undp.org/undp/hdro/e90over.htm (1 December 1998).
2. Terry Collingsworth, J. William Goold and Pharis J. Harvey, "Labor and Free Trade: Time for a Global New Deal," *Foreign Affairs*, 73, no. 1 (January/February 1994) p. 9.
3. Ibid.
4. See John Gerard Ruggie, "At Home Abroad, Abroad at Home: International Liberalisation and Domestic Stability in the New World Economy," *Millenium*, 24, no. 3 (1995) pp. 507–526; Steven Gill, "Globalisation, Market Civilisation and Disciplinary Neoliberalism," ibid., pp. 399–423; James Rosenau, "Sovereignty in a Turbulent World," in *Beyond Westphalia? State Sovereignty and International Intervention*, ed. Gene M. Lyons and Michael Mastanduno (Baltimore, MD: Johns Hopkins University Press, 1995) pp. 191–227; Robert Jackson, *Quasi-States: Sovereignty, International Relations and the Third World* (Cambridge: Cambridge University Press, 1990); and Susan Strange, *The Retreat of the State: The Diffusion of Power in the World Economy* (Cambridge: Cambridge University Press, 1996).
5. Philip Cerny, "Globalization and the Changing Logic of Collective Action," *International Organization*, 49, no. 4 (Autumn 1995) p. 610.
6. Richard Falk, "State of Siege: Will Globalization Win Out?" *International Affairs*, 73, no. 1 (January 1997) p. 125.
7. See Paul Q. Hirst and Grahame Thompson, *Globalisation in Question: The International Economy and the Possibilities of Governance* (Cambridge, England: Polity Press, 1996).
8. See Dani Rodrik, *Labour Standards and International Trade: Moving Beyond the Rhetoric* (Washington, DC: Institute for International Economics, 1995); Ethan B. Kapstein, "Workers and the World Economy," *Foreign Affairs*, 75, no. 3 (May/June 1996) pp. 16–37; Adrian Wood, *North-South Trade, Employment and Inequality: Changing Fortunes in a Skill-Driven World* (New York: Oxford University Press, 1994); Richard B. Du Boff, "Globalization and Wages: The Down Escalator," *Dollars and Sense*, no. 213 (September/October 1997) pp. 36–40; and Werner Sengenberger, "Local Development and International Economic Competition," *International Labour Review*, 132, no. 3 (1993) pp. 313–329.

9. Eric Bond and Larry Samuelson, "Strategic Behavior and Rules for International Taxation of Capital," *Economic Journal*, 99, no. 398 (December 1989) pp. 1099–1111; Herman E. Daly, "The Perils of Free Trade," *Scientific American*, 269, no. 5 (November 1993) pp. 24–29. See also Arik Levinson, "Environmental Regulations and Industry Location: International and Domestic Evidence," in *Fair Trade and Harmonization: Prerequisites for Free Trade*, ed. Jagdish Bhagwati and Robert E. Hudec (Cambridge: The MIT Press, 1996) pp. 429–457; and H. Jeffrey Leonard, *Pollution and The Struggle for World Product* (Cambridge: Cambridge University Press, 1988).

10. See Eddy Lee, "Globalization and Labour Standards: A Review of Issues," *International Labour Review*, 136, no. 2 (Summer 1997) pp. 173–189; Maureen Cropper and Wallace Oates, "Environmental Economics: A Survey," *Journal of Economic Literature*, 30, no. 2 (June 1992) pp. 675–740; and Charles S. Pearson, "Environmental Standards, Industrial Relocation, and Pollution Havens," in *Multinational Corporations, Environment, and the Third World: Business Matters*, ed. Charles S. Pearson (Durham, NC: Duke University Press, 1987) pp. 113–128.

11. See Cletis Coughlin, Joseph V. Terza and Vachira Arromdee, "State Characteristics and the Location of Foreign Direct Investment Within the United States," *Review of Economics and Statistics*, 73, no. 4 (November 1991) pp. 675–683; Timothy J. Bartik, "Business Location Decisions in the United States: Estimates of the Effects of Unionization, Taxes, and Other Characteristics of States," *Journal of Business and Economic Statistics*, 3, no. I (January 1985) pp. 14–22; Richard B. Freeman, "Comments," in *Labor Markets and Integrating National Economies*, ed. Ronald G. Ehrenberg (Washington, DC: The Brookings Institution, 1994) pp. 107–110; G. Knogden, "Environment and Industrial Siting," *Zeitschrift fur Umweltpolitik* (December 1979); and Gene M. Grossman and Alan B. Krueger, "Environmental Impacts of a North American Free Trade Agreement," Woodrow Wilson School Discussion Papers in Economics, no. 158 (November 1991).

12. David Vogel, *Trading Up: Consumer and Environmental Regulation in a Global Economy* (Cambridge: Harvard University Press, 1995).

13. For a discussion of mobility and its dangers, see Daly, pp. 24–29.

14. William A. Fischel, "Fiscal and Environmental Considerations in the Location of Firms in Suburban Communities," in *Fiscal Zoning and Land Use Controls*, ed. Edwin S. Mills and Wallace Oates (Lexington, MA: DC Heath & Co., 1975) pp. 119–174; and Michelle J. White, "Firm Location in a Zoned Metropolitan Area," in Mills and Oates, eds., pp. 175–201.

15. International Monetary Fund, *Balance of Payment Statistics Yearbook 1997*, Part 2 (Washington, DC: International Monetary Fund, 1998) p. 68.

16. Except, perhaps, to service these markets with lower transportation costs.

17. Joseph Freidman, Daniel A. Gerlowski and Johnathan Silberman, "What Attracts Foreign Multinational Corporations? Evidence From Branch Plant Location in the United States," *Journal of Regional Science*, 32, no. 4 (November 1992) pp. 403–418.

18. H. David Robison, "Who Pays for Industrial Pollution Abatement?" *Review of Economics and Statistics*, 67, no. 4 (November 1985) pp. 702–706; Cropper and Oates, p. 698.

19. For a discussion of sunk costs in multinational investment, see David B. Yoffie, "From Comparative Advantage to Regulated Competition," in *Beyond Free Trade: Firms, Governments, and Global Competition*, ed. David B. Yoffie (Boston: Harvard Business School Press, 1993) pp. 1–25.

20. Robert Wade, "Globalization and its Limits: Reports of the Death of the National Economy are Greatly Exaggerated," in *National Diversity and Global Capitalism*, ed. Suzanne Berger and Ronald Dore (Ithaca, NY: Cornell University Press, 1996) pp. 80–81.

21. Or as Vogel puts it, the "Delaware effect" is replaced by the "California effect." Businesses relocate to Delaware due to its low corporate taxation rate, while California's stringent environmental regulations raise the standards of regulation across the country. Vogel, pp. 5–6.

22. For more on Rousseau's idea of the stag hunt, see R. Harrison Wagner, "The Theory of Games and the Problem of International Cooperation," *American Political Science Review*, 77, no. 2 (June 1993) pp. 330–346.

23. See Debora L. Spar, *The Cooperative Edge: The Internal Politics of International Cartels* (Ithaca, NY: Cornell University Press, 1994); and Jock A. Finlayson and Mark W. Zacher, *Managing International Markets: Developing Countries and the Commodity Trade Regime* (New York: Columbia University Press, 1988).

24. Against this point, Paul Krugman argues that the case for free trade is a unilateral one. Regardless of other states' policies, he suggests, a single state always gains from trade liberalization. See Paul Krugman, "What Should Trade Negotiators Negotiate About?" *Journal of Economic Literature*, 35, no. 1 (March 1997) pp. 113–120. Jagdish Bhagwati also opposes common labor standards, though along different lines of reasoning. See Jagdish Bhagwati, "Policy Perspectives and Future Directions: A View From Academia," *Proceedings of a Symposium, United States Department of Labor, International Labor Standards and Global Economic Integration* (Washington, DC: Department of Labor, Bureau of International Labor Affairs, July 1994) pp. 57–62.

25. For an opposing viewpoint, see Alvin K. Klevorick, "Reflections on the Race to the Bottom," in Bhagwati and Hudec, eds., pp. 459–467.

26. For more on this relationship, see James Alt, Randall Calvert and Brian D. Humes, "Reputation and Hegemonic Stability: A Game Theoretical Analysis," *American Political Science Review*, 82, no. 2 (June 1988) pp. 445–466; Spar (1994).

27. See Yoffie, pp. 1–25.

28. See Raymond Vernon, Debora L. Spar and Glenn Tobin, *Iron Triangles and Revolving Doors: Cases in U.S. Foreign Economic Policymaking* (New York: Praeger, 1991) pp. 129–157.

29. See Peter J. Spiro, "New Global Communities: Nongovernmental Organizations in International Decision-Making Institutions," *Washington Quarterly*, 18, no.1 (Winter 1995) pp. 45–56; and Lester M. Salamon, "The Rise of the Nonprofit Sector," *Foreign Affairs*, 73, no. 4 (July/August 1994) pp. 109–122. For an argument that these concerns are linked solely to organized labor's disguised desire for protection, see International Labor Organization, *Extracts From Statements Made at the Ministerial Conference of the World Trade Organization*, Singapore: 9–13 December 1996 (Geneva: International Labor Organization, 1997).

30. Forest L. Reinhardt, "Business and the Environment," forthcoming manuscript (Boston: Harvard Business School Press, 1999) pp. 3–12.

31. M. Baram, "Multinational Corporations, Private Codes, and Technology Transfer for Sustainable Development," *Environmental Law*, 24 (1994) pp. 33–65.

32. David Victor, "The Operation and Effectiveness of the Montreal Protocol's NonCompliance Procedure," in *The Implementation and Effectiveness of International Commitments: Theory and Practice*, ed. David Victor, Kal Rustilia and Eugene B. Sholnikoff (Cambridge: MIT Press, 1998) pp. 137–176.

33. Steven Greenhouse, "Sporting Goods Concerns Agree to Combat Sale of Soccer Balls Made by Children," *New York Times*, 14 February 1997, p. A12.

34. Debora L. Spar, "The Spotlight and the Bottom Line," *Foreign Affairs*, 77, no. 2 (March/April 1998) pp. 7–12; and Michael Posner and Lynda Clarizio, An Unprecedented Step in the Effort to End Sweatshops," *Human Rights*, 24, no. 4 (Fall 1997) p. 14.

35. Hugh Williamson, "Stamp of Approval," *Far Eastern Economic Review*, 158, no. 5 (2 February 1995) p. 26.

36. For more on the provisions of SA8000, see Pamela Sebastian, "A Special Background Report on Trends in Industry and Finance," *Wall Street Journal*, 16 July 1998, p. Al; and Aaron Bernstein, "Sweatshop Police," *Business Week* (20 October 1997) p. 39.

37. Richard Freeman also suggests that private standards are more market-friendly, since they essentially allow consumers to determine which standards they deem acceptable. See Richard Freeman, "A Hard-headed Look at Labor Standards," in *International Labour Standards and Economic Interdependence*, ed. Werner Sengenberger and Duncan Campbell (Geneva: International Institute for Labor Studies, 1994) pp. 79–92.

38. See Victor; for an opposing argument, see Baram, pp. 33–65.

39. W. Douglas Ellis Jr., CEO of Southern Mills, Inc., cited in Paul Magnusson, De'Ann Weimer and Nicole Harris, "Clinton's Trade Crusade," *Business Week* (8 June 1998) p. 35.

Bottom Feeders

DANIEL W. DREZNER

The "race to the bottom" in global labor and environmental standards has captivated journalists, politicians, and activists worldwide. Why does this myth persist? Because it is a useful scare tactic for multinational corporations and populist agitators peddling their policy wares.

The current debates over economic globalization have produced a seemingly simple and intuitive conclusion: Unfettered globalization triggers an unavoidable "race to the bottom" in labor and environmental standards around the world. The reduction of restrictions on trade and cross-border investment frees corporations to scour the globe for the country or region where they can earn the highest return. National policies such as strict labor laws or rigorous environmental protections lower profits by raising the costs of production. Multinational corporations will therefore engage in regulatory arbitrage, moving to countries with lax standards. Fearing a loss of their tax base, nation-states have little choice but to loosen their regulations to encourage foreign investment and avoid capital flight. The inevitable result: a Darwinian struggle for capital where all other values—including workers' rights and the environment—are sacrificed upon the altar of global commerce.

The fear of such a race to the bottom has helped forge an unlikely coalition of union leaders, environmentalists, and consumer groups; together, they have spearheaded significant public resistance to several recent international economic initiatives. These include the North American Free Trade Agreement (NAFTA), the abortive Multilateral Agreement on Investment (MAI), the 1999 World Trade Organization (WTO) talks in Seattle, China's admission into the WTO, and the African Growth and Opportunity Act that U.S. President Bill Clinton signed into law last May. In each instance, protestors argued that unless globalization is reversed or at least slowed, a race to the bottom is inevitable.

At the opposite end of the political spectrum, the rhetoric and goals may differ, but the underlying imagery remains the same. Pro-market politicians and multinational corporations also cultivate the idea of an unstoppable global race—except they do so in order to advance environmental deregulation and "flexible" labor legislation that otherwise would become ensnared in fractious political debates. Multinational corporations argue that the pressures of the global marketplace force them to relocate or outsource their production to lower-cost facilities in poor nations.

The race-to-the-bottom hypothesis appears logical. But it is wrong. Indeed, the lack of supporting evidence is startling. Essayists usually mention an anecdote

From Daniel W. Drezner, "Bottom Feeders," *Foreign Policy* 121, November/December 2000, pp. 64–70. © 2000 *Foreign Policy*. Reproduced with permission of *Foreign Policy* in the format Textbook via Copyright Clearance Center.

or two about firms moving from an advanced to a developing economy and then, depending on their political stripes, extrapolate visions of healthy international competition or impending environmental doom. However, there is no indication that the reduction of controls on trade and capital flows has forced a generalized downgrading in labor or environmental conditions. If anything, the opposite has occurred.

Given this dearth of evidence, why does the race to the bottom persist in policy debates? Because the image is politically useful for both pro- and antiglobalization forces. Unfortunately, by perpetuating the belief in a nonexistent threat, all sides contribute to a misunderstanding of both the effects of globalization and how governments in developing and advanced economies should—or should not—respond.

RUNNING IN PLACE

If economic globalization really does trigger a race to the bottom in regulatory standards, two trends should be evident. First, countries that are more open to trade and investment should have fewer and less demanding regulations affecting corporate production costs. Once barriers to trade and investment are lowered, the logic goes, nation-states must eliminate burdensome regulations or risk massive capital flight. Over time, therefore, more open economies should display lower labor and environmental standards. Second, multinational corporations should flock to countries with the lowest regulatory standards. The core of the race-to-the-bottom hypothesis is that profit-maximizing firms will locate to places where the production costs are relatively low. Since any regulatory standard presumably raises these costs, corporations will seek out countries with the weakest possible standards.

These predicted trends are, in fact, nonexistent. Consider labor standards. There is no real evidence that economic openness leads to the degradation of workers. In fact, some evidence suggests that openness actually improves worker standards. A comprehensive 1996 study by the Organisation for Economic Co-operation and Development (OECD) found that "successfully sustained trade reforms" were linked to improvements in core labor standards, defined as nondiscrimination in the workplace, the right to unionize, and the prohibition of forced labor and exploitative child labor. This linkage occurs because multinationals often pay higher-than-average wages in developing countries in order to recruit better workers. Moreover, since corporations have learned to work efficiently under rigorous regulatory standards in their home countries, they favor improving standards in their foreign production sites in order to gain a competitive advantage over local competitors, who are not accustomed to operating under such conditions. A recent World Bank survey of 3,800 workers in 12 Nike factories in Thailand and Vietnam found that 72 percent of Thai workers were satisfied with their overall income levels, while a majority of Vietnamese workers preferred factory employment over lower-wage jobs in their country's agricultural sector.

The case of export processing zones (EPZs) in developing economies underscores the spuriousness of the race-to-the-bottom argument. EPZs are areas established in order to attract foreign investment. Typically, governments entice investors into EPZs with infrastructure investment and duty-free imports and exports. There are more than 850 export processing zones worldwide, employing some 27 million workers; in some developing nations, like Mauritius, EPZs account for a majority of a country's exports. If there is a race to the bottom in labor standards, it should be particularly evident in EPZs.

There are a few countries, such as Bangladesh and Zimbabwe, that have attempted to preempt competitive pressures by exempting their EPZs from regulations covering labor standards. However, contrary to the race-to-the-bottom hypothesis, such policies have not compelled other countries to relax labor standards in their own EPZs. Indeed, several nations, including the Dominican Republic and the Philippines, actually reversed course in the mid-1990s and established labor standards in their EPZs when none previously existed. A 1998 International Labour Organization report found no evidence that countries with a strong trade-union presence suffered any loss of investment in their EPZs, while a 1997 World Bank study noted a strong positive correlation between higher occupational safety and health conditions and foreign investment in EPZs. Analysts also have found that wages in EPZs actually tend to exceed average wages elsewhere in the host country.

Similarly, openness to trade and investment does not lead to a race to the bottom in environmental conditions or regulations. Countries most open to outside investment—OECD nations—also have the most stringent environmental regulations. Even developing countries such as Malaysia, the Philippines, Thailand, Argentina, and Brazil have liberalized their foreign investment laws while simultaneously tightening environmental regulations. In Latin America, there is clear evidence that more protectionist countries, such as pre-NAFTA Mexico and Brazil under military rule, have been the biggest polluters. This finding is hardly surprising; the most protectionist economies in this century—the Warsaw Pact bloc—displayed the least concern for the environment. Privatization programs in these countries, which help attract foreign direct investment, have contributed to improved environmental performance as multinational corporations have transferred cleaner technologies from the developed world. In Brazil, for instance, the privatization of the petrochemicals sector in the early 1990s led to a greater acceptance of environmentally safe practices.

Race-to-the-bottom critics counter that stringent labor and environmental standards in developing economies are backed by purely nominal enforcement capabilities. Although it is difficult to quantify compliance and enforcement in developing economies, the emergence of watchdog groups—analogous to election observers and human rights organizations—that scrutinize the enforcement of national labor and environmental legislation is a positive development. The United States has recently pursued this strategy by bolstering the role of the International Labour Organization in monitoring core labor standards around the world. And even in the absence of uniform national enforcement, many multinational corporations have embraced self-monitoring programs for the environment—an effective complement to government regulations.

Perhaps most damaging to the race-to-the-bottom proponents, there is no evidence that corporations direct their investment to developing countries with lower labor or environmental standards. Indeed, the relationship between foreign direct investment (FDI) and labor standards is strongly positive. During the 1990s, an overwhelming majority of global FDI was directed toward advanced economies (which tend to have higher labor standards), not to poor nations. A similar story can be told with environmental standards. Comparing data on U.S. FDI in developed and developing countries reveals that pollution-intensive U.S. firms tend to invest in countries with stricter environmental standards.

Profit-maximizing corporations invest in countries with high labor and environmental standards not out of a sense of obligation, but for hard-nosed business reasons. Consumption has gone global along with production; many firms base their investment decisions not just on likely production costs but also on access to sizable markets. A 1994 survey by the U.S. Department of Commerce found that more than 60 percent of the production of U.S. corporate affiliates in developing countries was sold in the host country and less than 20 percent was exported back to the United States. In Mexico, which provides an ideal platform for reexporting to the United States, only 28 percent of production by U.S. affiliates made it back to the United States; more than two thirds was marketed in Mexico. The great fear of the race-to-the-bottom crowd—that U.S. multinationals will locate production facilities in developing countries, exploit local resources, and reexport back to the United States—has not materialized. In fact, that type of activity characterizes less than 4 percent of total U.S. investment abroad. The oft-cited cases of garment facilities based in poor nations and geared to consumers in advanced economies are the exception, not the rule. This exception is largely due to the low capital investment and importance of labor costs in the textiles sector.

Since corporations invest overseas to tap into new, large markets, host countries actually wield considerable power. They can use that power to resist deregulatory pressures. Multinational corporations have invested large sums in China despite formidable regulatory hurdles, a blatant disregard for copyright laws, high levels of corruption, and strict requirements for technology transfers. The prospect of 1 billion consumers will cause that kind of behavior among chief executive officers. Mexico has enhanced its environmental protection efforts while trying to attract investment. The result? Foreign direct investment around Mexico City has exploded, while the air quality has actually improved.

Multinational firms are also well aware of the growing link between public opinion and profits. Increasingly, citizens care about the conditions under which their products are manufactured—an environmental or labor mishap can cripple a corporation's brand name. Thus, foreign investors in Costa Rican bananas or Asian lumber insist on higher standards than the local government in order to cater to environmentally savvy European consumers. And PepsiCo pulled out of Myanmar in 1997 because it did not want to be linked to that country's repressive regime. To be sure, some multinational corporations are hardly paragons of labor or environmental virtue, as the perilous labor conditions at Royal Dutch Shell and Chevron's operations in Nigeria make clear. But in general, corporations understand that it is smart business to stay in the good graces of their customers.

The lack of evidence for a race to the bottom is not surprising when put in historical perspective. In the late 19th century, there was an enormous increase in flows of capital, goods, and labor among countries in the Atlantic basin. On several dimensions, such as labor mobility and investment flows, the degree of market integration 100 years ago is much greater than today. Despite claims made at the time that these trends would lead to a world ruled by social Darwinism, the United States and Europe created national regulatory standards for consumer safety, labor, and the environment and developed regional institutions (including a predecessor to the European Central Bank) to cope with the vicissitudes of financial markets. Indeed, globalization does not eliminate the ability of sovereign states to make independent regulatory decisions. Nor does globalization render governments impervious to the preferences of their own citizens. Even authoritarian countries are not immune to public pressure; the beginning of the end of the Soviet bloc saw environmental protests against rising levels of pollution. Governments, particularly in democratic countries, must respond not only to domestic and foreign firms but also to the wishes of citizens who prefer stricter regulatory standards.

THE SCAPEGOAT FACTORY

Of course, one can hardly dispute that developing countries often display deplorable environmental and labor standards and conditions, far below those in the world's advanced economies. But the evidence thus far indicates that globalization itself does not cause or aggravate this disparity. If anything, the opposite is true. So why do so many people seem to believe in a hypothesis that has yet to attract any evidence? Because the myth is politically convenient for all sides. Nongovernmental organizations (NGOs), corporations, politicians, and academics use the race to the bottom as an excuse to peddle their policy wares.

Opponents of globalization—including environmentalists, labor unions, and a multitude of NGOs—advance the myth of a race to the bottom to oppose further global market integration. The race to the bottom is a wonderful rallying tool for fundraising and coalition building and also serves as the perfect bogeyman, allowing these groups to use scare tactics derived from previous domestic policy campaigns against nuclear power and acid rain. Such strategies are consistent with a pattern of exaggerating dangers to capture the attention of the press and the public: Only by crying that the sky is falling can antiglobalization forces rouse complacent citizens. For example, Public Citizen, one of the most vocal NGOs on trade issues, has argued that steps toward economic liberalization will have devastating social effects. Its Web site notes that the Multilateral Agreement on Investment would have "hasten[ed] the 'race to the bottom,' wherein countries are pressured to lower living standards and weaken regulatory regimes in an effort to attract needed investment capital." Whatever shortcomings the MAI may have displayed, it demanded discerning criticism, not knee-jerk attacks based on spurious reasoning.

The race to the bottom also provides a useful scapegoat for larger trends that adversely affect specific interest groups, such as labor unions. A recent statement by Philip Jennings, general secretary of the Geneva-based Union Network International, which represents more than 900 unions in 140 countries, provides an apt example. "Globalization is not working for working people," Jennings declared in

July 2000. "It needs a human face." Similarly, union leaders in the United States have argued that globalization and the race to the bottom are responsible for the 30-year stagnation in the median real wages and the growing income inequality in the United States. Such simplistic views disregard other key factors—particularly advances in technology and the subsequent demand for high-skilled labor—affecting wage and employment levels. If, as race-to-the-bottom proponents suggest, U.S. workers are being replaced by their counterparts in developing economies, then the 2.6 million employees laid off by manufacturing multinationals in the United States over the past three decades were replaced with a mere 300,000 workers hired in developing nations over the same period. In other words, Third World laborers would have to be nearly nine times as productive as those in the United States—hardly a persuasive proposition. In fact, the U.S. labor force displays the highest productivity levels in the world.

The race-to-the-bottom myth also helps pro-globalization forces sell deregulatory policies that may result in short-term economic pain. But rather than take the responsibility of pushing for deregulation directly, advocates invoke globalization as an excuse. It does not matter whether one favors deregulation or not; globalization will punish those who fail to deregulate, so there is little choice in the matter. For example, Pacific Telesis (now part of SBC Communications) used globalization as an excuse for cutbacks and layoffs in its San Francisco offices and to lobby Washington for deregulation. Unocal has argued that because of the competitive pressures of globalization, it should not be forced by U.S. sanctions to pull out of Myanmar.

Politicians also exploit the need to compete in the global marketplace and the myth of a race to the bottom as excuses to support policies that would otherwise trigger fierce public debate. State governments in the United States have often claimed that widespread deregulation must occur in order to attract capital. Meanwhile, European politicians trotted out the specter of globalization to justify the Maastricht criteria, a series of stringent economic prerequisites for a European monetary union. It was a clever tactic; governments across the European Union were able to push through deregulation and painful spending cuts without an overwhelming electoral backlash.

Perhaps the most potent reason for deploying the race-to-the-bottom myth is the psychological effect it has on individuals. By depicting a world without choices, the race to the bottom taps into the primal fear of a loss of control. Governments and citizens appear powerless in a world dominated by faceless, passionless capital flows. This perceived lack of control prompts unease for the same reason that many people prefer driving a car to flying in an airplane even though the latter is safer: Even if driving is riskier, at least we are behind the steering wheel.

A DURABLE MYTH

In his 1996 book *Jihad vs. McWorld*, Benjamin Barber warned that, by empowering owners of capital and disenfranchising voters, globalization would threaten democratic practices. Democracy may indeed be at risk, but not for the reasons Barber suggested. Globalization itself will not necessarily weaken democracy, but the rhetoric surrounding globalization may have that effect. If protestors persist in the indiscriminate trashing of multilateral institutions, they will only undermine the legitimacy of the mechanisms that democratic governments have established to deal with the very problems that concern them. And if enough leaders claim that globalization is an unstoppable trend demanding specific and formulaic policy responses, ordinary citizens will lose interest in a wide range of policy debates, believing their outcomes to be foregone conclusions determined by economic forces beyond their comprehension and control.

Can the race-to-the-bottom myth be debunked? In time, perhaps. As facts continue to contradict fiction, the claim will become untenable, much as the notion of Japan's global economic superiority died down by the mid-1990s. Ironically, some of the strongest voices speaking against the race-to-the-bottom myth emanate from the very developing countries that antiglobalization forces purport to defend. In a speech before the World Economic Forum in January 2000, Mexican President Ernesto Zedillo charged that antitrade activists wanted to save developing countries . . . from development. Even in Malaysia, where Prime Minister Mahathir Mohamad has become notorious for his diatribes against currency traders and global capitalism, the Federation of Malaysian Manufacturers recently stated that globalization and liberalization should be viewed "with an open mind and [in] an objective and rational manner." And economist Jagdish Bhagwati of Columbia University is spearheading the Academic Consortium on International Trade, a group of academic economists and lawyers arguing that the antisweatshop campaigns currently underway at several U.S. universities will only "worsen the collective welfare of the very workers in poor countries who are supposed to be helped."

Unfortunately, bad economics is often the cornerstone of good politics. The belief in a race to the bottom has helped cement an unwieldy coalition of interests and has enhanced the influence of antiglobalization activists both inside the corridors of power and in the mind of public opinion. Myths persist because they are useful; there is little incentive to abandon the race to the bottom now, even though there is no evidence to support it.

For those who wish to deepen the process of globalization, however, the implications are troubling. Historically, bouts of protectionism have occurred primarily during global economic downturns. But the rhetoric of a race to the bottom has gained adherents during a time of relative prosperity. If the current era has produced so many challenges for continued economic openness, what will happen when the economy hits the next speed bump? The image of a race to the bottom will likely endure in global policy debates well into the new century.

QUESTIONS FOR REVIEW AND DISCUSSION

1. According to Spar and Yoffie, under what conditions are we most and least likely to see a race-to-the-bottom dynamic? Can you think of specific industries that meet these most- and least-likely conditions?
2. What do Spar and Yoffie mean by the "race to the top"? Under what conditions are we likely to see such a race?

3. According to Spar and Yoffie, what role can private corporate self-regulation play in the contemporary global economy? What examples do they provide of such regulation? Do you believe that self-regulation is sufficient to manage MNC activities in the global economy? Why or why not?

4. Why does Drezner believe that the race to the bottom is a "myth"? Why does he believe that the argument retains currency despite its being a myth?

5. Do you believe that a race-to-the-bottom dynamic does exist in the contemporary global economy? Why or why not?

6. Assuming that a race-to-the-bottom dynamic does exist, what is the appropriate policy response? That is, should the race be allowed to proceed unchecked, or should national governments be encouraged to take steps to restrain it? If the latter, what steps should or could be taken?

SUGGESTIONS FOR FURTHER READING

There is a voluminous literature on MNCs. Three books provide excellent, detailed introductions to the general theories and issues: Richard E. Caves. *Multinational Enterprise and Economic Analysis*. New York: Cambridge University Press, 1996; John H. Dunning. *The Theory of Transnational Corporations*. London: Routledge, 1993; and Raymond Vernon. *In the Hurricane's Eye: The Troubled Prospects of Multinational Enterprises*. Cambridge: Harvard University Press, 1998.

Two accounts that are highly critical of the role of MNCs in the global economy are Alan Tonelson's *The Race to the Bottom: Why a Worldwide Worker Surplus and Uncontrolled Free Trade are Sinking American Living Standards*. Boulder: Westview Press, 2002; and David C. Korten's *When Corporations Rule the World*, 2nd edition. Bloomfield, CT: Kumarian Press and San Francisco: Berrett-Koehler Publishers, 2001. A more positive view is offered by John Micklethwait and Adrian Wooldridge in *A Future Perfect: the Challenge and Promise of Globalization*. New York: Random House, 2003.

David Vogel has written perhaps the most widely cited book about racing to the bottom and top. See: David Vogel. *Trading Up: Consumer and Environmental Regulation in a Global Economy*. Cambridge: Harvard University Press, 1995. For a more recent investigation, see the contributions in David Vogel and Robert Kagan, eds. *The Dynamics of Regulatory Change: How Globalization Affects National Regulatory Policies*. Berkeley: University of California Press, 2004.

CHAPTER 9
◖ MULTINATIONAL CORPORATIONS AND SWEATSHOPS

As American and European multinational corporations move manufacturing production to developing countries, they faced mounting home-country criticism about working conditions in developing-country factories. MNCs that hire developing-country workers to produce the goods they sell, or that contract with developing-country firms to produce for them, are often accused of running "sweatshops." While there is disagreement about what, exactly, a sweatshop is, an accepted definition is a manufacturing facility that requires its workers to work long hours for low wages, often in unsafe conditions. Researchers have documented many such practices in factories located in developing countries (see Graham 2000, pp. 99–104). Wages for the typical developing-country employee are quite low; sewers employed in the apparel industry in Bangladesh, for example, are paid only 12 to 18 cents per hour (National Labor Committee 2001). Long hours are also common; workers in an Indonesian factory that produces shoes for Nike, for example, worked 11 hours per day, seven days a week (Connor 2002, p. 20). Conditions are often unsafe; workers in a Chinese toy factory, for example, reported being exposed to chemical odors and paint dust that caused persistent headaches, dizziness, stomach aches, and nausea (The National Labor Committee 2002, p. 17).

MNCs, which sometimes own the factories but more often have contractual agreements with the factories, get the blame for these working conditions, all of which are substandard in comparison to conditions in the United States and the European Union.

No one has yet conducted an extensive and systematic survey to determine how many sweatshops exist. In the absence of a comprehensive study, we must rely on a body of somewhat anecdotal evidence compiled by individual researchers. This evidence suggests two conclusions. First, sweatshops appear to be concentrated in a limited number of labor-intensive manufacturing industries, particularly in footwear, apparel, toy making, and sporting goods (Graham 2000, p. 101). Second, sweatshop conditions appear to be more common in locally owned firms than in the affiliates of multinational corporations. According to the United Nations Conference on Trade and Development, "large well-established and visible MNCs are likely to comply with international standards and not to undercut the labor standards of their host (and home) countries. They adhere to minimum wage, working hours, overtime, and compensation regulations" (UNCTAD 1999). Critics point out, however, that the claim that MNCs behave better than locally owned firms is somewhat misleading, because locally owned firms often produce for MNCs under exclusive contract. MNCs consequently bear some responsibility for the conditions in locally owned factories.

What, if anything, should be done about sweatshops? Should governments negotiate and enforce global labor standards that would make it more difficult to run sweatshops? If so, should such standards be made part of the WTO? Currently, international labor standards fall under the authority of the International Labor Organization (ILO), an international organization created in 1919 as part of the League of Nations. During the 1990s the ILO developed, and its member governments adopted, a "Declaration on the Fundamental Principles and Rights at Work." This declaration requires ILO members to "respect and promote principles and rights in four categories." Often called "Core Labor Standards," the four categories are: freedom of association and the right to collective bargaining; the elimination of forced and compulsory labor; the abolition of child labor; and the elimination of discrimination in the workplace. Many in the antisweatshop movement would like to see these core standards expanded to include international regulation of pay and workplace conditions (see, for example, Scholars Against Sweatshop Labor 2001).

Critics of sweatshops, including labor unions based in the advanced industrialized world and most nongovernmental organizations active in the antiglobalization movement, also want governments to make labor standards an integral part of the WTO and regional trade arrangements. The desire to shift labor standards from the ILO to the WTO is based on the relative ability of these two organizations to enforce compliance with standards. The ILO has no mechanism through which to enforce compliance with labor standards. Consequently, compliance with these standards is largely voluntary. If labor standards were brought into the WTO, governments could use the organization's dispute-settlement mechanism to enforce compliance. Advocates of such a shift argue that this would give the labor standards greater import, as governments that refused to comply with standards would face higher barriers to trade.

Many developing-country governments, as well as many academic economists, have criticized the effort to link trade with labor standards, and are especially wary of the attempt to bring these standards into the WTO. Many developing-country governments believe that the link between trade and labor standards represents a new form of protectionism in the advanced industrialized countries. As Martin Khor, the Director of the Third World Network (and a prominent critic of many other aspects of globalization), has argued, "developing countries fear that the objectives of the northern and the international trade unions, and of the developed country governments that back [the push for core labor standards] are mainly protectionist in nature, that they want to protect jobs in the North by reducing the low-cost incentive that attracts global corporations to the developing countries" (Khor 1999). Many economists also think the link is ill-conceived, primarily because they believe that low-cost labor is the principal advantage that developing countries have, and efforts to force higher standards would diminish this advantage. Eliminating or reducing this labor-cost advantage would make it more difficult for developing countries to raise incomes.

The two articles presented in this chapter reflect these distinct perspectives on sweatshops and global labor standards. Paul Krugman, a prominent economist who teaches at Princeton University, argues that the concern about sweatshops is misplaced. He suggests that rather than lament sweatshops, we should recognize that they represent a positive step on the path of economic development. Working in such factories may not be pleasant, and the wages may not be high by American or European standards, but the jobs available in these factories are better than any of the other alternatives. Krugman argues that sweatshop conditions will eventually disappear as developing-country economies transition from low-skill labor-intensive industries toward more skill- and capital-intensive manufacturing. Moreover, he argues that instituting global labor standards in an attempt to improve conditions in these factories will not help. Rather than improving conditions, such standards will merely reduce the number of better-paying jobs that are available to developing-country workers.

John Miller, who teaches economics at Wheaton College, argues that mainstream economists like Krugman are wrong. He claims that available evidence does not suggest that global labor standards will reduce the number of manufacturing jobs available in developing countries. Nor does he believe that sweatshops will disappear as a natural consequence of economic development. Sweatshops will disappear only if governments use regulation, both national and global, to eliminate them.

REFERENCES

Connor, Timothy. "We Are Not Machines: Indonesian Nike and Adidas Workers." 2002. http://www.maquilasolidarity.org/campaigns/nike/pdf/Wearenotmachines.pdf

Graham, Edward M. *Fighting the Wrong Enemy: Antiglobal Activities and Multinational Enterprises*. Washington, DC: Institute for International Economics, 2000.

ILO. "What are International Labor Standards?" http://www.ilo.org/public/english/standards /norm/whatare/index.htm (accessed February 5, 2004).

Khor, Martin. "How the South is Getting a Raw Deal at the WTO." In *Views from the South: The Effects of Globalization and the WTO on the Third World*, edited by Sarah Anderson. San Francisco: International Forum on Globalization, 1999, pp. 41–49.

National Labor Committee. "Toys of Misery 2004," *A Joint Report by National Labor Committee and China Labor Watch* (February 2004) http://www.nlcnet.org/campaigns/ he-yi/he-yi.opt2.pdf (accessed June 23, 2004).

National Labor Committee. *Bangladesh: Ending the Race to the Bottom*. 2001. http://www.nlcnet.org/campaigns/shahmakhdum/1001/index.shtml (accessed February 5, 2004).

Scholars Against Sweatshop Labor (SASL). "Statement." 2001. http://www.umass.edu/peri /sasl/statement.PDF

United Nations Conference on Trade and Development (UNCTAD). *World Investment Report: Foreign Direct Investment and the Challenge of Development*. Geneva: The United Nations, 1999.

In Praise of Cheap Labor: Bad Jobs at Bad Wages are Better than No Jobs at All

PAUL KRUGMAN

For many years a huge Manila garbage dump known as Smokey Mountain was a favorite media symbol of Third World poverty. Several thousand men, women, and children lived on that dump—enduring the stench, the flies, and the toxic waste in order to make a living combing the garbage for scrap metal and other recyclables. And they lived there voluntarily, because the $10 or so a squatter family could clear in a day was better than the alternatives.

The squatters are gone now, forcibly removed by Philippine police last year as a cosmetic move in advance of a Pacific Rim summit. But I found myself thinking about Smokey Mountain recently, after reading my latest batch of hate mail.

The occasion was an op-ed piece I had written for the *New York Times*, in which I had pointed out that while wages and working conditions in the new export industries of the Third World are appalling, they are a big improvement over the "previous, less visible rural poverty." I guess I should have expected that this comment would generate letters along the lines of, "Well, if you lose your comfortable position as an American professor you can always find another job—as long as you are 12 years old and willing to work for 40 cents an hour."

Such moral outrage is common among the opponents of globalization—of the transfer of technology and capital from high-wage to low-wage countries and the resulting growth of labor-intensive Third World exports. These critics take it as a given that anyone with a good word for this process is naive or corrupt and, in either case, a de facto agent of global capital in its oppression of workers here and abroad.

But matters are not that simple, and the moral lines are not that clear. In fact, let me make a counter-accusation: The lofty moral tone of the opponents of globalization is possible only because they have chosen not to think their position through. While fat-cat capitalists might benefit from globalization, the biggest beneficiaries are, yes, Third World workers.

After all, global poverty is not something recently invented for the benefit of multinational corporations. Let's turn the clock back to the Third World as it was only two decades ago (and still is, in many countries). In those days, although the rapid economic growth of a handful of small Asian nations had started to attract attention, developing countries like Indonesia or Bangladesh were still mainly what they had always been: exporters of raw materials, importers of manufactures. Inefficient manufacturing sectors served their domestic markets, sheltered behind import quotas, but generated few jobs. Meanwhile, population pressure pushed desperate peasants into cultivating ever more marginal land or seeking a livelihood in any way possible—such as homesteading on a mountain of garbage.

Given this lack of other opportunities, you could hire workers in Jakarta or Manila for a pittance. But in the mid-'70s, cheap labor was not enough to allow a developing country to compete in world markets for manufactured goods. The entrenched advantages of advanced nations—their infrastructure and technical know-how, the vastly larger size of their markets and their proximity to suppliers of key components, their political stability and the subtle-but-crucial social adaptations that are necessary to operate an efficient economy—seemed to outweigh even a ten-fold or twentyfold disparity in wage rates.

And then something changed. Some combination of factors that we still don't fully understand—lower tariff barriers, improved telecommunications, cheaper air transport—reduced the disadvantages of producing in developing countries. (Other things being the same, it is still better to produce in the First World—stories of companies that moved production to Mexico or East Asia, then moved back after experiencing the disadvantages of the Third World environment, are common.) In a substantial number of industries, low wages allowed developing countries to break into world markets. And so countries that had previously made a living selling jute or coffee started producing shirts and sneakers instead.

Workers in those shirt and sneaker factories are, inevitably, paid very little and expected to endure terrible working conditions. I say "inevitably" because their employers are not in business for their (or their workers') health; they pay as little as possible, and that minimum is determined by the other opportunities available to workers. And these are still extremely poor countries, where living on a garbage heap is attractive compared with the alternatives.

And yet, wherever the new export industries have grown, there has been mea-surable improvement in the lives of ordinary people. Partly this is because a growing industry must offer a somewhat higher wage than workers could get elsewhere in order to get them to move. More importantly, however, the growth of manufactur-ing—and of the penumbra of other jobs that the new export sector creates—has a ripple effect throughout the economy. The pressure on the land becomes less intense, so rural wages rise; the pool of unemployed urban dwellers always anxious for work shrinks, so factories start to compete with each other for workers, and urban wages also begin to rise. Where the process has gone on long enough—say, in South Korea or Taiwan—average wages start to approach what an American teen-ager can earn at McDonald's. And eventually people are no longer eager to live on garbage dumps. (Smokey Mountain persisted because the Philippines, until recently, did not share in the export-led growth of its neighbors. Jobs that pay better than scavenging are still few and far between.)

The benefits of export-led economic growth to the mass of people in the newly industrializing economies are not a matter of conjecture. A country like Indonesia is still so poor that progress can be measured in terms of how much the average person gets to eat; since 1970, per capita intake has risen from less than 2,100 to more than 2,800 calories a day. A shocking one-third of young children are still malnourished—but in 1975, the fraction was more than half. Similar improvements can be seen throughout the Pacific Rim, and even in places like Bangladesh. These improvements have not taken place because well-meaning people in the West have done anything to help—foreign aid, never large, has lately shrunk to virtually nothing. Nor is it the result of the benign policies of national governments, which are as callous and corrupt as ever. It is the indirect and unintended result of the actions of soulless multinationals and rapacious local entrepreneurs, whose only concern was to take advantage of the profit opportunities offered by cheap labor. It is not an edifying spectacle; but no matter how base the motives of those involved, the result has been to move hundreds of millions of people from abject poverty to something still awful but nonetheless significantly better.

Why, then, the outrage of my correspondents? Why does the image of an Indonesian sewing sneakers for 60 cents an hour evoke so much more feeling than the image of another Indonesian earning the equivalent of 30 cents an hour trying to feed his family on a tiny plot of land—or of a Filipino scavenging on a garbage heap?

The main answer, I think, is a sort of fastidiousness. Unlike the starving subsistence farmer, the women and children in the sneaker factory are working at slave wages *for our benefit*—and this makes us feel unclean. And so there are self-righteous demands for international labor standards: We should not, the opponents of globalization insist, be willing to buy those sneakers and shirts unless the people who make them receive decent wages and work under decent conditions.

This sounds only fair—but is it? Let's think through the consequences.

First of all, even if we could assure the workers in Third World export industries of higher wages and better working conditions, this would do nothing for the peasants, day laborers, scavengers, and so on who make up the bulk of these countries' populations. At best, forcing developing countries to adhere to our labor standards would create a privileged labor aristocracy, leaving the poor majority no better off.

And it might not even do that. The advantages of established First World industries are still formidable. The only reason developing countries have been able to compete with those industries is their ability to offer employers cheap labor. Deny them that ability, and you might well deny them the prospect of continuing industrial growth, even reverse the growth that has been achieved. And since export-oriented growth, for all its injustice, has been a huge boon for the workers in those nations, anything that curtails that growth is very much against their interests. A policy of good jobs in principle, but no jobs in practice, might assuage our consciences, but it is no favor to its alleged beneficiaries.

You may say that the wretched of the earth should not be forced to serve as hewers of wood, drawers of water, and sewers of sneakers for the affluent. But what is the alternative? Should they be helped with foreign aid? Maybe—although the historical record of regions like southern Italy suggests that such aid has a tendency to promote perpetual dependence. Anyway, there isn't the slightest prospect of significant aid materializing. Should their own governments provide more social justice? Of course—but they won't, or at least not because we tell them to. And as long as you have no realistic alternative to industrialization based on low wages, to oppose it means that you are willing to deny desperately poor people the best chance they have of progress for the sake of what amounts to an aesthetic standard—that is, the fact that you don't like the idea of workers being paid a pittance to supply rich Westerners with fashion items.

In short, my correspondents are not entitled to their self-righteousness. They have not thought the matter through. And when the hopes of hundreds of millions are at stake, thinking things through is not just good intellectual practice. It is a moral duty.

Why Economists Are Wrong About Sweatshops and the Antisweatshop Movement

JOHN MILLER

The student-led antisweatshop movement that took hold on many college campuses during the late 1990s should have pleased economists. Studying the working conditions faced by factory workers across the globe offered powerful lessons about the workings of the world economy, the dimensions of world poverty, and most students' privileged position in that economy.

On top of that, these students were dedicated not just to explaining sweatshop conditions, but also to changing them. They wanted desperately to do something to put a stop to the brutalization and assaults on human dignity suffered by the women and men who made their jeans, t-shirts, or sneakers.[1] On many campuses, student activism succeeded in pressuring college administrators by demanding that clothing bearing their college logo not be made under sweatshop conditions, and, at best, that it be made by workers earning a living wage (Featherstone and United Students Against Sweatshops 2002). But most mainstream economists were not at all pleased. No, they did not dispute these tales from the factory floor, many of which had been confirmed in the business press (Roberts and Bernstein 2000) and by international agencies (ILO 2000). Rather, mainstream economists rushed to defend the positive role of low-wage factory jobs, the very kind we usually call sweatshops, in economic development and in alleviating poverty.

What is more, these economists were generally dismissive of the student-led antisweatshop movement. In summer 2000, the Academic Consortium on International Trade (ACIT), a group of advocates of globalization and free trade made up mostly of economists, took it upon themselves to write directly to the presidents of universities and colleges (see www.spp.umich.edu/rsie/acit/). The ACIT letter warned presidents that antisweatshop protesters on college campuses were often ill informed and that adopting codes of conduct requiring multinational corporations to pay higher wages recommended by the protesters may cost workers in poor countries their jobs.

The response of mainstream economists to the antisweatshop movement was hardly surprising. Economists have a penchant for playing the contrarian, and, for

From John Miller, "Why Economists Are Wrong About Sweatshops and the Anti-Sweatshop Movement" *Challenge*, vol. 46, no. 1, January-February 2003, pp. 93–122. © 2003 by M.E. Sharpe, Inc. Reprinted with permission.

the most part, they oppose interventions into market outcomes, even interventions into the labor markets of the developing world.

No matter how predictable, their response was profoundly disappointing. Although it contains elements of truth, what economists have to say about sweatshops misses the mark. . . . First, the propositions that mainstream economists rely on to defend sweatshops are misleading, rooted in an exchange perspective that obscures sweatshop oppression. Sweatshop oppression is not defined by labor market exchanges but by the characteristics of a job. Second, policy positions based on these propositions are equally flawed. Economists' claim that market-led economic development, independent of labor and social movements and government regulation, will put an end to sweatshop conditions distorts the historical record. Finally, their assertion that demands for better working conditions in the world-export factories will harm third-world workers and frustrate poverty alleviation is also suspect.

With that said, the challenge issued by mainstream economists to the antisweatshop movement remains a formidable one. What economists have to say about the sweatshops has considerable power in the way of persuasion and influence, the protestations of Bhagwati and the ACIT notwithstanding. Often it is their writings that are being distilled in what journalists, government officials, and the general public have to say about sweatshops.

Supporters of the antisweatshop movement, and instructors of sweatshop seminars, need to be able to answer each count of the economists' indictments of their movement with arguments that are equally persuasive.

Today a group of economists is dedicated to doing just that. In the fall of 2001, Scholars Against Sweatshop Labor (SASL) issued a response to the ACIT indictment of the antisweatshop movement (SASL 2001). Its lead author, economist Robert Pollin, made the case that "the anti-sweatshop movement is taking constructive steps toward improving living and working conditions for millions of poor people throughout the world."

Teaching about sweatshops also convinced me that supporters of the antisweatshop movement need to respond to the criticisms of mainstream economists with actions as well as words. We need to link antisweatshop campaigns for the betterment of the women and men who toil in the world-export factories with efforts to improve the lot of their brothers and sisters, who often work under even more oppressive conditions in the informal and agricultural sectors of the developing world.

JUST ENFORCE THE LAW

What to do about sweatshops? That is not a difficult question for most mainstream economists to answer. Just enforce the law, they say (Weidenbaum 1999, 26–28). And avoid other "institutional interventions" that might impair a market-led development that will enhance productivity and thereby raise wages and improve working conditions (Irwin 2002, 214; Sengenberger 1994, 10). By law, they mean local labor law, not some labor standard that ill-informed protesters (or even the

International Labor Organization, for that matter) would impose on multinational corporations and their subcontractors in developing economies.

No one in the antisweatshop movement would quarrel with the insistence that the law be obeyed. In fact, several U.S. antisweatshop groups define a sweatshop in legal terms. According to Feminists Against Sweatshops (2002), for instance, sweatshop operators are employers who violate two or more labor laws, from the prohibition of child labor, to health, safety, fire, and building codes, to forced overtime and the minimum wage.[2]

Effective enforcement of local labor law in the developing world, where labor legislation in many countries—on paper, at least—is quite extensive, would surely help to combat sweatshop abuse as well (Portes 1994, 163). For instance, *Made in China*, a report of the National Labor Committee, the leading U.S.-based antisweatshop group, found that subcontractors producing goods for U.S. corporations, including Wal-Mart and Nike, "routinely violate" Chinese labor law. In some of these factories, young women work as long as seventy hours a week and are paid just pennies an hour after pay deductions for board and room, clear violations of China's labor law (Kernaghan 2000). A three-month *Business Week* investigation of the Chun Si Enterprise Handbag Factory in southern China, which makes Kathie Lee Gifford handbags sold by Wal-Mart stores, confirmed that workers there confronted labor practices that included illegally collected fines, confiscated identity papers, and beatings (Roberts and Bernstein 2000).

But the limitations of this legal prescription for curing sweatshop abuse become obvious when we go to apply it to countries where local labor law, even on paper, does not measure up to the most minimal, internationally agreed-upon labor standards. Take the case of the high-performance economies of Southeast Asia, Indonesia, Malaysia, and Thailand. In those countries, several core labor conventions of the International Labor Organization (ILO) have gone unratified—including the right to organize. Minimum wages are well below the level necessary to lift a family of three above the poverty line, the usual definition of a living wage. And in those countries (as well as China), independent trade union activity is systematically and sometimes brutally suppressed.[3]

When labor law protections are limited and international labor conventions are neither ratified nor respected, then insisting "the law should be fully obeyed" will do little to prevent sweatshop abuse. In those cases, enforcing the law would seem to be a shaky foundation on which to build a strategy of alleviating sweatshop labor through improved market outcomes.[4]

A DEFENSE OF SWEATSHOPS?

The defense of sweatshops offered up by mainstream economists turns on two elegantly simple and ideologically powerful propositions. The first is that workers freely choose to enter these jobs, and the second is that these sweatshop jobs are better than the alternative employments available to them in developing economies. Both propositions have a certain truth to them.

An Exchange Perspective

From the perspective of mainstream economics, every exchange, including the exchange between worker and boss, is freely entered into and only takes place because both parties are made better off. Hiring workers to fill the jobs in the world-export factories is no exception.

Of course, in some cases, workers do not freely enter into sweatshop employment even by the usual standards of wage labor. Sometimes workers are held captive. For example, a 1995 police raid of a fenced-in compound of seven apartments in El Monte, California, found a clandestine garment sweatshop where some seventy-two illegal Thai immigrants were held in virtual captivity as they sewed clothes for brand-name labels (Su 1997, 143). Other times, workers find themselves locked into walled factory compounds surrounded by barbed wire, sometimes required to work fifteen hours a day, seven days a week, subject to physical abuse, and, after fines and charges are deducted from their paycheck, left without the money necessary to repay exorbitant hiring fees. That was the case for the more than 50,000 young female immigrants from China, the Philippines, Bangladesh, and Thailand who were recently discovered in Saipan (part of the Commonwealth of the Northern Mariana Islands, a territory of the United States) working under these near-slavelike conditions as they produced clothing for major American distributors bearing the label "Made in the United States" (ILO 2000).

But in most cases, workers do choose these jobs, if hardly freely or without the coercion of economic necessity. Seen from the exchange perspective of mainstream economics, that choice alone demonstrates that these factory job's are neither sweatshops nor exploitative.

Listen to how mainstream economists and their followers make this argument. In response to the National Labor Committee's exposé of conditions in the Honduran factories manufacturing Kathie Lee clothing for Wal-Mart, El Salvadoran economist Lucy Martinez-Mont assured us that "People choose to work in maquila shops of their own free will, because those are the best jobs available to them" (Martinez-Mont 1996, sec. A, p. 14). For economic journalist Nicholas Kristof (1998), the story of Mrs. Tratiwoon, an Indonesian woman, makes the same point. She sustains herself and her son by picking through a garbage dump outside of Jakarta in search of metal scraps to sell. She tells Kristof of her dreams for her three-year-old son as she works. "She wants him to grow up to work in a sweatshop."

Stories such as this one are powerful. The fact that many in the developing world are worse off than workers in the world-export factories is a point that economists supportive of the antisweatshop movement do not deny. For instance, a few years back, economist Arthur MacEwan . . . made much the same point. He observed that in a poor country like Indonesia, where women working in agriculture are paid wages one-fifth those of women working in manufacturing, sweatshops do not seem to have a hard time finding workers (MacEwan 1998). And the Scholars Against Sweatshop Labor statement (2001) admits that "Even after allowing for the frequent low wages and poor working conditions in these jobs, they are still generally superior to 'informal' employment in, for example, much of agriculture or urban street vending."

This is not meant to suggest that these exchanges between employers and poor workers with few alternatives are in reality voluntary or that world-export factory jobs are not sweatshops or places of exploitation. Rather, as political philosopher Michael Waltzer argues, these exchanges should be seen as "trades of last resort" or "desperate" exchanges that need to be protected by labor legislation regulating such things as limits on hours, a wage floor, and guaranteed health and safety requirements (Rodrik 1997, 35).[5]

Prevailing Wages and Working Conditions

What mainstream economists say in defense of sweatshops is limited in other ways as well. For instance, an ACIT letter (2000) misstates the argument. The ACIT writes that multinational corporations "commonly pay their workers more on average in comparison to the prevailing market wage for similar workers employed elsewhere in the economy." But, as the SASL authors correctly point out, "While this is true, it does not speak to the situation in which most garments are produced throughout the world—which is by firms subcontracted by multinational corporations, not the MNCs themselves." The ACIT authors implicitly acknowledge as much, for in the next sentence they write that, "in cases where subcontracting is involved, workers are generally paid no less than the prevailing market wage."[6]

The SASL statement also warns that the ACIT claim that subcontractors pay the prevailing market wage does not by itself make a persuasive case that the world export factories we commonly call sweatshops are anything but that. The SASL authors (2001) emphasize that "the prevailing market wage is frequently extremely low for garment workers in less developed countries. In addition, the recent university-sponsored studies as well as an October 2000 report by the International Labor Organization consistently find that serious workplace abuses and violations of workers' rights are occurring in the garment industry throughout the world."

The same can be said about other world-export factories. Consider for a minute the working conditions at the Indonesian factories that produce footwear for Reebok, the Stoughton, Massachusetts–based international corporation that "goes to great lengths to portray itself as a conscientious promoter of human rights in the Third World" (Zuckoff 1994). Despite its status as a model employer, working conditions at factories that make Reebok footwear became the focus of the *Boston Globe* 1994 series entitled "Foul Trade" (Zuckoff 1994). The *Globe* tells the story of Yati, a young Indonesian woman in Tangerang, Indonesia. She works sewing bits of leather and lace for tennis shoes sold as Reeboks.

Yati sits at a sewing machine, which is one of sixty in her row. There are forty-six rows on the factory floor. For working sixty-three hours a week, Yati earns not quite $80 a month—just about the price of a pair of Reeboks in the United States. Her hourly pay is less than 32 cents per hour, which exceeds the minimum wage for her region of Indonesia. Yati lives in a nearby ten-by-twelve-foot shack with no furniture. She and her two roommates sleep on the mud and tile floor.

A factory like the one Yati works in is typically owned by an East Asian company. For instance, PT Tong Yang Indonesia, a South Korean–owned factory, pumped out 400,000 pairs of Reeboks a month in 1993. In return, Reebok paid its owner, Tan Chuan Cheng, $10.20 for each pair of shoes and then sold them for $60 or more in the United States. Most of Tan's payment went to purchase materials. Tan told the *Globe* that wages accounted for as little as $1.40 of the cost of a pair of shoes (Zuckoff 1994).[7]

A MORE EFFECTIVE RESPONSE

As I taught my seminar on sweatshops, I settled on a more effective response to the mainstream economic argument. It is simply this: Their argument is irrelevant for determining if a factory is a sweatshop or if workers are exploited. Sweatshop conditions are defined by the characteristics of a job. If workers are denied the right to organize, suffer unsafe and abusive working conditions, are forced to work over-time, or are paid less than a living wage, then they work in a sweatshop, regardless of how they came to take their jobs or if the alternatives they face are worse yet.

A careful reading of what the mainstream exchange perspective suggests about sweatshop jobs is not they are "good news" for the world's poor but "less bad news" than the usual conditions of work in the agricultural and informal sectors. The oppressive conditions of the work in the world-export factories are not denied by their argument. For instance, ACIT leader Jagdish Bhagwati says sweatshop jobs are a "ticket to slightly less impoverishment" (Goldberg 2001, 30).

CONFRONTING CRITICS OF THE ANTISWEATSHOP MOVEMENT

Still, none of the above speaks directly to the contention of mainstream economists that imposing "enlightened standards" advocated by the antisweatshop activists onto conditions for employment in the export factories of the developing world will immiserate the very workers the movement intends to help (ACIT 2000).

Core Labor Standards

To begin with, as labor economist Richard Freeman (1994, 80) writes, "Everyone, almost everyone is for *some* standards" (emphasis in the original). Surely that includes economists who would combat sweatshops by insisting that local labor law be respected. Even their position recognizes that the "voluntary" exchange of labor for wages must be delimited by rules, collectively determined and obeyed by all.

The relevant question is: What are those rules, and are any so basic that they should be applied universally, transcending the normal bounds of sovereignty? For the most part, economists, trained after all as economists and not political philosophers, have little to say on this matter other than to caution that outside of the condemnation of slavery, there is no universal agreement about the appropri-ateness of labor standards even when it comes to bonded labor and child labor (Bhagwati 1995, 754; Brown 2001, 94; Irwin 2002, 216).

Nonetheless other economists, even some critical of the antisweatshop movement, are favorably disposed toward international labor standards about safety and health, forced labor, and the right to organize. For instance, Alice Amsden, an economist who opposes establishing wage standards on developing economies, favors the imposition of other labor standards. "The issue," she says, "is not health and safety conditions, the right of workers to be treated like human beings—not to be murdered for organizing unions, for example. These rights are inviolate" (Amsden 1995). At times, even Jagdish Bhagwati has taken a similar position (Bhagwati 2002, 60).

The International Labor Organization, in its 1998 Declaration on Fundamental Principles at Work, took a similar position. The ILO held that each of its 175 members (even if they have not ratified the conventions in question) was obligated "to respect, to promote and to realize" the fundamental rights of "freedom of association and the effective recognition of the right to collective bargaining, the elimination of all forms of forced or compulsory labour, the effective abolition of child labour and the elimination of discrimination in respect of employment and occupation" (2002a).

The empirical evidence of the effect of these core labor standards on economic development is ambiguous. For instance, the Organization for Economic Cooperation and Development (OECD) found that countries that strengthen these core labor standards "can increase economic growth and efficiency" (OECD 2000, 14). International trade economist Jai Mah, on the other hand, found that ratification of the ILO Conventions on freedom of association and on the right to nondiscrimination negatively affected the export performance of developing countries (Mah 1997, 781). And a study conducted by Dani Rodrik, another international trade economist, suggested that low core labor standards enhanced a country's comparative advantage in the production of labor-intensive goods but deterred rather than attracted direct foreign investment (Rodrik 1996, 59).

The Living Wage

Nevertheless, almost all mainstream economists draw the line at labor codes designed to boost wages as opposed to leaving the determination of wages to labor market outcomes. That surely goes for labor codes that call for the payment of a living wage, usually defined as a wage adequate to lift a worker and two dependents out of poverty. The ACIT worries that if multinational corporations are persuaded to increase their wages (and those of their subcontractors) "in response to what the ongoing studies by the anti-sweatshop movement may conclude are appropriate wage levels, the net result would be shifts in employments that will worsen the collective welfare of the very workers who are supposed to be helped" (2001). And ACIT leader Bhagwati dismisses the call for multinationals and their subcontractors to pay a living wage as so much first-world protectionism cloaked in the language of "social responsibility" (Bhagwati 2000, 11). As he sees it, students' demand that a "living wage" be paid in developing countries would dull the one competitive advantage enjoyed by these countries, cheap labor.

But, in practice, would a labor standard demanding that multinational corporations and their subcontractors boost their wages beyond the local minimum wage and toward a living wage be a jobs killer? On that point the ACIT letter is silent . . .

Still, we can ask just how responsive are the hiring decisions of multinational corporations and their subcontractors to higher wages. There is real reason to believe that the right answer is, not very responsive.

Economists Robert Pollin, James Heintz, and Justine Burns recently looked more closely at this question (Pollin et al. 2001). They examined the impact that a 100 percent increase in the pay for apparel workers in Mexico and in the United States would have on costs relative to the retail price those garments sell for in the United States. Their preliminary findings are that doubling the pay of nonsupervisory workers would add just 50 cents to the production costs of a men's casual shirt sold for $32 in the United States, or just 1.6 percent of the retail price. And even if the wage increase were passed on to consumers, which seems likely because retailers in the U.S. garment industry enjoy substantial market power, Pollin et al. argue that the increase in price is well within the amount that recent surveys suggest U.S. consumers are willing to pay to purchase goods produced under "good" working conditions as opposed to sweatshop conditions. (See Elliot and Freeman [2000] for a detailed discussion of survey results.) More generally, using a sample of forty-five countries over the period 1992–97, Pollin et al. found no statistically significant relationship between real wages and employment growth in the apparel industry. Their results suggest that the mainstream economists' claim that improving the quality of jobs in the world-export factories (by boosting wages) will reduce the number of jobs is not evident in the data (Pollin et al. 2001).

Even if this counterexample is not convincing, it is important to recall that the demand curve that defines the responsiveness of multinational corporations and their subcontractors to wage increases for factory workers is a theoretical device drawn while holding other economic circumstances constant, including public policy. In reality, those circumstances are neither fixed nor unalterable. In fact, to counteract any negative effect that higher wages might have on employment, the SASL statement calls for the adoption of new polices, which include "measures to expand the overall number of relatively high quality jobs; relief from excessive foreign debt payments; raising worker job satisfaction and productivity and the quality of goods they produce; and improving the capacity to bring final products to retail markets" (SASL 2001).

"Shifting the demand curve for labor outward," says economic sociologist Peter Evans (2002), "is almost the definition of economic development—making people more valuable relative to the commodities they need to live." This "high road" approach to development, adds Evans, has the additional benefit of augmenting the demand for the commodities that workers produce.

Historical Change and Social Improvement

A labor code that requires multinational corporations and their subcontractors to pay a living wage, provide safe and healthy working conditions, and allow workers to organize would be likely to have yet more profound effects on these developing economies. On this point, the antisweatshop activists and their critics agree. What they disagree about is whether these broader effects will be a help or hindrance to economic development and an improved standard of living in the developing world (Freeman 1992).

Mainstream critics argue that labor codes are likely to have widespread debilitating effects. The institutionalization of these labor standards proposed by activists, they argue, would derail a market-led development process (Irwin 2002, 214; Sengenberger 1994, 10–11).

As they see it, labor-intensive sweatshops are good starter jobs—the very jobs that successful developing economies and developed countries used as "stepping-stones" to an improved standard of living for their citizens. And in each case, these countries outgrew their "sweatshop phase" through market-led development that enhanced productivity, not through the interventions of an antisweatshop movement (Krugman 1994, 116).

These economists often use the Asian economies as examples of national economies that abandoned "sweatshop practices" as they grew. Their list includes Japan, which moved from poverty to wealth early in the twentieth century, and the tiger economies—South Korea, Hong Kong, Singapore, and Taiwan—which grew rapidly in the second half of the century to become middle-income countries (Irwin 2002; Krugman 1994; Krugman 1997; Lim 1990; Weidenbaum 1999). Paul Krugman (1997) allows that some tigers relied on foreign plant owners (e.g., Singapore) while others shunned them (e.g., South Korea). Nonetheless, he maintains that their first stage of development had one constant: "It's always sweatshops" (Meyerson 1997).

❋ ❋ ❋

But these arguments distort the historical record and misrepresent how social improvement is brought about with economic development. First, the claim that developed economies passed through a sweatshop stage does not establish that sweatshops caused or contributed to the enhanced productivity that they say improved working conditions. Second, in the developed world, the sweatshop phase was not extinguished by market-led forces alone but when economic growth combined with the very kind of social action, or enlightened collective choice, that defenders of sweatshops find objectionable.

Even Nobel Prize–winning economist Simon Kuznets, whose work did much to inspire economists' faith in the moderating effects of capitalist development on inequality, would find the mainstream economists' story of market-led social progress questionable. Kuznets based his famous hypothesis—that after initially increasing, inequality will diminish with capitalist economic development—not on the operation of market forces alone, but on the combined effect of economic growth and social legislation.[8] For instance, in his famous 1955 *American Economic Review* article, Kuznets writes, "In democratic societies the growing political power of the urban lower-income groups led to a variety of protective and supporting legislation, much of it aimed to counteract the worst effects of rapid industrialization and urbanization and to support the claims of the broad masses for more adequate shares of the growing income of the country" (1955, 17). The labor codes called for by the antisweatshop movement would seem to be an example of the "protective and supporting legislation" that Kuznets says is key to spreading the benefits of economic growth more widely.

To be sure, labor standards in the absence of economic growth will be hard put to make workers better off. Economist Ajit Singh and Ann Zammit of the South Centre, an intergovernmental organization dedicated to promoting cooperation among developing countries, make exactly this point in their article opposing compulsory labor standards (Singh and Zammit 2000, 37). As they note, over the last few decades, wages in rapidly growing South Korea increased much more quickly than those in slowly growing India, even though India had much better labor standards in the 1950s than South Korea did.[9]

❋ ❋ ❋

Finally, no matter how mistaken these mainstream economists might be about how societies have rid themselves of sweatshops, they are perhaps right that past economic developments have gone through a sweatshop stage. On that score, I would reply exactly as one well-known economist did to a 1997 *New York Times* article that made the same point. His letter read this way:

> Your June 22 Week in Review article on sweatshops quotes some prominent economists to the effect that sweatshops, which they confuse with "low-wage factories," are "an essential first step toward modern prosperity in developing countries." Sweatshops indeed existed in 19th-century Britain during early industrialization, leading to a burst of social legislation to rid the country of these ills. But nothing requires us to go that route again. Nations should join nongovernmental groups like the International Labor Organization to rid the world of sweatshops. In addition, we can require multinationals to apply our own labor, safety and environmental standards when they manufacture abroad. In Rome, they must do not as Romans do but as we do. Their example would spread.

Surprisingly, the author is none other than Jagdish Bhagwati (1997). I would only add to Bhagwati's powerful pre-ACIT letter that the student-led antisweatshop movement has increased the likelihood that future economic developments might avoid the sweatshop stage. Unlike earlier periods, when labor standards were imposed in response to the demands of labor organizations and an urban population of the developing world alone, first-world consumers today are also pushing multinational corporations to improve the working conditions in the factories of their subcontractors (Brunett and Mahon 2001, 70).

FASTIDIOUSNESS OR COMMODITY FETISHISM?

Mainstream economists have one last probing question for antisweatshop activists: Why factory workers? Krugman (1997) asks the question in a most pointed way: "Why does the image of an Indonesian sewing sneakers for 60 cents an hour evoke so much more feeling than the image of another Indonesian earning the equivalent of 30 cents an hour trying to feed his family on a tiny plot of land, or of a Filipino scavenging on a garbage heap?"

It is a good question. There are plenty of poor people in the world. Some 1.2 billion people, about one-fifth of the world population, had to make do on less than U.S. $1 a day in 1998 (World Bank 2001). The world's poor are disproportionately located in rural areas. Most scratch out their livelihood from subsistence agriculture or by plying petty trades, while others on the edge of urban centers work in the informal sector as street-hawkers or the like (Todaro 2000, 151). In addition, if sweat is the issue, journalist Kristof (1998) assures us that "this kind of work, hoeing the field or working in paddies, often involves more perspiration than factory work."

So why has the plight of these rural workers, who are often poorer and sweat more than workers in the world-export factories, not inspired a first-world movement dedicated to their betterment?

"Fastidiousness" is Krugman's answer. "Unlike the starving subsistence farmer," says Krugman, "the women and children in the sneaker factory are working at slave wages *for our benefit*—and this makes us feel unclean. And so there are self-righteous demands for international labor standards" (1997; emphasis in the original).

Ironically, Krugman's answer is not so different from the one Marx would have given to the question. Marx's answer would be commodity fetishism or that commodities become the bearers of social relations in a capitalist economy (Marx 1967). Purchasing commodities brings us in contact with the lives of the factory workers who manufacture them. Buying jeans, t-shirts, or sneakers made in Los Angeles, Bangkok, or Jakarta, or the export zones of southern China and Latin America, connected students in my seminar to the women and men who work long hours in unhealthy and dangerous conditions for little pay in the apparel and athletic footwear industries. And it was the lives of those workers that my most political students sought to improve through their antisweatshop activism. Beyond that, as consumers and citizens they are empowered to change the employment practices of U.S. corporations and their subcontractors.

Krugman's complaint is no reason to dismiss the concerns of the antisweatshop movement. Historically, the organization of factory workers has been one of the most powerful forces for changing politics in the democratic direction that Kuznets outlines. Krugman's complaint does, however, suggest that the plight of sweatshop workers needs to be seen in the context of pervasive world poverty and the gaping inequalities of the global economy.

The global economy, to the extent that we live in a truly unified marketplace, connects us not just with sweatshop workers, but with oppressed workers outside the factory gates as well. By pointing out these connections to my students, I hoped to demonstrate the need to build a movement that would demand more for working people across the multiple dimensions of the world economy. Campaigns to improve conditions in the world-export factories should, of course, be part of that movement. But that movement must also tackle the often worse conditions of low-wage agricultural workers, poor farmers, street vendors, domestic servants, small-shop textile workers, and prostitutes. Only when conditions for both groups of workers improve might economists be able to say honestly, as something other than a Faustian bargain, that more world factory jobs are good news for the world's poor.

REFERENCES

Academic Consortium on International Trade (ACIT). 2000. Letter to Presidents of Universities and Colleges, July 29 (www.spp.umich.edu/rsie/acit/).

Amsden, Alice. 1995. "International Labor Standards: Hype or Help?" *Boston Review* 20, no. 6 (bostonreview.mit.edu/BR20.6/amsden.html).

Begley, Sharon, et al. 1990. "The New Sweatshops." *Newsweek*, September 10: 50.

Benjamin, Medea. 1998. San Francisco: Global Exchange (www.globalexchange.org).

Bernstein, Aaron. 2000. "A World of Sweatshops: Progress Is Slow in the Drive for Better Conditions." *Business Week*, November 6: 84.

Bhagwati, Jagdish. 1995. "Trade Liberalization and 'Fair Trade' Demands: Addressing the Environmental and Labour Standards Issues." *World Economy* 18, no. 6: 745–59.

———. 1997. Letter. *New York Times*, June 23: sec. A, p. 18.

———. 2000. "Nike Wrongfoots the Student Critics." *Financial Times*, May 2: 11.

———. 2002. *Free Trade Today*. Princeton: Princeton University Press.

Brown, Drusilla K. 2001. "Labor Standards: Where Do They Belong on the International Trade Agenda?" *Journal of Economic Perspectives* 15, no. 3 (summer): 89–112.

Brunett, Erin, and James Mahon, Jr. 2001. "Monitoring Compliance with International Labor Standards." *Challenge* 44, no. 2 (March/April): 51–72.

Elliot, K.A., and R.B. Freeman. 2000. "White Hats or Don Quixotes? Human Rights Vigilantes in the Global Economy." National Bureau of Economic Research Conference on Emerging Labor Market Institutions (www.nber.org/~confer/ 2000/si2000/elliot.pdf).

Elson, Diane, and Ruth Pearson. 1997. "The Subornation of Women and the Internationalization of Factory Production." In *The Women, Gender, and Development Reader*, ed. Naline Visvanathan et al., pp. 191–202. London: Zed Books.

Evans, Peter B. 2002. Personal communication, April.

Featherstone, Liza, and Doug Henwood. 2001a. "Economists vs. Students." *Nation*, February 12: 5, 24.

———. 2001b. "Clothes Encounters: Activists and Economists Clash Over Sweatshops." *Lingua Franca* 11, no. 2 (March): 26–33 (www.linguafranca.com).

Featherstone, Liza, and United Students Against Sweatshops. 2002. *Students Against Sweatshops*. New York: Verso.

Feminists Against Sweatshops. 2002. www.feminist.org/other/sweatshops.html.

Foo, Lora Jo. 1994. "Immigrant Workforce." *Yale Law Journal* 103, no. 8 (June): 2179–2212.

Freeman, Richard B. 1992. "Labour Market Institutions and Policies: Help or Hindrance to Economic Development?" In *Proceedings of the World Bank Annual Conference on Development Economics*, pp. 117–56. Washington, DC: World Bank.

———. 1994. "A Hard-Headed Look at Labour Standards." In *International Labour Standards and Economic Interdependence*, ed. Werner Sengenberger and Duncan Campbell, pp. 79–92. Geneva: International Labor Organization (International Institute for Labor Studies).

Goldberg, Jonah. 2001. "Sweatshop Chic: The Know-Nothings Find a Cause." *National Review*, April 4.

Howard, Alan. 1997. "Labor, History, and Sweatshops in the New Global Economy." In *No Sweat: Fashion, Free Trade, and the Rights of Garment Workers*, ed. Andrew Ross, 151–72. New York: Verso.

International Labor Organization (ILO). 1998. *The Social Impact of the Asian Financial Crisis*. Bangkok, Thailand.

————. 1999a. *Toward Full Employment: Prospects and Problems in Asia and the Pacific*. Bangkok, Thailand.

————. 1999b. "Indonesia Ratifies Core ILO Conventions." Press release, June 7.

————. 2000. *Labour Practices in the Footwear, Leather, Textiles and Clothing Industries*. Geneva: International Labor Organization.

————. 2002a. Declaration on Fundamental Principles at Work. ilo.org/public/english/standards/deci/declaration/index.htm.

————. 2002b. Ratifications. ilolex.ilo.ch:1567/english/docs/declworld.htm.

Irwin, Douglas A. 2002. *Free Trade Under Fire*. Princeton: Princeton University Press.

Kernaghan, Charles. 2000. *Made in China: The Role of U.S. Companies in Denying Human and Worker Rights*. New York: National Labor Committee.

Kheel Center for Labor-Management Documentation and Archives. 1998. Cornell University, Industrial Labor Relations (www.ilr.cornell.edu/trianglefire.html).

Kristof, Nicholas. 1998. "Asia's Crisis Upsets Rising Effort to Confront Blight of Sweatshops." *New York Times*, June 15: sec. A, p. 1.

Krugman, Paul. 1994. "Does Third World Growth Hurt First World Prosperity?" *Harvard Business Review* (July–August): 113–21.

————. 1997. "In Praise of Cheap Labor: Bad Jobs at Bad Wages Are Better Than No Jobs at All." *Slate*, March 27.

Kuznets, Simon. 1955. "Economic Growth and Income Inequality." *American Economic Review* 45, no. 1 (March): 1–28.

Lim, Linda. 1990. "Women's Work in Export Factories." In *Persistent Inequalities*, ed. Irene Tinker, pp. 101–19. New York: Oxford University Press.

————. 1997. "Capitalism, Imperialism, and Patriarchy." In Visvanathan et al., ed., *The Women, Gender, and Development Reader*, pp. 216–29.

Lipsyte, Robert. 1995. "Voices from the 'Sweatshop of the Streets.'" *New York Times*, May 14: sec. A, p. 18.

MacEwan, Arthur. 1998. "Ask Dr. Dollar." *Dollars & Sense*, no. 219 (September/October): 51.

————. 1999. *Neo-Liberalism or Democracy? Economic Strategy, Markets, and Alternatives for the 21st Century*. London: Zed Books.

Mah, Jai S. 1997. "Core Labor Standards and Export Performance in Developing Countries." *World Economy* 20, no. 6 (September): 773–85.

Marx, Karl. 1967. *Capital*. Vol. 1. New York: International.

Martin, Douglas. 2001. "Rose Freedman, Last Survivor of Triangle Fire, Dies at 107." *New York Times*, February 17: sec. B, p. 8.

Martinez-Mont, Lucy. 1996. "Sweatshops Are Better Than No Shops." *Wall Street Journal*, June 25: sec. A, p. 14.

McClymer, John F. 1998. *The Triangle Strike and Fire*. New York: Harcourt Brace College.

Meyerson, Allen R. 1997. "In Principle, a Case for More 'Sweatshops,'" *New York Times*, June 22: sec. 4, p. 5.

Miller, John. 2001. "Teaching About Sweatshops and the Global Economy." *Radical Teacher*, no. 61: 8–14.

Organization for Economic Cooperation and Development (OECD). 2000. *International Trade and Core Labour Standards*. Paris: OECD.

Pasuk Phongpaichit and Chris Baker. 1998. *Thailand's Boom and Bust*. Chiang Mai, Thailand: Silkworm Books.

Piore, Michael. 1997. "The Economics of the Sweatshop." In Ross, ed., *No Sweat*, pp. 135–42.

Pollin, Robert, Justine Burns, and James Heintz. 2001. "Global Apparel Production and Sweatshop Labor: Can Raising Retail Prices Finance Living Wages?" Political Economy Research Institute, Working Paper series, no. 19.

Portes, Alejandro. 1994. "By-Passing the Rules: The Dialectics of Labour Standards and Informalization in Less Developed Countries." In Sengenberger and Campbell, ed., *International Labour Standards and Economic Interdependence*, pp. 159–76.

Reynolds, Christopher, and Dan Weikel. 2000. "For Cruise Ship Workers, Voyages Are No Vacations." *Los Angeles Times*, May 30: pt. A, p. A-1.

Roberts, Dexter, and Aaron Bernstein. 2000. "A Life of Fines and Beatings." *Business Week*, October 2: 122.

Rodrik, Dani. 1996. "Labor Standards in International Trade: Do They Matter and What Do We Do About Them?" In *Emerging Agenda for Global Trade: High Stakes for Developing Countries*, ed. Robert Z. Lawrence, Dani Rodrik, and John Walley, pp. 35–79. Washington, DC: Johns Hopkins University Press for the Overseas Development Council.

———. 1997. *Has Globalization Gone Too Far?* Washington, DC: Institute for International Economics.

Ross, Robert. 2002. "The New Sweatshops in the United States: How New, How Real, How Many, Why?" In *Free Trade and Uneven Development: The North American Apparel Industry*, ed. Gary Gereffi, David Spencer, and Jennifer Blair, pp. 100–22. Philadelphia: Temple University Press.

Scarff, Michelle. 2000. "The Full-Time Stress of Part-Time Professors: For the Pittance They're Paid, Adjunct Profs at Our Colleges Might as Well Be Sweatshop Workers." *Newsweek*, May 15: 10.

Scholars Against Sweatshop Labor (SASL). 2001. October (www.umass.edu/peri/ sasl/).

Sengenberger, Werner. 1994. "International Labour Standards in a Globalized Economy: The Issues." In Sengenberger and Campbell, ed., *International Labour Standards and Economic Interdependence*, pp. 3–16.

Singh, A., and A. Zammit. 2000. "The Global Labour Standards Controversy: Critical Issues for Developing Countries." Geneva: South Centre (www.southcentre.org/publicatons/ labour/toc.htm).

Stiglitz, Joseph. 2000. "Democratic Development as the Fruits of Labor." Keynote address of the annual meetings of the Industrial Relations Research Association, Boston (available at www.globalpolicy.org/socecon/bwi-wto/wbank/ stieg2.htm).

Su, Julie. 1997. "El Monte Thai Garment Workers: Slave Sweatshops." In Ross, ed., *No Sweat*, pp. 143–50.

Tierney, John. 1999. "The Big City: A 1911 Fire as Good TV, Bad History." *New York Times*, October 18: sec. B, p. 1.

Todaro, Michael. 2000. *Economic Development*. 7th ed. New York: Addison Wesley.

U.S. Department of Labor (DOL). 2001. *No Sweat: Garment Enforcement Reports*, October 1999–December 2000 (www.dol.gov/dol/esa/public/nosweat/ nosweat.htm).

Waldinger, Roger, and Michael Lapp. 1993. "Back to the Sweatshop or Ahead to the Informal Sector?" *International Journal of Urban and Regional Research* 17, no. 1: 6–29.

Weidenbaum, Murray. 1999. "A Defense of Sweatshops." In *Child Labor and Sweatshops*, ed. Mary Williams, pp. 26–28. San Diego: Greenhaven.

World Bank. 2001. *World Development Report 2000/2001*. New York: Oxford University Press.

Zuckoff, Mitchell. 1994. "Taking a Profit, and Inflicting a Cost." First part of a series titled "Foul Trade." *Boston Globe*, July 10: sec. A, p. 1.

ENDNOTES

1. While men and women suffer sweatshop abuse, young women overwhelmingly constitute the workforce of the "world market factories" in the developing world (Elson and Pearson 1997, 191). Women workers have also been the focus of the antisweatshop movement.

Female employment is generally high in the clothing industry and in export-processing zones. In 1995, women made up 74 percent of the global workforce in the clothing industry (ILO 2000, 26).

2. There is no universal agreement about the definition of a sweatshop in the antisweatshop movement. For instance, sociologists Roger Waldinger and Michael Lapp argue that sweatshop labor is a form of what the Organization for Economic and Cooperative Development (OECD) calls "concealed employment," which escapes state regulation (Waldinger and Lapp 1993, 8–9). Their definition would cover the return of sweatshops to the United States. It also covers subcontractors of first-world multinational corporations who employ workers in the formal sector of the third world under lax regulatory standards, as well as the minuscule firms in informal sectors of the developing world that are not subject to regulation. Other sweatshop critics, such as labor economist Michael Piore, insist that the term "sweatshop" should be reserved for "a specific organization of work" characterized by "very low fixed costs" (Piore 1997, 136). In sweatshops, workers are usually paid by the piece. Other fixed costs—rent, electricity, heat—are held to a minimum by operating substandard, congested, unhealthy factories, typically overseen by a "sweater" or subcontractor (Piore 1997, 135). Still others use the term sweatshop as a vivid metaphor to describe lousy jobs ranging from bicycle messengers who work in "Sweatshops of the Streets" (Lipsyte 1995), to cruise workers who endure "Sweatshops at Sea" (Reynolds and Weikel 2000), to adjunct professors at colleges "who might as well be sweatshop workers" (Scarff 2000).

3. In the case of China, the International Labor Organization writes that "the existence of a single trade union linked to the Communist Party [the All-China Federation of Trade Unions] in itself says much about freedom of association in the country" (ILO 2000, 66). The Organization for Economic Cooperation and Development reports that in China "the right to strike is not recognized" (OECD 2000, 101). In Indonesia, several core ILO conventions remained unratified until June 1999, when then President J. B. Habibie faced a national election. The Suharto regime never signed ILO labor convention 87, which recognizes the right of workers to organize; convention 138, establishing a minimum age of employment; convention 105, outlawing forced labor; and convention 111, banning discrimination in employment (ILO 1998; ILO 1999a; ILO 1999b). Thailand's and Malaysia's records are similarly dismal. Thailand has failed to ratify both ILO conventions recognizing the right of workers to organize (conventions 87 and 98) and the minimum age convention, 138. The right to strike is not recognized in Thailand's state enterprises, and authorities can prohibit strikes in the Thai private sector (OECD 2000, 104). Malaysia has not ratified ILO convention 87 and not only has failed to sign convention 105 calling for the abolition of forced labor, but has condemned it (ILO 1998). And the right to strike in Malaysia is "severely limited" (OECD 2000, 106). According to a study of wages at Indonesian factories producing Nike footwear, the minimum wage for Jakarta in 1997 provided a family of three less than $1 per day for each family member, the United Nations' definition of extreme poverty (Benjamin 1998). The same study found that to meet the minimum physical needs of a woman working for Nike in the Indonesian area required $35 month and that the usual wage paid by Nike subcontractors fell well below even that amount (Benjamin 1998). In Thailand, Bangkok's minimum wage, which kept pace with inflation during the 1990s boom, never extended to most of the 800,000 Thai garment workers, the great bulk of whom were employed by subcontractors (Pasuk and Baker 1998, 139–40).

4. These arguments also apply to countries in the developed world. For instance, the United States has failed to ratify six of the ILO's eight Fundamental Human Rights Conventions, covering freedom of association and collective bargaining, elimination of forced and

compulsory labor, elimination of discrimination in respect to employment and occupation, and the abolition of child labor (ILO 2002b). Bhagwati rightly complains that discussions of international labor standards have focused on conditions in the developing world while remaining silent about "the much-documented quasi-slavery conditions for migrant labor in American agriculture in Georgia and Mississippi" (Bhagwati 2002, 71–72). He adds that a recent Human Rights Watch report, *Unfair Advantage*, documents how U.S. legal doctrine violates internationally recognized workers' rights to organize by allowing employers to permanently replace workers on strike and by banning secondary boycotts (Bhagwati 2002, 77). Bhagwati's complaint makes it clear that merely enforcing local labor law, even in the United States, is insufficient for combating abusive working conditions.

5. This sort of "asymmetric bargaining power," actually any sort of bargaining power, goes unrecognized in standard economic models (Stiglitz 2000).

6. When correctly stated, the limitations of the claim that working for these manufacturing subcontractors is better than the other opportunities available to the sons and daughters of recyclers and other poor workers are evident in the writings of defenders of sweatshops. For instance, the writings of economist Linda Lim, an ACIT signatory who is dismissive of the efforts of the antisweatshop movement (which she describes as "patronizing white-man's-burden stuff"), convinced several students in my sweatshop seminar that women who work in the world's export factories are exploited (Featherstone and Henwood 2001b).

   In her earlier work, Lim reports that in East Asia, "the wages earned by women in export factories are usually higher than what they could earn as wage laborers in alternative low-skilled female occupations" (Lim 1990, 109). But at the same time, the wages of women in the export industries are lower than the wages of men who work in those industries and lower than those of first-world women who work in the same industries. That is true, even though third-world women's productivity "is acknowledged to be higher than that of either of these other groups" (Lim 1997, 223). Even for Lim, that makes these women "the most heavily exploited group of workers relative both to their output and other groups" (Lim 1997, 223). Whatever Lim's work suggests about the relative attractiveness of these factory jobs, it went a long way toward convincing my students that these workplaces are sites of exploitation and properly described as sweatshops.

7. How is Yati likely to be faring today? Thanks in part to aggressive consumer campaigns in the United States, spearheaded by such groups as Global Exchange, campus organizations, and unions, Reebok commissioned an independent Indonesian firm to study conditions in factories that do business with Reebok. Murray Weidenbaum acted as a consultant for that report. One of the factories investigated was PT Tong Yang. According to the London *Guardian* (October 19, 1999), the fourteen-month study "found evidence of health and safety abuses, sexual discrimination and communication problems. Safety notices were often handed out in English, for example." Other safety problems include "lack of labels for dangerous chemicals . . . and inadequate ventilation." According to the report, women face special problems, such as access to few toilets despite the fact that they represent 80 percent of the workforce, and under-representation among higher-ranking workers. In response, Tong Yang Indonesia introduced new machinery that used safer water-based solvents, installed a new ventilation system, and bought new chairs with backs that provided more support than the older ones. Despite those efforts, more basic problems remain. Wages still hover just above the inadequate Jakarta-area minimum wage, and workers continue to go without effective collective bargaining, denied the right to form independent unions (Bernstein 2000).

8. For a thoroughgoing analysis of the progressive underpinnings of Kuznets's article and its subversive implications for the neoliberal policy agenda, see the third chapter of

Arthur MacEwan's *Neo-Liberalism or Democracy? Economic Strategy, Markets, and Alternatives for the 21st Century* (1999).

9. For these reasons, Singh and Zammit favor measures intended to promote more equitable and stable economic growth in the developing world, such as managed world trade and controls on international capital movements, instead of compulsory labor standards (Singh and Zammit 2000, 67).

QUESTIONS FOR REVIEW AND DISCUSSION

1. Why does Krugman believe that sweatshop jobs should be seen as good rather than bad jobs? Is there an economic concept underlying this statement?
2. What does Krugman believe will happen if global standards are imposed in an attempt to improve wages and working conditions?
3. What arguments does Miller advance to counter Krugman's claims? How do you think Krugman would respond to Miller's arguments?
4. How does Miller define the concept "living wage"? Is this a good definition? Why or why not? What are the arguments for and against an internationally regulated minimum wage using the living wage as a standard?
5. Does Miller believe that higher wages would result in fewer jobs in developing countries? Is there an economic concept underlying his argument?
6. Should developing countries be required to have the same labor standards as the advanced industrialized countries? Why or why not?

SUGGESTIONS FOR FURTHER READING

For an in-depth developing-country perspective on global labor standards, see: Ajit Singh and Ann Zammit. *The Global Labour Standards Controversy: Critical Issues For Developing Countries.* Geneva: The South Centre, 2000. It is available on line at http://www.southcentre. org/publications/labour/labour1.pdf

The Academic Consortium on International Trade maintains a Web site about sweatshops. In addition to the letter discussed by Miller, there are many links to other material on sweatshops: http://www.fordschool.umich.edu/rsie/acit/Documents/Anti-SweatshopLetter Page.html

Scholars Against Sweatshop Labor (SASL) also maintain a useful Web site. Find their response to the ACIT letter, as well as other useful links, at: http://www.umass.edu/peri/sasl/

A number of reports on specific sweatshops are available online. See, for example: The National Labor Committee. *Made in China: The Role of U.S. Companies in Denying Human and Worker Rights.* http://www.nlcnet.org/campaigns/archive/chinareport/table_of_contents. shtml; The National Labor Committee. *Bangladesh: Ending the Race to the Bottom.* http:// www.nlcnet.org/campaigns/shahmakhdum/1001/index.shtml; The National Labor Committee. *Worker Rights in the Americas? A Rare Glimpse Inside.* http://www.nlcnet.org/campaigns/ archive/elsalvador/0401/index.shtml; Timothy Connor, 2002. *We Are Not Machines: Indonesian Nike and Adidas Workers.* http://www.maquilasolidarity.org/campaigns/nike/pdf/Wearenot machines.pdf; Oxfam Community Aid Abroad. *Like Cutting Bamboo: Nike and Indonesian Workers' Rights to Freedom of Association.* http://www.oxfam.org.au/publications/ briefing

The International Labor Organization maintains a Web site dedicated to international labor standards at: http://webfusion.ilo.org/public/db/standards/normes/index.cfm?lang=EN

CHAPTER 10

REGULATING MULTINATIONAL CORPORATIONS

As MNC activity has increased, calls for global regulation of MNCs have also increased. Indeed, a central issue in the debate over globalization has been whether foreign direct investment (FDI) and MNCs should be subject to international regulation, and if so, what this regulation should look like. The recent public visibility of calls for effective regulation of MNC activity suggests that the issue of international regulation of MNCs is a new one. Yet for more than 30 years, the world's governments have been debating and negotiating—but have not yet agreed upon—common rules for MNCs within the United Nations, the GATT and WTO, and the Organization for Economic Cooperation and Development (OECD).

Such negotiations have moved along two parallel tracks. Governments sought to, on one track, craft international rules that limit the ability of governments to restrict the activities of MNCs and on the other track, establish rules that constrain the activities of MNCs. The goal of the first track, pushed most forcefully by the capital exporting countries, particularly the United States, with support from other advanced industrialized countries, is to establish rules that make it easier for MNCs to operate in the global economy. The most recent such exercise was the abortive Multilateral Agreement on Investment (MAI), which was negotiated within the OECD in the 1990s (see Graham 2000). The MAI was intended to establish rules that would make it difficult for governments to discriminate against foreign firms. To that end, the MAI was based on two central principles. The first, *national treatment*, required governments to treat foreign-owned firms operating in their economy no differently than domestic firms. For example, the U.S. government, could not create domestic regulations that favored American businesses over foreign firms operating in the American market. The second principle, *most favored nation*, required governments to treat foreign firms from each party to the MAI the same as they treated firms from all other parties to the agreement. The French government could not, for example, offer more favorable treatment to a German firm than it did to an American firm.

Together, the two principles would have made it illegal for governments to discriminate against foreign firms from a particular country in favor of domestic firms or in favor of foreign firms from other countries. The MAI would also have provided greater security to foreign investors by guaranteeing prompt, effective, and adequate compensation in the event of a government expropriation. The agreement also contained provisions to ensure that firms could send profits, dividends, and proceeds from asset sales back to their home country. Finally, the MAI envisaged a dispute settlement mechanism that allowed for state-to-state claims and firm-to-state claims. While negotiations on the MAI were abandoned in the late 1990s, had it been successfully concluded, it would have imposed some important limitations on the ability of governments to restrict the activities of MNCs.

The second track has been pushed most forcefully by developing countries and, more recently, NGOs active in the antiglobalization movement. On this track, efforts have focused on creating international rules that oblige MNCs to act in socially responsible ways. During the 1960s and 1970s, developing countries used the United Nations to try to create a code of conduct to regulate MNC activities. The goal was to ensure that such activities "were compatible with the medium and long-term needs which the governments in the capital importing countries had identified in their development plans" (de Rivero 1980, p. 96). More recently, NGOs have advocated the creation of international rules that force MNCs to adopt high standards concerning the treatment of developing-country workers, human rights in general, and the environment. As Father Sergio Cobo, a member of the Catholic Agency for Overseas Development (CAFOD) wrote, "We cannot be too idealistic in what we press for, but [MNCs] should be providing at least a minimum of basic human rights in the workplace. The obligation of the companies should include respect for the dignity of the person and acknowledgment of their social, economic and cultural rights. That means, at the very least, dignified treatment, safe conditions, social security coverage and some contractual stability" (CAFOD n.d., p. 2).

In spite of this long history of negotiation, governments have never been able to agree on a set of comprehensive and binding rules with which to regulate FDI and MNC activity. As a consequence, the only such rules that do exist are based in large part on voluntary codes of conduct. Many MNCs, reacting to pressure from NGOs, have developed codes of corporate conduct. The United Nations has been developing voluntary codes of conduct that apply to MNC activities. The two articles presented in this chapter examine these emerging regulatory structures. In the first article, three professors from Duke University, Gary Gereffi, Ronie Garcia-Johnson, and Erika Sasser, trace the emergence and impact of private regulatory regimes, which are rules that are created and enforced not by governments but by MNCs and NGOs. Such codes of conduct have emerged as NGOs have increased their scrutiny of MNC activities. In the second article, Daniel Litvin focuses on the voluntary codes of conduct created by governments within the United Nations. Litvin argues that while these codes are a useful first step, the UN should develop a set of coherent and enforceable standards for MNC activities.

REFERENCES

CAFOD. "Rough guide to multinational corporations." A CAFOD Briefing. Available at http://www.cafod.org.uk/var/storage/original/application/phpDO7qiv.pdf (accessed February 16, 2004).

DeRivero, Oswaldo. *New Economy Order and International Development Law.* Oxford: Pergamon Press, 1980.

Graham, Edward. *Fighting the Wrong Enemy: Antiglobal Activities and Multinational Enterprises.* Washington, DC: Institute for International Economics, 2000.

The NGO-Industrial Complex

GARY GEREFFI, RONIE GARCIA-JOHNSON, AND ERIKA SASSER

In April 2000, Starbucks Corporation announced it would buy coffee beans from importers who pay above market prices to small farmers (so-called fair trade beans) and sell them in more than 2,000 of its shops across the United States. In August of the same year, the McDonald's Corporation sent a letter to the producers of the nearly 2 billion eggs it buys annually, ordering them to comply with strict guidelines for the humane treatment of hens or risk losing the company's business. And in 1998, De Beers Consolidated Mines, the company that controls two-thirds of the world trade in uncut diamonds, began investing heavily in Canada to distance itself from the controversy surrounding "blood diamonds"—gems sold to finance warring rebel factions in Africa.

Are these episodes sudden attacks of conscience on the part of the world's top CEOs? Not quite. Under increasing pressure from environmental and labor activists, multilateral organizations, and regulatory agencies in their home countries, multinational firms are implementing "certification" arrangements—codes of conduct, production guidelines, and monitoring standards that govern and attest to not only the corporations' behavior but also to that of their suppliers around the world. Champions of these new mechanisms include United Nations Secretary-General Kofi Annan, who in January 1999 exhorted world business leaders to "embrace and enact" the U.N. Global Compact, whose nine principles covering human rights, labor, and the environment "unite the powers of markets with the authority of universal ideals."

Certification has appeared in almost every major industry targeted by environmentalists, including the chemical, coffee, forest products, oil, mining, nuclear power, and transportation sectors. Certification is also prevalent in the apparel, diamond, footwear, and toy industries, to name a few. A recent inventory by the Organisation for Economic Co-operation and Development (OECD) listed 246 codes of corporate conduct, while the Global Reporting Initiative, an organization dedicated to standardizing corporate sustainability reporting, estimates that more than 2,000 companies voluntarily report their social, environmental, and economic practice and performance.

Supporters believe that certification efforts embody a new model for global corporate governance—no mean feat when national governments appear unable to

From Gary Gereffi, Ronie Garcia-Johnson, Erika Sasser, "The NGO-Industrial Complex," *Foreign Policy* 125, July/August, 2001, pp. 56–65. © *Foreign Policy* in the format Textbook via Copyright Clearance Center.

constrain powerful multinational corporations. Nevertheless, even while early signs suggest that certification arrangements may indeed improve working conditions and promote more environmentally friendly production, certification remains a blunt and imperfect tool for augmenting the accountability of global firms. Proliferating certification arrangements compete for legitimacy with non-governmental organizations (NGOs) and consumers, as well as for adoption by multinationals. And there is no guarantee that the most effective standards—in environmental or labor terms—will win these battles. Some observers even fear that certification driven by activists and corporations will preempt or supplant altogether the role of states and international organizations in addressing corporate accountability as free trade expands around the globe.

MANUFACTURING SHAME

Certification institutions have two key components: a set of rules, principles, or guidelines (usually in the form of a code of conduct) and a reporting or monitoring mechanism (often a corporate environmental report, or a "social audit"). Certification can be broken down into four broad categories, according to who produces the guidelines and conducts the monitoring:

First-party certification is the most common variety, whereby a single firm develops its own rules and reports on compliance. For instance, the Johnson & Johnson company credo that General Robert Wood Johnson wrote in 1943, which bolstered the company during the Tylenol® crises of the 1980s, now includes environmental and social concerns. The company published its first Social Contributions Report in 1992 and its first Environmental, Health & Safety Report in 1993.

Second-party certification involves an industry or trade association fashioning a code of conduct and implementing reporting mechanisms. The chemical industry's global Responsible Care® program provides an apt example. During the initiative's early years in the United States, the Chemical Manufacturers Association (now known as the American Chemistry Council) developed environmental, health, and safety principles and codes, required participating firms to submit implementation reports, and reported aggregate industry progress.

Third-party certification involves an external group, often an NGO, imposing its rules and compliance methods onto a particular firm or industry. The Council on Economic Priorities (CEP), the pioneering New York–based NGO, has collected data on corporate activities since its creation in 1969 and publishes reports on corporate behavior. The CEP (recently renamed the Center for Responsibility in Business) created an accreditation agency that designed auditable standards and an independent use accreditation process for the protection of workers' rights, dubbed Social Accountability 8000 (SA8000). As of April 2001, the group certified 66 manufacturing facilities around the world that mainly make toys and apparel as SA8000-compliant.

Fourth-party certification involves government or multilateral agencies. The United Nations' Global Compact, for instance, lists environmental, labor, and human rights principles for companies to follow; participating corporations must submit online updates of their progress for NGOs to scrutinize.

The earliest efforts to set and monitor voluntary standards in the United States were prompted, quite literally, by accident; they were responses to industrial mishaps in the environmental arena. After the Three Mile Island incident in 1979, the U.S. nuclear power industry created the Institute of Nuclear Power Operations, an organization that privately evaluates the industry through the provision of standards and inspections. Similarly, the 1986 Chernobyl accident prompted a handful of nuclear power associations from the United States and Europe to create the World Association of Nuclear Operators. And the chemical industry's Responsible Care initiative emerged in Canada and then the United States after the 1984 disaster that killed some 2,500 people and injured many more at a Union Carbide subsidiary in Bhopal, India. By April 2001, chemical industry associations in 46 countries had adopted the initiative, which promotes improvement in environment, health, and safety performance for the industry.

Over time, however, certification arrangements became more proactive and preemptive, with NGOs no longer waiting for accidents but rather seeking out ongoing corporate wrongdoing. Labor-based certification in particular emerged in response to exposés against top brand-name companies that use international contractors and sub-contractors, such as Wal-Mart Stores in Honduras and Bangladesh, the Walt Disney Company in Haiti, Mattel in China, Nike in Indonesia, J.C. Penney Company and Kmart Corporation in Nicaragua, and Liz Claiborne Inc. and Gap Inc. in El Salvador. The most typical abuses included abysmally low wages, use of child labor, mistreatment of female workers, and the suppression of labor unions. Levi Strauss & Co. issued a code of conduct in 1991, and other apparel industry giants such as Liz Claiborne, Nike, Reebok, and Gap Inc. soon followed. These codes included prohibitions on child labor and forced labor, guarantees of nondiscrimination in the workplace, respect for prevailing national legislation, and "decent" remuneration at or above the local minimum wage. Industry associations and other groups developed similar policies: For instance, the International Federation of Football Association (FIFA) created a licensing program in 1996 to prevent members from using soccer balls made with child labor.

While this history shows that most certification institutions began as creations of advanced industrial countries—particularly the United States, where direct government intervention is universally maligned and corporate accountability movements are increasingly powerful—it should come as no surprise that businesses and NGOs alike are taking their U.S.-based certification solutions global. As activist networks expand and social and environmental concern spreads in country after country, major multinationals hope to reassure their customers at home while surpassing the expectations of overseas governments that have weak or unenforced laws. Creating or participating in voluntary certification initiatives may allow entire industries to preempt the development of international labor and environmental laws directed at multinational companies, and to avoid a nightmarish scenario of stringent and often contradictory regulations in country after country.

IT'S NOT EASY BEING GREEN

Do certification arrangements really affect corporate behavior? The answer depends on the particular industry, the ability of NGOs to mobilize effectively, and the unique interests of the groups involved. Although still relatively recent phenomena, the certification experiences of the forest products and apparel industries reveal how certification can compel companies to rethink their practices.

Forest Certification

As the extent of global forest destruction became more apparent during the 1970s and 1980s, so did concerns over the environmental impacts of deforestation, clear-cutting, loss of bio-diversity, and the effluent from pulp and paper mills. However, well-organized, developed-country NGOs that focused on protecting tropical forests in developing economies found it difficult to identify which firms operating in endangered forests were actually inflicting damage. Forest certification emerged in response to this need.

The race to certify began in 1993, when powerful NGOs such as the World Wildlife Fund and Greenpeace created the Forest Stewardship Council (FSC). The FSC accepts no funding from industry and has developed a set of core principles guiding on-the-ground timber management and harvesting operations, including restrictions on pesticide use and requirements for bio-diversity protection and erosion control. Firms seeking FSC approval must undergo an audit by one of a few accredited "certifiers"—private firms such as SmartWood and Scientific Certification Systems in the United States and the Silva Forest Foundation in Canada—which can verify compliance with FSC requirements. The FSC also offers "chain-of-custody" certification, which traces the amount of certified wood in a product from the forest floor to the consumer shelf. (Chain-of-custody accounting is particularly difficult for products, such as paper, made from multiple sources.) Corporations meeting the chain-of-custody requirements are allowed to display the FSC logo on their products.

Arguing that the FSC guidelines are onerous and unwieldy, the timber industries in the United States, Canada, and Europe quickly countered with their own templates for appropriate forestry practices. Today, more than 40 certification programs exist worldwide, most of them at the national level. Timber companies often establish umbrella certification programs through their national industry associations rather than develop firm-specific certification programs because they face a "shared reputation" problem: Consumers don't necessarily distinguish between wood harvested by Georgia-Pacific and International Paper, for instance, so individual action does little to solidify a green reputation.

The contrast between industry-led certification and the NGO variety is stark. Consider the differences between the FSC and the Sustainable Forestry Initiative (SFI) program, established by the industry's American Forest and Paper Association in 1994. As originally conceptualized, the SFI program required firms only to develop internal mechanisms to meet the SFI program's broad, overarching objectives of ensuring long-term forest productivity and conservation of forest resources. Firms themselves conducted monitoring and enforcement. And because the original SFI program standards mandated few particular forest-management techniques, firms enjoyed tremendous freedom to set their own management specifications. This leeway led to significant differences in the environmental standards established by different firms. Furthermore, the SFI program has not conducted chain-of-custody monitoring and has only recently revealed plans to introduce a labeling system for products. Since the firms supply compliance reports privately to the industry association, accountability to consumers and the public remains minimal.

However, under heavy criticism from environmental groups, the industry has gradually encompassed more stringent standards and encouraged independent monitoring. The firms that felt the pressure most keenly were not timber extractors such as Georgia-Pacific, Weyerhaeuser, and International Paper, but retailers, specifically the big do-it-yourself centers such as The Home Depot and Lowe's Home Improvement Warehouse stores. The Rainforest Action Network, Greenpeace, Natural Resources Defense Council, and other NGOs launched major grass-roots campaigns against these retail giants in the late 1990s. Ultimately, both Home Depot (August 1999) and Lowe's (August 2000) declared their preference for FSC-certified products, a blow to the industry groups who hoped for the adoption of the SFI program. With the credibility of their certification program at stake, the industry had little choice but to push standards toward FSC levels.

Apparel Certification

Aggressive campaigns by labor groups, NGOs, and student activists have compelled apparel corporations to adopt stringent codes of conduct and establish independent monitoring as well. The revelation in 1995 of the virtual enslavement of Thai workers in a garment factory in El Monte, California, prompted the Clinton administration to form a task force called the Apparel Industry Partnership (AIP). Made up of manufacturers, NGOs, unions, and U.S. Department of Labor representatives, the AIP forged a code of conduct for apparel firms, stipulating that companies pay the local minimum or prevailing wage, that workers be at least 14 years old, and that employees work no more than 60 hours per week (although they could work unlimited voluntary hours). In November 1998, the AIP created the Fair Labor Association (FLA) to implement and monitor this code of conduct.

Controversy arose when several unions and NGOs withdrew from the AIP, claiming that its provisions were too weak (they relied on voluntary enforcement and set no standard for a living wage) and that its monitoring was neither independent nor transparent (its external-inspection system gave manufacturers too much control over which factories were investigated and by whom, and its monitoring reports did not have to be released to the public). The industry-backed FLA has attempted to address the concerns of the student antisweatshop movement that gained momentum through demonstrations at several U.S. universities such as Duke, Georgetown, Notre Dame, and Wisconsin in 1997 and 1998. The FLA, which plans to begin certifying manufacturers by the end of 2001, calls for internal monitoring as well as external surveillance from an FLA-approved list of monitors, who will conduct announced and unannounced factory visits.

Some student activists sided with the criticisms of the unions and NGOs, leading the United Students Against Sweatshops (in collaboration with university administrators and labor-rights experts) to establish the Worker Rights Consortium (WRC) in 2000 as a more radical alternative. With support from the AFL-CIO and the Union of Needleworkers, Industrial, and Textile Employees (UNITE), the WRC advocates a living wage for garment workers, independent unions, unannounced factory investigations, and full disclosure of factory conditions. The WRC has support from more than 80 universities, compared with the 155 universities that have signed on with the FLA.

Notwithstanding the infighting among competing certification groups, codes of conduct and effective independent monitoring have led global apparel firms to change their behavior. Take the case of Gap Inc., which acquires a portion of its clothing in Central America. In 1995, one of Gap Inc.'s apparel contractors in El Salvador, Mandarin International, fired 350 workers when they formed a union to protest working conditions. This dismissal, plus numerous other abuses exposed in the factory, violated Gap Inc.'s well-publicized code of conduct. Instead of simply rescinding its contract with Mandarin, which would have left the garment workers without jobs, Gap Inc.—under considerable pressure from NGOs such as the National Labor Committee, a union-backed worker advocacy group that organized a U.S. speaking tour for several of the fired female Salvadoran workers— became the first retailer to agree to independent monitoring of a foreign contractor. This agreement was considered a major breakthrough in apparel certification. While the monitoring agency (called the Independent Monitoring Group of El Salvador) has improved working conditions in the Mandarin factory in El Salvador, Gap Inc. has so far allowed independent monitoring of its codes of conduct in only a handful of the 55 countries where it does business (other sites are monitored in Honduras and Guatemala).

The WRC recently adopted a similar interventionist approach with Nike in Mexico. In January 2001, a large number of the 850 workers at the Korean-owned-and-operated Kukdong International factory in Puebla, Mexico—which produces Nike and Reebok sweat shirts for the $2.5 billion annual collegiate market—staged a work stoppage to protest the firing of five workers who opposed poor labor conditions. Operations in the Kukdong apparel factory violated a number of provisions in Nike's code of conduct, including freedom of association, harassment and abuse, and health and safety conditions. By early February, the independent monitoring organization, Verité, an Amherst, Massachusetts, nonprofit, sent a five-person team to Kukdong to examine the factory's workplace practices. The Verité factory evaluation report was completed and made public in a matter of weeks, and on March 14, 2001, Nike released its plan outlining the corrective actions and a timetable for Kukdong to comply with Nike's code of conduct. Just one week after the strike, nearly two thirds of the factory workers were back on the job.

Of course, companies do not always deal with factory abuses so readily. In February 2001, the Global Alliance for Workers and Communities released a 106-page, Nike-funded report on the labor conditions at nine Nike contract factories in Indonesia. The report detailed a variety of labor problems, including low wages, denial of the right to unionize, verbal and physical abuse by supervisors, sexual harassment, and forced overtime. The contents of the report are not surprising; similar findings were asserted throughout the 1990s. What is new about this report is that Nike paid for it, released it—and can't deny it. Nike's response to these problems will set new benchmarks that other apparel and footwear companies must match or else risk incurring relentless scrutiny by industry critics.

Although definitive conclusions may be premature, the forestry and apparel experiences underscore the growing power of NGOs to compel corporations to adopt new environmental and labor standards. In particular, NGOs have become highly sophisticated in using market-campaigning techniques to gain leverage over recalcitrant firms. Market campaigning, which focuses protests against highly visible branded retailers, is only about 10 years old, but in the words of one Greenpeace activist, "it was like discovering gunpowder for environmentalists." By targeting firms such as Gap Inc. or Home Depot—firms at the retail end of the supply chain with direct links to customers—NGOs are able to wield the power and vulnerability of corporate brand names to their advantage. Where resource-extractive firms like timber giant Georgia-Pacific may be isolated from consumers and thus insulated from negative press, companies such as Staples Inc. (a current Rainforest Action Network target) are much more vulnerable. By using tactics such as boycotts, banner hangings, leafleting, and other direct action, NGOs force retailers to take proactive labor and environmental stances.

THE CERTIFICATION SOLUTION

The strength and influence of certification programs seem to be increasing. Third-party certification and monitoring may soon become the norm in many global industries. The battles over forest-product certification show that consumers and NGOs can quickly delegitimize weak standards and inadequate enforcement mechanisms, and they can also mobilize effectively for more stringent codes of conduct and more reliable monitoring. Corporations in the apparel industry are making concessions that would have been unthinkable just a few years ago as they too advocate third-party arrangements. Even the chemical industry's Responsible Care initiative is considering third-party verification

Yet, watchdog activists cannot press for change in every industry and at all times. In the absence of their efforts, market forces and the drive toward standardization may lead firms to accept lowest-common-denominator certification, particularly when industry moves first and establishes a certification arrangement with widespread global membership. While competition can foster higher industry standards, less pressure will leave companies room to dictate their own terms of compliance. And even the most stringent certification initiatives may fail to address fundamental questions about industry structures, such as the international sub-contracting system that allows brand-name companies, such as Nike or Gap Inc., to control their suppliers through large orders without the legal responsibilities that go with factory ownership.

More fundamentally, the rise of certification institutions poses profound dilemmas for the progressive notion popular during the 20th century that the remedy for social and environmental problems was a stronger and more interventionist state. When the state proved unable to meet all the demands placed upon it, particularly as firms and business transactions moved outside national territorial boundaries, alternative solutions were sought. Trends in the past decade suggest a new response in the 21st century: the certification solution. Whether certification programs are developed by business associations or pushed by activist NGOs, the development of voluntary governance mechanisms is transforming traditional power relationships in the global arena. Linking together diverse and often antagonistic actors from the local, national, and international levels, certification institutions have arisen to govern firm behavior in a global space that has eluded the control of states and international organizations.

While certification will never replace the state, it is quickly becoming a powerful tool for promoting worker rights and protecting the environment in an era of free trade. These new mechanisms of transnational private governance exist alongside and within national and international regimes like the North American Free Trade Agreement, complementing and, in some cases, bolstering their efforts. In countries with stringent, rigorously enforced labor and environmental laws, certification provides a private layer of governance that moves beyond state borders to shape global supply chains. In countries with nascent or ineffective labor and environmental legislation, certification can draw attention to uneven standards and help mitigate these disparities. The challenge is for states to accept certification not as a threat but as an opportunity to reinforce labor and environmental goals within their sovereign territory and beyond.

"Needed: A Global Business Code of Conduct"

DANIEL LITVIN

MEMORANDUM:

TO: U.N. Secretary-General Kofi Annan

FROM: Daniel Litvin

RE: Raising Human Rights Standards in the Private Sector

Ensuring that companies respect human rights is an important and controversial challenge, one in which the United Nations has a unique role to play. As you, Mr. Secretary-General, have recognized, maintaining broad political consensus in favor of globalization and increased flows of foreign investment is crucial to raising living standards in the developing world. In addition to being inexcusable, human rights transgressions by multinational corporations threaten this consensus by giving ammunition to the many groups opposed to further global integration.

This memorandum argues that the United Nations must develop new standards concerning the relationship between corporations and human rights. It recommends drafting a set of principles that is tough on multinationals and backed by an enforcement mechanism but that also recognizes the difficulties companies face. The two most recent U.N. initiatives in this area, the so-called "Global Compact" and the Human Rights Norms for Businesses (the "Norms," as they are now known), both lack this balanced approach.

The failure of these initiatives to set reasonable and well-defined limits on the human rights responsibilities of companies helps explain the current hostility of business lobbies to any effort to create an enforceable code of conduct. A more realistic and fair approach can resolve this problem and win the support of both businesses and nongovernmental organizations (NGOs).

What follows is a detailed look at the problem of human rights and multinationals; at the failure of U.N. efforts to address the problem; a proposed solution; and suggestions for that solution's implementation.

THE PROBLEM

Multinationals confer many benefits, but they also can cause or exacerbate a range of problems in the places they invest, particularly developing countries. At worst, these problems may include civil conflict, repression of minorities, abuse of workers' rights, and the perpetuation of abusive regimes (which obviously draw sustenance from foreign investment).

Only a tiny proportion of the world's 50,000-plus multinationals explicitly include respect for human rights in their codes of conduct, and among those that do, not many can claim to have honored this commitment in every aspect of their operations. Fully implementing a policy of social responsibility in a large, globally dispersed organization presents a genuine management challenge.

Even if multinationals were able to guarantee complete adherence to such a policy, how they would go about upholding human rights in practice is unclear, for the boundaries of their responsibility—where it begins and where it ends—are often undefined. This ambiguity is the nub of the problem.

Take the issue of labor exploitation. Most of the Western multinationals that have been accused in recent years of abusing workers (by employing underage children, for instance) did not actually commit violations themselves; rather, the guilty party was a supplier, or a supplier of a supplier. Multinationals certainly have some duty to try to prevent these abuses, but how far down the supply chain do their obligations extend?

Many human rights controversies involving multinationals can be attributed to the lack of a clear dividing line between the responsibilities of a company and a host government. No one disputes that companies ought to do everything they can to uphold the rights of their employees and of local communities and to generally be a force for good wherever they operate. But what that means in practice is unclear.

Should a company investing in a country where union organization is restricted—China, for example—contravene the law by hosting unauthorized unions in its factories? Is a company operating in a politically repressive state such as Burma, where a number of Western firms still have investments, obliged to petition the government on behalf of jailed dissidents?

Companies cannot simply ignore these issues, but limits to their responsibilities need to be set. At the root of these problems is the failure of states to protect adequately the rights of citizens. Profit-making enterprises have neither the expertise nor the capacity to supplant the role of government in this regard. Moreover, if a multinational were to intervene heavily in the internal affairs of a country, it would rightly be accused of neocolonialism.

INADEQUATE SOLUTIONS

The United Nations has made two recent attempts to establish a set of human rights and broader ethical standards for multinationals: the "Global Compact," which you unveiled at Davos in 1999 and which has now been embraced by over

1,000 companies; and the "Norms," adopted in August 2003 by the U.N. Sub-Commission on the Promotion and Protection of Human Rights. The first has been attacked for being too soft on business, the latter for being too tough, and unfortunately, these criticisms are well founded.

The "Global Compact" has had various successes. For example, it has encouraged many fruitful local partnerships on development issues among companies, labor organizations, and other groups. But the objection raised by NGOs—that the compact is toothless and allows multinationals to "blue-wash" themselves (that is, to gain favorable publicity by associating themselves with the United Nations without actually improving their behavior)—has merit, too.

Companies wishing to participate in this voluntary initiative face a relatively low set of hurdles: Their CEOs must write you a letter expressing support for the nine principles enunciated in the compact. The corporations must then "set in motion changes to business operations so that the Global Compact and its principles become part of strategy, culture, and day-to-day operations." But enforcement, such as it currently is, consists of a requirement that firms describe in their annual reports the ways in which they are fulfilling their commitments.

Moreover, the two human rights provisions do little to define boundaries for companies in this area, merely declaring that firms should support human rights "within their sphere of influence" and not be "complicit" in abuses. The supporting literature on the compact's Web site offers some suggestions for "possible actions" by companies in this respect—for example, that they undertake a "human rights assessment" of the situation in countries where they intend to do business. But obligations are not defined in any concrete fashion.

As for the "Norms," their weakness lies not so much in failing to define companies' responsibilities but in defining them too expansively. While declaring that governments have the "primary responsibility" for upholding human rights, the "Norms" list an array of rights that companies themselves must protect. However, little is said about how firms should behave when fulfillment of these obligations would force them to violate local laws or to demand changes in host government policy.

For instance, the "Norms" say that firms should not directly or indirectly benefit from abuses and that they should "contribute" to the realization of, among other things, "freedom of thought, conscience, and religion, and freedom of opinion and expression." This goal sounds admirable, but what does it actually mean? As a practical matter, how far is General Motors supposed to go in trying to support human rights in China? Should it break the law? Should it permit, for example, Falun Gong meetings at its Shanghai plant?

Furthermore, the "Norms" recommend that companies be subject to periodic monitoring by the United Nations and other national and international bodies and provide "reparation" should they fail to meet their responsibilities.

The long list of obligations, coupled with the threat of sanctions, suggests that even ethical firms could be held financially liable for myriad human rights abuses in countries in which they invest. Put another way, the "Norms" potentially could deter responsible firms from investing in precisely those developing countries where governance and human rights problems are most acute—a perverse result, given that these countries are also most likely to be in urgent need of foreign capital and of integration with the global economy.

The "Norms" approach has not been received warmly by business lobbies and is likely to encounter even stronger resistance when put before the full U.N. Commission on Human Rights. It confirms the corporate sector's worst fears: that multinationals will be held accountable for problems over which they have little, if any, influence.

A BETTER SOLUTION

Corporations are generally averse to regulation and to proposals for binding international rules governing human rights. On the other hand, most CEOs are intelligent people; they understand that the issue of social responsibility is not going to disappear. They also recognize that without a more detailed code of conduct and some means of enforcement, charges leveled against companies will be adjudicated in the court of public opinion, where mitigating details count for little, where boundaries of corporate responsibility are defined by NGOs and other critics, and where firms are easily cast as ogres.

High-profile multinationals such as Shell and McDonald's have been vilified in recent years. Surely, it is a source of consternation to them that they are sometimes blamed for problems that are really the responsibilities of a host government and that they have been made symbols of corporate greed and callousness while less familiar firms often get away with worse sins.

In short, large, prominent firms have a strong incentive to create a global set of rules by which all multinationals should play—a set of rules that is fair, realistic, and, above all, clear. And obviously, corporate backing for any such initiative is essential if it is to work.

It is possible for the United Nations to develop a set of principles that is strict as well as enforceable and that commands the support of both NGOs and the business community. The details would need to be discussed carefully and hammered out partly through a process of consultation with the various lobbies and interests concerned. But the obligations and boundaries that might be placed on firms can be envisaged in general terms.

With regard to labor rights and supply chains, for example, companies above a certain size could be expected to demand appropriate standards of their immediate suppliers and to put in place basic monitoring systems to help guarantee these standards are being met. But they would have no obligation under these principles to ensure similar adherence from their suppliers' suppliers.

It would also be reasonable to expect companies to report to the United Nations substantial abuses perpetrated by host governments against local communities and to state publicly their opposition to such practices—but that should be the extent of their overt political involvement. With this issue and other equally knotty ones, the key will be to define obligations in such a way that they are politically and economically realistic but do not absolve multinationals of their responsibilities.

MAKING IT HAPPEN

The need for the United Nations to develop a balanced set of principles that elicit more than just a public relations response from multinationals is obvious. The question is how you, as secretary-general, can help the organization accomplish this task.

I would suggest you begin by establishing a timetable—by declaring that within, say, five years, you want the United Nations to have completed work on a new body of human rights commitments for multinationals and to have also conceived a means of enforcement to ensure compliance. You will need to mention enforcement to signal the seriousness of this endeavor but should not discuss the form it might take. (For the foreseeable future, the only politically practical enforcement mechanism may be a modest one—a U.N. rapporteur, for instance, to assess the behavior of a select number of firms each year.)

Drafting the new principles should be entrusted to a small, carefully selected group of experts from the business community, the NGO sector, the labor movement, and the United Nations itself. The participants should be equally drawn from the North and the South.

Once new standards have been agreed upon, the United Nations will need to secure the backing of the many multinationals and NGOs that have not participated in the drafting process. Assuming that the principles adequately address their interests and worries, it should be possible to get both sides to support the new rules. Governments will follow—although some developing countries may need reassurance that the code of conduct is not a rich world conspiracy to exclude them from Western markets but rather a means of ensuring the capital inflows they need.

If a way is found to bridge business and human rights concerns, the United Nations will have taken a big step toward building public trust in globalization and tempering some of its ill effects. And you, Mr. Secretary-General, will have secured a large part of your legacy.

QUESTIONS FOR REVIEW AND DISCUSSION

1. What are the four types of certification that Gereffi, Garcia-Johnson, and Sasser discuss? Can you provide an example of each type?
2. According to Gereffi, Garcia-Johnson, and Sasser, what factors have driven the development of these certification arrangements?
3. What are the strengths and weaknesses of the third-party certification arrangements that Gereffi, Garcia-Johnson, and Sasser discuss?
4. On what grounds does Litvin criticize the United Nations' "Global Compact" and "Norms"? Find these documents on the Web (see URLs below). Do you agree or disagree with Litvin's critique?
5. What standards does Litvin encourage the United Nations to develop? Do you think the development of such standards is politically feasible?
6. What is the correct balance of responsibility between MNCs and national governments when it comes to ensuring respect for basic human rights?

7. Is there a compelling case for international rules to regulate MNC activities? Why or why not? If we assume that such a need does exist, should such rules be created by governments or are nongovernmental arrangements, such as those discussed by Gereffi, Garcia-Johnson, and Sasser sufficient? Justify your answer.

SUGGESTIONS FOR FURTHER READING

An in-depth examination of the Multilateral Agreement on Investment can be found in Edward Graham's *Fighting the Wrong Enemy: Antiglobal Activities and Multinational Enterprises*. Washington, DC: Institute for International Economics, 2000.

A more detailed examination of codes of conduct can be found in Rhys Jenkins. *Corporate Codes of Conduct: Self Regulation in a Global Economy*. Geneva: The United Nations, 2001.

A Duke University Colloquia explored the impact of certification arrangements. The papers presented at this meeting are available at: http://www.nicholas.duke.edu/solutions/colloquia-7th.html#Publications

Ronie Garcia-Johnson explores how the interaction between ideas, technology, and NGO activity alters the behavior of MNCs in *Exporting Environmentalism: U.S. Multinational Chemical Corporations in Brazil and Mexico*. Cambridge, MA: MIT Press, 2000.

The United Nations Global Compact Web site can be found at: http://www.unglobalcompact.org/Portal/Default.asp

The draft United Nations "Norms" are: United Nations Economic and Social Council Commission on Human Rights, Sub-Commission on the Promotion and Protection of Human Rights. "Norms on the responsibilities of transnational corporations and other business enterprises with regard to human rights." E/CN.4/Sub.2/2003/12/Rev.2, 2003. This document is available at: http://www.unhchr.ch/Huridocda/Huridoca.nsf/(Symbol)/E.CN.4.Sub.2.2003.12.Rev.2.En?Opendocument

PART

V

Exchange Rates

CHAPTER 11

STRONG DOLLAR
OR WEAK DOLLAR?

The value of the dollar against other major international currencies has fluctuated dramatically ever since the United States floated its currency in 1973. The dollar depreciated sharply throughout the 1970s, losing more than 20 percent of its value against the German mark and the Japanese yen. Dollar depreciation reversed itself in the first half of the 1980s. Between 1980 and 1985, the American currency appreciated by more than 50 percent against the yen and mark. From this peak, the dollar began to lose value and in the first half of the 1990s fell to historic lows against both the yen and the mark. The dollar then surged in value after 1995 as the American economy boomed. Between 1995 and 1998 the dollar increased in value by more than 70 percent against the yen and mark. The dollar began to weaken once again late in 2001, losing value against the yen and the euro. By the summer of 2003, the dollar was standing at its lowest ever value against the euro, having fallen from about 89 cents per euro in 2001 to $1.13 per euro.

Such great and persistent changes in the value of the dollar against foreign currencies have a large impact on the American economy. The exchange rate is a very important price in an economy that is open to trade. It establishes the prices of American goods in foreign markets and of foreign goods in American markets. As with any price, dramatic changes in the value of the dollar affect the fortunes of people engaged in economic activity. As the dollar's value rises, the price of American goods in foreign markets rises as well, making it more difficult for American businesses to export. As the dollar loses value, the price of American goods in foreign markets falls, making it easier for American businesses to export. A strong dollar also reduces the American price of foreign goods, thereby exposing American producers to tougher competition from imports. Conversely, a weak dollar raises the American price of foreign goods, thereby reducing competition from imports in the American market.

The dollar's value also affects broader measures of economic performance, such as economic growth. The United States depends upon foreign capital to finance a portion of growth-inducing investment by selling dollar-denominated financial assets such as stocks, government and corporate bonds, certificates of deposit, and other financial instruments, to foreigners. The willingness of foreigners to purchase these financial assets is partly determined by the dollar's exchange rate. Most foreigners that buy dollar-denominated financial assets will eventually sell them, use the resulting dollars to purchase their domestic currency, and then spend the proceeds at home. Thus, the full value of a dollar-denominated asset to a foreigner depends in part on the exchange rate between the dollar and their home currency. If the dollar gains in value against the euro, for example, then the value of American financial assets when sold and transferred into euros rises. If the dollar loses value against foreign currencies, then the euro value of dollar-denominated financial assets falls. If for some reason foreigners begin to believe that the dollar will lose value in the future, they will either purchase fewer American financial assets or demand higher interest rates for doing so. If foreigners become less willing to buy dollar-denominated financial assets, or demand higher interest rates to do so, then the amount of investment in the American economy, and thus the rate of economic growth in the United States, will fall.

The value of the dollar against foreign currencies thus has significant but crosscutting effects on American economic activity. A strong dollar can boost investment by encouraging foreign capital inflows, but also creates severe problems for American manufacturing industries. A weak dollar benefits American manufacturers, but may also limit the amount of foreign capital available to finance investment, thereby slowing economic growth. Because the dollar's external value has crosscutting effects, and has been so prone to rise and fall, debate over the "correct" exchange rate for the dollar has been a recurrent theme in American policy circles.

The two articles presented in this chapter, although written prior to the dollar's recent decline, are broadly representative of the two sides in this debate. Lawrence Lindsey, who at the time this article was written was the leading voice in the Bush administration's economic policy team, and served as a Federal Reserve Governor during the 1990s, argues in favor of a strong dollar policy. He places most of his emphasis on the need to maintain foreign confidence in the dollar. Such confidence is important, he argues, to ensure that the dollar continues to play the preeminent role in the international monetary system and to continue to attract foreign capital to the United States. C. Fred Bergsten, a senior economist at the Institute of International Economics, argues that given current economic conditions in the United States, the Bush administration should seek to reduce the dollar's value.

In the Dollar We Trust

LAWRENCE LINDSEY

Since the end of the Second World War, the dollar has been the world's pre-eminent currency. Fifty years ago that position was held by default. The rest of the industrial world was suffering from the devastation of war. The United Kingdom, issuer of the dominant currency before the war, was wracked by huge war related debts and focused on the challenge of adjusting to a diminished role in the world. Accounting for nearly half of the world GNP, the dollar was chosen by common agreement as the benchmark currency. The Bretton Woods system came into being.

By 1970, the arrangements of the post-war years were no longer ideal. Global growth had removed the dollar's monopoly role. More importantly, fixed exchange rates were creating too rigid a box for growing global trade and capital markets. The attraction of flexible exchange rates grew, because macroeconomic divergences at the nation-state level were worked out by the currency markets without creating periodic balance of payments crises.

Indeed, the notion of a "balance of payments crisis" became nearly obsolete among developed countries. Instead of asking whether a nation could service its international obligations, the question became, at what price? Flexible exchange rates both allowed and necessitated the development of thick, liquid, currency markets. This permitted global trade to continue to expand at a rapid pace in spite of the currency risks involved for buyers and sellers of traded goods and services. There more liquid markets also allowed vastly increased movements of capital as the risks involved in transnational lending could also be hedged.

The role of the dollar has been tested in each of these regimes. Today the dollar's pre-eminence can no longer be taken for granted, but must be earned. It continues to be the case that the great majority of all foreign trade conducted on the planet is invoiced in dollars. But this is a matter of consent between the contracting parties, a choice, which could be altered if confidence in the dollar as a stable medium of exchange were lost.

Of even more importance, people all over the world look to the dollar as a reliable store of wealth. They are convinced that it provides a secure and portable asset that will hold its value over time. As a consequence, more than 70 percent of the value of all U.S. currency circulates outside the United States. Equally important, the U.S. capital markets offer global investors the opportunity to invest their funds in dollar-denominated assets valued in the trillions.

From Lawrence Lindsey, "In the Dollar We Trust," *The International Economy* 15 March/April, 2001, pp. 6–9, 52.

Again, this has become a matter of choice, reflecting the confidence of millions of individual investors and portfolio managers. It is not something that we should take for granted.

During the 1970s, the world's confidence in the dollar declined as faith in our currency's purchasing power slipped. The decisions in the early 1980s to opt for a "hard" non-inflationary currency led to a twenty-year expansion of confidence in the dollar and in foreign willingness to hold dollar assets. This includes the currency itself, as the number of dollars in circulation has risen by 25 percent more quickly than American GDP in spite of a proliferation of alternative non-cash methods of making payments. Obviously the willingness of Americans and others to hold dollars, and dollar-denominated financial assets, has increased.

This global willingness to hold dollars and dollar denominated assets is fundamentally what is meant by a "strong dollar" policy. The Bush administration is committed to maintaining global confidence in our currency. The reason for such a commitment is straightforward. America benefits from the willingness of foreign investors to hold both our currency and assets denominated in it. Foreign investors thicken our capital markets making them more liquid and, by increasing the total supply of funds available to dollar-denominated borrowers, lower the net cost of borrowing.

The administration's commitment to a strong dollar policy is linked to our belief that the best way to underpin a strong currency is to follow policies that make investments in America and in dollar denominated assets attractive. There are three fundamental policy pillars behind such a policy.

First, the Bush administration is committed to continuing support for a non-inflationary monetary policy. A fundamental prerequisite for maintaining the confidence of foreign investors in any currency is faith that it will hold its purchasing power. The Federal Reserve has done an outstanding job in carrying out a non-inflationary monetary policy during the past two decades. In this regard, not only does the administration recognize the Fed's independence, it also shares and supports the Fed's objective of maximum obtainable growth with low inflation.

The second policy pillar behind a strong dollar is making sure that the United States is an attractive place in which to invest capital. We are fortunate to be endowed with secure political, legal, and constitutional foundations. It is incumbent on the government to maintain a regime of sensible regulation and moderate taxation in order to maintain the attractiveness of America as a place to invest. We must also work to make sure our legal system protects property, assigns liability only to those who have committed a wrong, and assesses damages that are commensurate with the harm done. Again, the Bush administration is committed to maintaining a healthy business climate that attracts capital from around the world to our shores.

The President's first months in office are proof of this commitment to a sound business climate. Each of the administration's first three major economic initiatives was designed to enhance our competitive position. The President's first priority is to our nation's schools. He is determined to make sure that all children in America are prepared to participate in the rewarding high-technology economy of the Twenty-first Century. An educated workforce will attract investment. The President has also made clear his commitment to enhancing the energy available to run that economy. We have learned in the past five years that the high-tech economy is one that will use more, not less, electricity, and the President has committed his administration to finding ways to generate and transmit that power to where it is needed. Finally, the President has laid out a tax reform and relief plan that will return about a quarter of the projected federal budget surplus to the taxpayer. Equally important, the tax reductions will reduce the most burdensome parts of our tax system and thereby encourage labor supply, capital formation, and innovation. Prudent management of fiscal policy will also contribute to a strong economy and strong dollar.

Aside from maintaining a sound business environment and promoting an anti-inflationary monetary policy, the third key to maintaining confidence in the dollar is establishing an open and robust trading environment. Goods, services, and capital must flow freely between trading partners with minimum encumbrance. Confidence in a currency that is the world's choice for trade invoicing matters little if no trade takes place. Again, the Bush administration is committed to maintaining the principle of free trade and to opening markets around the world.

America's interest in a strong dollar is not academic. We obtain some very practical benefits from our currency's position in the world. First, as the world leading trading nation, we benefit enormously from our ability to use our own currency in international transactions. Even though foreign currency markets have developed sufficiently to allow buyers and sellers of goods to hedge their currency risks, such hedging is not without cost. The advantages to a firm in having its costs and revenue denominated at no added cost in the same currency provides a clear competitive advantage.

Second, the government of the United States benefits from seignorage, which we obtain from having more than $400 billion of Federal Reserve notes held by non-citizens. At the current average cost of borrowing, the interest saved on this foreign holding of currency amounts to roughly $20 billion annually.

Third, our capital market benefits from its unparalleled ability to attract capital from around the world. The depth of our capital market and the enormous liquidity it provides allows U.S. firms unrivaled access to capital. This provides both a direct cost advantage to domestically domiciled firms and a large indirect benefit to the economy in the form of high quality, high paying jobs.

The advantages of a deep and highly liquid capital market have also benefited our country in pursuit of international objectives. During the 1980s, for example, confidence in the dollar allowed the government to borrow the large sums necessary to rebuild our country's defenses. That investment was undoubtedly crucial to our ultimate success in the Cold War and in ending the specter of Soviet imperialism.

The same capital market advantage has been deployed to peaceful economic development. During the 1990s, the willingness of investors around the world to participate in our capital markets led to the greatest capital-spending boom in history. That boom allowed America to make enormous technological advances in telecommunications infrastructure and computer technology. The surge in U.S. productivity during the late 1990s was no doubt attributable to that investment.

Of course, these benefits also carry with them some responsibilities. Unilateral efforts to manipulate exchange rates have, in the past, contributed to misalignments in the dollar relative to other currencies, particularly the yen. For example, this mispricing of exchange rates played a role in skewing investment to third countries that were linked to the dollar, but which traded actively with Japan. When these currencies became more appropriately valued, these investments proved unprofitable. This played a part in the ensuing Asian financial crisis.

The costs of this crisis are still being borne by the people of East Asia and the taxpayers of the developed world. Borrower nations that act upon the main lessons of that experience will reform and strengthen the regulation and transparency of domestic financial markets. This will enable economic growth to put the costs of the crisis quickly behind. As for creditor nations and institutions, a policy of bailouts by international institutions cannot be a substitute for basic responsibilities in maintaining respect for and the value of the currency to which other nations look as a numeraire for their own currencies.

The Bush administration recognizes that the benefits of having a strong currency are not free, and they require careful and responsible attention to the formation and articulation of national economic policy. However, the benefits of having a strong currency for our country far outweigh the costs. Thus, a commitment to a stable, non-inflationary currency, a good business environment, and open trade will remain the cornerstones of American economic policy.

Strong Dollar, Weak Dollar

C. FRED BERGSTEN

Lawrence B. Lindsey, President George W. Bush's chief economic adviser, affirmed and articulated in the March/April 2001 issue of *The International Economy* the new administration's endorsement of the "strong dollar" policy maintained by the Clinton administration since 1995. Secretary of the Treasury Paul O'Neill has reiterated the same position since experimenting briefly with an alternative formulation in February. Their doing so raises two fundamental questions: the substantive issue of whether a strong dollar promotes the national interests of the United States at this point in time and the meaning of the term "strong dollar."

A "strong dollar" has never been defined by the relevant officials and the mantra was indeed uttered both when the dollar fell to 80 to 1 against the yen in 1995 and when it soared to 145 to 1 against that same currency in 1998. Those same officials have always taken great care to avoid espousing a "stronger" dollar and never suggested that the currency should rise in value except when the formulation was first introduced in 1994. Nor did they do anything to strengthen it after their market intervention when it hit record lows in 1995. In fact, they sold dollars against the yen in 1998 and again against the euro in 2000, all the while repeating the "strong dollar" rhetoric.

Hence there was never much substance to the "strong dollar" pronouncements. Nevertheless, their frequent utterances clearly comforted the currency markets and avoided the risk of embarrassment for Treasury officials. Thus, these pronouncements could be justified, pragmatically if not intellectually, during a period when an appreciating and even overvalued dollar in terms of the underlying international competitiveness of our economy, as reflected in the current account balance, was in the national interest of the United States.

The second half of the 1990s represented such a period. The economy boomed at a rate that clearly exceeded the growth of potential output. Unemployment fell to unanticipated lows, raising cost-push pressures. Inflation remained in check but there was widespread fears, as the economy continued to soar past all previous estimates of "full employment" level, that price surges might be just around the corner. The Federal Reserve was under continuing pressure to tighten monetary policy (which Chairman Alan Greenspan and the Board, to their great credit, resisted far longer into the cycle that any of their predecessors would have dared).

From C. Fred Bergsten, "Strong Dollar, Weak Dollar," *The International Economy* 15, July/August, 2001, pp. 8–10, 40–41

Under these circumstances, a rising dollar and the growing current account deficits that it substantially exacerbated were useful safety valves. The dollar has certainly risen substantially: by 75 percent against the yen from its trough of 1995 to its peak in 1998 (by 50 percent to the level of June 2001), and by 70 percent against the DM and other key European currencies from 1995 until mid-2001. This currency appreciation directly reduced the prices of imports and, much more importantly, competing domestic products. The rising external imbalance, at the same time, provided the additional supply of goods and services that was essential to meet a domestic demand that was expanding much faster than domestic output. The commensurately large net inflow of foreign capital that both caused and financed the trade deficit helped to hold down interest rates and thus to spur investment to record levels.

The truly strong dollar and the sizable imbalances in the external sector were therefore essential ingredients in permitting the United States to achieve its "economic miracle" in the late 1990s. The rest of the world gained too; booming U.S. growth provided a sorely needed locomotive for a sluggish global economy and was central to enabling Mexico, then East Asia, and then Brazil and the emerging market economies more generally to recover swiftly from the financial crises that plagued the period. It was no wonder that U.S. officials found it useful to reiterate the "strong dollar" mantra, despite its intellectual shortcomings, and their counterparts around the world were usually happy to let them do so despite the unsustainable imbalances that everyone knew were being created for the future.

The arrival of the Bush administration coincided with a fundamental reversal of the underlying economic situation in the United States. Growth plummeted by four to five percentage points and the economy avoided recession, as officially defined, only because of the abnormally high pace of growth during the previous four years. The equity markets and public confidence dropped sharply. Unemployment began to climb and will surely rise further. Any extant inflationary pressures are likely to recede. Short-term interest rates have come down dramatically as a result of aggressive easing by the Fed.

The case for a "strong dollar" has thus disappeared. There is no need for its anti-inflationary impetus. There is no need to promote even lower interest rates. The structural benefits for the United States from global use of the dollar cited by Dr. Lindsey, our ability to finance international transactions in our own currency and the financial gains from currency seignorage, have continued for more than forty years during periods of acute dollar weakness as well as dollar strength.

The impact of the "strong dollar" has in fact become quite negative. The drag of the trade deficit on the economy now becomes significant and the National Association of Manufacturers has importuned the administration that "at current levels, the exchange value of the dollar is having a strong negative impact on manufacturing exports, production and employment." As unemployment rises, these conditions are bound to add to Congressional pressure for protectionist trade policies. They will clearly make it even harder, in the face of an anti-globalization backlash that has already stalemated our trade policies since 1994, for the administration to win authorization for the new liberalization that it is courageously seeking.

Even more ominously, maintenance of the "strong dollar" posture will steadily increase the risk of a precipitous freefall of the currency. Such a rapid depreciation, even of only 20–25 percent a la 1971–73, let alone the 50 percent or more as in 1985–87, could ignite an acceleration of price pressures despite the economic slow-down and reverse the fall in interest rates that is so crucial for achieving sustainable recovery. The stock market could plunge anew, as it did when the dollar tanked in 1987, further weakening the economy.

The current account deficit is approaching $500 billion or 5 percent of GDP. This is unprecedented terrain for the United States; the sharp dollar declines of 1971–73, 1977–78, 1985–87, and 1994–95 came with the external deficit at far lower levels. (Note that the United States has faced such declines about once per decade.) In her comprehensive study, *Is the U.S. Trade Deficit Sustainable?*, Dr. Catherine L. Mann of the Institute for International Economics showed that OECD countries have typically had to correct their external balances when they hit 4 percent of GDP.

As a result of these imbalances, the United States must import about $2 billion of foreign currency every working day. Even a slight decline in that net inflow, let alone in cessation or reversal, would send the dollar tumbling and the economy reeling. The huge deficits come on top of a net international debtor position for the United States that now probably exceeds $2 trillion. Gross foreign holdings of dol-lar assets exceed $10 trillion and could easily produce enough selling to drive the dollar down sharply in any given time period.

These problems are further intensified by the tax cut passed by the Congress and signed by the President this past June. The resulting drop in the budget sur-plus, and thus net government saving, will lead to a further decline in our already low level of national savings unless there is a wholly unanticipated pickup in private saving. Our domestic investment will thus have to be financed increasingly by the rest of the world. This will require even larger net capital inflows and even larger current account deficits. The day of reckoning is brought ever closer.

It is stunning that Dr. Lindsey failed to even mention these issues in his article on the dollar, since they represent the means through which the currency situation affects the real economy. He indeed implies that the United States should wel-come any level of capital inflow that the rest of the world is willing to supply because he regards it solely as a vote of confidence in the American economy and ignores the costs thereof, despite the resulting further increase in the external deficit and debt. He has even publicly criticized his predecessors' intervention last fall to support the euro, which helped to keep the problem from getting worse.

This is precisely the mistake made by the Reagan administration, with its huge tax cuts, and "benign neglect" of the exchange rate—a "strong dollar" policy with-out using the term. That approach, which Dr. Lindsey extols because it "allowed the government to borrow the large sums necessary to rebuild our country's defenses" converted the balanced current account position it inherited into huge deficits and took the United States from being the world's largest creditor to largest debtor country. Secretary of the Treasury Baker acknowledged publicly that the dollar overvaluation spawned the most widespread adoption of trade protection (quotas on autos, steels, machine tools, and numerous other products) by any administration in the Twentieth Century despite President Reagan's obvious mar-ket and free-trade orientation. It set the dollar up for a "hard landing" that almost occurred in 1987, despite two years of effort by Baker to get the currency back down with his Plaza Agreement, and contributed mightily to Black Monday in the stock market that October.

It would be a mistake for the Bush administration to adopt a "weak dollar" policy or to drive the dollar down, as its Republican predecessors did in 1971–73 (with President Nixon's two devaluations) and 1985–87 (with President Reagan's Plaza Agreement), because a freefall would be so costly as noted above. But it is sheer folly for the administration to seek to maintain the dollar at its currently overvalued levels, let alone to push it higher or even to let it rise in the markets due to renewed weakening of the euro and the yen. The Bush administration should thus develop a "sound dollar" policy under which it and its G7 partners would ease the currency down gradually, by perhaps 20 percent or so over a couple of years, both to reduce the risk of a "hard landing" and to counter the inevitable protectionist pressures (as well as to make a modest contribution to economic recovery).

Such a shift in policy could begin with direct intervention in the foreign exchange markets to support the euro, which is grossly undervalued but has declined steadily over the past few months. This would at least keep the dollar from getting stronger and could be used to signal a change in U.S. and G7 intentions. The United States and the G7 should also resist any further weakening of the yen, since Japan is still running large trade surpluses, especially if it fails to adopt the necessary domestic reforms (especially of its banking system) and seeks to rely on renewed increases in those surpluses to avoid another recession. Such intervention by the United States and G7 could avoid a repeat of the 1984–85 experience, when a further rise in an already overvalued dollar was "pure bubble" with no conceivable economic justification even in retrospect.

Unfortunately, substantial depreciation of the dollar is the only way (other than prolonged and deep recession) to cut the U.S. external deficit to sustainable levels—perhaps around $200–250 billion, or to 2 to 2.5 percent of GDP, about half of where it now stands. Fortunately, we know that this remedy works; the sharp fall of the dollar in the middle 1980s virtually eliminated the deficit by the early 1990s. Fortunately too, it is also clear that direct intervention in the currency markets, including through rhetorical shifts ("Jawboning") as proposed here, works when conducted systematically and skillfully; the modest but totally successful U.S. interventions against the yen in 1995 and 1998 are the latest cases in point.

Such a policy could hardly be attacked as mercantilist by the rest of the world since all analysts, including the International Monetary Fund in publication after publication, agree that the dollar is substantially overvalued in trade terms and because it is quite clear that no other major industrial country would have permitted its external debt and deficits to become so large in the first place. If the new approach turned out to be too successful, in the sense that the dollar threatened to decline too fast or too far, the G7 could simply intervene on the other side of the market to buy dollars, just as the Louvre Accord in 1987 stopped the fall of the dollar triggered by the Plaza Agreement, when it seemed to accelerate too sharply.

The Bush administration clearly needs an exit strategy from the "strong dollar" stance that it inherited from its predecessors. Hence Secretary O'Neill was correct when, in the administration's early days, he said, "We do not follow . . . a policy for a strong dollar" and emphasized instead that "a strong dollar is the result of a strong economy." The obvious implication was that the slowdown in U.S. growth, both in absolute terms and relative to Europe and elsewhere, should produce a decline in the dollar. The Secretary unfortunately lost his nerve and immediately retreated to the "strong dollar" refuge, however, despite the fact that the resulting sell-off in the markets amounted to only about one percent against the euro (and nothing against the yen) and could in fact have become the start of the needed process of gradual correction.

The administration will simply have to try again, with a carefully calibrated strategy and greater resolve. An alteration in its rhetoric, perhaps by starting to espouse a "sound dollar" or offer a studious "no comment" when queried about the currency, can help push the foreign exchanges in the needed direction in light of their sensitivity to any change in the "strong dollar" mantra. Direct intervention vis-à-vis the euro and perhaps the yen, initially to stop their declines rather than to weaken the dollar, would help even more and would convey new guidance to the markets. Further reduction in interest rates would, of course, promote the correction and should be implemented if called for by domestic economic conditions.

The "strong dollar" approach provided a major boon to the United States and world economies for the past half decade. It has outlived its usefulness, however, and the new position proposed here can provide similar benefits for the period ahead. We can only hope that Secretary O'Neill will not really feel that he has to "hire on Yankee Stadium and some rousing brass bands," as he has put it, when the administration faces the inevitable need to change dollar policy as its Republican predecessors did in the early 1970s and the middle 1980s.

QUESTIONS FOR REVIEW AND DISCUSSION

1. Why, according to Lindsey, must the United States maintain confidence in the dollar? How does Bergsten respond to this argument? More broadly, is "foreign confidence" in the dollar the same thing as a "strong" dollar? How do you think each author would answer this question?
2. According to Lindsey, what policies should the United States pursue to maintain confidence in the dollar?
3. According to Bergsten, why was the strong dollar appropriate for economic conditions in the late 1990s? Why, again according to Bergsten, is a strong dollar no longer appropriate?
4. What policies does Bergsten suggest the Bush administration adopt in order to bring about the devaluation of the dollar?
5. Why has the dollar lost value against the euro and yen since 2001? Has this been brought about through the adoption of the policies Bergsten promotes, or for other reasons? Given your answer, how much ability does the U.S government have to influence the dollar's value against foreign currencies?
6. Is it merely a coincidence that the call for a strong dollar comes from a Republican administration while the call for devaluation comes from a member of a previous Democratic administration (Bergsten was a member of President Jimmy Carter's economic team in the 1970s)? If not, does this suggest anything about the source of different exchange-rate policy preferences?

SUGGESTIONS FOR FURTHER READING

For a detailed examination of the politics of American exchange-rate policy through the late 1980s, see: I.M. Destler and C. Randall Henning. *Dollar Politics: Exchange Rate Policymaking in the United States*. Washington, DC: Institute for International Economics, 1989.

An in-depth discussion of the impact of the dollar's overvaluation in the late 1990s can be found in C. Fred Bergsten and John Williamson (eds.). *Dollar Overvaluation and the World Economy*. Washington, DC: Institute for International Economics, 2003.

C. Fred Bergsten's reaction to the recent dollar decline is elaborated in "The Correction of the Dollar and Foreign Intervention in the Currency Markets." Testimony before the Committee on Small Business, United States House of Representatives. Washington, DC, June 25, 2003. Available at http://www.iie.com/publications/papers/bergsten0603–2.htm

CHAPTER 12

THE DOLLAR VERSUS THE EURO?

The dollar has served as the world's principal currency throughout the postwar period, a role that it took over from the British pound. The dollar was the currency that was used more than any other, both by governments outside the United States and by private individuals, as a unit of account, a medium of exchange, and a store of value. In the private sector, the dollar was the currency most often used to invoice international trade, to denominate international financial transactions, and to purchase foreign currencies in the foreign-exchange market. Among the world's governments, the dollar was the currency of choice when it came time to select a currency against which to peg the national currency, to intervene in foreign-exchange markets, and to hold as foreign-exchange reserves. While the dollar's dominance did decline somewhat as the postwar period progressed, ceding some ground to the German mark and the Japanese yen, its preeminence has not yet been challenged.

Could the launch of the euro by the European Union in 1999 represent such a challenge? Some observers, including the Nobel Prize winner Robert Mundell, who is seen by many to be the euro's "grandfather" because of his innovative research on the economics of currency areas, believe that the creation of the euro is the most significant event in the international monetary system since President Richard M. Nixon took the United States off the gold standard in 1971. In particular, these scholars argue that the creation of the euro has transformed the international monetary system. The postwar unipolar system dominated by the dollar has now been replaced by a bipolar system. In this new monetary system, "the euro is likely to challenge the position of the dollar [and hence] this may be the most important event in the history of the international monetary system since the dollar took over from the pound the role of dominant currency in World War I."[1]

Will there be a struggle for dominance between the dollar and euro, and thus between the EU and the United States? Is the euro already emerging as a challenger to the dollar's preeminent role in the global economy? The two articles presented in this chapter explore this issue in detail. The first article, written by Patricia S. Pollard, an economist at the Federal Reserve Bank in St. Louis, provides a detailed and cautious examination of the potential for the euro to challenge the dollar's dominance. Pollard first explains what functions a currency must fulfill in order to serve as an international currency, and then presents data to examine the relative importance of the dollar and the euro for these functions. She concludes that while the euro's international role is likely to grow, it is unlikely to supplant the dollar as the dominant currency in the international monetary system. C. Fred Bergsten adopts the opposite position. Pointing in particular to the combined economic size of the countries that are members of the EU monetary union, and to their large share of world trade, he argues that the euro will rapidly emerge as an important international currency that can, and most likely will, challenge the dollar's dominance.

ENDNOTES

1. Mundell, R. "The case for the euro—I and II." *Wall Street Journal*, March 24 and March 25, 1998.

The Creation of the Euro and the Role of the Dollar in International Markets

PATRICIA S. POLLARD

During the nineteenth and the first half of the twentieth centuries, the British pound was the preeminent international currency. It was used in both international trade and financial transactions and circulated throughout the British empire. With the decline of British economic power in the 20th century, the U.S. dollar replaced the pound as the leading international, currency. For over 50 years the U.S. dollar has been the leading currency used in international trade and debt contracts. Primary commodities are generally priced in dollars on world exchanges. Central banks and governments hold the bulk of their foreign exchange reserves in dollars, in addition. In some countries dollars are accepted for making transactions as readily as (if not more so than) the domestic currency.

On January 1, 1999, a new currency—the euro—was created, culminating the progress toward economic and monetary union in Europe. The euro replaced the currencies of 11 European countries: Austria, Belgium, Finland, France, Germany, Ireland, Italy, Luxembourg, the Netherlands, Portugal, and Spain. Two years later Greece became the 12th member of the euro area.

Although the Japanese yen and particularly the German mark have been used internationally in the past several decades, neither currency approached the international use of the dollar. With the creation of the euro, for the first time the dollar has a potential rival for the status as the primary international currency. What changes in the international use of the dollar have occurred in the first two years of the euro's existence? What changes are likely over the next decade? Moreover, what are the implications for the United States and the euro area as a result of these changes? To answer these questions, this article begins with an overview of the functions of an international currency and the major factors that determine whether a currency will be used outside its borders. It then examines the use of currencies in international markets prior to the establishment of the euro and the changes brought about by the creation of the euro.[1]

FUNCTIONS OF AN INTERNATIONAL CURRENCY

Economists define money as anything that serves the following three functions: a unit of account, a store of value, and a medium of exchange. To operate as a unit of

From Patricia S. Pollard, "The Creation of the Euro and the Role of the Dollar in International Markets," *Federal Reserve Bank of St. Louis Review* 83, September/October, 2001, pp. 17–36.

TABLE 1 ■ FUNCTIONS OF AN INTERNATIONAL CURRENCY

	Sector	
Function	*Private*	*Official*
Unit of Account	Invoice	Exchange Rate Peg
Store of Value	Financial Assets	Reserves
Medium of Exchange	Vehicle/Substitution	Intervention

account, prices must be set in terms of the money. To function as a store of value, the purchasing power of money must be maintained over time.[2] To function as a medium of exchange, the money must be used for purchasing goods and services. For an international currency, one used as money outside its country of issue, these functions are generally divided by sector of use—private and official as listed in Table 1.[3]

A currency serves as a unit of account for private international transactions if it is used as an invoice currency in international trade contracts. It serves as a store of value if international financial assets are denominated in this currency. It serves as a medium of exchange internationally if it is used as a vehicle currency through which two other currencies are traded, and as a substitute for a domestic currency.

A currency serves as a unit of account for official international purposes if it is used as an exchange rate peg. It serves as a store of value if governments and or central banks hold foreign exchange reserves in this currency and as a medium of exchange if it is used for intervening in currency markets.

The three functions of an international currency reinforce each other. For example, the use of a currency for invoicing trade and holding financial assets increases the likelihood that the currency will be used as a vehicle currency. In the official sector, if a country pegs its exchange rate to another currency, it is likely to hold reserves in that currency and conduct its interventions in exchange markets in that currency. In addition, the use of an international currency by one sector reinforces its use by the other sector. For example, using a currency as an exchange rate peg facilitates the use of that currency in debt contracts and foreign trade.

DETERMINANTS OF AN INTERNATIONAL CURRENCY

What determines the likelihood that a currency will be used in the international exchange of goods, services, and assets? Five key factors are as follows:

- Size of the economy
- Importance in international trade
- Size, depth, liquidity, and openness of domestic financial markets
- Convertibility of the currency
- Macroeconomic policies

The size of a country's economy is important because it determines the potential use of the currency in international markets. Economic size is linked with the importance of a country in international trade and the size of its financial markets. For example, exports account for a much greater share of the output of the Korean economy than for the U.S. economy. Nevertheless, because the U.S. economy is nearly 14 times larger than the Korean economy U.S. exports comprise a much larger share of world exports.

Clearly the dominance of the U.S. economy and the decline of the U.K. economy in the twentieth century were related to the rise of the dollar and the decline of the pound as international currencies. Likewise, the growth of the German and Japanese economies in the last several decades of the twentieth century prompted the use of their currencies in international markets. As a result, the overwhelming dominance the dollar held in international markets in the 1950s and 1960s diminished.

Table 2 compares the relative size of the U.S., the euro-area, and Japanese economies. The U.S. economy is the largest in the world, accounting for about 22 percent of world output. The establishment of economic and monetary union in Europe, linked through the euro, has created the world's second largest economy. The Japanese economy is less than half the size of the euro area.[4]

The share of a country in international trade as well as the size and openness of its financial markets are determinants of the demand for that country's currency in world markets. The United States accounts for a lower share of world exports than does the current euro area, as shown in Table 2. The size of U.S. financial markets as measured by the sum of bank assets, outstanding domestic debt securities, and stock market capitalization, however, is much larger than in the euro area. Japan is a distant third in terms of its share of world exports, but its financial markets are close in size to those in the euro area.

TABLE 2 ■ COMPARISON OF UNITED STATES, EURO-AREA, AND JAPANESE ECONOMIES IN 1999

	United States	Euro Area	Japan
Share of World GDP	21.9	15.8	7.6
Share of World Exports (%)	15.3	19.4	9.3
Financial Markets ($ billions)	40,543.8	24,133.4	20,888.5
Bank Assets ($ billions)	7,555.3	12,731.3	6,662.5
Domestic Debt Securities Outstanding ($ billions)	15,426.3	5,521.9	6,444.9
Stock Market Capitalization ($ billions)	17,562.2	5,880.2	7,781.4

Note: GDP is based on purchasing power parity equivalents. World exports excludes intra-euro-area trade.

Source: GDP: IMF, *World Economic Outlook*, October 2000. Exports: IMF, *Direction of Trade Statistics Quarterly*, September 2000. Bank Assets: European Central Bank, *Monthly Bulletin*; Board of Governors of the Federal Reserve System, *Flow of Funds Accounts*; IMF, *International Financial Statistics*, Debt Securities: Bank for International Settlements, *Quarterly Review of International Banking and Financial Market Developments*. Stock markets: Eurostat.

The convertibility of a country's currency is another important determinant of its use in international markets. Restrictions on the ability to exchange a currency for other currencies limits its global use. At the end of World War II almost every country, with the exception of the United States, restricted the convertibility of its currency. This inconvertibility persisted for the first decade after the war. The convertibility of the U.S. dollar prompted its use as the currency in which international trade was conducted.

Macroeconomic policies also play an important role in determining whether a country's currency will be used internationally. These policies affect a country's economic growth and its openness to the world economy. Policies fostering a low inflation environment are especially important. Countries experiencing hyper-inflation and/or political crises often see the use of their currencies collapse not only internationally but also within the domestic economy, as residents turn to a substitute currency.

Clearly the size and openness of the U.S. economy have been major factors in encouraging the international use of the dollar in the post-World War period. Its use as an international currency in the private sector and the effect of the emergence of the euro in this sector is examined in the next section.

THE PRIVATE USES OF AN INTERNATIONAL CURRENCY

As stated above, a currency operates as an international currency in the private sector (i) if international trade-and-debt contracts are priced in this currency: (ii) if this currency is used to facilitate the exchange of other currencies and (iii) if this currency is used as a substitute currency.

Invoice Currency

The dollar is the main currency that functions as a unit of account for private international transactions. Although data on the currency of invoice in international trade are limited, the available data confirm the dominance of the dollar. In 1995 the U.S. dollar was used as the invoice currency for more than half of world exports, down only slightly from 1980, as shown in Table 3. The Deutsche mark was the next most popular invoice currency, used for approximately 13 percent of world exports, followed by the French franc and the British pound. While the yen's use in world trade lagged behind these European currencies, its share had more than doubled since 1980. The combined share of the four major EU currencies was less than half that of the U.S. dollar.

More importantly, there is a clear distinction between the use of the dollar and other invoice currencies. The U.S. dollar is the only currency whose use in world trade far surpasses its country share in world trade, as shown by its internationalization ratio in Table 3. An internationalization ratio less than 1.0, as with yen, lira, and guilder, indicates that not all of that country's exports are denominated in

TABLE 3 ■ TRADE INVOICED IN MAJOR CURRENCIES

Currency	Percent of World Exports		Internationalization Ratio	
	1980	*1995*	*1980*	*1995*
U.S. dollar	56.4	52.0	4.5	3.9
Japanese yen	2.1	4.7	0.3	0.6
Deutsche mark	13.6	13.2	1.4	1.4
French franc	6.2	5.5	0.9	1.0
British pound	6.5	5.4	1.1	1.1
Italian lira	2.2	3.3	0.5	0.8
Netherlands guilder	2.6	2.8	0.7	0.9
Euro-4	24.6	24.8	NA	NA

Note: Euro-4 is the share of the four euro-area currencies listed in the table. No data were available for the other euro-area currencies. World exports includes intra-euro-area trade. The internationalization ratio is the ratio of the share of world exports denominated in a currency to the share of the issuing country in world exports.

Source: Bekx (1998, Table 3, p. 8).

the local currency. An internationalization ratio greater than 1.0, as with the dollar, the mark, and the pound, indicates that other countries use that currency to invoice some (or all) of their exports.[5]

What determines the currency of invoice in world trade? A number of studies including those by Grassman (1973), Page (1981), and Black (1990) revealed the following patterns. Trade in manufactured goods among the industrial economies is most often priced in the currency of the exporter. If the exporter's currency is not used, then the importer's currency is the most frequent choice. Only rarely is a third country's currency used. Trade between industrial and developing countries is generally priced in the currency of the industrial country or that of a third country. Trade between developing countries is often priced in the currency of a third country. When a third country's currency is used for invoicing trade, the U.S. dollar is the most likely choice. Trade in primary commodities is almost always invoiced in U.S. dollars because these products are predominantly priced in dollars on international exchanges.

∗ ∗ ∗

The mere creation of the euro as a currency should provide ample incentive for its use as an invoice currency. Replacing the currencies of 12 countries with a single currency reduces the transaction costs involved in currency exchanges. Although only a small number of firms within the euro area have already switched to invoicing in euros, the advent of euro notes and coins, along with the withdrawal from circulation of the notes and coins of the legacy currencies in 2002 will prompt several changes. According to Page (1981), the use of the dollar is negligible in intra-European Union trade, so the creation of the euro should not have had a noticeable effect on invoicing in the region. Where its effect is likely to be largest is in extra-euro-area trade, where most exports are likely to be invoiced in euros. It is unlikely, however, that trade currently invoiced in dollars and involving neither the euro area nor the United States will shift in the near term to euros. This argument is supported by the European Central Bank (ECB), which estimates that the percent of world exports denominated in euros "is likely not to differ significantly from that of euro area exports" (ECB 1999, p. 36). Thus, the internationalization ratio for the euro area will be close to 1.

❖ ❖ ❖

The dollar is also the main currency used for pricing internationally traded commodities, with the British pound being the only other currency used. As Tavlas (1997) notes, the commodity exchanges on which these products are traded are located in countries "that have a comparative advantage as financial centers," thus explaining the dominance of the United States and the United Kingdom and hence the currency choice.

The creation of the euro is unlikely to lead to any change in the pricing of these commodities. The location of major commodity exchanges in the United States, while not a necessary requirement for dollar pricing, does increase the likelihood that these commodities will continue to be priced in dollars. Although it is possible that an integrated Europe will develop commodity exchanges to rival those of the United States, such a shift is likely to be gradual. Any shift in pricing of these commodities is unlikely to occur until the stability of Europe's new monetary system is well established.[6]

❖ ❖ ❖

Financial Assets

In international bond markets the U.S. dollar was the currency of choice for nearly all issues in the 1950s. By the 1970s, however, the currency denomination of bond issues had become more diversified, as shown in Table 4. Nevertheless, the U.S. dollar has remained the most popular currency choice for issuing bonds

TABLE 4 ■ FUNDS RAISED IN INTERNATIONAL BOND MARKETS BY CURRENCY OF ISSUE (PERCENT)

Currency	1950–59	1960–69	1970–79	1980–89
U.S. dollar	78.2	69.9	49.2	50.7
Japanese yen	0.0	0.0	5.2	8.9
Swiss franc	7.1	5.4	17.5	11.4
Euro area*	3.2	20.3	24.1	15.8
Deutsche mark	2.0	16.3	17.9	8.0
Other E.U.[†]	8.7	3.1	0.7	6.8
Pound sterling	8.3	2.9	0.6	6.4

*Euro area includes the currencies of all current members of the euro area and currency composites, such as the ecu.
[†]Other E.U. includes the currencies of Denmark, Greece, Sweden, and the United Kingdom.

Source: OECD, *International Capital Market Statistics*, 1996, and *Financial Statistics Monthly*, June 1997.

TABLE 5 ■ INTERNATIONAL DEBT SECURITIES BY CURRENCY OF ISSUE (PERCENT)

	Amounts Outstanding			Share of New Issues		
	1993	*1998*	*2000*	*1998*	*1999*	*2000*
Total securities						
U.S. dollar	41.1	45.9	48.7	54.1	45.2	44.0
Japanese yen	13.2	11.3	8.2	5.6	5.3	8.3
Swiss franc	7.3	3.8	2.2	3.3	2.0	1.7
Euro Area*	24.8	27.2	30.1	24.6	36.8	33.9
Other EU[†]	7.9	8.5	8.2	8.9	8.0	9.2
Pound Sterling	7.6	7.9	7.8	8.3	7.7	9.1
Bonds and notes						
U.S. dollar	38.9	45.3	48.7	51.1	43.8	42.3
Japanese yen	14.0	11.7	8.6	6.3	6.7	11.4
Swiss franc	7.7	3.8	2.2	2.7	1.6	1.4
Euro Area*	25.7	27.6	30.0	28.0	38.3	34.2
Other EU[†]	8.1	8.5	8.1	9.0	7.3	8.4
Pound Sterling	7.8	7.9	7.7	8.2	7.0	8.2
Money Market						
U.S. dollar	79.4	59.9	49.1	61.0	48.8	47.5
Japanese yen	0.2	2.5	2.3	4.0	1.4	1.9
Swiss franc	1.8	4.5	2.3	4.7	2.9	2.3
Euro Area*	8.5	19.2	32.4	17.2	32.9	33.2
Other EU[†]	4.1	8.4	9.5	8.8	9.8	11.0
Pound Sterling	4.0	8.3	9.3	8.7	9.7	11.0

*Euro area includes the currencies of the 11 original members of the euro area and currency composites, such as the ecu.
[†]Other EU includes the currencies of Denmark, Sweden, and the United Kingdom.

Source: Bank for International Settlements, *Quarterly Review of International Banking and Financial Market Developments*, March 2001.

in international markets, as shown in Table 5.[7] By the 1960s the euro legacy currencies, taken together as a group, had become the second most widely used currency in international bond markets, a status that continues today. The Japanese yen was not used at all until the 1970s and its share of new issues lags far below that of the dollar or euro. The use of the Swiss franc in international bond markets, which rivaled the Deutsche mark in the 1970s, declined precipitously in the 1990s.[8]

In international money markets as well, the dollar is the currency of choice, but again its dominance has declined, as noted in Table 5. The increased use of the euro legacy currencies in these markets during the 1990s is particularly noteworthy. In 1993 these currencies accounted for 8.5 percent of the outstanding debt in international money markets. By 1998 this share had increased to 19.2 percent.

The creation of the euro led to a sharp rise in its use in international debt markets relative to its legacy currencies. The share of new issues of international securities denominated in the euro legacy currencies was 24.6 percent in 1998. In the following year, the share denominated in euros was 36.8 percent. Although the use of the euro relative to its legacy currencies rose strongly in both the bond and money market, the increase was highest in the money market. In international debt markets there is now a clear alternative to the use of the dollar.[9]

In international banking there is also evidence of currency diversification over the last two decades. Table 6 shows the assets and liabilities of banks accounted for by transactions with foreign residents (either in the domestic or foreign currencies). During the 1980s, 60 percent of the cross-border assets of banks were in dollars and 1 percent in the euro legacy currencies. In the 1990s, the dollar's share fell to 47 percent and the euro legacy currencies' share rose to 27 percent. A similar pattern is noted for cross-border liabilities. The advent of the euro, however, has had little initial effect on international banking. The dollar's share of cross-border assets remained nearly constant while its share of cross-border liabilities increased slightly. The opposite pattern held for euros. There was a slight increase in the share of cross-border assets denominated in euros, relative to the euro legacy currencies, and virtually no change in liabilities.[10]

The use of a country's currency in international capital markets is determined by the size, openness, and liquidity of that country's financial markets and the stability of its currency. The decline in the dollar's dominance in world capital markets, prior to the creation of the euro is a result of the emergence of other strong economies that, in conjunction with the liberalization and deregulation of financial systems worldwide, increased the attractiveness of assets denominated in

TABLE 6 ■ BANKS' CROSS-BORDER POSITIONS: AMOUNTS OUTSTANDING* (PERCENT)

	1983–89	1990–99	1998	1999	2000:Q3
Assets					
U.S. dollar	59.7	47.0	45.2	45.4	47.0
Japanese yen	10.0	12.0	11.6	10.3	9.9
Euro area[†]	18.6	27.4	28.1	31.8	30.7
Pound Sterling	3.4	4.3	4.9	4.9	5.3
Liabilities					
U.S. dollar	62.4	49.3	47.6	49.9	51.9
Japanese yen	7.9	8.0	8.4	7.8	7.4
Euro area[†]	17.2	26.8	26.3	26.9	25.4
Pound Sterling	4.3	5.6	6.5	6.7	6.9

*Includes both domestic and foreign currency assets and liabilities.
†Euro area includes the banks of the 11 original members of the euro area.

Source: Bank for International Settlements, *Quarterly Review of International Banking and Financial Market Developments*, March 2001.

other currencies. This is particularly evident in the bond markets where there has been a rapid increase in the number of currencies used.

* * *

For now U.S. financial markets continue to lead the world in both size and liquidity. As a result, the U.S. dollar remains the major currency in international bond markets. The euro, however, has already become a major player in these markets, and its use will likely expand as euro-area financial market integration proceeds. The development of a euro-area capital market similar to the U.S. market should produce benefits to both economies by increasing the options available to borrowers and lenders on both sides of the Atlantic.

Vehicle Currency

There are no direct data available on vehicle currencies, but this information can be gleaned from the shares of currencies in foreign exchange transactions, as shown in Table 7.[11] In 1998 the dollar was involved in 87 percent of all currency exchanges.[12] The euro legacy currencies were involved in 52 percent of all exchanges, with the Deutsche mark the most often traded of these currencies. The yen was used in 21 percent of all currency trades. The dollar's dominance was especially clear in forward and swap transactions. The dollar was involved in 81 percent of all forward trades compared with the mark's and yen's shares of 28 and 27 percent respectively. In swaps the contrast was even greater. The dollar was involved in 95 percent of all swaps, with the mark and yen taking part in 20 and 17 percent, respectively, of all trades.

The use of the dollar in foreign exchange transactions was well above its use in international trade and debt contracts, indicating its role as a vehicle currency. The BIS (1999) notes that evidence of the dollar's role as a vehicle currency is provided by its use in seven of the ten most heavily traded currency pairs. The report also notes that it is standard practice for the dollar to be used as a vehicle currency in swaps, which explains the high percentage of swaps involving the U.S. dollar and the low use of the yen and mark in these trades.

TABLE 7 ■ FOREIGN EXCHANGE MARKET TRANSACTIONS INVOLVING SELECT CURRENCIES (PERCENT OF TOTAL) APRIL 1998

	U.S. dollar	Japanese yen	Deutsche mark	French franc	Euro area*	Pound sterling
Spot	78.8	24.7	42.7	3.3	56.8	11.6
Forwards	81.4	26.7	28.0	5.1	50.7	12.3
Swaps	95.2	16.7	20.0	6.5	48.8	10.2
Total	87.4	20.8	29.8	5.1	52.2	11.0

*Euro area includes the currencies of the current member countries plus the Danish krone and the ecu.

Source: Bank for International Settlements, *Central Bank Survey of Foreign Exchange and Derivatives Market Activity, 1998.* Basle: BIS, May 1998.

The use of a currency as a vehicle currency is determined primarily by transactions costs. Transactions costs are inversely related to volume in each bilateral currency market.[13] This volume is in turn determined by a currency's share in international trade and capital flows. Thus, the use of a currency in invoicing international trade, in international capital markets, and as a reserve currency lowers the transactions costs associated with the use of that currency.

A vehicle currency emerges whenever the indirect exchange costs through the vehicle are less than direct exchange costs between two non-vehicle currencies. For example, given the depth of the exchange market for dollars, it may be less costly to exchange Mexican pesos for U.S. dollars and then exchange U.S. dollars for Korean won rather than to exchange pesos directly for won. Indeed, the existence of transaction costs may reinforce the use of the dollar as an invoice currency.

The extent of liquidity in asset markets also affects the development of a vehicle currency. Banks prefer to hold most off their foreign-currencies in the form of interest-earning assets rather than cash. The liquidity of these assets is a key determinant of the transaction costs involved in switching from one currency to another. Liquidity is determined not simply by the size of a country's capital markets but also by the extent to which secondary markets operate.

The prospects of the euro becoming an important vehicle currency thus depend primarily on the transactions costs associated with euro exchanges. Clearly the size of the euro currency market relative to the markets for individual euro currencies will result in lower relative transactions costs for the euro. These transactions costs will also depend on the extent to which the euro is adopted as (1) an invoice currency, (2) a reserve currency, and (3) a prevalent currency in international capital markets.

Preliminary data indicate that the euro has not increased its role as a vehicle currency to a level beyond that of the mark. According to the BIS (2000), the market share of the euro in currency markets during 1999 was close to the share of the Deutsche mark in 1998. Indeed, because a vehicle currency is no longer needed to facilitate exchanges among the euro currencies, the use of the euro as a vehicle currency has probably declined relative to that of the mark. Evidence on the limited use of the euro as a vehicle currency is also provided by data from foreign exchange markets in emerging market countries. The use of the euro in these markets during 1999 was concentrated in Eastern Europe, again similar to that of the mark in 1998. In Thailand and Korea for example, the euro was involved in less than 1 percent of local currency trades.

Substitute Currency

Another role that an international currency may play is as a substitute for domestic currency transactions. Uncertainty surrounding the purchasing power of a domestic currency can lead to the use of a foreign currency as a unit of account, store of value, and medium of exchange in the domestic economy. This generally occurs as a result of hyperinflation and/or political instability.

In the decades prior to the creation of the euro, the dollar and the mark were the only currencies used extensively outside their respective borders, with the dollar being the predominant substitute currency. In part, this predominance of the dollar was a result of the links between the United States and countries using a substitute currency. Nevertheless, the ease of availability of the dollar, which both determines and encourages its other uses as an international currency, continues to facilitate the use of the dollar as a substitute currency.

Measures of the extent to which currencies are used as substitute currencies are not easily obtained. However, the best estimates indicate that about 55 percent of the total U.S. currency held by the non-bank public was held abroad at the end of 1995. About 35 percent of Deutsche mark holdings were abroad (Seitz 1995).

The use of the U.S. dollar as a substitute currency began in earnest in the 1920s as a result of hyperinflations in several European countries.[14] Its use in Latin America expanded in the 1980s also as a result of hyperinflation. Most recently, the collapse of the Soviet Union expanded the use of the dollar in that region.[15] Although the dollar is the preferred substitute currency in the former Soviet Union, the German mark is more prevalent in some Eastern European countries as well as in the former Yugoslav republics.

The use of the dollar as a substitute currency provides a direct benefit to the United States through seignorage earnings. These earnings are generally estimated by calculating the amount the U.S. government would have to pay if, rather than holding cash, individuals in these countries held U.S. Treasury securities. [A] rough estimate of the real seignorage earned by the United States as a result of foreign holdings of U.S. currency during the period 1973–99 [suggests that] . . . seignorage revenues have averaged $8.7 billion [per year].[16] . . . One method of estimating the importance of these seigniorage revenues is to calculate the share of government expenditures accounted for by these revenues. . . . On average less than 1 percent of the expenditures' of the U.S. federal government have been financed by seigniorage revenues and currency held abroad.[17]

The euro is not likely to rapidly replace the dollar as the substitute currency of choice. In fact, the use of the euro as a substitute currency is likely to lag behind its use as an international currency. Foreign holders of a substitute currency want a stable, secure currency. Uncertainty surrounding the value of the euro, particularly given its decline against the dollar during the first two years of its existence, will limit the near term attractiveness of the euro as a substitute currency.

✿ ✿ ✿

THE OFFICIAL USES OF AN INTERNATIONAL CURRENCY

Exchange Rate Peg

Under the Bretton Woods system that existed from 1946 to 1973, most currencies in the world were tied to the U.S. dollar. With the demise of the Bretton Woods system, many countries chose to let their currencies float while others set the value of their currency against that of another country. Of those countries choosing the

TABLE 8 ■ CURRENCY PEGS

Year	U.S. Dollar		Euro Currencies		Other E.U.	
	Number	Percent	Number	Percent	Number	Percent
1975	52	40.6	14	10.9	8	6.3
1980	39	27.7	15	10.6	1	0.7
1985	31	20.8	14	9.4	1	0.7
1990	25	16.2	15	9.7	0	0.0
1995	22	12.2	17	9.4	0	0.0
2000	23	12.6	24	13.2	0	0.0

Source: IMF, *Annual Report on Exchange Arrangements and Exchange Restrictions,* various issues.

latter option, most continued to peg their currency to the U.S. dollar. In 1975, 52 member countries (about 41 percent) of the International Monetary Fund (IMF) pegged their currency to the dollar, as shown in Table 8. The euro legacy currencies were the second most popular choice. The French franc was the peg for the African Financial Community (CPA) franc, the currency used by the then 13 members of the CFA; and the Spanish peseta was the exchange rate peg for the currency of Equatorial Guinea. The pound was the only other European Union currency to be used as an exchange rate peg.

Over time the popularity of currency pegs has declined. However, both the number and percentage of member countries pegging their currencies to the euro have risen. In 2000, 24 IMF member countries tied their currencies to the euro.[18] The 14 CFA members continue to constitute the majority of countries whose currencies are tied to the euro. Most of the remaining 10 countries whose currencies are pegged to the euro hope to be in the first or second wave of enlargements of the European Union. In addition, Denmark which is one of the three members of the European Union who are not currently members of the euro area, ties its currency to the euro through the Exchange Rate Mechanism (ERM) II.[19]

According to these data the U.S. dollar is now the second most popular choice for a currency peg, with 23 countries tying their currencies to the dollar.[20] In practice, however, the dollar remains the currency against which most countries limit movements in their domestic currencies. For example, 20 countries in addition to those listed in Table 8 strictly limit the movement of their domestic currencies against the dollar. Some of these currencies are officially tied to another currency. Jordan, for example, officially pegs its currency to the SDR but in practice pegs to the U.S. dollar.

The primary reason countries choose to peg their currency to another currency is to reduce exchange rate risk and/or to control inflation. Keeping the currency stable against the peg, or setting limits on exchange rate changes, minimizes the risk to those borrowing or lending in foreign currencies or engaged in international trade. For those countries who do peg, the currency choice is usually determined by trade and financial links. This explains why, among countries with currency pegs, Latin American and Caribbean countries are pegged to the dollar while most European and African countries peg to the euro. Likewise, because oil is priced in dollars on world markets, many oil exporting countries either officially or in practice limit the fluctuations of their currency against the dollar.

The introduction of the euro has not resulted in any countries shifting their peg from the dollar to the euro. Nonetheless, it is likely that the share of currencies pegged to the euro will rise as more of the countries hoping to be admitted to the European Union may peg their currencies to the euro. In addition, any European Union country wanting to enter the euro area will have to first peg to the euro.

❋ ❋ ❋

Reserve Currency

In 1973 the dollar accounted for 76.1 percent of the official foreign currency reserves held by the member countries of the IMF. . . . The euro legacy currencies had an 8.7 percent share of foreign currency reserves and the pound sterling had a 5.6 percent share. Holdings of yen were only 0.1 percent of total reserves.

The dollar's share in foreign currency reserves declined in the late 1970s as some countries diversified their holdings, shifting primarily into euro legacy currencies, particularly Deutsche marks. Although the dollar's share fell again in the late 1980s, it has increased somewhat since 1991 to stand at 66.2 percent in 1999.[21] The share of the euro currencies peaked in 1989 at 31.1 percent and has fallen steadily since then, standing at 12.5 percent in 1999. The share of the yen rose slowly through most of the 1970s and 1980s, reaching a peak of 8.5 percent in 1991. Since then the yen's share has fallen, reaching 5.1 percent in 1999.

In the 1970s the developing countries as a group had more diversified holdings of foreign currencies than did the industrial countries. . . . Throughout most of the 1980s and 1990s, however, the developing countries held a greater share of their reserves in dollars than did the industrial countries. Currently there is little difference in the currency composition of reserves across developing and industrial countries. These changes can be explained by examining why countries hold reserves. Governments and central banks hold reserves for three main purposes: (i) to finance imports: (ii) to finance foreign debt; and (iii) to intervene in currency markets to manage the exchange rate. In advanced economies, private markets generally fulfill the role of financing trade and debt. Hence, reserves are held primarily for intervention purposes.

In developing countries all three purposes are important. The currencies in which imports are invoiced in developing countries is a key determinant of the composition of reserves. Similarly, because reserves also are important for financing foreign debt, the currency composition of this debt will affect the currency composition of reserves. . . . [T]he long-term debt of developing countries is most commonly denominated in U.S. dollars.

Euro-area-currencies are the next preferred choice. But this share has declined slightly over the past 30 years. Most noticeable has been the decline in the use of the pound in debt contracts of developing countries. This decline is partly reflected in the relative fall in pound reserves held by developing countries. In contrast, the rise in use of the yen in debt contracts between 1979 and 1990 is reflected in the rise in yen foreign exchange reserves.

The currency choice of reserves for intervention purposes depends in part on a country's exchange rate regime. Heller and Knight (1978) showed that if a country pegged its exchange rate to a particular currency, that currency's share in its reserves rose. Dooley et al. (1989) showed that industrial economies with flexible exchange rates had a high share of dollar reserves and a low share of Deutsche mark reserves. Among industrial economies, the main fixed exchange rate regime was the ERM. The establishment of the ERM in 1979 coincides with the sharp rise in the share of euro legacy currencies (particularly marks) in the foreign currency reserves of industrial economies.[22] The importance of the exchange rate arrangement in determining this currency composition of a country's reserves is linked to the use of these reserves for intervening in the currency markets.

The risk and return on currencies is also a factor in determining the currency composition of reserves. Most reserves are held in the form of government securities. Thus, changes in the relative return on these securities in conjunction with the depreciation risk, particularly if sustained over a long period, may cause shifts in a country's composition of reserves. In addition, the liquidity of government securities markets is a factor in determining the choice of reserve-currency because reserves may need to be sold quickly for intervention purposes.

What has been the initial effect of the creation of the euro on the currency composition of reserves? . . . [T]he dollar's share has risen and the euro's share has fallen. This occurred for two reasons: the elimination of ECU reserves and the reclassification of intra-euro area holdings of euro-currency reserves.[23] At the end of 1997, ECU reserves accounted for 10.7 percent of the foreign currency reserves of industrial countries and 5.0 percent of the reserves of all countries. Most of these ECU reserves were claims on the European Monetary Institute (the predecessor to the European Central Bank). They had been issued to the central banks of the European Union countries in exchange for gold and dollar deposits. In late 1998 the deposits were returned to these central banks and the ECU reserves were eliminated. This explains the sharp drop in euro legacy currency reserves in the industrial countries in 1998. With the advent of the euro in 1999 holdings by euro-area countries of the euro legacy currencies ceased to be foreign currency reserves. This led to a further decline in the share of the euro in the foreign currency reserves of industrial countries.

The importance of the transition to the euro in driving movements in the currency composition of worldwide reserves over the last two years is further indicated by looking at the developing countries. . . . [T]he euro share of reserves held by developing countries rose slightly in the last few years. In 1997 the euro legacy currencies accounted for 12 percent of the reserves of developing countries. At the end of 1999, the euro accounted for 13.6 percent of the reserves. Thus, while there is no evidence that the creation of the euro has led to a drop in the relative holdings of euros outside the euro area, neither is there evidence of a marked rise in these holdings.

The lack of a noticeable shift in the composition of world reserves is not surprising. The trade and debt financing needs of the developing countries remain primarily in dollars. Certainly, as the euro's use as an international medium of exchange rises, countries are likely to increase their holdings of euro reserves. It is also unlikely that the creation of the euro has had a noticeable effect on the demand for reserves for intervention purposes.[24] Central banks are unlikely to sell much of their dollar holdings to buy euros without good cause. The ECB notes "central banks traditionally refrain from abrupt and large changes in the level and composition of their foreign exchange reserves" (ECB 1999, p. 41). Johnson (1994) argues that as long as the Federal Reserve achieves an acceptable degree of price stability in the United States, changes in reserve holdings should occur gradually.

❋ ❋ ❋

Intervention Currency

A corollary to the dollar's role as the primary international reserve-currency is its use as the main currency for intervening in foreign exchange markets. This latter role is also aided by the use of the dollar as a vehicle currency and by the liquidity of the U.S. bond market. . . . Although data on interventions are limited, it is believed that nearly all intervention in the currency markets, with the exception of those undertaken by the United States, takes place in dollars.[25]

The most important determinants of the choice of intervention currency are liquidity and acceptability. In countries that peg their exchange rate, the currency peg will determine the intervention currency. Since countries prefer to hold their reserves in the form of interest-earning assets, the liquidity of these assets is extremely important. The relative illiquidity of the euro-area and Japanese bond markets gives the dollar an advantage over the use of these two currencies.[26]

The acceptability of an international currency is related to its role as a medium of exchange for private transactions. The more frequently a currency is used for private transactions the larger is the exchange market for that currency, which increases the ease with which a country can use the currency for intervention purposes.

CONCLUSION

Factors determining whether a country's currency will be used readily outside its border include the size and openness of its economy and financial markets as well as its macroeconomic policy environment. In the postwar period, these factors have favored the use of the U.S. dollar as the predominant international currency. In the early postwar period there were few alternatives to the dollar in international markets as a result of restrictions on convertibility and limits on capital mobility. In the last several decades, as other major economic powers emerged (notably

Germany and Japan) and markets opened, the dollar's dominance has been reduced. Nonetheless, the dollar has remained the most important international currency.

On January 1, 1999, the euro was created, linking an economic area nearly the size of the U.S. economy. The euro's impact will be felt in markets throughout the world economy. For the first time the dollar faces a potential challenge to its role as the world's major international currency. In the first two years of its existence, the euro's presence has been felt most in international securities markets. . . . Little change, however, has occurred in the use of the euro relative to the dollar in the other functions of an international currency.

In the short-term there is unlikely to be much change in this pattern. Over time, however, the use of the euro relative to the dollar will likely increase, particularly as euro-area financial markets become more integrated and more liquid. Nevertheless, the decline in the dollar's share and the rise in the euro's share in international transactions is likely to occur gradually. In part, this is because the more often a currency is used in international transactions the lower are the costs associated with using that currency and hence the more attractive is the currency for conducting international exchanges. Thus, there is much inertia in the choice of an international currency. The British pound, for example, continued to play a major role as an international currency long after its dominance of the global economy waned.

⁂

The ultimate determinants of the continued use of the dollar as an international currency are the economic policies and conditions in the United States. As Lawrence Summers noted when he was Deputy Secretary of the U.S. Treasury, "Ultimately, the dollar's relative standing in the international financial system will always depend more on developments here than on events elsewhere." In the absence of an economic crisis in the United States, the dollar is not likely to lose its standing as the most popular international currency.

⁂

REFERENCES

Bank for International Settlement. *BIS Quarterly Review.* Basle: BIS, February 2000.

Bank for International Settlement. Central Bank Survey of Foreign Exchange and Derivatives Market Activity 1998. Basle: BIS, May 1999.

Bekx, Peter. "The Implications of the Introduction of the Euro for Non-EU Countries," Euro Papers Number 26, European Commission, Directorate General Economic and Financial Affairs, July 1998.

Benassy, Agnes and Deusy-Fournier, Pierre. "Competition Among the World's Dominant Currencies Since Bretton Woods Collapsed," Unpublished manuscript, Centre for International Economics (CEPII), Paris, April 1994.

Benassy-Quere, Agnes, Mojon, Benoit, and Schor, Armand-Denis. The International Role of the Euro, Working Paper 98/03, CEPII, July 1998.

Bergsten, Fred C. "The Dollar and the Euro," *Foreign Affairs,* July/August 1997, 76(4), pp. 83–95.

Black, Stanley W. "The International Use of Currencies," in Yoshi Suzuki, Junichi Miyake, and Mitsuake Okabe, eds. *The Evolution of the International Monetary System: How Can Efficiency and Stability Be Achieved?* Tokyo: University of Tokyo Press, 1990.

Chrystal, K. Alec. "On the Theory of International Money," in John Black and Grame S. Dorrance, eds., *Problems of International Finance.* New York: St. Martin's Press, 1997.

Cohen, Benjamin J. *The Future of Sterling as an International Currency.* London: MacMillan Press, 1971.

Dooley, Michael P., Lizondo, J. Saul, and Mathieson, Donald J. "The Currency Composition of Foreign Exchange Reserves," *IMF Staff Papers,* June 1989, 36(2), pp. 385–434.

European Central Bank. "The International Role of the Euro," *ECB Monthly Bulletin,* August 1999, pp. 31–53.

Giavazzi, Francesco. "The European Monetary System: Lessons from Europe and Perspectives in Europe." *Economic and Social Review,* January 1989, 20(2), pp. 73–90.

Grassman, Sven. "A Fundamental Symmetry in International Payments Patterns," *Journal of International Economics,* May 1973, 3(2), pp. 105–16.

Hartmann, Phillip. "The Future of the Euro as an International Currency: a Transactions Perspective," London School of Economics *Financial Markets Group Special Papers,* November 1996.

Heller, H. Robert and Knight, Malcom. "Reserve Currency Preferences of Central Banks," *Princeton Essays in International Finance,* December 1978, (131).

Johnson, Karen H. "International Dimensions of European Monetary Union: Implications for the Dollar," *International Financial Discussion Paper* No. 469, Board of Governors of the Federal Reserve System, May 1994.

Kenen, Peter B. "EMU, Exchange Rates and the International Monetary System," *Recherches Economiques de Louvain,* 1993, 59(1.2), pp. 257–83.

Kool, Clemens J. M. "International Bond Markets and the Introduction of the Euro," *Federal Reserve Bank of St. Louis Review,* September/October 2000, 82(5), pp. 41–56.

Krugman, Paul. "Vehicle Currencies and the Structure of International Exchange," *Journal of Money, Credit, and Banking,* August 1980, 12(5), pp. 513–26.

Laxton, Douglas and Prasad, Eswar. "Possible Effects of European Monetary Union on Switzerland: A Case Study of Policy Dilemmas Caused by Low Inflation and the Nominal Interest Rate Floor." Working Paper WP/97/23, International Monetary Fund, March 1997.

Masson, Paul R. and Turtelboom, Bart G. "Characteristics of the Euro, the Demand for Reserves, and Policy Coordination Under EMU," Working Paper No. 97/58, International Monetary Fund, May 1997.

Page S. "The Choice of Invoicing Currency in Merchandise Trade," *National Institute Economic Review,* November 1981, 85, pp. 60–72.

Pollard, Patricia S. "The Role of the Euro as an International Currency," *The Columbia Journal of European Law,* Spring 1998, pp. 395–420.

Porter, Richard D. and Judson, Ruth A. "The Location of U.S. Currency: How Much is Abroad?" *Federal Reserve Bulletin,* October 1996, 82(10), pp. 883–903.

Portes, Richard and Rey, Helene. "The Emergence of the Euro as an International Currency," in *EMU: Prospects and Challenges for the Euro.* Oxford: Blackwell Publishers, 1998.

Seitz, Franz. "The Circulation of Deutsche Mark Abroad," Discussion Paper No. 1/95, Economic Research Centre of the Deutsche Bundesbank, May 1995.

Tavlas, George. "The International Use of the U.S. Dollar: An Optimum Currency Area Perspective." *The World Economy,* September 1997, 20(6), pp. 709–47.

United States Treasury Department and the Board of Governors of the Federal Reserve System. *The Use and Counterfeiting of United States Currency Abroad.* Washington, D.C., February 2000.

ENDNOTES

1. Between the time that the Treaty on European Union established the process for the completion of economic and monetary union and the creation of the euro, many economists studied the likely international role of the euro. Among these are Bekx (1996), Benassy-Quere, Mojon, and Schor (1998), Bergsten (1997), Hartmann (1996), Johnson (1994), Kenen (1993), Pollard (1998), and Portes and Rey (1998). Most of these studies concluded that the euro would be a major international currency but that the process would be gradual. Begsten and Portes and Rey, however, expected a quick ascent for the euro.

2. This is the most difficult for currency (sic) to achieve. Inflation reduces the purchasing power of money. As long as inflation is moderate, the ability of money to operate as a unit of account and medium of exchange ensures its continued use. Hyperinflation causes money to lose its store of value function and is associated with an increase in the use of barter and substitute currencies.

3. This sectoral division of the three functions of international money was first adopted by Cohen (1971).

4. In 1994 the Chinese economy surpassed the size of Japanese economy, based on purchasing power parity valuations of GDP. China accounted for 11.2 percent of the world's output in 1999. Nevertheless, Japan remains the world's third major economic power.

5. An internationalization ratio greater than or equal to 1.0 does not imply that all of the home country's exports are priced in its currency. According to data provided in Bekx (1998) in 1995, 92 percent of U.S. exports, 75 percent of German exports, 62 percent of British exports and 52 percent of French exports were invoiced in their domestic currencies.

6. In October 2000, Iraq began requiring payment for its oil exports in euros. There is no indication that this move will be followed by other major oil producers. A general shift to requiring payment in euros would probably hasten a switch to pricing oil in euros, but such a dual system is not without precedent. Benassy and Deusy-Fournier (1994) state that until 1974 oil was priced in dollars, but payment was made in pounds sterling.

7. The data in Tables 4 and 5 rely on different sources and hence may not be directly comparable.

8. Some policymakers in Switzerland were concerned that the creation of the euro might result in a sharp rise in demand for assets denominated in Swiss francs. See Laxton and Prasad (1997) for an analysis.

9. Kool (2000) addresses the use of the euro in international bond markets.

10. The data in Table 6 do not exclude bank transactions between members of the euro area.

11. These data were gathered from a triennial survey of foreign exchange markets conducted by the BIS.

12. Since there are two currencies involved in an exchange, the total share of all currencies traded on international exchanges will equal 200 percent. However, a single currency can, at most, be involved in 100 percent of all exchanges.

13. The use of transactions cost theory to explain the rise of a vehicle currency was developed by Krugman (1980) and Chrystal (1984).

14. The dollar was preferred to the British pound as the latter had yet to return to the gold standard after World War I.

15. According to the U.S. Treasury (2000), Argentina and Russia are believed to have the largest holdings of U.S. currency outside the United States.

16. These seignorage revenues are estimated by using the interest rate on one-year Treasury bills and adjusting nominal revenues using the GDP deflator.

17. The seignorage benefits must be weighed against the problems the foreign holdings of currency create for monetary policy. As Porter and Judson (1996) note, if foreign demand for a country's currency is unrelated to domestic demand, then the interpretation of movements in monetary aggregates becomes more difficult.
18. These 24 include San Marino, which uses the Italian lira as its currency, and Greece, which is now a member of the euro area.
19. Established in 1979, ERM was the fixed exchange rate system of the European Monetary System. With the creation of the euro, ERM was replaced by ERM II, linking the currencies of Denmark and Greece (until January 2001) to the euro.
20. These 23 include five countries (Ecuador, Marshall Islands, Micronesia, Palau, and Panama) that use the U.S. dollar as the local currency. In January 2001, El Salvador (which is not included in the 23) also adopted the U.S. dollar.
21. These shifts in holdings of reserves are affected both by changes in the physical holdings of currency and changes in exchange rates. Since the IMF measures reserve holdings in U.S. dollars, a rise in the exchange value of the dollar *ceteris paribus* will raise the dollar share of foreign exchange reserves.
22. Data in Masson and Turtelboom (1997) indicate that the European Union countries held 69 percent of the Deutsche mark reserves held by industrial countries in 1995.
23. The ecu, or more formally, the European currency unit, was a weighted average of the European Union currencies. Although it never existed as a paper currency, it was used as the unit of account for official European Union activities and a small ecu private bond market existed. The ecu was superceded by the euro.
24. Hong Kong, however, announced in late 1999 that it was increasing the share of the euro in its foreign currency reserves.
25. Under the rules of the ERM, mandatory interventions (when the exchange rate reached its upper or lower limit) had to take place in one of the member currencies. Non-mandatory (intra-band) interventions could take place in any currency, and generally dollars were used. See Giavazzi (1989) for details.
26. The existence of swap arrangements between central banks can offset some of these liquidity problems.

The Dollar and the Euro

C. FRED BERGSTEN

THE NEW GLOBAL CURRENCY

The creation of a single European currency will be the most important development in the international monetary system since the adoption of flexible exchange
rates in the early 1970s. The dollar will have its first real competitor since it surpassed the pound sterling as the world's dominant currency during the interwar
period. As much as $1 trillion of international investment may shift from dollars to
euros. Volatility between the world's key currencies will increase substantially,
requiring new forms of international cooperation if severe costs for the global
economy are to be avoided.

The political impact of the euro will be at least as great. A bipolar currency
regime dominated by Europe and the United States, with Japan as a junior partner,
will replace the dollar-centered system that has prevailed for most of this century.
A quantum leap in transatlantic cooperation will be required to handle both the
transition to the new regime and its long-term effects.

The global economic roles of the European Union and the United States are
nearly identical. The EU accounts for about 31 percent of world output and
20 percent of world trade. The United States provides about 27 percent of global
production and 18 percent of world trade. The dollar's 40 to 60 percent share of
world finance far exceeds the economic weight of the United States. This total also
exceeds the share of 10 to 40 percent for the European national currencies
combined. The dollar's market share is three to five times that of the deutsche
mark, the only European currency now used globally.

Inertia is a powerful force in international finance. For half a century, the
pound sterling retained a global role far in excess of Britain's economic strength.
The dollar will probably remain the leading currency indefinitely. But the creation
of the euro will narrow, and perhaps eventually close, the present monetary gap
between the United States and Europe. The dollar and the euro are each likely to
wind up with about 40 percent of world finance, with about 20 percent remaining
for the yen, the Swiss franc, and minor currencies.

Even an initial Economic and Monetary Union (EMU) comprising only
the half-dozen assured core countries would constitute an economy about two-
thirds the size of the United States' and almost equal to Japan's. The global trade

From C. Fred Bergsten, "The Dollar and the Euro," *Foreign Affairs* 76 July/August 1997, pp. 83–95. ©
1997, Institute for International Economics.

of this group would exceed that of the United States. If the gap between the current market share of the dollar and that of the European currencies were closed only halfway, that would produce an enormous shift in global financial holdings.

Substantial implications emerge for the functioning and management of the world economy. There will probably be a portfolio diversification of $500 billion to $1 trillion into euros. Most of this shift will come out of the dollar. This in turn will have a significant impact on exchange rates during a long transition period. The euro will move higher than will be comfortable for many Europeans. Europe will probably try to defend itself against this prospect by engineering a further substantial weakening of its national currencies between now and the euro's start-up.

In the long run, the dollar-euro exchange rate is likely to fluctuate considerably more than have the rates between the dollar and individual European currencies. This fluctuation could cause prolonged misalignments that would not only have adverse effects in both Europe and the United States but also provoke protectionist pressures on the global trading system. Creation of the euro will raise many policy issues that will require intensive cooperation, both across the Atlantic and in multilateral settings such as the Group of Seven (G-7) and the International Monetary Fund.

Europe has always accounted for a share of world trade comparable to that of the United States. In addition, Europe has had a common trade policy from the outset of its integration process. Trade policy thus has been bipolar for almost four decades, as evidenced by the necessity of Europe and the United States agreeing on all multilateral trade rounds in the General Agreement on Tariffs and Trade and recent sectoral agreements in the World Trade Organization.

The prospective developments on the monetary side would mirror that evolution, equating Europe's market position and institutional arrangements with those of the United States to produce a similarly bipolar regime. The United States, Europe, and global financial institutions are not prepared for these events. The initial blueprints for EMU ignored the issue, and there has been little subsequent discussion in Europe. The United States and the G-7 have failed to address the rise of the euro seriously, as they failed to address EMU's predecessor, the European Monetary System, even when it spawned currency crises with global effects in 1992–93. It is essential that the United States, Europe, and international financial institutions begin to prepare for the euro's global impact.

✿ ✿ ✿

GLOBAL MONEY

Five key factors determine whether a currency will play a global role: the size of its underlying economy and global trade; the economy's independence from external constraints; avoidance of exchange controls; the breadth, depth, and liquidity of the economy's capital markets; and the economy's strength, stability, and external position.

On the first two criteria, a unified Europe is superior to the United States. The European Union's GDP was $8.4 trillion in 1996, compared with $7.2 trillion for the United States. Growth of potential output is similar in the two regions, so their relative position should hold. The European Union also has a larger volume of global trade. EU external trade totaled $1.9 trillion in 1996, compared with $1.7 trillion for the United States.

In terms of openness, the share of exports and imports in total output is now about 23 percent in both the EU and the United States. This ratio has doubled for the United States over the past 25 years while rising only modestly in Europe, but it is also likely to remain broadly similar. Both regions are thus largely independent of external constraints and can manage their policies without being thrown off course by any but the most severe external shocks.

It is almost inconceivable that either the EU or the United States would unilaterally resort to exchange or capital controls. Globalization of capital markets has reached the point where all major financial centers, including many in the developing world, would have to act together to alter international capital flows effectively. Hence the two regions will remain parallel on this key currency criterion as well.

It is less clear when Europe will reach full parity with the United States in terms of the breadth, depth, and liquidity of its capital markets. The American market for domestic securities is about twice as large as the combined European markets. The European financial markets are highly decentralized. There will be no central governmental borrower like the U.S. Treasury to provide a fulcrum for the market. It may take some time to align the relevant standards and practices across the EU, especially if London is included. Germany may oppose wholesale liberalization, as the Bundesbank has traditionally done in Germany, on the grounds that it would weaken the ability of the ECB to conduct an effective monetary policy.

On the other hand, the total value of government bond markets in the EU is 2.1 trillion euros, compared with 1.6 trillion euros in the United States. Moreover, international bonds and equities are much more frequently issued in the European markets than in the United States. Futures trading in German and French government bonds, taken together, exceeded that in U.S. notes and bonds in 1995. Expectations over the launch of EMU have already produced a substantial convergence in the yields of government bonds throughout Europe. An integrated European capital market for private bonds shows clear signs of developing. So European parity on this key criterion is likely to occur eventually.

The final criterion is the strength and stability of the European economy. There is no risk of hyperinflation or any of the other extreme instabilities that could disqualify the euro from international status. On the contrary, the ECB is likely to run a responsible monetary policy. On the other hand, Europe may not carry out the structural reforms needed to restore dynamic economic growth. But markets prize stability more than growth, as indicated by the continued dominance of the dollar through extended periods of sluggish American economic performance. Hence the euro should qualify on these grounds as well.

In addition, America's external economic position will continue to raise doubts about the future stability and value of the dollar. The United States has run current account deficits for the last years. Its net foreign debt exceeds $1 trillion and is rising annually by 15 to 20 percent. The EU, in contrast, has a roughly balanced international asset position and has run modest surpluses in its international accounts in recent years. On this important criterion, the EU is decidedly superior to the United States.

The relative size of countries' economies and trade flows is of central importance in determining currencies' global roles. A large economy has a naturally large base for its currency and thus enjoys important economies of scale and scope. A high volume of trade gives a country's firms considerable leverage to finance in their own currency. Large economies are less vulnerable to external shocks and thus offer a safe haven for investors. They are more likely to have the large capital markets required for major currency status.

There is a clear historical correlation between size and currency status. Sterling and the dollar became dominant during the periods when the United Kingdom and the United States were the world's main economies and traders. The only global currencies today are those of the world's three largest economies and traders: the United States, Germany, and Japan.

The relevant comparison for present purposes is between the EU and the euro, on the one hand, and Germany and the deutsche mark on the other. It would be improper to compare the euro, which will meet all of the key currency criteria, with the sum of the individual European currencies, most of which do not. The comparison must be with the deutsche mark, the only European currency that is now used on a global basis.

Hence there will be a quantum leap in the size of the economy and trading unit in question. Germany accounts for nine percent of world output and 12 percent of world trade. The euro core group accounts for 8 and 19 percent, respectively. The full EMU accounts for 31 and 20 percent, respectively. The relevant unit will thus increase immediately by at least 50 to 100 percent. Eventually, the rise will be about 65 to 250 percent.

Crude econometric efforts suggest that every rise of 1 percent in a country's share of global output and trade raises its currency share by roughly the same amount. On this premise, the global role of the euro would exceed that of the deutsche mark by 50 to 100 percent if EMU included only the core group and by 65 to 250 percent if all Europe were included. The deutsche mark, by most calculations, accounts for about 15 percent of global financial assets in both private and official markets. The euro's role could thus reach 20 to 30 percent of world finance if EMU included only the core countries and 25 to 50 percent if the entire EU were involved. The midpoints of these ranges, 25 and almost 40 percent, provide rough indicators of the likely future global role of the euro. If these shifts into the euro came largely out of the dollar, they would eliminate half to all of the present gap between the dollar and the deutsche mark.

This evolution could produce a major diversification of portfolios into euros, mainly out of dollars. Official reserve shifts into euros could range between $100 billion and $300 billion. Private portfolio diversification could be much larger. Excluding intra-EU holdings, global holdings of international financial assets, including bank deposits and bonds, are about $3.5 trillion. About 50 percent are in dollars and only about 10 percent in European currencies. A complete balancing of portfolios between dollars and euros would require a shift of about $700 billion. A combination of official and private shifts suggests a potential diversification of between $500 billion and $1 trillion.

Such a shift, even spread over a number of years, could drive the euro up and the dollar down substantially. The extent of the shift will depend on whether the supply of euros rises in tandem with demand. It will also depend on the relationship between the dollar and the European national currencies when the euro is issued. While most Europeans want a strong euro, they also want to avoid an overvalued currency that deepens their economic difficulties. Many believe that their national currencies are already overvalued despite recent substantial declines against the dollar. The only way they can avoid the dilemma is to depreciate the European national currencies further before the launch of the euro. The EMU would then be able to set the initial exchange rate below the fundamental equilibrium exchange rate for the euro. The euro could appreciate modestly without undermining the long-term competitive position of the European economy.

Exchange market developments from now until the early part of the next century could be a mirror image of the first half of the 1980s. During that period, U.S. budget deficits soared. The elimination of Japanese exchange controls triggered a large portfolio diversification from yen into dollars. Fiscal tightening in Europe and Japan further enhanced the dollar's appreciation. The opposite conditions may apply in the period ahead: further reductions in, or even elimination of, the American budget deficit could coincide with European fiscal expansion and a large diversification out of the dollar triggered by the euro's creation. Substantial euro appreciation and dollar depreciation could thus occur in the transition to EMU.

Many analysts agree that the euro will rival the dollar as the world's leading currency. Most believe, however, that such a shift will take considerable time, since any redistribution of international portfolios occurs incrementally. But there is evidence from the history of major currencies that major shocks can produce rapid changes in portfolio composition. The devaluation of the pound sterling in 1931 permanently reduced the international role of that currency and propelled the dollar into the dominant position. The onset of double-digit inflation in the United States in the late 1970s produced a sharp drop in the dollar's role in just a few years.

These shocks, however, have derived more from poor policy and performance by the lead currency than from the improved position of the new rival. The euro's rise may have to await a serious policy lapse by the United States, as in the late 1970s, or a renewed explosion of America's external debt position, as in the 1980s. Even the most successful and best-managed countries undergo occasional setbacks, and the euro's rough parity with the dollar is probably inevitable.

JAPAN AS JUNIOR PARTNER

The yen will continue to play an important but smaller role, maintaining its 10 to 15 percent market share. But the world is not likely to see a tri-polar monetary system. The Japanese Ministry of International Trade and Industry's latest report on the topic concludes that "the yen is nowhere near achieving the status of a truly international currency." Japan will need to be included in any new EU-U.S. arrangements but will probably remain a junior partner in the management of the international monetary regime.

Japan's economy is about twice the size of Germany's. Its trade is only slightly smaller, and it has an even better record of price stability over the past 15 years. Yet its currency plays a much smaller role than the deutsche mark, suggesting a significant deficiency when it comes to the other key currency criteria—notably the capabilities of its financial markets. Japan's continued failure to deregulate and modernize those markets is likely to remain a barrier for the yen. Indeed, the fragility of Japan's financial sector is more likely to repel than attract international interest.

Many analysts have hypothesized the emergence of three north-south regional blocs centered around Europe, Japan, and the United States. So far, however, major trade groupings have developed around Europe and the United States but not around Japan. With the Asia-Pacific Economic Cooperation forum linking the United States and Japan, bipolarity may be evolving not only in monetary affairs but in trade as well.

THE NEW TRANSATLANTIC AGENDA

The euro's rise will convert an international monetary system that has been dominated by the dollar since World War II into a bipolar regime. Hence the structure and politics of international financial cooperation will change dramatically.

The exchange rate between the euro and the dollar will pose a significant policy challenge. The United States and the rest of the world should reject any attempt by Europe to substantially undervalue the euro's start-up rate. It would represent a blatant effort by Europe to export its high unemployment and to enable the euro to become a strong currency without any significant cost to its competitive position.

France is running sizable trade and current account surpluses, even adjusted for its high level of unemployment. Germany has the world's second-largest trade surplus and is the world's second-largest creditor country. The EU is a surplus region. By contrast, the United States is the world's largest debtor nation. Its trade and current account deficits are headed well above $200 billion in 1997. These facts hardly suggest that the European currencies are too strong or that the dollar is too weak. The G-7 should, at a minimum, actively resist further European depreciation and dollar appreciation.

Portfolio diversification's impact on the exchange rate between the dollar and the euro will also pose a challenge. Unfortunately, there is no way to assess the precise magnitude or timing of that impact, and it is impossible to predict the fundamental equilibrium exchange rate that will emerge for the euro and the dollar. It would, therefore, be a mistake to use target zones or any other predetermined mechanisms to limit dollar-euro fluctuations during the transition period.

However, markets could become extremely unstable. It will be important for the G-7 and the International Monetary Fund to monitor events closely, to form judgments on the likely outcome as the process evolves, and to intervene to limit unnecessary volatility. This monitoring will require much closer cooperation than exists today.

Over the longer run, availability of a more attractive alternative to the dollar could reduce the ability of the United States to finance its large external deficits. With more than $4 trillion in external liabilities and an array of alternative assets available to international investors, however, the United States' policy autonomy already faces considerable limits. Such constraints were felt in Washington in the late 1970s—even though the United States was then the world's largest creditor country—when the dollar's free fall signaled the need to tighten monetary policy and triggered the $30 billion dollar support package of October 1978. They were felt again in early 1987 and early 1995 when the dollar fell sharply against the deutsche mark and the yen.

European countries already pay relatively little attention to fluctuations in their national currencies vis-à-vis the dollar. But external events will play an even smaller role in the larger, unified European economy. Larger and even more frequent changes in the exchange rate of the euro could be accepted with equanimity. The EU might even promote greater currency movements to achieve external adjustment, as the United States has done on occasion.

The euro and the dollar will dominate world finance, but both Europe and the United States will often be tempted to practice benign neglect. If left to market forces, the two currencies will likely experience increased volatility and misalignments. Both outcomes would be destabilizing for other countries and the world economy.

The European Union and the United States must recognize that prolonged misalignments would be costly for their economies too. The United States learned this in the mid-1980s, when dollar overvaluation caused an extended recession in manufacturing and agriculture. Given the pivotal role of the EU and the United States in global trade policy, such lapses would be extremely harmful to the world economy. A structured exchange rate regime should be developed to manage the relationship that will emerge between the dollar and the euro. The EU, Japan, and the United States should negotiate a target zone system with broad currency bands, perhaps 10 percent on both sides of a nominal midpoint, that would avoid large current account imbalances and their attendant problems.

Many Europeans believe that EMU will facilitate such cooperation. Europe will speak with a single voice, enabling it to force the United States to be more cooperative. Some Europeans view this outcome as an important goal of EMU, and one that will offset the continent's enhanced ability to ignore external events.

Trade policy provides support for their logic. The multilateral trading system has been essentially bipolar since the creation of the Common Market in 1958, which has always spoken with a single voice on most trade matters. The united Europe could have chosen to raise barriers against the world, with only modest costs because of its considerable size, but has largely opted to support further global liberalization. Most observers believe that this negotiating structure facilitated the success of the three major rounds of the General Agreement on Tariffs and Trade. It has recently been on display in the forging of the two most important liberalizing measures since the end of the Uruguay Round, the agreement on trade in telecommunications services and the Information Technology Agreement on trade in high-tech goods.

While this pattern may hold, several scenarios can be envisioned. The United States could react defensively to its loss of monetary dominance and seek to create a formalized dollar area, like the United Kingdom's sterling area in the 1930s. The EU could adopt a strategy of benign neglect, arguing that the United States has done so repeatedly and that its turn has now come. Trade protection could result from either course.

When French President Valery Giscard d'Estaing and German Chancellor Helmut Schmidt decided to create the European Monetary System in 1978, one of their goals was to foster a more stable global monetary regime. The creation of EMU could bring that vision closer to reality. However, in the absence of cooperation between the European Union and the United States, the euro could create greater instability. It is up to the governments of the two regions to achieve a smooth transition from the sterling—and dollar-dominated monetary regimes of the nineteenth and twentieth centuries to a stable dollar and euro system in the early 21st century. The underlying strength and history of the North Atlantic relationship bodes well, but achieving a successful outcome will be a major policy challenge in the years ahead.

QUESTIONS FOR REVIEW AND DISCUSSION

1. According to Pollard, what functions must a currency fulfill in order to be considered an international currency? Does Bergsten agree with these criteria, or does he use different measures?
2. According to Bergsten, what factor, more than any other, is likely to raise questions in the minds of governments and private sector actors about the future stability and value of the dollar? What impact might this have on the dollar's use as an international currency?
3. Bergsten argues that the creation of the euro poses a "significant policy challenge." What is the nature of this challenge, and what policy solutions does he propose?
4. Will the creation of the euro make it more or less likely that EU governments and the United States begin to manage the exchange rates? What factors make such cooperation more likely, and what factors make is less likely?
5. What, if anything, can a government do to promote or maintain their currency's use in the international economy?
6. What are the stakes in the competition between the euro and the dollar? That is, what does the United States gain, and therefore stand to lose, from the dollar's role as the primary international currency?

SUGGESTIONS FOR FURTHER READING

For an in-depth treatment by prominent economists of the potential for a struggle for dominance between the euro and the dollar see: *The Journal of Policy Modeling* (July 2002).

For a more recent discussion, see remarks offered by Ben S. Bernanke (a member of the U.S. Federal Reserve's Board of Governors): "The Euro at 5—Ready for a Global Role?" Available at http://www.bis.org/review/r040304d.pdf. C. Fred Bergsten offers an updated evaluation in his "The Euro and the Dollar: Toward a Finance G-2?" Available at http://www.iie.com/publications/papers/bergsten0204-2.pdf

The European Central Bank examines the international role of the euro in *Review of the International Role of the Euro*. Frankfurt: European Central Bank, 2002. This publication is available on line at http://www.ecb.int/pub/pdf/euro-international-role2002.pdf

For an historical examination of the transition from a pound-centered to a dollar-centered system, see: Susan Strange. *Sterling and British Policy: A Political Study of an International Currency in Decline*. New York: Oxford University Press, 1971.

CHAPTER 13

DEVELOPING COUNTRIES AND DOLLARIZATION

While the world's major currencies have floated against each other since 1973, most developing countries continued to maintain fixed exchange rates since the collapse of the Bretton Woods system. Most developing countries adopted some type of fixed-but-adjustable exchange rate regime. As late as 1991 only 10 out of 37 emerging-market countries had adopted floating exchange rate regimes, while 21 had adopted fixed-but-adjustable exchange rates and 3 had adopted what the International Monetary Fund calls a "hard peg"—that is, a permanently fixed exchange rate (Fischer 2001). Many developing-country governments pegged their currencies to the dollar; others pegged to the British pound, the French franc, or the Japanese yen. Such arrangements provided the medium-term exchange rate stability they desired and yet allowed governments to change the exchange rate when it proved necessary to do so in the wake of economic shocks.

The last ten years have brought dramatic changes to these exchange rate arrangements as governments have increasingly abandoned fixed-but-adjustable exchange rates in favor of hard pegs or floating exchange rates. In 1999, 16 out of 33 emerging market countries had adopted floating exchange rates, and 6 had adopted hard pegs. Only 14 countries continued to maintain a fixed-but-adjustable exchange rate. This shift away from fixed-but-adjustable exchange rates has been driven in large part by the emergence of large international capital flows to emerging-market countries. Many economists have argued that fixed-but-adjustable exchange rates are unsustainable in a world of highly mobile capital. The very premise of such exchange rates, that the national currency can and will be devalued, creates instability in international financial markets. Currency devaluation reduces the value of assets denominated in that currency. Suppose an American resident holds a bond issued by a Mexican business that is denominated in pesos. If the Mexican government devalues the peso against the dollar, the dollar value of that Mexican corporate bond has fallen by the amount of the devaluation. Individuals and businesses will attempt to avoid such losses by selling peso-denominated assets whenever they believe the Mexican government is about to devalue the peso. The resulting volume of sales, or capital outflows, can be so large that a government's foreign exchange reserves are exhausted and it is forced to float its currency. Such dynamics were evident in many of the financial crises that struck emerging-market countries during the 1990s, including Mexico in 1994 and

Thailand, Indonesia, South Korea, and other East Asian countries in 1997, as well as in the speculative crisis that struck the European Monetary System in 1992.

The emerging policy consensus is that given the current high level of international capital mobility, fixed-but-adjustable exchange rates are no longer a viable policy option. Any government that adopts such a regime tempts fate by inviting a financial and currency crisis. Consequently, governments are left with only two options: float their currency or adopt a hard peg. As the two readings presented in this section make clear, however, there is substantially less consensus on which of these options is the better choice. Ricardo Hausmann, the chief economist at the Inter-American Development Bank, argues in favor of one form of a permanently fixed exchange rate, dollarization. Dollarization entails the elimination of the national currency and the adoption of the dollar (or another international currency such as the euro) in its place. Hausmann's case for dollarization is based on his understanding of why emerging-market countries regularly suffer financial crises. He focuses particularly on the weakness of emerging-market currencies. The typical emerging-market currency cannot be borrowed in international markets, and even at home can usually be borrowed only for the short term. Investors who want to make long-term investments must therefore choose between long-term borrowing in foreign currencies and short-term borrowing in the local currency. Either choice renders the financial system vulnerable to crisis. Borrowing in foreign currencies to finance domestic investments exposes investors to currency mismatch between their assets (denominated in the local currency) and their liabilities (denominated in a foreign currency). Borrowing short-term in the local currency in order to finance a long-term investment exposes investors to maturity mismatch between their assets (which pay off over the long term) and their liabilities (which must be paid off in the short term). Either mismatch can be a source of financial fragility by itself; Hausmann argues that the two mismatches interact in a way that render emerging markets highly susceptible to financial crises. The solution to the financial fragility that causes crises, therefore, is to replace national currencies with a strong foreign currency such as the dollar. Dollarization eliminates both mismatches, creating stable financial systems for emerging-market countries.

Jeffrey Sachs, an economist and the director of The Earth Institute at Columbia University, and Felipe Larrain, a Chilean economist, argue that countries should maintain flexible exchange rates. Sachs and Larrain argue that governments must use monetary policy and exchange-rate changes to respond to economic shocks. Dollarization, like other forms of fixed exchange rates, would prevent the government from devaluing in response to a fall in the price of the country's exports, and it would prevent the government from expanding the money supply in response to slowing economic growth. Without monetary and exchange-rate changes, adjustment can occur only through a rise in unemployment and, over time, a reduction of domestic wages. Dollarization would also occasionally require governments to adopt monetary policies that were inappropriate for local conditions. If the United States were to tighten monetary policy, perhaps because inflation was rising, countries that had dollarized would have to tighten their monetary policies as well, even if a tighter monetary policy was inappropriate for their economic conditions. Thus, while Sachs and Larrain recognize that dollarization, as well as other hard pegs, are sometimes appropriate, they argue that the typical emerging market country will be better off with a flexible exchange rate.

REFERENCE

Fischer, Stanley. "Exchange Rate Regimes: Is the Bipolar View Correct?" *Journal of Economic Perspectives*, 15 (spring, 2001): 3–24.

Currencies: Should There Be Five or One Hundred and Five?

RICARDO HAUSMANN

It was not supposed to turn out this way. The collapse of communism in the former Soviet Union and the abandonment of the interventionist and populist state in Latin America more than a decade ago were supposed to usher in a period of unparalleled prosperity. The invisible and efficient hand of the market, now made more powerful through globalization, would succeed where the incompetent and often bloody hand of government had failed. But more than a decade after the annunciation of this "end of history," country after country among the new emerging-market economies has fallen into financial crisis, the likes of which have not been seen since the Great Depression of the 1930s or the Latin American debt crisis of the 1980s. Economic turmoil has afflicted not only those countries with poor policy records, but also those held up as models (such as Mexico before 1994 and the East Asian Tigers until 1997), destroying livelihoods, crushing hopes, and increasing human suffering.

This cataclysm has also shattered the consensus among bankers, policymakers, academics, and ideologues about appropriate economic policy in emerging markets. As economic professionals now return to the drawing board, one question is generating particularly fierce debate: Should emerging-market countries allow their currencies to float freely, or should they abandon them altogether in favor of strong international or supranational currencies such as the U.S. dollar or the euro? Interestingly, the debate has quickly become polarized: Both sides seem to accept that there can be no middle ground, no halfway arrangement between allowing a currency to float freely and bolting it down completely.

MORAL HAZARD VERSUS ORIGINAL SIN

The debate between "floaters" and "dollarizers" reflects the broader debate over the precise causes of the recent financial turmoil. Two opposing explanations have emerged: a dominant view based on what economists call "moral hazard" and an alternative theory based on what might be called "original sin."

Just about anyone who has read about the financial crises in Asia, Latin America, and Russia has become familiar with the concept of moral hazard: the increase in recklessness that takes place when people are somehow protected

From Ricardo Hausmann, "Should There Be 5 Currencies Instead of 105?" *Foreign Policy*, Fall, 1999, pp. 65–79.

against the consequences of their risky behavior. For example, car insurance may make people more likely to drive faster or to park their cars in neighborhoods where the chances of vandalism or theft are higher. By the same logic, the readiness of governments and international institutions to provide bailouts in times of emerging-market (and other) financial crises may make investors less vigilant about weighing all the risks involved.

The view that moral hazard is to blame for the recent financial turmoil has inspired an ambitious roster of reforms for the international financial architecture. This agenda includes moves to upgrade the financial supervision and regulation of individual countries, to eliminate or reduce the provision of international bailouts by the International Monetary Fund (IMF), and to develop "bailing in" procedures to ensure that the investors themselves play a role in resolving future crises.

In addition to bailouts, there is another element of moral hazard that is often overlooked in the headlines: exchange rate regimes. Fixed exchange rates can serve as an implicit guarantee that a government will protect the value of its currency, thus keeping investments safe as well. Consequently, some economists advocate the adoption of floating exchange rates so that investors face the real risks of speculating in emerging-market currencies.

But is moral hazard really the core of the problem? After all, although car insurance may lead to some degree of increased recklessness, we still seem to believe that a world that offers such insurance is better than one that does not (otherwise the protection would not exist). In addition, the moral-hazard view of financial crises must answer the Jerry Maguire "Show me the money" critique. Moral hazard implies there is too much capital flooding the international financial system; it would explain excessive rather than surprisingly low international capital flows. Yet, in spite of the Internet and electronic wire transfers, there is proportionally less capital flowing across borders today than there was a century ago. In short, if moral hazard is so important, then "Show me the money!"

The alternative theory, original sin, seeks to explain why many emerging markets are volatile and prone to crisis by focusing on three characteristics that such countries often share: good economic prospects, a certain degree of openness to international capital flows, and a national currency that cannot be used by local firms or the government to borrow abroad, and cannot be used, even at home, for long-term borrowing—a weakness, or sin, shared by the currencies of almost all emerging-market economies.

If a country is economically promising and reasonably open, then people will want to invest. But if its currency cannot be used for either foreign or long-term borrowing, would-be investors must choose between borrowing in a foreign currency, such as the dollar, or borrowing short-term. If a company borrows in dollars to finance a project that generates pesos, a subsequent devaluation of the peso could lead to bankruptcy. If instead the company undertakes a longer-term project and finances it with short-term loans, it will go bust if liquidity dries up and if it cannot get the loans renewed. In other words, investments will suffer either from a currency mismatch (because projects that generate local currency are financed with dollar loans) or a maturity mismatch (because longer-term investments have been financed with short-term loans).

This scenario is a recipe for financial fragility. Such systems will be extremely vulnerable to sudden declines in the amount of liquidity in the banking system and to sudden depreciations of the currency. In fact, as the domestic currency starts to decline, companies fearful of further depreciation will attempt to buy foreign currency in order to cover their exposures. This decision will only make matters worse by causing the domestic currency to depreciate even further—a dynamic that can take place even in a floating exchange rate country. For its part, the government will seek to defend the currency by using its international reserves. But using those reserves will dry up the amount of money in the domestic banking system, and as liquidity declines, banks will be forced to call in their loans, precipitating a banking crisis caused by the maturity mismatches. So the two mismatches interact. In fact, such a system is subject to self-fulfilling crises, as in a bank run: If people fear that others may take their money out, they will want to be the first out the door.

The competing theories of moral hazard and original sin suggest two very different sets of options for countries with respect to monetary systems. The moral-hazard explanation suggests that letting exchange rates float would limit volatility by making investors bear the full risk of moving capital in and out of a country. But if the problem is rooted in original sin rather than moral hazard, allowing the currency to float will not have much of an impact: As long as the national currency, whether fixed or floating, is one that cannot be used for foreign or long-term borrowing, financial stability will remain elusive.

THE FALSE PROMISE OF FLOATING RATES

One idea embraced by almost all economists is that the choice of a monetary system involves a trilemma: There is an inherent trade-off among choosing the level of the exchange rate, choosing the level of the interest rate, and allowing capital to move freely in and out of a country. Governments can control two out of three, but not all three. If a government decides to fix the exchange rate and allow capital to move freely, it must accept whatever interest rate the market demands. If instead it decides to control the interest rate and allow capital to move freely, it must let the exchange rate float. Finally, if it wants to control both the exchange rate and the interest rate, then it must impose effective capital controls.

The terms of the trilemma have shifted over time, with floating exchange systems a relatively recent phenomenon. Before the twentieth century, most governments maintained their currencies pegged to the value of some underlying asset, typically gold or silver. During periods of war, countries often abandoned convertibility to gold or silver but returned to it as quickly as they could, as happened, for example, in Europe after World War I.

When the Bretton Woods Conference was convened in 1944 to plan the monetary system for the postwar period, the signatory countries opted for a system of fixed but adjustable exchange rates with the U.S. dollar at its core. In part, the choice of a fixed system was in response to the ruinous competitive currency devaluations of the 1930s. The IMF was created in order to assist countries with the financing necessary to ease payments crises and to sustain the pegs. These were times when capital could not move freely across borders, so countries could control both exchange rates and interest rates. Under the influence of economist John Maynard Keynes, monetary policy was thought of as an instrument to dampen cyclical booms and recessions. It was monetary policy that acted as speed control: Interest rates were increased to slow down a boom and lowered to prevent a recession.

This fixed system eventually collapsed in 1971, in part because the United States—reluctant to raise taxes as it was simultaneously paying for the Vietnam War and for Great Society social programs—pursued lax fiscal and monetary policies. But the system also collapsed because the increasingly free movement of capital meant that the terms of the trilemma had shifted: Governments now had to choose between controlling the exchange rate or the interest rate, as they could no longer control both. The Bretton Woods system was replaced by a regime in which the world's major currencies floated against one another. It was thought that this approach would allow countries to gain control over interest rates and avoid importing U.S. inflation through rising import prices. Instead, they could compensate for rising dollar prices by strengthening their domestic currency and, thus, keep inflation in check at home.

The floating system was also supposed to eliminate currency misalignments. Exchange rates would move in an orderly and automatic fashion to compensate for differences in inflation, keeping relative competitiveness stable. The system would permit countries to absorb shocks more easily through movements of the exchange rate. It would allow countries to choose their own mix of inflation and unemployment based on their sovereign preferences. With hindsight, in the words of Harvard economist Richard Cooper, these views appear "charmingly naive."

Instead of smoothness and orderliness, the system of floating rates among the major countries has produced large and unpredictable exchange rate movements. The perception of severe currency misalignments led the Group of Seven (G-7) to attempt policy coordination in the mid-1980s, as the strong dollar had produced a huge U.S. trade deficit and enormous protectionist pressures. Despite almost 15 years of G-7 coordination, however, the volatility of exchange rates remains enormous. For example, over the past few years, the yen-dollar rate has moved from 81 to 148 yen to the dollar, almost a 100 percent increase.

Emerging markets never voluntarily opted for floating regimes. Most of their currencies were fixed to the dollar during the Bretton Woods period and only came off the pegs after various economic crises. Many of these countries then opted for regimes that had limited flexibility of different sorts, such as exchange rate bands and "crawling pegs." In the wake of the recent financial crises, a number of countries—Brazil, Indonesia, Mexico, Papua New Guinea, South Korea, and Thailand have abandoned these schemes in favor of purely floating regimes. Given that such emerging-market countries are entering uncharted territory, it is fair to ask what they can really expect from a world of floating exchange rates.

The answers are not encouraging. Recent experience in Latin America suggests that the new popularity of floating rates may reflect yet another form of charming naivete. Floating regimes have not delivered much in the areas they were supposed to help: They have failed to provide more autonomy in the determination of interest rates, they have not facilitated more stabilizing monetary policies, and they have not led to an increased ability to absorb shocks.

Domestic interest rates in fact seem more sensitive to foreign rates under floating rather than fixed regimes, which implies less, not more, monetary independence. When the cost of foreign borrowing goes up by 1 percent, for example, domestic interest rates go up by 1.4 percent under Argentina's fixed-rate currency board and by 5.9 percent under Mexico's floating regime. Floating has also undermined monetary policy as an effective tool to stabilize the economy. For instance, domestic interest rates tend to go up instead of down during a recession (even more drastically than they would under a fixed regime). And floating in Latin America has increased the volatility of domestic interest rates, making banking a riskier industry.

Finally, the experiences of Chile, Mexico, Peru, or Venezuela—after the Asian Crisis of 1997 and the collapse in commodity prices in 1998—suggest that emerging-market countries with formal floating regimes do not allow their currencies to move much, even after huge external shocks. Instead, they react by raising interest rates, thereby dramatically worsening the domestic downturn. Therefore, floating rates in Latin America have failed to deliver the speed control and shock absorption qualities they promised.

On top of all this, floating can entail huge costs. It could be the catalyst for a shrinking financial system, as residents move their assets out of the domestic currency. A recent study by the Inter-American Development Bank suggests that Latin American countries with floating currencies end up with financial systems that are 15 to 30 percent smaller than they otherwise would have been. One reason is that letting the exchange rate appreciate in good times and depreciate in bad times reduces the incentive of residents to hold their assets in the domestic currency because it does not help diversify the income risk they already bear. In good times, when incomes are high and people are in a position to save, the value of their previously accumulated savings goes up through currency appreciation. In bad times, when income is low and people might wish to dip into their savings, they find their assets are worth increasingly less because of currency depreciation. Hence, residents of these emerging-market countries will want to hedge their savings by moving them out of the domestic currency. It will become apparent in coming years if this is also true of savers in Asian countries that have recently chosen floating rates.

Floating entails a second significant cost: Depositors demand a higher return to compensate for the greater instability in the value of their assets, thereby producing a much higher level of average real interest rates. In the 1990s, Latin American floater countries have averaged 9 percent real interest rates compared with 5 percent for countries with fixed exchange rates.

Finally, floating regimes tend to produce more wage indexation (salaries that are adjusted for inflation). When workers negotiate labor contracts in an unstable currency, they ask for protection from fluctuations. As wages become indexed, devaluations tend to have high inflationary effects because higher import prices lead to higher wages and thus to a wage-price spiral. For this reason, devaluations end up having limited effects on competitiveness. Knowing this, central banks try not to let the exchange rate move much and therefore have to rely on interest rates instead, which makes these same interest rates volatile. Thus, the real-life experience of Latin America shows that floating rates can generate quite unsavory results.

What about the idea that floating reduces moral hazard because it forces investors to bear the real risks of moving in and out of emerging markets? Floating regimes might help increase stability by making some capital shy away from emerging markets, but they will also cause domestic savings to flee, leaving countries with fewer resources to finance growth. In addition, highly volatile domestic interest rates will make banking riskier and will conspire against the development of long-term markets. New Asian floaters may find it impossible to return to the rates of growth that their countries were able to achieve over the last two decades. A system of floating rates does not solve the problem of original sin, which means emerging-market countries will remain crisis-prone.

An alternative to floating, strongly implied by the theory of original sin, would be for emerging markets to abandon national currencies altogether in favor of an international currency such as the dollar or a supranational currency such as the euro. This decision would expand the menu of financial options open to emerging-market governments and firms and, in doing so, would increase overall financial stability.

SURMOUNTABLE OBSTACLES

Original sin suggests that countries with weak national currencies will become financially fragile, no matter how they manage their exchange rates. Abandoning a weak national currency in favor of a stronger international or supranational currency would eliminate currency and maturity mismatches, because debts would be denominated in the same unit as a company's cash flow. It would also allow countries to take out long-term loans. In spite of its checkered political history, for example, dollarized Panama has the largest domestic credit market in Latin America. It is also the only Latin country to offer 30-year fixed-rate mortgages. (No wonder the Mexican business community wants to dollarize after only four years' experience with a floating currency.)

In a financial sense, a world of international or supranational currencies would be more stable and safer for capital mobility. Long-term interest rates would decline and become less volatile—as we have seen in Europe, where interest rates have gone down in Ireland, Italy, Portugal, and Spain—making it easier to cut budget deficits and promote growth. This scenario seems almost too good to be true, and of course, there are several hitches.

First is the issue of seignorage. Because currency is worth more than its printing costs, printing money generates revenue for whoever owns the printing machine. Called seignorage, this income usually accrues to national governments. Under current conditions, any government giving up its currency would forgo this revenue. How big an obstacle is this? Yearly, seignorage in most countries currently accounts for perhaps .5 percent of the gross domestic product; this is not a huge amount, and the benefits of adopting a supranational currency may well exceed the costs. There is also the possibility that in the interest of maintaining the overall system, enlightened "owners" of international or supranational currencies (such as the United States and the European Union) may be willing to share their seignorage with countries that adopt their currencies.

The second apparent obstacle involves a nation's ability to act as a lender of last resort. Banking systems require a mechanism to guarantee their ability to cope with sudden withdrawals of deposits, since depositors may otherwise end up pulling their money for fear that others may do so before them. This is the reason that central banks usually act as lenders of last resort in domestic banking systems, giving loans against good collateral to commercial banks. Abandoning the national currency means eliminating the central bank's ability to print money, which is currently how last-resort lending is usually provided. An alternative therefore needs to be found that does not involve transferring the risks to other countries. The solution to this problem requires some sort of collateral. If a country could put credible collateral on the table, it could even contract out the lender-of-last-resort function to the international private market.

With good collateral, countries could most likely negotiate credit lines for use in times of trouble, as Argentina has recently done. The collateral could come from several sources, but obviously a sharing of the seignorage would provide a good starting point. If a country such as Argentina were to put up the equivalent of its seignorage as collateral—by being allowed to exchange its current stock of peso bills for U.S. dollars at no cost—it could then dedicate its international reserves not to backing up its currency, but to assuring the liquidity of its banking system. The lender-of-last-resort issue would thus seem manageable.

The issue of asymmetric shocks appears more difficult. Adopting an international or supranational currency would not be a panacea: Countries would still undergo shocks, and they would be unable to devalue or lower interest rates in response. Yet they might not be any worse off than at present. We have already seen that emerging-market countries in Latin America with floating regimes seem powerless to use monetary and exchange rate policy to cushion and absorb shocks. Moreover, many of the shocks that emerging markets suffer are a consequence of the financial fragility that comes from having a domestic currency. In a world of fewer national currencies, this financial turbulence would presumably be smaller.

In addition, deeper and longer-term financial markets would allow companies and firms to cope with other kinds of shocks. On balance, the system may in fact tend to be more stabilizing than at present, and of course, more could still be done to tame the effects of potential shocks on emerging-market economies. In a system of fewer currencies, factors such as fiscal policy, the hedging of commodity prices, and labor market flexibility would likely play a larger policy role than they do today.

Finally, there is the issue of sovereignty and governance. Who would set policy in whatever central banks remain? This issue is probably less important than it appears. The last 20 years have been marked by the increasing independence of monetary authorities and a narrowing of the objectives of these institutions to the achievement of price stability. The members of the Executive Board of the

European Central Bank (ECB) are not there to represent their countries of origin. In spite of Germany's leading role in the ECB (the bank is located in Frankfurt), Germany's ex-finance minister Oskar Lafontaine could not get the bank to lower interest rates to help combat high German unemployment. What consideration would the finance minister of Portugal or Luxembourg expect to receive? Ultimately, the monetary authorities' autonomy and accountability are much more important than their national origins.

FEWER CURRENCIES: A MATTER OF TIME

Throughout history, currencies were not considered an acceptable means of exchange unless they could be converted at a known rate into gold or silver. Such convertibility was suspended only in times of war and crisis. Even the framers of Bretton Woods conceived of a system tied to the dollar. A world of over 100 floating currencies is a relatively new phenomenon that is unlikely to be stable or compatible with globalization. In Europe, 11 countries already have opted out of such a regime, instead going for a supranational currency.

Emerging markets will follow a similar course, adopting currencies in which they can borrow abroad and long-term. This scenario also implies that emerging currency areas will want to create their own international monetary institutions and to do away with the IMF. If the Czechs, Hungarians, and Poles opt for the euro, neither they nor the ECB will want the Japanese and Americans involved in their monetary issues. Similarly, if Mexico dollarizes, the United States will be loathe to negotiate related issues with the Japanese and Europeans. The IMF was created for a dollar-centric world: It is unlikely to survive in its present form in a world of regional currencies.

One final problem with abandoning national currencies is the symbolism involved. National currencies, like flagship airlines, are emblems of national identity. But as more and more airline customers are foreigners, the national character of airlines is no longer viewed as an asset: We are now seeing the emergence of a few huge global alliances in the industry. Similarly, flagship telecommunications and energy companies are downplaying their national roots and instead positioning themselves as global players. Should the U.S. Bureau of Engraving and Printing take the hint? Could something other than drawings of Founding Fathers and past presidents eventually find its way onto the U.S. dollar bill? How about great artists or scientists, with their more universal appeal? And by the way, how about a woman?

Why Dollarization Is More Straitjacket Than Salvation

JEFFREY SACHS AND FELIPE LARRAIN

The recent wave of financial crises has prompted some observers to argue that developing countries should abandon their own currencies and instead adopt the U.S. dollar (or perhaps the euro or yen, depending on their location). This conclusion is unwarranted, even reckless. Dollarization is an extreme solution to market instability, applicable in only the most extreme cases. The opposite approach—a flexible exchange rate between the national currency and the dollar—is much more prudent for most developing countries, including those hardest hit by recent crises.

There are two main arguments in favor of flexible exchange rates and two main arguments in favor of fixed ones. The first argument for flexibility is that an exchange rate depreciation (or appreciation) can act like a shock absorber for an economy. Take the case of an oil exporter, faced with declining prices. The drop in oil revenues would lead to weaker demand for a range of domestic goods and services, an overall slowing of the economy, and a rise in unemployment. Under a fixed exchange rate system (e.g., dollar-peso) one solution would be for wages to decline, so that non-oil industries would be able to cut prices in world markets and thereby increase sales. But as economist John Maynard Keynes famously pointed out over 70 years ago to Winston Churchill, then chancellor of the exchequer, that would be a messy business. It would require the renegotiations of thousands of separate wage contracts, and any such wholesale drop in wages would likely be accompanied by severe social stress. A much simpler solution would be to allow the peso to depreciate vis-a-vis the dollar. By changing just this one price (the number of pesos per dollar), all of the country's export products would suddenly become cheaper in world markets and therefore more attractive to foreign buyers. Increased demand for the country's non-oil exports would compensate for the fall in oil earnings, the shock would be absorbed, and the economy would continue to hum.

The second argument for flexible exchange rates is that what is good for the United States is not necessarily good for other countries. For legitimate reasons of its own (perhaps to lend pesos to the government to cover a budgetary shortfall, or perhaps to spur the domestic economy), country X may need a monetary expansion even if the United States does not. Under a fixed exchange rate system, this policy will lead immediately to a decline in reserves and eventually to a reversal of the monetary expansion itself (since the central bank has to reabsorb the public's increased holdings of pesos, as the counterpart to the sale of its dollar reserves). A country that pegs its currency to the dollar is, in effect, tying its monetary policy wholly to U.S. monetary policy. That decision makes sense only if U.S. monetary policy is wholly appropriate for its national economy, which is rarely the case.

The main argument for a pegged exchange rate system, by contrast, is that it enforces discipline. If an irresponsible central bank is given freedom to issue pesos without worrying about the consequences for the exchange rate, it will simply print pesos to its heart's content to fund a large budget deficit or to provide cheap credits to the banking system. These will be popular moves in the short run, but they will soon lead to inflation and a collapsing exchange rate. All prices, including the price of dollars in terms of pesos, will soar. In this light, a fixed exchange rate system forces the central bank to avoid issuing excessive pesos, since doing so will deplete its reserves. A currency board is an even tighter form of pegged-rate discipline, since the central bank is not allowed to issue credits to the government or to the private sector.

The second argument for a fixed exchange rate system is equally straight-forward: A stable exchange rate reduces business transactions costs. There is no risk in changing currencies if the exchange rate remains stable, and the costs of switching between the peso and the dollar (measured by the difference between the buying and selling price in the currency market) are also likely to be very low. Business executives like the certainty they associate with a pegged rate.

Thus, in theory at least, flexible rates are appropriate in some conditions and fixed rates in others. A flexible rate is probably better if a country is often hit by shocks to its exports for instance, by sharp price fluctuations. A fixed rate is probably better if shocks to the economy are rare or relatively small, or if the central bank or government either is politically irresponsible or lacks strong institutional controls.

Where you stand on flexible versus fixed rates may depend on where you sit. Businesspeople naturally tend to prefer the predictability promised by stable exchange rates, and it is true that some elements of the Mexican business community have come out in favor of dollarization. But businesspeople may underestimate the indirect costs, such as higher unemployment, which can result when the central bank pursues exchange rate stability to the exclusion of other goals. They also tend to forget that a pegged exchange rate is a conditional promise, not an unconditional guarantee: The exchange rate might still collapse, even if the central bank does everything in its power to prevent that from happening. If enough households and businesses try to convert their pesos to dollars, for example, the central bank will almost surely run out of reserves, since the number of pesos in circulation plus bank deposits is almost always higher than the dollar reserves held at the central bank. If bank depositors and currency holders try to shift out of pesos and into dollars en masse, only one of two things can happen: Either the banks will become illiquid, unable to provide the pesos to households that want to remove their funds, or the central bank will run out of reserves as it sells dollars in return for the public's mass flight from pesos. Of course, both a banking crisis and a currency collapse can occur together. That, indeed, is what has happened in many countries in the last three years. A currency board can help prevent this scenario, but it cannot stave it off altogether if households and businesses are determined to convert their holdings into dollars.

EXPERIENCE FAVORS FLEXIBLE RATES

The arguments against fixed exchange rates were vividly demonstrated 70 years ago by the problems that the nearly universal gold standard created for countries at the onset of the Great Depression. Countries that needed to increase their money supplies in 1929–32 to fight the growing depression—but that found themselves strapped into a gold straitjacket—tightened monetary policy rather than loosening it, despite surging unemployment. Only as countries left the gold standard one by one in the 1930s did their economies begin to recover from the global crash.

Seventy years later, we have again seen many countries bound to the dollar standard undertake extremely contractionary policies to preserve the pegged exchange rate at the cost of high unemployment and falling domestic output. Although in theory fixed exchange rates may be appropriate under some conditions and flexible rates under others, recent practical experience suggests that most emerging markets are better off with the latter.

First, many countries in the last several years have been unable to resist the pressure that builds up when markets come to expect that their exchange rates will depreciate. Mexico in 1994, Thailand and South Korea in 1997, and Russia and Brazil in 1998–99 all experienced the collapse of pegged exchange rates, even though the governments and central banks were committed to defending them to the bitter end of reserve holdings. Expectations of a currency collapse can become a self-fulfilling prophecy. As rumors of a currency depreciation circulate, money holders convert their pesos into dollars, since they do not want to be caught holding pesos that are going to fall in value. The rush out of pesos is often greater than the reserves held by the central bank; the central bank is then unable to mount an effective defense.

Second, a failed defense can be very costly. A country will find itself in serious trouble if its central bank runs out of reserves trying to defend the national currency. In such scenarios, foreign banks often flee, knowing that they will no longer be protected if something goes wrong. If a domestic bank collapses, for example, the central bank will not have the dollars to help that bank meet its foreign obligations. In Mexico in 1994, and in Thailand and South Korea in 1997, the collapse of the pegged exchange rate was followed by a financial panic, in which foreign banks abruptly demanded repayment of loans. Domestic banks could not meet the demands and had to default.

Third, U.S. monetary policy is seldom appropriate for countries whose currencies are pegged to the dollar. For several years, the U.S. economy has been booming. With high rates of return in the United States and the excitement of the information technology (IT) revolution leading to a surge of new IT investments, capital has flowed into the United States from the rest of the world, and the dollar has surged in value relative to the euro and the yen. Therefore, developing countries that pegged their currencies to the U.S. dollar (such as Thailand until July 1997 or Brazil until January 1999) have also seen their currencies soar in value relative to the euro and the yen. But what was good for America was not so good for these other economies. They needed weaker currencies to maintain their export competitiveness. To keep their currencies linked to the dollar, they had to tighten their monetary policies, even though that was not called for by their economic conditions. The defense of rates pegged to the dollar helped bring on recessionary conditions in a number of countries, including Brazil, Russia, South Korea, and Thailand.

Fourth, many emerging markets have experienced sharp declines in world prices for their commodity exports. Especially after the start of the Asian Crisis in 1997, countries selling oil, timber, gold, copper, and many other primary commodities experienced a sharp loss of income. They needed either a currency depreciation or a fall in wage levels. The first is typically easier to achieve, but during the Asian Crisis it was often blocked by commitments to maintain a pegged exchange rate. Commodity exporters such as Argentina and Venezuela, which suffered terms-of-trade losses on world markets but whose currencies were pegged to the dollar, ended up with sharp rises in unemployment and sharp declines in real economic output. The case for exchange rate flexibility is even stronger if we look at Australia and New Zealand, which depend to a large extent on commodity exports. When these economies were hit by sharp declines in commodity prices in the wake of the Asian Crisis, their floating exchange rates helped them absorb the shocks without significant damage to domestic output and employment.

A fifth point seals the practical case against fixed exchange rates in most countries. One vigorous argument has been that central banks cannot be trusted with floating exchange rates—that they will simply print too much money if given the chance. Pegged rates, or even dollarization, are seen as the remedy to chronic, irremediable irresponsibility. Although many developing-country governments or central banks are certainly not blameless, their actual practices are much less irresponsible and irremediable than often claimed. Countries with significant degrees of exchange rate flexibility, such as Chile, or Mexico since 1995, have actually behaved responsibly, keeping money growth low and inflation under control, even without the straitjacket of a pegged rate or dollarization.

WHAT MAKES DOLLARIZATION DIFFERENT?

If a country abandons its national currency in favor of the U.S. dollar, the result is very much like a pegged exchange rate, only with less room to maneuver. First, of course, there is no longer the "shock absorber" of exchange rate depreciation. The only alternative is a cut in wage levels, which is likely to be a long, drawn out affair, with lots of interim unemployment. Second, there is no scope for independent monetary policy. Monetary policy would be determined in Washington, by the U.S. Federal Reserve Board. Having the Fed make such decisions is a good thing if the national central bank involved is highly irresponsible. But it is a bad thing if the country needs a more expansionary monetary policy than the Fed wants to provide. (It hardly needs emphasizing that the Fed will choose monetary policies based on U.S. conditions, not on the conditions of the dollarizing country.)

There are, however, some important differences, both positive and negative. One sharp minus to dollarization is its cost. In opting to dollarize, a country would be forgoing its seignorage, the income it receives when the value of its currency exceeds the cost of producing the currency. Instead of making a profit from its national currency, the dollarizing country would be faced with the expense of buying dollars to swap for its national pesos. It would have to pay for these dollars either with its foreign reserves or with money from a large dollar-denominated loan. Either way, the cost in terms of forgone interest payments on its reserves, or new interest payments on its borrowings, would be significant. Argentina, for example, would have to spend $15 billion initially to swap its peso currency notes for U.S. dollars. As the economy grows and needs more greenbacks, there would be a continuing price to pay. In theory, these costs could be offset if the United States agreed to share its seignorage with dollarizers, but this seems a particularly distant political prospect.

Another sharp minus is the absence of a lender of last resort to the banking sector. Suppose that households in a country do decide to take their money out of the banks en masse, perhaps because of rumors about the banking sector's lack of safety. When a country has its own currency, the central bank can lend domestic banks the money needed to satisfy the sudden increase in withdrawals by depositors. The depositors can therefore be confident that the banks will have their deposits available for withdrawal. When a country has dollarized, however, there is no longer a national central bank that can make dollars available in the event of a sudden withdrawal of bank deposits. And there is no reason to expect the U.S. Federal Reserve Board to be the lender of last resort for banks in another country, even if that country has adopted the dollar as its currency. Dollarizing countries could try to establish contingent lines of credit, but producing adequate collateral could prove difficult.

A final sharp difference (one that is a plus, but also a significant minus) between dollarization and a pegged exchange rate is that dollarization is nearly irreversible. This factor is good in that it allays any fears of a possible collapse of a pegged rate or even of a currency board. However, it can be equally bad if a country gets hit by a rare but extreme shock and desperately needs a currency depreciation. With a pegged exchange rate, a depreciation would be possible. The government would tell the public that it has to renege on its promise to keep the exchange rate stable, given the extreme circumstances facing the country. If the country has abandoned its own currency, however, this extreme step (meant for extreme emergencies) might not be available. Dollarization does result in certainty—the lack of worry about exchange rate changes—but that certainty comes from strapping the economy into a monetary straitjacket.

IS DOLLARIZATION EVER WARRANTED?

Dollarization only makes sense under the following circumstances:

- A country's economy is very tightly integrated with that of the United States and thus would experience very similar shocks. In such a case, U.S. monetary policy might be a good fit. Commodity exporters whose products are subject to sharp swings in world prices rarely fit this criterion.
- A country has a very small economy in which most prices are set in dollars and most goods are used in international trade. In fact, there are only four independent countries that are currently dollarized: the Marshall Islands, Micronesia, Palau, and Panama. Of these, only Panama is of a significant

size in terms of population (2.7 million) and gross domestic product (GDP) ($8.7 billion). The other three are islands with populations between 17,000 and 120,000 and GDPs of between $100 million and $200 million.

- A country has very flexible labor markets. If domestic wages have to decline, they can do so without high levels of labor market strife and without a prolonged period of unemployment.
- A country's central bank cannot be trusted to run its own currency in a stable way, perhaps because local politics is too populist or because social demands are too high to resist pressures for money-financed budget deficits.

Very few countries fit this profile; Mexico and Argentina certainly do not. Both countries have relatively inflexible economies and heavy commodity dependence. They face shocks quite different from those that hit the United States and therefore might need monetary policies quite distinct from those of the United States. Argentina has been on a kind of dollar standard since April 1991, when the Argentine peso was pegged one-to-one with the dollar. In spite of some significant achievements, Argentina experienced a sharp recession in 1995 following the Mexican peso crisis and is currently enduring another one. The objective conditions call for monetary ease, but Argentina's pegged rate will not allow it. Mexico had a pegged rate until December 1994, when the rate was destabilized by a combination of economic shocks and inconsistent monetary policies, which caused the country to run out of foreign exchange reserves. Since 1995, Mexico has operated a floating exchange rate system. In 1999, it was able to absorb shocks in world markets by allowing its currency to depreciate rather than by tightening monetary policy (as Argentina did). The result is that Mexico continues to enjoy economic growth in 1999, even as Argentina sinks deeper into recession.

Halfway around the world, a similar comparison between Hong Kong and Singapore also puts in relief the risks of a dollarized system. When the Asian Crisis hit in 1997, both Hong Kong and Singapore experienced a sharp fall in demand for their exports in the rest of the region. Singapore countered this external shock by allowing its currency to depreciate. Hong Kong, by contrast, maintained a fixed exchange rate with the U.S. dollar, a rate that has been stable since 1984. Singapore, therefore, escaped recession in 1998 and 1999, while Hong Kong has experienced the sharpest decline in its output in recent history (about an 8 percent drop in real GDP from the peak until mid-1999).

Are Regional Currencies the Answer?

There may be a golden mean for some countries between the gains from a common currency (reduced transactions costs, depoliticized monetary management) and the gains from flexibility—a shock absorber for terms-of-trade fluctuations or other shifts in world trade patterns. That is the regionalization, rather than dollarization, of national currencies, as in the case of the euro. Suppose countries that are close neighbors have approximately the same economic structure, face the same international shocks, and do a lot of business with one another. They might want to adopt a common currency within the neighborhood, but one that remains flexible vis-a-vis other major currencies such as the U.S. dollar. Many members of the European Union made precisely that choice. Several additional candidate regions around the world come immediately to mind, and two in Latin America especially: MERCOSUR countries in South America and the Central American countries other than Panama (which is already dollarized).

The gains from regionalization of currencies could be quite large. First, there would be the reduction of transactions costs for doing business within the neighborhood. Second, there would be the creation of a supranational central bank run by designated representatives from each of the participating countries, which would take monetary policy out of the domain of populist national politics, while still preserving accountability of the monetary authorities to the political process of the member countries. Third, there would be the great savings of such a scheme compared with dollarization, because the seignorage problem would not be a factor. Suppose the Central American countries, for example, adopted a common currency. Since they would be the issuers, the countries could print the money at low cost and swap it for the outstanding currencies already in circulation. If the countries were to dollarize, by contrast, they would have to sell interest-earning dollar reserves or borrow new dollars at high interest rates in order to swap dollars for the existing currencies.

The obstacles to regionalization of national currencies would of course be significant, even where regionalization might be warranted by underlying economic realities. Take the case of MERCOSUR, for example. Argentina and Brazil would seem to have a common monetary stake: The depreciation of the Brazilian real early in 1999 threw Argentina into a very deep recession. And yet, Argentina apparently remains wedded to fixed parity with the U.S. dollar, if not outright dollarization. Brazil seems to many Argentines to be an unlikely, and unworthy, monetary partner. The probable result is a floating real in Brazil, an overvalued peso in Argentina, and little movement toward either dollarization or regionalization of the national currencies. In Central America, the situation is similar. Each country looks with doubt at its neighbors as plausible monetary partners. There would need to be considerable economic coordination among the countries to prepare for a common currency. The distinct lack of movement in this direction makes such a currency a distant prospect.

REDUCING THE RISKS OF GLOBALIZATION

The world financial system has become treacherous in recent years, especially since many players have not yet learned the ins and outs of globalization. Emerging markets are whipsawed by huge swings in lending from international banks: Sometimes money floods in; other times it floods out. All countries need to learn how to manage financial risks, and a good exchange rate system is part of good risk management. Under these circumstances, the following three principles can be recommended.

First, except in the extreme cases outlined earlier, flexible exchange rates (either at a national or regional level) are a useful absorber for external shocks. It is not good enough to have a pegged rate that is right most of the time. Countries have to plan for eventualities—natural disasters, collapses in world market prices, abrupt shifts in international capital—that might require the shock absorber role of the exchange rate.

Second, countries should attempt to limit inflows of hot money, especially very short-term loans from international banks. Money that pours into a country can just as easily pour out. Highly volatile shortrun capital, often moved by self-fulfilling waves of euphoria or panic, can disrupt economies and cause massive swings in exchange rates. Such flows can be limited through appropriate regulation of the banking system or through some restriction on inflows of short-term capital (once the foreign money has come in, however, it is not a good idea to limit its exit). Countries should also pay close attention to the ratio of short-term foreign debt to international reserves. Most countries that have recently endured currency crises had more short-term debt than international reserves on the eve of the crisis. Under these conditions, it is rational for foreign investors to try to be first to the door, and a speculative attack against the currency can easily happen.

Finally, countries should strengthen the operating capacity of their central banks and give such banks sufficient independence, so that they can resist political pressures for excessive monetary expansion. Advocates of dollarization are wrong to think that developing countries are congenitally incapable of managing a noninflationary currency. There are many developing countries that maintain good internal discipline without the straitjacket of dollarization. These advocates are correct, however, to warn of the risks and to emphasize the importance of institutional design to ensure the central bank has the professionalism and protection from daily politics that it needs to do a responsible job.

QUESTIONS FOR REVIEW AND DISCUSSION

1. Ricardo Hausmann offers two explanations for financial instability in developing countries, one based in moral hazard and one that he calls original sin. What are the essential characteristics of each explanation? On what does each approach focus to explain financial instability in developing countries?
2. Hausmann argues that original sin is the primary cause of financial instability. What mechanism links the characteristics of original sin to financial instability? How, according to Hausmann, would dollarization prevent such instabilities?
3. Outline the costs and benefits of a floating and a fixed exchange rate. Do you think that one approach is inherently better than the other? What type of policy problem do governments face, therefore, in selecting an exchange rate regime?
4. How is dollarization different from a pegged (or fixed-but-adjustable) exchange rate?
5. What do you think accounts for the different perspectives offered by Hausmann on the one hand and Sachs and Larrain on the other?
6. Should more developing countries dollarize (or euro-ize) their economies? Why or why not?

SUGGESTIONS FOR FURTHER READING

Two detailed studies of dollarization can be found on line: Andrew Berg and Eduardo Borensztein. *Full Dollarization: Pros and Cons.* Washington, DC: International Monetary Fund, 2000. Available at http://www.imf.org/external/pubs/ft/issues/issues24/index.htm; and Joint Economic Committee, Staff Report. *Basics of Dollarization.* 2000. Available at http://users.erols.com/kurrency/basicsup.htm

For a recent paper examining the dollarization trend see: Carmen M. Reinhart, Kenneth Rogoff, and Miguel A. Savastano. "Addicted to Dollars." *NBER Working Paper* no. 10015 (October 2003).

For a longer treatment, see: Dominick Salvatore, James W. Dean, and Thomas D. Willett. *The Dollarization Debate.* New York: Oxford University Press, 2003.

For a detailed study of Ecuador's experience with dollarization, see: Paul Beckerman, Andres Solimano, and Luc J. Christiaensen, eds. *Crisis and Dollarization in Ecuador: Stability, Growth, and Social Equity.* Washington, DC: The World Bank, 2002.

You can visit two good Web sites that provide a lot of dollarization-related links. The first is maintained by economist Nouriel Roubini at New York University's Stern Business School. The dollarization section of this Web site is available at http://www.stern.nyu.edu/globalmacro/exchange_rates/dollarization.html. The second Web site is maintained by Kurt Schuler and can be found at http://www.dollarization.org/

Developing Countries and Capital Flows

CHAPTER 14

DEVELOPING COUNTRIES AND CAPITAL FLOWS

In the 1990s, many developing countries began removing barriers to the flow of financial capital into and out of their economies; as they did, financial markets began funneling large quantities of short-term funds to these new markets. Data reported by the International Monetary Fund illustrate the rapid growth of capital flows to emerging-market countries during the decade. While little private capital flowed to developing countries during the late 1980s and early 1990s, by 1997, the eve of the Asian financial crisis, over $100 billion was being channeled to emerging-market countries. In a very short period of time, countries that had been able to attract few funds from foreign lenders, and therefore had little experience with international financial markets, were transformed into prized investment locations and offered more funds than they could productively use. The emergence of such capital flows provided new opportunities, by making it possible to increase investment beyond what would be possible otherwise, thereby increasing economic growth and raising per capita incomes.

Also in the 1990s, many of these emerging-market countries experienced dramatic and serious financial crises. Some of the most prominent of these crises include the Mexican peso crisis of 1994; the East Asian crisis of 1997 that affected Indonesia, Thailand, South Korea, Hong Kong, Singapore, the Philippines, and Malaysia; the Russian and Brazil crises of 1998; the Argentinean crisis of 1999–2000; and the Turkish crisis of 2000. In each case, enthusiasm by private investors about the investment opportunities in these emerging markets, combined with growing government willingness to ease policies that restricted the free flow of capital into and out of their countries, initially produced a wave of capital inflows. Most countries lacked sound financial regulations that could ensure that domestic financial institutions made sensible use of the funds they were borrowing from foreign lenders. Moreover, the lack of experience with international lending made it difficult for governments and private financial institutions to adequately judge the risks posed by such borrowing. Consequently, many countries developed precarious financial positions in which a deep crisis was kept at bay only by the continued willingness of foreign lenders to roll over their existing short-term loans. When foreign lenders ceased rolling over their loans, as they almost always did, countries found themselves facing severe financial and economic crises. Many domestic banks could not raise the funds they needed to repay their foreign creditors; even when they could find the needed funds, often the government could not provide the foreign currencies required to repay the foreign debt. Domestic financial systems thus came under extreme stress, national currencies lost value as governments were forced to float, and real economic activity collapsed as interest rates rose and demand fell. In Indonesia, for example, national output shrank by 13 percent in 1998.

The record of the 1990s provoked a debate about the degree to which developing countries should seek to integrate themselves into the international financial system. While most students of development agree that developing countries need to import capital from industrialized countries, there is considerable disagreement about how such funds should be transferred.

Behind this disagreement lies a broader debate about the inherent stability (or instability) of financial markets. Some people argue that financial markets in general and international financial markets in particular are inherently unstable. Financial markets are prone to "manias, panics, and crashes." Developing countries are particularly vulnerable to these perverse dynamics because they have weak financial institutions, thin (or illiquid) financial markets, and inadequate financial regulations. Consequently, developing countries should not be encouraged to integrate into the international financial system but should instead tightly regulate the flow of capital into and out of their economies. In addition, governments should strive to attract foreign direct investment and other forms of long-term investments that will not expose them to the instabilities generated by short-term capital flows.

Others argue that financial markets are not inherently unstable. According to this group, financial crises like those of the last ten years are not caused by perverse market behavior; they are caused by bad policies. Sometimes the bad policies are as simple as too much foreign debt accumulated by the government. Sometimes the bad policies involve financial regulations that do little to promote prudent behavior by domestic financial institutions. Because financial crises result from bad policies, crisis prevention does not require countries to insulate themselves from the international financial system. Instead, to prevent crises governments must simply adopt good policies.

The two articles presented in this chapter reflect this debate. Jagdish Bhagwati, Arthur Lehman Professor of Economics at Columbia University, argues that it is incorrect to equate trade in goods with capital flows. Unlike goods markets, financial markets are prone to sudden changes in market sentiment. He advocates, therefore, that developing countries retain capital controls. Sebastian Edwards, the Henry Ford II Professor of International Economics at UCLA's Anderson Graduate School of Management, and a former chief economist for Latin America at the World Bank, advances the opposite perspective. Edwards argues that the empirical record indicates that capital controls are ineffective. Governments that adopt them are not more successful at avoiding crises, nor at recovering quickly from them.

The Capital Myth

JAGDISH BHAGWATI

THE DIFFERENCE BETWEEN TRADE IN WIDGETS AND DOLLARS

In the aftermath of the Asian financial crisis, the mainstream view that dominates policy circles, indeed the prevalent myth, is that despite the striking evidence of the inherently crisis-prone nature of freer capital movements, a world of full capital mobility continues to be inevitable and immensely desirable. Instead of maintaining careful restrictions, we are told, the only sensible course is to continue working toward unfettered capital flows; the favored solution is to turn the IMF even more firmly into an international lender of last resort that dispenses bailout funds to crisis-afflicted countries. The IMF took an important step in this direction at its annual meeting in Hong Kong last September, when the Interim Committee issued a statement virtually endorsing an eventual move to capital account convertibility—which means that you and I, nationals or foreigners, could take capital in and out freely, in any volume and at any time—for IMF members. The obligations originally listed in 1944 in the Articles of Agreement, on the other hand, included only "avoidance of restrictions on payments for current transactions" and did not embrace capital account convertibility as an obligation or even a goal.

This is a seductive idea: freeing up trade is good, why not also let capital move freely across borders? But the claims of enormous benefits from free capital mobility are not persuasive. Substantial gains have been asserted, not demonstrated, and most of the payoff can be obtained by direct equity investment. And even a richer IMF with attendant changes in its methods of operation will probably not rule out crises or reduce their costs significantly. The myth to the contrary has been created by what one might christen the Wall Street-Treasury complex, following in the footsteps of President Eisenhower, who had warned of the military-industrial complex.

CAPITAL MOBILITY IDEOLOGY

Until the Asian crisis sensitized the public to the reality that capital movements could repeatedly generate crises, many assumed that free capital mobility among all nations was exactly like free trade in their goods and services, a mutual-gain phenomenon. Hence restricted capital mobility, just like protectionism, was seen to be

From Jagdish Bhagwati, "A Capital Myth," *Foreign Affairs*, Vol. 77, No. 3, May/June, 1998, pp. 7–12. Reprinted by permission of *Foreign Affairs*. © 1998 by the Council on Foreign Relations, Inc.

harmful to economic performance in each country, whether rich or poor. That the gains might be problematic because of the cost of crises was not considered.

However, the Asian crisis cannot be separated from the excessive borrowings of foreign short-term capital as Asian economies loosened up their capital account controls and enabled their banks and firms to borrow abroad. In 1996, total private capital inflows to Indonesia, Malaysia, South Korea, Thailand, and the Philippines were $93 billion, up from $41 billion in 1994. In 1997, that suddenly changed to an outflow of $12 billion. Hence it has become apparent that crises attendant on capital mobility cannot be ignored.

Although it is conceded that this downside exists, many claim that it can be ameliorated, if not eliminated, and that free capital mobility's immense advantages can be enjoyed by all. Conservatives would do this by letting the markets rip, untended by the IMF, which could then be sidelined or even disbanded. Liberals would do it instead by turning the IMF into the world's lender of last resort, dispensing funds during crises with several sorts of conditions, and overseeing, buttressing, and managing the world of free capital mobility.

To understand why neither of these modifications is enough, it is necessary to understand why the original version of the myth, which has steadily propelled the IMF into its complacent and dangerous moves toward the goal of capital account convertibility, was just that. True, economists properly say that there is a correspondence between free trade in goods and services and free capital mobility: interfering with either will produce efficiency losses. But only an untutored economist will argue that, therefore, free trade in widgets and life insurance policies is the same as free capital mobility. Capital flows are characterized, as the economic historian Charles Kindleberger of the Massachusetts Institute of Technology has famously noted, by panics and manias.

Each time a crisis related to capital inflows hits a country, it typically goes through the wringer. The debt crisis of the 1980s cost South America a decade of growth. The Mexicans, who were vastly overexposed through short-term inflows, were devastated in 1994. The Asian economies of Thailand, Indonesia, and South Korea, all heavily burdened with short-term debt, went into a tailspin nearly a year ago, drastically lowering their growth rates. Sure enough, serious economic downturns and crises can arise even when governments are not particularly vulnerable due to short-term borrowing: macroeconomic mismanagement in Japan has restrained its growth rate for nearly seven years now, and Japan is still a net lender of capital. But it is a non sequitur to suggest, as the defenders of free capital mobility do, that this possibility somehow negates the fact that short-term borrowings under free capital mobility will be, and have been, a source of considerable economic difficulty.

DOWNSIZING GAINS

When a crisis hits, the downside of free capital mobility arises. To ensure that capital returns, the country must do everything it can to restore the confidence of those who have taken their money out. This typically means raising interest rates, as the IMF has required of Indonesia. Across Asia this has decimated firms with large amounts of debt. It also means having to sell domestic assets, which are greatly undervalued because of the credit crunch, in a fire sale to foreign buyers with better access to funds. (Economists have usually advised the exact opposite in such depressed circumstances: restricting foreign access to a country's assets when its credit, but not that of others, has dried up.) Thus, Thailand and South Korea have been forced to further open their capital markets, even though the short-term capital inflow played a principal role in their troubles in the first place.

Besides suffering these economic setbacks, these countries have lost the political independence to run their economic policies as they deem fit. That their independence is lost not directly to foreign nations but to an IMF increasingly extending its agenda, at the behest of the U.S. Congress, to invade domestic policies on matters of social policy—as with the 1994 Sanders-Frank Amendment, which seeks to attach labor standards conditions to any increase in bailout funds—is small consolation indeed.

Thus, any nation contemplating the embrace of free capital mobility must reckon with these costs and also consider the probability of running into a crisis. The gains from economic efficiency that would flow from free capital mobility, in a hypothetical crisis-free world, must be set against this loss if a wise decision is to be made.

None of the proponents of free capital mobility have estimated the size of the gains they expect to materialize, even leaving out the losses from crises that can ensue. For free trade, numerous studies have measured the costs of protection. The overwhelming majority of trade economists judge the gains from free trade to be significant, coming down somewhere between Paul Krugman's view that they are too small to be taken seriously and Jeffrey Sachs' view that they are huge and cannot be ignored. But all we have from the proponents of capital mobility is banner-waving, such as that of Bradford De Long, the Berkeley economist and former deputy assistant secretary for economic policy in the Clinton administration:

> So now we have all the benefits of free flows of international capital. These benefits are mammoth: the ability to borrow abroad kept the Reagan deficits from crushing U.S. growth like an egg, and the ability to borrow from abroad has enabled successful emerging market economies to double or triple the speed at which their productivity levels and living standards converge to the industrial core.

And of Roger C. Altman, the investment banker, who served in the Treasury Department under Presidents Clinton and Carter:

> The worldwide elimination of barriers to trade and capital . . . have created the global financial marketplace, which informed observers hailed for bringing private capital to the developing world, encouraging economic growth and democracy.[1]

These assertions assume that free capital mobility is enormously beneficial while simultaneously failing to evaluate its crisis-prone downside. But even a cursory glance at history suggests that these gains may be negligible. After all, China and Japan, different in politics and sociology as well as historical experience, have registered remarkable growth rates without capital account convertibility. Western Europe's return to prosperity was also achieved without capital account convertibility. Except for Switzerland, capital account liberalization was pretty slow at the outset and did not gain strength until the late 1980s, and some European countries, among them Portugal and Ireland, did not implement it until the early 1990s.

Besides, even if one believes that capital flows are greatly productive, there is still an important difference between embracing free portfolio capital mobility and having a policy of attracting direct equity investment. Maybe the amount of direct foreign investment that a country attracts will be reduced somewhat by not having freedom of portfolio capital flows, but there is little evidence for this assertion. Even then such a loss would be a small fraction of the gains from having a pro-foreign investment strategy.

A WALL STREET–TREASURY COMPLEX

That brings us to the myth that crises under capital account convertibility can be eliminated. We have, of course, heard this assertion before as each crisis has been confronted, and then we have been hit by yet another one. Like cats, crises have many lives, and macroeconomists, never a tribe that enjoyed a great reputation for getting things right or for agreeing among themselves, have been kept busy adding to the taxonomy of crises and their explanations. None of the solutions currently propounded can really rid the system of free capital mobility of instability.

Thus, while no one can disagree with Secretary of the Treasury Robert Rubin's contention that reform of banking systems around the world will help, few should agree with him that it will eliminate the crises that unregulated capital flows inherently generate. Nor can the abolition of the IMF and its lender of last resort bailouts be the magic bullet: there were crises before the writer Walter Bagehot invented this function for domestic central banks in the nineteenth century. Nor can making the IMF more powerful kill the crises or give it the nonexistent macroeconomic wisdom to manage them at least cost when they arise.

In short, when we penetrate the fog of implausible assertions that surrounds the case for free capital mobility, we realize that the idea and the ideology of free trade and its benefits—and this extends to the continuing liberalization of trade in goods and financial and other services at the World Trade Organization—have, in effect, been hijacked by the proponents of capital mobility. They have been used to bamboozle us into celebrating the new world of trillions of dollars moving about daily in a borderless world, creating gigantic economic gains, rewarding virtue and punishing profligacy. The pretty face presented to us is, in fact, a mask that hides the warts and wrinkles underneath.

The question, then, is why the world has nonetheless been moving in this direction. The answer, as always, reflects ideology and interests—that is, lobbies. The ideology is clearly that of markets. The steady move away from central planning, overregulation, and general overreach in state intervention toward letting markets function has now reached across many sectors and countries. This is indeed all to the good and promises worldwide prosperity. But this wave has also lulled many economists and policymakers into complacency about the pitfalls that certain markets inherently pose even when they were understood in the classroom. Free capital mobility is just one example of this unwarranted attitude. Indeed,

Stanley Fischer, the deputy managing director of the IMF, admitted in a February appearance on the Charlie Rose show on PBS that he had underestimated the probability of such crises arising in a world of capital mobility.

But interests have also played a central role. Wall Street's financial firms have obvious self-interest in a world of free capital mobility since it only enlarges the arena in which to make money. It is not surprising, therefore, that Wall Street has put its powerful oar into the turbulent waters of Washington political lobbying to steer in this direction. Thus, when testifying before the Senate Foreign Relations Committee on South Asia in March 1995, right after the Mexican peso crisis, I was witness to the grilling of Undersecretary of Commerce Jeffrey E. Garten on why India's financial system was not fully open to U.S. firms. To his credit, Garten said that this was not exactly a propitious time for the United States to pressure India in this direction.

Then again, Wall Street has exceptional clout with Washington for the simple reason that there is, in the sense of a power elite a la C. Wright Mills, a definite networking of like-minded luminaries among the powerful institutions—Wall Street, the Treasury Department, the State Department, the IMF, and the World Bank most prominent among them. Secretary Rubin comes from Wall Street; Altman went from Wall Street to the Treasury and back; Nicholas Brady, President Bush's Secretary of the Treasury, is back in finance as well; Ernest Stern, who has served as acting president of the World Bank, is now managing director of J.P. Morgan; James Wolfensohn, an investment banker, is now president of the World Bank. One could go on.

This powerful network, which may aptly, if loosely, be called the Wall Street–Treasury complex, is unable to look much beyond the interest of Wall Street, which it equates with the good of the world. Thus the IMF has been relentlessly propelled toward embracing the goal of capital account convertibility. The Mexican bailout of 1994 was presented as necessary, which was true. But so too was the flip side, that the Wall Street investors had to be bailed out as well, which was not. Surely other policy instruments, such as a surcharge, could have been deployed simultaneously to punish Wall Street for its mistakes. Even in the current Asian crisis, particularly in South Korea, U.S. banks could all have been forced to the bargaining table, absorbing far larger losses than they did, but they were cushioned by the IMF acting virtually as a lender of first, rather than last, resort.

And despite the evidence of the inherent risks of free capital flows, the Wall Street–Treasury complex is currently proceeding on the self-serving assumption that the ideal world is indeed one of free capital flows, with the IMF and its bailouts at the apex in a role that guarantees its survival and enhances its status. But the weight of evidence and the force of logic point in the opposite direction, toward restraints on capital flows. It is time to shift the burden of proof from those who oppose to those who favor liberated capital.

ENDNOTE

1. Bradford DeLong, "What's Wrong with Our Bloody Economies?" January 11, 1998, from his World Wide Web page, http://econ 161. berkeley.edu/; Roger C. Altman, "The Nuke of the 90's," *The New York Times Magazine*, March 1, 1998, p. 34.

A Capital Idea?

SEBASTIAN EDWARDS

RECONSIDERING A FINANCIAL QUICK FIX

Massive capital flows have been at the heart of every major currency crisis in the 1990s. Whether Mexico in 1994, Thailand in 1997, Russia in 1998, or Brazil in 1999, the stories are depressingly similar. High domestic interest rates, perceived stability stemming from rigid exchange rates, and apparently rosy economic prospects all attracted foreign funds into these emerging markets, lifting stock prices and helping finance bloated current account deficits. When these funds eventually trickled to a halt or reversed direction, significant corrections in macro-economic policies became necessary. But governments often watered down or delayed reform, which increased investor uncertainty and nervousness over risk. As a result, more and more capital poured out of the countries and foreign exchange reserves dropped to dangerously low levels. Eventually, the governments had no choice but to abandon their pegged exchange rates and float their currencies. In Brazil and Russia, runaway fiscal deficits made the situation even more explosive.

In the aftermath of these crises, a number of influential academics have argued that the wild capital movements wrought by globalization have gone too far. In the words of Paul Krugman, "sooner or later we will have to turn the clock at least part of the way back" to limit the free mobility of capital. Bolstered by the growing number of capital-controls advocates, proposals for a new international financial architecture have focused on two types of controls: restrictions on short-term capital inflows, similar to those implemented in Chile between 1991 and 1998; and controls on capital outflows, like those Malaysia imposed in 1998. Both schemes try to reduce the "irrational" volatility inherent in capital flows and foster longer-term forms of investment, such as direct foreign investment, including investment in equipment and machinery.

Despite their good intentions, these proposals share a common flaw: they ignore the discouraging empirical record of capital controls in developing countries. The blunt fact is that capital controls are not only ineffective in avoiding crises, but also breed corruption and inflate the costs of managing investment.

From Sebastian Edwards, "A Capital Idea," *Foreign Affairs*, Vol. 78, No. 3, May/June 1999, pp. 18–22. Reprinted by permission of *Foreign Affairs*. © 1999 by the Council on Foreign Relations, Inc.

DON'T BANK ON IT

Chile, which experimented with short-term capital controls during 1978–82 and 1991–98, has become a favorite test case for proponents of such measures. In both episodes, foreigners wishing to move short-term funds into Chile were required to first deposit their money with Chile's central bank for a specified amount of time—at no interest. By stemming inflows, the policy aimed to mitigate capital volatility, prevent the currency from rising too quickly (a common result of accelerated capital inflows), and increase the central bank's control over domestic monetary policy. From 1978 to 1982, the controls were particularly stringent; foreign capital was virtually forbidden from entering the country for less than five and a half years. In this way, it was thought, the country would not be vulnerable to short-term speculation.

Proponents of controls cite all the above facts but miss the bigger picture. Indeed, their brand of wishful thinking misreads Chile's history and oversells the effectiveness of this policy. What you do not hear from them is that the draconian restrictions on capital inflows could not prevent Chile from going through a traumatic economic crisis from 1981 to 1982, which caused a peso depreciation of almost 90 percent and a systemic banking collapse. The problem lay with the largely unregulated banking sector, which used international loans to speculate on real estate and lend generously to bank owners, ultimately creating an asset-price bubble. When it burst, loans could not be repaid. Hence, many banks went under and had to be rescued by the government at a very high cost to taxpayers. A massive 1986 banking reform finally put an end to that by establishing strict guidelines on bank exposure and instituting rigorous on-site inspections. A healthy, strong, and efficient banking system emerged as a result, which to this day has helped Chile withstand the most recent global turmoil.

This historical episode underscores a key factor in evaluating restrictions on capital mobility: without effective prudential banking regulations, restrictions on capital inflows alone are unlikely to reduce a country's vulnerability. Moreover, capital controls may foster a false sense of security, encouraging complacent and careless behavior by policymakers and investors alike. South Korea's recent experience is a case in point. Until late 1997, international market players and local policymakers believed that Seoul's restrictions on capital mobility would inoculate the country from a currency crisis. Indeed, even after giving South Korea's central bank and private banks their next-to-lowest rating in early 1997, Goldman Sachs still argued that the nation's "relatively closed capital account" necessitated the exclusion of such gloomy data from its overall assessment of South Korea's financial vulnerability. Hence, Goldman Sachs played down the extent of the Korean won crisis throughout most of 1997. Had it correctly recognized that capital restrictions cannot truly protect an economy from financial turbulence, it would have accurately anticipated the South Korean debacle just as it forecast the Thai meltdown.

Brazil is another example that capital-control advocates should reconsider. Restrictions on short-term capital inflows in 1997 and 1998 lulled Brazilian policymakers into complacency. They repeatedly argued that their controls would preclude a Mexican-style currency crisis. As it turned out, they were wrong. Once the collapse of the Brazilian real became imminent in the autumn of 1998, domestic and foreign investors alike rushed to flee the country—just as in Mexico in 1994.

CONTROL FREAKS

Not surprisingly, most supporters of capital controls have focused only on Chile's experience during the 1990s, when 30 percent of all capital inflows had to be deposited for one year, at no interest, with the central bank, and direct foreign investment was required to stay in the country for at least one year. This policy was implemented in June 1991, when the newly elected democratic government of President Patricio Aylwin became concerned over the exchange rate and inflationary effects of the rapidly growing capital inflows. Aylwin sought the support of exporters, who resisted a strengthening of the currency, while taking a firm anti-inflationary stance. Accordingly, he turned to capital controls.

Despite positive media coverage and popularity with some academics, there is no firm evidence that this policy actually achieved its goals. First, Chile's short-term foreign-denominated debt was almost 50 percent of all debt from 1996 to 1998. Second, capital controls failed to slow the strengthening of Chile's currency. Throughout the 1990s, Chile's real exchange rate rose more than 30 percent despite capital controls. Finally, the argument that restrictions on inflows help increase central bank control over domestic monetary policy is tenuous at best. Tightening restrictions increases domestic interest rates only slightly and temporarily.

Chile's capital controls have also carried another price—by inflating the cost of capital. Large firms, with their easy access to international financial resources, can always find ways to circumvent the controls; smaller firms are not so fortunate. As a result, a prohibitively high cost of capital not only distorts the true cost of investment but discriminates against small- and medium-sized businesses. In fact, some analysts have calculated that investment costs for smaller firms exceeded 20 percent in dollar terms in 1996 and 1997; larger firms, on the other hand, could access the international market with dollar loans at a cost of only 7 or 8 percent per annum.

GO WITH THE FLOW

As their advocates would have it, temporary controls on capital outflows would allow stricken countries to lower interest rates and implement pro-growth policies without worrying about investors pulling out for fear of devaluation. Controlling capital outflows would also buy economies time to restructure their financial sector in an orderly fashion. Once the economy is back on its feet, so goes the argument, controls can be dismantled.

Again, the historical evidence flies in the face of this reasoning. According to two studies of 31 major currency crises in Latin America, countries that tightened controls after a major devaluation did not post better performances in economic growth, job creation, or inflation than those that did not. The Latin American debt crisis of the 1980s illustrates how ineffective these controls really were. Nations that imposed controls on capital outflows—Argentina, Brazil, Mexico, and Peru—muddled through but suffered rising inflation, worsening unemployment, and a long and painful decline in growth. Moreover, the stricter controls encouraged neither macro-economic restructuring nor orderly reforms aimed at increasing efficiency and competitiveness. In fact, the opposite happened: politicians experimented with populist policies that ultimately deepened the crisis. Mexico nationalized the banking sector and confiscated dollar-denominated deposits. Argentina and Brazil launched new currencies while setting price controls and expanding public spending. In Peru, stricter controls on outflows allowed President Alan Garcia to whittle away the basis of a healthy and productive economy, squandering international reserves and pursuing a hyperinflationary policy. To make things even worse, in none of these countries did controls on capital outflows successfully stem capital flight.

Chile and Colombia, which did not tighten controls on capital outflows, provide an interesting contrast. These two states attempted to restructure their economies. Chile even implemented a modern bank supervisory system that greatly reduced domestic financial fragility. Accordingly, both countries emerged from the debt crisis significantly better off than the rest of the region. In fact, they were the only two large Latin American countries to experience positive growth in per capita gross domestic product and real wages during the "lost decade" of the 1980s.

DISCIPLINARY MEASURES

The recent financial crises have dealt a severe blow to the International Monetary Fund's credibility. The IMF badly miscalculated the Mexican collapse of 1994, prescribed the wrong policies in East Asia in 1997, and offered vastly inadequate rescue packages to Russia and Brazil in 1998. This succession of embarrassments reflects the fact that the IMF's structure does not allow it to operate effectively in the modern world economy, where investor confidence and the frank, uncensored, and prompt dissemination of information are crucial. Sadly, international politics is likely to stand in the way of true IMF reform. After much talk about a new architecture, we will probably end up with a slightly embellished IMF that will continue to miss crises, throw good money after bad, and ultimately try to rationalize why currency crises persist.

Economists have long recognized that the issue of international capital movements is highly complicated. In the absence of strong financial and banking supervision in both lending and borrowing countries, unregulated capital flows may indeed be misallocated, generating major disruptions in the receiving nations. Many academics have rightly argued that relaxing controls on capital movement should therefore follow, not precede, market-oriented macroeconomic reform and the establishment of a reliable supervisory system for domestic financial markets. Governments should lift controls on capital movements carefully and gradually—but they should be lifted.

We must understand what capital controls can and cannot do. The historical record shows convincingly that, despite their new popularity, controls on capital outflows and inflows are ineffective. The best prescriptions to combat financial turmoil, now as then, are sound macroeconomic policies, sufficiently flexible exchange rates, and banking reforms that introduce effective prudential regulations and reduce moral hazard and corruption. Without a solid financial groundwork, emerging markets will remain as fragile as a house of cards, easily blown down by the first breezes of turbulence.

QUESTIONS FOR REVIEW AND DISCUSSION

1. Why, according to Jagdish Bhagwati, is free trade in financial capital not equivalent to free trade in goods? Would Edwards agree with Bhagwati on this point?
2. What factors does Bhagwati point to in order to explain the pace of financial liberalization in developing countries? Do you think he is correct? Why or why not?
3. Why does Sebastian Edwards oppose the use of capital controls? Do you find his argument convincing? Why or why not?
4. While neither author is explicit about this, the analysis that each presents is based on their understanding of the causes of financial crises. What factors do you think Bhagwati would stress in explaining these crises? What factors would Edwards stress? Where do they agree? Where do they disagree?
5. If we accept the main arguments of each author, then what policy advice should one give to governments in emerging-market countries? What policy advice would you give such governments?

SUGGESTIONS FOR FURTHER READING

For a detailed examination of emerging market financial crises of the 1990s, see: Miles Kahler's edited volume, *Capital Flows and Financial Crises*. Ithaca: Cornell University Press, 1998. Stephan Haggard's *The Political Economy of the Asian Financial Crisis*. Washington, DC: Institute for International Economics, 2000, offers a detailed analytical treatment of this episode. A more popular treatment of these many crises can be found in Paul Blustein's *The Chastening: Inside the Crisis that Rocked the Global Financial System and Humbled the IMF*. New York: Public Affairs, 2001.

Three books that examine emerging-market financial crises in detail include: Martin Feldstein, ed. *Economic and Financial Crises in Emerging Market Economies*. Chicago: University of Chicago Press, 2003; Sebastian Edwards and Jeffrey A. Frankel (eds.). *Preventing Currency Crises in Emerging Markets*. Chicago: University of Chicago Press, 2002; and Michael P. Dooley and Jeffrey A. Frankel (eds.). *Managing Currency Crises in Emerging Markets*. Chicago: University of Chicago Press, 2003.

CHAPTER 15

THE INTERNATIONAL MONETARY FUND

The International Monetary Fund (IMF) was established at the 1944 Bretton Woods conference and has since occupied a prominent and controversial role in the international financial system. Its principal mission is to promote international cooperation to help ensure the smooth operation of the international monetary and financial systems. The IMF is most visible when it helps governments manage and resolve economic and financial crises. Developing countries constitute the vast majority of the IMF's clients. Typically, a developing country will turn to the IMF when it is not able to pay for its imports or to service its foreign debt. The IMF then lends from a pool of currencies contributed by its members.

IMF loans are usually conditional upon the willingness of the borrowing government to implement economic policy reforms designed to correct the underlying cause of its economic crisis. In most instances, the required policy changes involve eliminating macroeconomic imbalances by cutting government budget deficits and reducing the rate of growth of the money supply. Since the mid-1980s, these stabilization measures typically have been accompanied by far-reaching structural reforms, including trade liberalization, privatization of state-owned industries, and the liberalization of foreign investment. The combination of financial resources and economic policy reforms is generally known by the term "conditionality."

Conditionality has long been central to the controversy concerning the IMF. Critics argue that the economic policy reforms embodied in IMF conditionality agreements force governments to accept harsh austerity measures that reduce economic growth, raise unemployment, and push vulnerable segments of society deeper into poverty. Moreover, the IMF has been accused of adopting a "one size fits all" approach when designing conditionality agreements, relying on the same economic model and recommending a similar set of policy changes for each country that comes to it for assistance. Consequently, critics allege, IMF policy reforms are often inappropriate given a particular country's unique characteristics. The IMF defends itself against such criticisms by arguing that the vast majority of crises that strike developing countries share common causes: the government is running too large a budget deficit, which is usually financed by the central bank. The result is a current account deficit that is larger than private foreign lenders are willing to finance. Because the underlying cause of most crises is identical, the solution to these crises should also be identical in broad outlines: governments must bring spending back in line with revenues and they must adopt structural reforms to establish a stable base for participation in the international economy.

While critics have attacked, and the IMF has defended, conditionality agreements since the 1950s, the debate over the role of the IMF in the international financial system gained vigor following the 1997 East Asian financial crisis. Most of the countries afflicted by this financial crisis, including Thailand, Indonesia, South Korea, the Philippines (as well as Russia, Turkey, Brazil, and Argentina as the crisis moved into its second phase), turned to the IMF for assistance. The IMF provided financial support to the crisis countries and demanded that they adopt standard conditionality agreements. The combination of the financial crisis and IMF conditionality measures pushed the crisis countries into deep recessions, which led critics to question the IMF's approach. Some critics argued that the IMF's standard recipe of budget cuts and higher interest rates was wildly inappropriate. The crisis countries did not have large budget deficits or inflationary monetary policies prior to the crisis, and were now sliding into recession. Instead of austerity, these critics argued, the IMF should have urged the crisis countries to adopt expansionary fiscal and monetary policies to stem the sharp contraction of economic activity. Other critics indicted the IMF on a broader scale, claiming that IMF "bailouts" of countries in distress was an important cause of international financial instability because it encouraged too much capital to flow to risky emerging-market countries.

The two readings presented in this chapter reflect this debate. The first article is written by the Nobel-prize winning economist Joseph Stiglitz. Stiglitz is an economics professor at Stanford University but was chief economist and vice president of the World Bank during the Asian crisis. Stiglitz has since emerged as a leading critic of the IMF for its approach to the Asian crisis, its unwillingness to listen to outside advice, and for its closed decision-making process. In the second article, Kenneth Rogoff, who is the director of the IMF's research department, defends the IMF. Rogoff argues that while some criticisms have merit, many are misguided and others have been vastly exaggerated.

What I Learned at the World Economic Crisis

JOSEPH STIGLITZ

Next week's meeting of the International Monetary Fund will bring to Washington, D.C., many of the same demonstrators who trashed the World Trade Organization in Seattle last fall. They'll say the IMF is arrogant. They'll say the IMF doesn't really listen to the developing countries it is supposed to help. They'll say the IMF is secretive and insulated from democratic accountability. They'll say the IMF's economic "remedies" often make things worse—turning slowdowns into recessions and recessions into depressions.

And they'll have a point. I was chief economist at the World Bank from 1996 until last November, during the gravest global economic crisis in a half-century. I saw how the IMF, in tandem with the U.S. Treasury Department, responded. And I was appalled.

The global economic crisis began in Thailand, on July 2, 1997. The countries of East Asia were coming off a miraculous three decades: incomes had soared, health had improved, poverty had fallen dramatically. Not only was literacy now universal, but, on international science and math tests, many of these countries outperformed the United States. Some had not suffered a single year of recession in 30 years.

But the seeds of calamity had already been planted. In the early '90s, East Asian countries had liberalized their financial and capital markets—not because they needed to attract more funds (savings rates were already 30 percent or more) but because of international pressure, including some from the U.S. Treasury Department. These changes provoked a flood of short-term capital—that is, the kind of capital that looks for the highest return in the next day, week, or month, as opposed to long-term investment in things like factories. In Thailand, this short-term capital helped fuel an unsustainable real estate boom. And, as people around the world (including Americans) have painfully learned, every real estate bubble eventually bursts, often with disastrous consequences. Just as suddenly as capital flowed in, it flowed out. And, when everybody tries to pull their money out at the same time, it causes an economic problem. A big economic problem.

The last set of financial crises had occurred in Latin America in the 1980s, when bloated public deficits and loose monetary policies led to runaway inflation. There, the IMF had correctly imposed fiscal austerity (balanced budgets) and

From Joseph Stiglitz, "What I Learned at the World Economic Crisis," *The New Republic*, April 17, 2000. Reprinted by permission of *The New Republic*. © 2000, The New Republic, LLC.

tighter monetary policies, demanding that governments pursue those policies as a precondition for receiving aid. So, in 1997 the IMF imposed the same demands on Thailand. Austerity, the fund's leaders said, would restore confidence in the Thai economy. As the crisis spread to other East Asian nations—and even as evidence of the policy's failure mounted—the IMF barely blinked, delivering the same medicine to each ailing nation that showed up on its doorstep.

I thought this was a mistake. For one thing, unlike the Latin American nations, the East Asian countries were already running budget surpluses. In Thailand, the government was running such large surpluses that it was actually starving the economy of much-needed investments in education and infrastructure, both essential to economic growth. And the East Asian nations already had tight monetary policies, as well: inflation was low and falling. (In South Korea, for example, inflation stood at a very respectable four percent.) The problem was not imprudent government, as in Latin America; the problem was an imprudent private sector—all those bankers and borrowers, for instance, who'd gambled on the real estate bubble.

Under such circumstances, I feared, austerity measures would not revive the economies of East Asia—it would plunge them into recession or even depression. High interest rates might devastate highly indebted East Asian firms, causing more bankruptcies and defaults. Reduced government expenditures would only shrink the economy further.

So I began lobbying to change the policy. I talked to Stanley Fischer, a distinguished former Massachusetts Institute of Technology economics professor and former chief economist of the World Bank, who had become the IMF's first deputy managing director. I met with fellow economists at the World Bank who might have contacts or influence within the IMF, encouraging them to do everything they could to move the IMF bureaucracy.

Convincing people at the World Bank of my analysis proved easy; changing minds at the IMF was virtually impossible. When I talked to senior officials at the IMF—explaining, for instance, how high interest rates might increase bankruptcies, thus making it even harder to restore confidence in East Asian economies—they would at first resist. Then, after failing to come up with an effective counterargument, they would retreat to another response: if only I understood the pressure coming from the IMF board of executive directors—the body, appointed by finance ministers from the advanced industrial countries, that approves all the IMF's loans. Their meaning was clear. The board's inclination was to be even more severe; these people were actually a moderating influence. My friends who were executive directors said they were the ones getting pressured. It was maddening, not just because the IMF's inertia was so hard to stop but because, with everything going on behind closed doors, it was impossible to know who was the real obstacle to change. Was the staff pushing the executive directors, or were the executive directors pushing the staff? I still do not know for certain.

Of course, everybody at the IMF assured me they would be flexible: if their policies really turned out to be overly contractionary, forcing the East Asian economies into deeper recession than necessary, then they would reverse them. This sent shudders down my spine. One of the first lessons economists teach their graduate students is the importance of lags: it takes twelve to 18 months before a change in monetary policy (raising or lowering interest rates) shows its full effects. When I worked in the White House as chairman of the Council of Economic Advisers, we focused all our energy on forecasting where the economy would be in the future, so we could know what policies to recommend today. To play catch-up was the height of folly. And that was precisely what the IMF officials were proposing to do.

I shouldn't have been surprised. The IMF likes to go about its business without outsiders asking too many questions. In theory, the fund supports democratic institutions in the nations it assists. In practice, it undermines the democratic process by imposing policies. Officially, of course, the IMF doesn't "impose" anything. It "negotiates" the conditions for receiving aid. But all the power in the negotiations is on one side—the IMF's—and the fund rarely allows sufficient time for broad consensus-building or even widespread consultations with either parliaments or civil society. Sometimes the IMF dispenses with the pretense of openness altogether and negotiates secret covenants.

When the IMF decides to assist a country, it dispatches a "mission" of economists. These economists frequently lack extensive experience in the country; they are more likely to have firsthand knowledge of its five-star hotels than of the villages that dot its countryside. They work hard, poring over numbers deep into the night. But their task is impossible. In a period of days or, at most, weeks, they are charged with developing a coherent program sensitive to the needs of the country. Needless to say, a little number-crunching rarely provides adequate insights into the development strategy for an entire nation. Even worse, the number-crunching isn't always that good. The mathematical models the IMF uses are frequently flawed or out-of-date. Critics accuse the institution of taking a cookie-cutter approach to economics, and they're right. Country teams have been known to compose draft reports before visiting. I heard stories of one unfortunate incident when team members copied large parts of the text for one country's report and transferred them wholesale to another. They might have gotten away with it, except the "search and replace" function on the word processor didn't work properly, leaving the original country's name in a few places. Oops.

It's not fair to say that IMF economists don't care about the citizens of developing nations. But the older men who staff the fund—and they are overwhelmingly older men—act as if they are shouldering Rudyard Kipling's white man's burden. IMF experts believe they are brighter, more educated, and less politically motivated than the economists in the countries they visit. In fact, the economic leaders from those countries are pretty good—in many cases brighter or better-educated than the IMF staff, which frequently consists of third-rank students from first-rate universities. (Trust me: I've taught at Oxford University, MIT, Stanford University, Yale University, and Princeton University, and the IMF almost never succeeded in recruiting any of the best students.) Last summer, I gave a seminar in China on competition policy in telecommunications. At least three Chinese economists in the audience asked questions as sophisticated as the best minds in the West would have asked.

As time passed, my frustration mounted. (One might have thought that since the World Bank was contributing literally billions of dollars to the rescue packages, its voice would be heard. But it was ignored almost as resolutely as the people in the affected countries.) The IMF claimed that all it was asking of the East Asian countries was that they balance their budgets at a time of recession. All? Hadn't the Clinton administration just fought a major battle with Congress to stave off a balanced-budget amendment in this country? And wasn't the administration's key argument that, in the face of recession, a little deficit spending might be necessary? This is what I and most other economists had been teaching our graduate students for 60 years. Quite frankly, a student who turned in the IMF's answer to the test question "What should be the fiscal stance of Thailand, facing an economic downturn?" would have gotten an F.

As the crisis spread to Indonesia, I became even more concerned. New research at the World Bank showed that recession in such an ethnically divided country could spark all kinds of social and political turmoil. So in late 1997, at a meeting of finance ministers and central-bank governors in Kuala Lumpur, I issued a carefully prepared statement vetted by the World Bank: I suggested that the excessively contractionary monetary and fiscal program could lead to political and social turmoil in Indonesia. Again, the IMF stood its ground. The fund's managing director, Michel Camdessus, said there what he'd said in public: that East Asia simply had to grit it out, as Mexico had. He went on to note that, for all of the short-term pain, Mexico emerged from the experience stronger.

But this was an absurd analogy. Mexico hadn't recovered because the IMF forced it to strengthen its weak financial system, which remained weak years after the crisis. It recovered because of a surge of exports to the United States, which took off thanks to the U.S. economic boom, and because of NAFTA. By contrast, Indonesia's main trading partner was Japan—which was then, and still remains, mired in the doldrums. Furthermore, Indonesia was far more politically and socially explosive than Mexico, with a much deeper history of ethnic strife. And renewed strife would produce massive capital flight (made easy by relaxed currency-flow restrictions encouraged by the IMF). But none of these arguments mattered. The IMF pressed ahead, demanding reductions in government spending. And so subsidies for basic necessities like food and fuel were eliminated at the very time when contractionary policies made those subsidies more desperately needed than ever.

∘∘∘

By January 1998, things had gotten so bad that the World Bank's vice president for East Asia, Jean Michel Severino, invoked the dreaded r-word ("recession") and d-word ("depression") in describing the economic calamity in Asia. Lawrence Summers, then deputy treasury secretary, railed against Severino for making things seem worse than they were, but what other way was there to describe what was happening? Output in some of the affected countries fell 16 percent or more. Half the businesses in Indonesia were in virtual bankruptcy or close to it, and, as a result, the country could not even take advantage of the export opportunities the lower exchange rates provided. Unemployment soared, increasing as much as tenfold, and real wages plummeted—in countries with basically no safety nets. Not only was the IMF not restoring economic confidence in East Asia, it was undermining the region's social fabric. And then, in the spring and summer of 1998, the crisis spread beyond East Asia to the most explosive country of all—Russia.

The calamity in Russia shared key characteristics with the calamity in East Asia—not least among them the role that IMF and U.S. Treasury policies played in abetting it. But, in Russia, the abetting began much earlier. Following the fall of the Berlin Wall, two schools of thought had emerged concerning Russia's transition to a market economy. One of these, to which I belonged, consisted of a melange of experts on the region, Nobel Prize winners like Kenneth Arrow and others. This group emphasized the importance of the institutional infrastructure of a market economy—from legal structures that enforce contracts to regulatory structures that make a financial system work. Arrow and I had both been part of a National Academy of Sciences group that had, a decade earlier, discussed with the Chinese their transition strategy. We emphasized the importance of fostering competition—rather than just privatizing state-owned industries—and favored a more gradual transition to a market economy (although we agreed that occasional strong measures might be needed to combat hyperinflation).

The second group consisted largely of macroeconomists, whose faith in the market was unmatched by an appreciation of the subtleties of its underpinnings—that is, of the conditions required for it to work effectively. These economists typically had little knowledge of the history or details of the Russian economy and didn't believe they needed any. The great strength, and the ultimate weakness, of the economic doctrines upon which they relied is that the doctrines are—or are supposed to be—universal. Institutions, history, or even the distribution of income simply do not matter. Good economists know the universal truths and can look beyond the array of facts and details that obscure these truths. And the universal truth is that shock therapy works for countries in transition to a market economy: the stronger the medicine (and the more painful the reaction), the quicker the recovery. Or so the argument goes.

Unfortunately for Russia, the latter school won the debate in the Treasury Department and in the IMF. Or, to be more accurate, the Treasury Department and the IMF made sure there was no open debate and then proceeded blindly along the second route. Those who opposed this course were either not consulted or not consulted for long. On the Council of Economic Advisers, for example, there was a brilliant economist, Peter Orszag, who had served as a close adviser to the Russian government and had worked with many of the young economists who eventually assumed positions of influence there. He was just the sort of person whose expertise Treasury and the IMF needed. Yet, perhaps because he knew too much, they almost never consulted him.

We all know what happened next. In the December 1993 elections, Russian voters dealt the reformers a huge setback, a setback from which they have yet really to recover. Strobe Talbott, then in charge of the noneconomic aspects of Russia policy, admitted that Russia had experienced "too much shock and too little therapy." And all that shock hadn't moved Russia toward a real market economy at all. The rapid privatization urged upon Moscow by the IMF and the Treasury Department had allowed a small group of oligarchs to gain control of state assets. The IMF and Treasury had rejiggered Russia's economic incentives, all right—but the wrong way. By paying insufficient attention to the institutional infrastructure that would allow a market economy to flourish—and by easing the flow of capital in and out of Russia—the IMF and Treasury had laid the groundwork for the oligarchs' plundering. While the government lacked the money to pay pensioners, the oligarchs were sending money obtained by stripping assets and selling the country's precious national resources into Cypriot and Swiss bank accounts.

The United States was implicated in these awful developments. In mid-1998, Summers, soon to be named Robert Rubin's successor as secretary of the treasury, actually made a public display of appearing with Anatoly Chubais, the chief architect of Russia's privatization. In so doing, the United States seemed to be aligning itself with the very forces impoverishing the Russian people. No wonder anti-Americanism spread like wildfire.

At first, Talbott's admission notwithstanding, the true believers at Treasury and the IMF continued to insist that the problem was not too much therapy but too little shock. But, through the mid-'90s, the Russian economy continued to implode. Output plummeted by half. While only two percent of the population had lived in poverty even at the end of the dismal Soviet period, "reform" saw poverty rates soar to almost 50 percent, with more than half of Russia's children living below the poverty line. Only recently have the IMF and Treasury conceded that therapy was undervalued—though they now insist they said so all along.

Today, Russia remains in desperate shape. High oil prices and the long-resisted ruble devaluation have helped it regain some footing. But standards of living remain far below where they were at the start of the transition. The nation is beset by enormous inequality, and most Russians, embittered by experience, have lost confidence in the free market. A significant fall in oil prices would almost certainly reverse what modest progress has been made.

East Asia is better off, though it still struggles, too. Close to 40 percent of Thailand's loans are still not performing; Indonesia remains deeply mired in recession. Unemployment rates remain far higher than they were before the crisis, even in East Asia's best-performing country, Korea. IMF boosters suggest that the recession's end is a testament to the effectiveness of the agency's policies. Nonsense. Every recession eventually ends. All the IMF did was make East Asia's recessions deeper, longer, and harder. Indeed, Thailand, which followed the IMF's prescriptions the most closely, has performed worse than Malaysia and South Korea, which followed more independent courses.

I was often asked how smart—even brilliant—people could have created such bad policies. One reason is that these smart people were not using smart economics. Time and again, I was dismayed at how out-of-date—and how out-of-tune with reality—the models Washington economists employed were. For example, microeconomic phenomena such as bankruptcy and the fear of default were at the center of the East Asian crisis. But the macroeconomic models used to analyze these crises were not typically rooted in microfoundations, so they took no account of bankruptcy.

But bad economics was only a symptom of the real problem: secrecy. Smart people are more likely to do stupid things when they close themselves off from outside criticism and advice. If there's one thing I've learned in government, it's that openness is most essential in those realms where expertise seems to matter most. If the IMF and Treasury had invited greater scrutiny, their folly might have become much clearer, much earlier. Critics from the right, such as Martin Feldstein, chairman of Reagan's Council of Economic Advisers, and George Shultz, Reagan's secretary of state, joined Jeff Sachs, Paul Krugman, and me in condemning the policies. But, with the IMF insisting its policies were beyond reproach—and with no institutional structure to make it pay attention—our criticisms were of little use. More frightening, even internal critics, particularly those with direct democratic accountability, were kept in the dark. The Treasury Department is so arrogant about its economic analyses and prescriptions that it often keeps tight—much too tight—control over what even the president sees.

Open discussion would have raised profound questions that still receive very little attention in the American press: To what extent did the IMF and the Treasury Department push policies that actually contributed to the increased global economic volatility? (Treasury pushed liberalization in Korea in 1993 over the opposition of the Council of Economic Advisers. Treasury won the internal White House battle, but Korea, and the world, paid a high price.) Were some of the IMF's harsh criticisms of East Asia intended to detract attention from the agency's own culpability? Most importantly, did America—and the IMF—push policies because we, or they, believed the policies would help East Asia or because we believed they would benefit financial interests in the United States and the advanced industrial world? And, if we believed our policies were helping East Asia, where was the evidence? As a participant in these debates, I got to see the evidence. There was none.

Since the end of the cold war, tremendous power has flowed to the people entrusted to bring the gospel of the market to the far corners of the globe. These economists, bureaucrats, and officials act in the name of the United States and the other advanced industrial countries, and yet they speak a language that few average citizens understand and that few policymakers bother to translate. Economic policy is today perhaps the most important part of America's interaction with the rest of the world. And yet the culture of international economic policy in the world's most powerful democracy is not democratic.

This is what the demonstrators shouting outside the IMF next week will try to say. Of course, the streets are not the best place to discuss these highly complex issues. Some of the protesters are no more interested in open debate than the officials at the IMF are. And not everything the protesters say will be right. But, if the people we entrust to manage the global economy—in the IMF and in the Treasury Department—don't begin a dialogue and take their criticisms to heart, things will continue to go very, very wrong. I've seen it happen.

The IMF Strikes Back

KENNETH ROGOFF

Vitriol against the IMF, including personal attacks on the competence and integrity of its staff, has transcended into an art form in recent years. One bestselling author labels all new fund recruits as "third rate," implies that management is on the take, and discusses the IMF's role in the Asian financial crisis of the late 1990s in the same breath as Nazi Germany and the Holocaust. Even more sober and balanced critics of the institution—such as *Washington Post* writer Paul Blustein, whose excellent inside account of the Asian financial crisis, *The Chastening*, should be required reading for prospective fund economists (and their spouses)—find themselves choosing titles that invoke the devil. Really, doesn't *The Chastening* sound like a sequel to 1970s horror flicks such as *The Exorcist* or *The Omen?* Perhaps this race to the bottom is a natural outcome of market forces. After all, in a world of 24-hour business news, there is a huge return to being introduced as "the leading critic of the IMF."

Regrettably, many of the charges frequently leveled against the fund reveal deep confusion regarding its policies and intentions. Other criticisms, however, do hit at potentially fundamental weak spots in current IMF practices. Unfortunately, all the recrimination and finger pointing make it difficult to separate spurious critiques from legitimate concerns. Worse yet, some of the deeper questions that ought to be at the heart of these debates—issues such as poverty, appropriate exchange-rate systems, and whether the global financial system encourages developing countries to take on excessive debt—are too easily ignored.

Consider the four most common criticisms against the fund: First, IMF loan programs impose harsh fiscal austerity on cash-strapped countries. Second, IMF loans encourage financiers to invest recklessly, confident the fund will bail them out (the so-called moral hazard problem). Third, IMF advice to countries suffering debt or currency crises only aggravates economic conditions. And fourth, the fund has irresponsibly pushed countries to open themselves up to volatile and destabilizing flows of foreign capital.

Some of these charges have important merits, even if critics (including myself in my former life as an academic economist) tend to overstate them for emphasis. Others, however, are both polemic and deeply misguided. In addressing them,

I hope to clear the air for a more focused and cogent discussion on how the IMF and others can work to improve conditions in the global economy. Surely that should be our common goal.

THE AUSTERITY MYTH

Over the years, no critique of the fund has carried more emotion than the "austerity" charge. Anti-fund diatribes contend that, everywhere the IMF goes, the tight macroeconomic policies it imposes on governments invariably crush the hopes and aspirations of people. Yet, at the risk of seeming heretical, I submit that the reality is nearly the opposite. As a rule, fund programs lighten austerity rather than create it. Yes, really.

Critics must understand that governments from developing countries don't seek IMF financial assistance when the sun is shining; they come when they have already run into deep financial difficulties, generally through some combination of bad management and bad luck. Virtually every country with an IMF program over the past 50 years, from Peru in 1954 to South Korea in 1997 to Argentina today, could be described in this fashion.

Policymakers in distressed economies know the fund will intervene where no private creditor dares tread and will make loans at rates their countries could only dream of even in the best of times. They understand that, in the short term, IMF loans allow a distressed debtor nation to tighten its belt less than it would have to otherwise. The economic policy conditions that the fund attaches to its loans are in lieu of the stricter discipline that market forces would impose in the IMF's absence. Both South Korea and Thailand, for example, were facing either outright default or a prolonged free fall in the value of their currencies in 1997—a far more damaging outcome than what actually took place.

Nevertheless, the institution provides a convenient whipping boy when politicians confront their populations with a less profligate budget. "The IMF forced us to do it" is the familiar refrain when governments cut spending and subsidies. Never mind that the country's government—whose macroeconomic mismanagement often had more than a little to do with the crisis in the first place—generally retains considerable discretion over its range of policy options, not least in determining where budget cuts must take place.

At its heart, the austerity critique confuses correlation with causation. Blaming the IMF for the reality that every country must confront its budget constraints is like blaming the fund for gravity.

Admittedly, the IMF does insist on being repaid, so eventually borrowing countries must part with foreign exchange resources that otherwise might have gone into domestic programs. Yet repayments to the fund normally spike only after the crisis has passed, making payments more manageable for borrowing governments. The IMF's shareholders—its 184 member countries—could collectively decide to convert all the fund's loans to grants, and then recipient countries would face no costs at all. However, if IMF loans are never repaid, industrialized countries must be willing to replenish continually the organization's lending resources, or eventually no funds would be available to help deal with the next debt crisis in the developing world.

A HAZARDOUS CRITIQUE

Of course, in so many IMF programs, borrowing countries must pay back their private creditors in addition to repaying the fund. Yet wouldn't fiscal austerity be a bit more palatable if troubled debtor nations could compel foreign private lenders to bear part of the burden? Why should taxpayers in developing countries absorb the entire blow?

That is a completely legitimate question, but let's start by getting a few facts straight. First, private investors can hardly breathe a sigh of relief when the fund becomes involved in an emerging-market financial crisis. According to the Institute of International Finance, private investors lost some $225 billion during the Asian financial crisis of the late 1990s and some $100 billion as a result of the 1998 Russian debt default. And what of the Latin American debt crisis of the 1980s, during which the IMF helped jawbone foreign banks into rolling over a substantial fraction of Latin American debts for almost five years and ultimately forced banks to accept large write-downs of 30 percent or more? Certainly, if foreign private lenders consistently lose money on loans to developing countries, flows of new money will cease. Indeed, flows into much of Latin America—again the current locus of debt problems—have been sharply down during the past couple of years.

Private creditors ought to be willing to take large write-downs of their debts in some instances, particularly when a country is so deeply in hock that it is effectively insolvent. In such circumstances, trying to force the debtor to repay in full can often be counterproductive. Not only do citizens of the debtor country suffer, but creditors often receive less than they might have if they had lessened the country's debt burden and thus given the nation the will and means to increase investment and growth. Sometimes debt restructuring does happen, as in Ecuador (1999), Pakistan (1999), and Ukraine (2000). However, such cases are the exception rather than the rule, as current international law makes bankruptcies by sovereign states extraordinarily messy and chaotic. As a result, the official lending community, typically led by the IMF, is often unwilling to force the issue and sometimes finds itself trying to keep a country afloat far beyond the point of no return. In Russia in 1998, for example, the official community threw money behind a fixed exchange rate regime that was patently doomed. Eventually, the fund cut the cord and allowed a default, proving wrong those many private investors who thought Russia was "too nuclear to fail." But if the fund had allowed the default to take place at an earlier stage, Russia might well have come out of its subsequent downturn at least as quickly and with less official debt.

Since restructuring of debt to private creditors is relatively rare, many critics reasonably worry that IMF financing often serves as a blanket insurance policy for private lenders. Moreover, when private creditors believe they will be bailed out by the IMF, they have reason to lend more—and at lower interest rates—than is appropriate. The debtor country, in sum, is seduced into borrowing too much, resulting in more frequent and severe crises, of exactly the sort the IMF was designed to alleviate. I will be the first to admit the "moral hazard" theory of IMF lending is clever (having introduced the theory in the 1980s), and I think it is surely important in some instances. But the empirical evidence is mixed. One strike against the moral hazard argument is that most countries generally do repay the IMF, if not on time, then late but with full interest. If the IMF is consistently paid, then private lenders receive no subsidy, so there is no bailout in any simplistic sense. Of course, despite the IMF's strong repayment record in major emerging-market loan packages, there is no guarantee about the future, and it would certainly be wrong to dismiss moral hazard as unimportant.

FISCAL FOLLIES

Even if IMF policies are not to blame for budget cutbacks in poor economies, might the fund's programs still be so poorly designed that their ill-advised conditions more than cancel out any good the international lender's resources could bring? In particular, critics charge that the IMF pushes countries to increase domestic interest rates when cuts would better serve to stimulate the economy. The IMF also stands accused of forcing crisis economies to tighten their budgets in the midst of recessions. Like the austerity argument, these critiques of basic IMF policy advice appear rather damning, especially when wrapped in rhetoric about how all economists at the IMF are third-rate thinkers so immune from outside advice that they wouldn't listen if John Maynard Keynes himself dialed them up from heaven.

Of course, it would be wonderful if governments in emerging markets could follow Keynesian "countercyclical policies"—that is, if they could stimulate their economies with lower interest rates, new public spending, or tax cuts during a recession. In its September 2002 "World Economic Outlook" report, the IMF encourages exactly such policies where feasible. (For example, the IMF has strongly urged Germany to be flexible in observing the budget constraints of the European Stability and Growth Pact, lest the government aggravate Germany's already severe economic slowdown.) Unfortunately, most emerging markets have an extremely difficult time borrowing during a downturn, and they often must tighten their belts precisely when a looser fiscal policy might otherwise be desirable. And the IMF, or anyone else for that matter, can only do so much for countries that don't pay attention to the commonsense advice of building up surpluses during boom times—such as Argentina in the 1990s—to leave room for deficits during downturns. According to some critics, though, a simple solution is staring the IMF in the face: If those stubborn fund economists would only appreciate how successful expansionary fiscal policy can be in boosting output, they would realize countries can simply wave off a debt crisis by borrowing even more. Remember former U.S. President Ronald Reagan's economic guru, Arthur Laffer, who theorized that by cutting tax rates, the United States would enjoy so much extra growth that tax revenues would actually rise? In much the same way, some IMF critics—ranging from

Nobel Prize-winning economist Joseph Stiglitz to the relief agency Oxfam—claim that by running a fiscal deficit into a debt storm, a country can grow so much that it will be able to sustain these higher debt levels. Creditors would understand this logic and happily fork over the requisite extra funds. Problem solved, case closed. Indeed, why should austerity ever be necessary? Needless to say, Reagan's tax cut during the 1980s did not lead to higher tax revenues but instead resulted in massive deficits. By the same token, there is no magic potion for troubled debtor countries. Lenders simply will not buy into this story.

The notion that countries should reduce interest rates—rather than raise them—to fend off debt and exchange-rate crises is even more absurd. When investors fear a country is increasingly likely to default on its debts, they will demand higher interest rates to compensate for that risk, not lower ones. And when a nation's citizens lose confidence in their own currency, they will require a large premium to accept debt denominated in that currency or to keep their deposits in domestic banks. No surprise that interest rates in virtually all countries that experienced debt crises during the last decade—from Mexico to Turkey—skyrocketed even though their currencies were allowed to float against the dollar.

The debate over how far interest rates should be allowed to rise in defending against a speculative currency attack is a legitimate one. The higher interest rates go, the more stress on the economy and the more bankruptcies and bank failures; classic cases include Mexico in 1995 and South Korea in 1998. On the other hand, since most crisis countries have substantial "liability dollarization"—that is, a lot of borrowing goes on in dollars—an excessively sharp fall in the exchange rate will also cause bankruptcies, with Indonesia in 1998 being but one example among many. Governments must strike a delicate balance in the short and medium term, as they decide how quickly to reduce interest rates from crisis levels. At the very least, critics of IMF tactics must acknowledge these difficult trade-offs. The simplistic view that it can be solved by just adopting softer "employment friendly" policies, such as low interest rates and fiscal expansion is dangerous as well as naive in the face of financial maelstrom.

CAPITAL CONTROL FREAKS

Although currency crises and financial bailouts dominate media coverage of the IMF, much of the agency's routine work entails ongoing dialogue with the fund's 184 member countries. As part of the fund's surveillance efforts, IMF staffers regularly visit member states and meet with policymakers to discuss how best to achieve sustained economic growth and stable inflation rates. So, rather than judge the fund solely on how it copes with financial crises, critics should consider its ongoing advice in trying to help countries stay out of trouble. In this area, perhaps the most controversial issue is the fund's advice on liberalizing international capital movements—that is, on how fast emerging markets should pry open their often highly protected domestic financial markets.

Critics such as Columbia University economist Jagdish Bhagwati have suggested that the IMF's zeal in promoting free capital flows around the world inadvertently planted the seeds of the Asian financial crisis. In principle, had banks and companies in Asia's emerging markets not been allowed to borrow freely in foreign currency, they would not have built up huge foreign currency debts, and international creditors could not have demanded repayment just as liquidity was drying up and foreign currency was becoming very expensive. Although I was not at the IMF during the Asian crisis, my sense from reading archives and speaking with fund old-timers is that although this charge has some currency, the fund was more eclectic in its advice on this matter than most critics acknowledge. For example, in the months leading to Thailand's currency collapse in 1997, IMF reports on the Thai economy portrayed in stark terms the risks of liberalizing capital flows while keeping the domestic currency (the baht) at a fixed level against the U.S. dollar. As Blustein vividly portrays in *The Chastening*, Thai authorities didn't listen, still hoping instead that Bangkok would become a financial center like Singapore. Ultimately, the Thai baht succumbed to a massive speculative attack. Of course, in some cases—most famously South Korea and Mexico—the fund didn't warn countries forcefully enough about the danger of opening up to international capital markets before domestic financial markers and regulators were prepared to handle the resulting volatility.

However one apportions blame for the financial crises of the past two decades, misconceptions regarding the merits and drawbacks of capital-market liberalization abound. First, it is simply wrong to conclude that countries with closed capital markers are better equipped to weather stormy financial markers. Yes, the relatively closed Chinese and Indian economies did not catch the Asian flu, or at least not a particularly bad case. But neither did Australia nor New Zealand, two countries that boast extremely open capital markets. Why? Because the latter countries' highly developed domestic financial markets were extremely well regulated. The biggest danger lurks in the middle, namely for those economies—many of which are in East Asia and Latin America—that combine weak and underdeveloped financial markers with poor regulation.

Moreover, a country needs export earnings to support foreign debt payments, and export industries do not spring up overnight. That's why the risks of running into external financing problems are higher for countries that fully liberalize their capital markets before significantly opening up to trade flows. Indeed, economies with small trading sectors can run into problems even with seemingly modest debt levels. This problem has repeatedly plagued countries in Latin America, where trade is relatively restricted by a combination of inward-looking policies and remote location.

Perhaps the best evidence in favor of open capital markets is that, despite the financial turmoil of the last decade, most developing countries still aim to liberalize their capital markets as a long-term goal. Surprisingly few nations have turned back the clock on financial and capital account liberalization. As domestic economies grow increasingly sophisticated, particularly regarding the depth and breadth of their financial instruments, policymakers are relentlessly seeking ways to live with open capital markers. The lessons from Europe's failed, heavy-handed attempts to regulate international capital flows in the 1970s and 1980s seem to have been increasingly absorbed in the developing world today.

Even China, long the high growth poster child for capital-control enthusiasts, now views increased openness to capital markets as a central long-term goal. Its economic leaders understand that it's one thing to become a $1,000 per capita economy, as China is today. But to continue such stellar growth performance—and one day to reach the $20,000 to $40,000 per capita incomes of the industrialized countries—China will eventually require a world class capital market.

Even though a continued move toward greater capital mobility is emerging as a global norm, absolutely unfettered global capital mobility is not necessarily the best long-term outcome. Temporary controls on capital outflows may be important in dealing with some modern-day financial crises, while various kinds of light-handed taxes on capital inflows may be useful for countries faced with sudden surges of inflows. Chile is the classic example of a country that appears to have successfully used market-friendly taxes on capital inflows, though a debate continues to rage over their effectiveness. One way or another, the international community must find ways to temper debt flows and at the same time encourage equity investment and foreign direct investment, such as physical investment in plants and equipment. In industrialized countries, the pain of a 20 percent stock market fall is shared automatically and fairly broadly throughout the economy. But in nations that rely on foreign debt, a sudden change in investor sentiment can breed disaster. Nevertheless, financial authorities in developing economies should remain wary of capital controls as an easy solution. "Temporary" controls can easily become ensconced, as political forces and budget pressures make them hard to remove. Invite capital controls for lunch, and they will try to stay for dinner.

STRIKING A GLOBAL BARGAIN

Should the international community just give up on global capital mobility and encourage countries to shut their doors? Looking further ahead in the 21st century, does the world really want to adopt greater financial isolationism?

Perhaps the greatest challenge facing industrialized countries in this century is how to deal with the aging bulge in their populations. With that in mind, wouldn't it be more helpful if rich countries could find effective ways to invest in much younger developing nations, and later use the proceeds to support their own increasing number of retirees? And let's face it, the world's developing countries need funds for investment and education now, so such a trade would prove mutually beneficial—a win-win. Yes, recurring debt crises in the developing world have been sobering, but the potential benefits to financial integration are enormous. Full scale retreat is hardly the answer.

Can the IMF help? Certainly. The fund provides a key forum for exchange of ideas and best practices. Yes, one could go ahead and eliminate the IMF, as some of the more extreme detractors wish, but that is not going to solve any fundamental problems. This increasingly globalized world will still need a global economic forum. Even today, the IMF is providing such a forum for discussion and debate over a new international bankruptcy procedure that could lessen the chaos that results when debtor countries become insolvent.

And there are many other issues where the IMF, or some similar multilateral organization, seems essential to any solution. For example, the current patchwork system of exchange rates seems too unstable to survive into the 22nd century. How will the world make the transition toward a more stable, coherent system? That is a global problem, and dealing with it requires a global perspective the IMF can help provide.

And what of poverty? Here, the IMF's sister organization, the World Bank, with its microeconomic and social focus and commensurately much larger staff, is appropriately charged with the lead role. But poor countries in the developing world still face important macroeconomic challenges. For example, if enhanced aid flows ever materialize, policymakers in emerging markets will still need to find ways to ensure that domestic production grows and thrives. Perhaps poor nations won't need the IMF's specific macroeconomic expertise—but they will need something awfully similar.

QUESTIONS FOR REVIEW AND DISCUSSION

1. According to Joseph Stiglitz, the IMF should have encouraged Asian governments to adopt what kinds of macroeconomic policies? According to Kenneth Rogoff, what consequences would such policies have had on the Asian-crisis countries? What policies do you think the IMF should have recommended to the Asian-crisis countries? Why?
2. Stiglitz suggests that the severity of the recessions that followed the Asian financial crisis were a result of IMF conditionality programs. How would Rogoff respond to this criticism? More broadly, to what extent are IMF policies the cause of growth slowdowns in the countries that turn to the fund for assistance?
3. What is "moral hazard," and how, according to some critics, do IMF operations create this problem in the international financial system?
4. Stiglitz argues that the IMF decision-making process should be more open and democratic. How could this be achieved, what would such a decision-making process look like, and how would it alter the kinds of policies the IMF includes in conditionality agreements? Would reform of the decision-making process have any negative impact on the ability of the IMF to move quickly to address emerging financial crises?
5. Would developing countries be better off with or without the IMF? Use economic *and* political arguments to support your answer.

SUGGESTIONS FOR FURTHER READING

Joseph Stiglitz develops his criticism of the IMF at much greater length in Joseph Stiglitz. *Globalization and its Discontents*. New York: W.W. Norton and Company, 2002.

For a more detailed account of the IMF and the recent international financial crises, see: Paul Blustein. *The Chastening: Inside the Crisis that Rocked the Global Financial System and Humbled the IMF*. New York: Public Affairs, 2001.

Some of the strongest criticisms of the IMF were advanced by the Meltzer Commission, a policy group established in 1998 by the Joint Economic Committee of the United States Congress. You can download their report at http://www.house.gov/jec/imf/meltzer.pdf

For a good overview of the reform process that followed the Asian crisis, see: Peter B. Kenen. *The International Financial Architecture: What's New? What's Missing?* Washington, DC: Institute for International Economics, 2001.

CHAPTER 16

DEBT RELIEF

Rock stars do not usually travel the world campaigning for global economic issues. But, during the last five years, Bono, the lead singer of the Irish rock group U2, has been on a quest to convince governments throughout the advanced industrialized world to forgive the debt owed by the world's poorest countries. Bono has not traveled this path alone. In fact, he has been in very good company. The pope, the Dalai Lama, Jeffrey Sachs (a prominent economist who heads Columbia University's Earth Institute), and a global group called Jubilee 2000 (which claims to have collected 24 million signatures on its petitions calling for debt forgiveness) have also been calling for significant debt relief for the world's poorest countries.

As a group, the world's poorest countries, the majority of which are located in sub-Saharan Africa, collectively owe about $200 billion. Most of this debt is owed to official creditors, that is, the World Bank, the International Monetary Fund, other regional development banks, and governments in the advanced industrialized world. Payments to service this debt in 1999 (before the latest debt-relief initiatives had taken effect) equaled slightly more than $3 billion, an amount equal to 21 percent of government revenue and 15 percent of export earnings. The countries that owe this debt are poor; roughly half of their combined population of 615 million people live on less than one dollar per day, and for at least ten of these countries, per capita income was lower in 1999 than it was in 1960.

Proponents of debt relief argue that the world's poorest countries simply can't afford to repay the money they have borrowed. Moreover, money they use to service foreign debt could be put to better use financing critical social expenditures such as health care and education. According to the IMF, governments in a group of 26 heavily indebted poor countries devoted a larger share of their revenues to servicing foreign debt than to health care and education combined. Others argue that high levels of foreign debt in the world's poorest countries have greatly reduced the incentives for investment, and thereby greatly reduced the possibility for economic growth in these countries. The result is a poverty trap from which they cannot escape. Other debt-relief proponents argue that it is simply wrong to ask the world's poorest to repay such large amounts of debt, especially debt incurred by authoritarian governments spent on palaces and other extravagances, as well as on political repression. Such debt is "odious debt," that is, it is incurred without the public's consent and not spent in ways that benefit the public.

The major creditors—including the International Monetary Fund, the World Bank, other regional development banks, and governments in the advanced industrialized countries—responded to debt-relief requests by creating "The Heavily Indebted Poor Country (HIPC) Initiative." Launched in 1996, and substantially reformed and expanded in 1999, the HIPC Initiative was the first comprehensive approach to the least-developed-country debt problem and marked the first time that the IMF and World Bank agreed to reduce their claims on developing countries. The HIPC Initiative has a limited country coverage, as only the world's poorest countries—those that can borrow from the World Bank's International Development Association—are eligible for the program. Currently, 42 least-developed countries are eligible to participate in the program. HIPC offers only a limited amount of debt relief and does not forgive all debt, but instead strives to create a "sustainable" foreign debt position for participating countries. The IMF and World Bank estimate that the typical least-developed country that completes the program will see its debt level fall by two-thirds and its debt-service-to-export-earnings ratio cut in half.

Like other IMF and World Bank programs, the HIPC Initiative involves a high degree of policy conditionality. The Initiative is structured around a two-stage process. In the first stage, which is to last no longer than three years, the government must work with domestic groups, the IMF, and the World Bank to develop a Poverty Reduction Strategy Paper (PRSP). The PRSP describes the macroeconomic, structural, and social policies the government will adopt in order to foster economic growth and reduce poverty, and also details how the government will spend the money it no longer needs to dedicate to debt service. The country must also establish a track record of implementing this strategy. At the end of this first stage, the country reaches the "decision point" at which the IMF and World Bank conduct a debt-sustainability analysis to determine the country's eligibility for relief under the HIPC Initiative. If the country's foreign debt is above 150 percent of its export earnings, the country is eligible, and the World Bank, the IMF, and individual governments commit to forgive enough of the country's debt to restore it to a sustainable position. In addition, countries begin to receive debt relief once they pass the decision point in the form of lower debt-service payments. The country then passes into the second stage. According to the IMF, "the length of this second period . . . is not time bound, but depends on the satisfactory implementation of key structural policy reforms agreed at the decision point, the maintenance of macroeconomic stability, and the adoption and implementation of a poverty reduction strategy." Countries exit the HIPC Initiative at the "completion point," where the full amount of debt relief committed at the decision point is granted. As of mid-2003, eight countries had reached the completion point and have together received a total of $14.6 billion in nominal debt relief ($8.3 billion in net present value terms). Eighteen other countries are currently between the decision and the completion points.

The HIPC Initiative has been the subject of considerable criticism. Jubilee Research (the current name of the former Jubilee 2000 campaign) argues that the amount of debt relief offered under the program is inadequate. They estimate that a total of $300 billion of debt must be cancelled, while the HIPC Initiative will only cancel about $100 billion. Critics also question the need for least-developed countries to qualify for the program and to develop and implement IMF-sponsored PRSPs. The two articles presented here criticize debt relief for other reasons. William Easterly, formerly a World Bank economist and now a professor at New York University, develops a fundamental criticism of debt relief. He argues that countries given debt relief during the last 20 years merely accumulated additional debt, thereby quickly returning to unsustainable debt levels and the need for further relief. He attributes this dynamic to the willingness of many developing-country governments to take on debt in order to pay for the current consumption of their standard of living and questions why irresponsible governments should get more assistance than responsible governments. Jeffrey D. Sachs, a leading advocate of debt relief, agrees with Easterly's claim that previous efforts have failed, but points to a different reason. Past debt relief has failed because creditors failed to relieve enough debt to give countries a truly fresh start. He sees similar problems in the HIPC Initiative, in particular in its reliance on what he calls arbitrary standards. For debt relief to work, he argues that it must be based on a thorough analysis of each country's individual needs, with a particular focus on how much debt reduction is required to enable each country to achieve the Millennium Development Goals.

Forgive Us Our Debts

WILLIAM EASTERLY

Haiti, a poor country, has a high foreign debt and is not growing. The ratio of foreign debt service to exports has reached 40 percent, well above the 20 to 25 percent thought to be "sustainable" (World Bank 1998a, p. 56). Unfortunately, the debt was incurred not to expand economic production capacity, but to finance the government's patronage employment and large military and police forces. Corruption has been endemic, so there is the strong suspicion that some of the proceeds of foreign loans found their way into the pockets of the rulers. This is a description of Haiti's experience in the nineties. However, the decade to which these facts refer is not the 1990s but the 1890s (Dupuy 1988, p. 116; Lundahl 1992, pp. 39, 41, 244).

The problem of poor countries with high foreign debts is not a new one. Its history stretches from the two Greek city-states that defaulted on loans from the Delos Temple in the fourth century B.C., to Mexico's default on its first foreign loan after independence in 1827, to Haiti's 1997 ratio of foreign debt to exports of 484 percent (Dommen 1989; Winkler 1933, p. 22; Wynne 1951, pp. 5–7).

But the problems of poor countries with high foreign debts are very much in the news today. Many aid advocates call for a forgiveness of all debt of poor countries on the occasion of the turning of the millennium. This campaign to forgive the debt is called Jubilee 2000. Support for Jubilee 2000 has been expressed by such diverse figures as Bono from the rock group U2, the economist Jeffrey Sachs, the Dalai Lama, and the pope. I saw a webcast of unlikely companions Bono and Sachs consulting the pope about Third World debt on September 23, 1999. In April 2000, thousands gathered on the Mall in Washington, D.C. to demonstrate for "dumping the debt." Even Hollywood has taken notice. In the recent hit movie *Notting Hill*, Hugh Grant mentions "cancellation of Third World debt" to woo Julia Roberts.

The World Bank and IMF already have a program, the HIPC (Highly [sic] Indebted Poor Countries) Initiative, to provide debt forgiveness for poor countries with good policies. This program includes, for the first time, partial forgiveness of IMF and World Bank debts. The summit of the seven largest industrial countries (the G-7) in Cologne in June 1999 called for an expansion of the HIPC program, speeding up the process of receiving relief and increasing the amount of debt relief provided for each country. The membership of the World Bank and IMF—about every country's government in the world—approved

From William Easterly, "Forgive Us Our Debts" *The Elusive Quest for Growth: Economists' Adventures and Misadventures in the Tropics*, MIT Press: Cambridge, MA, 2002, pp. 123–137.

the expansion in September 1999. The expansion will increase the total cost (in terms of today's money) of the HIPC Initiative from $12.5 billion to $27 billion.[1] So debt forgiveness is the latest panacea for relieving poverty of poor countries. As the official web site for the Jubilee 2000 campaign puts it, "Millions of people around the world are living in poverty because of Third World debt and its consequences." If only the Jubilee 2000 debt forgiveness plan goes through, "the year 2000 could signal the beginning of dramatic improvements in healthcare, education, employment and development for countries crippled by debt" (http://www.jubilee2000uk.org/main.html).

There is just one problem: the little recognition among the Jubilee 2000 campaigners, such as Bono, Sachs, the Dalai Lama, and the pope, that debt relief is not a new policy. Just as high debt is not new, efforts to forgive debtors their debts are not new. We have already been trying debt forgiveness for two decades, with little of the salutary results that are promised by Jubilee 2000.

TWO DECADES' HISTORY OF DEBT FORGIVENESS

Although there were intimations as long ago as 1967 that "debt-service payments have risen to the point at which a number of countries face critical situations," the current wave of debt relief for poor countries really got underway in 1979 (UNCTAD 1967, p. 3). The 1979 World Debt Tables of the World Bank noted "lagging debt payment" on official loans to poor countries, although "debt or debt service forgiveness has eased the problems for some." The 1977–1979 UNCTAD meetings led to official creditors' forgiving $6 billion in debt to forty-five poor countries. The measures by official creditors included "the elimination of interest payments, the rescheduling of debt service, local cost assistance, untied compensatory aid, and new grants to reimburse old debts" (World Bank 1979, pp. 7–8; UNCTAD 1983, p. 3).

The 1981 Africa report by the World Bank noted that Liberia, Sierra Leone, Sudan, Zaire, and Zambia (all of which would become HIPCs) had already experienced "severe debt-servicing difficulties" in the 1970s and "are likely to continue to do so in the 1980s." The report hinted of debt relief: "longer-term solutions for debt crises should be sought" and "the present practice of [donors'] separating aid and debt decisions may be counterproductive" (World Bank 1981, p. 129). The 1984 World Bank Africa report was more forthright, at least as forthright as bureau-speak can get: "Where monitorable programs exist, multi-year debt relief and longer grace periods should be part of the package of financial support to the program" (World Bank 1984, p. 46). The wording got even stronger in the World Bank's 1986 Africa report: low-income Africa's financing needs will "have to be filled by additional bilateral aid and debt relief" (World Bank 1986, p. 41). The World Bank noted in 1988 that "the past year has brought increasing recognition of the urgency of the debt problems of the low-income countries of Sub-Saharan Africa" (World Bank 1988a, p. xix).[2] The Bank's 1991 Africa report continued escalating the rhetoric: "Africa cannot escape its present economic crisis without reducing its debt burden sizably" (World Bank 1991a, p. 176).

THE G-7 ALL WORLD TOUR

The rich countries were responding to World Bank calls for debt forgiveness for poor countries. The June 1987 summit of the G-7 in Venice called for interest rate relief on debt of low-income countries. The G-7 agreed on a program of partial debt forgiveness that became known as the Venice terms (beginning an onslaught of technocrat-speak that would name the latest debt relief program after the site of the most recent G-7 summit). One year later, the June 1988 G-7 summit in Toronto agreed on a menu of options, including partial forgiveness, longer maturities, and lower interest rates. These became known as the Toronto terms (World Bank 1988b, p. xxxviii).

Meanwhile, in order to help African countries service their official debt, the World Bank in December 1987 initiated a Special Program of Assistance (SPA) to low-income Africa. The IMF complemented the SPA with the Enhanced Structural Adjustment Facility (ESAF). Both programs sought to provide "substantially increased, quick-disbursing, highly concessional assistance to adjusting countries" (World Bank 1989, p. 31).

The 1990 Houston G-7 summit considered "more concessional re-schedulings for the poorest debtor countries." The United Kingdom and the Netherlands proposed "Trinidad terms" that would increase the grant element of debt reduction to 67 percent, from 20 percent under the Toronto terms (World Bank 1990, p. 29). The 1991 London G-7 summit agreed "on the need for additional debt relief measures . . . going well beyond the relief already granted under Toronto terms" (World Bank 1991b, p. 31). Through November 1993, the Paris Club (the club of official lenders) applied Enhanced Toronto Terms that were even more concessional (World Bank 1993c, p. 6). In December 1994, the Paris Club announced "Naples terms" under which eligible countries would receive yet additional debt relief (World Bank 1994a, p. 42).

Then, in September 1996, the IMF and World Bank announced the HIPC Debt Initiative, which was to allow the poor countries to "exit, once and for all, from the rescheduling process" and to resume "normal relations with the international financial community, characterized by spontaneous financial flows and the full honoring of commitments." The multilateral lenders for the first time would "take action to reduce the burden of their claims on a given country," albeit conditional on good policies in the recipient countries.

The Paris Club at the same time agreed to go beyond the Naples terms and provide an 80 percent debt reduction (Boote et al. 1997, pp. 126, 129). By September 1999 and the time of the meeting of Bono, Sachs, the Dalai Lama, and the pope, debt relief packages had been agreed for seven poor countries, totaling more than $3.4 billion in debt relief in today's money (World Bank 1999, p. 76).[3] Then, there were renewed calls in 1999 for expansion of this program, an expansion that Jubilee 2000 said did not go far enough. As of October 2000, the World Bank said that twenty poor countries will receive "meaningful debt relief" by the end of the year.

Besides explicit debt relief, there also has been an implicit form of debt relief going on throughout the period, which is the substitution of concessional debt (debt with interest rates well below the market rate) for nonconcessional (market interest rate) debt. It's remarkable that the burden of debt service for HIPCs rose throughout the period despite the large net transfers of resources from concessional lenders like the International Development Association of the World Bank and the concessional arms of bilateral and other multilateral agencies.

The necessity to provide continuing waves of debt relief one after another, all the while substituting concessional for nonconcessional debt, all the while having Jubilee 2000 call for even more debt relief, all the while having Bono, Sachs, the Dalai Lama and the pope wring their hands in dismay, may suggest something is wrong with debt relief as a panacea for development. There is the paradox that a large group of countries came to be defined as highly indebted at the end of two decades of debt relief and increasingly concessional financing.

The rest of this chapter reviews possible explanations for what went wrong over the past two decades of attempted debt relief. The revealed preference of debtors for high debt may simply lead to new borrowing to replace old canceled debts. The granting of progressively more favorable terms for debt relief may also have perverse incentive effects, as countries borrow in anticipation of debt forgiveness. High debt may remain a persistent problem simply because it reflects "irresponsible governments" that remain "irresponsible" after debt relief is granted.

SELLING OFF THE FUTURE

The Jubilee 2000 debt campaigners treat debt as a natural disaster that just happened to strike poor countries. The truth may be less charitable. It may be that countries that borrowed heavily did so because they were willing to mortgage the welfare of future generations to finance this generation's (mainly the government clientele's) standard of living.

This is a hypothesis that we can test. If it is true, it has explosive implications. If "people respond to incentives," then some surprising things will happen in response to debt relief. Any debt forgiveness granted will result in new borrowing by irresponsible governments until they have mortgaged the future to the same degree as before. Debt forgiveness will be a futile panacea in that case; it will not only fail to spur development, it won't even succeed in lowering debt burdens.

There are more subtle signs of mortgaging the future that we can check to see if the "irresponsible borrowing" hypothesis holds. We can see if in addition to incurring high debt, the poor countries also sold off national assets at a disproportionately high rate, another way of expropriating future generations. Just as a profligate heir in Victorian novels turns from running up debts to selling off the family silver, we should expect to see "irresponsible governments" both incurring new debt and depleting assets.

To examine the response of new debt and assets to debt relief, I examine the forty-one HIPCs as so classified by the IMF and World Bank: Angola, Benin, Bolivia, Burkina Faso, Burundi, Cameroon, Central African Republic, Chad, Congo (Democratic Republic), Congo (Republic), Cote d'Ivoire, Equatorial Guinea, Ethiopia, Ghana, Guinea, Guinea-Bissau, Guyana, Honduras, Kenya, Laos, Liberia, Madagascar, Malawi, Mali, Mauritania, Mozambique, Myanmar, Nicaragua, Niger,

Rwanda, Sao Tome and Principe, Senegal, Sierra Leone, Somalia, Sudan, Tanzania, Togo, Uganda, Vietnam, Yemen, and Zambia.

The data on debt relief from the World Bank's World Debt Tables go back only to 1989. The relationship between debt relief and new borrowing over this period is interesting: total debt forgiveness for forty-one highly indebted poor countries from 1989 to 1997 totaled $33 billion, while their new borrowing was $41 billion. This seems to confirm the prediction that debt relief will be met with an equivalent amount of new borrowing.

New borrowing was the highest in the countries that got the most debt relief. There is a statistically significant association between average debt relief as a percentage of GDP and new net borrowing as percentage of GDP. Consistent with the mortgaging-the-future hypothesis, governments replaced forgiven debt with new debt.

Another bit of evidence that debt forgiveness did not lower debt significantly is to look at the burden of the debt over the period 1979 to 1997. Debt relief over this period should have lowered debt burdens, unless governments were replacing forgiven debt with new debt. For the burden of the debt, I use the present value of debt service as a ratio to exports. The present value of debt service is simply the amount that the government would have to have in the bank today (earning a market interest rate) to be able to meet all their future debt service. That doesn't mean that it should have such an amount in the bank; it's just an illustrative calculation that allows us to summarize in one number the whole stream of future interest and debt repayments.

I again use 1979 as a base year because it was the year the UNCTAD summit inaugurated the current wave of debt relief. I have data for twenty-eight to thirty-seven highly indebted poor countries over the period 1979 to 1997. Despite the ongoing debt relief, the typical present value debt to export ratio rose strongly from 1979 to 1997. We see three distinct periods: (1) 1979 to 1987, when debt ratios rose strongly; (2) 1988 to 1994, when debt ratios remained constant; and (3) 1995 to 1997, in which debt ratios fell. The behavior in periods 1 and 2 is consistent with failed debt relief, while the fall in the last period may indicate that the 1996 HIPC debt relief program has been more successful than earlier efforts.

Despite the fall in the last period, however, the typical debt to export ratio was significantly higher in 1997 than it was in 1979. This suggests that for the forty-one highly indebted countries, new borrowing (more than) kept pace with the amount of debt relief, as would have been predicted by the mortgaging-the-future view of how high debt came about.

I next turn to data on selling off assets, a more subtle sign of mortgaging the future. One type of asset important for some HIPCs is oil reserves. Pumping out and selling oil is a form of running down assets, since it leaves less oil in the ground for future generations. There are ten HIPCs that are oil producers, for which we have data for 1987 to 1996. Did HIPCs have higher oil production growth over this period of debt relief than did the non-HIPC oil producers? Yes. The average growth in oil production is 6.6 percentage points higher in the HIPCs than in the non-HIPCs, which is a statistically significant difference. The average log growth in oil production in HIPCs was 5.3 percent; in non-HIPCs, it was −1.3 percent.

Another form of selling off assets taking place at this time was sales of state enterprises to private foreign purchasers ("privatization"). We have data on privatization revenues for 1988 through 1997. Over this period, total sales of state enterprises in the HIPCs amounted to $4 billion. This is an underestimate, because not all privatization revenues are recorded in the official statistics. Even using these flawed data, there is a positive and significant association across the forty-one HIPCs between the amount of debt forgiveness and the amount of privatization of foreign exchange revenues. Privatization may have been done for efficiency reasons or even as a condition for debt relief, but it also may suggest a profligate government running down its assets.

The most general sign of running down assets is also the most worrisome. The per capita income of the typical HIPC declined between 1979 and 1998. This is worrisome first of all because two decades of debt relief failed to prevent negative growth in HIPCs. This is not good news for Jubilee 2000 campaigners who claim that debt relief will bring growth.

Second, the decline in income is an indirect sign of the governments' running down their economies' productive capacity. The governments' policies may have favored present consumption over future investment. The decline in income may have been an indirect sign that governments were running down public infrastructure like roads, schools, and health clinics, lowering returns to private investment, and contributing to the general depression in the HIPCs.

HIGH DEBT FROM BAD POLICY OR BAD LUCK?

Another sign of irresponsible governments that we would expect to see—in particular with high-debt countries—are high external and budget deficits. Indeed, the average levels of external deficits and budget deficits (with or without grants) between 1980 and 1997 were worse for HIPCs than for non-HIPCs, controlling for per capita income.

Nor are these the only signs of irresponsible behavior by high-debt governments. They are also more likely to follow shortsighted policies that create subsidies for favored supporters while penalizing future growth. For example, they may control interest rates below the rate of inflation, granting subsidized credits to government favorites. However, the poor depositors, seeing that inflation is eroding their deposits in real terms, will take their money out of the financial system and put it into real estate or foreign currency. This shrinks the size of the total financial sector, which is too bad since a large and healthy financial sector is one of the prerequisites for growth. Indeed, we find that HIPCs have smaller financial systems than do other economies, controlling for per capita income.

Irresponsible governments will also tend to subsidize imports to their favored clients. They can do this by keeping the exchange rate artificially low (that is, keeping their currency at an artificially high value), making imports cheap. Unfortunately, an exchange rate that keeps imports cheap will also depress the domestic currency price that exporters receive for their exports, lowering their incentive to export their products. Since exports are an important engine of growth, an artificially overvalued currency will tend to depress growth. Private investors will not invest in what would have been profitable export activities but for the misaligned exchange rate. I indeed find that HIPCs tend to have a more overvalued currency relative to non-HIPCs, controlling for income. This is another way that HIPCs mortgage the future in favor of the present: subsidizing consumption of imported goods at the cost of future growth.

But what if HIPCs suffered worse luck than other countries? Could that explain why they became highly indebted, instead of the "irresponsible governments" hypothesis? We can test this alternative hypothesis directly. One form of bad luck is to have import prices climb faster than export prices (terms of trade deterioration, in technocrat jargon). Did HIPCs see their terms of trade deteriorate more than did non-HIPCs? No.

Another form of bad luck is war. Many poor countries had war over the period in which HIPCs became HIPCs. Did HIPCs suffer from the collapse of output that often accompanies war, making their debts more burdensome? No. HIPCs were not any more likely than non-HIPCs to be at war over this period. The "irresponsible governments" hypothesis explains much more how the poor countries' high debt came about than does the "bad luck" hypothesis.

SHOWDOWN AT FINANCING GAP

So far I have been looking at irresponsible behavior from the viewpoint of the borrower. However, someone had to be willing to lend to these irresponsible borrowers. Was there irresponsible lending as well as irresponsible borrowing? I think you can guess the answer.

Let us examine the composition of financing the irresponsibly high external deficits in HIPCs. There are some intriguing patterns First, HIPCs received less foreign direct investment (FDI) than other less developed countries (LDCs), controlling for income. This may be an indirect indicator of the bad policies found on the other indicators: investors don't want to invest in an economy with high budget deficits and high overvaluation. Investors may also have worried what debt relief may have meant for other external liabilities like the stock of direct foreign investment.

Second, despite their poor policies, HIPCs received more in World Bank and IMF financing than other LDCs. The result on World Bank financing is controlling for initial income (negatively related to World Bank financing). The additional amount of World Bank financing for HIPCs (0.96 percent of GDP) is small relative to the size of the current account deficit but large relative to the average amount of World Bank financing in all LDCs (1.1 percent of GDP). The share of World Bank financing in new external loans also was significantly higher (by 7.2 percentage points) in HIPCs than in non-HIPCs.

The results are similar for the IMF. The IMF did lend more to HIPCs than to non-HIPCs, controlling for initial income. Like the World Bank HIPC effect, the effect is small relative to current account deficits (0.73 percent of GDP) but large relative to the non-HIPCs' average IMF financing (0.5 percent of GDP). The HIPC effect for the IMF's share of new external loans is of the same sign and significant: the IMF had 4.4 percentage points higher share of new external loans to HIPCs than to non-HIPCs, controlling for income. The HIPCs got to be HIPCs in part by borrowing from the World Bank and IMF.

Third, the results are similar examining the trends in composition of new lending to HIPCs over 1979 to 1997. Private credit disappears and multilateral financing assumes an increased share. World Bank low-interest-rate loans, termed International Development Association (IDA) loans, alone more than tripled their share in new lending. The share of private credit in new lending began the period 3.6 times higher than the IDA share; by the end of the period, the share of IDA was 8.6 times higher than that of private financing.

Fourth, we can examine the net flow of resources to the HIPCs, that is, the new loans minus debt repayments and interest. During the period in which the debt burden increased (1979–1987), the bulk of the net transfer of resources was from concessional sources (IDA) other multilaterals, and the bilateral donors like USAID, although there were also positive transfers of resources from private lenders. Concessional sources made total net transfers to the HIPCs of $33 billion. This huge concessional transfer makes it all the more striking that these countries became increasingly indebted in net present value terms over this period.

There was then a huge shift in net transfers from 1979–1987 to 1988–1997, a period in which debt ratios stabilized. Large positive net transfers from IDA and bilateral donors offset negative net transfers for IBRD (nonconcessional World Bank loans), bilateral non-concessional, and private sources. This was another form of debt relief, since it exchanged low-interest-rate, long-maturity debt—debt that has a large grant element—for nonconcessional debt. However, remarkably, the net present value of debt remained roughly unchanged over this period, at least until the past few years. IDA and bilateral donors were bailing out all the nonconcessional lenders, piling on new debt fast enough that the debt burden remained constant even though the nonconcessional lenders were getting their money out.

The bottom line is that the debt burden of the poor countries came about because of lending by the IMF, World Bank (IDA), and bilateral donors, in the face of withdrawal by private and nonconcessional lenders. How did this happen?

The lending methodology of the donor community (the IMF, the World Bank, and the bilateral donors) encouraged granting of new loans to irresponsible governments, a methodology known as filling the financing gap. . . . Here the financing gap is defined as the gap between the "financing requirement" in the external balance of payments and the available private financing. The financing requirement is equal to the sum of the trade deficit, the interest payment on the old debt, and the repayment of maturing old debt. "Filling the financing gap" implies giving more concessional aid to countries with higher trade deficits, higher current debt, and lower private lending. This perversely rewards the "irresponsible governments," whose policies scare away private lenders and lead to higher trade deficits and higher debt. Filling the financing gap pours good money after bad, creating an official debt spiral in which the inability of countries to service their existing debt is the reason that they are granted new official loans.

Then in the ultimate folly, the donor community calculates the amount of "necessary" debt relief to "close the financing gap." The reward for having a large financing gap is to have the debt wiped off the books, erasing the memory of irresponsible behavior of both borrowers and lenders.

By 1997, with the coming of the new multilateral debt relief initiative, HIPCs received 63 percent of the flow of resources devoted to poor countries despite accounting for only 32 percent of the population of those countries.

THE CURIOUS CASE OF COTE D'IVOIRE

Including debt reduction as aid, Cote d'Ivoire received 1,276 times more per capita aid net flow than India in 1997. It would be interesting to explain to the poor in India why Cote d'Ivoire, whose government has twice created lavish new national capitals in the hometowns of successive leaders, should receive over a thousand times more aid per capita than they do.

This explanation grows all the more difficult when we examine how Cote d'Ivoire got into trouble. From 1979 to 1997, it ran a deficit on the current account of the balance of payments that averaged over 8 percent of GDP. That is, on average, it spent more on imports and interest on debt than it received on exports, by 8 percent of GDP. The most likely suspect for this excess spending is the government, which ran a budget deficit over this period of over 10 percent of GDP.

How did this big government budget deficit come about? The government benefited from a rise in international coffee and cocoa prices in the 1970s, since it required all domestic coffee and cocoa producers to deliver their products to its "marketing board" at a fixed price. This "marketing board" price to producers did not increase with international prices, leading to a huge windfall for the government, which was buying low and selling high. (Between 1976 and 1980, cocoa farmers got only 60 percent and coffee producers only 50 percent of the world price. [World Bank 1988c, vol. 2, p. 78].) The government used these extra revenues to go on a spending spree that continued even after the windfall revenues from cocoa and coffee vanished as international cocoa and coffee prices dropped sharply in 1979 (Chamley and Ghanem, 1994). With unchanged spending and sharply diminished revenue, the Ivorian government began to run large budget deficits.

The government's excess spending on such things as new national capitals caused domestic inflation to be faster than foreign inflation, which caused the currency to appreciate in real terms since the exchange rate was fixed. The average overvaluation of the currency over this period was 75 percent, which made for cheap imports for consumers but strong disincentives for exporters—reinforcing the large external deficit. The profligate government caused the burden of the external debt to double over this period, from 60 percent of GDP in 1979 to 127 percent of GDP in 1994, when debt forgiveness began.

We can tell that the loans were not used for anything very productive, because the income of the average Ivorian fell in half between 1979 and 1994. Ivorians in poverty—in whose name the loans would be made and the loans forgiven—rose from 11 percent of the population in 1985 (the earliest date for which we have data) to 37 percent in 1995 (International Monetary Fund 1998, p. 29). There was some output recovery after the currency was devalued, in 1994, but it was a long road back after the steep economic decline.

And who was doing the lending to Cote d'Ivoire over the period of irresponsible policies in which its debt burden doubled? As a 1988 World Bank report put it, "On the questionable assumption that sufficient foreign financing could be secured, the ratio of public foreign debt to GDP would rise to around 130 percent by 1995" (World Bank 1988c, vol 1). Note how close this prediction is to the actual outcome, so the "questionable" financing was indeed found. On average, the World Bank and IMF accounted for 58 percent of new lending to Cote d'Ivoire between 1979 and 1997. The IMF alone made eight adjustment loans to the Ivorian government over this period, and the World Bank made twelve adjustment loans. The share of the World Bank and IMF trended up over time from 10 percent in 1979 to 76 percent in 1997.

Within the World Bank lending to Cote d'Ivoire, there was an important shift away from nonconcessional lending (known as IBRD lending) to concessional lending (known as IDA lending). One of the perverse incentives in the foreign assistance business is that the more irresponsible governments become eligible for more favorable lending terms.

Most of the rest of the lending was from rich country governments, with a key role for France (whose government must also bear some of the blame for postponing Cote d'Ivoire's necessary devaluation). Meanwhile, private foreign loans plummeted from 75 percent of all new lending in 1979 to near zero from 1989 on. The private lenders did indeed consider lending to Cote d'Ivoire questionable by the time of the 1988 World Bank report. The official lenders did not have the same common sense as private ones.

So it was only fitting that in March 1998, the World Bank and IMF announced a new debt forgiveness program for Cote d'Ivoire that forgave some of their own past loans. The debt forgiveness was subject to Cote d'Ivoire's fulfilling a few conditions like reining in its budget deficit and cleaning up its act on cocoa and coffee pricing. The IMF gave a new three-year loan to Cote d'Ivoire in March 1998, again subject to these conditions. World Bank lending continued as well, with about $600 million in new loan commitments in 1999 (http://www. worldbank.org/afr/ci2htm).

For awhile, the Ivorian government met key conditions. Then things began to go wrong. The IMF noted in July 1999, "Performance under the 1998 program was mixed, and there were some difficulties in its implementation" (International Monetary Fund 1999). The currency was still overvalued by 35 percent in 1998. In 1998, Cote d'Ivoire was rated as being in the most corrupt third of countries in the world. The European Union suspended aid to Cote d'Ivoire in 1999 after its previous aid was embezzled. The embezzlement was so imaginative as to perform "vast over-billing of basic medical equipment purchased, such as a stethoscope costing about $15 billed at $318, and $2,445 for a baby scale costing about $40" (Economist Intelligence Unit 1999). The IMF suspended disbursements of its program in 1999. The army finally put the latest corrupt government out of its misery with a coup just before Christmas 1999.

CONCLUSION

We should do everything in our power to improve the lives of the poor, in both high-debt and low-debt nations. It seems to make sense that high debt could be diverting resources away from health and education spending that benefits the poor. Those who tell us to forgive the debt are on the side of the angels, or at least on the side of Bono, Sachs, the Dalai Lama, and the pope. Our heart tells us to forgive debts to help the poor.

Alas, the head contradicts the heart. Debt forgiveness grants aid to those recipients that have best proven their ability to misuse that aid. Debt relief is futile for countries with unchanged government behavior. The same mismanagement of funds that caused the high debt will prevent the aid sent through debt relief from reaching the truly poor.

A debt relief program could make sense if it meets two conditions: (1) it is granted where there has been a proven change from an irresponsible government to a government with good policies; (2) it is a once-for-all measure that will never be repeated. Let's look at the case for these two conditions.

It could be that the high debt is inherited from a bad government by a good government that truly will try to help the poor. We could see wiping out the debt in this case. This tells us that only governments that display a fundamental shift in their behavior should be eligible for debt relief. To assess whether countries have made such a fundamental shift, the international community should see a long and convincing record of good behavior prior to granting debt relief. There were important steps in this direction in the 1996 HIPC initiative, which unfortunately may have been weakened by subsequent proposals such as the 2000 World Bank IMF annual meetings proposals that speeded up the process of debt relief and made more countries eligible.

In the absence of a change in government behavior, official lenders should not keep filling the financing gap. The concept of financing gap should be abolished, now and for all time, since it has created perverse incentives to keep borrowing. Although loans are made and loans are forgiven all in the name of the poor, the poor are not helped if the international community creates incentives simply to borrow more.

To avoid the incentive to borrow more, the debt relief program has to attempt to establish a credible policy that debt forgiveness will never again be offered in the future. If this is problematic, then the whole idea of debt relief is problematic. Governments will have too strong an incentive to keep borrowing in the expectation that their debt will be forgiven.

A debt relief program that fails either of these two conditions results in more resources going to countries with bad policies than poor countries with good policies. Why should the HIPCs receive four times the aid per capita of less indebted poor countries, as happened in 1997? If there is any expectation that donors will continue to favor the irresponsible governments in the future, then debt relief will run afoul of peoples' (governments') response to incentives. Debt forgiveness will then be one more disappointing elixir on the quest for growth.

REFERENCES

Boote, Anthony, Fred Kilby, Kamau Thugge, and Axel Van Trotsenburg. 1997. "Debt Relief for Low-Income Countries and the HIPC Initiative," in Z. Iqbal and R. Kanbur, eds., *External Finance for Low-Income Countries*. Washington, D.C.: International Monetary Fund.

Brooks, Ray, Mariano Cortes, Francesca Fornasari, Benoit Ketchekmen, Ydahlia Metzgen, Robert Powell, Saqib Rizavi, Doris Ross, and Kevin Ross. 1998. "External Debt Histories of Ten Low-Income Developing Countries: Lessons From their Experience." IMF Working Paper WP/98/72.

Chamley, Christophe and Hafez Ghanem. 1994. "Cote d'Ivoire: Fiscal Policy with Fixed Nominal Exchange Rates." In W. Easterly, C. Rodriguez, and K. Schmidt-Hebbel, eds., *Public Sector Deficits and Macroeconomic Performance*. Oxford: Oxford University Press.

Dommen, Edward. 1989. "Ligthening the Debt Burden: Some Sidelights from History," *UNCTAD Review* 1, no. 1: 75–82.

Dupuy, Alex. 1988. *Haiti in the World Economy: Class, Race, and Underdevelopment Since 1700*. Boulder, Colo: Westview Press.

Economist Intelligence Unit. 1999. Cote d'Ivoire Country Report, Fourth Quarter.

Greene, Joshua. 1989. "The External Debt Problem of Sub-Saharan Africa," *IMF Staff Papers* 36 (December): 836–874.

Humphreys, Charles and John Underwood. 1989. "The External Debt Difficulties of Low-Income Africa." In Ishrat Husain and Ishac Diwan, eds., *Dealing with the Debt Crisis*. Washington, D.C.: World Bank.

Husain, Ishrat, and John Underwood, eds. 1991. *African External Finance in the 1990s*. Washington, D.C.: World Bank.

International Monetary Fund. 1998. *Cote d'Ivoire: Selected Issues and Statistical Appendix*. IMF Staff Country Report No. 98/46. Washington, D.C.

International Monetary Fund. 1999. "IMF Concludes Article IV Consultation with Cote d'Ivoire." Public Information Notice 99/63, July 16.

Iqbal, Z. and R. Kanbur, eds. 1997. *External Finance for Low-Income Countries*. Washington, D.C.: International Monetary Fund.

Lancaster, Carol and John Williamson, eds. 1986. *African Debt and Financing*. Washington, D.C.: Institute for International Economics.

Lundahl, Mats. 1992. *Politics or Markets: Essays on Haitian Underdevelopment*. London: Routledge.

Mistry, Percy S. 1988. *African Debt: The Case for Relief for Sub-Saharan Africa*. Oxford: Oxford International Associates.

Nafziger, E. Wayne. 1993. *The Debt Crisis in Africa*. Baltimore: Johns Hopkins University Press.

Parfitt, Trevor W. and Stephen P. Riley. 1989. *The African Debt Crisis*. London: Routledge.

United Nations Conference on Trade and Development. 1967. *The Terms, Quality, and Effectiveness of Financial Flows and Problems of Debt Servicing*. Report TD/B/C.3/35, February 2.

United Nations Conference on Trade and Development. 1983. *Review of Arrangements Concerning Debt Problems of Developing Countries Pursuant to Board Resolution 222 (XXI)*, Paragraph 15. Report TD/B/945, March 23.

Winkler, Max. 1933. *Foreign Bonds: an Autopsy*. Philadelphia: Roland Swain Company.

World Bank. 1979. *World Debt Tables 1979*. Washington, D.C.

World Bank. 1981. *Accelerated Development in Sub-Saharan Africa: An Agenda for Action*. Washington, D.C.

World Bank. 1984. *Toward Sustained Development in Sub-Saharan Africa: A Joint Program of Action*. Washington, D.C.

World Bank. 1986. *Financing Adjustment with Growth in Sub-Saharan Africa, 1986–90*. Washington, D.C.

World Bank. 1988a. *World Debt Tables 1987–88*, Vol. 1. Washington, D.C.

World Bank. 1988b. *World Debt Tables 1988–89*, Vol. 1. Washington, D.C.

World Bank. 1988c. *Cote d'Ivoire: Mobilizing Domestic Resources for Stable Growth*. Report 7372-RCI, vols. 1 and 2. Washington, D.C.

World Bank. 1989. *World Debt Tables 1989–90*, Vol. 1. Washington, D.C.

World Bank. 1990. *World Debt Tables 1990–91*, Vol. 1. Washington, D.C.

World Bank. 1991a. *Sub-Saharan Africa: From Crisis to Sustainable Growth*. Washington, D.C.

World Bank. 1991b. *World Debt Tables 1991–92*, Vol. 1. Washington, D.C.

World Bank. 1993c. *World Debt Tables 1993–94*, Vol. 1. Washington, D.C.

World Bank. 1994a. *World Debt Tables 1994–95*, Vol. 1. Washington, D.C.

World Bank. 1998a. *Global Development Finance 1998*, Vol 1. Washington, D.C.

World Bank. 1999. *Global Development Finance 1999*, Vol 1. Washington, D.C

Wynne, William H. 1951. *State Insolvency and Foreign Bondholders: Selected Case Histories of Government Foreign Bond Defaults and Debt Readjustments*. New Haven: St. Martin's Press.

ENDNOTES

1. *International Herald Tribune*, June 14 1999, p.1; *Financial Times*, June 21 1999. p. 2. See the World Bank website on the HIPC Initiative: www.worldbank.org/hipc

2. The general literature started noticing low-income African debt at about the same time. See Lancaster and Williamson 1986; Mistry 1988; Greene 1989; Parfitt and Riley 1989; Humphreys and Underwood 1989; Husain and Underwood 1991; Nafziger 1993. For more recent compilations of analysis, see Iqbal and Kanbur 1997; Brooks et al. 1998.

3. [See also] the web site www.worldbank.org/hipc. The seven countries are Bolivia, Burkina Faso, Cote d'Ivoire, Guyana, Mali, Mauritania, Mozambique, and Uganda. According to the [World] Bank's web site, "Ethiopia, Guinea-Bissau, Nicaragua, Mauritania, and Tanzania have completed a preliminary review and could qualify for billions more in debt relief."

Resolving the Debt Crisis of Low-Income Countries

JEFFREY D. SACHS

The idea of bankruptcy for insolvent sovereign borrowers has been around a long time, at least since Adam Smith's favorable mention of it in the *Wealth of Nations*.[1] Kenneth Rogoff and Jeromin Zettlemeyer have recently reviewed the history of the idea, as has Ann Pettifor.[2] The current international framework for workouts of distressed sovereign borrowers is woefully inadequate, lacking both the efficiency and the equity protections that characterize well-designed bankruptcy systems. This paper focuses on one part of the problem, namely, the plight of the world's most highly indebted poor countries, and illustrates the serious problems that have arisen because of the weakness of international institutional arrangements. I conclude with several recommendations for reform.

MOTIVATIONS FOR BANKRUPTCY LAWS

Bankruptcy laws have two somewhat distinct motivations. The first is to overcome the collective action problems that arise when multiple creditors confront an insolvent debtor.[3] In the absence of a bankruptcy law, a creditor "grab race" can undermine the value of the assets of an insolvent debtor. The bankruptcy law forestalls the grab race through devices such as the automatic stay on debt collection that is triggered by the filing of a bankruptcy petition. In bankruptcy reorganizations under Chapter 11 of the U.S. bankruptcy code, further protections against a grab race are implemented, such as debtor-in-possession financing and provisions for confirmation of a restructuring plan in the absence of unanimity among creditors; the latter weaken the power of an individual creditor to hold out for special treatment.

The second motivation of bankruptcy law is to offer a "fresh start" to an insolvent debtor. Whereas the motivation to avoid a grab race applies in principle to all kinds of insolvent debtors—businesses, individuals, and municipalities—the motivation for a fresh start applies only to individuals (Chapters 7, 12, and 13) and municipalities (Chapter 9) rather than to businesses.[4] The key instrumentality of the fresh start is the discharge of debt, which frees the debtor from future collection efforts while leaving the debtor with some exempt assets and with a future

From Jeffrey D. Sachs, "Resolving the Debt Crisis of Low-Income Countries," *Brookings Papers on Economic Activity* 1, 2002, pp. 1–28. Reprinted by permission of The Brookings Institute.

income stream. An insolvent debtor may seek the discharge of debt even when there is only one creditor, and thus no possibility of a creditor grab race.

The motivation for forestalling a creditor grab race is efficiency. The motivations for offering a fresh start, however, include both efficiency and equity. The creditors' claims are superseded by the higher interest of protecting the autonomy of the individual vis-à-vis the creditors,[5] and analogously, of ensuring that a debt-strapped municipality maintains the sovereignty needed to provide public services to its residents. For example, under Chapter 9, a municipality's assets cannot be liquidated to pay creditors, because that would undermine sovereignty. Moreover, "[n]either creditors nor the court may control the affairs of a municipality indirectly through the mechanism of proposing a plan of adjustment of the municipality's debts that would in effect determine the municipality's future tax and spending decisions."[6] Indeed, the powers of the court and of creditors are deeply circumscribed. "[T]he debtor's day to day activities are not subject to court approval," and "the debtor may borrow money without court authority. . . . The court also cannot interfere with the operations of the debtor or with the debtor's use of its property and revenues."[7] Most important, neither under individual bankruptcy (Chapter 7 or Chapter 13) nor under municipal bankruptcy (Chapter 9) do creditors obtain the maximum discounted value of income and property potentially collectable from the debtor. Individuals and municipalities are allowed to keep important property out of the creditors' reach, such as a homestead up to a certain value, as well as keep most or all future income.[8]

The idea of the fresh start can be framed variously in terms of ethics (preserving the autonomy of the individual or the sovereign), equity (preserving an acceptable standard of living for an insolvent debtor), or ex ante efficiency (bankruptcy mechanisms as a way to spread risks between a debtor and world financial markets when other risk-spreading mechanisms such as contingent contracts are incomplete). In any case, the debtor is not reduced to destitution and permanent servitude to creditors. The borrowing costs to a debtor rise in anticipation of the possibility of bankruptcy, but the downside risks of extreme adverse shocks are thereby limited.

INTERNATIONAL SOVEREIGN BORROWERS

For hundreds of years, sovereign borrowers have experienced repayment crises, including defaults and restructuring of debts.[9] Despite the repeated experience of sovereign debt crises, and despite the important efficiency and equity issues they pose, no international system of sovereign bankruptcy has been devised. In the age of imperialism in the nineteenth and early twentieth centuries, creditors often resorted to force or the threat of force to collect debts, including the removal of insolvent sovereigns from power. Since the Great Depression, however, sovereign debt crises have generally been worked out in negotiations between creditors and debtors, often with the heavy political engagement of major creditor powers or international institutions such as the International Monetary Fund (IMF), where creditors predominate. These negotiations have been characterized by a high degree of ad hockery and a low degree of systematization of international rules.

This ad hockery has come at a very high cost. Insolvent countries have often been locked into decades of instability and impoverishment. There is certainly no guarantee of a fresh start. The creditor grab race has often undermined economic stability in debtor countries, to the detriment of both creditors and debtors. Debtor nations complain bitterly about the loss of sovereignty to creditor-led institutions, especially the IMF and the World Bank. And ad hoc bailouts of private creditors by official lenders—for example, through IMF loans to debtor governments to maintain debt servicing to private lenders in the creditor countries—have been widely seen as creating moral hazard, encouraging future indiscriminate lending by creditors to weak borrowers on the basis of expected future bailouts.

The absence of a fresh start for sovereign debtors can have a particularly pernicious effect on economic and social development. In a country whose government is insolvent, but that has not been released from extremely onerous debt servicing, the provision of public goods is likely to be severely curtailed. Macroeconomic stability and even public order (in the case that services such as health, police, and fire services are limited) can easily be lost. Prolonged political uncertainty and instability may result, as the sovereign power has limited means to defend itself against internal insurgencies and external military threats.

The IMF's recent recognition of the need for more-formal processes is without doubt a breakthrough in and of itself, as well as a major spur for new ideas in this area.[10] Any specific bankruptcy proposals launched in response to the IMF initiative should recognize the two intertwined motivations of bankruptcy: addressing the collective action problems and gaining a fresh start. For the world's middle-income countries, with multiple classes of creditors including important private sector creditors (banks, bondholders, suppliers), the collective action problems probably loom largest and are the most complex.[11] For the low-income countries, the issue of a fresh start—suitably interpreted—is probably even more important. Dozens of low-income countries have been stuck for two decades or more in a persistent debt trap from which they are not recovering. For these countries, bankruptcy procedures will have to be considered in the much larger context of the overall foreign assistance strategy of the creditor-debtor community.

✵ ✵ ✵

POVERTY TRAPS AND THE DEBT OVERHANG

One key hypothesis of this paper is that poor countries are vulnerable to a poverty trap, which can be caused or exacerbated by an excessive foreign debt burden. The basic idea of a poverty trap is that nonlinearities in saving, investment, and production can lead some low-income countries to remain stuck at low or even falling levels of GNP per capita, despite the forces of economic convergence that are also at play in the world economy, such as the potential for capital inflows into capital-scarce countries and the diffusion of technology from rich to poor countries.

✵ ✵ ✵

What kinds of economies are likely to find themselves in a poverty trap? First—and for present purposes critical—poor countries with a heavy inherited debt burden are likely to be in the zone of negative growth. Second, and very important, economies with intrinsically low productivity . . . are especially vulnerable. Low-productivity economies include geographically isolated regions (such as landlocked states and countries with a small internal market, especially those that are remote from larger markets) and regions with adverse ecologies (such as tropical rainforests and regions with high rates of malaria transmission, fragile soils, or water stress). Third, economies with low initial levels of reproducible capital, . . . perhaps the result of previous war or natural disaster, are obviously vulnerable. Fourth, countries with very high fertility rates, for cultural reasons or in response to high infant and child mortality rates, are especially vulnerable as well.

Not all very poor countries fall into a poverty trap. Indeed, countervailing forces, the most important of which are inflows of technology and capital from the rich countries, can promote very high growth rates in poor settings. In particular, if a poor country has an adequate mix of favorable geography (good ports, proximity to major markets), physical ecology (fertile soils, plentiful rainfall, absence of tropical diseases), little inherited debt, large internal markets (to spur domestic and foreign investment aimed at the home market), and good governance (to promote private sector investment and provide essential public services), the prospects for rapid growth are likely to be high and the risk of a poverty trap is likely to be remote.

THE DEBT OVERHANG AND THE POVERTY TRAP IN LOW-INCOME COUNTRIES

The rich creditor governments that "own and operate" the principal international financial institutions—such as the IMF, the World Bank, and the Paris Club—have failed to acknowledge the pervasive risks of poverty traps for very low-income countries. During the late 1970s and early 1980s, several dozen developing countries, including a large number of very poor countries, fell into serious sovereign debt crises. And although debt service burdens were rising, inflation-adjusted foreign assistance per capita in the recipient countries was declining. The squeeze of rising debt burdens and falling aid levels threw a large number of poor countries into persistent stagnation or economic decline. For roughly twenty years the standard interpretation of this phenomenon was that the countries needed yet more "structural adjustment" rather than debt relief or increased foreign assistance.

As debt burdens became more and more untenable, and as sustained growth in dozens of low-income countries proved elusive, the official creditors wrote off increasingly large portions of the debts owed them. But throughout the process, creditors failed to put sufficient political will or serious analysis into the debt reduction operations. Debt reduction targets were set and reset arbitrarily—writing off 30 percent, then 50 percent, and so on—rather than based on serious assessments of the needs of each country. To examine the debt restructuring process more formally, Table 1 lists those countries that required Paris Club restructurings during the period from 1975 to 1996. For these purposes I exclude the transition economies,

TABLE 1 ■ DATES OF RESTRUCTURINGS AND IMF PROGRAMS, AND ECONOMIC OUTCOMES IN COUNTRIES THAT RESCHEDULED PARIS CLUB DEBT[a] (UNITS AS INDICATED)

Country	Year of First post-1975 Paris Club restructuring	Follow-up Paris Club restructurings	Years under IMF lending program	Recovery Status	Average growth of GNP per capita[b] (percent a year)	
					1975–99	1990–99
Algeria	1994	1995	1994–98	Remission	−0.4	−0.5
Angola	1989	HIPC eligible[c]		Chronic Crisis	−2.1	−2.8
Argentina	1985	1987, 1989, 1991, 1992	1983–2001	Remission	0.3	3.6
Benin	1989	1991, 1993, 1996, 2000 HIPC eligible	1989–2001	Chronic Crisis	0.4	1.8
Bolivia	1986	1988, 1990, 1992, 1995(x2), 1998,2001 HIPC eligible	1986–2001	Chronic Crisis	−0.6	0.8
Brazil	1983	1987, 1988, 1992	1983–86, 1988–90, 1992–93, 1998–2001	Remission	0.8	1.5
Burkina Faso	1991	1993, 1996, 2000 HIPC eligible	1991–2001	Chronic Crisis	1.0	1.4
Cambodia	1995		1994–97, 1999–2001	Remission	1.9	1.9
Cameroon	1989	1992, 1994, 1995, 1997, 2001 HIPC eligible	1988–90, 1992, 1994–2001	Chronic Crisis	−0.6	−1.5

(continued)

TABLE 1 ■ CONTINUED

Country	Year of First post-1975 Paris Club restructuring	Follow-up Paris Club restructurings	Years under IMF lending program	Recovery Status	Average growth of GNP per capita[b] (percent a year)	
					1975–99	1990–99
Central African Rep.	1981	1983, 1985, 1988, 1990, 1994, 1998	1981, 1983–90, 1994–95, 1998–2001	Chronic Crisis	−1.6	−0.3
Chad	1989	HIPC eligible 1995, 1996, 2001	1987–90, 1994–2001	Chronic Crisis	0.0	−0.9
Chile	1985	HIPC eligible 1987	1983–90	Cured	4.1	5.6
Congo (Brazzaville)	1986	1990, 1994, 1996	1986–88, 1990–92, 1994–99	Chronic Crisis	0.3	−3.3
Congo (Kinshasa)	1976	HIPC eligible 1977, 1979, 1981, 1983, 1985, 1986, 1987, 1989	1978–82, 1984–90	Chronic Crisis	−4.7	−8.1
Costa Rica	1983	HIPC eligible 1985, 1989, 1991, 1993	1980–83, 1985–97	Cured	1.1	3.0
Cote d'Ivoire	1984	1985, 1986, 1987, 1989, 1991, 1994, 1998	1981–92, 1994–2001	Chronic Crisis	−2.1	0.6
Dominican Rep.	1985	HIPC eligible 1991	1983–86, 1991–94	Cured	1.4	3.9

Ecuador	1983	1985, 1988, 1989, 1992, 1994, 2000	1983–92, 1994–95, 2000–01	Chronic Crisis	0.3	0.0
Egypt	1987		1991–98	Remission	2.9	2.4
El Salvador	1990		1990–2000	Remission	−0.2	2.8
Equatorial Guinea	1985	1989, 1992, 1994	1993–96	Cured	8.4	16.3
Ethiopia	1992	1997, 2001 HIPC eligible	1992–99, 2001	Chronic Crisis	−0.3	2.4
Gabon	1987	1988, 1989, 1991, 1994, 1995, 2000	1987–2001	Chronic Crisis	−1.7	0.6
Gambia	1986	HIPC eligible	1988–91, 1998–2001	Chronic Crisis	−0.3	−0.6
Ghana	1996	2001 HIPC eligible	1983–92, 1995–2001	Chronic Crisis	0.0	1.6
Guatemala	1993		1993–94	Cured	0.0	1.5
Guinea	1986	1989, 1992, 1995, 1997, 2001 HIPC eligible	1982–83, 1986–2000	Chronic Crisis	1.4	1.5
Guinea-Bissau	1987	1989, 1995, 2001	1995–98, 2000–01	Chronic Crisis	0.3	−1.9
Haiti	1995	n.a. HIPC eligible	1995–99	Remission	−1.8	−1.2
Honduras	1990	1992, 1996, 1999	1990–97, 1999–2001	Chronic Crisis	0.1	0.3
Jamaica	1984	1985, 1987, 1988, 1990, 1991, 1993	1978–96	Cured	0.1	−0.6
Jordan	1989	1992, 1994, 1997, 1999	1989–90, 1992–2001	Chronic Crisis	0.4	1.1
Kenya	1994	2000	1988–94, 1996–2001	Chronic Crisis	0.4	−0.3
Liberia	1980	1981, 1983, 1984 HIPC eligible	1979–85	Chronic Crisis	n.a.	n.a.

(continued)

TABLE 1 ■ CONTINUED

Country	Year of First post-1975 Paris Club restructuring	Follow-up Paris Club restructurings	Years under IMF lending program	Recovery Status	Average growth of GNP per capita[b] (percent a year)	
					1975–99	1990–99
Madagascar	1981	1982, 1984, 1985, 1986, 1988, 1990, 1997, 2000, 2001 HIPC eligible	1980–92, 1996–2001	Chronic Crisis	−1.8	−1.2
Malawi	1982	1983, 1988, 2001 HIPC eligible	1979–86, 1988–99, 2001	Chronic Crisis	−0.2	0.9
Mali	1988	1989, 1992, 1996, 2000 HIPC eligible	1982–2001	Chronic Crisis	−0.7	1.1
Mauritania	1985	1986, 1987, 1989, 1993, 1995, 2000 HIPC eligible	1985–2001	Chronic Crisis	−0.2	1.3
Mexico	1983	1986, 1989	1983–93, 1995–97, 1999–2000	Remission	0.8	1.0
Morocco	1983	1985, 1987, 1988, 1990, 1992	1980–93	Cured	1.4	0.4
Mozambique	1984	1987, 1990, 1993, 1996, 1997, 1999, 2000 HIPC eligible	1987–2001	Chronic Crisis	1.3	3.8
Nicaragua	1991	1995, 1998 HIPC eligible	1991–2001	Chronic Crisis	−3.8	0.4

Country					
Niger	1983	1984, 1985, 1986, 1988 (2x), 1990, 1994, 1996, 2001 HIPC eligible	1983–91, 1994–99, 2001	Chronic Crisis	−2.2	−1.0
Nigeria	1986	1989, 1991, 2000	1987–92, 2000–01	Chronic Crisis	−0.8	−0.5
Pakistan	1981	1999, 2001, 2001	1980–83, 1989–91, 1993–2001	Chronic Crisis	2.9	1.3
Panama	1985	1990	1978–87, 1992–2001	Remission	0.7	2.4
Peru	1978	1983, 1984, 1991, 1993, 1996	1979–80, 1982–85, 1993–2001	Remission	−0.8	3.2
Philippines	1984	1987, 1989, 1991, 1994	1978–81, 1983–2000	Remission	0.1	0.9
Senegal	1981	1982, 1983, 1985, 1986, 1987, 1989, 1990, 1991, 1994, 1995, 1998, 2000 HIPC eligible	1979–92, 1994–2001	Chronic Crisis	−0.3	0.6
Sierra Leone	1977	1980, 1984, 1986, 1992, 1994, 1996 HIPC eligible	1978–82, 1984–89, 1994–98	Chronic Crisis	−2.5	−7.0
Somalia	1985	1987 HIPC eligible	1985–90	Chronic Crisis	n.a.	n.a.
Sudan	1979	1982, 1983, 1984 HIPC eligible	1979–85	Chronic Crisis	n.a.	n.a.
Tanzania	1986	1988, 1990, 1992, 1997, 2000, 2002 HIPC eligible	1980–82, 1986–94, 1996–2001	Chronic Crisis	n.a.	−0.1

(continued)

TABLE 1 ■ CONTINUED

Country	Year of First post-1975 Paris Club restructuring	Follow-up Paris Club restructurings	Years under IMF lending program	Recovery Status	Average growth of GNP per capita[b] (percent a year)	
					1975–99	1990–99
Togo	1979	1981, 1983, 1984, 1985, 1988, 1989, 1990, 1992, 1995 HIPC eligible	1979–98	Chronic Crisis	−1.3	−0.5
Trinidad and Tobago	1989	1990	1989–91	Cured	0.4	2.0
Turkey	1978	1979, 1980	1978–85, 1994–96, 1999–2001	Remission	2.1	2.2
Uganda	1981	1982, 1987, 1989, 1992, 1995, 1998, 2000 HIPC eligible	1980–84, 1987–2001	Chronic Crisis	2.5[d]	4.0
Yemen	1996	1997, 2001	1996–2001	Chronic Crisis	n.a.	−0.4
Zambia	1983	1984, 1986, 1990, 1992, 1996, 1999 HIPC eligible	1978–87, 1995–2001	Chronic Crisis	−2.4	−2.4

Source: World Wide Web site of the Paris Club (www.clubdeparis.org); Muntaz Hussein, IMF; IMF, *Annual Report,* various years; IMF, *Debt Relief for Poverty Reduction: The Role of the Enhanced HIPC Initiative,* 2001; United Nations Development Programme (2002).

a. Includes all developing countries that rescheduled debt with the Paris Club on at least one occasion during 1975–96, but excludes counties with 1980 population less than 1 million; former socialist economies in Eastern Europe, the former Soviet Union, and other economies that were closely tied with the Soviet Union; and countries that were not sovereign as of January 1, 1980.

b. In dollars at purchasing power parity.

c. Classified as a HIPC but expected to achieve debt sustainability after receiving debt relief under traditional mechanisms.

d. Data for [19XX–XX].

because the debt and restructuring problems of Eastern Europe, the former Soviet Union, and other economies once closely linked to the Soviet Union pose special issues. I also exclude very small economies . . . and countries that were not sovereign as of January 1, 1980. Fifty-nine developing countries in the included group rescheduled their debts in the Paris Club during this period; only thirty-one did not, of which eight were oil-exporting states.

For all Paris Club reschedulers during 1975–96, the countries are classified according to the outcome of the debt restructuring operations. Since a debt crisis signifies a kind of macroeconomic pathology, a three-way medical analogy is used: countries are either cured, in remission, or in chronic crisis. The criteria for this classification are as follows:

- A country is considered *cured* of its debt crisis if it is current on its debt servicing, did not restructure its debt in the Paris Club during 1997–2001, is not a candidate for relief under the Heavily Indebted Poor Countries (HIPC) initiative, and was not under an IMF lending program during 1999–2001.
- A country is considered *in remission* if it meets the conditions for "cured" except that it is currently under a lending program with the IMF.
- A country is considered to be in a *chronic crisis* if it required a Paris Club restructuring during 1997–2001, or is a candidate for HIPC relief, or is in default on its Paris Club debts.

Note that all countries deemed eligible for further debt relief under the enhanced HIPC program are considered to be in a chronic crisis, since these countries are acknowledged to require further debt cancellation to bring their debts to sustainable levels.

Of the fifty-nine countries shown in Table 1 that required a Paris Club restructuring of their debt during 1975–96, only eight have been cured: Chile, Costa Rica, Equatorial Guinea, Guatemala, Jamaica, Morocco, and Trinidad and Tobago. Twelve more are in remission, and the remaining thirty-nine are in chronic crisis. Also notable is the sensitivity of countries' outcomes to their initial income: the low-income countries have generally failed to come out of their debt crises, requiring continued debt restructurings, including under the new HIPC terms, whereas most of the middle-income countries have been cured or at least gone into remission. Equatorial Guinea is the only least-developed country . . . to achieve a "cure," and it did it in style: by discovering massive offshore oil reserves, which led to the fastest per capita growth rates in the world during the 1990s. But apart from that anomalous outcome, all of the very poor countries fell into a persisting debt trap.

The countries in chronic debt crisis not only failed to reestablish a viable debt profile, but also failed to achieve sustained economic growth in the 1990s (Table 2). The unweighted mean annual growth rate during 1990–99 of the countries in crisis was –0.2 percent, and the median growth rate was only 0.3 percent; this compares with mean annual growth in the cured economies of 4.0 percent and median growth of 2.5 percent. Sixteen of the thirty-nine countries in chronic crisis experienced absolute declines in income, and only three experienced a per capita growth rate above 2.0 percent a year.

TABLE 2 ■ OUTPUT GROWTH IN COUNTRIES THAT RESTRUCTURED
PARIS CLUB DEBT, 1990–99 (UNITS AS INDICATED)

Recovery status	No. of countries	Average growth of GNP per capita[a] (percent a year)	
		Mean	Median
In chronic crisis	39	−0.2	0.3
In remission	12	1.7	2.1
Cured	8	4.0	2.5
All countries	59	0.8	0.9

Source: table 1.
[a] In dollars at purchasing power parity.

The unrealism of the current debt treatment of the poorest countries is also evidenced by endless and thankless rounds of debt renegotiation and IMF agreements. As Table 1 shows, seventeen countries—all of which except Ecuador are in the low-income category—have experienced six or more Paris Club debt restructurings following the initial onset of crisis . . . and fourteen of these countries are now in line for yet another cancellation of debts in the enhanced HIPC process. Accompanying these endless rounds of debt restructurings have been nearly continuous IMF programs, going on for twenty years or more, despite the fact that under its Articles of Agreement (Article I, Section V) the IMF is supposed to make funding "temporarily available" for emergency relief, not continuously available for a country with unpayable debts.[12]

One can almost say that, for a poor country, requiring an IMF program has been an absorbing state: once in the IMF's clutches, it has been almost impossible to escape. That is the main reason why the number of countries under IMF programs has continued to soar during the past thirty years. In 1978 there were twenty-two countries in IMF lending programs. By 1996 that figure had reached seventy-five, and as of 2001, sixty-three. Dozens of these countries have experienced nearly a quarter century of continuous IMF lending.

Several authors have recently studied the remarkably long-term use of IMF resources, finding as one might suppose that the problem is especially serious among low-income countries.[13] The IMF's new Independent Evaluation Office has recently taken up the issue.[14]

REFORMING THE DEBT RELIEF PROCESS FOR LOW-INCOME COUNTRIES

Poor countries that fell into a debt crisis got neither sufficient help to restore economic growth, nor deep enough debt reduction to reestablish normal relationships with creditors. There has been neither an economic recovery nor a fresh start.

When one looks closely at the modalities of debt rescheduling, it is not hard to understand why. The guiding principle of official debt relief in the past twenty years has been to do the minimum possible to prevent outright disaster, but never enough to solve the debt crisis. In particular, the official creditors (both in their capacity as bilateral creditors in the Paris Club and as multilateral creditors through the IMF and the World Bank) have used arbitrary formulas rather than a serious analysis of country needs to decide on the level of relief. That remains the case today. Even now the so-called debt sustainability analysis of the enhanced HIPC initiative is built on the flimsiest of foundations.

The guiding principles of the Paris Club debt restructurings for low-income countries since 1975 are shown in Box 1. Two things are striking about these principles. The first is that they have repeatedly been eased over time, both in the extent of relief and in the number of countries covered, as the terms of debt reduction have consistently proved inadequate to give a fresh start to the vast majority of these poor countries. The second is that the quantitative guidelines are across-the-board indicators, not based on an assessment of each country's charac- teristics and circumstances. For a decade after the outbreak of the developing- country debt crisis in the late 1970s, creditor countries denied the need for debt cancellation altogether. That changed for the first time in 1988, with the introduction of debt reduction in Paris Club agreements equal to one-third of the outstanding debt. The one-third limit was arbitrary and was soon relaxed, then relaxed again, and then again, and then for a fourth time in the enhanced HIPC initiative.

The current definition of debt sustainability in the enhanced HIPC initiative is as arbitrary as the previous standards, if a bit more generous. A ratio of debt to exports of 150 percent or a ratio of debt to government revenue of 250 percent cannot truly be judged to be sustainable or unsustainable except in the context of each country's needs, which themselves must be carefully spelled out. It is per- fectly possible, and indeed is currently the case, for a country or region to have a "sustainable" debt (and significant debt servicing) under these formal definitions while millions of its people are dying of hunger or disease.

For twenty-five years the creditor nations and the IMF in effect defined debt sustainability as the amount of debt servicing that could be maintained in practice while still achieving a modicum of macroeconomic stability. If the country was maintaining a roughly balanced budget, with low inflation, the debt was considered manageable, even if economic growth was negligible or negative, and even if debt reschedulings had to be repeated every couple of years. And with creditors deter- mining what was or was not sustainable, the flagrantly excessive demands on the impoverished debtor nations could not be challenged in the corridors of power. Only in the past couple of years has the inadequacy of this approach become widely recognized.

Looking forward, debt reduction for the HIPCs should not be based on arbi- trary criteria such as a 150 percent debt-exports ratio, but rather on systematic assessment of each country's needs for debt reduction and increased foreign assis- tance, measured against explicit development objectives. The right starting point for assessing needs should be the internationally accepted targets for economic

PARIS CLUB RESTRUCTURING TERMS FOR LOW-INCOME COUNTRIES, 1975–2001

1975–88.
Paris Club debt is rescheduled but not cancelled or reduced in present value by reductions in interest.

October 1988.
Toronto terms are introduced. For the first time, bilateral debts can be reduced in present value terms by as much as 33.3 percent. This can be accomplished through a debt reduction option or a debt service reduction option. Twenty countries benefit. Multilateral debts are not reduced.

December 1991.
London terms raise the allowable debt reduction for low-income countries to 50 percent. Once again, debt reduction and debt service reduction options are offered. Twenty-three countries benefit, including many that had benefited from the Toronto terms. Multilateral debts are not reduced.

December 1994.
Naples terms raise the allowable debt reduction for low-income countries to 67 percent and set the minimum debt reduction for "the poorest and most indebted countries" at 50 percent. In September 1999 the 67 percent threshold is applied to all heavily indebted poor countries. Thirty countries benefit. Multilateral debts are not reduced.

December 1996.
Lyon terms (also known as the Heavily Indebted Poor Countries, or HIPC, initiative) raise the allowable debt reduction for heavily indebted poor countries to 80 percent. For the first time, debts owed to the multilateral institutions (mainly the IMF, World Bank, and the regional development banks) may also be reduced. The concept of debt sustainability is introduced. Debts are to be cancelled to bring countries' debts to between 200 and 250 percent of exports of goods and services, or, for countries with a high export–GNP ratio, to no more than 280 percent of annual government revenue.[1]
    Five countries benefit.

November 1999.
Cologne terms (also known as the enhanced HIPC initiative) raise the allowed debt reduction to 90 percent or more "if necessary within the framework of the HIPC initiative." Debts of bilateral and multilateral official creditors are also to be reduced sufficiently to establish debt sustainability, as redefined by the initiative. Debt sustainability is now defined as debt no greater than 150 percent of exports, or, in countries with a high export–GNP ratio, no greater than 250 percent of net annual government revenue.[2] Forty-one countries are potentially eligible for the enhanced HIPC initiative, and fifteen countries have benefited to date.

[1]Technically, the debt–export limit applied to countries with export–GNP ratios below 40 percent. The alternative measure could apply for countries with an export–GNP ratio above 40 percent, as long as government revenue was above 20 percent of GNP.
[2]The thresholds for the government revenue alternative were eased slightly as well. The government revenue-based measure could apply for countries with an export–GNP ratio above 30 percent and with a government revenue–GNP ratio above 150 percent.

development that are (ostensibly) the guiding framework for the global development partnership between rich and poor countries. The targets are enshrined in the Millennium Development Goals (MDGs), a set of eight major goals and eighteen intermediate targets endorsed by all U.N. members at the Millennium Summit in New York in September 2000 and recently reconfirmed by the U.N. membership in the Monterrey Consensus of the United Nations Conference on Financing for Development in Monterrey, Mexico, in March 2002. The MDGs are quantified goals for poverty alleviation, reduction of hunger, reduction of disease burden, and other targets, mostly for the year 2015.[15]

In principle, if the MDGs are taken as the baseline, and if there is a working economic model of growth and poverty for each country, it is possible to calculate a level of net resource transfers . . . needed to achieve a given level of output per capita in the target year 2015. In practice, what is needed is nothing short of a country-specific "business plan" for scaling up essential public services (health, education, basic infrastructure) as part of an overall strategy for meeting the MDGs. In addition, each government—in conjunction with civil society—should articulate an overall development strategy that includes economic reforms and improved governance and accountability. The country-level business plan would provide an assessment of the financial gaps that must be bridged by development assistance and debt cancellation so that the country can scale up essential services. The Commission on Macroeconomics and Health of the World Health Organization (WHO) recently completed such an exercise for the health sector. For low-income countries in Sub-Saharan Africa, for example, it was found that spending on health care services needs to increase from 3.9 percent of GNP in 2002 to 13.2 percent of GNP in 2015, in order to extend the coverage of essential health services to roughly two-thirds of the population.[16] The commission assumed that these countries could muster an increase of 2.0 percentage points of GNP for health out of their own domestic revenues, leaving a gap of nearly 8 percent of GNP to be provided by donors (a sum estimated to equal $26 billion a year as of 2015).[17]

Annual debt service owed by a HIPC rarely exceeds 5 percent of its GNP. Thus, even if all of the HIPCs' debts were cancelled, the savings would not be enough to fund the increased outlays needed just for health, much less the sums also needed for expanded education and basic infrastructure, such as water and sanitation, and feeder roads to villages. For the twenty-four countries that had reached the "decision point" of the HIPC process by the end of 2000,[18] the average level of debt servicing was scheduled to decline from 4 percent of GNP in 1998 to 3 percent in 2000, and 2 percent during 2002–05.[19] Thus, even if all remaining debt servicing were cancelled, for a saving of 2 percent of GNP, the HIPCs would still likely need large increases in foreign assistance.

The idea of linking debt reduction to a detailed assessment of the financial requirements for meeting the debtors' essential needs may seem obvious, even trivial, but it is radically different from what the creditor-donor nations have done during the past quarter century. Debts owed by low-income countries have been collected, or partially cancelled, without any serious assessment of actual country needs anchored in specific development targets. And as we have seen, the

TABLE 3 ■ PROGRESS TOWARD DEVELOPMENT GOALS IN COUNTRIES
THAT RESCHEDULED PARIS CLUB DEBT AS OF 2002

Country	Undernourishment	Under-five mortality rate	No. of goals either "on track" or "achieved"
In chronic crisis			
Angola	On track	Slipping back	1 / 2
Benin	On track	Far behind	1 / 2
Bolivia	Lagging	On track	1 / 2
Burkina Faso	On track	Far behind	1 / 2
Cameroon	On track	Slipping back	1 / 2
Central African Rep.	Far behind	Far behind	0 / 2
Chad	On track	Far behind	1 / 2
Congo (Brazzaville)	Far behind	Far behind	0 / 2
Congo (Kinshasa)	Slipping back	Far behind	0 / 2
Côte d'Ivoire	On track	Slipping back	1 / 2
Ecuador	On track	On track	2 / 2
Ethiopia	n.a.	Far behind	0 / 1
Gabon	On track	Far behind	1 / 2
Gambia	On track	Far behind	1 / 2
Ghana	Achieved	Lagging	1 / 2
Guinea	On track	On track	2 / 2
Guinea-Bissau	n.a.	Far behind	0 / 1
Honduras	Far behind	On track	1 / 2
Jordan	On track	Lagging	1 / 2
Kenya	Far behind	Slipping back	0 / 2
Liberia	Slipping back	Far behind	0 / 2
Madagascar	Slipping back	Far behind	0 / 2
Malawi	On track	Lagging	1 / 2
Mali	Far behind	Far behind	0 / 2
Mauritania	On track	Far behind	1 / 2
Mozambique	On track	Far behind	1 / 2
Nicaragua	Far behind	On track	1 / 2
Niger	Far behind	Far behind	0 / 2
Nigeria	Achieved	Far behind	1 / 2
Pakistan	On track	Far behind	1 / 2
Senegal	Far behind	Far behind	0 / 2
Sierra Leone	Lagging	Far behind	0 / 2
Somalia	Slipping back	Far behind	0 / 2
Sudan	On track	Far behind	1 / 2
Tanzania	Slipping back	Far behind	0 / 2
Togo	On track	Far behind	1 / 2
Uganda	Far behind	Lagging	0 / 2
Yemen	Far behind	Far behind	0 / 2
Zambia	Far behind	Slipping back	0 / 2
Subtotal			24 / 76
In Remission			
Algeria	On track	Slipping Back	1/2
Argentina	n.a	On track	1/1

Country	Undernourishment	Under-five mortality rate	No. of goals either "on track" or "achieved"
Brazil	On track	On track	2/2
Cambodia	On track	Slipping back	1/2
Egypt	On track	On track	2/2
El Salvador	Far behind	On track	1/2
Haiti	Lagging	Far behind	0/2
Mexico	On track	On track	2/2
Panama	On track	On track	2/2
Peru	Achieved	On track	2/2
Philippines	Far behind	On track	1/2
Turkey	n.a.	On track	1/2
Subtotal			16/22
Cured			
Chile	Achieved	On track	2/2
Costa Rica	On track	On track	2/2
Dominican Republic	Far behind	On track	1/2
Equatorial Guinea	n.a.	On track	1/2
Guatemala	Slipping back	On track	1/2
Jamaica	On track	Far behind	1/2
Morocco	On track	On track	2/2
Trinidad and Tobago	Far behind	On track	1/2
Subtotal			11/15
Total			51/113

Source: United Nations Development Programme (2002).

results have been quite miserable. The vast majority of the HIPCs have suffered chronically from low or negative economic growth rates, and many have experienced a serious deterioration of social conditions. Almost all of the countries listed as in chronic crisis in Table 2 are far off track from meeting many if not most of the MDGs by 2015.[20]

Table 3 highlights just how poorly the economies in crisis are doing in terms of two central MDGs, those relating to child mortality and hunger, according to the most recent assessment made by the United Nations Development Program (UNDP). (The table singles these two MDGs out because they are the goals for which current data are most complete.) The child mortality goal is to reduce the child mortality rate by two-thirds by 2015 from its 1990 level. As Table 3 shows, only five of the thirty-nine countries in chronic crisis are in a position to achieve that MDG. Meanwhile, nine of the twelve economies in remission are on track or have already achieved the target, and among the eight cured economies only Jamaica is not on track. Regarding hunger, the goal is to halve the proportion of malnourished people on a country-by-country basis by 2015 from the 1990 level. Only nineteen of the thirty-seven crisis economies for which data are available are deemed to be on track for this goal or have achieved it. Of the ten countries in remission for which data are available, seven are on the desired trajectory. Among the cured economies, the corresponding figure is four out of seven. The crisis countries are clearly struggling, whereas the in-remission and cured economies are in vastly better shape.

REFORMING THE TREATMENT OF
HIGHLY INDEBTED POOR COUNTRIES

* * *

What kind of institutional changes are required to reorient the international system in the recommended direction? I suggest the following:

- The creditors should understand that, in a sovereign insolvency, whether under Chapter 9 in the United States or an international sovereign insolvency, the systemic goal is not the simple maximization of debt repayments to the creditors. Repayments to creditors must be placed in the context of additional objectives: a fresh start for an insolvent sovereign, preservation of its public functions, and achievement of broad development objectives. For low-income countries, the basic standard for debt collection should be to restructure debts in order to provide a macro-economic framework within which the countries can achieve the MDGs.
- Each HIPC should be encouraged—indeed, required, in order to obtain comprehensive debt cancellation—to prepare medium-term plans for scaling up its investments in health, education, and basic infrastructure during the period from now until 2015. The targets should be set in order to meet the MDGs. These plans should be designed in conjunction with civil society, as part of the ongoing poverty reduction strategy process.
- The key U.N. agencies, including the UNDP, WHO, and UNICEF, and the Bretton Woods institutions should support the countries in this costing exercise, but they should also carry out independent estimates of the countries' financing needs and incorporate those estimates into their own key country strategy documents.
- An independent review panel, with representatives appointed by both creditor and debtor countries but not representing either, should review the evidence from the countries and from the international agencies and make recommendations on the scale of debt cancellation and increased foreign assistance that should be granted to each country. For most HIPCs, the objective evidence will support a complete cancellation of debts, plus an increase in foreign assistance, all on a conditional basis to ensure that the increased net resource flow in fact supports the desired development objectives. The review panel could be convened under IMF auspices, but the recommendations should not be subject to a vote by the IMF's creditor-dominated executive board. In principle, such

recommendations should be binding. In practice, it is almost certain that the rich countries will concur with such a system only if such a review panel operates on an advisory basis.

- The United Nations and the Bretton Woods institutions should provide published yearly updates on the progress of each country toward each of the MDGs. These assessments would help not only in monitoring the low-income countries, but in monitoring the creditor-donor countries as well.

To the extent that the new system is merely advisory to the creditors, these recommendations may seem unnecessarily modest and might not resolve many of the political economy barriers that have blocked a more realistic approach to debt cancellation for the poorest countries. But they might just do the trick. A transparent process would shine important public light on the shortcomings of the creditor-dominated approach of the past quarter century. The objective evidence would underscore that the poorest countries are utterly impoverished and face multiple challenges of education, hunger, water and sanitation, and basic health that cannot be met without vastly larger flows of resources from the creditor countries. With the world just now recommitted to the MDGs after the Monterrey conference, an organized and intensive spotlight on the shortfall of practice relative to aspiration might help the international community come much closer to meeting its avowed aims.

REFERENCES

Azariadis, Costas, and Allan Drazen. 1990. "Threshold Externalities in Economic Development." *Quarterly Journal of Economics* 105(2): 501–26.

Bankruptcy Judges Division. 2000. Bankruptcy Basics. Public Information Series. Washington (June). (www.uscourts.gov/bankbasic.pdf, accessed May 6, 2002.)

Ben-David, Dan. 1998. "Convergence Clubs and Subsistence Economies." *Journal of Development Economics* 55(1): 155–71.

Bird, Graham, Mumtaz Hussain, and Joseph P. Joyce. 2000. "Many Happy Returns? Recidivism and the IMF." Working Paper 2000–04. Wellesley College (March).

Borchard, Edwin M., and William H. Wynne. 1951. *State Insolvency and Foreign Bondholders*. Yale University Press.

Elbadawi, Ibrahim, and Francis Mwega. 1998. "Can Africa's Saving Collapse be Reverted?" Presented at a World Bank conference on "Savings across the World," September 16–18. (www.worldbank.org/research/projects/savings/pdffiles/mwega2.pdf, accessed May 6, 2002.)

Independent Evaluation Office. 2002. *Prolonged Use of IMF Resources: Terms and References for an Evaluation by the Independent Evaluation Office*. Washington: International Monetary Fund.

International Monetary Fund. 2001. *Impact of Debt Reduction under the HIPC Initiative on External Debt Service and Social Expenditures*. Washington.

Krueger, Anne. 2001. "International Financial Architecture for 2002: A New Approach to Sovereign Debt Restructuring." Address given at the National Economists' Club, November 26. (www.imf.org/external/np/speeches/2001/ 112601.htm, accessed on May 6, 2002.)

Loayza, Norman, Klaus Schmidt-Hebbel, and Luis Serven. 2000. "What Drives Private Saving across the World?" *Review of Economics and Statistics* 82(2): 165–81.

Nelson, Richard. 1956. "A Theory of the Low-Level Equilibrium Trap in Underdeveloped Economies." *American Economic Review* 46(5): 894–908.

Pettifor, Anne. 2002. "Chapter 9/11? Resolving International Debt Crises—The Jubilee Framework for International Insolvency." London: New Economics Foundation (February). (www.jubileeplus.org/analysis/reports/jubilee_framework.pdf, accessed May 6, 2002.)

Rogoff, Kenneth, and Jeromin Zettelmeyer. 2002. "Early Ideas on Sovereign Bankruptcy Reorganization: A Survey." Working Paper 02/57. Washington: International Monetary Fund (March).

Sachs, Jeffrey D. 1984. "Theoretical Issues in International Borrowing." *Princeton Studies in International Finance* 54. Princeton University (July).

Sachs, Jeffrey D. ed. 1989. *Developing Country Debt and Economic Performance*. University of Chicago Press.

Sachs, Jeffrey D. 1995. "Do We Need an International Lender of Last Resort." Frank D. Graham Lecture, Princeton University. (www2.cid.harvard.edu/cidpapers/ intllr.pdf, accessed May 6, 2002.)

Sachs, Jeffrey D., and Erika Jorgensen. 1989. "Default and Renegotiation of Latin American Foreign Bonds in the Interwar Period." In *The International Debt Crisis in Historical Perspective*, edited by Barry Eichengreen and Peter H. Lindert. MIT Press.

Smith, Adam, and Edwin Cannan. 2000. *Wealth of Nations*. New York: Modern Library.

United Nations Development Programme. 2002. "How Many Countries Are on Track? The Millennium Declaration's Goals for Development and Poverty Eradication." *Human Development Report* (March). New York.

World Health Organization. 2002. Macroeconomics and Health: Investing in Health for Economic Development: Report of the Commission on Macroeconomics and Health. Geneva.

ENDNOTES

1. "When national debts have once been accumulated to a certain degree, there is scarce, I believe, a single instance of their having been fairly and completely paid. The liberation of public revenue, if it has ever been brought about at all, has always been brought about by a bankruptcy; sometimes by an avowed one, but always by a real one, though frequently by a pretended payment [in a depreciated currency] . . . When it becomes necessary for a state to declare itself bankrupt, in the same manner as when it becomes necessary for an individual to do so, a fair, open, and avowed bankruptcy procedure is always the measure which is both least dishonourable to the debtor, and least harmful to the creditor" (Smith and Cannan, 2000, Book V, Chapter III, pp. 466 and 468).
2. Rogoff and Zettlemeyer (2002); Pettifor (2002).
3. I have previously discussed these issues in many places, including for example Sachs (1984, 1995).
4. Under Chapter 11, businesses are allowed a fresh start only to the extent that creditor interests are thereby protected. Creditors can force the conversion of a Chapter 11 restructuring into a Chapter 7 liquidation by failing to confirm the reorganization plan.
5. For a similar reason, individuals may not voluntarily sell themselves into slavery. The autonomy of human beings takes precedence over any contractual obligations, even those voluntarily and knowingly made.
6. Bankruptcy Judges Division (2000, p. 51).
7. Bankruptcy Judges Division (2000, p. 48).

8. Thus, in an individual bankruptcy under Chapter 7, creditors are paid out of the property of the bankruptcy estate, and remaining debts are discharged. The individual's future income stream is protected against any future collection efforts. Thus repayment of debts is limited to the amount available from the liquidation of nonexempt property and does not extend to the discounted value of the debtor's future labor income.

9. Borchard and Wynne (1951); Sachs (1989); Sachs and Jorgensen (1989).

10. Krueger (2001).

11. The key complexity, of course, is the reconciliation of national laws on creditor-debtor relations that govern outstanding loan agreements, with the global objective of avoiding the creditor grab race. It seems likely that the IMF Articles of Agreement will need amending so that international treaty law supersedes national law in the event of a sovereign bankruptcy.

12. The continual Paris Club reschedulings and IMF programs go hand in hand, since an IMF agreement is generally a precondition for a Paris Club rescheduling. Thus, if an unpayable debt burden must constantly be renegotiated, the country is also obliged to remain within an IMF program (and the IMF is similarly obliged to continue lending to the country).

13. See, for example, Bird and others (1999).

14. Independent Evaluation Office (2002).

15. The goals are listed at www.undp.org/mdg/Millennium%20Development%20Goals.pdf.

16. WHO (2002, table A2.9, p. 170).

17. As shown in WHO (2002, table A2.11, p. 173).

18. The decision point marks the beginning of interim relief under the HIPC initiative. Following successful implementation of a poverty reduction program for a few more years (up to three), the completion point is reached, under which the negotiated cancellation of the debt is completed.

19. IMF (2001, table 2, p. 8).

20. UNDP (2002).

QUESTIONS FOR REVIEW AND DISCUSSION

1. Both authors highlight the failure of pre-HIPC debt-relief initiatives to yield lasting debt reductions for developing countries. What factors do each author emphasize in explaining this failure? Which author's account do you find most convincing? Why?

2. What is a "poverty trap"? How does a high level of foreign debt push a country into a poverty trap? What impact, then, would debt forgiveness have on the indebted economy?

3. Jeffrey Sachs criticizes the HIPC Initiative for its "arbitrary standards." What does he propose in place of current standards, and does he envisage such a process would work?

4. How do you think William Easterly would respond to Sachs' alternative approach to debt relief? Does the program satisfy Easterly's two conditions for sensible debt relief? Why or why not?

SUGGESTIONS FOR FURTHER READING

You can get current information and detailed descriptions of the HIPC Initiative at www.worldbank.org/hipc and http://www.imf.org/external/np/exr/facts/hipc.htm

Jubilee Research (formerly Jubilee 2000) maintains a Web site dedicated to the debt problem at http://www.jubilee2000uk.org

For an in-depth treatment of the debt problem, the HIPC Initiative, and proposals for reform, see: Nancy Birdsall and John Williamson. *Delivering on Debt Relief: From IMF Gold to a New Aid Architecture*. Washington, DC: Center for Global Development and Institute for International Economics, 2002. See also David M. Roodman's *Still Waiting for the Jubilee: Pragmatic Solutions for the Third World Debt Crisis*, Worldwatch Paper 155. Washington, DC: Worldwatch Institute, 2001.

CHAPTER 17

FOREIGN AID

In the last ten years, governments and multilateral lending agencies have made important changes in the way they think about foreign aid. For most of the postwar period, the rationale for foreign aid was based on an economic model called the "finance gap." According to this approach, poverty was largely a result of insufficient physical and human capital. Creating such capital, largely by making investments in critical infrastructure and manufacturing industries, would thus generate rapid growth and rising per capita incomes. Lending agencies encouraged developing-country governments to create development plans that established a target rate of economic growth. They then calculated how much investment was required to reach this target growth rate. The difference between the amount of investment required and the amount the country could finance from its own resources produced a finance gap, which was then filled with foreign aid. Based on this model, foreign-aid flows provided the single largest source of foreign capital to developing countries during the 1960s and the early 1970s, and aid flows continued to increase during the 1980s. Much of the aid provided to developing countries during this period financed large infrastructure projects, such as building roads and increasing electrical capacity.

During the 1990s, governments in the advanced industrialized world and multilateral lending agencies such as the World Bank became disenchanted with foreign aid and the finance-gap model upon which aid flows had been based. Experience with almost four decades of foreign aid made it clear that aid based on this approach was failing to deliver results. Studies conducted by researchers at the World Bank during the 1990s found little relationship between the amount of foreign aid a country received and its subsequent economic performance. While foreign aid did contribute to rapid growth in some countries, there was little evidence to suggest that the postwar aid regime was hugely successful.

Why was aid not more effective? Analysts pointed to a range of factors. Donor governments often used aid to cultivate allies in the context of the Cold War conflict and were less concerned about how recipient governments used the aid. Many developing-country leaders took advantage of this opportunity and used foreign aid to fund lavish lifestyles. Even where donors and recipients were well intentioned, the lack of consensus about development strategies led to a lack of coordination. As a result, the number of aid-giving agencies and the number of separate projects within the recipient countries proliferated. During the 1990s, Mozambique had

405 donor-funded projects ongoing in the Ministry of Health alone, while Tanzania had 2,000 projects funded by 40 different agencies. Moreover, many of the projects lacked local "ownership," that is, there was little belief in the recipient country that the projects being funded, often at the behest of the World Bank or another external agency, would yield measurable improvements in the quality of life. Consequently, the recipient country had few incentives to implement the projects effectively.

As disenchantment with the results from aid grew, and as the strategic motivation for foreign aid diminished with the end of the Cold War, the amount of foreign aid that the advanced industrialized countries channeled to developing countries fell. According to the World Bank, by the late 1990s foreign-aid flows, measured as a share of the wealthy countries' gross national products, had fallen to a postwar low. It is only recently that the advanced industrialized countries have begun to exhibit renewed enthusiasm for foreign aid. The Bush administration, for example, initiated the "Millennium Challenge Account" in 2001, which promised to increase U.S. foreign aid expenditures by 50 percent between 2002 and 2005, bringing total U.S. aid to more than $15 billion.

Renewed interest in foreign aid is accompanied by the recognition that reform is required. The emerging foreign-aid regime places substantially less emphasis on providing money for investment in physical capital and substantially more emphasis on using foreign aid to promote good policies, good institutions, and good public services. In other words, rather than using aid to finance investments in infrastructure projects, donors should use aid to encourage developing-country governments to establish strong property rights, root out corrupt practices within government bureaucracies, and develop government agencies capable of delivering high-quality public services. Once high-quality institutions are in place, additional foreign aid can be put to work on infrastructure projects—with a much greater chance of success.

The articles presented in this chapter examine the foreign-aid regime from two different perspectives. David Dollar, director of development policy in the Development Economics Vice Presidency of the World Bank, provides a concise statement of current official thinking on foreign aid. He argues that the finance-gap model placed too much emphasis on the symptoms of poverty, such as too little physical and human capital, and too little emphasis on the causes of poverty—low-quality institutions. For foreign aid to succeed, he argues that it must be used to promote the development of high-quality institutions. He is cautious, however, about whether aid agencies can promote such reforms, stressing that most instances of successful reform have been home grown. William Easterly, formerly of the World Bank and now an economics professor at New York University, argues that successful foreign aid will also require reform of the structure through which aid is delivered. Focusing on what he calls the "foreign aid cartel," he argues that the bureaucratic agencies responsible for delivering and administering foreign aid are accountable solely to politicians in the wealthy donor countries. They therefore concentrate on projects that please these constituents rather than on projects that would generate higher returns for developing countries. Making foreign aid more effective will require donor agencies to be made accountable to their developing-country clients. He suggests that bringing market competition into the distribution of foreign aid could create such accountability.

Eyes Wide Open: On the Targeted Use of Foreign Aid

DAVID DOLLAR

Conventional wisdom on international development holds that "the rich get richer while the poor get poorer." This saying does not capture exactly what has happened between the rich and poor regions of the world over the past century, but it comes pretty close. In general, poor areas of the world have not become poorer, but their per capita income has grown quite slowly. On the other hand, income in the club of rich countries (Western Europe, the United States, Canada, Japan, Australia, and New Zealand), has increased at a much more rapid pace. As a result, by 1980 an unprecedented level of worldwide inequality had developed. The richest fifth of the world's population—which essentially corresponds to the population of the rich countries—produced and consumed 70 percent of the world's goods and services, while the poorest fifth of the global population, in contrast, held only two percent.

There has been a modest decline in global inequality since 1980 because two large poor countries—China and India—have outperformed the rich countries economically. This shift represents an interesting change that has important lessons for development. However, if one ignores the performance of China and India, much of the rest of the developing world still languishes, and there continues to be an appalling gap between rich countries and poor countries.

Inequality within countries is an important issue as well, but it pales in comparison with inequality between countries across the world. A homeless person panhandling for two US dollars a day on the streets of Boston would sit in the top half of the world income distribution. Without traveling through rural parts of the developing world, it is difficult to comprehend the magnitude of this gap, which is not just one of income. Life expectancy in the United States has risen to 77 years whereas in Zambia it has fallen to 38 years. Infant mortality is down to seven deaths per 1,000 live births in the United States, compared to 115 in Zambia. How can these gaps in living standards be understood? And, more importantly, what can be done about it?

Traditionally, one part of the answer to the latter question has been foreign aid. Since the end of the Cold War, aid has been in decline, both in terms of volume (down to about 0.2 percent of the gross national product of the rich countries) and popularity as an effective policy. However, since before September 11, 2001, aid has made something of a comeback, with a number of European countries, notably the

From David Dollar, "Eyes Wide Open: On the Targeted Use of Foreign Aid" *Harvard International Review* 25, Spring 2003, pp. 48–52.

United Kingdom, arguing for the importance of addressing global poverty by implementing reforms to make aid more effective. Since September 11, the US government has shown renewed interest as well.

What can come from this renewed interest in foreign aid? Foreign aid bureaucracies have a long history of mistaking symptoms for causes. If this trend continues uncorrected, then it is unlikely that greater volumes of aid will make much of a dent in global poverty and inequality. On the other hand there is much more evidence about what leads to successful development and how aid can assist in that process. Thus, the potential exists to make aid a much more important tool in the fight against poverty. My argument on this matter is comprised of four points.

First, countries are poor primarily because of weak underlying institutions and policies. Features such as lack of capital, poor education, or absence of modern industry are symptoms rather than causes of underdevelopment. Aid focused on these symptoms has not had much lasting impact.

Second, local institutions in developing countries are persistent, and foreign aid donors have little influence over them. Efforts to reform countries through conditionality of aid from the Bretton Woods organizations have generally failed to bring about lasting reform within developing country institutions. It is difficult to predict when serious movements will emerge, but the positive developments in global poverty in the past 20 years have been the result of home-grown reform movements in countries such as China, India, Uganda, and Vietnam.

Third, foreign aid has had a positive effect in these and other cases, and arguably its most useful role has been to support learning at the state and community level. Countries and communities can learn from each other, but there are no simple blueprints of institutional reform that can be transferred from one location to the next. Thus, helping countries analyze, implement, and evaluate options is useful, whereas promoting a "best-practice" approach to each issue through conditionality is not.

Fourth, the financial aspect of foreign aid is also important. In poor countries that have made significant steps toward improving their institutions and policies, financial aid accelerates growth and poverty reduction and helps cement popular support for reform. Hence, large-scale financial assistance needs to be "selective," targeting countries that can put aid to effective use building schools, roads, and other aspects of social infrastructure.

INSTITUTIONS AND POLICIES

Economists have long underestimated the importance of state institutions in explaining the differences in economic performance between countries. Recent work in economic history and development is beginning to rectify this oversight. In their 2001 study, "Colonial Origins of Comparative Development: An Empirical Investigation," Daron Acemoglu, Simon Johnson, and James Robinson find that much of the variation in per capita income across countries can be explained by differences in institutional quality. They look at a number of different institutional measures, which generally capture the extent to which the state effectively provides a framework in which property is secure and markets can operate. Thus, indicators of institutional quality try to measure people's confidence in their property rights and the government bureaucracy's ability to provide public services relatively free of interest group appropriation and corruption. All countries have some problems with appropriation and corruption, so the practical issue is the extent of these problems. While these differences are inherently hard to measure, some contrasts are obvious; there is, for example, no doubt that Singapore or Finland has a better environment of property rights and clean government than Mobutu's Zaire or many similar locations in the developing world.

Differences in institutional quality explain much of the variation in per capita income across countries, an empirical result that is very intuitive. In a poor institutional environment, households must focus on day-to-day subsistence. The state fails to provide the complementary infrastructure—such as roads and schools—necessary to encourage long-term investment, while the lack of confidence in property rights further discourages entrepreneurial activity. In this type of setting, any surplus accumulated by individuals is more likely to fund capital flight, investment abroad, or emigration than to be reinvested in the local economy.

In addition, there is evidence that access to markets is also important as well for economic growth. If a region is cut off from larger markets either because of its natural geography or because of man-made trade barriers, then the incentives for entrepreneurial activity and investment are again reduced. In 1999, Jeffrey Frankel and David Romer cautiously concluded that the converse holds as well: better trading opportunities do lead to faster growth. There is still some debate among economists about the relative importance of institutions and trade, but it seems likely that both are important and that in fact they complement each other. Several years ago, Kenneth Sokoloff found that rates of invention were extremely responsive to the expansion of markets during the early industrialization of the United States by examining how patenting activity varied over time and with the extension of navigable waterways. For example, as the construction of the Erie Canal progressed westward across the state of New York, patenting per capita rose sharply county-by-county. The United States had a good system of protecting these intellectual properties, and the development of transport links to broader markets stimulated individuals and firms to invest more in developing new technologies.

Indeed, looking back over the past century, locations with access to markets and good property rights have generally prospered, while locations disconnected from markets and with poor property rights have remained poor. Many of the features that we associate with underdevelopment are therefore results of these underlying weaknesses in institutions and policies. In such environments, there is little incentive to invest in equipment or education and develop modern industry.

But these symptoms have often been mistaken by aid donors as causes of underdevelopment. If low levels of investment are a problem, then give poor countries foreign aid to invest in capital. If a lack of education is a problem, finance broad expansion of schools. If modern industry is absent, erect infant-industry protection to allow firms to develop behind a protected wall. All of these approaches have been pushed by aid donors. In poor countries with weak underlying institutions, however, the results have not been impressive.

Over several decades, Zambia received an amount of foreign aid that would have made every Zambian rich had it achieved the kind of return that is normal in developed economies. If lack of capital was the key problem in Zambia, then that was certainly addressed by massive amounts of aid; but the result was virtually no increase in the country's per capita income. Similarly, large amounts of aid targeted at expanding education in Africa yielded little measurable improvement in achievement or skills. Donors financed power plants, steel mills, and even shoe factories behind high levels of protection, but again there was virtually no return on these investments.

The recent thinking in economic history and development suggests that these efforts failed because they were aimed at symptoms rather than at underlying causes. If a government is very corrupt or dominated by powerful special interests, then giving it money, or schools, or shoe factories will not promote lasting growth and development. These findings suggest that much of the frustration about foreign aid comes from the many failed efforts to develop social infrastructure in weak institutional environments where governments and communities cannot make effective use of these resources—not from the intrinsic inability of aid itself to generate positive results.

There are a number of important caveats about these findings on aid effectiveness. First, humanitarian or food aid is a different story. When there is a famine or humanitarian crisis, international donors have shown that they can bring in short-term relief effectively. Second, there are some health interventions that can be delivered in a weak institutional environment. In much of Africa, donors have collaborated to eradicate river blindness, a disease that can be controlled by taking a single pill each year. That intervention—and certain types of vaccinations—can be carried out in almost any environment. But many other social services require an effective institutional delivery system; other health projects in countries with weak institutions have tended to fail without producing any benefits.

PERSISTENT INSTITUTIONS

A second important finding from recent work in economic history is that institutions are persistent. Last year, Stanley Engerman and Sokoloff showed how differences in the natural endowments of South and North American colonies centuries ago led to the development of different institutions in the two environments. Furthermore, many of these institutional differences have persisted to this day. If institutions are important and if they typically change slowly over time, then it is easy to understand the pattern of rising global inequality over the past century. Locations with better institutions have consistently grown faster than ones with poor institutions, widening inequalities. Because it is relatively rare for a country to switch from poor institutions and policies to good ones, countries that began at a disadvantage only fell further behind in the years that followed.

The importance of good institutions and policies for development in general and for aid effectiveness in particular is something that donors have gradually realized through experience and research. International donors' first instincts were to make improved institutions and policies a condition of their assistance. In the 1980s in particular, donors loaded assistance packages with large numbers of conditions concerning specific institutional and policy reforms. Some World Bank loans, for example, had more than 100 specific reform conditions. However, the persistence of institutions and policies hints at the difficulty of changing them. There are always powerful interests who benefit from bad policies, and donor conditionality has proved largely ineffective at overcoming these interest groups. A 2000 study that I coauthored with Jakob Svensson examined a large sample of World Bank structural adjustment programs to find that the success or failure of reform can largely be predicted by underlying institutional features of the country, including whether or not the government is democratically elected and how long the executive has been in power. Governments are often willing to sign aid agreements with large amounts of conditionality, but in many low-income countries the government is either uninterested in implementing reform or politically blocked from doing so. "Aid and Reform in Africa," a set of case studies written by African scholars on 10 African states, reaches similar conclusions: institutional and policy reform is driven primarily by domestic movements and not by outside agents.

PROSPECTS FOR REFORM

The good news is that a number of important developing countries have accomplished considerable reforms in the past two decades. In 1980, about 60 percent of the world's extreme poor—those living on less than one US dollar per day—lived in just two countries: China and India. At that time, neither country seemed a particularly likely candidate for reform. Both had rather poor property rights and government efficiency according to the measures used in cross-country studies, and both were extremely closed to the world market. Over the past two decades, however, China has introduced truly revolutionary reforms, restoring property rights over land, opening the economy to foreign trade and investment, and gradually making the legal and regulatory changes that have permitted the domestic private sector to become the main engine of growth. Reforms in India have not been quite as dramatic, but have still been very successful at reducing the government's heavy-handed management of the economy and dismantling the protectionist trade regime. Among low-income countries, there have been a number of other notable reformers as well; Uganda is a good example in Africa, and Vietnam in Southeast Asia.

The general point about all of these low-income reformers is that outside donors were not particularly important at the start of these reform efforts. These movements are home-grown and each has an interesting and distinct political-economy story behind it. Once these reforms began, however, foreign assistance played an important supporting role in each case. Institutional reform involves much social and political experimentation. The way that China has gradually strengthened private property rights is an excellent example, as is the way India reformed its energy sector. Foreign assistance can help governments and communities examine options, implement innovations, and evaluate them. To do this effectively, donor agencies need to have good technical staff, worldwide experience, and an open mind about what might work in different circumstances.

The World Bank is often criticized for giving the same advice everywhere, but this simply is not true. World Bank reports on different countries show that the World Bank typically makes quite different recommendations in different countries. The criticism that comes from government officials in the developing world is a different and more telling one: that the World Bank tends to make a single strong recommendation on each issue, instead of helping clients analyze the pros and cons of different options so that communities can make up their own minds about what to do. We do not know much about institutional change, so it is more useful to promote community learning than to push particular institutional models.

For example, the Education, Health, and Nutrition Program—known by its Spanish acronym, PROGRESA—is a successful program of cash transfers that encourages poor families to keep their children in school that was developed and evaluated in Mexico without any donor support. A number of donors now have helped communities in Central American countries to implement similar programs. In each case, communities need to tailor the program to their particular situation. Systematic re-evaluation is important because the same idea will not necessarily work everywhere. But this is a good example of how donors can promote learning across countries and support institutional change by presenting a variety of reform options for developing countries to follow.

MONEY MATTERS

While supporting country and community learning is probably the most useful role for aid, and the one that will have the largest impact, there is still a role for large-scale financial aid. Studies have shown that there is little relationship between aid amounts and growth rates in developing countries, but there is a rather strong relationship between growth and the interaction of aid and economic policies. This finding, as well as microeconomic evidence about individual projects, suggests that the growth effect of aid is greater in countries with reasonably good institutions and policies. The success of the Marshall Plan is a classic historical example. More recently, states such as Uganda show that the combination of substantial reform and large-scale aid goes together with rapid growth and poverty reduction. In a poor institutional environment, however, large-scale aid seems to have little lasting economic impact and may even make things worse by sustaining a bad government.

What follows from this is that aid is going to have more impact on poverty reduction if it is targeted to countries that are poor and have favorable institutions and policies. This philosophy underlies a number of new initiatives in foreign aid— European countries, including the United Kingdom and the Netherlands, have reformed and expanded their aid program along these lines. The new US Millennium Challenge Account is based on these principles as well.

Using aid to support learning and being selective in the allocation of large-scale financial resources are linked. When donors tried to push large amounts of money into weak institutional environments, they naturally wanted to have large numbers of conditions dictating how institutions and policies would change. But this neither promoted effective learning nor led to good use of money. The new model argues for much less conditionality—encouraging countries and communities to figure out what works for them—but retaining some form of selectivity in the allocation of financial resources.

Keeping in mind the persistence of institutions and the difficulty of changing them, one should have modest hopes for what foreign aid can accomplish. But as long as there are countries and communities around the world struggling to change, the international community must support them. Afghanistan today is a good example. The country is trying to develop new institutions at the national and local levels, and the world has a big stake in helping it succeed. The international community does not know for sure what will work, but outsiders dictating a new set of institutions will almost certainly fail. On the other hand, donor agencies can help both national and local governments learn about options, implement policies, evaluate results, and re-design if necessary. As a sound institutional framework develops, there will be increasing scope for large-scale funding of roads, schools, and other social infrastructure. The effort may fail. No doubt the lack of good institutions in Afghanistan reflects extensive historical and political factors that will be hard to overcome. It is important to go in with eyes wide open; trying to reform aid based on what we know is preferable to giving up on aid and closing our eyes to the massive poverty that remains throughout the developing world.

The Cartel of Good Intentions

WILLIAM EASTERLY

The world's richest governments have pledged to boost financial aid to the developing world. So why won't poor nations reap the benefits? Because in the way stands a bloated, unaccountable foreign aid bureaucracy out of touch with sound economics. The solution: Subject the foreign assistance business to the forces of market competition.

The mere mention of a "cartel" usually strikes fear in the hearts and wallets of consumers and regulators around the globe. Though the term normally evokes images of greedy oil producers or murderous drug lords, a new, more well-intentioned cartel has emerged on the global scene. Its members are the world's leading foreign aid organizations, which constitute a near monopoly relative to the powerless poor.

This state of affairs helps explain why the global foreign aid bureaucracy has run amok in recent years. Consider the steps that beleaguered government officials in low-income countries must take to receive foreign aid. Among other things, they must prepare a participatory Poverty Reduction Strategy Paper (PRSP)—a detailed plan for uplifting the destitute that the World Bank and International Monetary Fund (IMF) require before granting debt forgiveness and new loans. This document in turn must adhere to the World Bank's Comprehensive Development Framework, a 14-point checklist covering everything from lumber policy to labor practices. And the list goes on: Policymakers seeking aid dollars must also prepare a Financial Information Management System report, a Report on Observance of Standards and Codes, a Medium Term Expenditure Framework, and a Debt Sustainability Analysis for the Enhanced Heavily Indebted Poor Countries Initiative. Each document can run to hundreds of pages and consume months of preparation time. For example, Niger's recently completed PRSP is 187 pages long, took 15 months to prepare, and sets out spending for a 2002–05 poverty reduction plan with such detailed line items as $17,600 a year on "sensitizing population to traffic circulation."

Meanwhile, the U.N. International Conference on Financing for Development held in Monterrey, Mexico, in March 2002 produced a document—"the Monterrey Consensus"—that has a welcome emphasis on partnership between rich donor and poor recipient nations. But it's somewhat challenging for poor countries to carry out the 73 actions that the document recommends, including such ambitions as establishing democracy, equality between boys and girls, and peace on Earth.

Visitors to the World Bank Web site will find 31 major development topics listed there, each with multiple subtopics. For example, browsers can explore 13 subcategories under "Social Development," including indigenous peoples, resettlement, and culture in sustainable development. This last item in turn includes the music industry in Africa, the preservation of cultural artifacts, a seven-point framework for action, and—well, you get the idea.

It's not that aid bureaucrats are bad; in fact, many smart, hardworking, dedicated professionals toil away in the world's top aid agencies. But the perverse incentives they face explain the organizations' obtuse behavior. The international aid bureaucracy will never work properly under the conditions that make it operate like a cartel—the cartel of good intentions.

ALL TOGETHER NOW

Cartels thrive when customers have little opportunity to complain or to find alternative suppliers. In its heyday during the 1970s, for example, the Organization of the Petroleum Exporting Countries (OPEC) could dictate severe terms to customers; it was only when more non-OPEC oil exporters emerged that the cartel's power weakened. In the foreign aid business, customers (i.e., poor citizens in developing countries) have few chances to express their needs, yet they cannot exit the system. Meanwhile, rich nations paying the aid bills are clueless about what those customers want. Nongovernmental organizations (NGOs) can hold aid institutions to task on only a few high-visibility issues, such as conspicuous environmental destruction. Under these circumstances, even while foreign aid agencies make good-faith efforts to consult their clients, these agencies remain accountable mainly to themselves.

The typical aid agency forces governments seeking its money to work exclusively with that agency's own bureaucracy—its project appraisal and selection apparatus, its economic and social analysts, its procurement procedures, and its own interests and objectives. Each aid agency constitutes a mini-monopoly, and the collection of all such monopolies forms a cartel. The foreign aid community also resembles a cartel in that the IMF, World Bank, regional development banks, European Union, United Nations, and bilateral aid agencies all agree to "coordinate" their efforts. The customers therefore have even less opportunity to find alternative aid suppliers. And the entry of new suppliers into the foreign assistance business is difficult because large aid agencies must be sponsored either by an individual government (as in the case of national agencies, such as the U.S. Agency for International Development) or by an international agreement (as in the case of multilateral agencies, such as the World Bank). Most NGOs are too small to make much of a difference.

Of course, cartels always display fierce jostling for advantage and even mutual enmity among members. That explains why the aid community concludes that "to realize our increasingly reciprocal ambitions, a lot of hard work, compromises and true goodwill must come into play." Oops, wait, that's a quote from a recent OPEC meeting. The foreign aid community simply maintains that "better coordination among international financial institutions is needed." However, the difficulties of organizing parties with diverse objectives and interests and the inherent tensions in a cartel render such coordination forever elusive. Doomed attempts at coordination create the worst of all worlds—no central planner exists to tell each agency what to do, nor is there any market pressure from customers to reward successful agencies and discipline unsuccessful ones.

As a result, aid organizations mindlessly duplicate services for the world's poor. Some analysts see this duplication as a sign of competition to satisfy the customer—not so. True market competition should eliminate duplication: When you choose where to eat lunch, the restaurant next door usually doesn't force you to sit down for an extra meal. But things are different in the world of foreign aid, where a team from the U.S. Agency for International Development produced a report on corruption in Uganda in 2001, unaware that British analysts had produced a report on the same topic six months earlier. The Tanzanian government churns out more than 2,400 reports annually for its various donors, who send the poor country some 1,000 missions each year. (Borrowing terminology from missionaries who show the locals the one true path to heaven, "missions" are visits of aid agency staff to developing countries to discuss desirable government policy.) No wonder, then, that in the early 1990s, Tanzania was implementing 15 separate stand-alone health-sector projects funded by 15 different donors. Even small bilateral aid agencies plant their flags everywhere. Were the endless meetings and staff hours worth the effort for the Senegalese government to receive $38,957 from the Finnish Ministry for Foreign Affairs Development Cooperation in 2001?

By forming a united front and duplicating efforts, the aid cartel is also able to diffuse blame among its various members when economic conditions in recipient countries don't improve according to plan. Should observers blame the IMF for fiscal austerity that restricts funding for worthy programs, or should they fault the World Bank for failing to preserve high-return areas from public expenditure cuts? Are the IMF and World Bank too tough or too lax in enforcing conditions? Or are the regional development banks too inflexible (or too lenient) in their conditions for aid? Should bilateral aid agencies be criticized for succumbing to national and commercial interests, or should multilateral agencies be condemned for applying a "one size fits all" reform program to all countries? Like squabbling children, aid organizations find safety in numbers. Take Argentina. From 1980 to 2001, the Argentine government received 33 structural adjustment loans from the IMF and World Bank, all under the watchful eye of the U.S. Treasury. Ultimately, then, is Argentina's ongoing implosion the fault of the World Bank, the IMF, or the Treasury Department? The buck stops nowhere in the world of development assistance. Each party can point fingers at the others, and bewildered observers don't know whom to blame—making each agency less accountable.

THE $3,521 QUANDARY

Like any good monopoly, the cartel of good intentions seeks to maximize net revenues. Indeed, if any single objective has characterized the aid community since its inception, it is an obsession with increasing the total aid money mobilized. Traditionally, aid agencies justify this goal by identifying the aid "requirements" needed to achieve a target rate of economic growth, calculating the difference between existing aid and the requirements, and then advocating a commensurate aid increase. In 1951, the U.N. Group of Experts calculated exactly how much aid poor countries needed to achieve an annual growth rate of 2 percent per capita, coming up with an amount that would equal $20 billion in today's dollars. Similarly, the economist Walt Rostow calculated in 1960 the aid increase (roughly double the aid levels at the time) that would lift Asia, Africa, and Latin America into self-sustaining growth. ("Self-sustaining" meant that aid would no longer be necessary 10 to 15 years after the increase.) Despite the looming expiration of the 15-year aid window, then World Bank President Robert McNamara called for a doubling of aid in 1973. The call for doubling was repeated at the World Bank in its 1990 "World Development Report." Not to be outdone, current World Bank President James Wolfensohn is now advocating a doubling of aid.

The cartel's efforts have succeeded: Total assistance flows to developing countries have doubled several times since the early days of large-scale foreign aid. (Meanwhile, the World Bank's staff increased from 657 people in 1959–60 to some 10,000 today.) In fact, if all foreign aid given since 1950 had been invested in U.S. Treasury bills, the cumulative assets of poor countries by 2001 from foreign aid alone would have amounted to $2.3 trillion. This aid may have helped achieve such important accomplishments as lower infant mortality and rising literacy throughout the developing world. And high growth in aid-intensive countries like Botswana and Uganda is something to which aid agencies can (and do) point. The growth outcome in most aid recipients, however, has been extremely disappointing. For example, on average, aid-intensive African nations saw growth decline despite constant increases in aid as a percentage of their income.

Aid agencies always claim that their main goal is to reduce the number of poor people in the world, with poverty defined as an annual income below $365. To this end, the World Bank's 2002 aid accounting estimates that an extra $1 billion in overseas development assistance would lift more than 284,000 people out of poverty. (This claim has appeared prominently in the press and has been repeated in other government reports on aid effectiveness.) If these figures are correct, however, then the additional annual aid spending per person lifted out of poverty (whose annual income is less than $365) comes to $3,521. Of course, aid agencies don't follow their own logic to this absurd conclusion—common sense says that aid should help everyone and not just target those who can stagger across the minimum poverty threshold. Regrettably, this claim for aid's effect on poverty has more to do with the aid bureaucracy's desperate need for good publicity than with sound economics.

A FRAMEWORK FOR FAILURE

To the extent that anyone monitors the performance of global aid agencies, it is the politicians and the public in rich nations. Aid agencies therefore strive to produce outputs (projects, loans, etc.) that these audiences can easily observe, even if such outputs provide low economic returns for recipient nations. Conversely, aid bureaucrats don't try as hard to produce less visible, high-return outputs. This emphasis on visibility results in shiny showcase projects, countless international meetings and summits, glossy reports for public consumption, and the proliferation of "frameworks" and strategy papers. Few are concerned about whether the show-case projects endure beyond the ribbon-cutting ceremony or if all those meetings, frameworks, and strategies produce anything of value.

This quest for visibility explains why donors like to finance new, high-profile capital investment projects yet seem reluctant to fund operating expenses and maintenance after high-profile projects are completed. The resulting problem is a recurrent theme in the World Bank's periodic reports on Africa. In 1981, the bank's Africa study concluded that "vehicles and equipment frequently lie idle for lack of spare parts, repairs, gasoline, or other necessities. Schools lack operating funds for salaries and teaching materials, and agricultural research stations have difficulty keeping up field trials. Roads, public buildings, and processing facilities suffer from lack of maintenance." Five years later, another study of Africa found that "road maintenance crews lack fuel and bitumen . . . teachers lack books . . . [and] health workers have no medicines to distribute." In 1986, the Word Bank declared that in Africa, "schools are now short of books, clinics lack medicines, and infrastructure maintenance is avoided." Meanwhile, a recent study for a number of different poor countries estimated that the return on spending on educational instructional materials was up to 14 times higher than the return on spending on physical facilities.

And then there are the frameworks. In 1999, World Bank President James Wolfensohn unveiled his Comprehensive Development Framework, a checklist of 14 items, each with multiple subitems. The framework covers clean government, property rights, finance, social safety nets, education, health, water, the environment, the spoken word and the arts, roads, cities, the countryside, microcredit, tax policy, and motherhood. (Somehow, macroeconomic policy was omitted.) Perhaps this framework explains why the World Bank says management has simultaneously "refocused and broadened the development agenda." Yet even Wolfensohn seems relatively restrained compared with the framework being readied for the forth-coming U.N. World Summit on Sustainable Development in Johannesburg in late August 2002, where 185 "action recommendations"—covering everything from efficient use of cow dung to harmonized labeling of chemicals—await unsuspect-ing delegates.

Of course, the Millennium Development Goals (MDGs) are the real 800-pound gorilla of foreign aid frameworks. The representatives of planet Earth agreed on these goals at yet another U.N. conference in September 2000. The MDGs call for the simultaneous achievement of multiple targets by 2015, involving poverty, hunger, infant and maternal mortality, primary education, clean water, contraceptive use, HIV/AIDS, gender equality, the environment, and an ill-defined "partnership for development." These are all worthy causes, of course, yet would the real develop-ment customers necessarily choose to spend their scarce resources to attain these particular objectives under this particular timetable? Economic principles dictate that greater effort should be devoted to goals with low costs and high benefits, and less effort to goals where the costs are prohibitive relative to the benefits. But the "do everything" approach of the MDGs suggests that the aid bureaucracy feels above such trade-offs. As a result, government officials in recipient countries and the foreign aid agency's own frontline workers gradually go insane trying to keep up with proliferating objectives—each of which is deemed Priority Number One.

ALL PAYIN', NO GAIN

A 2002 World Bank technical study found that a doubling of aid flows is required for the world to meet the U.N. goals. The logic is somewhat circular, however, since a World Bank guidebook also stipulates that increasing aid is undoubtedly "a primary function of targets set by the international donor community such as the [Millennium] Development Goals." Thus increased aid becomes self-perpetuating—both cause and effect.

FOREIGN AID AND ABET

Pity the poor aid bureaucracy that must maintain support for foreign assistance while bad news is breaking out everywhere. Aid agencies have thus perfected the art of smoothing over unpleasant realities with diplomatic language. A war is deemed a "conflict-related reallocation of resources." Countries run by homicidal warlords like those in Liberia or Somalia are "low-income countries under stress." Nations where presidents loot the treasury experience "governance issues." The meaning of other aid community jargon, like "investment climate," remains elusive. The investment climate will be stormy in the morning, gradually clearing in the afternoon with scattered expropriations.

Another typical spin-control technique is to answer any criticism by acknowledging that, "Indeed, we aid agencies used to make that mistake, but now we have corrected it." This defense is hard to refute, since it is much more difficult to evaluate the present than the past. (One only doubts that the sinner has now found true religion from the knowledge of many previous conversions.) Recent conversions supposedly include improved coordination among donors, a special focus on poverty alleviation, and renewed economic reform efforts in African countries. And among the most popular concepts the aid community has recently discovered is "selectivity"—the principle that aid will only work in countries with good economic policies and efficient, squeaky-clean institutions. The moment of aid donors' conversion on this point supposedly came with the end of the Cold War, but in truth, selectivity (and other "new" ideas) has been a recurrent aid theme over the last 40 years.

Unfortunately, evidence of a true conversion on selectivity remains mixed. Take Kenya, where President Daniel arap Moi has mismanaged the economy since 1978. Moi has consistently failed to keep conditions on the 19 economic reform loans his government obtained from the World Bank and IMF (described by one

NGO as "financing corruption and repression") since he took office. How might international aid organizations explain the selectivity guidelines that awarded President Moi yet another reform loan from the World Bank and another from the IMF in 2000, the same year prominent members of Moi's government appeared on a corruption "list of shame" issued by Kenya's parliament? Since then, Moi has again failed to deliver on his economic reform promises, and international rating agencies still rank the Kenyan government among the world's most corrupt and lawless. Ever delicate, a 2002 IMF report conceded that "efforts to bring the program back on track have been only partially successful" in Kenya. More systematically, however, a recent cross-country survey revealed no difference in government ratings on democracy, public service delivery, rule of law, and corruption between those countries that received IMF and World Bank reform loans in 2001 and those that did not. Perhaps the foreign aid community applies the selectivity principle a bit selectively.

DISMANTLING THE CARTEL

How can the cartel of good intentions be reformed so that foreign aid might actually reach and benefit the world's poor? Clearly, a good dose of humility is in order, considering all the bright ideas that have failed in the past. Moreover, those of us in the aid industry should not be so arrogant to think we are the main determinants of whether low-income countries develop—poor nations must accomplish that mainly on their own.

Still, if aid is to have some positive effect, the aid community cannot remain stuck in the same old bureaucratic rut. Perhaps using market mechanisms for foreign aid is a better approach. While bureaucratic cartels supply too many goods for which there is little demand and too few goods for which there is much demand, markets are about matching supply and demand. Cartels are all about "coordination," whereas markets are about the decentralized matching of customers and suppliers.

One option is to break the link between aid money and the obligatory use of a particular agency's bureaucracy. Foreign assistance agencies could put part of their resources into a common pool devoted to helping countries with acceptably pro-development governments. Governments would compete for the "pro-development" seal of approval, but donors should compete, too. Recipient nations could take the funds and work with any agency they choose. This scenario would minimize duplication and foster competition among aid agencies.

Another market-oriented step would be for the common pool to issue vouchers to poor individuals or communities, who could exchange them for development services at any aid agency, NGO, or domestic government agency. These service providers would in turn redeem the vouchers for cash out of the common pool. Aid agencies would be forced to compete to attract aid vouchers (and thus money) for their budgets. The vouchers could also trade in a secondary market; how far their price is below par would reflect the inefficiency of this aid scheme and would require remedial action. Most important, vouchers would provide real market power to the impoverished customers to express their true needs and desires.

Intermediaries such as a new Washington-based company called Development Space could help assemble the vouchers into blocks and identify aid suppliers; the intermediaries could even compete with each other to attract funding and find projects that satisfy the customers, much as venture capital firms do. (Development Space is a private Web-based company established last year by former World Bank staff members—kind of an eBay for foreign aid.) Aid agencies could establish their own intermediation units to add to the competition. An information bank could facilitate transparency and communication, posting news on projects searching for funding, donors searching for projects, and the reputation of various intermediaries.

Bureaucratic cartels probably last longer than private cartels, but they need not last forever. President George W. Bush's proposed Millennium Challenge Account (under which, to use Bush's words, "countries that live by these three broad standards—ruling justly, investing in their people, and encouraging economic freedom—will receive more aid from America") and the accompanying increase in U.S. aid dollars will challenge the IMF and World Bank's near monopoly over reform-related lending. Development Space may be the first of many market-oriented endeavors to compete with aid agencies, but private philanthropists such as Bill Gates and George Soros have entered the industry as well. NGOs and independent academic economists are also more aggressively entering the market for advice on aid to poor countries. Globalization protesters are not well informed in all areas, but they seem largely on target when it comes to the failure of international financial institutions to foment "adjustment with growth" in many poor countries. Even within the World Bank itself, a recent board of directors paper suggested experimenting with "output-based aid" in which assistance would compensate service providers only when services are actually delivered to the poor—sadly, a novel concept. Here again, private firms, NGOs, and government agencies could compete to serve as providers.

Now that rich countries again seem interested in foreign aid, pressure is growing to reform a global aid bureaucracy that is increasingly out of touch with good economics. The high-income countries that finance aid and that genuinely want aid to reach the poor should subject the cartel of good intentions to the bracing wind of competition, markets, and accountability to the customers. Donors and recipients alike should not put up with $3,521 in aid to reduce the poverty head count by one, 185-point development frameworks, or an alphabet soup of bureaucratic fads. The poor deserve better.

QUESTIONS FOR REVIEW AND DISCUSSION

1. David Dollar emphasizes the importance of high-quality institutions. What specific institutions does he mean? Why, according to Dollar, does aid have more of a positive impact in countries with high-quality institutions than it does in countries with low-quality institutions?

2. Does Dollar believe that traditional forms of aid conditionality can be used to promote high-quality institutions in developing countries? What are the consequences of this for the distribution of foreign aid across developing countries? That is, which countries will get aid and which will not?

3. What does Easterly mean by the "foreign aid cartel"? How, and in what ways, does the existence of this "cartel" affect the kinds of projects that are funded by aid agencies?

4. What solutions does Easterly propose to solve the problems created by the "foreign aid cartel"? Do you think these solutions would work if put into practice? Do you think that donor governments have an incentive to implement such solutions? Why or why not?

5. Which of the two changes, that is, either Dollar's proposal to change the purposes for which aid is given or Easterly's proposal to change the structure through which aid is given, would do the most to improve the performance of foreign aid?

SUGGESTIONS FOR FURTHER READING

For a good discussion of the origins and development of postwar foreign aid, see: Robert Wood. *From Marshall Plan to Debt Crisis: Foreign Aid and Development Choices in the World Economy*. Berkeley: University of California Press, 1986.

For an in-depth examination and justification of the new approach to foreign aid, see: The World Bank. *Assessing Aid—What Works, What Doesn't, and Why*. Oxford: Oxford University Press, 1998.

PART

VII

Globalization

CHAPTER 18

◖ GLOBALIZATION: WHY NOW, AND WHAT IMPACT?

W e live in a global economy. This is an oft-stated but rarely defined claim. What does globalization mean? While the precise definition will differ depending upon which dimension of globalization we focus on, economic globalization generally refers to the integration of previously independent national economies into a single, tightly connected international economy. The economic integration of national economies has been brought about by the growth of international trade, foreign direct investment (investment by MNCs), and international capital flows (Bhagwati 2004, p. 3). Each of these economic activities has increased sharply in the last 20 years.

World trade has grown at historically unprecedented rates during the last 50 years. Between 1950 and 1999, world trade grew at an average rate of six percent per year (Oatley 2004). What is perhaps more impressive than the simple growth of world trade, however, is the fact that international trade has consistently grown more rapidly than total world economic production. In almost every year since 1950, world trade has grown at a faster rate than world economic output. Thus, countries are becoming progressively more open to trade each year. Stated slightly differently, each year a little bit more of the world's total economic production is produced in one country but consumed in another.

Foreign direct investment (FDI) has also grown rapidly, especially during the last 20 years. As we saw in a previous chapter, annual flows of FDI rose from $180 billion in the mid-1980s to more than $1 trillion in 2000 (UNCTAD 2001). In addition, the nature of FDI changed over the same period. From the end of the Second World War until the mid-1980s, FDI was oriented largely toward advanced industrial economies. To the extent that FDI flowed to developing countries, it did so either to extract natural resources or to produce locally in order to sell in the domestic market in which the MNC was investing.

Since the mid-1980s, the emerging markets have attracted an increasing share of world FDI. The character of FDI has also changed. Relatively less emphasis is placed on natural-resource extraction, and substantially more emphasis is placed on manufacturing investment. Moreover, manufacturing investments in emerging markets are now less often undertaken to gain access to the domestic market, and more often undertaken to establish export-oriented facilities. As a consequence, economic production in the advanced-industrialized and the emerging-market countries have become more tightly linked.

Financial flows have also increased substantially since the mid-1980s. While no single statistic can capture this tremendous growth, one statistic is illustrative: between 1986 and 1998, the average daily turnover in foreign-exchange markets grew from $850 billion to $1.5 trillion (Oatley 2004). The volume of international lending transactions has also risen sharply. New international bank loans and bond issues grew from $100 billion in 1975 to almost $900 billion in 1998 (Oatley 2004). Many analysts argue that the growth of international capital flows has greatly reduced national economic autonomy, as governments increasingly must make policy decisions under the watchful eye of international financial markets.

The expansion of crossborder economic activity and the consequent deepening of economic interdependence during the last 20 years raises a number of questions that have been the focus of study during the last 10 years. Perhaps most fundamentally, analysts have tried to understand why globalization emerged in the late twentieth century. Most analysts agree that this process has been driven by a combination of technological change and changes in government policy. Technological change, in particular changes in information processing and transmission and in transportation, have vastly reduced the costs of organizing global economic activities. In addition, many developing countries began to change their economic-development strategy in the late 1980s. This policy change has been characterized by a move away from inward-looking strategies, in which governments attempt to develop industrialized economies by isolating themselves from the global economy, to more outward-looking strategies in which industrialization is pursued through opening to and taking advantage of the international economy. Students of the global economy have also attempted to evaluate how far globalization has progressed. There is substantially less agreement about the answer to this question, with some scholars suggesting that the world economy is already a single global market, while others argue that such a position exaggerates the depth of globalization. The answer to this question matters, in part, because the depth of globalization determines how much autonomy governments retain in their national economic policymaking.

The two articles presented in this chapter examine these dimensions of globalization. Jeffrey D. Sachs accepts the claim that globalization has progressed quite far, and then focuses on explaining why it has occurred. In doing so, he explains how dramatic changes in technology and government economic policies combined to produce the rapid growth of international economic activity. Robert M. Dunn Jr., a professor of economics at The George Washington University, argues that globalization has not progressed as far as global enthusiasts claim. Focusing exclusively on the United States, Dunn argues that linkages between the American and the world economy have not deepened substantially over the last 20 years. Consequently, he argues, the American economy has not been globalized and the world economy imposes few constraints on American policymakers.

REFERENCES

Bhagwati, Jagdish. *In Defense of Globalization*. New York: Oxford University Press, 2004.

Oatley, Thomas. *International Political Economy: Interests and Institutions in the Global Economy*. New York: Longman, 2004.

United Nations Conference on Trade and Development. *World Investment Report*. Geneva: The United Nations, 2001.

The Geography of Economic Development

JEFFREY D. SACHS

In the waning days of the Soviet Empire, when the linkages between flagging economic power and the changing state of national security in the Soviet Union were becoming obvious, one story really hit home. It was the story of a gentleman waiting in one of the interminable bread queues in Moscow. Late in the Mikhail Gorbachev era, of course, the lines were getting longer, as the economic chaos in the Soviet Union worsened. Finally the bedraggled Muscovite reached the counter, where the clerk told him, "I'm sorry, we've run out of bread." The poor man exploded. The clerk said, "Now wait a minute, mister. If it weren't for Gorbachev, you would have been shot for saying something like that." The Muscovite went home and lamented to his wife, "Dear, it's much worse than I thought. They've run out of bullets, too."

There was a lot of grim humor in those days, and it has not been much less grim in the last few years. The Russian transformation has been bumpy, to say the least. More accurately, that transformation has been unsuccessful in recent years. This is a topic that I obviously ponder often, having served for two years, 1992 and 1993, as a senior economic advisor to the Russian government. I reflect on what might have been done differently, what we might have advised differently, whether there was another course of action that would have led to a more stable and prosperous society—something that I believe to be in not only Russia's interest but that of the United States as well.

But before getting to particular times and places, it would be useful to take up a very broad theme—nothing less than global economic dynamics—as a way to understand somewhat the nature of the world economy right now: the ways different regions fit into a fast-changing picture, the real economic struggles that engage most of the world.

Without question, the buzzword of our era is globalization. Some say this term is now so hackneyed as to be without content. In fact, it is a real phenomenon, one that is important for us to understand. But it is also important that different parts of the world fit into this fast, globalizing system in thoroughly different ways and have equally different economic prospects. One part of our analysis, then, is the shape of the world system as it is evolving; there is also the important question of why different parts of the world, different geographies or ecologies, face such different futures in it. Let us start, therefore, with some basic ideas about globalization, and then turn to the differences, which I think is the more interesting subject.

From Jeffrey D. Sachs, "The Geography of Economic Development," *Naval War College Review*, Autumn, 2000, pp. 93–105.

GLOBALIZATION

Globalization is a dynamic process of the economic integration of virtually the entire world. At least four aspects of this increased economic integration are worth bearing in mind. What most of us think of as the first part of globalization is increased international trade. There is no doubt that the role of international trade within any individual economy, and therefore for the world as a whole, has been increasing in importance relative to other kinds of economic activity. A typical measure that economists use is an economy's ratio of exports or imports to total output—that is, gross domestic product, GDP. If we look at the ratio of either exports or imports to GDP for virtually any economy in the world, we find that it has been rising; in a number of economies it has been rising particularly rapidly in the last fifteen years. On a day-to-day basis, economies today feel the effect of the international system much more heavily than they did forty years ago. Firms increasingly are directly engaged overseas as exporters or importers, and producers are exposed to competition of imports from the rest of the world.

In general, economic theory has taught—and the idea is very much confirmed by the evidence—that this growth in international trade is a source of increased productivity for all participants. Trade, as economists have been emphasizing ever since Adam Smith in 1776, is not a zero-sum game, where one side wins and the other side loses; rather, it is an opportunity for increased diversity of products, increased specialization, transmission of information and technology, and the like, and therefore a positive-sum game. The most obvious aspect of globalization, then, is simply the increased interpenetration of markets through the trade of goods and services.

A second point, one that is absolutely pivotal, is the increased interpenetration of markets by capital flows. Headlines in the last three years about globalization have been much more about capital flows than about trade. We have witnessed a recurring, sharp, and important kind of economic crisis, that is, crises undergone by countries in the process of globalization—a type of crisis closely linked to the international financial system. We saw them in East Asia beginning in 1997, in Thailand in July, then in Indonesia and Korea. The chaos that continues in Indonesia is rooted not only in geopolitics and local politics but also in the economic collapse that struck the nation at the end of 1997—a collapse clearly rooted in international financial flows. Huge amounts of money poured into Indonesia in the mid 1980s; then, just as suddenly, huge amounts of money flowed out in the fall of 1997. That rapid withdrawal of capital brought down the economy and with it the Suharto regime (which had its own weaknesses, to be sure) and led to cascading political and social change of incredible dynamism and risk.

The third aspect of globalization is the globalization of economic production. Economics textbooks, at least older ones, speak of, say, American products and Japanese products, and give the impression that countries simply trade their products with each other. But international trade today involves more and more not merely the exchange of one nation's products for another's but the exchange of products representing work done in ten, twenty, or even thirty countries. This process has become so complex that we can no longer say that this particular car is Japanese or this computer is American; the components are invariably from half a dozen or more countries—two dozen or more in a typical automobile or computer.

What has happened is that an increasing proportion of international production is carried out by major multinational firms. These firms typically locate their headquarters in the world's wealthiest regions—the United States, the European Union, Japan, in a few cases Korea or Southeast Asia—but their production sites are all over the world. Production itself is a rich logistical process that involves bringing components from one place, shipping them to another, dividing up what economists and business consultants call the "value chain" (itself a process of ever-increasing complexity) and then farming out the individual parts of the production process to areas of comparative advantage. In one region one handles logistical functions; in another region one takes advantage of low wages, in yet another of particular natural resources; and so forth. What this means is that a country's geographic relationship to major markets is crucial to how it is integrated—or why it is not integrated—into an increasingly globalized production structure. The determination of who wins and who loses, or at least who falls farther behind, is very much determined by geography. The importance of location for economic success has been enhanced by the globalization of production processes.

A fourth and quite fascinating dimension of globalization is the increasing institutional harmonization of economic policies, legislation, and structure. Not only are countries becoming integrated into a web of production, a network of capital flows, and an international market for goods and services, but they engage in these activities increasingly in a common structure of national and international institutions. By far the most dramatic example of this is the collapse of communism as a rival economic system, followed by the adoption, though as yet incomplete, by most postcommunist countries of imported, or derivative, legal and institutional structures that are compatible with those of the major markets. There are, for example, 135 countries in the World Trade Organization, created in 1995 to harmonize global trading rules and procedures. Underpinning the World Trade Organization is a corpus of international law setting forth in excruciating detail how international trade is to proceed: what kinds of regulations are fair game, which ones are not, even how sanitary standards can be applied. For example, when can a nation impose trade barriers if it thinks another is violating environmental norms? How should intellectual property standards be enforced? Patent law is now being "harmonized" internationally for the first time. Similarly, countries now regulate the convertibility of their currencies according to standards they accept as members of the International Monetary Fund, a body even more universal than the World Trade Organization.

All this has the effect of making international law without an international government—a highly difficult, challenging, and so far only partially successful venture. There are those in the United States who feel that it is ceding too much sovereignty by allowing international standards to determine what it does. There are others, closer to my own outlook, who feel that such standards are what prevents the rule of the jungle in international economic affairs and that the nation should be striving for such shared agreements. But whatever one's normative stance, the positive, or diagnostic, view of the world scene is that institutional harmonization—of how markets are organized, how banks are regulated, how food standards are imposed, even how intellectual property rights are organized—is now proceeding faster and is extending over more of the globe, by far, than at any other time in world history. Here we see more than 130 countries announcing that they want to live by a common set of economic codes and standards and to organize their own internal politics and policies according to them.

That encapsulates what globalization is about. It is a very deep process, involving not simply trade but finance, production, and even the rules of national economies and how they relate to each other. What is driving it, and why so dramatically? Several forces are at play, and they are both pervasive and persistent. This phenomenon is not going to disappear because of some local derangement. The trend is not irreversible, but to knock it off course will take more than a protectionist's winning an election, or an economic crisis in Colombia, Thailand, or Brazil.

WHY NOW?

At bottom, what is pushing globalization is that most of the world, particularly the developing countries, tried just about everything else first. They have now arrived, by elimination, at the realization that they must join the world economy. This has not been a linear process, in which countries recognized the advantages of participating in the international marketplace and decided to sign up. It has been distinctly nonlinear. During the last 150 to two hundred years, governments went in very different directions.

For most of world history, the vast majority of countries were poor. There was not much variation in economic performance or wealth until around 1800. At that point, one small part of the world took off—the Western European and the North Atlantic nations. There a dynamic process of industrialization built on new forms of harnessing power, particularly steam and coal, and new mechanized technologies. These states—primarily Britain and the United States, for quite a while—so accelerated their economic development that the military imbalances in their favor with respect to the rest of the world became even more marked than they had been for the preceding century or two. That translated, of course, into a very rapid carving-up of the world into the imperial property of, mainly, the European powers.

Why then did not worldwide institutional harmonization come easily? One reason is an interlude of about a century in which Western industrialization produced a profoundly skewed balance of power. Europe now owned a very large part of the world: Africa was completely gobbled up in the 1870s and 1880s, India by 1857, much of Southeast Asia in the 1850s and 1860s, Indochina about that same time, North Africa in the 1830s, and so on.

This state of affairs was thought in 1910 to be the permanent shape of the world (warning us, by the way, that however deep and persistent a state of affairs globalization may be, we should not simply extrapolate). In 1911, a book, *The Great Illusion*, by Norman Angell, was published in Britain and became famous. Its thrust was that the world economic system was in place: it was owned by Europe, and

Europe was the industrial center. While industry would slowly diffuse to the rest of the world, the system was stable. War, Angell argued, had become so costly and devastating as to be unthinkable. As might be imagined, Angell's book was a terrific best-seller in 1912 and 1913, but it quickly fell off the best-seller list in 1914. What had seemed an unshakable, permanent international system disappeared.

Mr. Angell tried again in 1934, when he wrote another book. This one had quite a realistic hypothesis. In it Angell said, in effect, "I told you so back in 1911. And I was right. War was devastating for our civilization. Human beings sometimes have to learn through experience. Now you've seen it. We are done with this." He proclaimed, again, the end of war in Europe. This book also was soon remaindered, unfortunately. But by 1945, with Europe devastated and war-torn, the end of the imperial era was in sight. Europe had so weakened itself that its imperial holdings of the world soon broke away, in a series of anticolonial wars—India in 1947, Indonesia in 1948, Egypt in 1952, and so on.

What is interesting is that what became known as the "developing world" did not, as it became independent, simply jump to the global system. To understand why not, let us put ourselves in the position of Jawaharlal Nehru, Gamal Abdel Nasser, or Sukarno at the moment of independence. If one has been struggling for decades against British domination in India, and if the first British colonizing power in India had not been even the Raj but the East India Company, a private multinational firm, the idea that the way to sovereignty and development is to open the doors to foreign multinationals might not seem convincing. All over the developing world, a simple logic prevailed: "Look, we are weak, they are strong. They used to own us; we have just got rid of them. We have to develop and industrialize quickly so that we can rebalance power in the world. But we cannot risk inviting them in to do that. What we need is a development strategy that will protect us while we gain our strength."

There were two variants of this strategy—soft and hard. The hard variant, of course, was Bolshevism, as spread first within Russia after the chaos of World War I, then by the Red Army after World War II, and later by imitators in other parts of the world, including the Maoist revolutionaries in China. The softer variant of this strategy was pursued not by one-party socialist-Leninist states but by regimes that chose not to monopolize the means of production but instead to spur industrialization by planting and protecting the seeds of industry—an approach that came to be known as "state-led industrialization."

A third of the world lived under "hard" socialism through the mid-1980s; another 40 percent or so lived under some kind of state-led industrialization. Both failed spectacularly. They failed for reasons that Adam Smith identified in 1776: closing doors means losing access to world knowledge. They lost the ability to tap into world technologies that they would otherwise have acquired through open trade and foreign investment. At the most fundamental level, this is the biggest problem with any kind of closed regime; the world moves on without you. Conceivably the United States, given its incredible dynamism and inventiveness, could go it alone—but probably not. Certainly for any other country in the world, the vast majority of the technologies needed for development must come from outside. However dynamic a nation is, it can develop only a small fraction of the technologies, manufacturing processes, and capital goods that it needs. International trade and foreign direct investment are absolutely fundamental to any successful development strategy.

Most of the regimes that tried state, and state-led, socialism went bankrupt. Bankruptcy is an interesting process and a systemic one. It could be seen in the nineteenth century when Europe threatened the sovereignty and survival of competitors, like the Ottoman Empire. Those empires usually ended up going bankrupt rather than being defeated militarily. They went bankrupt because when countries fall behind they tend to borrow in order to purchase foreign technology, military equipment, and even mercenary armies, in an effort to rectify the balance. The Ottomans borrowed heavily in the 1850s and 1860s trying to modernize; in the 1870s they went broke. Most of the state-led industrializers and most of the socialist countries (not all—China is a particular exception) did the same and went bankrupt—not morally, economically, or technologically but literally. The Soviet Union ran out of dollars in 1991. Gorbachev, for example, had borrowed about forty billion dollars from West German banks and Western governments between 1986 and 1990, and by 1991 that flow of funds was drying up. The result was hyperinflation, intensification of shortages, weakness and desperation of the regime, perhaps the tempting of the 1991 coup plotters, and the quick downward spiral.

Why did Solidarity emerge as a powerful political force in Poland in 1980?—because Poland had gone bankrupt in 1978. Being somewhat closer to the West, Poland had started borrowing earlier than the Soviet Union, when Edward Gierek instituted reforms in the early 1970s. The financial squeeze came later in the decade, and Polish living standards plummeted. People took to the streets. An electrician, Lech Walesa, jumped the fence at Gdansk's Lenin Shipyards, and Solidarity was born. Financial crisis was the precursor of political revolution.

Some seventy governments went bankrupt in the 1980s and early 1990s. A famous banker, Walter Wriston, the chairman of Citibank, once proclaimed that countries never go bankrupt; it was, accordingly, part of Citibank's strategy to lend to countries—in the years before it almost went bankrupt itself. In one sense, what Wriston said is correct: countries do live on. But it is absolutely a fact that governments can go bankrupt, can find themselves without the funds to pay their bills. This is not a rarity; it happens frequently. It results in part from the great imbalances of economic power that cause countries, especially poor and poorly organized ones, to borrow desperately to offset weaknesses, thereby digging themselves deeper.

This historical excursion answers the question posed earlier: why did globalization start so late, and then so dramatically? After a series of events that started in about 1840, dozens of governments went bankrupt, fairly simultaneously, in the 1980s. They reached a dead end, looked for success stories to emulate, and found one—the incredible economic, financial, and military power of the United States. The American model and its influence quickly assumed such dominance that the reform process itself has become known as the Washington Consensus. Countries have abandoned the failed strategy of closure and are joining the international system.

THE TECHNOLOGICAL REVOLUTION
AND GLOBALIZATION

The other deep force at work, aside from globalization, is the technological revolution, which steadily raises the dividends of being part of the international system. Not only is staying out costly, but getting in yields higher and higher returns. The underlying information, communications, logistics, and transport technologies are making it possible for more countries to globalize, and in deeper ways.

Who are the real winners now? They are a handful of developing countries, primarily of Southeast Asia and Northeast Asia, that did not opt for state socialism or state-led development—South Korea, Hong Kong, Singapore, and Malaysia. They went a different way. The way they went, of course, brought them under the U.S. security umbrella; in response, they integrated their economies into the U.S. production system.

Singapore is a classic example. Even in the British Empire, it was a free port. After its independence in 1965, it maintained itself as essentially a free port, strongly linked to American production. Singapore's strategy was to hook into U.S. industry, mainly in electronics but also to some extent in textiles and apparel, importing components and exporting assembled, integrated products for the American market. Advances in information technology and transport allowed Singapore, although it is halfway around the world, to do this in a cost-effective manner. Singapore has built state-of-the-art port facilities, which turn around containerships in just six hours. Its firms are electronically linked to U.S.-based multinationals. Orders and design specifications are received through computer-aided design and manufacturing systems; firms know exactly what template to use or which motherboard to install. Computerized data transmission has enabled Singapore's firms to become deeply enmeshed in the U.S. production process.

These technological developments, especially the widespread use of containerization (computerization and the Internet came much later), made the East Asian boom possible. Without containerization it would not have been possible for East Asia to incorporate itself into the U.S. economy as deeply as it did. Containerization drastically reduced the costs of merchandise shipments, particularly for capital goods, thereby greatly facilitating the globalization of production.

On one side, then, there were failed, old systems. On the other side there was the underlying dynamism of the technologies of global networking in the fields of information, computerization, communication, and transport. The push and pull of globalization has been so compelling that by the late 1980s, it is fair to say, almost no part of the world, and almost no world leader, dared to stay on the sidelines. That is the main reason why we have seen such a dramatic move toward institutional harmonization in the last ten years. These forces are so deep that nothing of less than worldwide impact—not a recession in the United States, or financial crisis in a country or two—is likely to divert them. Events that could undo this process would be of the kind that undid the pre-1914 system and that occurred between 1914 and 1945—a combination of war and profound economic crisis resulting in deep rupture on a global scale. Globalization is not set and assured, but it is moving in a very deep channel, where it is felt strategically by almost all leaders. The presidents and prime ministers of developing countries, even those in the midst of crises, are not asking how to escape globalization or how to protect their countries by closing their economies. They are asking how it can be made to work for them.

THE GEOGRAPHY OF GLOBALIZATION

In some places globalization is working, and in others it is not. What are some of the structural underpinnings of success or failure in this world system? What do they suggest about U.S. economic strategy and about tactics the United States can use to help incorporate countries into the world system, for its interests as well as their own? Are there policies that will make this process more equitable?

Let us start with the crucial fact that globalization is taking place in a world of astounding inequality—the greatest inequality in world history. We can say that with confidence, without having explored every era since civilization began some ten thousand years ago, because, as noted earlier, through 1800 everybody was poor. Not until the last two hundred years did vast inequalities of income develop, because only in the last two hundred years did industrialization and science-based economic growth emerge.

When it did, a huge increase in the gap between rich and poor arose. In 1820, according to estimates by the leading economic historian of long-term growth, the richest part of the world was Western Europe, with a per capita income of around $1,200. The poorest part of the world was Sub-Saharan Africa, with an income of about four hundred dollars per capita. (These numbers are adjusted to be somewhat comparable to our sense of dollars today in terms of purchasing power.) The ratio was about three to one. Over the course of the next 180 years, Western European income grew twentyfold; in the United States as well, income, in very rough terms, also increased twentyfold. In Sub-Saharan Africa, per capita income grew only threefold; shockingly, that region has only now arrived at something like the income level of Britain in 1820. The gap between richest and poorest has grown to around twenty, or even twenty-five, to one, now; if we take only the very richest countries and the very poorest, the differential is forty, fifty, or sixty to one.

If these income gaps were entirely random, a graphic representation of per capita income in the world would show a random distribution of the rich countries and poorer ones. But in fact there are geographical gradients in the distribution of world income. First of all, there is the basic gradient that virtually all of the rich countries of the world are outside of the tropics, and virtually all of the poor countries are in them. Temperate-zone countries are either rich, socialist and therefore poor now, or deeply landlocked—and maybe also socialist, and therefore deeply in trouble. Except for Singapore and Hong Kong, virtually all of the tropic zone remains poor today. Tropical countries are not necessarily desperately or uniformly poor, but they are poor. Climate, then, accounts for a quite significant proportion of the cross-national and cross-regional disparities of world income.

Another geographical gradient that is quite important is proximity to markets. That has been true ever since Adam Smith wrote. The "name of the game" in international trade, as it has been in world power, often has been naval access. Coastal countries routinely do better than interior, landlocked parts of the world. Even today, despite air, rail, the Internet, and everything else, the largest proportion of international trade still travels by sea. For a landlocked country the cost of moving a container to a port is ferociously high. That is true because it must not only go over land, which is expensive, but cross political borders, which is often even more expensive. Studies conducted by Harvard's Center for International Development have consistently shown that proximity, especially political proximity, to the sea is very important. Which are the poorest countries of the world? They are the tropical, landlocked countries: Chad, Mali, Niger, Central African Republic, Rwanda, Burundi, and Bolivia.

There are, then, two major barriers to international development—a climatic barrier and a geographical, or physical transport, barrier. These are real problems, with real implications for the success or failure of globalization. First, the countries that tend to be successful are those that are near major markets; a country that is proximate to major markets and has a coastline is in especially good shape, once it opens up. Let us think about what that means in some specific cases.

For a number of reasons, Mexico and Central America, North Africa, and Eastern Europe fell far behind their developed neighbors, before globalization began. Some were colonized by their neighbors; others absented themselves from the world economy. Some faced physical, geographical, or resource barriers, and some had bad luck. Today, in the age of globalization, new underlying forces are flowing in favor of some of these nations.

Mexico is an example. Certainly, it has experienced serious problems with financial flows—the banking crisis of 1994 comes to mind. Also, its political system is only now in the process of reform, after a long period of one-party rule. But to the north, across the Rio Grande, is the United States, with a per capita income of some thirty thousand dollars; Mexico has a per capita income of three thousand dollars. The result is a powerful force bringing technology and investment to Mexico; that is exactly what is happening. Mexico's economic prospects are quite good; the underlying geography supports its development.

North Africa has been culturally and, for a long time, economically and politically cut off from its northern neighbors across the Mediterranean. Rome and Carthage fought each other more than two thousand years ago; the Christian-Islamic divide prevented the establishment of normal relations for about seven hundred years. But Tunisia, for example, is only about a hundred kilometers away from Italian territory. With Italian per capita income at twenty thousand dollars and Tunisia's at two thousand, there will be a very powerful economic flow between the two countries. Italian firms will take advantage of the income differential by investing in Tunisia; Fiat, for instance, will make automotive components in Tunis and then re-export them to Italy. Indeed, Tunisia is growing quite well right now, as is its neighbor, Morocco. Greek Cypress, which unlike its Turkish counterpart has not been subjected to a Western European embargo, is booming right now. That is the result of geographic proximity.

Among the transition economies, the most successful are those located along the border of Western Europe. History and culture play roles, but geographic proximity, facilitating trade and investment, is an important factor. The Baltic States are becoming workshops for Scandinavia. Scandinavian and German firms are investing in Estonia to produce components for re-export, thereby raising Estonia's living standards. Poland's boom can be ascribed to geographic proximity. The Czech Republic, Slovakia, Croatia, and Slovenia are experiencing the same phenomenon of proximity. Go inland a thousand kilometers to Moldavia or the Balkans, however, or two thousand kilometers into the heartland of Russia, or five thousand kilometers into Central Asia, and one finds none of that economic pull. Why, after all, would an Italian textile company outsource stitching to Turkmenistan?

The other developmental barrier is climate. Why is climate so important in this day and age? It is because poor countries still face problems that wealthier countries left behind long ago. The tropics pose tremendous difficulties for basic food production. Growing rice or maize in a lowland tropical environment is generally very tough; farmers are plagued by pests, veterinary disease, weak soils, rapid soil erosion, and other environmental barriers. Another profound challenge, particularly in Africa, is health. Diseases like malaria still impose huge economic, social, and health burdens on the tropical world.

A large part of the tropics has been trapped in a vicious circle. The tropics were poorer in the last century than the temperate zones, because of a variety of deep problems. The larger markets in the rich temperate zones supported more research and technological development. Advances pushed income even higher in those zones but could not be readily diffused to the tropics; ecological conditions were too different. Whether in areas of medicine, public health, food productivity, construction, or energy use, the gap widened. Tropical countries experienced a massive brain drain. People with critical skills packed up and went to work in Cambridge, Silicon Valley, or elsewhere, further widening the gap between underlying national and regional capabilities.

Countries that are both tropical and far from markets face the most profound problems. It is in tropical, geographically disadvantaged countries and regions that we see some of the biggest humanitarian challenges and social disasters. It is no accident that genocide took place in Rwanda. Obviously, we must avoid crude geographic determinism, but Rwanda's location poses near-insurmountable problems for economic development. It is plagued by intense crowding, environmental stress, and vast struggles among groups over resources for survival; further, it is without the port that could turn its capital, Kigali, into an export processing zone and otherwise contribute to economic development.

These ecological and geographical factors are very important and deserve greater attention from analysts and policy makers alike. Countries that are favorably located generally tend to make it, unless their politics are so deeply skewed as to pose a fundamental barrier—and there are such cases. We have not yet begun to address the implications of the profound problems that tropical countries and landlocked regions represent for international economic institutions, foreign assistance programs, and the way we think about development.

This is obviously a mixed assessment. For significant parts of the world, there is reason for considerable optimism. Despite all the wonders of globalization, however, serious risks remain for others. Not all of the world will be fruitfully touched by the processes of globalization.

For even the "proximate" countries—the ones blessed by geographic location, with the wind at their backs—the process of escaping from the damage of the past, from weak institutions, from economic atrophy, and from financial bankruptcy remains a heavy burden. They must meet the challenges both of catching up and of successful transformation. Not all manage, and when governments go bankrupt, societies cannot function. One of the legacies of the last fifty years is bankrupt governments all over the world. We sometimes use that fact tactically, as a lever by which friendly governments can be kept in place, or by which regimes can be controlled and manipulated. That approach is a mistake. At the edge of bankruptcy, even the consolidation of political power sufficient to maintain internal order is in jeopardy. American foreign-policy makers trying to work with "difficult" countries find that things explode in their faces. Things seem to be going fine, just before a quite dramatic collapse of authority and civil power. At the roots of these collapses often lie economic problems, problems severe enough to pull down governments and therefore open the way to anarchy.

What this means is that in our approach to globalization, we need a sensitivity to geography, to climate, to the history of how we got where we are, and to the financial and political struggles of countries. If we adopt this broader view, we can more effectively ensure that much more of the world will partake of the unbelievable bounty that modern science and technology provide.

Has the U.S. Economy Really Been Globalized?

ROBERT M. DUNN JR.

It is difficult to read an academic or popular analysis of the U.S. economy without encountering the "fact" that it has been globalized, with the clear implication that this country no longer has an independent national economy but instead is merely part of a single world entity. Debates occur as to whether this melding of the U.S. economy into a global economy is desirable or undesirable, but whether it has actually happened is seldom raised. In reality, the evidence of a globalized economy is quite weak, indicating instead that the U.S. economy retains a large part of its historic national independence.

This issue has become increasingly important because fear of the effects of globalization on the United States have become widespread. The World Trade Organization (WTO) meetings in Seattle were disrupted by groups opposing a globalized U.S. economy, Pat Buchanan and Ralph Nader ran for president largely on the basis of such fears, and congressional debates frequently revolve around this issue. Perhaps most important, opposition to the increasingly globalized U.S. economy was a major factor in the defeat of President William Clinton's request for fast-track authority to negotiate the expansion of the North American Free Trade Agreement (NAFTA) and to pursue other trade agreements. This is the first time that a president has been refused such authority, and this defeat represents Congress's movement away from its past willingness to liberalize international trade. As long as fears of the effects of globalization on our economy play a major role in debates over trade and other international economic issues, there is little prospect for the expansion of NAFTA or for U.S. participation in another multilateral WTO negotiating round. These fears presume, however, that the U.S. economy actually has been globalized. Four economic indicators are used here to show that these fears are largely groundless. As this becomes more widely understood, the international economic policy of the United States may return to its previous, and more productive, pattern.

THE CRITERIA FOR GLOBALIZATION

What statistics might measure the extent to which the U.S. economy is more integrated into the rest of the world than in the past? A number of indicators could be suggested, but this study relies on the following concepts:

From Robert M Dunn, Jr., "Has the U.S. Economy Really Been Globalized?" *The Washington Quarterly*, 24:1, Winter, 2001, pp. 53–64. © 2001 by the Center for Strategic and International Studies (CSIS) and the Massachusetts Institute of Technology.

1. The role of international trade in the economy

    If the U.S. economy has actually been globalized, the share of trade in its gross domestic product (GDP) should be much higher than in the past. This share merely returning to, or moving slightly above, previous levels would not be evidence of global integration; the role of trade in the U.S. economy should be an order of magnitude greater than in the past.

2. Real interest rates

    If capital markets are globalized, real interest rates in the major industrialized countries would have been arbitraged together and should now be quite similar. U.S. real yields should now be determined primarily in Europe, Canada, and Japan rather than exclusively in U.S. capital markets.

3. U.S. macroeconomic policies

    If the U.S. economy is globalized, both U.S. fiscal and monetary policies should be constrained by policies in the other major industrialized countries. It should no longer be possible for the United States to pursue macroeconomic policies that differ significantly from those in other large countries of the Organization for Economic Cooperation and Development (OECD).

4. Business cycles

    A globalized economy should mean a global business cycle, of which the United States is merely a part. The timing of U.S. business cycles should have become similar to the timing of cycles of other industrialized countries in recent decades. The close ties among markets here and abroad, both for goods and for financial assets, should make it impossible for the United States to avoid either the recessions or the macroeconomic expansions that occur in other major OECD countries.

HISTORY AS A YARDSTICK

Despite discussion of the enormous growth in the role of trade in the U.S. economy, this share has only recently returned to the levels of the late nineteenth century.

    As column 4 of Table 1 shows, merchandise trade constituted 16.4 percent of U.S. gross national product (GNP) in 1880 and matched that level only at the end of the 1970s. The striking event of this 120-year period is its collapse in the 1920s and its very slow recovery after World War II, not the recent growth of trade. As recently as 1970, merchandise trade was only 9.1 percent of U.S. GNP, slightly more than half of the share prevailing in 1880.

    The United States maintained a relatively open economy in the late nineteenth and early twentieth centuries, moved sharply toward autarky in the 1920–1940 period, and then maintained a small and largely unchanged role for trade in the 1940–1970 period. In the 1970s, trade recovered sharply and then grew slowly as a share of the economy in the next 19 years. In 1999, the role of merchandise trade in U.S. GDP was only 2.5 percentage points higher than it was in 1880.

    International trade in goods and services as a share of GNP followed a similar pattern, but the growth in recent years has been slightly more rapid than for trade

TABLE 1 ■ THE ROLE OF FOREIGN TRADE IN THE U.S. ECONOMY, 1870–1999

Year	Gross National Product[A]	Merchandise $(X + M)^B$	Goods & Services $(X + M)^B$	Merchandise/GNP	G&S/GNP
1870	6,710	829	1,115	12.4	16.6
1880	9,180	1,504	1,811	16.4	19.7
1890	12,300	1,647	2,069	13.4	16.8
1900	17,300	2,244	2,865	13.0	16.6
1910	31,600	3,302	4,274	10.4	13.5
1920	88,900	13,506	17,005	15.2	19.1
1930	91,100	6,904	9,864	7.6	10.8
1940	100,600	6,646	8,991	6.6	8.9
1950	284,600	19,127	26,525	6.7	9.3
1960	515,300	34,408	50,627	6.7	9.8
1970	1,015,500	92,338	119,871	9.1	11.8
1980	2,732,000	473,019	560,000	17.3	20.5
1990	5,463,000	887,644	1,155,200	16.2	21.1
1999	9,256,100	1,748,100	2,250,500	18.9	24.3

[A]GDP for 1999 [B] X + M = exports plus imports

Sources: *Historical Statistics of the United States: Colonial Times to 1957*, U.S. Department of Commerce, 1960; *Economic Report of the President*, U.S. Government Printing Office, various issues; *Survey of Current Business*, April 2000.

in merchandise alone. As column 5 of Table 1 shows, this broader measure of trade was more than 19 percent of GNP in both 1880 and 1920, but then fell to only 10.8 percent in 1930 and 8.9 percent in 1940. Recovery was very slow in the 1940–1970 period, but considerably more rapid in the 1970s. By the 1980s, it had recovered to slightly more than the late nineteenth and early twentieth-century levels, and by 1999 it was 4.6 percentage points above the 1880 level. The share of U.S. GNP (GDP in 1999) that is now exported or imported is higher than that in the late nineteenth century, but the increase is far too small to suggest a globalized economy.

The lack of major trade growth as a share of U.S. GNP is surprising in light of the sharp decline in tariff rates in the past 130 years. In 1870, the average tariff rate on U.S. imports was 44.9 percent; in recent years it has been less than 2 percent.[1] Despite this reduction in tariffs, the U.S. economy has not become globalized.

Not only has trade failed to globalize the U.S. economy thus far, but it is unlikely to do so in the future if remaining trade barriers are reduced. A recent statistical study by the U.S. International Trade Commission concludes that, if this country were to remove all of its remaining statutory import restraints, total employment losses in import-competing sectors would be only 135,000 jobs. This is less than the number of new jobs created in this country in a typical month in the recent boom. Predicted efficiency gains from the removal of remaining trade barriers are less than one-half of 1 percent of GDP. The likely effects of removing the remaining barriers are modest because there are not many left. The United States is already close to free trade, retaining high tariffs or other major barriers only in textiles, garments, sugar, dairy products, and coastal shipping (the Jones Act).[2] Trade has not globalized the U.S. economy and would not do so even if the few remaining barriers to imports were removed.

Although trade has not globalized the U.S. economy, it may have done so in many other countries. The 24 percent role of trade in U.S. GDP contrasts rather strikingly with the data for nations whose economies are smaller and therefore more open. The trade-to-GDP ratio in the United Kingdom is 54 percent, in Canada it is 81 percent, and in the Netherlands it is 104 percent. Ireland, at 157 percent, is an even more open economy, but Singapore's 254 percent is probably the record. Among industrialized countries, only Japan, with a trade-to-GDP ratio of 20 percent, is less integrated with the world economy than the United States, due to high Japanese import barriers.

This country really is different. The United States has an enormous economy and a wide range of natural resources, making trade less vital than elsewhere. Distance from European and Asian industrialized countries is sufficient for transportation costs to be a modest but significant barrier to trade. The concept of economic globalization through trade is relevant for small industrialized countries, but not for the United States.

THE MYTH OF THE SINGLE CAPITAL MARKET

Articles in the U.S. financial press would lead one to conclude that there is now a world capital market, or at least a single capital market for the major industrialized countries. According to these reports, flows of funds are large enough to have destroyed national distinctions. There is no longer a U.S. capital market, but instead merely a U.S. segment of a much larger market consisting of all the major industrialized countries.

If there were such a single capital market for the industrialized countries, rates of return across those countries should have converged. Because many of these countries maintain flexible exchange rates and therefore may experience quite different rates of inflation, nominal interest rates may not be driven together through an arbitraging process, but real interest rates should have converged.

Because the real interest rate is the nominal rate minus the expected rate of inflation over the lifetime of an asset, such real yields are difficult to observe for long-term debt instruments. Because there is no way of knowing the rate of inflation that investors expect over the next decade or more, one cannot be certain what real yields are foreseen. For short-term assets, this is less of a problem. One cannot be certain what inflationary expectations are, but, for a period as brief as 90 days, it is not unreasonable to assume that people typically expect approximately the same rate of inflation that has prevailed during the previous three months. This means that the short-term real interest rate can be approximated as the nominal short-term interest rate minus the annual rate of inflation prevailing during the previous 90 days. Early 2000 observations for this estimate of real short-term yields in the G-10 industrialized countries are found in Table 2.

TABLE 2 ■ SHORT-TERM REAL INTEREST RATES IN
G-10 COUNTRIES[A]

Belgium	1.34%	Italy	0.64%
Switzerland	0.33%	Canada	3.78%
Japan	−1.15%	United Kingdom	4.46%
France	2.34%	Netherlands	0.74%
United States	2.15%	Germany	3.64%
Sweden	2.75%		

[A]As of January 2000; note that 11 countries are referred to as the G-10, analogous to the Big Ten Athletic Conference.

Source: *Economist*, January 8, 2000, pp. 98–99.

The globalized capital market is not apparent in these numbers. Even among the G-10 countries that are members of the European Monetary Union (EMU), there is a range of real yields of 300 basis points. For all 11 countries, the range of real yields is a high of 4.46 percent in the United Kingdom to a low of –1.15 percent in Japan, or 561 basis points. These data strongly suggest the continued existence of national capital markets with considerable degrees of autonomy.

Although real yields differed significantly in January 2000, evidence of some convergence of U.S. real interest rates toward those of other major industrialized countries during recent decades may exist. This would indicate some globalization of U.S. capital markets. In Figure 1 are data on the absolute value of the difference between the U.S. real interest rate and the average of real yields in four other countries during the 1960–1998 period.[3] To eliminate the impact of the EMU, only one entering country (Germany) is included with Great Britain, Japan, and Canada. If U.S. capital markets have actually been globalizing, the data should show a clear declining trend in recent years as U.S. real yields became very similar to those in the other four countries.

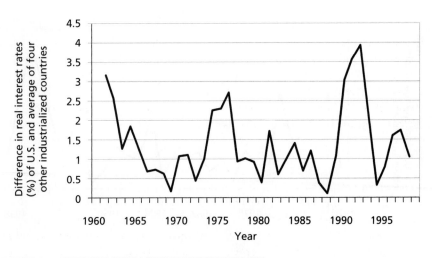

FIGURE 1 ■ DIFFERENCE IN REAL SHORT-TERM INTEREST RATES

There is no evidence in Figure 1 to support the globalization of U.S. short-term capital markets. Real short-term yields converged in the late 1960s but sharply diverged when the Bretton Woods system collapsed in the early 1970s. Convergence in the early 1980s was reversed later in the decade, a pattern that was repeated at the end of the 1980s and in the early 1990s. U.S. capital markets, as represented by real short-term interest rates, have not become more closely linked to those of other major industrialized countries in recent decades.

CONVERGING MACROECONOMIC POLICIES?

If the United States and the other major industrialized countries now constitute a single economy, their macroeconomic policies should have converged. That would suggest that the rates of growth of the money supplies of these countries had become more similar. Short-term interest rates might be viewed as an alternative monetary policy tool, but it has already been argued that there is no evidence of convergence in real interest rates. Using narrow money (M1) supply growth as another indicator of monetary policy, the same statistical exercise was performed as for short-term real interest rates. A 1970–1998 time series was prepared for the absolute value of the difference between the rate of growth of the U.S. money supply and the average of that of the other four countries. This time series is found in Figure 2. Again, if U.S. monetary policy had been globalizing, this time series should show a clear trend toward zero.

Evidence for the convergence of U.S. monetary policy toward that in the other four countries is difficult to discover in these data. Once again, convergence at the beginning of the 1970s was reversed when the Bretton Woods system ceased to operate. Convergence at the beginning of the 1980s was followed by sharp divergences in the late 1980s and the mid-1990s.

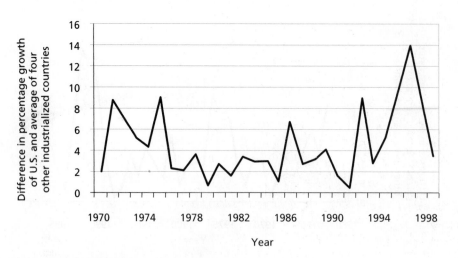

FIGURE 2 ■ DIFFERENCE IN MONEY SUPPLY GROWTH

Further evidence for the continuing independence of U.S. monetary policy is provided by the manner in which the Taylor rule was estimated. This rule, developed by John Taylor of Stanford University, is the most widely used monetary policy rule explaining the policies of the Federal Reserve System, as represented by the federal funds rate.[4] The rule, which was estimated from U.S. data, includes only two explanatory variables: the U.S. rate of inflation and the domestic unemployment rate relative to a full employment norm. The Taylor rule does an impressive job of explaining data for the U.S. federal funds rate in recent decades, without any foreign or international variables. Federal Reserve System targets for the federal funds rate can be explained solely by U.S. rates of inflation and unemployment. The Open Market Committee of the Federal Reserve System does not appear to be constrained in any significant way by pressures of globalization.

If U.S. fiscal policy had been globalized, budget deficits as a share of GDP should also have become increasingly similar to those in other industrialized countries. The same time series was prepared for the absolute value of the difference between the U.S. budget deficit as a share of GNP and the average of the same number for the four industrialized countries that appeared in previous exercises. These data are in Figure 3.

This graph leads to the conclusion that U.S. fiscal policy has actually become more dissimilar to that prevailing abroad in recent decades, with similarities existing in the 1960s, but not after the early 1970s. The breakdown of the Bretton Woods system appears to have triggered greater national independence in budgetary policies. U.S. macroeconomic policies have not been globalized.

Business Cycles: Timing Is Everything

If a globalized economy, of which the United States is part, really exists, the major industrialized countries should share the timing of business cycles. National patterns of expansion and recession should have been replaced by a single pattern,

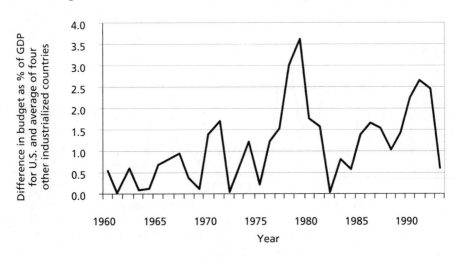

FIGURE 3 ■ DIFFERENCE IN BUDGET DEFICITS AS A SHARE OF GDP

TABLE 3 ■ COUNTRIES REAL GDP GROWTH RATES IN 1999[A]

Belgium	4.6%	Italy	2.1%
Switzerland	2.5%	Canada	4.7%
Japan	0.0%	United Kingdom	3.0%
France	3.1%	Netherlands	4.2%
United States	5.0%	Germany	2.3%
Sweden	3.8%		

[A]Note: 11 countries are referred to as the G-10.

Source: OECD, *Main Economic Indicators*, May 2000, p. vi.

largely shared across these economies. The data in Table 3 indicate that this was not the case in 1999.

The range of growth rates was 5.0 percentage points, from a high of 5.0 percent in the United States to a low of zero in Japan. The fact that the 10 non-U.S. countries had an average growth rate of only 3 percent did not preclude the United States from enjoying 5 percent growth in its eighth consecutive year of expansion. Serious constraints do not seem to be placed on U.S. economic growth by a global business cycle.

It might be argued that, although 1999 saw large differences in growth rates among the industrialized countries, there has still been a trend toward convergence in the business cycles of the major industrialized countries. Evidence on that issue can be found in Figure 4, which presents the absolute value of the difference between U.S. GDP growth and the average growth rate in the four countries used in the discussions above.

Once again, there is very little evidence for convergence. Similar rates of growth after the end of the Bretton Woods era were followed by sharp divergence in the

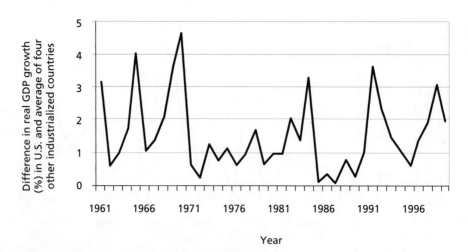

FIGURE 4 ■ DIFFERENCE IN REAL GDP GROWTH

early 1980s. Convergence in the mid-1980s was followed by very different growth rates in the early 1990s. Similarity followed in the mid-1990s, but divergence returned late in the decade. The United States retains its own macroeconomy, and business cycles in this country frequently differ sharply in timing and amplitude from those of other major industrialized countries.

Many other industrialized countries have far less independent macro-economies than does the United States. The absence of independent macro-economies is particularly true of members of the EMU, who have not only given up any national control of monetary policy but have also had their control of fiscal policy severely compromised by Maastricht rules. These countries should not run budget deficits in excess of 3 percent of GDP and may be fined for doing so. All members of the European Union (EU), including the four that are not members of the EMU, have to abide by rules that greatly constrain economic independence. Many European economies therefore have not been globalized, but have been EU/EMU-ized.

Even a country such as Canada, which is not a member of the EU or EMU, has considerably less macroeconomic freedom than does the United States. A depreciation in the Canadian dollar will cause the acceleration of inflation in our northern neighbor, meaning that the Bank of Canada may feel compelled to follow U.S. monetary policy to maintain stability in the Canadian exchange rate and price level. By contrast, in the United States, trade is a sufficiently small share of GDP that the linkage from the exchange rate to the price level is quite weak, meaning that the Federal Reserve System is not constrained to follow policies being pursued abroad to stabilize the exchange rate.

The previous arguments are not meant to imply that the United States has become isolated from the rest of the world. Our culture, society, and economy are affected more by the rest of the world than they were previously. The sharp decline in the cost of international telephone calls and other communications means that Americans have more regular contact with citizens of foreign countries than they did a few years ago. International travel by Americans and foreign visits to this country have grown significantly, due to higher incomes and a decline in air fares relative to other prices. Flows of investment funds in and out of this country have grown enormously, and trade is a slightly larger part of the economy than it was a century ago. These factors indicate that the society, culture, and economy of the United States have become more connected to the rest of the world, but our national economic independence has remained largely intact.

MORE THAN ENOUGH HYSTERIA

Evidence of a fully globalized U.S. economy is sparse. The role of foreign trade has only recently recovered to levels present in the latter part of the nineteenth century, and, even at the end of the 1990s, it was only modestly above those levels. U.S. interest rates, both nominal and real, are frequently different from those in other major industrialized economies, and both fiscal and monetary policies remain independent. The timing of our business cycles is often entirely different from those abroad, and there is no evidence that these cycles have converged in recent decades.

Some of the macroeconomic indicators discussed above were similar in the industrialized countries in the late 1960s, but diverged sharply in the early 1970s. The collapse of the Bretton Woods system at the beginning of the 1970s, and the subsequent maintenance of a system of floating exchange rates by the United States and many other industrialized countries, represented a shift away from globalization. A regime of flexible rates makes it possible for macroeconomic policies to differ more than was possible with the fixed parities of the Bretton Woods system and loosened the linkages among the timing patterns of business cycles. The move to flexible exchange rates increased national economic independence in these matters.[5]

If the Bretton Woods system were still in operation, or if the United States returned to a fixed parity, the potential for a globalized economy would probably have more meaning for this country. As long as the United States retains a flexible exchange rate, which it now appears virtually certain to do, this economy will largely retain its independence.

Because the U.S. economy is not globalized, economic policy should not be based on fears of its effects. The fiasco in Seattle, the defeat of fast-track authority, and the unfortunate tenor of recent public discussion of international economic policy all result from fear of something that does not exist. Gertrude Stein's description of an unfortunate city in California applies equally to the globalization of the U.S. economy: "There's no there, there."

As Americans come to understand that the globalization fears of the past few years were irrational, it should again be possible for this country to pursue traditional international economic policies. It can at least be hoped that the new administration will be granted fast-track authority to expand NAFTA and move toward another WTO round. The "globalized U.S. economy" is largely a myth.

ENDNOTES

1. U.S. Department of Commerce, *Historical Statistics of the United States: Colonial Times to 1957*, 539; and *Economic Report of the President: 2000*, 399.
2. U.S. International Trade Commission (USITC), *The Economic Effects of Significant U.S. Import Restraints: Second Update 1999* (Washington, D.C.: USITC, 1999).
3. Figure 1 contains average annual data, so the entries are annual average short-term interest rates minus the average rate of inflation during that year. All the data in this and the later time series and graph come from the International Financial Statistics of the International Monetary Fund.
4. John B. Taylor, "The Inflation/Output Variability Tradeoff Revisited," in J. Fuhrer, ed., *Goals, Guidelines, and Constraints on Monetary Policy* (Boston: Boston Federal Reserve Bank, 1994).
5. Robert Mundell, "The Monetary Dynamics of International Adjustment Under Fixed and Flexible Exchange Rates," *Quarterly Journal of Economics*, May 1960. See also "Capital Mobility and Stabilization Policy Under Fixed and Flexible Exchange Rates," *Canadian Journal of Economics and Political Science*, November 1963.

QUESTIONS FOR REVIEW AND DISCUSSION

1. What factors does Jeffrey D. Sachs emphasize in his explanation of why globalization occurred in the late twentieth century? How does Sachs treat the relative importance of these factors? Do you think other factors were important? If so, what are they?
2. According to Sachs, how does geography shape the extent to which countries or regions benefit from globalization? Do you agree that geography plays such an important role? What are the implications of focusing on geography as an explanation for which countries can benefit from globalization?
3. Given the factors that Sachs emphasizes in his explanation for why globalization has occurred, do you think that he believes that globalization is reversible? Do you think that globalization is reversible? Why or why not?
4. What economic indicators does Robert Dunn rely upon to evaluate the depth of American integration into the global economy? Do you think that his conclusions are in any way sensitive to his choice of these indicators rather than others? If yes, what other indicators would you want to examine?
5. Would the conclusions that Dunn draws from his examination of the American case apply to other countries, such as countries in the European Union or in Latin America? Why or why not?

SUGGESTIONS FOR FURTHER READING

There is a large body of literature on globalization. David Held, Anthony McGrew, David Goldblatt, and Jonathan Perraton's *Global Transformations: Politics, Economics, and Culture*. Stanford: Stanford University Press, 1999, is considered by many to offer the most comprehensive discussion of the multiple dimensions of globalization. Some of the better contributions that argue strongly for globalization include Jagdish Bhagwati's *In Defense of Globalization*. New York: Oxford University Press, 2004 and John Micklethwait and Adrian Wooldridge's *A Future Perfect: The Challenge and Promise of Globalization*. New York: Random House, 2003. Thomas Friedman's *The Lexus and the Olive Tree*. New York: Anchor Books, 1999 is also a fascinating read. For a more cautious view, see Dani Rodrik's *Has Globalization Gone Too Far?* Washington, DC: Institute for International Economics, 1997 and Joseph E. Stiglitz's *Globalization and its Discontents*. New York: Norton & Co., 2002. Harold James's *The End of Globalization: Lessons for the Great Depression*. Cambridge, MA: Harvard University Press, 2001 examines contemporary globalization through the lens of the first wave of globalization in the late nineteenth and early twentieth century.

For a more detailed examination of the impact of globalization on the American economy, see Gary Burtless, Robert Z. Lawrence, Robert E. Litan, and Robert J. Shapiro's *Globaphobia: Confronting Fears About Open Trade*. Washington, DC: The Brookings Institution, 1998.

CHAPTER 19

◖ GLOBALIZATION AND GOVERNANCE

Is globalization weakening the nation-state? More specifically, can a national government maintain the ability to set many of its various policies autonomously as the national economy integrates into the international economy? In theory, national governments could lose policy autonomy in many areas. At perhaps the broadest level, governments could lose the ability to pursue autonomous macroeconomic policies. Suppose, for example, that a government wanted to run a budget deficit or a relatively loose monetary policy in order to counter a recession. While such a policy could easily be sustained in a closed national economy, once the economy becomes integrated into the global financial and trade systems, such policies might not be implemented readily. A fiscal expansion might simply lead to increased imports rather than domestic production; the combination of fiscal and monetary expansion might generate capital outflows that force domestic interest rates higher. Thus, globalization might greatly weaken the ability of a government to use macroeconomic policy to manage the domestic economy.

Governments might also lose the ability to pursue policies that promote a desired income distribution. Suppose, for example, that a government is committed to limiting the gap between society's wealthiest and poorest individuals. To do so, the government levies taxes on the wealthy and uses these revenues to fund programs that benefit the less well-off. Such policies might be easily implemented in a closed economy, but may be more difficult in an open economy. As taxes on high incomes rises, the wealthy might decide that they would be better off living somewhere else. A wealthy Swede, for example, who faces a very high tax rate, might decide to emigrate to the United Kingdom where his tax bill would be lower. If the government taxed corporate profits, corporations might find it beneficial to relocate their operations to a country with a lower tax rate. Thus, globalization, by making it easier for wealth to move from one country to another, may erode the ability of governments to perform what is the most basic of government tasks.

Globalization may also limit the ability of a government to impose regulations to achieve particular objectives. In a closed economy, governments can use regulations to raise labor standards, to protect consumers from fraud, to protect the environment, and to achieve a host of other goals. Once the national economy opens to the global economy, however, corporations facing such national regulations might find them too onerous and relocate to a country that imposes fewer such regulations. If this dynamic is at play, governments lose an important instrument of policy through which they can achieve objectives that society wants. It is this logic that stands at the center of the so-called race to the bottom.

While it is probably more accurate to say that globalization may have raised the cost of autonomous national policies rather than prevented governments from adopting policies, the implication is essentially the same. In a globalized economy, national governments find it increasingly difficult to use policies to achieve desired outcomes. The tension inherent in markets that increasingly are organized globally and politics that remain organized along national lines raises a number of questions to which we don't currently have complete answers. Perhaps the most important is whether nation-states are in fact being weakened by globalization. It is relatively easy to claim that nations are being weakened, and not much more difficult to produce a logic that shows why this must be true. It is much more difficult to find systematic evidence to show that they are being weakened. Second, if national governments are being weakened by globalization, is political power flowing to other organizations at higher or lower levels? Is political power flowing up, so that international economic organizations like the WTO, the IMF, and the World Bank are gaining power? Or is political power flowing down, so that the real winners of globalization are local and regional governments? Finally, perhaps nothing will arise to take the place of national governments, and power will simply shift to multinational corporations and nongovernmental organizations. More broadly, then, what impact is globalization having on the organization of political authority?

The two articles presented in this chapter examine this question. Robert Wright, a contributing editor at the *New Republic,* argues that globalization is bringing about a gradual shift in political power. While he focuses mostly on the WTO, his broader argument is that national governments are gradually transferring authority, sometimes willingly and sometimes less so, to international organizations. Moreover, he asserts that there is little that governments can do to reverse this shift in political authority—it is simply driven by the logic of global markets and technology. Martin Wolf, Associate Editor and Chief Economics Commentator at the *Financial Times,* is more skeptical of claims that globalization is weakening national governments. He argues that governments have chosen globalization, that globalization has not eroded their ability to implement that most important of government functions—taxing their citizens. And, in contrast to Wright, Wolf believes that globalization is reversible.

Continental Drift

ROBERT WRIGHT

In recent years, more and more people have raised the specter of world government. Ralph Nader, protesters in Seattle, Pat Buchanan, militiamen in the heartland—all sense an alarming concentration of planetary power in one or more acronyms: WTO, U.N., IMF, and so forth.

Of course, these people have something else in common: They are widely considered fringe characters—flaky, if not loony. And their eccentric visions have been punctured by legions of sober observers. "The WTO is not a world government," an economist wrote in a *Wall Street Journal* op-ed last month after the Seattle protests against the World Trade Organization. His verdict has been echoed by various academics and pundits.

But this may be one of those cases when the flaky are closer to the truth than the sober. Much power now vested in the nation-state is indeed starting to migrate to international institutions, and one of these is the WTO. This doesn't mean that two or three decades from now we'll see world government in the classic sense of the term—a single, central planetary authority. But world government of a meaningful if more diffuse sort is probably in the cards. It follows from basic technological trends and stubborn economic and political logic. And, what's more, it's a good idea. Among other virtues, it could keep a sizable chunk of the liberal coalition from veering off toward Buchananism.

If the political forces driving the WTO toward firmer and broader authority seem less than overwhelming, one reason is that the key political players have a love-hate relationship with world government and tend to dwell on the hate part.

Many on the left, when denouncing the WTO, talk as if national sovereignty were sacred. The WTO, Nader has long complained, "means foreign regulation of America. It means any two dictatorships can out-vote us. . . . It means secret tribunals can rule against our laws." Yet Nader and most of the Seattle left would gladly accept a sovereignty-crushing world body if it followed the leftish model of supranational governance found in the European Union. Indeed, it was partly to please the Seattle activists that President Clinton espoused a future WTO whose member nations would meet global environmental and labor standards or else face sanction.

Many centrist and conservative free-traders also talk as if national sovereignty should be inviolable. They were aghast at Clinton's proposal to take the WTO "beyond its proper competence," as an editorial in *The Economist* sternly put it.

From Robert Wright, "Continental Drift," *The New Republic* 222, January 17, 2000, pp. 18–23. Reprinted by permission of *The New Republic*. © 2000, The New Republic, LLC.

But they can live with sovereignty infringement of a less leftish variety—the kind that erodes a nation's power to erect subtle trade barriers via environmental or health policy. They certainly didn't lose sleep over the famous 1998 case in which the United States, under threat of WTO sanction, relaxed its ban on shrimp caught in nets that kill sea turtles.

Of course, these free-traders deny that this sort of ruling amounts to world government. *The Economist* editorial said that "the WTO is not a global government" but merely a place where nations "make agreements, and then subject themselves to arbitration in the event of a dispute." But isn't that a large part of what a government is: a body whose constituents agree to respect its authority, to accept punishment if they're deemed to have broken the rules?

Assorted other players, such as human rights hawks, also have mixed feelings about world government. After Seattle, William Safire wrote a column backing Clinton's view that the WTO should someday punish nations that exploit child labor. This is quite a turnaround: Safire, a longtime free-trader and something of a libertarian, now believes that foreigners in Geneva should decide whether you can buy a soccer ball made in Pakistan. Struggling to contain his cognitive dissonance, Safire issued a disclaimer: "I am not a global warmnik. . . . Indeed, laissez-fairies have always been dancing in my garden." If I were Safire, I'd peek out at my garden to see whether the fairies are still in a festive mood.

For all these people—traditional leftists, centrist and right-wing free-traders, and assorted single-issue agitators (everyone except the Buchananites, basically)—the fundamental question has been settled. They agree that sometimes nations should surrender an appreciable chunk of sovereignty to a central authority. They just disagree on when. Even as they heap scorn on the notion of world government, they're really arguing about what kind of world government we should have.

The evolution of world government has two basic engines—stubborn economic logic and stubborn political logic, both fueled by technology's relentless shrinking of the economic distance between nations.

The economic logic is pretty simple. You could describe it as a series of non-zero-sum games—a series of cases in which nations, to achieve win-win outcomes or avoid lose-lose outcomes, enmesh themselves in common governance. The series starts with that elementally human non-zero-sum game, mutually profitable exchange. Nations trade with one another. Then they see further gains in agreements that will mutually lower tariffs (game number two). Then they decide all would benefit by dampening quarrels over what constitutes a violation of the rules, so they set up a way to handle disputes (game number three). Crossing this last threshold—forming an inchoate judiciary—is what turned the General Agreement on Tariffs and Trade into the World Trade Organization.

But adjudication entails tricky questions. For example: How do you handle covert trade barriers? When a country makes it illegal to import shrimp caught in nets that kill sea turtles, is that just an environmental law? Or is it de facto protectionism, as the WTO claimed when it demanded that the United States quit barring shrimp imports from several Asian nations? In theory, the United States could have ignored the ruling. All the WTO would have done in response would have been to approve retaliatory tariffs by aggrieved countries. Still, the United States has benefited from so many WTO rulings that it has a stake in preserving respect for them. That's the way good government works: A central authority, by solving non-zero-sum problems, gives out in benefits more than it exacts in costs, thus justifying its existence. This net benefit is why WTO rulings will probably become more binding, whether through sheer custom or through tougher sanctions.

The WTO isn't breaking new ground here. It's following in the footsteps of a body that's much further down the road of supranational governance: the European Union. Europe is the most geographically dense conglomeration of high-tech nations in the world. So, as technology shrinks economic distance, Europe is on the leading edge of the trend. That doesn't mean that its political present is the world's political future. The EU has been shaped by various elements peculiar to European history (including a dogged post-1945 desire to avoid war). Still, it may offer a hint of things to come.

For example: With transnational commerce growing, all of Europe's national currencies became a bother. There was costly currency conversion and uncertainty about exchange rates. So the EU opted for a single currency. And one currency meant one central bank; each nation lost its autonomous central bank and, at a more symbolic level, its currency (or, as they aptly say in Britain, its sovereign). At this point—with nations surrendering control over their monetary policy—the line between a loose association of nations and an outright confederacy has arguably been crossed.

As Europe was unifying its currencies, *The Economist* published an article called "One World, One Money," noting the analogously powerful logic behind global monetary union. The article stressed the political difficulty of such a goal, and some economists doubt its economic wisdom as well. Still, as exchange rates gyrated after the Asian financial crisis, there was talk in both Argentina and Mexico about adopting the U.S. dollar as official currency.

The EU also gets involved in regulatory issues, from food labeling to health and labor law. (It decided that member states could—and, indeed, must!—permit the sale of Viagra.) Right-wing free-traders claim there is no sound economic rationale for this sort of meddling. They say that the EU's attempt to specify everything from cheese labels to the maximum length of the workweek represents the triumph of interest-group politics. In some cases, at least, this is true; a maximum workweek doesn't follow from Econ 101 principles about maximizing GDP. But so what? Interest-group politics has always been part of governance. At the local and national levels, much of government consists of services rendered to various groups in order to maintain their support for the larger governmental enterprise. The question is whether at the global level, too, politics will dictate the construction of a substantial body of law.

There is reason to think so, and much of it was on display in Seattle. Well-organized interest groups in affluent nations fear—correctly, in many cases—that they'll be hurt by the continued lowering of trade barriers. So they want to thwart further lowering unless they get global rules that will blunt its impact, such as the rules Clinton has now embraced.

Can these groups really hold trade liberalization hostage to their agenda? Absolutely. In 1997, Clinton introduced fast-track legislation, which denies Congress the power to amend negotiated trade deals before voting on them—and which, practically speaking, is a prerequisite for passing most trade accords. Bowing to Republican pressure, Clinton phrased the legislation narrowly: it wouldn't have allowed U.S. negotiators to include labor and environmental rules in trade agreements. Liberal interest groups responded by defeating the bill. So for now, at least, America's real-world political choice seems to be either trade liberalization that invites lefty supranational governance or no trade liberalization. Both Democratic presidential candidates seem to favor the former option, and, if elected, each of them would presumably seek the leftish fast-track authority that Clinton didn't seek.

In the short run, this authority would yield little. Developing nations generally oppose global environmental and labor law, which raises production costs and thus dulls their factories' competitive edge. Still, there are two reasons this obstacle will probably prove temporary. First, the United States and other rich nations, with markets that poorer nations lust after, have tremendous bargaining power. Second, as time passes, the developing nations will themselves develop strong constituencies for left-leaning world law.

This second point was lost in the post-Seattle commentary. Negotiators for developing nations went on television and alleged that American union leaders, with their poignant pleas for better working conditions abroad, were phonies; they were at heart worried not about protecting foreign workers but about making foreign labor more pricey and hence less competitive internationally.

Absolutely true. In fact, many American workers would love to price foreign workers out of the market entirely. But they never will. A more realistic goal is to slightly raise labor costs abroad. And, if they do that, they'll have most foreign workers on their side. Sure, a few children will lose their jobs if child labor is regulated. And, sure, if workers in poor nations are guaranteed the right to organize, the result could be a minimum wage that would put a few adult workers out of jobs. But the American minimum wage has the same effect, and most workers still support it, for quite rational reasons.

So, in coming years, expect workers in poor nations to link up with Western labor groups to pursue their common cause: higher wages in poor nations. The groups won't see eye-to-eye on everything. American workers would like to raise environmental standards abroad as a way to increase production costs, whereas foreign workers will prefer the sort of raised production costs that mean higher wages. Still, there will be enough common interest that, to some extent, workers of the world will unite—if not exactly in the context Marx envisioned.

Other international coalitions will also blossom. Western environmentalists, for example, share an interest with Third World tourist industries in cleaning up Third World cities.

As international lobby groups acquire power and start doing the things national lobby groups have long done, economists and industrialists will grumble about the costs. The special interests, they'll say, are gumming up the works, dulling capitalism's edge, slowing down globalization!

And it will be true. But is that so bad? Globalization has polluted developing nations, dislocated workers in developed nations, and radicalized some environmentalists and religious fundamentalists. And radicalism is a special problem when, thanks to advancing weapons technology, any two or three highly alienated people can create a pretty lethal terrorist cell.

Don't get me wrong. Globalization is great. On balance, it makes the world's poor people less poor (a fact that doesn't seem to have penetrated the brain of the average Seattle protester). And it fosters a fine-grained economic interdependence that makes war among nations less thinkable. But these benefits are all the more reason to keep globalization from getting derailed by the reactionary backlash it incites when it moves too fast. And derailment is possible. As Paul Krugman recently noted in *The New York Times,* the "First Global Economy"—the one that took shape in the late nineteenth century—foundered early this century in part because its constituency didn't extend very far beyond a cosmopolitan elite.

Nor is the derailment of globalization per se the only thing to worry about. Some historians trace the virulence of twentieth-century German nationalism to the nineteenth century, when industrialization swept from west to east, leaving bewilderment in its wake. And Russia, even more than Germany, had to fast-forward from an age of serfs into the industrial revolution—and, in a sense, it never recovered, never got fitting governance. It got Stalin instead.

In a way, it's a misnomer to speak of slowing globalization. After all, the things that might do the slowing—supranational labor or environmental groups, global bodies of governance—are themselves part of globalization. What is really happening is that political globalization is catching up to economic globalization.

This has a precedent on a smaller scale. In the United States during the early twentieth century, as economic activity migrated from the state to the national level, the national government grew powerful enough to regulate it. Some of these regulations made simple economic sense, but some of them—labor laws in particular— were political in rationale and had the effect of subduing capitalism, dulling its harsher edges. This was, among other things, a preemptive strike against Marxist revolution—against the turmoil that unbridled modernization can bring—and a successful one. Enlightened capitalists realized that giving labor a seat at the table would help make the world safe for capitalism.

By the same token, enlightened capitalists should today invite the Seattle protesters indoors. One way or another, people who feel threatened by globalization will make their influence felt. Either they'll modulate globalization by linking up with like-minded groups abroad to help shape international rules or they'll take the economic-nationalist route and lobby for the sort of trade barriers that, in addition to starting trade wars, often involve xenophobia and nativism. The way to keep these people from being sheer protectionists—and, in some cases, from morphing into full-fledged Buchananites—is to turn them into WTO lobbyists, which means making the WTO a body worth lobbying. Put suits on those scraggly rabble-rousers and send them to Geneva!

The WTO, though the topic of world governance du jour, is hardly the only global institution with real economic power. The International Monetary Fund (IMF) makes loans to troubled nations to prevent panics—the rough analogue of a nation's bank-deposit insurance—and in return asks for sound management and transparent bookkeeping. This may not sound very forceful. But to lend when the private sector refuses to do so is to subsidize, and with subsidy comes power. Much of the U.S. government's power over states, after all, consists not of legalized coercion but of strings attached to subsidies.

After the Asian crisis, some economists argued that the IMF had been too heavy-handed—that it shouldn't demand fiscal austerity so single-mindedly and that by too readily bailing out bad investors it encouraged more bad investment. But almost no one is saying the IMF should quit lending altogether, and almost no one is saying it should quit using its lending as leverage of one sort or another. As with the WTO, the mainstream argument isn't about whether to have a form of world government but about what form of it to have.

And, as with the WTO, the reason to expect the IMF's ongoing solidification is simple. Its authority results from shrinking economic distance. This shrinkage is the reason economic downturns can be contagious, the reason rich nations suddenly care about the financial soundness of poor nations. And if there is one thing the basic direction of technological change clearly implies, it is continued shrinkage— more interdependence among nations.

For that matter, the shrinkage of noneconomic distance will also continue. A decade from now, global laws regulating the prescription of antibiotics could make sense, if the too-casual use of these drugs creates strains of super-bacteria that can cross oceans on airplanes. And then there is cyberspace, that notorious distance-shrinker and sovereigntysapper. It empowers offshore tax-evaders, off-shore libelers, offshore copyright-violators. Nations will find it harder and harder to enforce more and more laws unless they coordinate law enforcement and, in some cases, the laws themselves.

But, even given all these reasons for firmer and broader global governance, will it ever get as firm and broad as the governance of nation-states? Probably not. World government may well always rely on member states to levy its sanctions. It will probably never inspire the patriotic fervor nations do. And it may always be diffuse, consisting of lots of partly overlapping bodies: some regional, some global; some economic, some environmental; some comprising national governments, some comprising nongovernmental organizations.

Why won't world government ever be as taut as old-fashioned national government? For one thing, governments have traditionally drawn internal strength from external opposition. If you scan the historical and prehistoric record for distant parallels to the current moment, the nearest approximations you'll find are when agrarian villages have united to form "chiefdoms" or when chiefdoms evolved into ancient states. And there are no clear examples of such transitions happening in the absence of external hostility. For a full-fledged global political conglomeration to take place without the threat of war against a common foe would mark a contrast with all of the known past. And, barring an invasion from outer space, no such threat will be available.

Still, we do face what you could call planetary security problems, and they will help sustain the current drift toward real, if loose, world government. Impending climate change may not have quite the viscerally galvanizing effect of troops massed on your border, but it does qualify as a common peril best combated by concerted action. Terrorism is also a common peril (and, actually, a pretty galvanizing one). As more compact, lethal, and long-range weapons make terrorists tougher, national governance will become less and less adequate to the task of national security.

Already, with the Chemical Weapons Convention, the United States has agreed to international inspections intrusive enough to have filled the Senate chamber with plaints about surrendered sovereignty. But the surrender (a minor one, in truth) was rational; permitting such inspections on our soil is the only way to get them to happen on foreign soil. And chemical weapons are just the beginning. Biological weapons are orders of magnitude more lethal and much easier to make covertly. The encroachment on sovereignty that combating them will require is, to current sensibilities, shocking. But the idea of trauma—say, 20,000 deaths in an American city—has a way of making the unthinkable widely thought.

As technology pulls and pushes nations together, it highlights an irony: world government, which for so long was a pet cause of the idealistic left—the "woolly minded one-worlders"—isn't getting much support from the left. True, some Seattle activists profess a willingness to work with a left-leaning WTO. But when Naderite Lori Wallach declared, "We're the coalition that's going to tell the WTO, 'You're going to be fixed or you're going to be nixed,'" her heart seemed to be with the "nixed" part. Certainly that was the sentiment of the average Seattle protester.

But, even if nixing were within the left's power, it would be a mistake. Stopping the WTO in its tracks wouldn't turn back the clock. Under current tariff levels, globalization would continue (and, besides, tariffs would probably keep dropping via bilateral trade deals). The various problems that exercise the left—environmental decline, an exodus of low-skill jobs from high-wage nations, human rights violations—would persist.

And these problems are just about impossible to solve without an enforcement mechanism—without the power of sanction that the WTO, more than any other world body, has to offer. The Rio accords on global warming, for example, lack an enforcement mechanism and are notable for the blithe disregard with which various signatories have treated them. The history of international labor accords tells the same story. After the Seattle talks, a *New York Times* editorial said that "the administration can urge other groups, like the International Labor Organization, to pursue the issue with or without the WTO's participation." Which is to say, with or without effect. The ILO has been in existence for 81 years and, lacking the force of sanction, has been unable to do much of anything.

One oddity in contemporary political nomenclature is the tendency of leftist economic nationalists, who favor raising tariffs, to call themselves "progressives." Early this century, progressives were people who realized that communications and transportation technologies were pushing the compass of economic activity outward, from individual states to the United States. In response, they pushed economic regulation from the state to the federal level. The modern-day successors to these progressives should be advocating supranational regulation, not impeding it with unilateral tariffs.

Seattle may have moved them in that direction. At the end of the week, however virulent the anti-WTO rhetoric remained, the "progressive" left was thinking more seriously about using the WTO as a vehicle for its agenda. One big reason was Bill Clinton. For an American president to say that global laws on the treatment of workers should be enforced with real sanctions authorized by a worldwide body was a milestone in the evolution of global governance.

Clinton's remarks have been dismissed as a transparent ploy to lock up the labor vote for Al Gore, as a nostalgic effort to bond with 1960s-esque protesters, and as a tactical blunder that alienated negotiators from poor nations. All of this may be true. But it's also true that these days Clinton is said to be preoccupied with his legacy, trying to pave the way for a thumbs-up verdict from historians a generation hence. If so, then one-worlders should be cheered by his Seattle performance. No one has ever accused Bill Clinton of not knowing which way the wind is blowing.

Will the Nation-State Survive Globalization?

MARTIN WOLF

DEFINING GLOBALIZATION

A specter is haunting the world's governments—the specter of globalization. Some argue that predatory market forces make it impossible for benevolent governments to shield their populations from the beasts of prey that lurk beyond their borders. Others counter that benign market forces actually prevent predatory governments from fleecing their citizens. Although the two sides see different villains, they draw one common conclusion: omnipotent markets mean impotent politicians. Indeed, this formula has become one of the cliches of our age. But is it true that governments have become weaker and less relevant than ever before? And does globalization, by definition, have to be the nemesis of national government?

Globalization is a journey. But it is a journey toward an unreachable destination—"the globalized world." A "globalized" economy could be defined as one in which neither distance nor national borders impede economic transactions. This would be a world where the costs of transport and communications were zero and the barriers created by differing national jurisdictions had vanished. Needless to say, we do not live in anything even close to such a world. And since many of the things we transport (including ourselves) are physical, we never will.

This globalizing journey is not a new one. Over the past five centuries, technological change has progressively reduced the barriers to international integration. Transatlantic communication, for example, has evolved from sail power to steam, to the telegraph, the telephone, commercial aircraft, and now to the Internet. Yet states have become neither weaker nor less important during this odyssey. On the contrary, in the countries with the most advanced and internationally integrated economies, governments' ability to tax and redistribute incomes, regulate the economy, and monitor the activity of their citizens has increased beyond all recognition. This has been especially true over the past century.

The question that remains, however, is whether today's form of globalization is likely to have a different impact from that of the past. Indeed, it may well, for numerous factors distinguish today's globalizing journey from past ones and could produce a different outcome. These distinctions include more rapid communications, market liberalization, and global integration of the production of goods and

From Martin Wolf, "Will the Nation-State Survive Globalization?" *Foreign Affairs*, Vol. 80, No. 1, January/February, 2001, pp. 178–190. Reprinted by permission of *Foreign Affairs*. © 2001 by the Council on Foreign Relations, Inc.

services. Yet contrary to one common assumption, the modern form of globalization will not spell the end of the modern nation-state.

THE PAST AS PROLOGUE

Today's growing integration of the world economy is not unprecedented, at least when judged by the flow of goods, capital, and people. Similar trends occurred in the late nineteenth and early twentieth centuries.

First, the proportion of world production that is traded on global markets is not that much higher today than it was in the years leading up to World War I. Commerce was comparably significant in 1910, when ratios of trade (merchandise exports plus imports) to GDP hit record highs in several of the advanced economies. Global commerce then collapsed during the Great Depression and World War II, but since then world trade has grown more rapidly than output. The share of global production traded worldwide grew from about 7 percent in 1950 to more than 20 percent by the mid-1990s; in consequence, trade ratios have risen in almost all of the advanced economies. In the United Kingdom, for example, exports and imports added up to 57 percent of GDP in 1995 compared to 44 percent in 1910; for France the 1995 proportion was 43 percent against 35 percent in 1910; and for Germany it was 46 percent against 38 percent in the same years. But Japan's trade ratio was actually lower in 1995 than it had been in 1910. In fact, among today's five biggest economies, the only one in which trade has a remarkably greater weight in output than it had a century ago is the United States, where the ratio has jumped from 11 percent in 1910 to 24 percent in 1995. That fact may help explain why globalization is more controversial for Americans than for people in many other countries.

Second, by the late nineteenth century many countries had already opened their capital markets to international investments, before investments, too, collapsed during the interwar period. As a share of GDP, British capital investments abroad—averaging 4.6 percent of GDP between 1870 and 1913—hit levels unparalleled in contemporary major economies. More revealing is that the correlation between domestic investment and savings (a measure of the extent to which savings remain within one country) was lower between 1880 and 1910 than in any subsequent period.

Historical differences exist, however. Although current capital mobility has precedents from the pre-World War I era, the composition of capital flows has changed. Short-term capital today is much more mobile than ever before. Moreover, long-term flows now are somewhat differently constituted than in the earlier period. Investment in the early twentieth century took the form of tangible assets rather than intangible ones. Portfolio flows predominated over direct investment in the earlier period (that trend has been reversed since World War II); within portfolios, stocks have increased in relative importance to roughly equal bonds today. And finally, before 1914, direct investment was undertaken largely by companies investing in mining and transportation, whereas today multinational companies predominate, with a large proportion of their investment in services.

Today's high immigration flows are also not unprecedented. According to economists Paul Hirst and Grahame Thompson, the greatest era for recorded voluntary mass migration was the century after 1815. Around 60 million people left Europe for the Americas, Oceania, and South and East Africa. An estimated ten million voluntarily migrated from Russia to Central Asia and Siberia. A million went from Southern Europe to North America. About 12 million Chinese and 6 million Japanese left their homelands and emigrated to eastern and southern Asia. One and a half million left India for Southeast Asia and Southwest Africa.

Population movement peaked during the 1890s. In those years, the United States absorbed enough immigrants to increase the U.S. population from the beginning of the decade by 9 percent. In Argentina, the increase in the 1890s was 26 percent; in Australia, it was 17 percent. Europe provided much of the supply: the United Kingdom gave up 5 percent of its initial population, Spain 6 percent, and Sweden 7 percent. In the 1990s, by contrast, the United States was the only country in the world with a high immigration rate, attracting newcomers primarily from the developing world rather than from Europe. These immigrants increased the population by only 4 percent.

As all of this suggests, despite the many economic changes that have occurred over the course of a century, neither the markets for goods and services nor those for factors of production appear much more integrated today than they were a century ago. They seem more integrated for trade, at least in the high-income countries; no more integrated for capital—above all for long-term capital—despite important changes in the composition of capital flows; and much less integrated for labor.

So why do so many people believe that something unique is happening today? The answer lies with the two forces driving contemporary economic change: falling costs of transport and communications on the one hand, and liberalizing economic policies on the other.

THE TECHNOLOGICAL REVOLUTION

Advances in technology and infrastructure substantially and continuously reduced the costs of transport and communications throughout the nineteenth and early twentieth centuries. The first transatlantic telegraph cable was laid in 1866. By the turn of the century, the entire world was connected by telegraph, and communication times fell from months to minutes. The cost of a three-minute telephone call from New York to London in current prices dropped from about $250 in 1930 to a few cents today. In more recent years, the number of voice paths across the Atlantic has skyrocketed from 100,000 in 1986 to more than 2 million today. The number of Internet hosts has risen from 5,000 in 1986 to more than 30 million now.

A revolution has thus occurred in collecting and disseminating information, one that has dramatically reduced the cost of moving physical objects. But these massive improvements in communications, however important, simply continue the trends begun with the first submarine cables laid in the last century. Furthermore, distances still impose transport and communications costs that continue to make geography matter in economic terms. Certain important services still cannot be delivered from afar.

Diminishing costs of communications and transport were nevertheless pointing toward greater integration throughout the last century. But if historical experience demonstrates anything, it is that integration is not technologically determined. If it were, integration would have gone smoothly forward over the past two centuries. On the contrary, despite continued falls in the costs of transport and communications in the first half of the twentieth century, integration actually reversed course.

Policy, not technology, has determined the extent and pace of international economic integration. If transport and communications innovations were moving toward global economic integration throughout the last century and a half, policy was not—and that made all the difference. For this reason, the growth in the potential for economic integration has greatly outpaced the growth of integration itself since the late nineteenth century. Globalization has much further to run, if it is allowed to do so.

CHOOSING GLOBALIZATION

Globalization is not destined, it is chosen. It is a choice made to enhance a nation's economic well-being—indeed, experience suggests that the opening of trade and of most capital flows enriches most citizens in the short run and virtually all citizens in the long run. (Taxation on short-term capital inflows to emerging market economies is desirable, however, particularly during a transition to full financial integration.) But if integration is a deliberate choice, rather than an ineluctable destiny, it cannot render states impotent. Their potency lies in the choices they make.

Between 1846 and 1870, liberalization spread from the United Kingdom to the rest of Europe. Protectionism, which had never waned in the United States, returned to continental Europe after 1878 and reached its peak in the 1930s.

A new era of global economic integration began only in the postwar era, and then only partially: from the end of World War II through the 1970s, only the advanced countries lowered their trade barriers. The past two decades, by contrast, have seen substantial liberalization take root throughout the world. By the late 1990s, no economically significant country still had a government committed to protectionism.

This historical cycle is also apparent in international capital investments. Capital markets stayed open in the nineteenth and early twentieth centuries, partly because governments did not have the means to control capital flows. They acquired and haltingly solidified this capacity between 1914 and 1945, progressively closing their capital markets. Liberalization of capital flows then began in a few advanced countries during the 1950s and 1960s. But the big wave of liberalization did not start in earnest until the late 1970s, spreading across the high-income countries, much of the developing world, and, by the 1990s, to the former communist countries. Notwithstanding a large number of financial crises over this period, this trend has remained intact.

In monetary policy, the biggest change has been the move from the gold standard of the 1870–1914 era to the floating currencies of today. The long-run exchange-rate stability inherent in the gold standard promoted long-term capital flows, particularly bond financing, more efficiently than does the contemporary currency instability. Today's vast short-term financial flows are not just a consequence of exchange-rate instability, but one of its causes.

Yet governments' control over the movement of people in search of employment tightened virtually everywhere in the early part of the last century. With the exception of the free immigration policy among members of the European Union (EU), immigration controls are generally far tighter now than they were a hundred years ago.

The policy change that has most helped global integration to flourish is the growth of international institutions since World War II. Just as multinational companies now organize private exchange, so global institutions organize and discipline the international face of national policy. Institutions such as the World Trade Organization (WTO), the International Monetary Fund (IMF), the World Bank, the EU, and the North American Free Trade Agreement underpin cooperation among states and consolidate their commitments to liberalize economic policy. The nineteenth century was a world of unilateral and discretionary policy. The late twentieth century, by comparison, was a world of multilateral and institutionalized policy.

TRADEOFFS FACING STATES

Ironically, the technology that is supposed to make globalization inevitable also makes increased surveillance by the state, particularly over people, easier than it would have been a century ago. Indeed, here is the world we now live in: one with fairly free movement of capital, continuing (though declining) restrictions on trade in goods and services, but quite tight control over the movement of people.

Economies are also never entirely open or entirely closed. Opening requires governments to loosen three types of economic controls: on capital flows, goods and services, and people. Liberalizing one of the above neither requires nor always leads to liberalization in the others. Free movement of goods and services makes regulating capital flows more difficult, but not impossible; foreign direct investment can flow across national barriers to trade in goods without knocking them down. It is easier still to trade freely and abolish controls on capital movement, while nevertheless regulating movement of people.

The important questions, then, concern the tradeoffs confronting governments that have chosen a degree of international economic integration. How constrained will governments find themselves once they have chosen openness?

THREE VITAL AREAS

Globalization is often perceived as destroying governments' capacities to do what they want or need, particularly in the key areas of taxation, public spending for income redistribution, and macroeconomic policy. But how true is this perception?

In fact, no evidence supports the conclusion that states can no longer raise taxes. On the contrary: in 1999, EU governments spent or redistributed an average of 47 percent of their GDPS. An important new book by Vito Tanzi of the IMF and Ludger Schuknecht at the European Central Bank underlines this point. Over the course of the twentieth century, the average share of government spending among Organization for Economic Cooperation and Development (OECD) member states jumped from an eighth to almost half of GDP. In some high-income countries such as France and Germany, these ratios were higher than ever before.

Until now, it has been electoral resistance, not globalization, that has most significantly limited the growth in taxation. Tanzi claims that this is about to change. He argues that collecting taxes is becoming harder due to a long list of "fiscal termites" gnawing at the foundations of taxation regimes: more cross-border shopping, the increased mobility of skilled labor, the growth of electronic commerce, the expansion of tax havens, the development of new financial instruments and intermediaries, growing trade within multinational companies, and the possible replacement of bank accounts with electronic money embedded in "smart cards."

The list is impressive. That governments take it seriously is demonstrated by the attention that leaders of the OECD and the EU are devoting to "harmful tax competition," information exchange, and the implications of electronic commerce. Governments, like members of any other industry, are forming a cartel to halt what they see as "ruinous competition" in taxation. This sense of threat has grown out of several fiscal developments produced by globalization: increased mobility of people and money, greater difficulty in collecting information on income and spending, and the impact of the Internet on information flows and collection.

Yet the competitive threat that governments face must not be exaggerated. The fiscal implications of labor, capital, and spending mobility are already evident in local jurisdictions that have the freedom to set their own tax rates. Even local governments can impose higher taxes than their neighbors, provided they contain specific resources or offer location-specific amenities that residents desire and consume. In other words, differential taxation is possible if there are at least some transport costs—and there always are.

These costs grow with a jurisdiction's geographic size, which thus strongly influences a local government's ability to raise taxes. The income of mobile capital is the hardest to tax; the income of land and immobile labor is easiest. Corporate income can be taxed if it is based on resources specific to that location, be they natural or human. Spending can also be taxed more heavily in one jurisdiction than another, but not if transport costs are very low (either because distances are short or items are valuable in relation to costs). Similarly, it is difficult to tax personal incomes if people can live in low-tax jurisdictions while enjoying the amenities of high-tax ones.

Eliminating legal barriers to mobility therefore constrains, but does not eliminate, the ability of some jurisdictions to levy far higher taxes than others. The ceiling on higher local taxes rises when taxable resources or activities remain relatively immobile or the jurisdiction provides valuable specific amenities just for that area.

The international mobility of people and goods is unlikely ever to come close to the kind of mobility that exists between states in the United States. Legal, linguistic, and cultural barriers will keep levels of cross-border migration far lower than levels of movement within any given country. Since taxes on labor income and spending are the predominant source of national revenue, the modern country's income base seems quite safe. Of course, although the somewhat greater mobility resulting from globalization makes it harder for governments to get information about what their residents own and spend abroad, disguising physical movement, consumption, or income remains a formidable task.

The third major aspect of globalization, the Internet, may have an appreciable impact on tax collection. Stephane Buydens of the OECD plausibly argues that the Internet will primarily affect four main areas: taxes on spending, tax treaties, internal pricing of multinational companies, and tax administration.

Purely Internet-based transactions—downloading of films, software, or music—are hard to tax. But when the Internet is used to buy tangible goods, governments can impose taxes, provided that the suppliers cooperate with the fiscal authorities of their corresponding jurisdictions. To the extent that these suppliers are large shareholder-owned companies, which they usually are, this cooperation may not be as hard to obtain as is often supposed.

It is also sometimes difficult to locate an Internet server. If one cannot do so, how are taxes to be levied and tax treaties applied? Similar problems arise with multinational companies' ability to charge submarket prices to their subsidiaries abroad (so-called "transfer pricing" within multinationals), which leaves uncertain the question of how and in which country to levy the tax. This scenario suggests that classic concepts in the taxation of corporations may have to be modified or even radically overhauled.

The overall conclusion, then, is that economic liberalization and technology advances will make taxation significantly more challenging. Taxes on spending may have to be partially recast. Taxation of corporate profits may have to be radically redesigned or even abandoned. Finally, the ability of governments to impose taxes that bear no relation to the benefits provided may be more constrained than before.

Nevertheless, the implications of these changes can easily be exaggerated. Taxation of corporate income is rarely more than ten percent of revenue, whereas taxes on income and spending are the universal pillars of the fiscal system. Yet even lofty Scandinavian taxes are not forcing skilled people to emigrate in droves. People will still happily pay to enjoy high-quality schools or public transport. Indeed, one of the most intriguing phenomena of modern Europe is that the high-tax, big-spending Scandinavian countries are leading the "new economy."

Governments will also use the exchange of information and other forms of cooperation to sustain revenue and may even consider international agreements on minimum taxes. They will certainly force the publicly quoted companies that continue to dominate transactions, both on-line and off, to cooperate with fiscal authorities. But competition among governments will not be eliminated, because the powerful countries that provide relatively low-tax, low-spending environments will want to maintain them.

The bottom line is that the opening of economies and the blossoming of new technologies are reinforcing constraints that have already developed within domestic politics. National governments are becoming a little more like local governments. The result will not necessarily be minimal government. But governments, like other institutions, will be forced to provide value to those who pay for their services.

Meanwhile, governments can continue the practice of income redistribution to the extent that the most highly taxed citizens and firms cannot—or do not wish to—evade taxation. In fact, if taxes are used to fund what are believed to be location-specific benefits, such as income redistribution or welfare spending, taxpayers will likely be quite willing to pay, perhaps because they either identify with the beneficiaries, fear that they could become indigent themselves, or treasure the security that comes from living among people who are not destitute. Taxpayers may also feel a sense of moral obligation to the poor, a sentiment that seems stronger in small, homogeneous societies. Alternatively, they may merely be unable to evade or avoid those taxes without relocating physically outside the jurisdiction. For all these reasons, sustaining a high measure of redistributive taxation remains perfectly possible. The constraint is not globalization, but the willingness of the electorate to tolerate high taxation.

Last but not least, some observers argue that globalization limits governments' ability to run fiscal deficits and pursue inflationary monetary policy. But macroeconomic policy is always vulnerable to the reaction of the private sector, regardless of whether the capital market is internationally integrated. If a government pursues a consistently inflationary policy, long-term nominal interest rates will rise, partly to compensate for inflation and partly to insure the bondholders against inflation risk. Similarly, if a government relies on the printing press to finance its activity, a flight from money into goods, services, and assets will ensue—and, in turn, generate inflation.

Within one country, these reactions may be slow. A government can pursue an inflationary policy over a long period and boost the economy; the price may not have to be paid for many years. What difference, then, does it make for the country to be open to international capital flows? The most important change is that the reaction of a government's creditors is likely to be quicker and more brutal because they have more alternatives. This response will often show itself in a collapsing exchange rate, as happened in East Asia in 1997 and 1998.

THE CONTINUING IMPORTANCE OF STATES

A country that chooses international economic integration implicitly accepts constraints on its actions. Nevertheless, the idea that these constraints wither away the state's capacity to tax, regulate, or intervene is wrong. Rather, international economic integration accelerates the market's responses to policy by increasing the range of alternative options available to those affected. There are also powerful reasons for believing that the constraints imposed on (or voluntarily accepted by) governments by globalization are, on balance, desirable.

For example, the assumption that most governments are benevolent welfare-maximizers is naive. International economic integration creates competition among governments—even countries that fiercely resist integration cannot survive with uncompetitive economies, as shown by the fate of the Soviet Union. This competition constrains the ability of governments to act in a predatory manner and increases the incentive to provide services that are valued by those who pay the bulk of the taxes.

Another reason for welcoming the constraints is that self-imposed limits on a government's future actions enhance the credibility of even a benevolent government's commitments to the private sector. An open capital account is one such constraint. Treaties with other governments, as in the WTO, are another, as are agreements with powerful private parties. Even China has come to recognize the economic benefits that it can gain from international commitments of this kind.

The proposition that globalization makes states unnecessary is even less credible than the idea that it makes states impotent. If anything, the exact opposite is true, for at least three reasons. First, the ability of a society to take advantage of the opportunities offered by international economic integration depends on the quality of public goods, such as property rights, an honest civil service, personal security, and basic education. Without an appropriate legal framework, in particular, the web of potentially rewarding contracts is vastly reduced. This point may seem trivial, but many developing economies have failed to achieve these essential preconditions of success.

Second, the state normally defines identity. A sense of belonging is part of the people's sense of security, and one that most people would not want to give up, even in the age of globalization. It is perhaps not surprising that some of the most successfully integrated economies are small, homogeneous countries with a strong sense of collective identity.

Third, international governance rests on the ability of individual states to provide and guarantee stability. The bedrock of international order is the territorial state with its monopoly on coercive power within its jurisdiction. Cyberspace does not change this: economies are ultimately run for and by human beings, who have a physical presence and, therefore, a physical location.

Globalization does not make states unnecessary. On the contrary, for people to be successful in exploiting the opportunities afforded by international integration, they need states at both ends of their transactions. Failed states, disorderly states, weak states, and corrupt states are shunned as the black holes of the global economic system.

What, then, does globalization mean for states? First, policy ultimately determines the pace and depth of international economic integration. For each country, globalization is at least as much a choice as a destiny. Second, in important respects—notably a country's monetary regime, capital account, and above all, labor mobility—the policy underpinnings of integration are less complete than they were a century ago. Third, countries choose integration because they see its benefits. Once chosen, any specific degree of international integration imposes constraints on the ability of governments to tax, redistribute income, and influence macroeconomic conditions. But those constraints must not be exaggerated, and their effects are often beneficial. Fourth, international economic integration magnifies the impact of the difference between good and bad states—between states that provide public goods and those that serve predatory private interests, including those of the rulers.

Finally, as the world economy continues to integrate and cross-border flows become more important, global governance must be improved. Global governance will come not at the expense of the state but rather as an expression of the interests that the state embodies. As the source of order and basis of governance, the state will remain in the future as effective, and will be as essential, as it has ever been.

QUESTIONS FOR REVIEW AND DISCUSSION

1. According to Robert Wright, what forces are driving the world toward global government?
2. What kind of world government does Wright see emerging? What problems does he see with the emergence of this form of government?
3. What trade-offs does Martin Wolf believe national governments currently face?
4. According to Wolf, how does globalization affect the ability of governments to tax? Are these constraints fundamentally different from the constraints that arise in a closed national economy? Why or why not?
5. Does a global economy require global government? Why or why not?

SUGGESTIONS FOR FURTHER READING

Most of the readings suggested in the previous chapter contain discussions of globalization and governance. They provide a useful starting place. For a classic statement about how globalization weakens the nation-state, see two of the books by Kenichi Ohmae, including *The Borderless World: Power and Strategy in the Interlinked World Economy*. New York: Harper Business, 1990 and *The End of the Nation State: The Rise of Regional Economies*. New York: Free Press, 1995. Benjamin R. Barber provides a more philosophical discussion in his *Jihad vs. McWorld*. New York: Times Books, 1995. For more recent treatments, see: James N. Rosenau's *Distant Proximities: Dynamics Beyond Globalization*. Princeton: Princeton University Press, 2003; Robert O. Keohane. *Power and Governance in a Partially Globalized World*. London: Routledge, 2002; and the volume edited by David Held and Anthony McGrew, *Governing Globalization: Power, Authority and Global Governance*. Cambridge: Polity Press, 2002.